Arab Political Demography

Revised and Expanded Second Edition

Arab Political Demography

POPULATION GROWTH, LABOR MIGRATION AND NATALIST POLICIES

Revised and Expanded Second Edition

Onn Winckler

SUSSEX
ACADEMIC
PRESS

Brighton • Portland

2 4 6 8 10 9 7 5 3 1

First published in 2009 in Great Britain by
SUSSEX ACADEMIC PRESS
P.O. Box 139
Eastbourne BN24 9BP

and in the United States of America by
SUSSEX ACADEMIC PRESS
920 NE 58th Ave. Suite 300
Portland, Oregon 97213-3786

British Library Cataloguing in Publication Data
A CIP catalogue record for this book is available from the British Library.

Library of Congress Cataloging-in-Publication Data
Winckler, Onn.
Arab political demography : population growth, labor migration and natalist policies / Onn Winckler. — Rev. and expanded 2nd ed.
p. cm.
Includes bibliographical references and index.
ISBN 978-1-84519-238-9 (h/c : alk. paper) —
ISBN 978-1-84519-240-2 (p/b : alk. paper)
1. Arab countries—Population. 2. Demography—Research—Arab countries.
3. Arab countries—Economic conditions. 4. Fertility, Human—Arab countries.
5. Arab countries—Population policy. I. Title.
HB3660.A3W56 2009
304.60917′5927—dc22

2008031492

Mixed Sources
Product group from well-managed forests and other controlled sources
www.fsc.org Cert no. SGS-COC-2482
© 1996 Forest Stewardship Council

Typeset and designed by SAP, Brighton and Eastbourne.
Printed by TJ International, Padstow, Cornwall.
This book is printed on acid-free paper.

Contents

List of Tables, Figures and Charts

Tables

Figures

Charts

To
Iris, Hadar and Yael

Preface and Acknowledgments

Since the 1970s, but particularly with the end of the "bonanza" period of the "oil decade," the "demographic problem," also frequently named the "demographic challenge," has become the most acute socioeconomic problem for an increasing number of Arab countries. This book examines the connection between demography and politics in the Arab countries from three major perspectives: internal political dimensions; inter-Arab political dimensions; and the nature of relationships between the Arab and the developed Western countries. A better understanding of the "demographic factor" is crucial for broadening our understanding of the modern politics of the Arab countries, which, as noted by Farzaneh (Nazi) Roudi from the Population Reference Bureau, "is full of surprises and its demography is no exception."

Specifically, the book aims to describe and analyze four major areas. The first relates to the various demographic sources of the Arab countries during the twentieth century and the early 2000s, their limitations, and the reasons for these limitations. The second focus of the book is on the process of the intensified rapid population growth of the Arab countries since the early twentieth century, but particularly since the 1950s, following their independence. The third area is the fundamental socioeconomic consequence of the extremely high natural increase rates, namely, the emergence of the structural unemployment problem and its various socio-political implications for the short and the longer terms. The fourth and most important focus is on the natalist policies of the Arab countries since the mid-twentieth century.

Many people helped me during the process of writing this second edition. First and foremost, I am deeply indebted to Professor Gad G. Gilbar from the Department of Middle Eastern History at the University of Haifa, and the former Rector of the University, for his ongoing support and guidance during the past two decades. I am also sincerely thankful to my teacher and colleague Professor Uri M. Kupferschmidt from the Department of Middle Eastern History at the University of Haifa for the time and effort he devoted to reading the manuscript and for his valuable comments; to Professor Israel Gershoni from the Department of Middle Eastern and African History at Tel Aviv University who "forced" me to precisely define the meaning of "*political demography*" in its Middle Eastern context.

Parts of Chapter 3 are based on my article, "The Demographic Dilemma of the Arab World: The Employment Aspect," *Journal of Contemporary History*, Vol. 37, No. 4 (October 2002), pp. 617–36. Parts of Chapter 4 are based on two of my articles: "Was it Worth It? A Reexamination of the Cost/Benefit Balance of the Inter-Arab Labor Migration," *Journal of South Asian and Middle Eastern Studies*, Vol. 29, No. 4

(Summer 2006), pp. 38–59; and "Labor and Liberalization: The Decline of the GCC *Rentier* System," in Joshua Teitelbaum (ed.), *Political Liberalization in the Persian Gulf* (New York: Columbia University Press, forthcoming 2009). Parts of Chapter 5 are based on an article written with Professor Gad G. Gilbar, "Nasser's Family Planning in Perspective," in Elie Podeh and Onn Winckler (eds.), *Rethinking Nasserism: Revolution and Historical Memory in Modern Egypt* (Gainesville: University Press of Florida, 2004), pp. 282–304. The sections dealing with Syria and Jordan's fertility policies are based on my previous two books, published by Sussex Academic Press: *Population Growth and Migration in Jordan, 1950–1994* (1997); and *Demographic Developments and Population Policies in Ba'thist Syria* (1999).

Regarding the transliteration of the Arabic names, I follow the most common rules employed by *Middle Eastern Studies*, *The Middle East Journal* and other leading Middle Eastern journals. However, for personal names, I follow the most common usage rather than the transliteration rules.

This book was financially supported by **The Meir & Miriam Ezri Center for Iran & Persian Gulf Studies** at the **University of Haifa**.

I have been fortunate in receiving help in the process of collecting the sources for this book from the librarians in the Middle East Documentation Unit at Durham University, UK; the Arab World Documentation Unit in the University of Exeter, UK; the Cairo Demographic Center; the Newspaper Archive of the Moshe Dayan Center at Tel Aviv University; and the University of Haifa Library. I would also like to thank Ms. Livia Goldenblatt for editing the manuscript and Mr. Shai Spiler for preparing the tables, the figures and the cartoons for publication.

Above all, special thanks to my wife **Iris** and my two daughters **Hadar** and **Yael**, to whom this book is dedicated.

List of Abbreviations

ALO	Arab Labor Organization
BMA	Bahrain Monetary Agency
CAPMAS	Egypt, Central Agency for Public Mobilisation and Statistics
CBR	Crude Birth Rate
CBS	Central Bureau of Statistics
CDR	Crude Death Rate
DHS	Demographic and Health Surveys
ECWA/ESCWA	UN Economic (and Social) Commission for Western Asia
EIU	Economic Intelligence Unit
ECA	UN Economic Commission for Africa
EU	European Union
FAO	UN Food and Agricultural Organization
FDI	Foreign Direct Investment
GCC	Gulf Cooperation Council
GCHS	Gulf Child Health Survey
GDP	Gross Domestic Product
GFHS	Gulf Family Health Survey
GNP	Gross National Product
IBRD	International Bank for Reconstruction and Development
IJMES	International Journal of Middle East Studies
ILO	International Labour Office
IMF	International Monetary Fund
IOM	International Organization for Migration
IPPF	International Planned Parenthood Federation
MECS	Middle East Contemporary Survey
MEED	Middle East Economic Digest
MEES	Middle East Economic Survey
MENA	Middle East and North Africa
NGO	Non-Governmental Organization
NRR	Net Reproductive Rate
PNA	Palestinian National Authority
PRB	Population Reference Bureau
OECD	Organization for Economic Cooperation and Development
OPEC	Organization of Petroleum Exporting Countries
PCBS	Palestinian Central Bureau of Statistics

PLO	Palestinian Liberation Organization
PPP	Purchasing Power Parity
PRB	The Population Reference Bureau
SAMA	Saudi Arabian Monetary Agency
SR	Saudi Riyal
TFR	Total Fertility Rate
UNDP	United Nations Development Programme
UNFPA	United Nations Fund for Population Activities
UNICEF	United Nations Children's Fund
UNRWA	United Nations Relief and Works Agency
UNESCO	United Nations Educational, Scientific, and Cultural Organization
UNPF	United Nations Population Fund
USAID	United States Agency for International Aid
WB	The World Bank
WHO	UN World Health Organization

Introduction
The Methodological Framework of Arab Political Demography

1 The Emergence of "Poor" and "Rich" Arab States

During recent decades, the Arab region became one of the most diverse socioeconomic areas worldwide with very poor and very rich countries co-existing side by side. For example, Yemen and Sudan are among the poorest countries worldwide with a per capita GDP of $879 and $1,949, respectively, in 2004, while in the United Arab Emirates (UAE), it was more than $24,000 (in PPP terms[1]).

This huge economic gap between the Arab countries is a relatively new phenomenon. Even in the late 1960s, the economic gap between the Arab countries was quite narrow, with the exception of Kuwait and Libya which were in a class of their own as early as 1960s.[2] In 1968, the per capita GNP was $130 in Sudan, $190 in Egypt, $240 in Tunisia, $250 in Oman, $290 in Syria, $300 in Algeria, and $500 in Saudi Arabia (current prices).[3] Thus, except for Kuwait and Libya, the economic gap between the various Arab countries was no more than three-fold. This relatively small gap, however, has widened dramatically since the early 1970s mainly due to the following five factors:

(a) Oil export revenues Oil exports constituted the major factor impacting on the economies of the Arabian/Persian Gulf countries,[4] Libya and Algeria since the late 1950s. The dramatic increase in oil prices following the October 16, 1973 "oil boom" transformed the major Arab oil exporters not only into the wealthiest Arab states but also into some of the wealthiest countries worldwide within the very short period of time of only several years. Thus, whereas in 1972, the last year prior to the "oil boom," the oil exports of the ten Middle Eastern OPEC members (including Iran) amounted to $10 billion, in 1980, at the peak of oil prices, they reached $217 billion (in current prices), representing an increase of almost twenty-two fold in only eight years.[5] One year later, in 1981, Kuwait's per capita GNP amounted to $20,900 and that of the UAE to $24,660, compared, for example, to $10,210 in Japan and $12,820 in the United States (US).[6]

Although the non-oil Arab countries had the highest economic growth rates in their history during the 1973–1982 "oil decade" (see Chapter 3), the per capita GNP in 1981 remained quite low at $650 in Egypt, $860 in Morocco, $1,420 in Tunisia, $1,570 in

Syria and $1,620 in Jordan.[7] Since that time, the paramount factor determining the economic situation in each of the Arab countries has been the value of per capita oil exports.

(b) Internal political stability The second major determinant distinguishing the level of socioeconomic development between the various Arab countries was and still is the degree of political stability. The most important underlying reason accounting for the poor socioeconomic conditions in Yemen and Sudan is the political instability hampering the implementation of socioeconomic development plans. Thus, despite the substantial natural resources that these two countries have – Yemen's oil and Sudan's Nile water – they remain the two poorest Arab countries.

(c) Involvement in the Arab–Israeli conflict The third important issue affecting the economic gap between the various Arab countries was the degree of direct involvement in the Arab–Israeli conflict. Generally speaking, the degree of involvement in the Arab–Israeli conflict had five major impacts on the economies of the countries that were directly involved in the conflict: (1) the amount of defense allocations; (2) both direct and indirect damages from the wars and the continuation of the conflict; (3) a decline in potential foreign investments; (4) the pro-natalist environment; and above all, (5) attention by the leadership directed to the conflict rather than to socioeconomic development (see Chapter 5).

Naturally, the more intense the involvement in the conflict, the more devastating the economic damage, both direct and indirect. It must be emphasized, however, that the huge military expenditures of the Arab countries were not allocated for the sole purpose of dealing with the Arab–Israeli conflict. The very existence of the current Arab regimes, both the military and the monarchy, depend on the loyalty of their armies and the various security forces, which are often called upon to protect the regime. Examples of this were the cases of the 1970 "Black September" incidents in Jordan between the PLO and the Hashemite regime and the February 1982 clashes between the Ba'thi-'Alawi regime and the "Muslim brothers" in Syria. Moreover, the army and the civilian security forces have served as a major source for alleviating the employment pressures since the 1970s (see Chapter 3).

Until the June 1967 War, the economic implications of the conflict on the Arab countries directly involved in it were quite marginal. Moreover, in the case of Jordan and Egypt, the wars even brought about substantial economic levers: the control over the West Bank and Arab/East Jerusalem to Jordan as a result of the 1948 War; and control over the Suez Canal for Egypt as a result of the 1956 Suez War. However, the June 1967 War constituted a turning point not only from political and geo-strategic points of view, but even more so from a purely economic one, as the "economic price" of the military conflict with Israel became unbearable.

Jordan was the hardest hit of all the countries involved in the June 1967 War. First and foremost, Jordan lost the West Bank and Arab/East Jerusalem, thereby losing almost 40% of the Kingdom's population, valuable agricultural land and water sources, as well as the vast majority of the Kingdom's tourism sites.[8]

Egypt lost the oil fields of Sinai. In addition, due to the instability along the Suez Canal from the June 1967 War and until the signing of the Sinai Interim Agreement between Egypt and Israel in September 1975, Egypt could not develop the oil fields and the petrochemical industry on the west bank of the canal. This alone damaged Egyptian revenues by billions of dollars annually. Furthermore, between June 1967 and June 1975, the Suez Canal was closed, meaning that during these eight years,

Egypt lost its most important source for hard currency. To this direct damage should be added the indirect damages, primarily the small number of tourists and the small scale of foreign investments relative to the potential in these areas.[9] As a result, during the 1966–1973 period, Egypt's GDP grew by less than 1% on annual average,[10] representing a decline of almost 2% on annual average in per capita terms.

In the case of Syria, the economy was also considerably damaged from the June 1967 and the October 1973 wars, albeit substantially less than both Egypt and Jordan. The main damage of the conflict with Israel resulted from the huge defense burden, amounting to more than half of the government's budget during the first half of the 1980s,[11] and the high priority accorded to the conflict in the leadership agenda at the expense of socioeconomic development.

The Arab oil states, on the other hand, benefited from the huge increase in oil prices brought about by the October 1973 War (see Table 4.3) without having to shoulder any economic burden, as they were not directly involved in it. From their viewpoint, the October 1973 War was "a blessed occasion" as it served as the catalyst for the huge increase in oil prices (see Table 4.2).

The withdrawal from the conflict through the peace agreements by Israel with Egypt in March 1979 and with Jordan in October 1994, however, reaped tremendous economic dividends, both direct and indirect. For Egypt, these dividends included a huge increase in tourism revenues;[12] the return of the oil fields in Sinai; the reopening of the Suez Canal; massive US financial and military aid; and an influx of foreign investments.[13]

In the case of Jordan, the economic bonuses of peace included the cancellation of a large part of the external debt; a sharp increase in tourism revenues; a rise in financial foreign aid;[14] increased foreign investments; and privileged access to the US market through the Qualifying Industrial Zones (QIZs), which resulted in a tremendous increase in Jordan's exports to the US.[15]

There is no doubt, however, that the most important economic dividend of the peace treaty with Israel for both Egypt and Jordan is the US obligation to guarantee the economic survival of both regimes. Thus, the true value of the free trade agreement signed between Jordan and the US lies in "securing the political allegiance of Amman and preserving the cold peace between Jordan and Israel."[16] In a very similar way, following the US-led invasion of Iraq in March 2003 and the subsequent halt of the Iraqi imports from Egypt,[17] the US and the World Bank provided Egypt with $3.3 billion in assistance so as to ensure that Egypt's balance of payments deficit would "remain at a manageable level . . ."[18]

(d) Adoption of macroeconomic reforms In retrospect, in almost all of the developing countries worldwide, the economic crisis associated with socialist policies and authoritarian regimes has constituted the major lever for economic liberalization reforms. Since the ability of the regime to secure finances from rental sources – in the case of the Arab countries, the exports of oil and gas as well as the contribution of massive foreign aid, particularly following the collapse of oil prices in the mid-1980s[19] – diminished, the regime has been forced to collect more direct and indirect taxes while simultaneously narrowing the socioeconomic benefits given to the population in exchange for more political participation.[20] This represents a withdrawal from Myrdal's "soft state,"[21] at least in part, and a move toward the western-democratic formula of "no taxation without representation." Regarding this process in the Middle East, Harik claimed that:

> The main drive for change came from the fact that regimes were losing credibility and legitimacy among the general public in proportion to their inability to deliver. Having total control over the national economy deprived political leaders of sharing the burden and the responsibility for failure with others . . . Thus, the state moved toward economic liberalization both in order to partition the blame and responsibility and in the hope that an injection of fresh economic actors and capital would help a declining economy to regain its fortunes.[22]

Many of the Arab countries witnessed a gradual shift from *étatism* to more economic liberalization, starting in Tunisia in 1970 and then in Egypt in 1974 with Anwar al-Sadat's "open door" policy (*al-Infitah al-Iqtisadi*), and continuing during the 1980s and 1990s in the vast majority of the other Arab countries. This economic liberalization consisted mainly of trade and financial liberalization, exchange rate reforms, as well as privatization of public sector industries.

The change in economic approach was mainly due to the deepening economic pressure resulting from the basic imbalance between economic and population growth. The economic history of the Arab countries since the early 1970s indicates that the more extensive the economic reforms, the greater the foreign investments and the higher the economic growth rates. Tunisia, it should be emphasized, was the first country outside Europe to sign a partnership agreement with the European Union (EU), paving the way not only to increasing trade with the EU member countries, but also to attracting larger EU investments.[23]

While the majority of the Arab countries have adopted substantial economic reforms during the past two decades, a group of six Arab countries – Syria, Iraq, Yemen, Sudan, Algeria and Libya – has only implemented minor reforms toward economic liberalization. Henry and Springborg dubbed these countries "bunker states." They claimed that:

> In each of these cases except Algeria, the social forces that have penetrated and come to control these states are tribal or religious minorities, typically ones despised by much of the remainder of the population . . . In these circumstances, coercion is necessarily the primary and in some cases, such as that of Iraq or in much of Sudan, virtually the only means by which government can ensure the public's compliance.[24]

Under the formula of "bunker states," implementing macroeconomic reforms in order to revive economic performance was not possible, as they require political reforms as well. Thus, the *étatist* policy remained in force and hampered socioeconomic improvement. The end result was that the economic growth rates in these countries remained much lower than the potential and even negative in per capita terms in periods of low oil prices which continue to constitute the major source for governmental revenues.

(e) Implementation of efficient anti-natalist measures The final factor determining the degree of the socioeconomic gap between the Arab countries during the past generation was their natalist policies. In the early 1960s, fertility levels in the various Arab countries were quite similar, with only insignificant variations between them. Four decades later, at the dawn of the twenty-first century, fertility gaps between the Arab countries were huge, ranging from a total fertility rate (TFR) of replacement-level[25] in Tunisia and Lebanon to as high as almost six in Oman and above 3.5 in many Arab countries (see Table 2.4). The history of the non-oil Arab countries reveals that since the 1970s, the lower the fertility rates, the better the economic performances.

These five factors together, to a large extent, explain the socioeconomic variability of the Arab countries at the beginning of the twenty-first century. The oil states hold the position at the top of the Arab economic pyramid, in line with their per capita oil revenues. At the bottom of the pyramid, far behind the other Arab countries, are Yemen and Sudan with their typically sub-Saharan socioeconomic patterns: high infant and child mortality rates; low life expectancy; high illiteracy rates; and an overall low living standard.

The rest of the Arab countries are located in the middle of the pyramid. Tunisia leads this middle group with a per capita GDP (PPP terms) in 2004 of $7,768, followed by Lebanon with $5,837, Jordan with $4,688, and Egypt and Morocco with approximately $4,200 (see Appendix I). Thus, although Tunisia does not have a considerable amount of natural resources, in PPP terms, its per capita GDP at the start of the twenty-first century was almost double that of the other non-oil Arab countries. This is a combined result of its having the lowest fertility rates of all of the Arab countries; its implementation of economic reforms since the early 1970s, many years prior to the other Arab countries; its avoidance of direct involvement in the Arab–Israeli conflict; its political stability since its independence in 1956; and above all, top political priority to socioeconomic issues.

At the bottom of the middle group is Syria, with a per capita GNI of $1,380 in 2005, compared to almost $1,700 in the early 1980s (current prices).[26] This decline was mainly due to the failure of the Syrian regime to implement macroeconomic reforms and decisive anti-natalist measures, as well as the continuing involvement in the Arab–Israeli conflict up to the present. Egypt, on the other hand, started to adopt effective anti-natalist steps in the mid-1980s and substantial macroeconomic reforms a decade earlier, in the mid-1970s. Thus, despite the fact that at the peak of the "oil boom" in the early 1980s, Syria's per capita GDP was almost three-fold that of Egypt's, by the beginning of the twenty-first century, Syria was lagging behind Egypt in almost every socioeconomic indicator. Even with substantial oil exports and considerable water and agricultural land resources, Syria's economic performance has not kept pace with the progress made through Egypt's "good governance," combined with the economic dividends from its peace treaty with Israel.

From among the above-mentioned five factors, the focus of this book is on the fifth factor – the demographic aspect – as seen through the prism of **political demography.**

2 The Concept of Political Demography

> Although demography is a sometimes central component of politics and political argument, "*political demography*" as an acknowledged science does not exist.
>
> Philippe Fargues[27]

Generally speaking, the term "population" raises a variety of images. To some, "population" is a set of numbers and tables. To others, it is a target group for companies, businesses and other commercial organizations attempting to sell products and services. Both views approach "population" as a static entity. To the demographer, on the other hand, "population" also has a dynamic aspect, since the "population" never remains the same and is always changing in many respects. First and foremost, the number of people is always changing through fertility, mortality, and migration of both in-migration (immigration) and out-migration (emigration). Other dynamic demographic aspects are the spatial distribution and the various socioeconomic characteristics of the population that affect each of the demographic indicators of any given society.[28] These dynamics constitute the core of demographic research.

John Graunt's (1620–1674)[29] *Natural and Political Observations Mentioned in a following Index, and Made upon the Bills of Mortality*, published in 1662, is considered to be the first demographic research ever. Graunt was a merchant and used book-keeping principles to construct the first life table, drawing data on mortality from the records of deaths in London.[30] In this research, Graunt tried to find systematization in the two most important demographic phenomena, namely, births and deaths. Graunt found differences in the birth patterns between the city of London itself and its countryside. He also recorded the biological fact that the number of male births is systematically higher than the number of females. The two terms included in Graunt's book title, "natural" and "political," demonstrates that Graunt already recognized the two major factors affecting demographic trends: the biological and the socio-political.[31]

It should be mentioned that until Graunt's time, there was hardly any research interest in the demography issue. The few censuses that were conducted aimed only to count the population in a specific territory for the purposes of tax collection or military conscription, but not for learning about the health situation of the population or their service and infrastructure needs (see Chapter 1). Thus, Graunt opened the way for a new research discipline: "the population study."[32] Since Graunt, researchers have attempted to compare various demographic data between periods, regions, and later, countries, in order to understand mankind's demographic behavior.[33] Since the late eighteenth century, researchers have been trying to discover not only mankind's demographic behaviors, but even more important, the factors which influence each of the demographic phenomena, the most significant among them being births, deaths, and migration.[34]

At the initial stage of the demographic research, the main focus was on mortality rates and building life tables. This emphasis was mainly due to the fact that fertility levels in the pre-Industrial Revolution period were more or less stable at the highest biological limit while mortality rates often fluctuated due to frequent famines and epidemics. In addition, a substantial decline in mortality rate was a clear sign for "good governance." Since the nineteenth century, however, the interest of the demographers was expanded to include changes in fertility levels which had started to decline in the more developed European societies.

During the twentieth century, the worldwide demographic attention turned to fertility. This was characterized not only through the implementation of an enormous number of researches on fertility levels and behavior in the developing societies around the world, but also through the increased interest since the 1970s in the new demographic phenomenon of constant fertility decline in the developed societies worldwide, particularly the causes for this constant decline. Overall, modern demographic research mainly concentrates on fertility behavior and primarily on the core factors affecting the changes in fertility behaviors in developed and developing societies alike.

As the two basic mechanisms for detailed demographic research are censuses and civil registration systems, both of which are controlled by the state itself, implementing modern demographic research does not depend solely on academic ability and resources, but rather on the ability and the willingness of the state to collect and publish the demographic data. The importance of the demographic research is not merely academic, but poses many important practical aspects. Understanding the phases, the causes, and the level of population growth, immigration, emigration, changes in life expectancy, and many other demographic phenomena are the most basic needs for any future socioeconomic plans. Thus, knowledge of the demographic situation is one of the most important aims of any regime: municipal, regional, and above all, national.

Although, according to Fargues, *political demography* as a scientific disciplinary method did not yet exist, in the following section, the connection between *demography* and *politics* in the context of the Arab countries will be examined from a historical prism, as "demography is too important to be left to demographers."[35] This examination will be carried out in line with three basic categories:

The first category is **the ethno-religious composition of the society**. The ethno-religious composition of the Lebanese population has constituted the most important single factor in its political history since the nineteenth century, rendering its entire modern political history "a religious conflict history." In the case of the other Arab countries, although the ethno-religious composition has not been as crucial as in the Lebanese case, it still has immense political consequences. The most recent example of the ethno-religious political influence is that of Iraq following the March 2003 US-led invasion. At the heart of the Iraqi internal political dispute is the ethno-religious division, particularly the bloody revival between the Sunnis and the Shi'is.

The political "fingerprints" on the demographic records in each of the Arab countries can be seen even in the early stages of data collection, namely, in the decision-making as to what to include and what to exclude in the censuses and the civil registration records in terms of ethno-religious categories. Almost each of the Arab countries is "hiding" something: either the religious or the ethnic composition. There are a wide range of political reasons for this which varies from one country to another. Thus far, the only Middle Eastern country that publishes official data on a regular basis regarding both the ethnic and the religious composition of its population is Israel (see Chapter 1). However, in the case of Israel as well, some basic socioeconomic data collected by official agencies are not published according to religion, such as unemployment rates, the composition of public sector employees and the composition of those living below the "poverty line."

The second category of the Middle Eastern *political demography* is that of **the national political struggle based on the ethno-religious quantity factor**. The most representative case of this category in the Middle East is the Palestinian-Zionist conflict. The demographic quantity factor has played a major role in the conflict since its onset more than a century ago, insofar as each side is trying to increase the number of members in its community at the expense of the other side. This effort is based on the fundamental assumption that the demographic advantage will prove to be one of the most important factors, if not the most, determining the outcome of the struggle, whether through a peace treaty or through another cycle of war. Thus, the two sides, the Palestinians and the Zionists, adopted a pro-natalist concept from the very beginning of the conflict.[36] With their constant emphasis on the "demographic factor," the authorities on both sides have indeed succeeded in creating a "pro-natalist environment" among the populations themselves.

The third category of the *Arab political demography* deals with **the political influence on the demographic policy per se**, in most cases on the natalist policy. This category refers to all of the various political factors influencing government natalist policy, including the regime's ideology; the political structure of the society; the religious impact on the political structure; and the influence of the relationship between the regime and the Islamic fundamentalist opposition.

Despite the different natalist and migration policies adopted by each of the Arab countries during the second half of the twentieth century, the political influence on both areas was and still is immense. Thus, one cannot deal with the modern political history of the Arab countries without taking "the demographic factor" into consideration. At the same time, it is impossible to deal with modern Arab demographic history without examining the various political aspects. Accordingly, it is the goal of this book to address the mutual influence of demography and politics in the case of the Arab countries.

In the mid-1970s, André Burguière wrote that: "Historical demography is a young science, barely thirty years old, and yet it already suffers from the ailments of old age: recent work has become repetitive, and seems always to come up against the same contradictions."[37] I hope that this book will not fall into that category.

In light of the aims described in the Preface, the book contains five chapters. The aim of Chapter 1 is two-fold: First, to examine the quantity and quality of the demographic records of the Arab countries. As will be illustrated in this chapter, the major barrier to conducting demographic research in the Arab countries until very recently was the limited sources and in many cases low reliability of the official demographic records themselves. The second aim is to analyze the political influence on the demographic records of the Arab countries, specifically in terms of which demographic records were either not collected or not published.

Chapter 2 deals with the causes of the rapid population growth in the Arab countries since the beginning of the twentieth century. The first part of the chapter compares the Arab countries with other developing and developed countries worldwide in order to "position" the Arab countries in the global demographic picture. It addresses the following: factors which account for the high fertility rates in the Arab countries; causes for the fertility decline in the Arab countries since the mid-1980s; and explanations for the immense fertility gaps between urban and rural areas, as well as the gaps due to differences in mothers' educational level and employment pattern. The second part of the chapter consists of the history of mortality trends in the Arab countries since the early twentieth century. The final part of the chapter examines the major differences between the Western demographic transition pattern and the pattern of developing countries as a whole, particularly in respect to the Arab countries.

Chapter 3 analyzes the most acute consequence of the high natural increase rates among the Arab countries, namely, the emergence of the immense employment pressure that has characterized the non-oil Arab countries since the 1970s and the oil-based Arab countries since the mid-1990s. The first part of the chapter deals with the short- and long-term consequences of the wide-based age pyramid. It concentrates on the labor force participation rates and on the "demographic momentum" and its influence on future population and labor force growth rates. The second part examines the emergence of the unemployment problem, both open and disguised, since the early 1960s. The final part examines the major differences between the unemployment patterns of the non-oil Arab countries and the unemployment characteristics of the developed countries.

Chapter 4 deals with the newly but extremely important demographic phenomenon of the intra-Arab labor migration. The first part of the chapter provides the theoretical framework of international labor migration and the prevailing perceptions on the cost/benefit balance of both the labor-exporting and the labor-importing countries. The second part examines the macroeconomic development strategy of the GCC countries following the October 1973 "oil boom" and the subsequent rapid growth of foreign labor. The third part examines the nature of the inter-Arab labor migration process from an historical perspective. The fourth part discusses the labor migration policy of both the labor-importing and the labor-exporting countries. The final part analyzes the overall cost/benefit balance of the intra-Arab labor migration for the major Arab labor-exporting countries.

Chapter 5 analyzes the natalist policies of the Arab countries. The first part of the chapter examines the different attitudes toward rapid population growth since this phenomenon first emerged in Europe in the late eighteenth century as a direct result of the Industrial Revolution. The second part discusses the various natalist policies implemented by the Arab countries since the 1950s, focusing on the differences between the various countries and the changing perceptions and policies within the countries themselves. The final part examines the crucial question of why some Arab countries have succeeded more than others in the implementation of national family planning programs.

The **Summary and Conclusions** first evaluates the balance of achievements and failures of the natalist policies of the Arab countries and relates the macroeconomic reforms to the changing natalist approaches adopted by the Arab countries since the mid-1980s. The final part of the book examines the effect of the ongoing rise in unemployment rates on the political stability of the Arab countries at the dawn of the twenty-first century.

1 Sources for Demographic Research of the Arab States

Numbers are not neutral: they are framed and defined by their creators, distorted and redefined by those responsible for their collection and reconstituted and reordered by those who select, display, use and analyze them for their purpose. Numbers are a powerful tool in the hands of those who decide to gather them and to use them.

Pat Hudson, 2000[1]

The extent and quality of statistical data are paramount indicators of the degree of the central authority's control over the population and the territory in a given country. Generally, the more extensive and accurate the statistical data, the better the regime's control over both the population and the territory. Thus, the improvement in the overall socioeconomic data, particularly the demographic data, of the Arab countries since the 1960s has occurred along with the increase in control of the central authorities over their populations and territories. However, in many cases, governments are trying to "hide" sensitive demographic facts and thus do not collect and publish particular data, usually related to the ethno-religious composition of the population.

I An Overview of Demographic Records in the Arab Countries

The word ***census*** has its origins in ancient Rome, coming from the Latin word *censere*, meaning "to assess" or "to estimate." The first known demographic census was taken by the Babylonians in 3800 BC, nearly 6000 years ago. In 2500 BC, Egypt conducted a census in order to assess the workforce available for building the Pyramids. From a very early period, China placed great importance on carrying out a demographic census. The Roman census, which took place every five years, was the most developed of any recorded in the Ancient World and provided a register of citizens and their property. Censuses and the recording of births and deaths were carried out in some of the city-states of Renaissance Italy.

The first modern record of demographic censuses was in Quebec (Canada) which held 15 censuses during the 1665–1754 period. In Europe, systematic records of population do not appear to have started until the eighteenth century. In 1719, Frederick William I of Prussia commenced half-yearly counts of the population. In the US, the first census was taken in 1790. Both England and France started conducting demographic censuses in 1801, and Norway censuses began in 1815. In 1837, the registration of births and deaths became compulsory in England and Wales.[2] Regular censuses began in Belgium in 1829, in the Netherlands in 1839, and in Switzerland in 1850. The first pan-Germanic census was held in 1852. These early censuses, however, suffered from two basic shortcomings: first, they failed to collect complete lists of names and addresses; and second, they did not conduct the whole census in one day.[3]

1.1 Sources for Demographic Research of the Arab Areas under the Ottoman Rule

Population censuses and registration of births, deaths, marriages, and divorces, as well as changes in place of residence – all of which constitute the most important sources for comprehensive demographic research – have had a very short history in most of the Arab countries. Modern censuses were carried out only in two Arab regions prior to the end of World War I – in Egypt, since 1882, colonized by Britain at the time, and in Algeria, since 1886, which was then colonized by the French.[4] In the rest of the Arab regions which were under Ottoman rule, in place of demographic censuses, there were only general population estimates, which were based on partial censuses or general enumerations that were conducted by the Ottoman regime. However, even the Egyptian and the Algerian censuses had basic limitations. For example, nomadic and semi-nomadic populations, as well as other segments of the population, such as young children, primarily young girls, may have been markedly underreported. Together with age misreporting, this produced noticeable distortions in the apparent age-sex distribution of the population.[5]

Generally, the Ottomans never took a real interest in counting the populations under their rule. Moreover, the flimsy rule of the Ottoman Empire over the Arab provinces until the mid-nineteenth century was not conducive to comprehensive population registration. Given that the Ottoman regime provided almost no social services to its subjects, there was no need to accurately determine their demographic characteristics. In addition, since the Ottoman tax collection system was based on the *Iltizam*,[6] the central and the provincial authorities did not need a specific record of the rural populations, which constituted the main target of tax collection.

Consequently, only very limited demographic data of the areas that were ruled by the Ottomans are available. Shaw noted in this regard that: "No problem has perplexed students of modern Ottoman history more than that of determining the state of the empire's population during its last century."[7] The only sources regarding the scope of the population in many Ottoman regions during the early nineteenth century are the sporadic estimates of European travelers, such as Volney, Seetzen and Burckhardt,[8] whose figures were, naturally, based on local observation, often exaggerated or inconsistent.[9] Thus, these estimates cannot serve as a primary source for comprehensive demographic research.

Since the mid-nineteenth century, as part of the reform movement (*Tanzimat*) that took place in the Ottoman Empire, the demographic data also improved accordingly. A census was carried out during the years 1831–1838 by Sultan Mahmud II (1808–1839) as part of his efforts to create a new army and bureaucracy following the destruction of the *Janissart* Corps in 1826. Only men were included in the census because only they served in the army and paid taxes. Although Christians and Jews did not serve in the Ottoman army at that time, they were also recorded, as they were subject to a head tax (*harac*). Females, however, were not recorded in this census at all.[10]

Knowledge of the size and changes in the spatial distribution of the population throughout the Empire became much more important during the latter part of the nineteenth century. This was due mainly to administrative reasons, as roads, railways, and a variety of professional schools were planned in accordance with the spatial distribution of the population in the Empire's provinces.[11] As the Ottoman control over the provinces improved during the last quarter of the nineteenth century, the population registrations improved accordingly. The Ottoman authorities kept the population registrations in the provincial capitals, where they were published in the *Salname* (provincial yearbook), as well as in the *Defter Nüfus* in the Empire's capital, Istanbul.[12]

1.2 The Demographic Records in the Arab States since the Mandatory Period

Since the beginning of the Mandatory period, following the end of World War I, there has been a steady improvement in the socioeconomic statistical database, including the demographic data, in all of the Arab countries, with the exception of Lebanon.[13] But Lebanon, it should be emphasized, is a unique case and in this respect, stands alone among all the Arab countries (see below).

In all of the other Arab countries, the socioeconomic data, including demographic data, were further improved following independence. The large-scale socioeconomic development plans, as well as the changing economic policy from the Mandatory capitalism to some form of socialism-étatism, also required accurate socio-demographic data, particularly in regard to age and sex composition, educational level and the spatial distribution of the population. This information on the age pyramid, which is considered as the most fundamental data for implementing demographic research, was needed because the socialism-étatism system provided, *inter alia*, a wide variety of public services, the most important of which were healthcare and education, which were either totally free of charge or highly subsidized. Thus, as one can see in Table 1.1, almost all of the Arab countries conducted population censuses during the 1950s and the first half of the 1960s.

A further improvement in the socioeconomic and demographic data in the vast majority of the Arab countries occurred in the 1960s and 1970s, as a result of both the implementation of the massive socioeconomic development plans, such as the Egyptian and the Syrian Five-Year Development Plans covering the 1960–1965 period, and the steady rise in awareness of many Arab governments regarding the "demographic issue." Thus, the population censuses conducted during the 1960s and 1970s also included information on fertility patterns that had largely been missing from the previous censuses of the 1940s and 1950s. Nevertheless, these population censuses also suffered from some basic shortcomings, such as the under-enumeration of the nomad populations and young girls, age misreporting, and the like. In the Gulf countries, the most prominent problems of the censuses were misreporting of age and nationality as well as large-scale undercounting of the nomadic population.

However, despite the above-mentioned shortcomings, these censuses constituted

Table 1.1 Demographic Censuses in Arab Countries, 1945–2005

Period Country	Before 1950	1950–1959	1960–1969	1970–1979	1980–1989	1990–2000	2001–1005
Algeria	31.10.1948	31.10.1954	1.2.1960 4.4.1966	11.2.1977	20.3.1987	25.6.1998	
Egypt	26.3.1947		20.9.1960 30.5.1966(a)	22/23.11.1976	17/18.11.1986	18/19.11.1996	
Libya		31.7.1954	31.7.1964	31.7.1973	31.7.1984	11.8.1995	
Morocco		15.4.1951	18.6.1960	20.7.1971	3/21.9.1982	2.9.1994	2.9.2004
Sudan		1.7.1955 2.9.1956		3.4.1973	1.2.1983	15.4.1993	
Tunisia	11.1.1946	1.2.1956	3.5.1966	8.5.1975	30.3.1984	20.4.1994	28.4.2004
Bahrain		3.3.1950 2.5.1959	13.2.1965	3.4.1971	5.4.1981	16.11.1991	7.4.2001
Iraq	19.10.1947	12.10.1957	14.10.1965	17.10.1977	17.10.1987	16.10.1997	
Jordan		8.9.1952	18.11.1961	10/11.11.1979		15.12.1994	2/8.10.2004
Kuwait		28.2.1957	20.5.1961 25.4.1965	19.4.1970 21.4.1975	20/21.4.1985	20.4.1995	20/21.4.2005
Lebanon	1932			15.11.1970(a)			
Oman						1.12.1993	7/8.12.2003
Qatar				4.5.1970	16.3.1986	1.3.1997	16.3.2004
Saudi Arabia				9/14.9.1974		27.9.1992	15.9.2004
Syria			20.9.1960	22.9.1970	3.9.1981	3/9.9.1994	22.9.2004
UAE			13.3/16.4.1968	30/31.12.1975	15.12.1980 17/23.12.1985	17.12.1995	5.12.2005
Yemen (United)						16/17.12.1994(b)	16.12.2004

(a) Sample Census.
(b) North and South Yemen were united into one country in May 1990.
Sources: The US, Department of Commerce, US Census Bureau. Available at: http:/www.census.gov; GeoHive. Available at: http://geohive.com; UN, Population Division, *Operational Aspects of Census Taking in the ESCWA Region: Results of ESCWA Questionnaire*, by Ahmed Hussein (New York, August 12, 2005); Eliance Domschke and Doreen S. Goyer, *The Handbook of National Population Censuses: Africa and Asia* (New York, Westport and London: Greenwood Press, 1986); UN, Statistics Division, "Population and Housing Censuses" (New York, October 5, 2005). Available at: http://unstats.un.org/UNSD/Demographic/sources/census/censusdates.htm.

the basic sources for the earlier demographic research on the Arab countries. In the case of Jordan, for example, although the first census was carried out in 1952, the 1961 census is considered the first comprehensive census in line with the modern type of census. In addition to the censuses, some of the Arab countries started to conduct specific demographic surveys during the 1970s (see below).

During the 1980s, but more so since the early 1990s, the acceleration of the devastating results of the rapid population growth led many Arab governments to adopt national family planning programs. The precondition for implementing these programs was accurate and detailed fertility data, mainly according to women's age, educational level and employment status, average and median age of first marriage for women, family income, and fertility differences between rural and urban dwellers.

Some of this information was obtained through international fertility surveys conducted in the late 1970s and early 1980s, such as the *1978 World Fertility Survey*, which among the Arab countries included Egypt, Tunisia, Morocco, Jordan, Syria and the Republic of Yemen (North Yemen). Other data were obtained from demographic and health surveys which were implemented under the auspices of the Arab League, the most prominent of which were: the *Pan-Arab Child Health Survey* initiated during the late 1980s; the *Pan-Arab Project for Family Health* (*al-Mashru' al-'Arabi li-Sihat al-Usra*) carried out during the early 2000s in seven member states of the Arab League, namely, Algeria, Djibouti, Lebanon, Morocco, Syria, Tunisia and Yemen;[14] or within the framework of the GCC organization,[15] such as the *Family Health Survey* which was conducted in the mid-1990s in each of the GCC states (see below).

2 Case Studies in the History of Demographic Records

Despite the considerable improvement in the overall demographic data of the vast majority of the Arab countries since the 1960s, a variety of basic demographic data is still absent. In most cases, this absence is not a result of the inability of the central regime to collect the data (as was the case during the Ottoman period), but rather purely due to political calculations. However, owing to limited space, this section examines the history of the demographic records in several Arab states only, namely, Egypt, Jordan, Syria and the GCC countries.

2.1 Egypt

Egypt had one of the longest history of demographic data worldwide, stretching back thousands of years. The official Egyptian argument is that Egypt's earliest census dates back to 3340BC.[16] In modern times, Egypt's first census was conducted during the French occupation in 1800. Regular censuses in Egypt started in 1882. This census was taken by the British following their occupation of Egypt. The next census was carried out in 1897. During the twentieth century, Egypt conducted ten censuses – more than any other Arab country – in 1907, 1917, 1927, 1937, 1947, 1960, 1966, 1976, 1986 and 1996. Egypt's latest census was carried out in December 2006.

In September 1964, the Central Agency for Public Mobilization and Statistics (CAPMAS) was established. According to Decree No. 2915 of 1964, CAPMAS is the only official source for providing statistical data for all the Egyptian public sector bodies. It soon became the largest and the most reliable statistical organization among all the Arab countries.

Following the censuses, the second important source for Egypt's demographic data is the ten national-level *Demographic and Health Surveys*. The first survey was the 1980 Egypt Fertility Survey (*1980-EFS*); the second was the 1984 Egypt Contraceptive Prevalence Survey (*1984-ECPS*). This was followed by the 1988 Egypt Demographic and Health Survey (*1988-EDHS*) after which there was the 1991 Maternal and Child Health Survey (*1991-EMCHS*). The next six surveys were the Egypt Demographic and Health Survey (*EDHS*) of 1992, 1995, 1997, 1998, 2000 and 2005 which were carried out within the framework of Demographic and Health Surveys (DHS) Program of ORC Macro.[17]

The primary aim of these surveys was to gather and analyze data on the key demographic and health indicators of Egypt's population, the most prominent of which were: the fertility patterns according to various characteristics of age, mothers' educational level, place of residence, parents' employment patterns, family income and infant and child mortality rates. Since the *1995-EDHS*, technical support for implementing the surveys was provided by Macro International Inc, and sponsored by the USAID.

2.2 *Jordan*

The 1952 housing census is considered the first enumeration of the Jordanian population following independence (1946). However, since it was a housing rather than a population census, it only ascertained the total number of males and females with no other demographic data. As a result, its overall usefulness for comprehensive demographic research is very limited.

The first comprehensive population census in Jordan was carried out in November 1961. The coverage of the census is considered reasonably complete. The reported annual natural increase rate of approximately 3% is also reasonable and is consistent with the demographic data of other sources, official and unofficial alike.[18]

The second population census in Jordan was conducted in November 1979 in order to establish a comprehensive demographic database for purposes of formulating the Kingdom's socioeconomic development plans. It was also the first census following the June 1967 War in which Jordan lost the West Bank and East/Arab Jerusalem and absorbed approximately 380,000 Palestinian refugees following their displacement from the West Bank and the Gaza Strip.[19]

The third census in Jordan was carried out in December 1994. There was some debate regarding the aim of this census, and there were some arguments in the Jordanian press that the decision to conduct it was politically motivated, aiming to divide the population between "Jordanians" and "Palestinians." This issue was a sensitive one, following the return of about 350,000 Jordanian citizens to the Kingdom after their deportation in 1991 from Kuwait and Saudi Arabia due to the refusal of King Husayn to support the US-led anti-Iraqi coalition in the Kuwait crisis (see Chapter 4). The Executive Director of the census, 'Abd al-'Aziz Zoubi, claimed that the only aim of the census was "to establish an accurate demographic picture of the Kingdom."[20]

The latest census in Jordan was conducted in October 2004. More than 16,000 persons participated in the field work of the census, most of them Ministry of Education employees. The coverage rate of the census was reported as 96.4%.[21]

In addition to the population censuses, the various demographic and health surveys constitute another important source for Jordanian demographic research. The *1972 National Fertility Survey* (*1972-NFS*) was the first demographic survey in the Kingdom, and its results were published in 1976. This was followed by the *Jordan Fertility Survey* conducted in 1976 (*1976-JFS*), with its results published in 1983. The third survey was the *1981 Jordan Demographic Survey* (*1981-JDS*) and its results were published in 1983. The fourth survey was the *1983 Jordan Fertility and Family Health Survey* (*1983-JFFHS*), and its results were published in 1985. The fifth survey was the *1985 Jordan Husbands' Fertility Survey* (*1985-JHFS*), with the aim of investigating the attitude of husbands regarding fertility patterns. The sixth survey was the *1990 Jordan Population and Family Health Survey* (*1990-JPFHS*), aimed at collecting data on fertility patterns, knowledge and use of contraceptives, and scale and patterns of infant and child mortality rates. The survey's results were published in 1992. The seventh survey was the *1997 Jordan Population and Family Health Survey* (*1997-JPFHS*), which had similar aims to the *1990-JPFHS*. Its results were published in 1998. The latest survey was the *2002 Jordan Population and Family Health Survey* (*2002-JPFHS*). The survey was conducted by the Jordanian Department of Statistics within the framework of the DHS Program. Data were collected from July to September 2002 from 7,825 households and complete interviews were carried out with 6,006 women aged 15–49.[22]

2.3 Syria

The first census in Syria following the collapse of the Ottoman Empire was conducted by the French Mandatory regime in 1921–1922.[23] However, there were many defects in the census. As Widmer commented: "The census of 1921–1922 . . . can scarcely be considered as even an approximation."[24] Even during the decade and a half after independence (1946), Syrian demographic data remained unreliable, preventing the carrying out of any comprehensive socio-demographic research. As Hansen wrote in the late 1960s: "Syrian population statistics are poor. The first modern census was made in 1960 and the population registration statistics are not very reliable."[25] Since that time, both the quality and the quantity of the Syrian socio-demographic and economic data have substantially improved. This improvement has found expression mainly in the following three areas:

(a) Population censuses Since its independence and up to the present, Syria has carried out five censuses. The first was conducted in 1947, with the sole aim of establishing an election list to the parliament. The results of the census have never been published, other than those relating to the distribution of the population by sex and religion.[26]

The need for reliable socio-demographic data was underscored in the late 1950s with the preparation of the First Five-Year Development Plan for the years 1960–1965. Therefore, the 1960 census, which was conducted under the United Arab Republic (UAR) regime,[27] constituted the first scientifically demographic census, which covered the entire Syrian population. However, there were apparently some serious defects in the census data, including a marked under-enumeration of nomads and semi-nomads.[28]

The third census took place in September 1970. The questionnaires, as well as the methods used for the organization of the census were similar to those used in the 1960 census. It was also flawed by under-enumeration, which was estimated at about 2% among the urban population and 11% in the rural areas. Nevertheless, it was believed that the 1970 census data were more accurate than those of the 1960 census and that more information was obtained about various demographic characteristics.[29] The 1970 census was the first in which the data were computer-tabulated.[30]

In 1976, the Syrian authorities conducted a sample census in order to draw a numerical picture of the structural composition of the Syrian population, to trace the socioeconomic factors affecting it, and to obtain indicators comparable to the data collected in the 1960 and 1970 censuses.[31] The fourth Syrian census was held in September 1981, followed by a census in September 1994. The most recent census was carried out on September 22, 2004.

(b) Demographic and health surveys The second important source for Syrian demographic research are the demographic surveys that were carried out by the Central Bureau of Statistics, the most important of which were: the *1973-Infant and Child Mortality Survey in Damascus*; the *1976–1979 Follow-Up Demographic Survey*; the *1978-Syrian Fertility Survey* (*1978-SFS*); the *1993-Syrian Maternal and Child Health Survey* (*1993-SMCHS*); and the *2001 Syrian Family Health Survey* (*2001-SFHS*), which was carried out within the framework of the *Pan-Arab Project for Family Health*. The main objective of the *2001-SFHS* was to provide policymakers with the needed information on socioeconomic, health and environmental characteristics of the Syrian population in order to formulate a comprehensive demographic policy.[32]

(c) The Civil Registration System The Syrian Civil Registration System, although established as early as 1923, in the early days of the French mandate, continued to suffer from high underreporting rates during the 1950s and 1960s, particularly in the area of death registration. This situation persisted for several reasons: First, it was impossible to register a birth unless both parents were on the population register. As many parents, particularly from the rural areas and the remote provinces were themselves not registered, they could not register their offspring. Second, it was a costly operation to the public, especially in those cases when the registration office was located a long distance away. Finally, and most importantly, there was no incentive for the population to register deaths – the opposite was the case, as the pro-natalist policy had created an incentive *not* to register deaths, particularly those of children (see Chapter 5).[33]

2.4 The GCC Countries

While there are numerous demographic data for the past three decades on many Arab countries, this is not the case in the GCC countries. Actually, up to and including the present, with the exception of Oman since 1993, the GCC countries do not publish official data even regarding certain basic demographic characteristics of the indigenous populations, such as crude birth rate (CBR), crude death rate (CDR) and TFR. In the case of Qatar, as will be examined below, the official demographic data do not even include a breakdown of the country's population according to nationals and foreigners. In contrast to the past, however, the reason for this lack of basic demographic data published by the GCC authorities during the past two decades is purely political, and serves mainly to disguise the huge percentage of foreign population within the total population.

Another major obstacle to implementing detailed demographic research on the

GCC countries is that the demographic data published by international organizations relating to these countries do not distinguish between the indigenous and the foreign populations and combine them together. Thus, for example, in the World Bank's *World Development Report–1990*, Kuwait's CBR in 1988 was put at 26 per 1,000.[34] In reality, however, while the CBR of the Kuwaiti nationals in that particular year was 42.2 per 1,000, it was only 18.4 for the foreign population.[35] In the case of the UAE, one can find the same pattern: While the World Bank's estimate for the CBR in 1988 was as low as 23 per 1,000,[36] in reality this rate was 39.6 per 1,000 among the indigenous population and 22.2 among its foreign population.[37] Consequently, the TFR data were distorted as well. For example, the World Bank put Kuwait's TFR in 1994 as 3.0 children per woman and that of the UAE at 4.1.[38] In fact, the TFR was 6.52 children per Kuwaiti national woman and as low as 2.0 for non-Kuwaiti woman.[39] In the case of the UAE, the estimates were 5.3 children for the UAE woman and only 3.0 for non-UAR woman.[40]

This mistaken approach of combining the demographic indicators of the foreign and the national GCC populations led, naturally, to mistaken conclusions as well. For example, Tabutin and Schoumaker claimed in an article published in 2005 that Bahrain, UAE, Qatar, Kuwait, Tunisia and Lebanon were a "very advanced model" of the demographic transition process.[41] This conclusion, although true regarding Tunisia and Lebanon, is a mistaken one regarding the oil-based countries, namely, Bahrain, UAE, Qatar and Kuwait. This is because the fertility rates of the indigenous populations of these countries, although lower during the past decade, are still very high in any regional and international comparison. Moreover, from a purely methodological viewpoint, it is a mistake to measure fertility level through CBRs in a society that is comprised mostly of males, as is the case in the GCC countries due to the fact that the vast majority of the foreigners are males.

In addition, some researchers who deal with the demographic connection of the GCC socioeconomic development during the oil era do not distinguish between the natural increase of the indigenous GCC populations and the overall population growth of these countries which also include the large-scale immigration and combine them together. Laipson for example, claimed that: "The Middle Eastern countries ranked highest on the Human Development scale also have the lowest population growth rates. Four Middle Eastern countries rank in the category of 'high human development': Bahrain, Kuwait, UAE and Qatar. While Kuwait's annual population growth rate has remained at 2.5% on average since 1975, the others are due to experience dramatic drops . . . "[42] In the case of the GCC countries, however, the period of rapid population growth, particularly during the "oil decade," was actually the "bonanza economic period," while the period of relatively low population growth rates, due to declining labor immigration following the end of the "oil decade," was characterized by a severe recession (see Chapter 4). Thus, by combining the natural increase rates of the indigenous populations and labor immigration together, Laipson, unfortunately, reached a mistaken conclusion. The best illustration for the *positive connection* between population and economic growth rates in the case of the GCC economies is Dubai, where its extremely rapid population growth rates during the past decade resulted in large-scale labor importation which was driven by the rapid economic expansion.[43]

Since the early 1990s, the demographic data which are published by the GCC authorities have been significantly improved and extended.[44] This improvement, it should be noted, was not only a result of the fact that since 2001 all of the GCC countries, without exception, have carried out a demographic census, but also due to the understanding of the GCC authorities (with the exception of that of Qatar) that a complete and updated socio-demographic database constitutes a precondition for any future socioeconomic planning. As the *Arab Human Development Report–2002* noted: "Any program is only as good as the information on which it is based."[45]

Nevertheless, despite the sharp improvement in the demographic data published by the GCC authorities in recent years, even today, with the exception of Oman, none of the other GCC countries publishes official data on a regular basis regarding the fertility and mortality rates of their indigenous populations. Such data can be obtained from one source only, the UNESCWA publications.[46] However, since 2001, ESCWA stopped publishing its most important demographic publication, *the Demographic and Related Socio-Economic Data Sheets.* Hence, in many demographic areas, the only sources left for recent demographic trends are the official publications of the countries themselves.

2.4.1 Bahrain

Among the GCC countries, Bahrain has the longest history of population censuses, dating back to 1941 and continuing until 2001, the most recent census. In addition to the population censuses, another important demographic source is the Civil Registration System, which has kept an almost complete record of births and deaths of the indigenous population since the early 1980s.[47] The third important source, as in the other GCC countries, is the fertility and health surveys, the first of which was the *1989 Bahrain Child Health Survey* conducted within the framework of the *Gulf Child Health Survey Program* (*GCHS*); and the second was the *1995 Bahrain Family Health Survey*, conducted within the framework of the *Gulf Family Health Survey* (*GFHS*).[48]

2.4.2 Kuwait

Among the GCC countries, Kuwait has the longest history of population censuses, after Bahrain. The first census was conducted in 1957 and was followed by eight others, usually at five year intervals until 1985. The 1990 census was not held due to the Iraqi invasion in August of that year. The next census was conducted in 1995 and the latest one was carried out from March 29 until April 20, 2005 by 2,500 census officers. It was a complete census for all citizens and expatriates living in the country as well as Kuwaitis who were temporarily abroad, studying or receiving medical treatment.[49] As in Bahrain, in Kuwait, too, the population censuses represent the most important demographic source.

Registration of births and deaths has been required in Kuwait since 1952. In 1960, the first law requiring the compulsory registration of births and deaths was issued. Although six health bureaus were subsequently established, this did not initially result in accurate registration because of the many births that did not take place in public hospitals, especially among desert dwellers.[50] By 1970, however, it seems that birth registration had become virtually universal and death registration almost complete as well.[51] In 1977, an automated information center was established in the Civil Service Department in order to modernize public administration through a personal information system. By 1982, a civil data system was set up, containing a complete registry of both nationals and foreigners residing in the country and other data on the entire population.[52]

The major source for fertility patterns among the indigenous Kuwaiti population during the 1980s is the *1987 Kuwait Child Health Survey* (*1987-KCHS*), which was conducted as part of the *GCHS*. The survey provides data on the levels, trends and differentials of child mortality in Kuwait. It also identifies the major diversities in bio-demographic patterns, preferences and behaviors. The survey also examines the way in which Kuwait's socioeconomic modernization has shaped these patterns. In 1996, Kuwait, like the other GCC countries, conducted a *Family Health Survey* that provides data on a wide variety of demographic issues, including fertility and marriage patterns and contraceptive prevalence rates among married indigenous Kuwaiti women.

2.4.3 Oman

Oman has the shortest history of population censuses and demographic surveys, not only among the GCC countries, but among all the Arab countries. As a result of the severe limitations on the entrance of foreigners into the country, combined with the absence of accurate and updated statistical data or any other official demographic publications, very little was known about Oman's socioeconomic situation until the 1970s. As Eickelman noted: "Oman was almost as isolated as Tibet until a British-supported palace coup in 1970 replaced the Sultan with his son, the present ruler, Qabus bin Sa'id."[53] The only source regarding the Omani demographic composition during the 1970s is the 1975 household survey, which was conducted in five towns and later extended to another six. The topics covered by this survey included name, sex, current age, place of birth, age at first marriage, number of children, educational level, relationship with the head of household, nationality and basic economic characteristics.[54]

From the late 1970s onward, however, the demographic data on Oman steadily improved. The improvement of the socioeconomic data collection in Oman was a direct outcome of the massive socioeconomic development plans, starting with the First Five-Year Development Plan, 1976–1980, which was carried out by Sultan Qabus. More accurate socioeconomic data, including demographic data, were also required for attracting foreign investments which, already from the early 1970s, were considered in Oman as crucial due to the Sultanate's relatively low oil reserves.[55]

However, despite the improvement in socioeconomic data collection, Oman held its first demographic census ever in December 1993. The second Sultanate's demographic census was conducted a decade later, in December 2003. 5,000 persons participated in the census' different operations. This census made it possible to compare its results with those obtained in the first one. In addition, the 2003 census was of extreme importance as, according to the Omani Ministry of National Economy, "It provided the most accurate and reliable demographic data which is a precondition for any future socioeconomic plans,"[56] namely, Oman's long-term socioeconomic plan, known as "Oman 2020" (see Chapter 4).

The second significant source on Oman's demography is the two demographic surveys, which provide data on fertility patterns and contraceptive prevalence rates: the *1989 Oman Child Health Survey* (*1989–OCHS*) and the *1995 Oman Family Health Survey* (*1995–OFHS*).

The third major demographic source for Oman is the *Five-Year Socio-Economic Development Plans*, extends from the first plan covering the 1976–1980 period, until the present plan, covering the years 2006–2010. These plans include data and official estimates regarding the labor force structure,[57] both national and foreign, as well as some demographic data on the indigenous population, mainly those related to the composition of the indigenous workforce. In addition, all of the development plans contain detailed data regarding educational services, including the number of students and their distribution according to age and sex at each educational level. Such information is extremely important for demographic research in any country, but particularly in a country like Oman, which lacked many of the basic demographic statistics until the first census was conducted.

Following the 1993 population census, the Omani demographic data became the most diverse, updated and accurate among all the GCC countries. Thus, Oman is currently the only GCC country publishing data on an annual basis regarding CBR and CDR, TFR and infant mortality rates of the Omani indigenous population,[58] as well as the number of foreign workers and the breakdown according to nationality.[59] However, in Oman as well, the ethno-religious composition of the indigenous population remains unknown, as the authorities did not include it in the two censuses that were carried out. It should be noted, however, that in contrast to the other Arab countries, where the absence of the ethno-religious composition in the official publications is a result of political sensitivity, in the case of Oman it is driven by the fact that the ethno-religious composition of the indigenous population "is a non-issue," in the form that it almost totally absent from the Sultanate's politics.

2.4.4 Qatar

The first national population census in Qatar was conducted in April-May 1970. According to the report of the British Embassy in Beirut, the general under-enumeration of the census was approximately 6%. Other serious shortcomings of the census were age misreporting, high under-enumeration of females, primarily young girls, and misreporting of nationality of older immigrants.[60] The second Qatar's population census was carried out in 1986. However, only a small number of tabulations were published. Moreover, the results that were published showed evidence of fundamental defects and inaccuracies.[61] Qatar's third population census was held in 1997 and the latest Qatar's census was carried out in 2004. The 2004 census covered all individuals residing within the boundaries of the state at the reference point of time of the census-taking.[62]

Other important source for Qatar's demographic research is the two health surveys: the *1987 Qatar Child Health Survey* and the *1998 Qatar Family Health Survey*. Both of these surveys provided information on fertility patterns and contraceptive prevalence rates among Qatari as well as non-Qatari women.

However, despite the implementation of the 1970 census, Qatar's socio-demographic data continued to be the poorest among the Gulf countries. A 1980 ECWA report on Qatar's demography noted that: "Qatar does not maintain a system of vital registration, and though there is some recording on births in the capital Doha, there is virtually no information on a national scale of births, deaths, migration, marriage and divorce."[63] Since 1982, Qatari nationals are required to inform the authorities of births, deaths, marriages and changes in place of residence. However, despite the improvement in the demographic records, during the 1980s Qatari authorities continued not to publish these data.[64]

Due to the merging of the indigenous and the foreign populations into one demographic entity, the demographic indicators published in Qatar's *Annual Statistical Abstract* do not appear to be "normal." Thus, for example, it is reported that males comprise far more than 50% of the population, as the vast majority of the foreign workers in Qatar are males. According to the 1997 census results, there were 522,023 people in Qatar, of whom 342,459 were males (65.6%). However, it is unknown how many of these males are Qatari nationals and how many foreigners.[65]

According to the official website of Qatar's Planning Council, following the 2004 census, "various population and demographic . . . data has become available for three separate time periods, allowing for conducting analytical studies and observing civilizational development of the society."[66] However, although in many areas Qatar's demographic data indeed substantially improved, even following the 2004 census, Qatar's authorities continue not to publish any data regarding the composition of the population according to nationality. This is apparently done with the aim of disguising the huge majority of the foreign population within the total population. Consequently, we know that according to the 2004 census results, Qatar's total population was 744,029, made up of 496,382 males (66.7%) and 247,647 females (33.3%).[67] However, how much of the total Qatari population are nationals? This crucial information is not included in the published data of the census. The only section of the 2004 census data which the Qatari authorities published according to nationality is that of the labor force composition.[68] From these data, however, it is impossible to calculate the total Qatari population according to nationality.

In the same way, Qatar's authorities publish birth and death records only in nominal figures without specifying whether these data are related to nationals only or to the total population, including foreigners.[69] This missing information precludes accurate demographic data on the indigenous Qatari population. Due to such a lack of data, demographic research on Qatar has to draw primarily on semi-official data (such as the publications of the various UN bodies) and on unofficial estimates.

2.4.5 UAE

The first census in the Emirates which comprise the UAE was conducted during March-April 1968, when it was still under British control.[70] This census was "little more than a brief breakdown of the population by age, sex, religion, occupation, literacy, and level of education."[71] However, similar to Qatar, the UAE authorities also combined nationals and foreigners in their published demographic data. Thus, as one can see in Chart 1.1, in the first *Statistical Handbook* of the UAE, published in 1973, the only demographic information from the 1968 census was the total population of each emirate, with a breakdown of males and females, but not according to nationality.

The second census of the UAE was carried out in 1975. Although this census was more detailed and comprehensive than the 1968 census, the most important demographic data, namely, the distribution of the population according to nationality, had not been released. Consequently, standard demographic indicators, such as CBR, CDR, TFR, and infant and child mortality rates, were of little value as they combined both nationals and foreigners.[72] Birks and Sinclair noted in this regard: "A very limited amount of data has been released on the composition of the population in 1975. We know that in 1978 there were about 115,000 nationals."[73] This means that although the UAE had carried out two censuses, the most basic data on the national population

Chart 1.1 The 1968 Census of the Seven Emirates which Comprise the UAE

	Males	Females	Total
Dubai	35,620	23,351	58,971
Abu Dhabi	34,863	11,512	46,375
Sharjah	17,660	14,008	31,668
Ras al Khaimah	13,249	11,138	24,387
Fujairah	5,220	4,515	9,735
Ajman	2,212	2,034	4,246
Um al Quaiwain	1,982	1,762	3,744
Trucial Oman Scouts	1,100	–	1,100
Total 1968 Census	111,906	68,320	180,226

Source: UAE, Ministry of Planning, *Statistical Handbook – 1973* (Abu Dhabi, 1973), p. 2, table 2.

continued to be unknown. Therefore, even in the mid-1970s, it was impossible to categorize the UAE indigenous population even according the most basic demographic indicators.[74]

During the 1980s, two censuses were carried out in the UAE, the first in 1980 and the second in 1985. The fifth census was conducted in 1995. The latest census was held in 2005. The uniqueness of the 2005 census was that for the first time, the authorities published the census data with the breakdown of the population according to nationality in many of the basic demographic indicators.[75] The UAE authorities are particularly proud of that census, as they used "the latest technological and analytical techniques, including satellite technology to map buildings and personal digital assistance (PSAs) to record data, resulting in the most accurate and comprehensive study of the social and economic makeup of the UAE."[76]

Other important source for demographic research in the UAE is the two health surveys: the *Child Health Survey* and the *1995 UAE Family Health Survey*. Both of these surveys collected baseline data on major social and demographic indicators.

3 The "Flickering" Nature of the Saudi Arabian Demographic Data[77]

There is no way to be sure of the true size of the Kingdom's demographic challenge.

Anthony Cordesman, 2003[78]

No country in the Middle East presents as great a challenge to those dealing with demography as Saudi Arabia. This challenge is not a result of a lack of official data as was the case in Oman for example until the implementation of the 1993 census, but is rather due to the questionable reliability of the official Saudi demographic data. Prior to the first demographic census of 1962–1963, the differences between the various estimates on the number of the Saudi population were extremely wide. For example, in his book on Saudi Arabia, published in 1959, Lipsky opened the section dealing with the Saudi population by stating that: "Estimates of the total [Saudi] population vary from 3 million to 7 million,"[79] namely more than 100% between the lowest and the highest estimates – certainly a unique phenomenon among the Middle Eastern countries.

According to the 1962–1963 census data, the Saudi national population numbered 3,302,330.[80] The 1962–1963 census, however, did not solve the problem of the accurate number of Saudi population. This is because while the Saudi authorities considered this census incomplete, mainly due to large-scale undercount of the nomadic population,[81] Birks and Sinclair on the other hand argued that "the 1962/63 census figure of 3.3 million was of the right order."[82] In any case, only parts of the census results, i.e. those pertaining to certain cities, were published by the Saudi Central Department of Statistics (CDS).[83] According to the Population Division of the UN, the 1962–1963 census results were not published "mainly because of largely incomplete enumeration."[84]

In general, during the 1960s and the early 1970s, the Saudi practical policy regarding publication of demographic data was that of omission. This policy is evident in many and varied examples, the most prominent of which is the absence of a demographic chapter from the *Statistical Yearbooks* of the CDS, published since 1965. This absence, however, is very unique, as normally, a country's general statistical abstract/yearbook contains a separate demographic chapter, usually the first or second. The logic for publication of the demographic chapter as one of the first two chapters of the statistical abstract/yearbook is that the demographic data is not only the most basic information regarding any given country, but in order to examine the socioeconomic situation of any society, many of the socioeconomic indicators, such as GDP, GNP and various social services, are measured in per capita terms.

The need for accurate and updated socioeconomic data became even more crucial in Saudi Arabia during the late 1960s, as a prerequisite for preparing the Kingdom's first Development Plan for 1970–1975 period. Indeed, in the plan itself, it was written that "Statistics that describe the operation of a country's economic and social forces are rightfully a matter of national concern."[85] Thus, the question of what could be useful for future social plans without even knowing the number of the country's population remained unanswered.

The second Saudi demographic census, carried out in September 1974, was considered by the Saudi authorities to be the first complete enumeration of the population. According to the census data, the Kingdom's total population numbered 7,012,643, including both nationals and foreigners.[86] However, some serious problems in the accuracy and reliability of the census data are apparent, primarily regarding the reported age-sex composition of the national population.[87] Moreover, many researchers claimed that the official figure for Saudi citizens, 6,218,361, is "too high." True indigenous Saudi population estimates in 1974–1975 varied, running from as low as 3.3 million to 5.6 million.[88] Thus, following the implementation of the second census, the number of Saudi citizens also remained considerably questionable. A joint study of the Saudi Ministry of Planning and the World Bank, published in 1984, noted in respect to the Saudi demographic data that: "Current estimates and reported figures are particularly perplexing when that early estimate and the two censuses of 1962–63 and 1974 are juxtaposed."[89]

According to the third Saudi census, carried out in September 1992, the Saudi national population numbered 12,310,302. However, as was the case in the 1974 census, the official data of the census regarding the number of Saudi citizens were doubtful and unofficial estimates put the true number of Saudi citizens in 1992 much below the census data. According to an estimate of Birks and Sinclair, for example, by mid-1992 Saudi national population numbered only 8.07 million.[90] The US Embassy in Riyadh estimated that the number of Saudi citizenry population in 1988 "ranged between 5 and 6 million."[91] Regarding the reliability of the Saudi official demography data in the early 1990s, Wilson and Graham claimed that: "Staffers at both the Ministry of Planning and the Ministry of Finance and National Economy told the authors that they regularly used padded figures on the orders of their superiors."[92]

This substantial gap between the various official, semi-official and the unofficial sources regarding the true number of the Saudi citizenry looks strange. This is particularly so because since the 1960s, but primarily following the "oil boom," the Saudi government has provided various services to its citizens, some of which, such as healthcare and education, require accurate data not only regarding the total citizenry population, but also according to age and sex. Moreover, many of the governmental direct payments, such as welfare payments, are directed to specific persons or families. Indeed, data on such governmental direct payments, for both individuals and families, have been published by the CDS since 1970. Thus, for example, according to CDS data, the number of the Saudi families who received social security assistance increased from 64,000 in 1970 to 306,000 in 1984. The corresponding number of individual beneficiaries increased during the corresponding period from 198,000 to 903,000.[93] It is obvious that the prerequisite for governmental direct payments to individuals is a precise demographic database of all potential beneficiaries.

Overall, the reasons which were raised by the researchers for the inflation of the number of the Kingdom's citizenry by the authorities are the following four:

(a) **The Saudi authorities desired to show that the Kingdom was not only rich in oil, but also had a large population** which constituted a major factor in the balance of power in the three major spheres, namely, the Gulf, particularly in relation to its traditional opponents – Iraq and Iran, the inter-Arab arena and OPEC. Birks and Sinclair noted in the late 1970s that: "Years of uncertainty and political pressures have led to the parlance of a series of population estimates of a much greater order."[94]

(b) **The Saudi authorities desired to minimize the declared share of the foreigners within both the Kingdom's total population and in the labor force.** In this respect, as was previously examined, Saudi Arabia was no different from the other Gulf labor-importing countries.

(c) **The absolute number of the population was an important factor in determining OPEC quotas** for oil production during the 1970s and the 1980s. This was particularly important following the end of the "oil decade" in 1983 when oil prices were low and each member of OPEC attempted to increase its quota at the expense of the others.[95]

(d) **The Saudi Wahhabi-Hanbali authorities wished to minimize the percentage of the Shi'a minority** within the total Saudi indigenous population.[96]

Following the 1992 census, however, the Saudi official demographic data, on both the indigenous and the foreign populations, have been largely expanded. The first *Statistical Yearbook* which included any demographic data was that of 1993 which provided the basic results of the 1992 census, namely, the total population with a breakdown into nationality and sex (see Chart 1.2).

The Thirty-Second *Statistical Yearbook*, published in 1996, was the first which had a separate demographic chapter. The chapter included the main results of the 1992 census, namely, the total Saudi population, with data on nationals and foreigners, sex,

Chart 1.2 Saudi Arabian Demographic Data Prior to 1999

Population and Housing:
Preliminary results of the population and housing census taken on 1/4/1413 A.H. (27/9/1992A.D.) show the following :

Total population is	16,929,294
Number of Saudis is	12,304,835 representing 72.7 % of total population.
Number of Saudi males is	6,211,213 representing 50.5% of Saudi population.
Number of Saudi females is	6,093,622 representing 49.5% of Saudi population.
Number of non-Saudis is	4,624,459 representing 27.3% of total population.
Number of non-Saudi males is	3,255,328 representing 70.4% of non-Saudi population
Number of non-Saudi females is	1,369,131 representing 29.6% of non-Saudi population.
Number of houses is	2,791,044, some of which are occupied by a large number of inhabitants.

Source: The Kingdom of Saudia Arabia, Ministry of Planning, CDS, *Statistical Yearbook – 1995* (Riyadh, 1996), p. 16.

age groups, marital status, administrative areas and households.[97] The next two issues, those of 1997 and 1998, included the same data as that of the 1996 issue.[98] Since 1999, the demographic chapter of the *Statistical Yearbook* presents the current demographic situation in the Kingdom as it is presented in Chart 1.3.

Chart 1.3 Saudi Arabian Demographic Data Since 1999

Population by Sex and Nationality in Administrative Areas, 1999

Administrative	Total			Non Saudi			Saudi		
Areas	T.	F.	M.	T.	F.	M.	T.	F.	M.
Riyadh	448528	1982290	2502738	1404717	465217	939500	3080311	1517073	1563238
Makka	5193149	2405369	2787780	1812933	697449	1115484	3380216	1707920	1672296
Jazan	1071478	528309	534169	102992	38958	64034	968486	489351	479135
Eastern Province	2886661	1246224	1640437	706951	196926	510025	2179710	1049298	1130412
Assyear	1563015	739564	823451	190913	45644	145269	1372102	693920	678182
Oaseem	933146	427507	505639	172764	42712	130052	760382	384795	375587
Hail	495769	234889	260880	65724	16881	48843	430045	218008	212037
Madinah Monawarah	1310448	611310	699138	302049	104836	197213	1008399	506474	501925
Baha	459172	236219	222953	40525	11343	29182	418647	224876	193771
Northern Bord	237074	111871	125203	26165	8371	17794	210909	103500	107409
Tabouk	560212	258348	301864	81051	24259	56792	479161	234089	245072
Najran	367672	162254	205418	59450	12887	46563	308222	149367	158855
Jowf	332408	145952	186456	56194	9169	47025	276214	136783	139431
Total	19895232	9090106	10805126	5022428	1674652	3347776	14872804	7415454	7457350

Source: The Kingdom of Saudi Arabia, Ministry of Planning, CDS, *Statistical Yearbook–1999* (Riyadh, 2000), p. 501, table 12-1.

The latest census in Saudi Arabia was carried out in September 2004. The results of the census showed that the Kingdom's total population numbered 22,673,538 people, 16,529,302 of whom were nationals (72.9%) and 6,144,236 foreigners (27.1%).[99] These data reveal that the Saudi national population increased by 4,224,467 nominally and by 34.3% during 12 years, 2.49% on annual average, compared to an annual average of 3.87% during the period between the 1974 and the 1992 censuses.[100] The 2004 census data, however, raises two main reservations:

First, according to the Saudi CDS data, by mid-2003, the Saudi citizenry population numbered 16.96 million (see Table 1.2). Taking into consideration a 2.49% annual growth rate, this means that the Saudi citizens were supposed to number 17.38 million in mid-2004. Since the census was held in September, we would expect that the Saudi citizens would be approximately 17.5 million at the time of the census – about one million more than the actual census results, equivalent to 6% of the total Saudi citizenry in 2004.

The second reservation regarding the 2004 census results is that both the Saudi official and the semi-official data on the natural increase rates of the Saudi citizenry population during the period between the 1992 and the 2004 censuses were constantly and significantly higher than 2.49%, which was the average annual population growth rate between the 1992 and the 2004 censuses (see Table 1.2).

As population growth is the sum of natural increase rate ± migration balance, one explanation for the wide gap between the population growth rates and the natural increase rates is a negative migration balance of the Saudi citizens which compensated for the much higher natural increase rates. This, however, as is well known, was not the case, as the migration balance of the Saudi citizenry was positive from the beginning of the oil era, but particularly following the "oil boom," although not in considerable numbers due to the strict Saudi naturalization regulations. The prohibition of the Saudi law on dual citizenship contributed to the positive migration balance, as Saudi citizens did not want to loose their citizenship, primarily in light of the various rental incomes driven directly from their Saudi citizenship.

Moreover, as the vast majority of those who became naturalized as Saudi citizens were and still are women who married Saudi males,[101] this by itself produced higher fertility rates of the Saudi national population. Therefore, if the migration balance was positive, or at least not substantially negative, the only remaining option which could explain the relatively low population growth rates during the 1992–2004 period is that the reported natural increase rates of the Saudi national population for the corresponding period were largely inflated.

As the natural increase rate is the sum of CBR minus CDR, either the reported CDRs were exaggeratedly low, or the reported CBRs were exaggeratedly high. Regarding the CDRs, the wide-based age pyramid (see Chapter 3), as a result of previous long-term high natural increase rates, combined with the steady life expectancy increase due to the tremendous living standard improvement following the "oil boom," produced an extremely low CDRs among the Saudi citizenry. In fact, this rate was one of the lowest worldwide – an average of 4–5 per 1,000 people throughout the 1990s and the early 2000s (see Table 2.4).

Thus, the only explanation left is a sharp CBRs decline to below 30 per 1,000 in order to achieve a natural increase rate of no more than 2.5% on an annual average during the 1992–2004 period. However, all of the available data, as indicated in Table 1.2, firmly contradict this level, and point to CBRs of much above 30 per 1,000 during most of the 1992–2004 period. Also the official CDS statistics pointed to a population growth of much above 2.5% annually during the 1992–2004 period. According to the 1992 census data, the natural increase rate of the Saudi indigenous population was 3.3%.[102] The CDS pointed to a growth rate of the Saudi national population during 1995–2000 of 3.5% on annual average.[103] Only the data for the early 2000s indicated that the population growth rate of the Saudi citizenry declined to below 3%, but certainly not to below 2.5%. According to the latest UN data, during the year prior to the September 2004 census, the births in Saudi Arabia totaled 499,734 and the death totaled 75,337. Thus, according to the UN data, in the year prior to the 2004 census, the CBR of the Saudi citizenry was 30.6 per 1,000 and the CDR was 4.6 per 1,000, that is, a natural increase rate of 2.6%.[104] According to Saudi official data, by 2004 the Saudi national population increased by 2.6%.[105] According to the latest Saudi official data, by mid-2006, the Saudi national population numbered 17.270 million, representing an increase of 2.5% from the previous year.[106] Unofficial sources, however, claim that the annual growth rate of the Saudi national population remained above 3% during the early 2000s as well.[107]

The statistics on the fertility level of the Saudi women during the 1992–2004 period, indeed confirm the available data on CBRs above 30 per 1,000. Thus, for example, according to a demographic survey which was carried out by the Saudi Ministry of Planning in 1999, the TFR of the Saudi national women averaged 4.53 children per woman.[108] This rate, according to another survey, slightly declined to 4.3 children per woman in 2002.[109] Also the findings of the *Health of the Saudi Family* research, carried out in early 2003, can be used as another indicator for the continuing high fertility rates among the Saudi national women in recent years as well. According to the research findings, only 10% of the participants wanted less than four children, 30% wanted 4–5 children, 30% wanted 6–7 children and 30%, 8 or more children.[110] Therefore, statistically, it is impossible in any given society with demographic characteristics such as those of the Saudi citizenry, namely, normal sex distribution, a wide-based age pyramid, TFR of above four children per woman and high life expectancy, that the natural increase rate would only be 2.5%.

Moreover, the Saudi socioeconomic development plans were based on a much higher projected population growth rate than 2.5% annually. Thus, for example, the Saudi Seventh Five-Year Development Plan for the 2000–2004 period predicted that during the years 1999–2004, the Saudi national population would increase from 15.658 million to 18.520 million, representing an increase of 18.28% within only five years, that is, an average annual growth rate of 3.4%.[111] For the 2000–2020 period, the predicted was that the average annual growth rate would be 3.0%.[112]

It should also be noted that the unofficial sources pointed to very high growth rates of the Saudi citizenry during the 1990s and the early 2000s. Thus, for example, Ramady wrote in 2005 that: "The Saudi population was not only one of the fastest growing, but also one of the most fertile; the proportion of infants per woman was considerably higher than in other regions of the world. Regardless of whether Saudi or non-Saudi estimates are absolutely correct, it is extremely clear that rapid population growth is taking place in Saudi Arabia."[113]

Not only does the available data not support the possibility of a sharp fertility decline of the Saudi national women in a period of only a decade, but this option is also in contradiction to the worldwide demographic experience that a sharp fertility decline could either be a result of a comprehensive family planning program, such as

Table 1.2 Saudi Arabian Demographic Indicators, 1992–2004

Year	**Saudi national population** (millions) (official and semi-official data)	CBR	CDR	NI (%)	TFR
1992 (census)	12.31	42.7	4.6	3.8	7.0
1994	13.05	37.8	4.5	3.3	6.1
1996	14.32	44.6	3.8	4.1	7.3
1998	14.47	35.5	4.3	3.1	5.0
1999	14.87	–	–	–	4.5
2000	15.58	28.9	4.0	2.5	4.4
2001	16.04	–	–	–	–
2002	16.49	–	–	–	4.3
2003	16.96	–	–	–	–
2004 (census)	16.53	30.2	4.6	2.6	–

– No data available.
CBR = Crude birth rate per 1,000 people.
CDR = Crude death rate per 1,000 people.
NI = Natural Increase Rate (%).
TFR = Total Fertility Rate.

Sources: The Kingdom of Saudi Arabia, CDS, *Statistical Yearbook*, various issues (Riyadh); al-Mamlaka al-'Arabiyya al-Sa'udiyya, Wizarat al-Iqtisad wal-Takhtit, *al-Nataij al-Awaliyya lil-Ta'dad al-'Amm lil-Sukan wal-Masakin – 1425A.H.* [2004] (Riyadh, 2004); SAMA, *Annual Report*, various issues (Riyadh); ESCWA, *Demographic and Related Socio-Economic Data Sheets for Countries of the Economic and Social Commission for Western Asia*, various issues (Amman and Beirut).

those implemented in Tunisia and Egypt in the case of the Arab countries for example, or due to a radical change in women's status, primarily in their employment opportunities, as has been the case in the developed countries. In both cases, however, the fertility rates declined gradually, stretching over a generation at least.

The reality in the case of Saudi Arabia in both areas was quite the contrary. Not only did the Saudi authorities not carry out a family planning plan, but they implemented some major pro-natalist measures (see Chapter 5). Insofar as women's employment opportunities, they discouraged them, and actually prevented women's employment through both social norms and legal regulations, such as the prohibitions on women driving or mixing together with males in the workplace (see Chapter 3). Hence, one can not escape the conclusion that rapid fertility decline did not occur in Saudi Arabia during the past decade and thus the option of radical fertility decline which led to a sharp reduction of the natural increase rates should be eliminated as well.

It is quite surprising, however, that neither the CDS, nor the semi-official and the unofficial sources have thus far raised any objections to, or at least expressed amazement at the 2004 census data regarding the number of Saudi citizens. Both the 2005 and 2006 SAMA annual reports only presented the census data.[114] Also the research department of the NCB (National Commercial Bank),[115] in its *Market Review & Outlook*, only presented the major results of the census.[116] In addition, the famous economic weekly, the *Saudi Economic Survey*, only reported the Kingdom's total population, breaking down the data into Saudi nationals and foreigners, but did not even mention the unexpected results regarding the number of Saudi nationals.[117] Thus far, the EIU is the only source that at least indicated "the discrepancy" between the 2004 census results and the CDS data regarding the growth rates of the Saudi citizenry during the two years prior to the census.

Therefore, the question remains: if the migration balance was positive, or at least not negative, and the annual natural increase rate was much above 2.5% during the 1990s and only declined to 2.5%–2.6% in the early 2000s, how is it that the Saudi national population increased by only 2.49% on an annual average during the 1992–2004 period? In light of this discrepancy, either the reported Saudi citizenry number was inflated in the 1992 census, or that of the 2004 census was deflated. My assumption is that the 2004 census data is the accurate figure, based on four main factors:

***(a)* The Saudi regime has no reason to "deflate" the number of the kingdom's citizenry**.

***(b)* The reasons, both internal and external, that might have brought the Saudi authorities to inflate the number of Saudi citizens, had become irrelevant during recent years.** In regards to the internal arena, the greatest internal political challenge of the Saudi regime is no longer the Shi'i opposition, but rather the Sunni fundamentalist opposition group of *al-Qa'ida*. Thus, there is no need to "minimize" the percentage of the Shi'a minority within the total Saudi citizenry as the previous undeclared approach had been (see below). In addition, the Saudi citizenry population was large enough in 2004 and even without inflating its number the percentage of the foreign population within the total Kingdom's population had declined to less than one-fourth.

From the international point of view, it seems that the two previous major reasons of the Saudi regime to "inflate" the number of citizens were also eliminated in the early 2000s. The first and most important factor, namely, the military balance with Iraq, was eliminated following the collapse of the Saddam Husayn regime in April 2004. The second factor, "the demographic connection" of OPEC oil production quotas, became irrelevant following the September 11, 2001 *al-Qa'ida* attacks on the US. This is because since then, from both the political and economical viewpoints, the Saudi regime has been eager to increase the Kingdom's oil production as much as possible in order to preserve their role as a "swing producer."[118]

***(c)* Growing socioeconomic problems, primarily increasing unemployment among young Saudis, require accurate demographic data** since they constitute the prerequisite for formulating long-term employment strategy (see Chapter 4). Therefore, the collection and publication of accurate socio-demographic data had become crucial for the Saudi authorities themselves.

***(d)* Under the leadership of King 'Abdallah, a profound change occurred in Saudi Arabia, allowing for open discussion on many previously taboo political, social and economic topics**. Moreover, in recent years, many indications suggest that Saudi authorities are more open to supplying information that they were previously reluctant to provide. The current Eighth Five-Year Development Plan, covering the 2005–2009 period, emphasizes the need for improving the collection of socioeconomic data: "The Kingdom continues to make efforts to develop its national statistical system and promote public awareness of the crucial importance of statistical data and information to the success of economic and social development."[119] Indeed, the EIU noted in this regard that:

> Official efforts to collect and publish employment data are in stark contrast to the recent past, when such information was never made available. The [Saudi] authorities aim to create a database that will enable them to place unemployed Saudis in work and penalize companies that fail to hire enough nationals.[120]

How much was the 1992 official data of the Saudi citizenry inflated? Taking into consideration the most accepted natural increase rates during the 1992–2004 period, namely an annual average of 3.3% for 1992–1999 and 2.6% for 2000–2004, calculations put the population at approximately 11.6 million for September 1992 – about 700,000 less than the actual census data. Even if we assume a higher population growth rate of 3.2% on annual average for the whole 1992–2004 period, then the Saudi citizenry numbered about 11.4 million in September 1992. In any case, it seems unreasonable that the Saudi citizenry numbered less than 11 million in September 1992. Thus, the previously-mentioned estimates, both of the US Embassy in Riyadh which estimated that the number of Saudi citizens in 1988 "ranged between 5 and 6 million" and of Birks and Sinclair, who put the number at 8.1 million in mid-1992, were both tens of percent less than the actual figure.

As for the 1974 census results, even assuming the lowest option of only 11 million Saudi citizens in September 1992 and an annual average growth rate of 3.87% between the 1974 and 1992 censuses, which is the most reasonable figure, then Saudi citizens in September 1974 numbered approximately 5.5 million. Thus, the figure that Birks and Sinclair suggested for 1975 – 4.593 million[121] – which was and still is widely quoted, including by myself in the first edition of this book, was probably 20–25% less than the actual number.

The surprising 2004 census data has probably solved the half-century debate on the Saudi citizenry number. A database can now be established, although in broad terms only, regarding the number of Saudi citizens since 1974 through deducing the most reasonable population growth rates from the 2004 census results (the "back projection method"). This database, in turn, will permit researchers for the first time ever to examine the Saudi socioeconomic history since the early 1970s not only at the national macro-level, but in per capita terms as well.

4 The "Missing" Ethno-Religious Composition of the Arab Countries

Like many other countries worldwide, in the Middle Eastern countries as well, there is no correlation between ethnicity and political borders. The major reason for this lack of correlation is the fact that many of the current Middle Eastern states were established following World War I through a series of agreements between the UK and France according to their own interests rather than the interests of the local populations. With time, the ethno-religious composition in many Arab countries has become a "hot" political issue. This political sensitivity was an outcome of frequent clashes between the regime and one or more of the minorities, or even more frequently in cases when the regime itself was of a religious minority, such as in Syria, Iraq, Bahrain and Lebanon. The most representative expression for this political sensitivity is the absence of the ethno-religious composition from the official demographic records of all of the Arab countries.

It should be mentioned that a lack of ethno-religious data characterizes many worldwide developed countries as well. For example, only a limited number of European countries publish data on the ethno-religious composition of their citizens.[122] The US and Canada do not publish any official data according to religion. The official reason why these countries do not collect and publish data according to religion is that they are "secular countries." In the case of some of the EU countries, in recent years the religious composition of the population, particularly the steady increase in the percentage of "non-Christians," has become a major political issue which has been expressed in each of the recent elections (see Chapter 2).

Why is the ethno-religious composition of the Arab countries so politically sensitive? The answer to this question changes from one country to another, as will be examined through a number of examples in the following section.

4.1 Lebanon

The most famous case among the Arab countries in this regard is Lebanon. According to the 1932 census, the only census which has been carried out until the present, Christians constituted a slight majority (51.7%) of the total population.[123] The Lebanese political structure, as outlined in the 1943 National Pact, was based on this small Christian majority, mandating that the head of the state, the President, would be a Christian-Maronite. Furthermore, every six of 11 seats in the Parliament were designated for Christians and five for Muslims (including both the Sunnis and the Shi'is), and the Druze, thus ensuring Christian domination of the Lebanese political life.[124] However, the percentage of the Christians within the total Lebanese population has markedly decreased, particularly following the onset of the Second Civil War in 1975, mainly due to the following two factors:

(a) **The large-scale emigration of Christians from Lebanon**, which actually began in the late nineteenth century,[125] substantially increased following the onset of the first Lebanese Civil War (1958), and turned into a "flood" following the start of the Second Civil War.[126]

(b) **The much lower fertility rates of the Christians than those of the Muslims**, particularly the Shi'is in southern Lebanon. The reason for this is that the Lebanese Christians, similar to many other Middle Eastern Christian communities, entered into the second phase of the Demographic Transition, namely a reduction in the death rates, much earlier than most of the Middle Eastern Muslim communities. As Fargues noted, "Having been the first to reduce their death rates . . . they were also the first to limit their birth rates, which now helps to diminish their proportion of the population."[127] Thus, throughout the second half of the twentieth century, the natural increase rates of the Lebanese Christians were remarkably lower than that of the Muslims. Moreover, the large-scale emigration also contributed to the much lower natural increase rates of the Lebanese Christians. This is because the vast majority of the emigrants were young people of childbearing age.

The October 1989 Taif Agreement, which ended the Lebanese Second Civil War, divided the 128 Parliament seats equally between the Christians and the Muslims. However, even this change does not really represent the true picture in Lebanon's religious composition, as it "a well-known secret" that the Muslims, not including the Palestinian refugees, represent much above 50% of the total population. How much above? By 1990, according to Held, 33% of the Lebanese population were Shi'is, 20%

Sunni-Muslims, 20% Maronite, 8% Greek Orthodox, 6% Greek Catholic, 4% Armenian-Christians and 8% Druze.[128] Thus, by 1990, according to Held's estimate, the percentage of the Christians within the total Lebanese population had declined to less than 40%. Taking into consideration the 392,000 Palestinian refugees that lived in Lebanon at that time,[129] of whom the vast majority – more than 90%, as in other Palestinian communities – were Sunni-Muslims,[130] the percentage of the Christians within the total Lebanese population at the dawn of the twenty-first century did not exceed 30%–34%, while that of the Muslims, both Sunnis and Shi'is, was above 60%. This being the case, it is understandable why the Lebanese Christian authorities have refrained until the present not only from carrying out a population census, but also from publishing basic demographic data, such as births and deaths, according to religion. Faour noted in this respect that:

> By controlling the vital registration system, Maronite public officers were able never to disclose or publish data on the birth and death rates of the various [religious] sects. Nor have they released the number of citizens registered by religion. As a result, most of the published statistics on population size and religious composition are estimates that have unknown margins of error.[131]

4.2 Syria

The latest census that enumerated the Syrian population according to their ethno-religious composition was conducted in 1960 during the rule of the UAR. However, since the rise to power of the Ba'th party in March 1963, the official Syrian statistics divided the population into three categories in line with the secular party's ideology of *al-Qawmiyya al-'Arabiyya* (Arab nationalism): Syrian citizens, Palestinian refugees and foreigners.

Since the 1960 census, however, some major developments occurred in Syria that substantially affected its ethno-religious composition. First, there was the large-scale emigration of Sunni-Muslims which, since the late 1950 and throughout the 1960s, involved hundreds of thousands of businessmen and professionals who resented the Arab Socialist policy (*al-Ishtiraqiyya al-'Arabiyya*)[132] adopted during the UAR period and which was followed by the Ba'thi regime, particularly following the February 1966 neo-Ba'th *coup d'état*.[133] This large-scale emigration, combined with the substantial fertility differences between the various Syrian regions, markedly affected Syria's ethno-religious composition as a result of the following factors:

(a) The majority of the Syrian 'Alawites are still rural dwellers. As in the other Arab countries, fertility rates in the Syrian rural areas are much higher than in the urban centers (see Chapter 2). Hence, it is reasonable to assume that the average fertility rates of the Syrian 'Alawites since the implementation of the 1960 census and up to the present were considerably higher than the national average.

(b) As the 'Alawites were almost totally absent from the urban middle class prior to the mid-1960s, not only were they hardly harmed by the "Socialist measures," they rather enjoyed it, as they were traditionally the lowest socioeconomic stratum in the Syrian society. Thus, it is reasonable to assume that the scale of emigration from Syria among them was very minor in comparison to both the Christian and the Sunni-Muslim urban middle class.

(c) A similar process was occurring among the Syrian Kurds and the Druze,

namely, small-scale emigration as opposed to higher than the national average fertility rates. Hence, it is reasonable to assume that their share in the total Syrian population also increased considerably since 1960.

(d) The fertility rates of the Syrian Christians were, and probably still are, considerably lower than the national average, *inter alia*, since almost all of them belong to the urban middle class.[134] Therefore, it is likely that since 1960 the percentage of the Christians within the total Syrian population has steadily decreased.

(e) Although the Syrian authorities do not publish migration data according to religion, it seems that the large-scale emigration of the urban middle class and professionals from Syria during the 1960s and early 1970s involved many Christians that were represented in considerable numbers in these two groups. This large-scale emigration led to further decline in the percentage of the Christians within the total Syrian population.

Taking into consideration the probably higher than average fertility rates among the 'Alawites, the Kurds, and the Druze on the one hand, and the probably lower than average fertility rates among the Christians and the Sunni-Muslim urban dwellers on the other, along with the large-scale emigration from Syria of these two strata, the end result is that Syria's religious composition at the start of the twenty-first century is remarkably different from the structure presented by the 1960 census results.

How much different? According to the 1947 census data, the Syrian 'Alawites numbered 339,466 and they constituted 11.2% of Syria's total population.[135] According to the 1960 census data, their number amounted to 495,000,[136] namely, 10.6% of the total Syrian population. This decline was probably a result of the higher than national average mortality rates of the 'Alawites as a result of their lower living standard. According to the EIU estimate, in the late 1990s, the Syrian population was comprised of some 70% Sunni-Muslims, while the rest of the population consisted of 'Alawites (12%), Christians of the Maronite, Greek, Armenian and Syrian Orthodox churches, as well as Protestant and Roman Catholic sects of Christianity (9%). In addition there were Druze (3.5%), and the rest were Isma'ilis and Shi'is. Was the percentage of the 'Alawites in the late 1990s indeed 12%, namely, almost without any change since the ascendancy of the Ba'th party to power in 1963? My estimate is that due to the above-mentioned factors, the current percentage of the 'Alawites within the total Syrian population is actually much above the traditional estimate of 12%, although we do not yet have the methodological tool to set a new percentage.

With regard to Syria's ethnic composition, the largest ethnic minority, located in the north of the country near the Syrian–Turkish border, is the Kurds, and they represent some 6.6% of the total Syrian population. While the vast majority of the Kurds in Syria are Sunnis, a small number are *Yazidis*.[137] The second ethnic minority is that of the Armenians, all of whom are Christians. There are also a small number of Turkman and Circassian minorities.[138] As in the case of the religious composition, in the case of the ethnic composition as well, we do not have any methodological tool to evaluate the accuracy of the common estimates, all of which are based on the 1960 census data.

4.3 Jordan

In sharp contrast to Syria, from a religious viewpoint, Jordan is one of the most homogenous of the Arab countries, with the Arab Sunni-Muslims constituting approximately 93% of the total population. The largest minority group is that of the Christians, which constituted approximately 6% of the total Jordanian population in 2003.[139] According to other estimates, their percentage in the Kingdom was much lower, assessed at only 3.6% in 2000.[140]

There are two major ethnic minorities in Jordan. One is the Circassians, who were deliberately planted in the area of current Jordan by the Ottomans during the late nineteenth century and early twentieth century. Indeed, modern Amman itself owes its revival to the Circassians.[141] By the early 1990s, their number was estimated at 35,000. The second important ethnic minority in the Kingdom is the Shishanis, most of them having arrived to Jordan during and following World War I. Their number was estimated at approximately 4,000 in the early 1990s.[142]

In Jordan, the "demographic sensitivity" is the division between "Jordanians" and "Palestinians." Generally speaking, the fear of the Hashemite regime in this respect is that if the regime would officially admit that the majority of Jordanian citizens are Palestinians, its legitimacy would disappear. Thus, the only two official demographic data on the Jordanian population are: first, the division of the population according to religion – given that this is not a sensitive political issue due to the homogeneity of the Kingdom's population in this respect – and second, the number of Palestinians living in the refugee camps and the total number of Palestinian refugees, both of which are published by UNRWA.[143]

The only methodological option to estimating the percentage of the "Jordanians," that is, those who were living on the East Bank of the Jordan River before the 1948 War and their offspring, within the total Jordanian population is to add the natural increase rates to the number of the East Bank population before 1948, assuming zero migration balance, as there are neither official nor unofficial figures regarding the scale of Jordanian citizens who permanently emigrated from the Kingdom according to their "ethnic origin." The rest are Palestinians. The only figure on the East Bank population prior to the 1948 War is the British data – 433,659 people in 1946.[144] Considering a 3% natural increase rate on annual average since 1948 until the year 2000, it seems that the number of "Jordanians" on the East Bank of Jordan by the year 2000 was no more than 2.1 million of the 5.039 million Jordanians.[145] The meaning of these calculations is clear: By the year 2000, the Palestinians constituted at least 60% of the Kingdom's total population.[146]

4.4 Egypt

From an ethnic point of view, Egypt is the most homogeneous among the Arab countries, as almost 100% of its population are Arabs. Egypt is homogeneous from a religious point of view as well. According to the 1986 census, 94.1% of Egypt's citizens were Muslims, almost all of whom were Sunnis, while the Christian Copts constituted 4.9% of the total population. In addition, approximately 50,000 Egyptians belong to other Christian sects.[147] According to one estimate from the mid-1980s, the Christians represented approximately 6.3% of the total Egyptian population.[148] Other unofficial estimates put the Copt percentage at much higher levels of more than 8% of the total Egyptian population in the mid-1980s.[149] The CIA estimates the percentage of the Copts within the total Egyptian population in the early 2000s at 6%.[150] Although the exact percentage of the Copts is still debatable, it is generally accepted that the share of the Copts within the Egyptian population is considerably higher than the official figures, estimated at roughly 6%–8%.[151]

4.5 *Saudi Arabia*

From ethno-religious points of view, almost 100% of the Saudi nationals are Arabs and Muslims. The dominant and the official Saudi religious sect is that of Wahhabi-Hanbali (Sunnis).[152] It should be noted, however, that officially the Saudi regime does not make any distinction between the four Sunni schools (*madhhab*, masculine plural *madhahib*). As noted by the founder of the Kingdom, 'Abdel 'Aziz ibn Sa'ud in a speech delivered in March 11, 1929: "We hold no preference between Malike and al-Safie, Ahmad and Abu-Hanifa; in our view they are all to be respected by us."[153] The vast majority of the Hejaz's population is Sunnis-Shafi'i, some of whom originated from South Arabia. In the southern areas, there are also Isma'ilis and Zaydis,[154] originally from Yemen.

The only official religious minority in Saudi Arabia is that of the Shi'is, with most of them concentrated in al-Hasa (the Eastern) province, mainly in the city of Qatif and around the city of Madina. The number of the Shi'is in Saudi Arabia is unknown as they are not distinguished from the Sunni majority in the civil registration system or in the censuses. Although they are officially estimated at 1 million,[155] according to unofficial sources they number approximately 1.5 to 2 million, namely between 10–15% of the current Saudi citizenry.[156]

4.6 *Bahrain*

Although 65%–70% of the Bahraini citizenry population are Shi'is, and the rest of the indigenous population, including the royal family, Al Khalifa, are Sunnis,[157] the Bahraini authorities have long insisted that the Shi'i community in the country comprises no more than 35% of the total indigenous population. The issue of Sunni-Shi'i relations rose to the forefront during the mid-1990s when Shi'i activists staged violent confrontations with the security forces due to domestic developments.[158]

5 The Lacuna of Accurate Employment Data

> Unfortunately, officially published data in ESCWA member countries are rather scanty, and the region has no strong tradition of regularly monitoring unemployment.
>
> ESCWA, *2004–5 Survey*[159]

The employment issue poses another prominent challenge for any socio-demographic and economic research on the Arab countries. This is because official unemployment data are either almost totally absent, as in the cases of Iraq and Yemen regarding most of the period examined in this book, or are reported as being much lower than they are in reality, as in the case of most of the other Arab countries.

Regarding the overall quality of the employment and unemployment data of the Middle Eastern countries, Richards and Waterbury noted in the mid-1990s that: "All data must be treated with considerable caution."[160] In the non-oil Arab countries, there is no system of unemployment insurance and therefore no reason for anyone to register as unemployed. Thus, as Wilson rightly claimed in the mid-1990s: "Any unemployment statistics which are published in the region are meaningless, even those reported to the ILO."[161] *The Middle East* monthly also noted in regard to the problematic employment data that: "Accurate figures are impossible to obtain since many states in the Middle East do not collect detailed labor statistics."[162]

Specifically, on Syria's official employment data, Kanovsky claimed in the mid-1980s that: "the unemployment figures are not very meaningful."[163] Almost two decades later, in the early 2000s, Syria's employment statistics remained unreliable. Thus, for example, by 2003, according to official Syrian figures, the unemployment rate amounted to 6.3%. The 2004–2005 ESCWA socioeconomic report, however, noted that: "ESCWA has reservations about this low unemployment rate, as the corresponding rate for 2002 was 11.7%, while the real Syrian GDP growth rate was only 2.6% in 2003."[164] In any case, an unemployment rate of 11.7% in Syria in 2002 also seems to be too low and unofficial sources claimed much higher rates of above 15% (see Chapter 3). Generally speaking, the misreporting of employment data in the Arab countries has four major dimensions:

(a) **The under-counting of female employment.** The reason for this is that in many cases, females work in agriculture within the rural household framework and thus are not taken into consideration when calculating the overall national female labor force participation rate. This is because the official female employment data is calculated only on the basis of those women who receive salaries, mainly in the urban formal sectors. Since the rural population continues to constitute a significant percentage of the population of the non-oil Arab countries, it is quite clear that the actual female labor force participation rates in the rural areas of the non-oil Arab countries are considerably higher than the official reported figures. In the 2004 ESCWA socioeconomic report, it was written in this regard that: "Because of measurement problems in estimating rural employment or the urban informal sector . . . , it is difficult to pin a number on the rates of women labor force participation."[165] Specifically regarding Oman's female labor force participation, Chatty noted that:

> Women from pastoral households are not included in official statistics on the economically active labor force in Oman. And in spite of their very active role in animal husbandry . . . , these women are categorized in the first Oman General Population Census as "housewives," and hence are excluded from enumeration.[166]

Large-scale women employment in the informal sector also exists in the urban centers of the poorer Arab countries (see below). Consequently, it is quite reasonable to assume that the official employment figures as well as the various semi-official estimates, primarily those of the ILO and other UN bodies, regarding female employment rates in the non-oil Arab countries are considerably lower than the actual figures.[167]

(b) **The inaccurate employment data relates to lower urban dwellers who are unable to find employment in the formal economy**, either in the public or in the private sector. These people work in jobs such as servants, porters, watchmen, and newspaper and cigarette vendors. In these varied capacities, they constitute another considerable segment of the urban informal employment, though many of them are included on the waiting list for public sector employment and thus officially categorized as "unemployed."

(c) **The deliberate under-reporting of actual unemployment rates by the**

authorities in an effort to hide the steady increase of unemployment rates. This phenomenon was particularly prevalent in the Gulf oil states. The lack of accurate and updated employment data on Saudi Arabia prompted 'Abd al-Rahman Al Rashid to write the article in late 1999 entitled "Saudi Arabia without Data."[168] The fear of the GCC royal families was that public acknowledgement of the high unemployment rates among nationals, parallel to the general deterioration in the living standard since the early 1990s would be tantamount to an admission of the failure in their basic role as "providers." This would put the basis of the "*rentier*" political system in danger (see Chapter 4). Thus, officials in the governmental bureaucracy as well as high-ranking politicians constantly denied the existence of high unemployment rates among the indigenous workforce.

For example, in an interview to the *MEED* in September 2002, the Secretary General of the Saudi Supreme Economic Council, 'Abd al-Rahman 'Abd al-'Aziz al-Tuwayjri, said as follows: "the unemployment rate in Saudi Arabia is not more than 8% for Saudis . . . I think this is a new and important figure to dispel all this nonsense about 20%–30% unemployment."[169] In another *MEED* interview published in mid-2003, al-Tuwayjri repeated his previous claim, stating that: "some people talk about an unemployment rate of 20%–30% – are simply incorrect."[170] However, in September 2002 al-Tuwayjri stated that: "One of the major challenges we face is providing jobs for the new generation."[171] Likewise, the discussion on the employment policy in the Saudi Seventh Five-Year Development Plan covering the period 2000–2004 also began by stating that: "Labor force development issues present some of the most important challenges for the Seventh Development Plan . . . "[172] Indeed, during the past decade, all of the Saudi as well as the socioeconomic development plans of the other GCC countries, without exception, have emphasized the issue of providing employment opportunities for the young generation as their major challenge. However, if in fact the unemployment rate among Saudi nationals is only 8%, surely the Saudi economy must have more severe socioeconomic challenges.

Unofficial and even semi-official figures, such as those of ESCWA, pointed to much higher unemployment rates, particularly among males, sometimes even as high as twice the official figures. For example, the 2001–2002 ESCWA socioeconomic report noted that: "a high-level Saudi Arabian official stated that the estimated unemployment in the country to be 20% in 2001."[173] In 2003, Saudi newspapers quoted a study conducted by SAMA which estimated the Saudi unemployment rate as high as 31.7%.[174]

This dichotomy between publishing low official unemployment rate on the one hand, and continuing to emphasize the acute employment challenge, particularly among young Saudis, on the other, has continued in recent years as well. While the Saudi official unemployment data for the Saudi national workforce were 7.0% for 2004 and 6.9% for 2005,[175] unofficial sources claimed much higher rates. For example, some Saudi bankers believed the unemployment rate in 2005 among Saudi national males was 20%. Some sources estimated the unemployment rate among the younger Saudis as closer to 30%.[176]

One can also find a very similar phenomenon in Bahrain, where the unemployment problem presents not only a socioeconomic challenge but a political one as well, insofar as the vast majority of the unemployed are rural Shi'is. In late 1998, according to unofficial estimates, while the unemployment rate among Bahraini nationals averaged 15%, it was as high as 30% among the Shi'a rural population.[177] According to an unofficial estimate, the unemployment rate in Bahrain in 2000 was as high as 17%, while the official Bahraini figure was only 3%[178] – lower than in all of the OECD countries.

If the unemployment rate in Bahrain was indeed as low as 3%, then it is puzzling as to why the Bahraini Minister of Finance and National Economy, 'Abdallah Sayf, said at the time that: "The most important challenge facing the Bahraini economy is job creation."[179] An economy with an unemployment rate of only 3% does not actually have an "unemployment problem" and thus could not consider unemployment to be its "most important challenge." Eventually, in early 2003, the Bahraini Crown Prince, Salman bin Hamed Al Khalifa, openly acknowledged that the actual unemployment rate in the country was 15%. The reality could no longer be avoided in light of the increasing visibility of the unemployment problem and in the wake of the demonstrations in which many of the unemployed participated, the vast majority of whom, it should be noted, were Shi'is.[180]

Among the poorer Arab countries, the same phenomenon of official unemployment rates being considerably lower than the actual rates prevails as well. For example, while the official Jordanian unemployment rate for 1998 was 15.2%, unofficial sources estimated the real rate as almost double the official figure.[181] In the case of Egypt, the official unemployment rate for the year 2000 was 8%,[182] yet unofficial sources estimated that the actual rate was more than double, between 15% and 25%.[183] Two years later, in 2002, the official number of the unemployed in Egypt was 1.9 million, while unofficial sources argued that this number was "far lower than reality."[184] In the case of Yemen, official figure indicated an unemployment rate of 11.5% in 2000; however, unofficial sources claimed that the rate "exceeded 23%".[185]

The unemployment data published by international official bodies were often based on the official figures and thus could not be useful. For example, in an article published in the IMF *Finance & Development* journal, Gardner used official unemployment data for the year 2000, with 7.9% for Egypt and 13.7% for Jordan.[186] Likewise, the ILO publishes the countries' official unemployment rates.[187] Using the official employment data as the basis for employment research is, of course, distorting the reality, thereby making the whole research useless.

(d) **The inconsistency in the number of migrant workers**, particularly in the case of Egypt, Jordan and North Yemen – the largest Arab labor-exporting countries. For example, according to an official Egyptian report for 1981, the number of Egyptian workers in other Arab countries was 1.149 million, while according to unofficial estimates the number was considerably higher – running between 1.5–2.5 million.[188] In the mid-1980s, according to the vast majority of sources, official and unofficial alike, the number of Egyptian workers abroad was approximately 3 million,[189] while according to the *MEED* reporter in Cairo, their real number was "about half" of the prevailing estimates.[190] Indeed, according to a survey conducted by the Egyptian National Population Council [*al-Majlis al-Qawmi lil-Sukan*], the number of Egyptians working abroad in 1985 was 1.4 million.[191] The HRD Base published quite a similar figure of 1.430 million Egyptian workers in other Arab countries in 1985.[192] With regard to the number of Egyptian workers abroad in the early 1980s, the EIU noted as follows:

> How many expatriates are there? . . . In the late 1970s the consensus was that the number was somewhere around 1 million. The 1976 census derived a figure of 1.6 million for Egyptian residents abroad, though this clearly included both workers and non workers, as well as temporary and permanent migrants . . . Last year [in 1983] the minister responsible for migra-

> tion produced figures showing 3.3 million Egyptians living abroad . . . Some people claimed that the numbers were even higher, the total for Egyptians in Iraq, for example, being nearer 2 million than the 1.25 million given by the minister. The counterclaim is that even 1.25 million is too high . . . [193]

Thus, if the actual number of Egyptian workers abroad in the mid-1980s was not over 3 million, but only half that number, then the real unemployment rate in Egypt at that time was higher than the prevailing estimates by as much as 7%–10%, considering that Egypt's total labor force at that time was approximately 11–12 million.

Regarding the other major Arab labor-exporting countries, mainly Jordan and North Yemen, one can also find considerable gaps between the various estimates regarding the real number of workers in the Arab oil countries. Fargues recently noted that: "Numbers of migrants [in the Arab region] vary according to who is counted as well as to who does the counting."[194] Overall, there are two major reasons for the inconsistent data on the number of Arab foreign workers in the Arab labor-importing countries. One is that some of the labor-exporting countries tend to inflate the number of migrants, while the labor-importing countries tend to underestimate their number.[195] The second factor is the huge number of illegal foreign workers, mainly in Saudi Arabia, where any Muslim worldwide is entitled to enter the Kingdom in order to fulfill the *Hajj* duty. Instead of returning to their home countries after completing the *Hajj* commitment, many of the pilgrims remain in the Kingdom as illegal workers. In Kuwait, the number of illegal foreign workers in 1979 was estimated at more than 100,000.[196] In the UAE, one also finds a similar phenomenon of large-scale illegal foreign workers.[197]

Another reason for the contradictory data on the number of workers abroad, perhaps, is that in many cases the sources unintentionally included the workers and their family members together.[198] In this respect, it should be taken into consideration that until the 1990–1991 Kuwaiti Crisis, the Gulf labor-importing countries maintained a liberalized policy regarding the entry of the family members of the foreign labor, particularly the Arab foreign labor. Whatever the reason, the result was the same, namely, contradictory estimates regarding the number of the labor abroad during the 1970s and the 1980s. This problem, however, was largely solved during the recent decade, as the labor-importing countries radically changed their policy and started to limit the entry of the accompanying family members (see Chapter 4).

With regard to conducting demographic research on the GCC countries, Bonine noted in the mid-1990s that: "It is particularly difficult because of the great number of foreigners within each country, some of whom may be working illegally."[199] Owen and Pamuk raised a very similar argument, claiming that: "so many workers entered the Gulf states illegally . . . "[200] Thus, due to the large unrecorded number of migrant workers who came from the poorer Arab countries to the Arab oil countries following the October 1973 "oil boom" and until the early 1990s, the employment data of both the Arab labor-exporting and the labor-importing countries are only partial.

6 The Research Implications of the "Informal (Hidden) Economy"

Another major obstacle to conducting socioeconomic and demographic research on the poorer Arab countries is the vast extent of the "informal economy," sometimes called a "cash," "underground" or "hidden economy." Although the definitions for the term "informal economy" are quite varied, it basically refers to an economy in which a significant percentage of its direct or indirect financial transactions and employment activities are not reported and thus do not appear in the official national accounts.[201] Roy noted that:

> The main components of the hidden economy represent economic activity – capital flows, imports, production, factor payments, rents, etc. – that is mostly unreported and unrecorded, legal [barters, home and small-scale industrial production], illegal [smuggling, tax evasion, and corruptions] or quasi-legal but have nevertheless the effects of which are not entirely invisible.[202]

In the non-oil Arab countries, in addition to the informal employment, there are three main dimensions of the widespread informal economy:

(a) **Low salaries paid in the public sector**, in most cases amounting to less than $100 per month, are not sufficient for supporting a family. Consequently, many public sector employees work in another workplace, as taxi drivers, tourist guides, waiters and the like, after, or even within, the formal working hours. All of these financial activities, naturally, go unreported and thus are not included in the official national accounts.

(b) **Workers' remittances** in the major Arab labor-exporting countries constituted the largest foreign exchange earner during the 1970s and 1980s, as well as a considerable percentage of the total GDP. In the case of Jordan, workers' remittances in the early 1980s constituted one-fourth to one-third of the total GDP, thus representing the largest non-governmental contributor to the national income.[203] Likewise, in Egypt, North Yemen, Syria and Sudan, the amount of the official workers' remittances during the 1970s and 1980s far exceeded earnings through the export of goods and services.[204]

However, a considerable percentage of the workers' remittances were not included in the official national accounts of the labor-exporting countries, due to the huge gap between the formal and the informal ("black market") exchange rates.[205] Rather, they were transferred through unofficial channels, mainly in cash by the workers themselves or by relatives and friends traveling home. In some cases, special agents dealt with these money transfers. Thus, the real scale of the workers' remittances during the 1970s and 1980s cannot be calculated due to the absence of both the actual number of migrant workers and the real wages of the migrant workers in the host countries.

Consequently, the unofficial estimates of the scale of the workers' remittances were remarkably varied. Choucri noted that: "Formally recorded remittances are only the tip of the iceberg. The size of that which remains submerged is not known."[206] Choucri claimed that in the mid-1980s, at the peak of the Egyptian labor emigration, the workers' remittances of the Egyptian workers did not only amount to the $4 billion recorded in the official statistics,[207] but were actually "closer to $20 billion."[208] Officials of the Ministry of Economy and the Egyptian Central Bank estimated that in addition to the official annual remittances of $2.2–$3.1 billion reported in the late 1980s,[209] there were approximately $3–$4 billion unofficial remittances per annum.[210] Wilson noted in regard to the scale of the Egyptian workers' remittances that:

> It is extremely difficult to estimate their worth as many do not pass through the formal banking system . . . Egyptian workers in neighboring Arab states return home for visits . . . Often they

> travel back with large amounts of cash . . . for their relatives in Egypt. Such transfers are not counted in official figures . . . [211]

However, if the real number of Egyptians working abroad at that time was actually less than 2 million, as we saw earlier, then Choucri's estimate that the real remittances of the Egyptian workers abroad was five-times higher than the official figures must be greatly exaggerated. In any case, whatever the real scale of the unofficial workers' remittances in the 1970s and the 1980s was, a difference of billions of dollars in workers' remittances, even only $3-$4 billion per annum, dramatically changed the whole picture of Egypt's macroeconomic condition at that time, including the employment situation.

In the other major Arab labor-exporting countries, one finds a similar phenomenon of large-scale unofficial workers' remittances due to the large gap between the official and unofficial exchange rates. In the case of Syria, while the official exchange rate in 1982 was US$1=£S (Syrian Pound) 3.95, the "free market rate" was as high as £S37 for US$1.[212] Consequently, the Syrian official workers' remittances fluctuated sharply from one year to the next not as a result of a change in the number of the Syrian workers abroad or their salaries, but in line with their ability to transfer their earnings through the unofficial channels according to the unofficial rate.

Thus, in 1979, the official workers' remittances of the Syrian workers abroad amounted to $901 million, declining to $774 million one year later, in 1980, and further declined to only $436 million in 1981.[213] However, according to the various sources and estimates, the number of Syrian migrant workers in the other Arab states during those years was more or less the same, and may have even slightly increased.[214] Moreover, there is no information indicating a sharp reduction in the wages of the Arab migrant workers in the GCC countries or in Libya at that time. Indeed, according to unofficial estimates, by the early 1980s, the scale of the Syrian workers' remittances amounted to more than $1 billion,[215] namely more than twice the official amount. Therefore, it seems that the only logical explanation for these sharp oscillations in the scale of the official Syrian workers' remittances during the late 1970s and the first half of the 1980s is the large-scale transfer through unofficial channels. Actually, in 1985, the Syrian Minister of Economy and Foreign Trade, Muhammad al-Atrash, admitted that a large percentage of the Syrian workers' remittances were not transferred to Syria through the official channels, but were sold in Beirut in the free market.[216]

In the case of Jordan, one can find a similar phenomenon. In 1983, for example, while the official workers' remittances of the Jordanian workers abroad amounted $1.1 billion,[217] it was estimated that undocumented remittances were as much as one-third this amount.[218] Thus, although in the Jordanian case the unofficial workers' remittances throughout the 1970s and the 1980s were substantial, their scale was much lower in comparison to the other major Arab labor-exporting countries. This is because Jordan did not adopt a socialist economic policy. Consequently, there was almost no gap between the official and the unofficial exchange rate of the Jordanian Dinar (JD). The source of the unofficial workers' remittances was that the Jordanian authorities did not establish sufficient financial incentives, such as a higher rate for workers' remittances, for the Jordanian workers abroad to transfer their remittances through the official channels. Consequently, in many cases the Jordanian workers abroad brought their earnings in cash when they came to Jordan for vacation or went back to Jordan after finishing their work abroad.

Since the mid-1980s, however, but particularly during the 1990s, almost all of the former socialist-étatist Arab countries conducted exchange rate reforms, narrowing, or even totally abolishing, the gap between the "black market" exchange rate and the official exchange rate. Consequently, there was a sharp decline in the amount of unofficial workers' remittances, as evidenced by the substantial increase in the scale of the recorded remittances, despite the sharp decrease in both the number of Arab foreign workers in the GCC countries and their wages (see **Chapter 4**).

In the case of Egypt, the scale of the recorded workers' remittances in 1994 was $5.1 billion[219] – the highest amount ever – while the number of Egyptian labor migrants at that time was considerably lower than in mid-1980s, at the peak of the Egyptian labor emigration.[220] Thus, it seems that Sullivan was wrong to conclude that "remittances to Egypt were going against the declining trend line of oil prices and oil revenues in the GCC."[221] This is because the sharp increase in the amount of the recorded remittances of the Egyptian workers abroad was simply due to the elimination of the gap between the official and the unofficial exchange rate of the £E which led to a sharp increase in the recorded remittances at the expense of the unrecorded remittances. The whole scale of the remittances, however, largely declined.

***(c)* Tourism receipts** constitute another significant part of the urban informal economy in the poorer Arab countries. In the countries where there is a considerable gap between the official and the unofficial exchange rates, many tourists are inclined to change their foreign currency on the "black market" rather than in the banks, a situation similar to the one of the workers' remittances. An additional unreported aspect of the informal economy in the tourism area is that of the services provided to tourists around the hotels and the major tourism sites, in many cases by public sector employees. Even children participate in these activities, for example, by carrying the tourists' suitcases. Not only do these activities go unreported, but it is impossible to calculate or even estimate their scale, which change from one instance to another. As the tourism industry in the non-oil Arab countries rapidly expanded during the past decade, and in some of them became the largest among the private sector activities, both in terms of employment and income, the unrecorded financial activities related to the tourism industry sharply increased accordingly.

Therefore, the major question is: What is the share of the informal economy in the poorer Arab countries? Richards and Waterbury estimated the share of informal urban employment in the Middle East in the mid-1990s as "at least one-third to one-half of the labor force."[222] In the Egyptian case, for example, in the early 2000s the World Bank estimated that the informal employment constituted 48% of the total employment, and as much as 65% to 70% of the total private sector employment.[223] According to a CAPMAS estimate, by 2003, as much as 6.9 million Egyptians found their living in the informal private sector.[224] Regarding the share of the informal economy in the overall Egyptian economy, it was written in the EIU in the late 1980s as follows:

> The 1988 US report points out that estimates of GDP, for which the government is the only source, are unreliable because of the growing "unofficial" economy in Egypt on which there are no statistics; actual activity could be as much as 25–50% higher than reported.[225]

According to research conducted by the National Bank of Egypt on the Egyptian underground economy, it appears that by 1990, while the official Egyptian national income was £E117.7 billion, the real national income was much higher, estimated at almost twice the official figures and running between £E196 and £E222 billion. This means that:

> Egypt's underground economy may be at least equal to the published figure of the country's national income . . . Even if an estimate can be made as to the size of the legal activities . . . it is almost impossible to know with some degree of reliability the extent of the illegal transactions.[226]

In many other non-oil Arab countries as well, one can find a similar structure with a widespread informal economy that hampers socioeconomic and demographic research. The widespread hidden economy leads to a situation in which the magnitude of the actual economic activities is largely unknown. As a result, macroeconomic analysis, which constitutes a paramount tool to evaluating employment data, is substantially distorted.

7 Summary and Conclusions

As for the Ottoman and the Mandatory periods, only a broad description on the demographic trends could be presented due both to the scarce demographic data as well as to their inconsistency and inaccuracy. However, the demographic data of the Arab countries following independence, particularly since the 1960s when almost all of the Arab countries carried out at least one modern demographic census, are without any doubt much more inclusive, accurate and most importantly, consistent, which is a prerequisite for any demographic research.

Despite the sharp improvement of the demographic data in the vast majority of the Arab countries since the early 1960s, many Arab governments even today do not publish all the demographic data collected. In contrast to the Ottoman and Mandatory periods, however, the missing demographic information in many Arab countries since the 1960s, primarily with regard to the ethno-religious composition, should be attributed to political factors rather than to the inability of the authorities to collect these data. The result, however, is quite similar: detailed research on the ethno-religious composition on the Arab countries is impossible to implement even today.

The second problematic area for carrying out comprehensive research is related to the composition of nationalities in the labor-importing Gulf countries (with the exception of Oman since 1993). In this respect, the most extreme example is that of Qatar, which does not publish even the most basic demographic indicator of the breakdown of the total population into nationals and foreigners.

As for the employment area, the situation is much more complicated than in the purely demographic arena. The most crucial problem in this respect is the huge gap between the official and the unofficial data. Is Egypt's unemployment rate 9%, as per the official data, or is the rate closer to 20% as per the unofficial estimates? The difference between an economy with 9% unemployment rate and one with a 20% unemployment rate is the difference between an economy with an employment problem that through massive macroeconomic and socio-demographic reforms has the potential of overcoming the employment problem, as opposed to an economy which is on "a collapsing track" with all of the political implications involved in this situation.

Nevertheless, with all of the above-mentioned barriers, in many demographic areas detailed research could be carried out on both the oil-based and the non-oil Arab countries, as satisfactory data is available, with the exception of Sudan, where, even today, the most basic demographic data are absent and/or inconsistent. Moreover, the censuses that are carried out by many Arab countries since the mid-1980s were computerized and their under-enumeration rates were much lower than in the previous censuses. The latest censuses of Saudi Arabia, Oman and the UAE are good examples of this improvement.

The sharp improvement of the demographic data collected and published by the Arab governments since the mid-1980s is the result not only of the fact that the control of the central authority on the population has sharply improved, but should be attributed to some other factors as well, the most important of which are the following:

***(a)* The more political openness of the Arab regimes since the mid-1980s** and certainly since the early 1990s, even of the traditionally "closed regimes" of the GCC countries, which included *inter alia*, more openness regarding public discussions on many issues that were previously regarded as "sensitive." The most prominent expression of this "new openness" was, and to a large extent still is, the publication of data that could reflect a failure of the authorities, such as the continuing high fertility rates despite the implementation of family planning programs.

***(b)* Intensification of the socioeconomic problems which is directly related to the steady increase of the "demographic pressure,"** primarily in the employment arena. In other words, the continuing "hiding" of the reality from the public and the world alike was not practical any more, as was illustrated in the unemployment problem among the GCC younger generation. The problem had become "too visible."

***(c)* The aim of many Arab regimes to substantially increase the scale of foreign investments**, which, as a precondition, required detailed socioeconomic data, including in the demographic arena.

***(d)* The decision of many Arab regimes, particularly the non-oil based, to "share" the responsibility for the socioeconomic problems with their own citizens** in order to increase their awareness of the crucial need for adopting a family planning plan and macroeconomic reforms in order to revive the economy. Thus, the publication of "the real situation" in both the demographic and economic arenas were aimed at presenting the unpleasant reality to the public. In this respect, it should be taken into consideration that in all the Arab countries, with the exception of Tunisia, the Islamist opposition consistently opposed any anti-natalist measures, either directly or indirectly. Their basic claim was and still is that the low living standard should be attributed not to the rapid population growth but rather to the failure of the socioeconomic and political policies of the current "secular regimes." Therefore, presenting the harsh socioeconomic situation to the public is part of the whole "war on public opinion" of the regimes against the Islamist opposition (see Chapter 5).

However, in contrast to the demographic data which radically improved during the past generation, the macroeconomic data of the poorer Arab countries at the dawn of the twenty-first century remains unreliable due to the large-scale of the hidden economy. The large percentage of the hidden economy imposes a "heavy shadow" on the official data, mainly in the area of GDP, current account balance, labor productivity, etc.

The large-scale hidden economy raises some major methodological questions, the most important of which for demographic research are as follows: What could a satisfactory definition for "job opportunity" in the poorer Arab economies be? What methodology could be useful in order to calculate the real number of "job opportunities"? Should the jobs in the informal urban economy also be taken into consideration in measuring the number of available work opportunities? In other words, can selling newspapers and cigarettes on a street corner be considered as "a job opportunity"? In practice, millions of those belonging to the lower urban stratum find their living in these kinds of occupations.[227] And if we decided to takes these informal occupations into consideration, what methodology should be used in order to evaluate their number?

What about the widespread phenomenon of underemployment which so prevails in the public sectors of the poorer Arab countries? How should the common phenomenon of working simultaneously in the public sector and in the informal urban sector be treated from a methodological point of view? Should we consider a position in the lower ranks of the public sector that produces a monthly wage of less than $100 a "job"? In reality, only a tiny percentage of those who work in the lower and even the middle ranks of the public sectors of the poorer Arab countries do not work simultaneously in the informal sector as well. Do these employees fill one or two positions?

All of these questions are crucial and thus dictate very cautious interpretations and calculations. Within these limitations the present research was conducted.

2 Beyond Expectations
Arab Population Growth in Retrospect

The total number of Egyptians is 22 million . . . In 50 years [i.e., in 2003] the population of Egypt will reach 44 million.

Gamal 'Abd al-Nasser, November 1953[1]

1 Introduction: Worldwide Population Growth in Retrospect

During most of human history, only a few million people were living on earth due to the limited ability of the hunting and gathering way of life to support more people.[2] However, with the development of agriculture approximately 10,000–12,000 years ago, the earth's "carrying capacity" grew substantially. Since then, the world's population has steadily increased, although at very low rates, as one can see in Table 2.1. Until modern times, during periods of epidemics, such as the Black Death from 1347–1350[3] and prolonged droughts, the world's population decreased, sometimes even substantially.

According to the prevailing estimates, the world's population numbered about 250 million at 1 AD, rose to between 245–275 million around the year 1000,[4] climbed to 545 million by 1650 and reached 728 million by 1750, on the eve of the Industrial Revolution. This means that during 1750 years, the world's population increased by less than three-fold and that there was almost zero population growth during the period 1 AD until the year 1000.[5]

The Industrial Revolution first started in Britain in the mid-eighteenth century and later spread to other European countries in the nineteenth century, leading to accelerated population growth in Western Europe. By the year 1900, the total world's population numbered 1.6 billion. This means that during the nineteenth century alone, the global population increased by 77.5%, representing a net increase of 702 million people.

During the twentieth century, particularly in the second half, the world's population grew more rapidly than ever before. By 1950, the world's population numbered 2.556 billion, an increase of 60% within only half a century, compared to 37.3% during the second half of the nineteenth century. During the second half of the twentieth century, world population growth rates accelerated, peaking at more than 2% on annual average during the first half of the 1960s.[6] Thus, the total world population numbered more than 4 billion by 1975, 6.2 billion by the end of the twentieth century and reached 6.6 billion in mid-2007 (see Table 2.1).

Consequently, the net population increase during the twentieth century amounted

Table 2.1 Estimation of World Population Growth (millions)

Year	Estimated World Population (millions)	Nominal Population Increase (millions)
1 AD	250	204
1650	545	183
1750	728	178
1800	906	265
1850	1,171	437
1900	1,608	948
1950	2,556	484
1960	3,040	667
1970	3,707	739
1980	4,446	76
1981	4,522	79
1982	4,601	81
1983	4,682	80
1984	4,762	81
1985	4,843	83
1986	4,926	86
1987	5,012	87
1988	5,099	86
1989	5,185	88
1990	5,273	83
1991	5,356	84
1992	5,440	80
1993	5,520	80
1994	5,600	81
1995	5,681	80
1996	5,761	79
1997	5,840	78
1998	5,918	77
1999	5,995	76
2000	6,071	75
2001	6,146	75
2002	6,221	75
2003	6,296	75
2004	6,371	76
2005	6,447	76
2006	6,523	77
2007	6,600	—

Sources: Michael P. Todaro, *Economic Development*, seventh edition (Reading, Mass.: Addison-Wesley, 1999), p. 212, table 6.1; WB, *World Development Report-2002*, p. 233, table 1; The US, Department of Commerce, US Census Bureau, *International Data Base*. Available at: http:/www.census.gov.

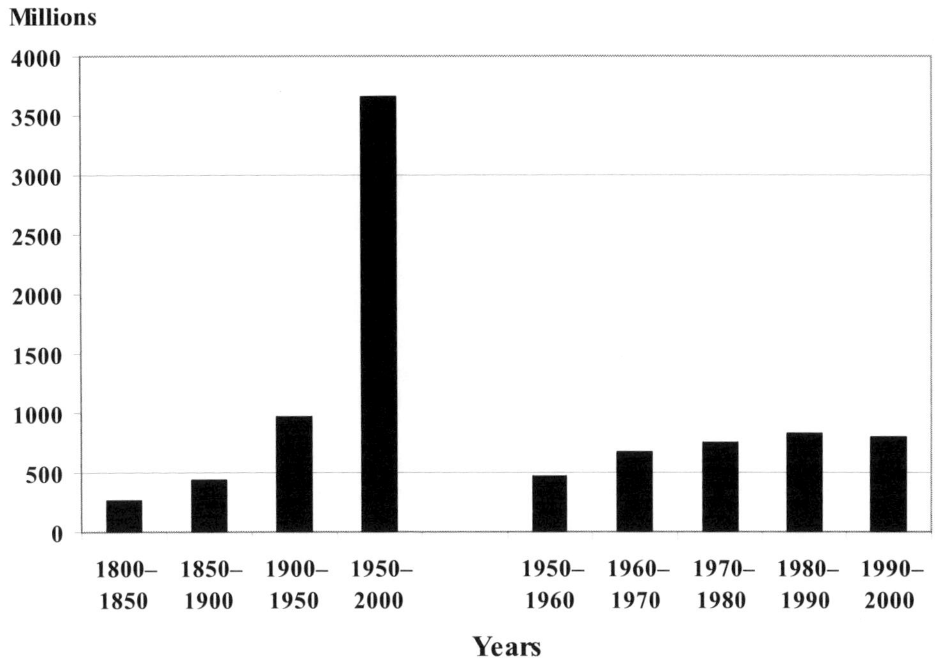

Figure 2.1 Nominal World Population Growth, 1800–2000 (millions)

to 4.463 billion – 3.5 billion in the second half of the century alone. As the data reveal, in nominal figures, the highest population growth ever was during the second half of the 1980s with a population growth of 86 million on annual average. Since the early 1990s, as a result of fertility decline in both the developed and the developing countries, the natural increase rates of the world's population substantially declined, leading to a drop in the world's population growth rates. Thus, in the first seven years of the twenty-first century, the world's population increased by 530 million, an annual average increase of 75.7 million (see Table 2.1), namely "another New York" every month and "another Egypt" every year.[7]

2 The Demographic Transition Theory and the Arab Countries

Since birth and death rates determine the natural increase rates, the connection between them, or the mutual influence of one on the other, was and still is a major research topic. The core factor dictating the search of a "grand demographic theory" which could explain the changing fertility regime from high fertility to low fertility was the alarming low fertility rates in the developed European countries during the period between the two world wars (see below). Thus, the demographic research in its initial stage was based almost entirely on the conditions in the developed countries, mainly those of Western Europe. Only in the 1950s and more so in the 1960s and 1970s did the core of worldwide demographic research attention move into the developing countries. This shift in research focus was an outcome of the recovery of the fertility rates in Western European countries following World War II on the one hand, and the evidence of the devastating consequences of the extremely high natural increase rates in the developing countries on the other. Since the early 1990s, however, the focus of the demographic research in the developed countries worldwide turned again to the developed countries. This "second turning" research focus was a result of the declining fertility rates in the vast majority of the developing countries worldwide on the one hand, and the extremely prolonged low fertility rates in the developed countries, in most cases much below the replacement-level rate of 2.1 children per woman,[8] on the other.

2.1 The Demographic Transition Theory

The basic theory on the relationship between birth and death rates is the *Demographic Transition Theory*.[9] The first signs of the theory had appeared in 1929 in an article written by Warren Thompson in which he classified three types of countries with different natural increase rates: The first group included countries with fertility rates which declined faster than death rates, namely, countries whose natural increase rate was in a declining process. The second group included countries where death rates declined earlier and faster than the birth rates, that is, countries where the natural increase rate was increasing. The third group included countries in which neither birth nor death rates were under control. These were countries whose demographic regime remained in its "traditional form."[10] Thus, by this classification, Thompson practically laid the three fundamental "stages" or "regimes" of the Demographic Transition. The theory was finally formulated, 16 years later, in 1945, by Frank Notestein, the director of the Office of Population Research at Princeton University.[11]

The basic assumption of the Demographic Transition Theory is that the number of births in any given society in any given period is based on a rational decision of the parents. Therefore, in pre-industrial agrarian societies, a large number of births was an inescapable necessity due to the high death rates, particularly among infants and children. Moreover, due to the lack of machinery, a large number of children was essential for cultivating the fields. The Industrial Revolution brought with it rapid machinery development, thus reducing the need for child labor. Improvements were made in nutrition, healthcare facilities, and both private and public sanitation. Furthermore, the development of the steam engine in boats and trains during the nineteenth century allowed for the transfer of food supplies from one place to another. A rapid urbanization process took place, accompanied by the spread of education from the elite to the middle class and later to the lower strata as well. All of these developments led to a steady decline in death rates, which, combined with rapid economic development, was followed by a decline in birth rates as well.

The basic theme of the Demographic Transition Theory is that "modernization," that is, the transformation from an autarkist pre-industrial economy[12] to the modern pattern of an industrial urban market economy also led to changes in the concept of the desired number of children. In the modern urban economy, a large number of children is considered an economic burden rather than an economic benefit. The importance of the Demographic Transition Theory in this respect is that it "rationalized" the fertility behavior in both pre-modern and modern societies, while previously the theme was that high fertility rates in pre-modern societies were the result of irrationality which characterized pre-modern societies in many respects, including in the area of fertility behavior.[13] As economic modernization originally occurred in the major cities, the process of fertility decline was first evident in the major urban centers and only subsequently in the countryside where their economic development was slower.

As Notestein argued, "There are abundant evidences that the [fertility] decline came about primarily through rational control . . . "[14] On the question of why death rates started to decline earlier than fertility rates in response to the modernization process, Notestein answers that: "The reduction of mortality is a universally acceptable goal and faced no substantial social obstacles. But the reduction of fertility requires a shift in social goals from those directed toward the survival of the group to those directed toward the welfare and development of the individual."[15]

In line with this basic assumption of "the rationalization of births," the demographic history of the Western developed countries can be divided into four main stages, with the transition from one stage to another explained as an outcome of macroeconomic and socio-cultural developments.

The first stage of the demographic transition was characterized by high birth and death rates, leading to low, or even negative natural increase rates. This stage ruled most of human history until the onset of the Industrial Revolution. During that period, the world was governed by "a cruel demographic regime" in which high fertility was necessary in order to offset the high mortality rates.[16] On the eve of the Industrial Revolution, both the CBRs and the CDRs fluctuated between 30 and 40 per 1,000 people. Thus, for example, Finland's CBRs were above 40 per 1,000 throughout the eighteenth century and slightly above 30 per 1,000 in Sweden and Denmark.[17] The average life expectancy was very low accordingly – less than 40 years.[18] Under this "primitive demographic regime," it was necessary to have at least five to six live-births per woman just to ensure population replacement. Although demographic censuses for that period do not exist, it seems that until the mid-eighteenth century, the natural increase rate of the world's population was marginal, averaging as low as 0.1% annually.[19]

The second stage of the demographic transition, which began following the Industrial Revolution, was characterized by a steady decrease in the death rates. Therefore, during the second half of the eighteenth century, the world's natural increase rate was estimated at 0.4% on an annual average[20] – much higher than the rates that prevailed prior to the onset of the Industrial Revolution, but still very low in comparison to later periods. During the first half of the nineteenth century, the world's population substantially increased, particularly in the developed Western European areas. This increase was a result of continuing high fertility rates despite the marked and steady decline of the death rates, particularly among infants and children. The continuing high fertility rates during the first stage of the Industrial Revolution was due to the fact that it took several decades until the population became aware of the changing of the "death regime." Sweden's CBR, for example, was estimated at 31.4 per 1,000 at the dawn of the nineteenth century and remained at that level until the 1860s. A similar trend prevailed in Germany, Austria and England as well.[21]

During the second half of the nineteenth century, with the widespread expansion of the Industrial Revolution, the trend of declining death rates was strengthened by the steady decrease of infant and child mortality rates along with a considerable increase in life expectancy. In the case of Norway, for example, CDRs declined from approximately 30 per 1,000 in the 1740s to less than 20 a century later, in the mid-nineteenth century, and further declined to less than 15 toward the end of the nineteenth century. A similar trend occurred in Sweden and Denmark as well.[22] The decline in the birth rates, however, was much slower than that of the death rates. In the case of Britain (including Wales) for example, the CBR at the beginning of the nineteenth century was estimated at 35 per 1,000,[23] while the TFR was 5.8 children per woman.[24] A century later, during the years 1908–1913, the CBR in England and Wales averaged 24.9 per 1,000,[25] namely, a decline of 30% in the CBRs compared to a decline of 50% in the CDRs.

Hence, the natural increase rates in the Western European developed countries substantially accelerated throughout the second half of the nineteenth century. For example, Sweden's annual natural increase rate grew from 0.7% at the start of the nineteenth century to 1.2% in 1870s, while that of England increased from 1.1% to 1.4% during the corresponding period.[26] During the first decade of the twentieth century, the annual natural increase rate in each of the Western European countries reached above 1%.[27] Overall, during the 1800–1914 period, despite the massive emigration from Europe to North America and to the European colonies around the world, Europe's population more than doubled, swelling from 188 million to 455 million.[28]

The third stage of the demographic transition in the developed countries started following World War I. This stage, which stretched until the late 1960s, was characterized by a steady fertility decline which occurred much faster than the drop in the death rates. By 1970, the TFR in all of the worldwide developed countries approached replacement-level, or slightly above that level (2.4 children per woman in France and Norway, 2.2 in Austria, 2.1 in Denmark and 2.0 in Switzerland and Sweden[29]). Although the CDRs continued to decline as well, reaching a level of 9 to 12 per 1,000 in the early 1970s,[30] that is, approximately 3 to 6 points less compared to the rates that prevailed during the early 1930s,[31] the fertility decline was much more substantial. This new transition from high to low fertility rates, like the earlier transition, involved enormous socioeconomic as well as political changes, the most prominent of which were the radical changes of women's status, primarily in their employment opportunities (see below). By the end of the third stage, however, the natural increase rate in developed countries was not zero, despite the reduction of the TFR to below the replacement-level, as a result of the "population momentum" (see Chapter 3).

The fourth stage of the demographic transition started in the 1970s when the TFR of the vast majority of the developed countries had dropped to below the replacement-level. By 1980, the TFR was 1.6 in Belgium, 1.8 in Norway, France and the UK and 1.9 in the US (see Table 2.4). Despite the extremely low age-specific death rates,[32] the CDRs not only did not decline accordingly, but even increased, due to the "population ageing phenomenon" (see Chapter 3). Consequently, during the past two decades, the natural increase rates in most of the developed countries worldwide, particularly in the more developed EU countries, have been very low, in most cases approaching zero. By 1998, the natural increase rate of the developed countries worldwide averaged 0.3%, down from 0.7% in 1970 (see Table 2.2). This new phenomenon of zero or even negative natural increase rates in many of the developed countries worldwide is called "the second demographic transition," or "the fourth stage of the demographic transition."[33]

It should be emphasized, however, that the rapid fertility decline in developed countries worldwide took place despite the governmental pro-natalist policies implemented by these countries since the 1970s.[34] The changing role of women from "mother" to "provider" on the one hand, and the extremely high cost of living, particularly in the major urban centers,[35] that called for dual salaries among the

Table 2.2 Natural Increase Rate in Different Parts of the World, 1970, 1998 (%)

Region / Year	1970			1998			Average Annual Growth, 1970–1990 (%)	Average Annual Growth, 1990–1998 (%)
	CBR	CDR	NI (%)	CBR	CDR	NI (%)		
Sub-Saharan Africa	48	21	2.7	41	16	2.5	2.8	2.6
Middle East and North Africa	45	17	2.8	28	7	2.1	2.9	2.3
South Asia	41	18	2.3	27	9	1.8	2.2	1.9
East Asia and Pacific	35	10	2.5	18	7	1.1	1.7	1.2
Latin America and Caribbean	37	10	2.7	23	6	1.7	2.2	1.7
East Europe and Baltic states	20	9	1.1	14	11	0.3	0.9	0.3
Developed countries	17	10	0.7	12	9	0.3	0.7	0.6
Developing countries	38	14	2.4	25	9	1.6	2.1	1.7
Least developing countries	48	22	2.6	38	15	2.3	2.5	2.5
World total	33	12	2.1	22	9	1.3	1.7	1.4

Source: UNICEF, *The State of the World's Children – 2000* (Published for UNICEF by Oxford University Press, 2000), p. 103, table 5.

predominant middle class, on the other,[36] led to this sharp fertility decline. Thus, as Chesnais noted regarding many young women in the developed countries, "most of them stick to the one-child pattern."[37] The common assumption of the modern demographic theories, in contrast to previous theories, is that the socioeconomic condition, rather than mortality rates, dictates fertility patterns.[38]

The steady decline in the "desired number of children" is well illustrated by the two demographic surveys conducted by the Spanish National Institute of Statistics in 1977 and in 1987: While according to the 1977 survey as much as 47.4% of the married women who had two children wished to have at least one more child, in the 1987 survey this rate dropped to only 4.4%.[39] This means that even under the optimal condition, namely, if the actual fertility rate indeed reaches the "desired number of children," Spain's fertility rate would not even exceed the minimum replacement-level of two children per woman. A similar trend of "desired number of children" of less than two has been spreading since the early 1990s in the vast majority of the developed countries, particularly in the more developed EU countries, as indicated by many surveys and demographic polls which were carried out in these countries.[40]

Another major factor for the sharp fertility decline in the developed countries is the widespread phenomenon of childless women. In the case of Australia, for example, this trend was estimated at as high as 20% by the late 1990s.[41] This extensive phenomenon is illustrated by the description of one 33-year-old Swedish woman regarding her attitude toward children:

> There are times when I think perhaps I will be missing something important if I don't have a child. But today women finally have so many chances to have the life they want. To travel and work and learn. It's exciting and demanding. I just find it hard to see where the children would fit in.[42]

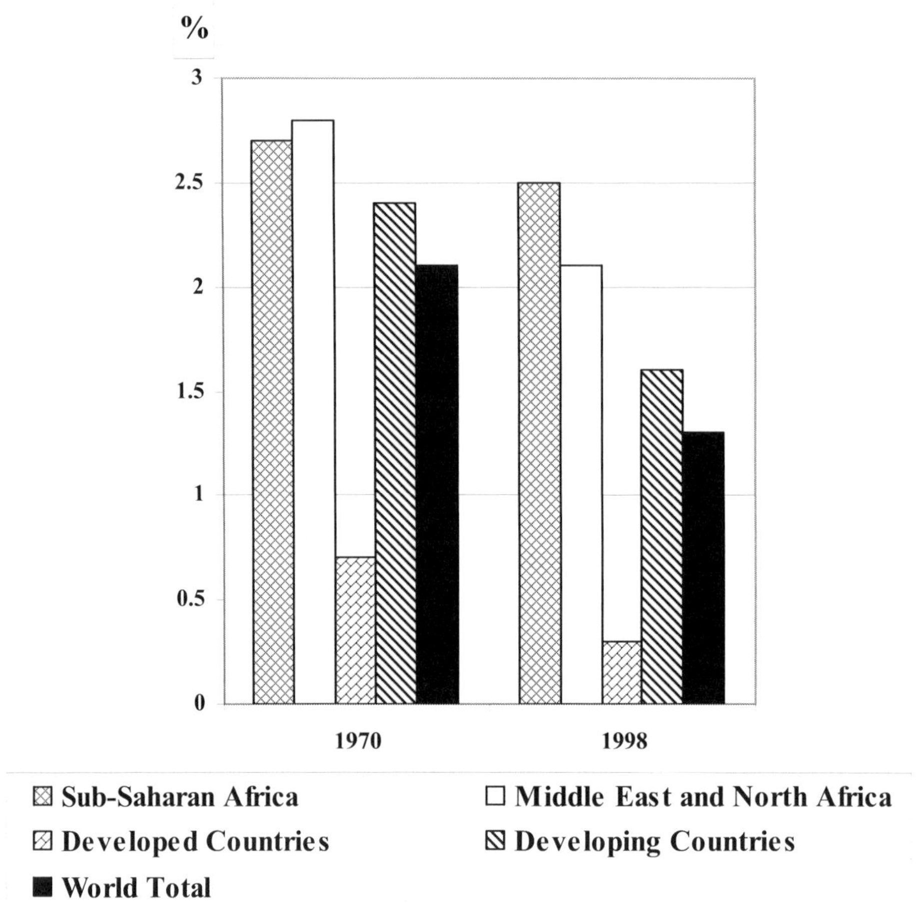

Figure 2.2 Natural Increase Rate in Different Parts of the World, 1970, 1998 (%)

The New York Times reporter who interviewed her characterized her as part of "a cadre in one of the fundamental social revolutions of the [twentieth] century."[43] The main conclusion from recent demographic developments in the developed countries worldwide is that the traditional explanation of the Demographic Transition Theory, namely, the transformation from high equilibrium of birth and death rates to low equilibrium of birth and death rates has broken. In other words, the Gordian-historical mutual dependence between death and birth rates has ended and each of these two basic demographic parameters acts independently of the other.

Such a turn of events raises the question of why the fertility rates in developed countries have declined so rapidly during the past four decades even in countries that have implemented extensive pro-natalist measures? Who benefits from these new demographic patterns and who does not? What are the consequences, both economically and politically, of such low fertility rates, particularly in the longer run?

2.2 The Pattern of Western European Demographic Transition

Couples are now able to choose their family size, free of the traditional pressures to bear children that was characteristic of most traditional societies. In fact, most societal pressures for the last generation have been distinctly anti-natalist . . .

Sarah Harbison and Warren Robinson, 2002[44]

The Western European demographic transition is well illustrated by the example of Finland. During the years 1785–1790, Finland's CBR averaged 38 per 1,000, while the CDR averaged 32 per 1,000, leading to an annual average natural increase rate of 0.6%. This was the end of the first stage of the demographic transition. During the years 1825–1830, Finland's CBR remained at the same level of 38 per 1,000, while the CDR dropped to 24 per 1,000. This means that Finland's annual natural increase rate more than doubled, from 0.6% to 1.4%. The third stage of Finland's demographic transition began in the early twentieth century. During the period 1910–1915, Finland's CBRs averaged 29 per 1,000, while the CDRs averaged 17 per 1,000, leading to an annual natural increase rate of 1.2% – a decline of 15% compared to the natural increase rate during the 1825–1830 period.[45]

Following World War I, the downward trend in both the CBRs and the CDRs in Finland continued, although the CBRs declined more rapidly than the CDRs, leading to a steady shrinking of natural increase rates. In 1960, Finland's CBR was 19 per 1,000 and the CDR was 9 per 1,000, which meant a natural increase rate of 1.0%[46] – a decline of 20% compared to the natural increase rate that had prevailed in the early twentieth century. Two decades later, in 1980, Finland's CBR and CDR were 14 and 9 per 1,000 respectively, namely, a natural increase rate of 0.5%, or half the rate of 1960.[47] Since then, due to a combination of declining fertility rates and increasing death rates, Finland's natural increase rates have steadily declined, amounting to only 0.3% (CBR of 13 per 1,000 and CDR of 10 per 1,000) in 1990.[48] By the year 2005, Finland's natural increase rate was zero with both the CBR and CDR of 10 per 1,000.[49] Considering that Finland's TFR is 1.7 children per woman, one can expect that Finland's natural increase rate will soon be negative with the CDR exceeding the CBR. Therefore, without massive immigration, Finland's population will soon begin to shrink.

A similar trend of shrinking natural increase rates prevails in all the developed EU countries in recent years. In the case of Germany, for example, the number of live births in 2002 was 725,000, while the number of deaths amounted to 845,000, leading to a negative natural increase rate. In Greece and Italy, one can find the same phenomenon of higher CDRs than CBRs.[50] Italy's TFR is stagnant at 1.1 during recent years – the lowest not only worldwide, but also the lowest rate ever documented in any given period in any given society. Thus, as noted by Eastebrook, "on paper at least, Italy will be a theme park in a few generations."[51]

Although the phenomenon of below replacement-level fertility is not new among the European societies and had already occurred in the early 1930s, the difference between then and the current low fertility rates is substantial: While the low fertility of the early 1930s was a direct result of the Great Depression and lasted for only a decade and a half, until the end of World War II,[52] the current European low fertility rates have continued for more than four decades and have lasted despite the rapid economic development and the various pro-natalist measures which were taken. Thus, in contrast to the past, the current low fertility rate in the developed societies is a "socio-cultural phenomenon."

The following numbers will illustrate the sharp decline in Europe's fertility rates during the twentieth century: while in 1900, at the beginning of the century, the number of births in Europe was 9.9 million for a total population of 300 million, this number declined to 5.9 million in 1996 for a total population of 500 million. This means that while Europe's population increased by two-thirds, the number of births declined by 40%.[53] Thus, while in 1960 the natural increase of the EU-15 countries[54] was 2.398 million with a total population of 314.8 million, this number declined to only 330,000 in 1995 with a total population of 371.6 million.[55] By 2002, the EU-15 TFR averaged 1.47 children per woman, declining from 1.82 in 1980.[56] Popescu noted in this respect that "the clichéd image of fertility in Europe is no longer true . . . [the] large Mediterranean family from Italy, Spain, Greece and Portugal is rather a stereotype . . ."[57] Paradoxically, while in the past there were a large number of unwanted pregnancies, in recent years, the actual fertility rates in the more developed countries are much below the desired number.[58]

The much below replacement-level fertility in the more developed countries represents a new demographic regime in the developed societies in which declining population is due to low fertility rates, rather than epidemics and diseases as it had been prior to the Industrial Revolution. Thus, as noted by Chesnais, "The EU is entering a new historical stage, the age of migration dependency,"[59] in line with "the Low Fertility Trap Hypothesis" of Lutz, Skirbekk and Testa.[60]

Actually, this stage of decreasing population already prevails in the new EU members which suffered from both extremely low fertility rates and large-scale young emigration to the more developed EU countries. Thus, for example, during the years 1995–2004, the population of the Czech Republic declined from 10.333 million to 10.211 million; Latvia's population decreased from 2.50 million to 2.31 million; while Hungary's population went from 10.34 million to 10.12 million.[61] The most extreme example of this new demographic stage is that of Russia whose population decreased during recent years by almost 700,000 persons per annum.[62]

Is there any chance of reversing Europe's current demographic regime to the one that prevailed a half a century ago with a fertility rate above the replacement-level?

2.3 The Applicability of the Demographic Transition Theory to the Arab Countries

From a historical perspective, the application of the Demographic Transition Theory to the demographic history of the Arab countries during the twentieth century raises five reservations:

(a) Even if the basic assumption of the Demographic Transition Theory on the relationship between "modernization" and "fertility behavior" is also correct in the case of the developing countries, it is clear that the patterns of both socioeconomic and political developments during the second half of the twentieth century in the developing countries, including the Arab countries, were different from those of the developed countries. Such was the case in a wide variety of aspects, including economic policy and structure, women's status, level of industrialization, governmental income sources, and above all, the political structure. All of these aspects, as will be examined in Chapter 5, have an immense influence on fertility patterns.

(b) In the Western developed countries, the socioeconomic development was the core explanation offered by the Demographic Transition Theory for the decline of death rates and later also the birth rates. In contrast, in the developing countries, the death rate decline has been caused primarily by external factors, first and foremost by the import of modern healthcare facilities, and not by internal socioeconomic development. Among the Arab countries, one can find some examples for this pattern, such as that of Yemen: While Yemen remains one of the poorest countries worldwide with a per capita GNI of only $600 in 2004 and ranks as low as 150 in the HDI (see Appendix 1), its CDR sharply declined from 29 per 1,000 in 1960[63] to 11 in 2000,[64] and to only 9 in 2005.[65]

In the Gulf oil countries, the overall living standard sharply improved since the 1960s. This was accompanied by a sharp decline in infant and child mortality rates and substantially improved female educational level. The fertility rate in these countries, however, did not decline (see below). Also in the case of Egypt, the demographic trends from the mid-1960s until the mid-1980s were opposed to what they should have been according to the Demographic Transition Theory. During the decade between the mid-1960s and until the October 1973 War, Egypt's fertility rates sharply declined despite the overall deterioration in the economic conditions as a result of the June 1967 War and the 1969–1970 War of Attrition. During the decade between the mid-1970s and the mid-1980s, although Egypt's socioeconomic condition substantially improved, with a doubling of the per capita income, fertility rates markedly increased (see Chapter 5). A similar trend can also be found among the Israeli-Arabs during the 1950s and 1960s.[66]

(c) The Demographic Transition Theory did not take into consideration "the emigration effect" on fertility behavior. When the population of Europe considerably increased during the nineteenth and the early twentieth centuries, Europe found a way to relieve its demographic pressure through emigration to "The New World." This option, however, was not relevant to the developing countries during the second half of the twentieth century, particularly during the last two decades when many developed countries started to limit the scale of migration.

(d) The Demographic Transition Theory did not take into account the effect of the natalist policy. While the "core explanation" for demographic changes according to the Demographic Transition Theory is "modernization," in many developing countries, including some Arab countries, a substantial fertility decline occurred without massive socioeconomic development, but was rather a response to comprehensive family planning policies (see Chapter 5).

(e) The Demographic Transition Theory did not take into consideration the cultural-religious factor, which was and still is subject to change, not only from one society to another, but also within the same society, and/or between parents and their children.[67] In the case of the Arab countries in particular, the cultural-religious factor is extremely important as a major barrier for fertility decline is the prevailing concept among the lower stratum that contraceptive use is prohibited according to the Islamic *Shari'a* (see Chapter 5).

With respect to the relevance of the Demographic Transition Theory to the developing countries, Caldwell noted that "there were no two demographic transitions," one spontaneous in the Western countries, namely without direct governmental involvement, and the other "a planned transition," engineered by the developing countries' authorities. In the developing societies, the fertility decline was basically an inevitable process as a response to changes in socioeconomic conditions and political regimes,[68] despite the above-mentioned differences. The main difference between the Western demographic transition pattern and the one that occurred in the developing countries is in the timing and the duration of the transition, but not the transition itself.

Hence, despite all the criticism of the Demographic Transition Theory, it still remains the most useful generalization framework for analyzing demographic changes from a historical perspective. Kirk noted regarding the Demographic Transition Theory that: "Its greatest strength is the prediction that the transition will occur in every society which is experiencing modernization."[69] Harbison and Robinson noted that the Demographic Transition Theory was "a major step forward in our understanding of the mechanics of population change, because it saw fertility and mortality as interacting with social and economic forces."[70]

The applicability of the Demographic Transition Theory to the demographic developments of the developing countries is not a mere academic debate, but has immense practical importance when choosing the preferred natalist policies. If socioeconomic development is the sole, or at least the paramount factor accounting for fertility decline, then anti-natalist policy should concentrate on socioeconomic development itself rather than devoting the limited resources to expensive family planning programs. However, if the socioeconomic development is not the only factor dictating fertility behavior, but other factors, such as the religious-cultural ones, are influential in determining fertility behavior, then developing countries would do well to allocate resources in this direction. Thus, those following Notestein's basic assumption contend that family planning programs, by themselves, would not be much help in bringing about fertility decline, while supporters of the other approach argue that well-designed family planning programs which also take care of other factors, rather than the socioeconomic condition itself, can effectively contribute to reducing fertility in developing countries (see Chapter 5).

In retrospect, the worldwide natural increase rate, which had averaged 1.7% during the 1950s, skyrocketed to more than 2% in the second half of the 1960s, at the peak of the second stage of the demographic transition in many developing countries. The meaning of an annual 2% growth rate is so great that "if the human race had begun with a single couple at the time of Christ and had grown steadily at 2% per year, since then, there would now be 20 million people for every person alive on the earth today."[71] Since the early 1970s, however, the decline in worldwide fertility rates has been higher than the decline in death rates, leading to a consistent decline in worldwide natural increase rates. During the 1970s, the worldwide natural increase rate had declined back to 1.7%, further declined to 1.4% during the 1990s, and 1.2% in 2006 (a CBR of 20.3 per 1,000 and a CDR of 8.5 per 1,000)[72] – representing the lowest rate ever since World War II.

By the end of the twentieth century, the vast majority of countries worldwide were still at the beginning of the third stage of the demographic transition, that is, their death rates were quite low, but their fertility rates, albeit considerably lower compared to those prevailing in the 1970s, were still far above replacement-level. Consequently, their natural increase rates were higher than 1.5% annually. According to UNICEF data, by the year 1998, of the 189 countries worldwide, the TFR was below replacement-level in only 30 countries, while it was above 3 in 53 countries and above 4 in 41 countries.[73]

3 An Historical Examination of Population Growth in the Arab States

Although demographic statistics on the Middle East prior to the nineteenth century are completely lacking, Issawi wrote that "It is possible to hazard educated guesses about magnitudes and trends."[74] Accordingly, in the second century AD., the population of the Middle East was estimated at 40–45 million – a fifth of the total global population at that time. Subsequently, the region's population fluctuated without a clear trend until the nineteenth century, when a steady rise in number became evident. During the 1840–1914 period, the Middle Eastern population doubled at an average annual growth rate of just under 1%[75] – it was the beginning of the second stage of the demographic transition which rapidly increased afterward.

By 1914, on the eve of World War I, the Middle Eastern population (including Iran and Turkey) was estimated at 68 million. By 2000, it reached 374 million (including Iran, Turkey, Israel and the Palestinians living in the Occupied Territories of the West Bank and the Gaza Strip).[76] Thus, within less than nine decades, despite the huge emigration from the region, the Middle Eastern population increased almost six-fold as a result of the accelerating natural increase rates. Similar to other developing regions worldwide, the Middle Eastern population grew by particularly accelerated rates during the two decades between the mid-1960s and the mid-1980s. As can be seen in Table 2.3, the population growth rates during the second half of the twentieth century and the early 2000s were extremely high in the Arab countries.

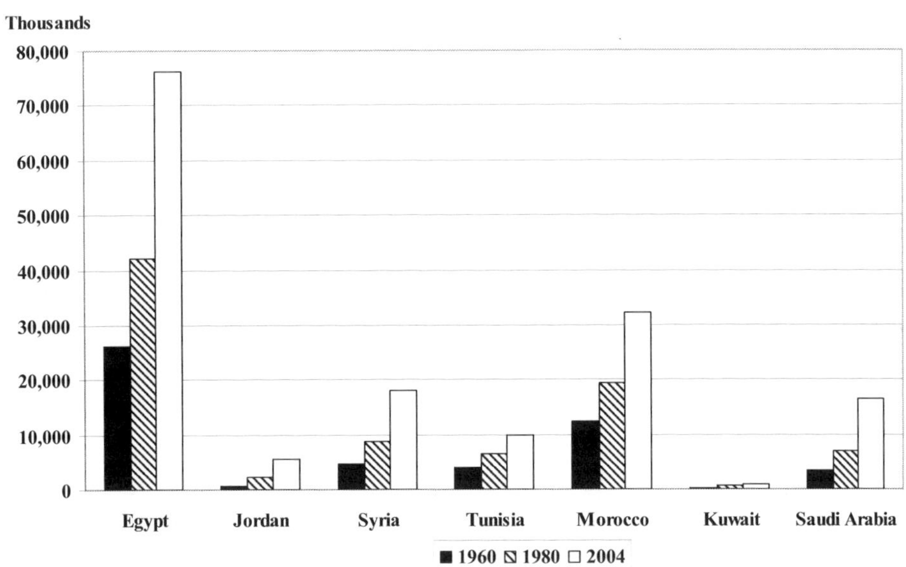

Figure 2.3 Population Growth in some Oil and non-Oil Arab Countries, 1950–2004 (thousands)

Table 2.3 Population Growth in some Oil and non-Oil Arab Countries, 1950–2004 (thousands)

Year / Country	1950	1960	1970	1980	1990	2000	2004
Egypt	21,437(b)	26,085	33,053	42,126	55,543	70,492	76,117
Jordan*	600	781	1,668	2,218	3,453	5,178	5,611
Syria	3,252	4,656	6,305	8,704	12,116	16,320	18,017
Tunisia	3,517	4,149	5,099	6,443	8,207	9,590	9,975
Morocco	9,343	11,626	15,379(f)	19,380	24,167	28,466	30,172
Saudi Arabia**	—	3,302(e)	5,935(g)	7,079	8,847(i)	16,210	16,529
Bahrain**	91	119(c)	178(f)	238 (h)	323(j)	391	438
Kuwait**	100(a)	162(d)	347	566	581	832	975

— No data available.
(a) Figure relates to 1949.
(b) Figure relates to 1952.
(c) Figure relates to 1959.
(d) Figure relates to 1961.
* East Bank only.
(e) Figure relates to 1962-3.
(f) Figures relate to 1971.
(g) Figure relates to 1974.
** Nationals only.
(h) Figure relates to 1981.
(i) Figure relates to 1988.
(j) Figure relates to 1991.

Sources: Egypt, CAPMAS, *Statistical Yearbook*, various issues (Cairo); The Hashemite Kingdom of Jordan, Department of Statistics, *Statistical Abstract*, various issues (Amman); Syrian Arab Republic, Office of the Prime Minister, CBS, *Statistical Abstract*, various issues (Damascus); State of Kuwait, Ministry of Planning, Statistics and Information Center, *Annual Statistical Abstract*, various issues (Kuwait); State (Kingdom) of Bahrain, Central Statistics Organization, Directorate of Statistics, *Statistical Abstract*, various issues (Manama); Bahrain Monetary Agency, *Annual Report*, various issues (Manama); al-Mamlaka al-Maghribiyya, al-Mandubiyya al-Samiyya lil-Takhtit, Qisem al-Ihsaiyyat al-'Amma, *al-Nashra al-Ihsaiyya al-Sanawiyya lil-Maghrib*, various years (Rabat); ECWA, *The Population Situation in the ECWA Region-Saudi Arabia* (Beirut, 1979); ECWA/ESCWA, *Demographic and Related Socio-Economic Data Sheets for Countries of the Economic and Social Commission for Western Asia*, various issues (Baghdad, Amman and Beirut); idem, *Statistical Abstract of the ESCWA Region*, various issues (New York); US Census Bureau, *International Data Base*; Jacqueline S. Ismael, *Kuwait: Social Change in Historical Perspective* (Syracuse: Syracuse University Press, 1982); The *NCB Economist*, Vol. 15, Issue 6 (April 26, 2005); R. McGregor, "Saudi Arabia: Population and the Making of a Modern State," in J. I. Clarke and W. B. Fisher (eds.), *Populations of the Middle East and North Africa: A Geographical Approach* (London: University of London Press, 1972).

3.1 The Causes for the High Fertility Rates in the Arab Countries

Despite the lack of population censuses and accurate demographic records in many of the Arab countries until the 1960s, from what is available, it appears that during the first half of the twentieth century, like other developing regions worldwide, the fertility rates in the Arab region were very high. For example, in 1907 Egypt's CBR was 45.9 per 1,000 and remained at that level throughout the three decades which followed.[77] In 1950, Egypt's CBR was 48.7 per 1,000,[78] slightly higher than what it had been at the beginning of the century. In the other Arab countries, one can find similar fertility patterns as well. Hence, the fertility level in the Arab societies during the first half of the twentieth century was "natural fertility,"[79] as there were no deliberate efforts to limit fertility other than "natural causes," such as prolonged breastfeeding and early widowhood.[80]

From the 1950s until the mid-1980s, the fertility rates in the Arab countries continued to be very high. Kuwait's TFR, for example, remained stable at 7.2–7.3 chil-

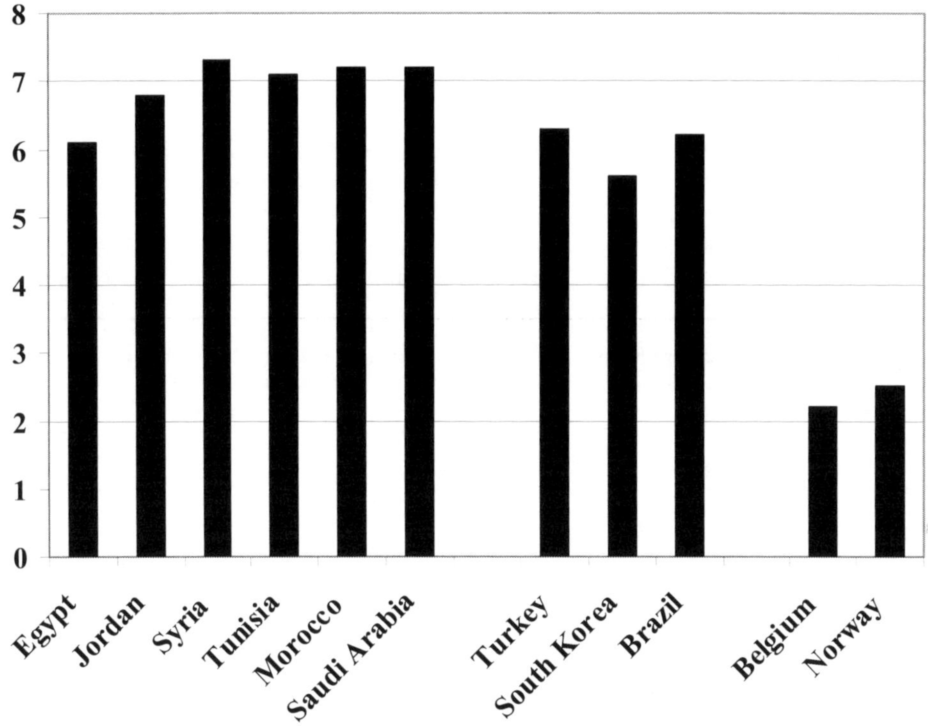

Figure 2.4 Total Fertility Rates in some Arab Countries, non-Arab Developing Countries and Developed Countries, 1960

dren per woman during that period despite the tremendous improvement in every aspect of living standard, driven by the rapid increase in oil revenues. A similar process had occurred in each of the other Gulf oil states. The phenomenon of continuing high fertility rates despite the massive socioeconomic development, it should be emphasized, characterized not only the Arab oil societies but semi-oil and non-oil Arab societies as well. In the cases of Syria and Jordan, for example, the CBR in 1960 was 48 per 1,000 and remained at the same level during the 1960s and the 1970s as well (see Table 2.4).[81]

In retrospect, the fertility patterns which characterized the Arab countries during the "bonanza oil decade," contradicted the prevailing fertility patterns in most of the non-Arab developing countries (not including those of Sub-Saharan countries), whose fertility rates, as one can see in Table 2.4, had already started to decline during the 1960s. In some of them, this fertility decline had begun to happen even earlier. Thus, for example, South Korea's CBR sharply declined from 43 per 1,000 in 1960 to 30 in 1970 and then to only 24 in 1980. During the corresponding period, South Korea's TFR declined from 5.6 children per woman to 3.0. In many non-Arab Muslim societies, the fertility rates during the 1960s and 1970s also substantially declined: In the case of Turkey, for example, the CBR declined from 45 per 1,000 in 1960 to 32 two decades later, in 1980. A similar process has occurred in Indonesia as well – the largest Muslim country worldwide – where the CBR went from 52 per 1,000 on annual average during the years 1951–1956,[82] to 30.7 in 1983.[83]

The crucial issue to consider, therefore, is why the Arab countries, the non-oil and the oil-based alike, did not follow the common transition pattern that characterized the majority of the worldwide developing societies during the 1960s and 1970s. Overall, it seems that there are nine major factors which account for the delay in the fertility decline in the Arab countries:

(a) Children as a cheap labor force In pre-industrial agrarian societies, children constituted an important workforce from a very early age, sometimes even from the age of four or five. Up to and including today, it is very common in Egypt to see small children working in the family fields. It should be remembered that until the 1970s all of the Arab countries, with the exception of Lebanon and the Gulf oil countries, were

Table 2.4 Natural Increase Rates and Total Fertility Rates in some Arab Countries, non-Arab Developing Countries and Developed Countries, 1960–2005

Country	1960				1970				1980			
	CBR	CDR	NI	TFR	CBR	CDR	NI	TFR	CBR	CDR	NI	TFR
Arab Countries												
Egypt	43	17	2.6	6.1	35	15	2.0	5.2	38	10	2.8	5.2
Jordan	48	20	2.8	6.8	48	16	3.2	7.1	47	11	3.6	7.3
Syria	48	18	3.0	7.3	48	16	3.2	7.6	46	8	3.8	7.3
Lebanon	43	14	2.9	6.3	35	11	2.4	5.5	30	8	2.2	4.1
Tunisia	49	21	2.8	7.1	41	15	2.6	6.5	35	10	2.5	5.3
Morocco	52	23	2.9	7.2	47	17	3.0	7.1	44	12	3.2	6.9
Algeria	50	23	2.7	7.3	48	17	3.1	7.4	48	14	3.4	7.3
Sudan	47	25	2.2	6.7	47	22	2.5	6.7	47	19	2.8	6.7
Saudi Arabia*	49	23	2.6	7.2	48	18	3.0	7.3	46	14	3.2	7.3
Kuwait*	44	10	3.4	7.3	48	6	4.2	7.2	48	6	4.2	7.2
Oman*	51	28	2.3	7.2	50	19	3.1	7.2	50	13	3.7	7.2
Bahrain*	46	15	3.1	7.1	43a	8a	3.5	6.7	–	–	–	–
Non-Arab Developing Countries												
Turkey	45	18	2.7	6.3	37	12	2.5	5.6	32	10	2.2	4.4
South Korea	43	14	2.9	5.6	30	10	2.0	4.2	24	7	1.7	3.0
Brazil	43	13	3.0	6.2	35	10	2.5	5.0	30	9	2.1	4.1
Mexico	46	12	3.4	6.8	45	10	3.5	6.6	37	7	3.0	5.1
Pakistan	49	24	2.5	7.5	48	19	2.9	7.1	47	24	2.3	6.1
Developed Countries												
Belgium	17	12	0.5	2.2	15	12	0.3	2.2	13	12	0.1	1.8
Norway	18	9	0.9	2.5	18	10	0.8	2.5	13	10	0.3	1.9
France	18	12	0.6	2.5	17	11	0.6	2.5	14	11	0.3	1.9
United States	24	9	1.5	2.5	17	9	0.8	2.5	16	9	0.7	1.9
United Kingdom	17	12	0.5	2.3	16	12	0.4	2.4	14	12	0.2	1.8

– No data available. CBR = crude birth rate per 1,000 people. CDR = crude death rate per 1,000 people. NI = Natural increase (%).
TFR = total fertility rate. * Nationals only. a. Figures relate to 1971. b. Figures relate to 1988.

Sources: Arab Republic of Egypt, CAPMAS, *Statistical Yearbook*, various issues (Cairo); The Hashemite Kingdom of Jordan, Department of Statistics, *Statistical Yearbook*, various issues (Amman); Syrian Arab Republic, Office of the Prime Minister, CBS, *Statistical Abstract*, various issues (Damascus); al-Jumhuriyya al-Tunisiyya, Wizarat al-Tanmiyya, al-Ma'had al-Watani lil-Ihsa, *al-*

still agrarian societies in which more than half of the population resided in rural areas and made their living through agriculture. By 1970, the rural population constituted 58% of Egypt's total population, 57% in Syria, 61% in Algeria, and 65% in Morocco. Even during the second half of the 1980s, the percentage of the rural population within the total population of the non-oil Arab countries remained relatively high by international comparison, amounting to 57% in Egypt, 51% in Syria, 52% in Morocco, and 49% in Algeria in 1990 (see Table 2.5). Consequently, the high percentage of the rural population within the total population had an overall impact on the national average fertility rates in these countries.

1990				2000				2005				
CBR	CDR	NI	TFR	CBR	CDR	NI	TFR	CBR	CDR	NI	TFR	
				Arab Countries								
33	8	2.5	4.3	26	7	1.9	3.3	25	6	1.9	2.9	Egypt
39	6	3.3	5.8	29	5	2.4	3.8	22	3	1.9	3.7	Jordan
44	6	3.8	6.5	28	4	2.4	3.8	28	5	2.3	3.5	Syria
27b	5b	2.2b	3.4b	21	7	1.4	2.4	19	6	1.3	1.9	Lebanon
29	7	2.2	3.7	20	7	1.3	2.5	17	6	1.1	1.8	Tunisia
34	9	2.5	4.5	25	6	1.9	3.1	22	6	1.6	2.7	Morocco
36	8	2.8	5.1	23	5	1.8	2.7	17	5	1.2	1.9	Algeria
44	15	2.9	6.3	39	10	2.9	5.5	35	9	2.6	4.8	Sudan
42	7	3.5	7.1	29	4	2.5	4.4	30	3	2.7	4.1	Saudi Arabia*
42b	3b	3.9	6.2 b	37	3	3.4	4.9	–	–	–	–	Kuwait*
45	8	3.7	–	39	4	3.5	6.2	37	4	3.3	5.8	Oman*
40b	5b	3.5	5.8b	28	4	2.4	3.5	–	–	–	–	Bahrain*
				Non-Arab Developing Countries								
28	8	2.0	3.5	19	6	1.3	2.2	17	6	1.1	1.9	Turkey
16	6	1.0	1.7	13	6	0.7	1.5	10	6	0.4	1.3	South Korea
27	8	1.9	3.3	19	6	1.3	2.1	17	6	1.1	1.9	Brazil
28	6	2.2	3.3	23	5	1.8	2.7	21	5	1.6	2.4	Mexico
44	12	3.2	6.2	32	10	2.2	4.6	30	8	2.2	4.1	Pakistan
				Developed Countries								
13	11	0.2	1.6	11	10	0.1	1.6	12	10	0.2	1.6	Belgium
13	10	0.3	1.8	13	10	0.3	1.8	12	9	0.3	1.8	Norway
13	10	0.3	1.8	13	9	0.4	1.9	12	9	0.3	1.8	France
17	9	0.8	1.9	14	9	0.5	2.1	14	8	0.6	2.1	United States
13	11	0.2	1.8	11	10	0.1	1.7	11	10	0.1	1.7	United Kingdom

Nashriyya al-Ihsa al-Sanawiyya Li-Tunis, various years (Tunis); The WB, *World Tables*, various issues (Published for the WB by Johns Hopkins University Press); idem, *World Development Report*, various issues (Published for the WB by Oxford University Press); UN, *Demographic Yearbook*, various issues (New York: UN Publications); ECWA/ESCWA, *Demographic and Related Socio-Economic Data Sheets for Countries of the Economic and Social Commission for Western Asia*, various issues (Beirut, Baghdad and Amman); idem, *Statistical Abstract of the ECWA/ESCWA Region*, various issues (New York, Baghdad and Amman); The US, Department of Commerce, US Census Bureau, *International Data Base*. Available at: http:/www.census.gov.

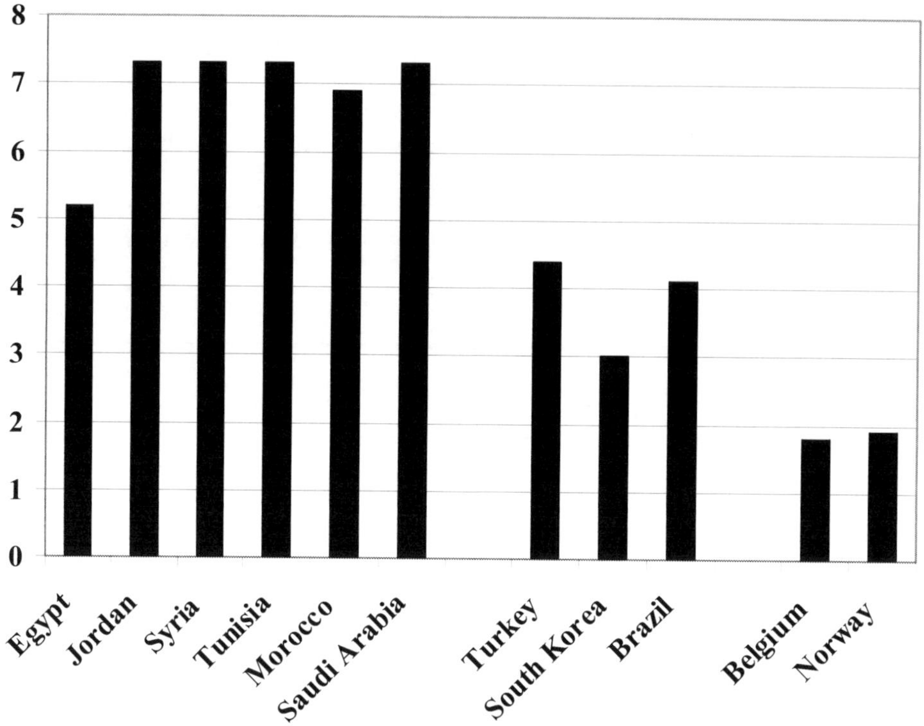

Figure 2.5 Total Fertility Rates in some Arab Countries, non-Arab Developing Countries and Developed Countries, 1980

Table 2.5 The Percentage of the Urban Population within the Total Population in some Arab Countries, 1950–2005 (%)

Year Country	1950	1960	1970	1980	1990	2000	2005*
Egypt	31.9	37.9	42.2	43.8	43.4	42.1	42.3
Syria	30.6	36.8	43.3	46.7	48.9	50.1	50.3
Jordan	35.9	50.9	56.0	60.2	72.2	78.7	79.3
Sudan	6.3	10.3	16.4	20.0	26.6	36.1	40.8
Tunisia	31.2	36.0	44.5	51.5	57.9	62.8	64.4
Morocco	26.2	29.2	34.6	41.3	48.4	55.5	58.8
Algeria	22.3	30.4	39.5	43.5	51.4	57.1	60.0
Saudi Arabia	17.5	30.2	48.7	65.9	78.2	86.2	88.5
Kuwait	59.2	72.3	77.8	90.8	94.9	96.0	96.4
Oman	2.4	3.5	11.4	31.5	62.1	76.0	78.6

* Projections

Source: UN, Population Division, *World Urbanization Prospects: The 2003 Revision* (New York, 2004).

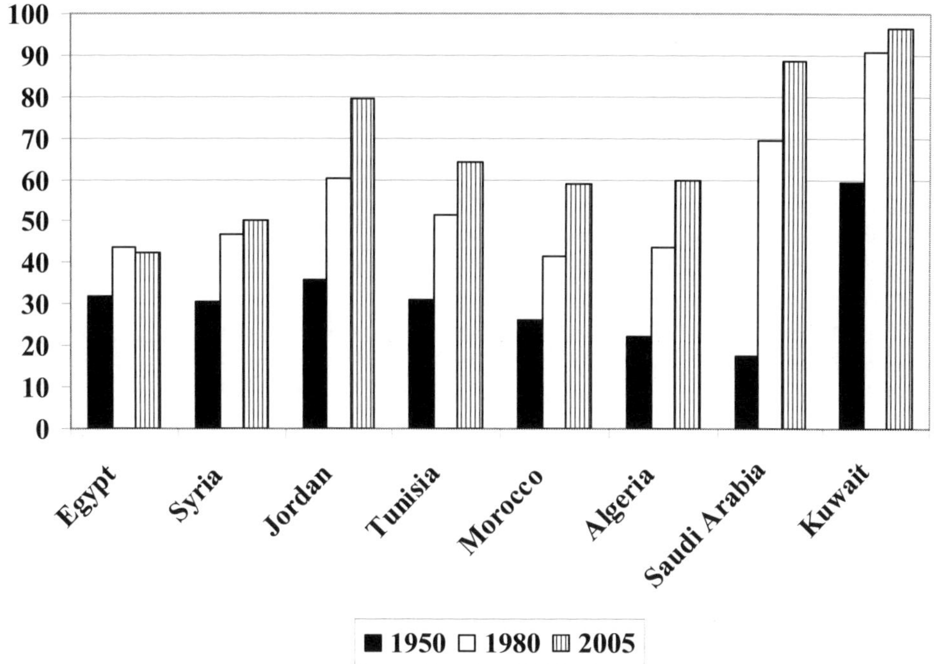

Figure 2.6 The Percentage of the Urban Population within the Total Population in some Arab Countries, 1950–2005 (%)

(b) Children as "social security" for the elder generation In most developing societies until very recently, and in many countries even today, a national social security system in the Western format of a "welfare state" either does not exist or is inadequate. This refers to the government's responsibility for providing a "minimum living standard" to its citizens through elder allowances, child allowances, allowances to poor people, allowances to the disabled, and the like. Such provisions are not available in the Arab countries, with the exception of the Gulf oil states. Moreover, in the poorer Arab agrarian societies, the average income is not enough so that one can save for a pension, as in Western developed societies. Thus, the major, and sometimes the only economic security of the elder population, mainly in the rural areas, is provided by their male children.[84] Consequently, parents attempt to produce the required number of adult boys in order to secure their own future. Three to four male adult children are generally considered as a minimum, meaning that parents in poor agrarian societies would need to have six to eight adult children.

(c) Women's status The status of women in any given society has a critical impact on fertility rates.[85] Generally speaking, one can say that as the status of women rises, fertility rates decline. As long as the woman's role is to raise children and as long as her status in the extended family is a function of the number of her children, particularly males, then it is in the very basic interest of the woman herself to bear as many children as possible.[86] The main argument of the modern feminist literature regarding the family planning issue is that: "Women must be the subjects, rather than the objects, of population policy – or population policy simply won't work."[87] Indeed, Western

Europe's fertility decline since the 1960s has occurred simultaneously with the changing family model from the traditional form of "one breadwinner" to "two breadwinners." As examined in Chapter 5, the Arab countries are no different in this respect. When women's status improves, mainly in the employment arena, fertility rates are lower. The prominent explanation for the huge fertility difference between Tunisia and Saudi Arabia focuses on the differences in women's status.[88]

(d) The cultural-religious factor Throughout history, societies have suffered from high infant and child mortality rates along with low life expectancy. The vast majority of the pre-industrial societies worldwide have adopted socio-cultural and religious concepts that encourage high fertility, including a ban on contraceptive use. In the case of Judaism, one of the religious commands is "Be fruitful and multiply." In many cultures, including Islamic culture, early marriage of females is a deeply rooted norm. As Weeks described it: "Once married, there is immediate pressure to bear a child, in order especially to prove the wife's fecundity to her husband's family . . . Youthful marriage is thus part and parcel of the traditional family system, reinforced by (but not necessarily caused by) Islam."[89]

Naturally, the vast majority of people conform to the prevailing norms of their own society, including those relating to age of marriage and fertility. With respect to "cultural fertility," it should be emphasized that in many Arab societies there is no apparent difference between urban and rural patterns. This is best demonstrated in the Gulf oil societies. Although they underwent a rapid urbanization process following the discovery of oil, the fertility rates did not decline in accordance with the demographic transition model until the mid-1990s, despite the tremendous socioeconomic development. One major reason for this, it appears, is that these societies have maintained their extended family arrangements and even tribal systems in the cities as well.

Another factor accounting for high fertility rates in traditional societies is the absence of openness regarding sex, including the proper use of contraceptives for married woman. Thus, a large number of unwanted pregnancies occur even among married couples (see Chapter 5). It can be said in general that the more traditional the society, the lower the willingness to use contraceptives and, consequently, the higher the fertility rates. This argument is supported by research conducted among elites, whose fertility rates traditionally were and still are considerably lower than those found among the lower strata. As noted by Moghadam: "As women from elite families are generally those with the most access to education and employment, fertility is also variable by class."[90] The question is whether the lower number of children among elites is a function of their higher educational level, accessibility to the contraceptives themselves and knowledge about their proper use, or whether it should be attributed to other factors, such as lower infant and child mortality rates or absence of the need for a large number of children from a purely economic viewpoint. Although this question remains open, it would appear that higher accessibility to contraceptives and family planning education would likely reduce fertility rates, given the considerable number of unwanted pregnancies in developing societies (see Chapter 5).

A related religious-cultural factor reinforcing high fertility levels in traditional societies is the fatalistic belief that everything is "a decree from Heaven," or *al-Qadar* in Arabic, and that "God will provide." As such, it is not seen as necessary or even desirable to attempt to control one's own fertility.

(e) Early age at first marriage Another important factor contributing to the high fertility rates in the Arab countries was the early marriage of women, which is clearly

evident from the population censuses and the demographic surveys which have been conducted in the Arab countries since the 1960s. For example, according to the 1960 Syrian population census, the average age at first marriage for females was 19.51 years. According to the *1978-SFS*, 52.5% of the females aged 45–49 were married before the age of 20.[91] According to the *2003–Egypt Interim Demographic and Health Survey (2003–EIDHS)*, 60.8% of the women aged 45–49 were married before the age of 20 and as high as 85.8% before the age of 25.[92]

However, the median and average age at first marriage for women in almost all of the Arab countries has increased considerably since the 1970s, with the exception of Yemen where early age at first marriage continues to be very common.[93] For example, whereas in 1956 only 43% of the women aged 15–24 in Tunisia were unmarried, this percentage dramatically increased to 75% in 1980.[94] By 1995, only 3% of the Tunisian women under 20 years old were married.[95] One finds a similar phenomenon of increased age at first marriage among Syrian women. According to the *1993–SMCHS*, the median age at first marriage increased from 18 years for women aged 35–39 to 20 years for women aged 25–29.[96] Also in Bahrain, the country with the lowest fertility rate among the Gulf countries, the median age at first marriage rose from 15 years for women currently aged 45–49, to 21 years for women currently aged 30–34 and to 23 years for women currently aged 25–29.[97]

It should be taken into consideration, however, that despite the increase in the average age of women at first marriage, in most of the Arab countries early marriages remained quite common during the 1990s as well. For example, according to the *1993–SMCHS*, 2.4% of women aged 20–24 were married between the ages of 10 to 14 years.[98] In the case of Egypt, according to the *2003–EIDHS*, as many as 36.3% of the women aged 20–24 were married before the age of 20 and 18.5% were married before the age of 18.[99] In the case of Morocco, despite the marked fertility decline during the past two decades, in 2004, the age specific fertility rate for the age group of 15–19 was still considerable at 19.1.[100]

The rise in age at first marriage, however, occurred at the same time as a considerable lengthening of the reproductive period due to the sharp increase in life expectancy (see below). Consequently, the older age at first marriage did not bring about a reduction in the length of the reproductive period within the marriage framework. As births outside the marriage system were and still continue to be very rare, the length of the reproductive period within the marriage framework is a crucial factor affecting fertility rates in the Arab societies. While in the Arab societies the increased age at first marriage did not reduce the overall length of the reproductive period within the framework of marriage, in Western developed societies, the reproductive period within the marriage framework considerably declined, as during the past two generations, the average age of women at first marriage increased by more than 10 years. The difference in the length of the reproductive period within the marriage framework constitutes an important factor for the huge fertility gaps between the Arab societies on the one hand, and the worldwide developed societies, on the other.

(f) High marriage stability Another prominent characteristic of Arab-Islamic societies that has implications for fertility rates is the low divorce rates. For example, according to the *1978–SFS*, 92.9% of the women who participated in the survey reported that they were still married to their first husbands. Among the remaining 7.1%, 3.7% were widows and only 3.1% were divorced. From the *1993–SMCHS* data, it appears that 95% of the women who participated in the survey were still married to

their first husbands.[101] The marriage stability in the Gulf oil societies was even higher than in the non-oil Arab societies. The *1987-SACHS* indicated that almost all of the Saudi women participating in the survey were still married to their first husbands.[102] According to the *GFHS* carried out during 1995–1998, the percentage of divorcees within the total participants was 2.9% in Bahrain and the UAE, 3.4% in Kuwait, 3.8% in Oman, 3.2% in Qatar and 2.1% in Saudi Arabia.[103]

(g) Wars and political instability In times of war and intensive international political conflicts, governing authorities tend to be more focused on managing the situation at hand rather than on operating in line with long-term socioeconomic calculations. Moreover, in many cases, it appears that the basic instinct of both the authorities and the public itself is to treat a large population as a security-political asset. The Arab–Israeli conflict, particularly the Palestinian-Israeli conflict, constitutes a good example in which each side has attempted to increase its population as a political-security asset (see the Introduction). Since many of the Arab countries were involved in the Arab–Israeli conflict, either directly or indirectly, or in other regional conflicts (such as the Iraq–Iran War, 1980–1988), the issue of family planning has been widely neglected until very recently (see Chapter 5).

Higher fertility levels are also desired in cases of local tribal conflicts or in rural areas where the presence of a central authority is ineffective in enforcing law and order, thereby creating the need for as many fighters as possible.[104] In the case of the Gulf oil societies in which the political structure was and to a large extent still is based on "tribal politics" and *Asabiyya* (group solidarity),[105] each tribe or extended family had an incentive to increase rather than to decrease the number of its members.

The phenomenon of a "pro-natalist environment" in periods of security-political tension, however, is not limited to the Arab states alone, and similar situations existed during the 1960s and 1970s in Southeast Asia as well as in South America. Thus, for example, in 1977, Shin Hyon Hwack, South Korea's Minister of Health and Social Affairs and later the Prime Minister, was worried that the success of South Korea's family planning policy would leave the country at a disadvantage in the conflict with North Korea, despite the fact that South Korea's population outnumbered North Korea's by 20 million! Likewise, the Thai leaders were worried that the larger population of neighboring Vietnam would give them the advantage in times of conflict between the two countries. A similar phenomenon prevailed during the 1960s and 1970s among South American leaders as well.[106]

(h) The socioeconomic policy A prominent contributor to high fertility rates in the Arab countries has been the pro-natalist socioeconomic policies that prevailed until the mid-1980s and even during the 1990s in some countries. The policy of *al-Ishtiraqiyya al-'Arabiyya* (Arab Socialism) adopted during the 1950s and 1960s in many Arab countries in effect promoted higher fertility, although it was not the initial intention. In retrospect, it seems that one of the major barriers for Egypt's successful first family planning plan in the second half of the 1960s was the high subsidies provided for basic foodstuffs, healthcare facilities, educational services, transportation, electricity, gasoline, housing and the like. In effect, this policy created a situation in which the government, rather than parents, was responsible for providing the basic needs of children.

Moreover, in many rural areas in the non-oil Arab countries, the new socioeconomic policy made it much cheaper for parents to raise a child than to pay an employee on their farm due to the high subsidies on basic foodstuffs and public services on the one hand and the introduction of a minimum wage on the other. It should be mentioned that even in the Arab countries which did not adopt the Arab Socialism policy, mainly the Gulf oil states, Jordan and Morocco, many of the socialist components were adopted, particularly in the area of massive governmental subsidies along with large-scale public sector employment.

(i) The absence of national family planning programs The Arab countries, with the exception of Tunisia, were among the latest worldwide to implement effective national family planning programs. In retrospect, it appears that avoiding the adoption of comprehensive national family planning programs contributed to the continuing high fertility rates in many of the Arab countries during the 1970s and 1980s, and in some, such as Syria, Jordan and Algeria, during the first half of the 1990s as well. A major factor accounting for this avoidance was the effects of the "oil boom" in both the oil-based and the poorer Arab countries (see Chapter 5).

3.2 Arab Fertility Decline since the mid-1980s

Since the mid-1980s, fertility rates in all of the Arab countries, even in Yemen and Sudan although to a lesser extent, started to decline. By 1990, the CBRs of all of the Arab countries were lower than they had been in 1980. This trend picked up speed throughout the past 15 years. By 2005, Egypt's CBR for example was 23 per 1,000, compared to 33 in 1990 and 38 in 1980. A similar trend was also evident in Syria, Jordan, Morocco and Algeria. Tunisia's CBR had declined from 41 per 1,000 in 1970 to 35 in 1980 and reached 16 in 2005 – the lowest level of all of the Arab countries. Thus, by 2005, Tunisia's CBR was only 4 points higher than the prevailing rate in the more developed EU countries. Even in the Gulf pro-natalist countries, fertility rates have substantially declined since the early 1990s. By 2005, the TFR of Saudi national women averaged 4.1 children per woman compared to 7.3 in 1980 and 7.1 in 1988, while the CBR of the Saudi national population declined from 42 per 1,000 in 1990 to 30 in 2005. A similar trend occurred in Oman as well, whose TFR declined from 7.2 children per woman in 1980 to 6.2 in 2000 and reached 5.8 in 2005 (see Table 2.4).

What factors are responsible for this general fertility decline among all of the Arab countries since the mid-1980s? Why has this process taken place almost simultaneously during the second half of the 1980s in almost all the Arab countries, regardless of whether they are pro-natalist oil states or poorer anti-natalist countries? It seems that the following seven factors can provide a satisfactory explanation to these questions:

(a) A sharp drop in infant and child mortality rates Since the 1950s, the infant and child mortality rates in all of the Arab countries substantially declined (see below). Consequently, the "desired number of children" could be reached by a much lower number of births compared to previous periods. Once the parents were convinced that the survival chances of their offspring indeed markedly increased, they reacted by reducing fertility. The period between the reduction of infant and child mortality rates and the beginning of fertility decline constituted the second stage of the demographic transition.[107] In the Arab countries, it should be noted, the pace of the decline in infant and child mortality rates during the 1970s and 1980s was faster than in most other developing countries worldwide – a direct result of the "oil boom" that led to a sharp improvement in the living standard and in healthcare facilities alike.[108]

(b) "Economic births" As noted earlier, in pre-industrial agrarian societies, children constituted an important labor force asset to their families from a very early age. This

situation, however, has rapidly changed with the improvement in salaries, the introduction of the "welfare state" and, most importantly, the enactment of child labor laws and compulsory education. Hence, whereas children in traditional societies provided economic services to their families, in modern urban societies, they represent an increasing economic burden in line with the advance of modernization.[109] This, in fact, is the major theme of the "Chicago School of thought" of the reduced demand for children as determined by income, costs and prices.[110] In other words, in modern society, in contrast to traditional society, the parents exchanged "quantity" for "quality" in their fertility behavior.

(c) Rapid urbanization All of the population censuses and demographic surveys conducted in developing societies, including the Arab countries, point to the fact that the fertility rates in the urban centers were and still are much lower than in the rural areas. The process of transformation from agrarian to modern urbanized economy not only led to a profound socioeconomic change, but influenced fertility patterns as well. This phenomenon prevailed in both the oil-based economies and the poorer countries alike. For example, according to the *1989–OCHS*, while the TFR in the urban centers averaged 5.3 children per woman, it was as high as 9.1 in the rural areas.[111] A similar fertility trend was found in the *1995–OFHS*, according to which the TFR in the urban centers averaged 6.6 children per woman, compared to 8.0 in the rural areas (see Table 2.6). According to the *1993–SMCHS* data, while the TFR in Syrian urban centers averaged 3.57 children per woman, this number increased to 5.06 in the countryside.[112] According to the *2001–SFHS*, the TFR in the urban centers averaged 3.4 children per woman, compared to 4.4 in the rural areas.[113] The Syrian 2004 census results record that the TFR in the urban centers was 3.2 compared to 4.1 in the rural areas.[114] According to *2002–JPFHS*, while the TFR in urban centers averaged 3.5, it was 4.2 in the rural areas (see Table 2.7). According to the latest official Jordanian data, by 2005, the TFR in the urban centers averaged 3.1 children per woman, compared to 3.5 in the rural areas.[115] Likewise, in Morocco, according to the *National Survey on Population and Health–1992*, the TFR in the urban areas averaged 2.5 children per woman – less

Table 2.6 Total Fertility Rate and Mean Number of Children Ever-born in Oman, According to Place of Residence and Female Educational Level, 1995

Background Characteristics	Total Fertility Rate (age 15–49)	Mean Number of Children Ever-born to All Women (age 40–49)
Place of Residence		
Urban	6.60	8.68
Rural	7.95	8.38
Women's Educational Level		
Illiterate	8.61	8.75
Less than primary	7.59	8.39
Primary	7.51	8.14
Preparatory	4.74	5.25
Secondary and above	3.81	3.95
Total	**7.05**	**8.57**

Source: Sultanate of Oman, Ministry of Health, *Oman Family Health Survey–1995*, edited by Ali J.M. Sulaiman, Asya al-Riyami and Samir Farid (Muscat, 1996), p. 30, table 7.3.

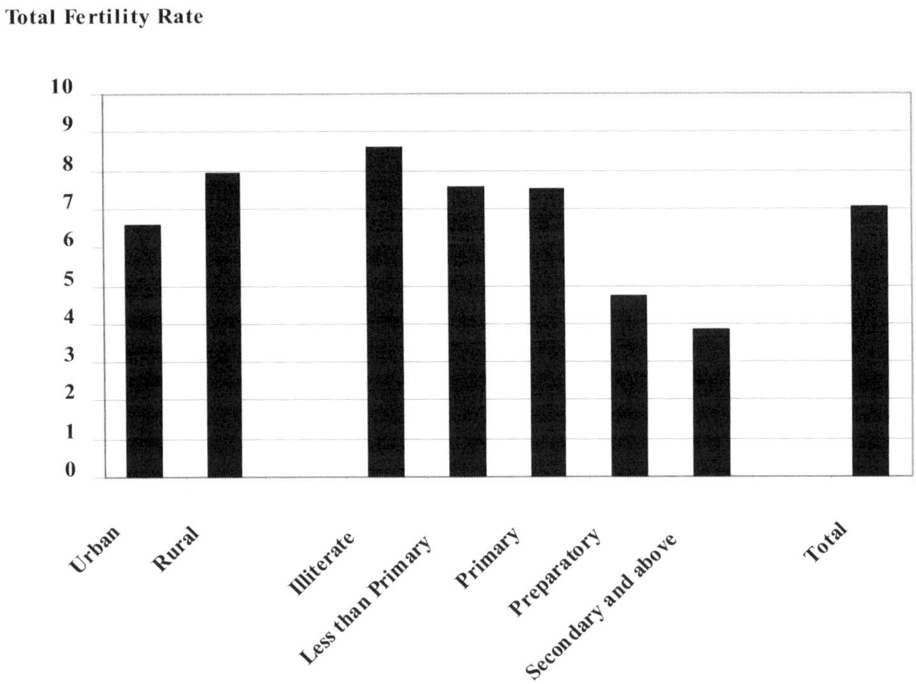

Figure 2.7 Total Fertility Rate in Oman, According to Place of Residence and Female Educational Level, 1995

than half of the 5.5 in the rural areas.[116] By 2004, the TFR in the Moroccan urban centers had declined to the replacement level of 2.1 children per woman, compared to 3.1 in the rural areas.[117] In the other North African countries, one can find a similar trend of much higher fertility rates in the rural areas than in the urban centers.[118]

Table 2.7 Total Fertility Rate in Jordan, According to Place of Residence and Female Educational Level, 2002

Background Characteristics	Total Fertility Rate (age 15-49)
Place of Residence	
Urban	3.5
Rural	4.2
Female Educational Level	
No education	3.6
Elementary	3.7
Preparatory	4.4
Secondary	3.9
Higher	3.1
Total	**3.7**

Source: The Hashemite Kingdom of Jordan, Department of Statistics, *Jordan Population and Health Survey–2002* (Amman, 2003), p. 38, table 4.3.

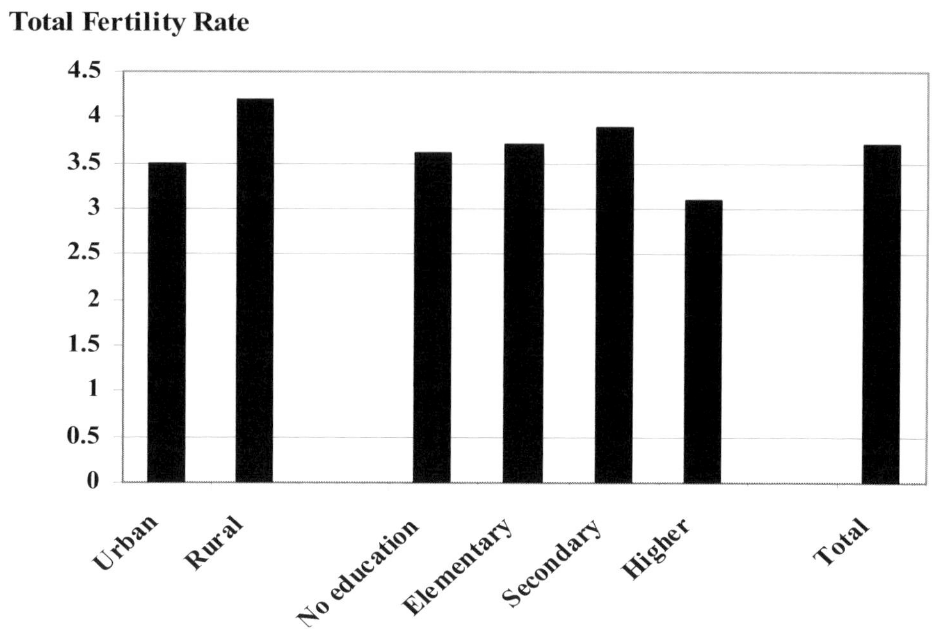

Figure 2.8 Total Fertility Rate in Jordan, According to Place of Residence and Female Educational Level, 2002

The reasons for the considerably lower fertility rates in the major cities than in the countryside are fivefold:

(1) **In the urban centers, the children, in most cases, no longer constitute an economic asset to their parents.**

(2) **The cost of housing in the major cities is much higher than in the countryside.** This factor is particularly important among the urban middle class which on the one hand wants better living standards, including better housing conditions, while on the other hand do not have the financial ability to acquire large apartments in the major cities due to their extremely high cost. This factor, it seems, is common to both developed and developing countries worldwide. Among the lower urban classes in the developing countries, as will be examined below, not only do many families live in informal housing in the cities' suburbs, but their children constitute a major economic asset. These children are usually employed in the "informal urban sector" as was examined in Chapter 1. On one of my visits to Cairo, there was a young child of around ten years old in front of my hotel who "pounced" on every visitor, offering to carry suitcases or summon a taxi. Monitoring his activities from the sidelines, I calculated that this child earned much more money in tips than the average salary of an adult male in the middle rank of the Egyptian public sector. No doubt, this child was a major contributor to his family's income.

In such cases, of course, all cost/benefit calculations of raising children in the cities are rendered irrelevant. According to World Bank figures, more than 18% of the children in Egypt aged 10 to 14 were working in 1980, though this rate declined to 11% in 1996.[119] Still, at the dawn of the twenty-first century, children's employment is a

Informal housing in Cairo: The City of Death *(Madinat al-Mawt)*

common phenomenon in the poorer Arab countries. According to data collected by the Arab League, this phenomenon has expanded in recent years, particularly in Morocco, Tunisia, Egypt, Jordan, Yemen, Syria and Lebanon,[120] as a result of increasing unemployment and decreasing real wages in these countries (see Chapter 3).

(3) In both the oil-based and the poorer Arab countries, **the higher education system is concentrated in the major cities**, making for greater accessibility to higher education in those areas. The result is a higher than average educational level of women in the cities, particularly in the capitals. Since women's educational level represents one of the two paramount factors impacting on fertility rates (see below), the increased percentage of the urban population within the total population has led to a decline in the national average fertility rates.

(4) **Women's employment patterns in the cities are not conducive to taking small children with them to their jobs**, as they tend to do on the household farm in the countryside.

(5) **The social and cultural environment in the rural areas is much more conductive to higher fertility than in the urban centers,** particularly the larger cities. This is due to three factors: the earlier age that rural women marry compared to urban women; the traditional higher status of large families; and the still common phenomenon of living within extended family households.[121]

(d) The sharp improvement in the educational level of women This is among the most important factors which account for the declining fertility in all the developing countries worldwide, including the Arab countries. As one can see in the following two

Table 2.8 Literacy Rates among Males and Females in some Arab Countries, 1970, 1985, 2000–2001 (%)

Year	1970		1985		2000-2001	
Country	Males	Females	Males	Females	Males	Females
Egypt	50	20	59	30	67	44
Syria	60	20	76	43	88	61
Jordan	64	29	87	63	95	84
Tunisia	44	17	68	41	81	61
Morocco	34	10	45	22	62	36
Algeria	39	11	63	37	78	57
Saudi Arabia	15	2	71	31	84	67
Kuwait	65	42	76	63	85	80
Oman	–	–	47	12	80	62

Sources: PRB, *Population Reference Bureau Data Finder*. Available at: http://www.worldpop.org/datafinder.htm; UNDP, *Human Development Report–1990* (Published for the UNDP by Oxford University Press, 1990).

tables (2.8 and 2.9), in each of the Arab countries since the 1960s "an educational revolution" has occurred at all levels. While until the 1950s, education was concentrated almost totally among the elites, since then, it has rapidly spread to the lower strata, as education at all levels has become free of charge. Hence, while the literacy rate among Egyptian women in 1970 was 20%, it increased to 44% in 2000. In Tunisia the increase was even sharper, from 17% to 61% during the corresponding period. The highest increase was, of course, in the Gulf oil countries. In the case of Saudi Arabia, women's

Table 2.9 Number of Students Enrolled in Universities per 100,000 People in some Arab Countries, 1965–1996

Year / Country	1965		1980		1990		1996	
	Males	Females	Males	Females	Males	Females	Males	Females
Egypt	936	246	2,205	1,048	1,869	1,025	2,316 (c)	1,472 (c)
Syria	994	212	2,231	946	2,166	1,402	1,814 (b)	1,297 (b)
Jordan	215	108	1,712	1,577	2,072	2,402	2,587	2,492
Tunisia	195	45	685	297	1,005	670	1,456	1,201
Morocco	120	17	886	273	1,353	773	1,332 (b)	931 (b)
Algeria	102	27	1,081	508	—	—	1,466 (c)	1,000 (c)
Saudi Arabia	103	4	863	393	955	965	1,396	1,528
Kuwait	322 (a)	395 (a)	739	1,330	—	—	1,926 (c)	2,590 (c)
Bahrain	—	—	555	542	1,071	1,859	1,056 (b)	1,972 (b)
Oman	—	—	2	3	354	340	539	524
Qatar	—	—	594	1,682	602	2,871	617	3,278

— No data available.
(a) Figures relate to 1970. (b) Figures relate to 1994. (c) Figures relate to 1995.

Sources: UNESCO, *Statistical Yearbook*, various issues, 1967–1998 (Paris).

Table 2.10 Total Fertility Rate in Egypt, According to Place of Residence and Female Educational Level, 2005

Background Characteristics	Total Fertility Rate (age 15–49)
Place of Residence	
Urban	2.7
Rural	3.4
Female Educational Level	
No education	3.8
Some primary	3.4
Primary complete/some secondary	2.9
Secondary complete/higher	3.0
Total	**3.1**

Source: Arab Republic of Egypt, Ministry of Health and Population, National Population Council and Macro International Inc., *Egypt Demographic and Health Survey–2005*, by Fatma El-Zanaty and Ann Way (Cairo, 2006), p. 46, table 4.2.

literacy rate increased from a mere 2% in 1970 to 67% at the start of the twenty-first century. In the other Gulf oil countries, the same phenomenon occurred.

As for higher education, while in 1965 the number of females enrolled in universities in Egypt was 246 per 100,000 people, this number increased to 1,472 in 1995. In Tunisia, the increase was much sharper, from 45 in 1965 to 1,201 in 1996. The highest growth rate has occurred, of course, in the Gulf oil countries. The most extreme growth has occurred in Oman: while in 1980 the number of females enrolled in universities was barely 3 per 100,000 people, this number increased to 524 in 1996.

From population censuses and demographic surveys conducted during the past four decades in developing societies worldwide, including the Arab countries, it appears that women's educational level is a paramount factor in determining fertility behavior. The higher the woman's educational level, the lower the number of children. For example, according to the *1995–EDHS*, while the TFR for illiterate women averaged 4.5 children per woman, this number sharply declined to 3.0 among women with secondary education and above.[122] A similar fertility gap which corresponds to women's educational level appeared in the *2005–EDHS*, in which the TFR of women without any formal education averaged 3.8 children per woman, compared to 3.0 for women with secondary education and above (see Table 2.10).

In terms of the huge fertility gap created by women's educational level, there were no differences between the oil-based and the poorer Arab countries.[123] Thus, for example, according to the *1995–OFHS*, while the TFR among illiterate women averaged 8.6 children per woman, this rate declined to 4.7 among women with preparatory education and even further declined to 3.8 among those with secondary education and above (see Table 2.6). A comparable trend can also be found in the *1987–Kuwait Child Health Survey*.[124] The correlation between women's education and fertility rates is so high that the fertility rate of minimally educated women, that is women with less than a complete primary education, is lower than among illiterate women.

The academic literature on the correlation between fertility rates and women's educational level in developing countries is immense, not only in demography, sociology and economics but in the field of gender studies as well. The high correlation

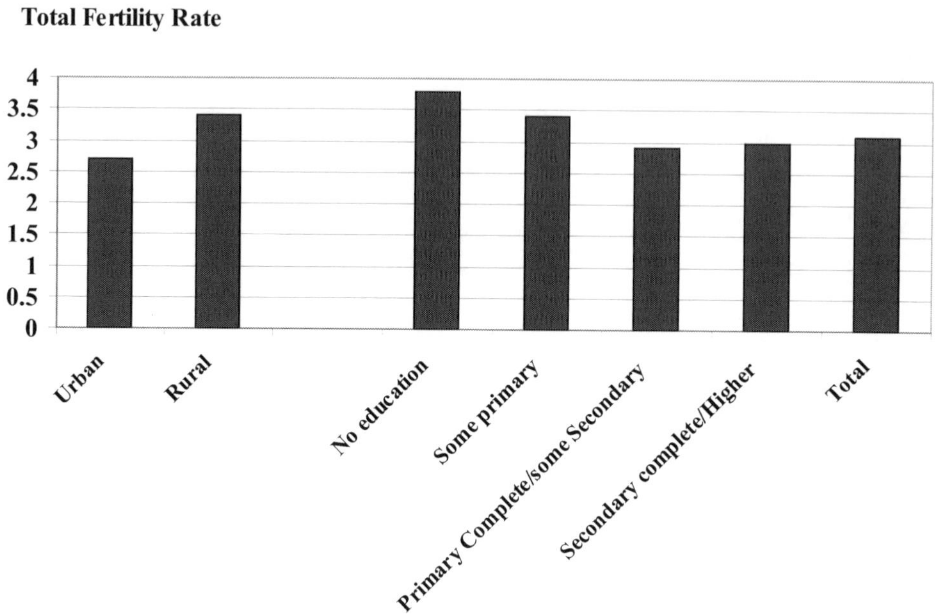

Figure 2.9 Total Fertility Rate in Egypt, According to Place of Residence and Female Educational Level, 2005

between women's educational level and fertility rates can be summarized by the following seven factors:

(1) **The higher the woman's educational level, the greater her tendency to marry at an older age**, in most cases after the completion of her education. This means that if she attended a university, she is more likely not to marry until her mid-twenties.

(2) **The higher the woman's educational level, the greater her tendency to work outside the home**. Since having a large number of small children acts as a hindrance to a woman's career, women working outside the household tend to have fewer children. According to the Syrian 1970 census, for example, the average number of children ever born to women who were economically active in non-agricultural occupations was 3.9, compared to 5.4 on average among women who were engaged in agriculture.[125]

(3) Since there is a high correlation between educational level and salary level, **the "lost income" of educated women for each additional child born is higher than that of uneducated women**, particularly those working in the family fields.

(4) **Educated women usually have a better understanding of the correlation between the number of children and their standard of living**. Consequently, they naturally tend to bear fewer children which correspond to the socioeconomic condition of the family and the "consumption aspiration model." This is particularly evident in the growing awareness of educated parents in the non-oil Arab countries of the need to send their children to higher educational institutions abroad in order to increase their opportunities for better private sector jobs. As such, a large number of children

impacts on the ability of the middle class parents to send their children abroad. Courbage noted that: "This entails not only planning a smaller family, but also longer intervals between births to avoid the financial drain of having two children being educated abroad at the same time."[126]

(5) **Educated women tend to be more aware of the various family planning options** and thus have better knowledge of contraceptive methods and their proper use, avoiding, to a large extent, the probability of unwanted pregnancies. Thus, the number of children ever born to educated woman is, in most cases, close to the desired number of children.

(6) **Educated women are more competent of taking care of their children**, who are, as a result, less exposed to illness. Consequently, the mortality rates among infants of educated women are considerably lower than those among infants of uneducated mothers. For example, according to the *1990–JPFHS*, while the infant mortality rate of illiterate mothers was 38.7 per 1,000 live births, this rate declined to only 23.9 among mothers with higher education.[127] According to the *2005–EDHS*, children born to women who never attended school were more than twice as likely to die by their fifth birthday compared to children born to mothers with a secondary or higher education (67.7 per 1,000 live births compared to 30.7 per 1,000 live births).[128] Educated women are thus more inclined to have a smaller number of children because they are not as fearful about losing their offspring.

(7) **Educated women in developing societies are more aware of the outside world.** They are fully aware of the basic contradiction between a modern lifestyle and having a large number of children. This basic contradiction has various aspects, but it is most illustrated through the basic contradiction between the acquisition of modern consumer goods on the one hand, and large families, i.e., smaller per capita income, on the other.[129]

The only exception to the high correlation between women's educational level and fertility rate among the poorer Arab societies is that of the Palestinians in the Occupied Territories, particularly in the Gaza Strip. Despite the average high educational level of the Palestinian women there, the fertility rates remain very high up to the present – in fact the highest worldwide, even surpassing those that prevail in sub-Saharan African countries. According to ESCWA figures, by the year 2000, the CBR in the Gaza Strip was 46.5 per 1,000, while the TFR was as high as 6.93 children per woman. In the West Bank, although the fertility rate is lower than in the Gaza Strip, it still remains very high relative to both Arab and international averages, with a CBR of 41.5 per 1,000 and a TFR of 5.6 children per woman in 2000.[130] In total contrast to the other Arab societies in general and the other Palestinian communities in particular, these fertility rates declined very slightly in the early 2000s. According to the *2004–Demographic and Health Survey*, which was carried out by the PCBS, the TFR was 4.1 children per woman in the West Bank and 5.8 in the Gaza Strip.[131]

The reasons for the continuing high fertility rates among the Palestinians in the Occupied Territories, despite the marked decline in the infant and child mortality rates[132] and the sharp rise in women educational level, are both political and economic. From the economic viewpoint, the aid policy of UNRWA was and still is based on the number of family members. Thus, one finds much higher fertility rates among the Palestinian refugees than among the settled population in the Occupied Palestinian Territories. According to a survey conducted by the PCBS in April–July 1995, while the TFR in the refugee camps (in both the West Bank and the Gaza Strip) averaged

6.84 children per woman, this rate declined to 6.18 among the rural population and 5.57 among the urban population.[133]

Fargues argued that the reason for the continuing high fertility rates among the Palestinians in the Occupied Territories is the low female labor force participation rates under the Israeli occupation, particularly since the onset of the first *Intifada* in December 1987. Since the improvement in the women's educational level did not bring about an increase in their labor force participation rates, there was no subsequent decline in the fertility rates.[134] Indeed, according to the December 1997 Palestinian population census, the labor force participation rate among females 15 years of age and over was 9.3% in the West Bank and only 5.2% in the Gaza Strip[135] – lower than any of the Arab countries, even Saudi Arabia and Kuwait. From a political viewpoint, the continuing high fertility rates of the Palestinians in the Occupied Territories is attributable to the fact that the Palestinian leadership treats rapid population growth as a political asset – hence the absence of any kind of family planning program.

(e) Increased employment opportunities for women In all of the developing countries worldwide, including both the oil-based and the poorer Arab countries, there is almost a complete correlation between women's employment outside the household and their fertility rates in the form of the higher the economic participation rate, the lower the fertility rate. As will be examined in Chapter 3, during the past two decades, there has been a steady rise in the economic active participation rates of women in all of the Arab countries. As discussed above in relation to Palestinian women in the Occupied Territories, the distinct contradiction between the high educational level of the young GCC women, on the one hand, and their high fertility rates, on the other hand, can be explained by the various limitations, both social and legal, on women's employment. In contrast to the GCC countries, Tunisia's women have a lower educational level, but a much higher crude economically active rate – in fact the highest among the Arab countries – thus explaining Tunisia's much lower fertility rates in comparison to any other Arab society.

(f) Increased family planning activities and contraceptive prevalence rates Since the mid-1980s, following the end of the "bonanza oil decade," the activities of the Arab governments in the family planning area, both direct and indirect, were largely intensified. Even in countries such as Syria, Jordan, Oman and Algeria, which had previously implemented hidden indirect anti-natalist measures, the family planning activities became more open and targeted. The Middle Eastern experience in the family planning area, as will be examined in Chapter 5, reveals a high correlation between the implementation of family planning plans and the pace of fertility decline.

(g) Changing socioeconomic policies The substantial macroeconomic policy changes in the entire world during the past two decades, namely, the adoption of the free market economy approach at the expense of *étatism* and socialism, have constituted a major factor in fertility decline among many developing societies worldwide, including the poorer Arab countries.[136] The basic assumption of the capitalist approach is that the fundamental responsibility for supporting children lies with their parents, as opposed to the state under the socialist approach. In this regard, it must be recognized that in many of the Arab countries, such as Egypt, Tunisia, and recently Syria and Yemen as well, the declining fertility rates and the withdrawal from the socialist socioeconomic policy occurred simultaneously. The adoption of the market economy involved the narrowing of many state subsidies, leading to a general increase in the cost of raising children.

Table 2.11 Contraceptive Prevalence Rates (all methods) among Married Women in some Arab Countries, 1983, 1993–2001 (%)

Country	1983	1993–2001
Egypt	30	56.1 (h)
Jordan	26	52.6 (e)
Syria	23	39.6 (a)
Tunisia	35	59.7 (b)
Morocco	26	58.4 (e)
Algeria	7	64.0 (h)
Saudi Arabia	—	31.8 (d)
Kuwait	—	52.0 (g)
Bahrain	—	61.8 (c)
Oman	—	23.7 (c)
Qatar	—	43.2 (f)

— No data available.
(a) Figure relates to 1993.
(b) Figure relates to 1994/95.
(c) Figures relate to 1995 (nationals only).
(d) Figure relates to 1996 (nationals only).
(e) Figures relate to 1997.
(f) Figure relates to 1998 (nationals only).
(g) Figure relates to 1999 (nationals only).
(h) Figures relate to 2001.

Sources: PRB, *2001 World Population Data Sheets*. Available at: http://www.worldpop.org/datafinder.htm; idem, *Family Planning Worldwide* (New York, 2002); WB, *World Development Report*, various issues (Published for the WB by Oxford University Press); UNDP, *Human Development Report–2006* (New York, 2006).

Therefore, the four most crucial factors for fertility decline are: female education, female employment opportunities, the socioeconomic policies, and the governmental family planning activities. When all of these four factors are combined, fertility rate rapidly declines. The case of Tunisia, as will be examined in Chapter 5, best illustrates this assertion.

The clearest expression of the declining fertility in the Arab countries during the past two decades is the sharp increase in the contraceptive prevalence rates.[137] The highest contraception prevalence rates recorded among the Arab countries were 64% in Algeria in 2001 and 60% in Tunisia in the year 1994/95. The lowest rate was 24% in Oman in 1995, though it has probably increased slightly since then as a result of the expanded anti-natalist measures taken by the Omani authorities. In Saudi Arabia, as well, the contraceptive prevalence rate has remained very low, at only 32% in 1996 (see Table 2.11).

3.3 *Fertility Differentials according to Religion*

A crucial question in the area of fertility patterns in the Arab countries is the "religion effect." Is there any correlation between fertility pattern and religion in the Arab countries?

This question, although crucial from a socio-political viewpoint, not to mention its academic interest, can not be answered, as none of the Arab countries, as was examined in Chapter 1, publish any data, including socio-demographic, according to an

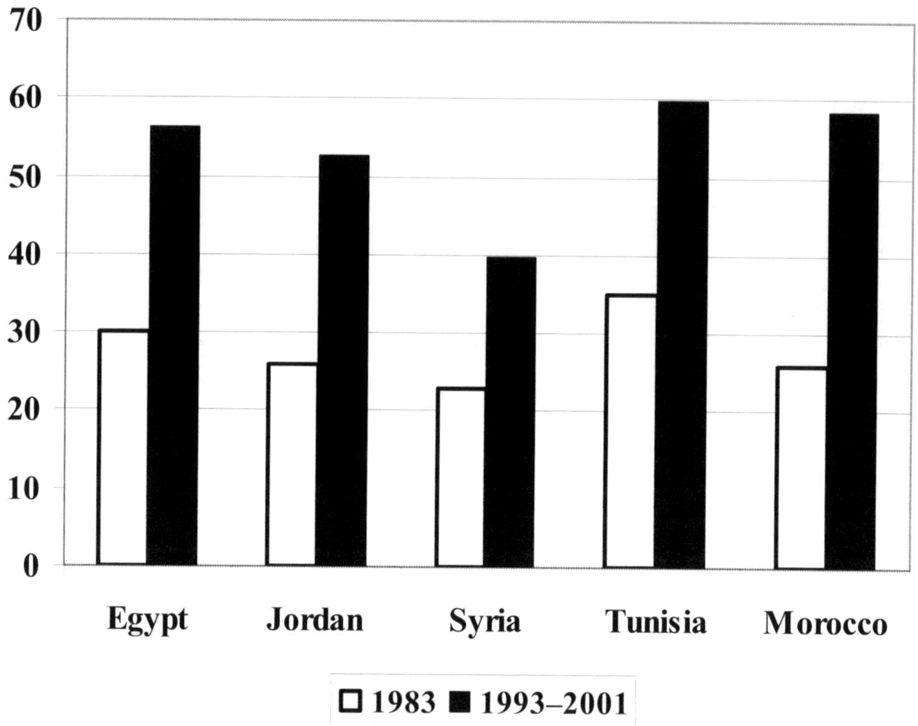

Figure 2.10 Contraceptive Prevalence Rates (all methods) among Married Women in some Arab Countries, 1983, 1993–2001 (%)

ethno-religious differential. Moreover, the rapid urbanization process that occurred in each of the Arab countries, combined with the internal migration between the various regions themselves, abolished the tradition of settlement according religion and ethnicity. Consequently, there is no possibility of identification according to the religious or ethnic fertility deferential, although there are some exceptions to this "shifting settlement pattern," such as the concentration of the Kurds in Northern Syria and Iraq, the Druze in the Syrian Jabel Druze and the Shi'a concentration in al-Hassa province in Saudi Arabia.

Israel is an exception in this respect, as it is the only Middle Eastern country which publishes fertility data according to religion. By 2005, the CBR of the Israeli-Muslims was 30.4 per 1,000 compared to 22.2 among the Druze and only 17.2 among the Christians – even lower than 18.9 of the Jews.[138] However, the crucial question in the "ethno-religion factor" is that of the "chicken and the egg": Are the significantly higher fertility rates among the Israeli-Muslims a result of the religious-cultural factors, or are they a factor of their different socioeconomic characteristics? In other words, do the high fertility rates among the Israeli-Muslims constitute the "core of their poverty" or are their higher fertility rates only a "response to their poverty"? Why has the fertility rate of the Israeli Druze, which was equivalent to the Muslims in the late 1950s and early 1960s, sharply declined since the late 1960s, while among the Muslims, despite some fertility decline, their TFR remained at the level of 4.0 children per woman in 2005, the highest among the non-oil Arab societies (with the exception of Yemen and Sudan)?[139] In the case of Israel, it seems that the "chicken and the egg" question is quite simple: The fertility behavior of the Israeli-Muslims, as that of the Druze and the Christians, was a direct response to their socioeconomic condition.[140]

Another interesting question relates to the "Sunna–Shi'a fertility differential: Are there any differences in the fertility patterns between Sunnis and Shi'is in the same country? In the case of Bahrain, although the authorities do not publish demographic data according to religion, the various informal sources reveal that the fertility rate among the Shi'is is substantially higher than among the Sunnis. Also in the case of Bahrain, it seems that the higher fertility rate among the Shi'is is a direct response to their lower socioeconomic condition.[141]

With respect to the Lebanese Shi'is, although the Lebanese authorities do not publish demographic data according to religion, it appears that the fertility rate of the Shi'is is quite low in comparison to any other Arab-Shi'a community. This assertion is based on the following logical assumption: As the Shi'is in Lebanon constitutes approximately half of the total population, and Lebanon's TFR was estimated at 1.9 in 2005,[142] it is not possible that the average TFR among the Lebanese Shi'is is currently higher than 2.5.

In general, in the case of the Arab countries, it appears that the "religious factor" by itself does not have any influence on fertility patterns. The fertility deferential between Sunnis and Shi'is in Bahrain, between the Druzes and the Christians on the one hand and the Muslims on the other hand in Israel, and between Christians and Muslims in Lebanon are a direct response to the substantial socioeconomic gaps rather than to a different religious approach toward fertility behavior.[143]

4 The Revolution of Mortality Rates in the Arab Countries

The tremendous increase in the natural increase rates in the Arab countries since the mid-twentieth century, as in other developing societies worldwide, was a result of the sharp decline in the death rates. The causes for the "Middle Eastern death rate revolution" were many and varied. It was a process that started in Egypt during the first half of the nineteenth century at a slow pace, and later spread over other regions of the Ottoman Empire in line with economic developments and the adoption of market agriculture. At that time, the most important factor accounting for the declining death rates in the Middle East was the improvement in the roads, which for the first time allowed for the transfer of food in considerable quantities, from one location to another. This provided the means for overcoming starvation as well as the accompanying diseases that had previously blighted the area. Another important factor was the stabilization of the political regimes in the area, first in Egypt under the rule of Muhammad 'Ali (1805–1848) and later in the other regions of the Ottoman Empire as part of the *Tanzimat*. According to prevailing estimates, the Middle Eastern average CDR declined from 42–44 per 1,000 at the end of the eighteenth century to 32–34 at the end of the nineteenth century.[144]

During the first half of the twentieth century, the rapid decline in death rates in the Middle East was mainly the result of the sharp improvement and expansion of health-care services, including preventive health services. The rise in the living standard also contributed to the declining death rates during the first half of the twentieth century.

For example, Egypt's CDR declined from 28.4 per 1,000 in 1907 to 21.4 in 1947.[145] Thus, the decline of Egypt's CDRs was slow but steady. A similar process of slow but steady decline in death rates occurred in other Arab countries during the Mandatory period as well.

During the second half of the twentieth century, however, the process of declining death rates strongly accelerated. By the end of the twentieth century, the CDRs in the Arab countries, with the exception of Sudan and Yemen, were among the lowest worldwide, running between 5 to 7 per 1,000. Egypt's CDR declined from 17 per 1,000 in 1960 to 7 in the year 2000. In Jordan, the decline was from 20 to 5 and in Tunisia from 21 to 7 during the corresponding period. The decline in the CDRs was the most prominent in the GCC oil economies, which changed from poor to rich states within only two decades. At the same time, fertility rates remained high, leading to a very wide-based age pyramid (see Chapter 3). Thus, for example, Oman's CDR declined from as high as 28 per 1,000 in 1960 to 13 in 1980 and only 4 in 2000. By the year 2000, the Kuwaiti national population had achieved the lowest CDR worldwide, with only 3 per 1,000 (see Table 2.4).

In general, three components have contributed to the sharp decline in the CDRs among the Arab countries since the mid-twentieth century. First was the marked drop in infant and child mortality rates; second was the considerable increase in life expectancy, which together constitutes the two most prominent indicators for the overall health situation of any given society. The third factor was the very young age pyramid, which was a direct consequence of the prolonged high natural increase rates (see Chapter 3). In the following section, the changes in these three components since the mid-twentieth century will be examined.

(a) The sharp decline in infant (0–1) and child (1–5) mortality rates Until the mid-twentieth century, infant and child mortality rates in the Arab countries were very high, amounting to almost one-third of live births. Since the 1950–1955 period, when the average under-5 mortality rates in the Arab countries was 312 per 1,000 live births, there has been a dramatic drop in these two indicators.[146] By 1999, the under-5 mortality rate per 1,000 live births was 62 in Morocco, 54 in Egypt, and 31 in Jordan. The highest rate among all of the Arab countries was in Yemen, with 97 deaths per 1,000 live births.[147] According to the latest available data, by 2004 the under-5 mortality rate was 25 per 1,000 live births in Tunisia, 27 in Jordan, 36 in Egypt and 43 in Morocco. As expected, the highest under-5 mortality rate was in the poorest Arab countries with 111 in Yemen and 91 in Sudan, while the lowest rates were in the Gulf oil countries with rates as low as 13 per 1,000 live births in Oman, 21 in Qatar and 27 in Saudi Arabia.[148]

The major factor for the sharp decline in the under-5 mortality rates was the sharp decline in infant mortality rates. Whereas the average infant mortality rate of the Arab countries during the 1950–1955 period was 181 per 1,000 live births, this rate declined to 81 on average during the years 1980–1985.[149] By 2005, the infant mortality rate was 33 in Egypt, 31 in Algeria, 42 in Morocco, and as high as 50 in Iraq – a direct result of the general poor socioeconomic conditions following the sanctions imposed on the country in 1991.[150] The best achievements in this area were made in the Gulf oil countries, where infant mortality rates in 2005 were 17 in Bahrain and as low as 10 in Kuwait. It should be emphasized in this respect that with the exception of Iraq, infant mortality rates declined to below 45 even in the poorer Arab countries (see Table 2.12). Thus, the infant mortality rates in the Arab countries declined from almost one-fifth of live births in the mid-twentieth century to approximately 4% at the dawn of the twenty-first century, and to only 1% in Kuwait!

(b) The increase in life expectancy During the 1920s and 1930s, the average life expectancy at birth in the Arab Middle Eastern societies was approximately 40 years. For example, the life expectancy of the Arabs in Mandatory Palestine averaged 38 years (for men and women) during the years 1924–1926 and increased to 50 years on

Table 2.12 Infant Mortality Rates and Life Expectancy (both sexes) in some Arab Countries, non-Arab Developing Countries and Developed Countries, 1960–2005

Year	1960		1970		1980		1990		2000		2005	
Country	IM	LE	IM	LE	IM	LE	IM	LE	IM	LE	IM	LE
Arab Countries												
Algeria	165	47	139	53	98	59	67	65	50	70	31	73
Tunisia	159	48	127	54	72	62	44	67	22	70	25	75
Morocco	163	47	120	52	99	56	67	62	41	68	42	71
Egypt	179	46	144	51	124	55	60	66	46	67	33	71
Jordan	135	47	90	52	58	63	40	69	30	70	17	78
Syria	132	50	98	55	67	65	43	66	25	71	30	70
Iraq	139	47	104	51	78	56	63	65	103	58	50	69
Saudi Arabia	185	43	128	52	91	60	65	65	18	73	13	76
Oman	193	39	158	44	128	49	66(a)	61(a)	18	72	20	73
Kuwait	89	60	49	66	34	70	14(a)	75(a)	9	76	10	77
Bahrain	128	56	74	62	75	64	33(a)	71(a)	16	74	17	74
Non-Arab Developing Countries												
Turkey	190	50	150	57	109	62	60	65	59	70	41	72
South-Korea	85	54	43	60	26	65	17	70	5	75	6	77
Brazil	116	55	95	59	67	63	57	66	32	68	30	72
Mexico	92	57	79	62	51	65	39	70	25	73	21	75
Pakistan	163	43	118	48	124	50	103	58	85	60	72	63
Developed Countries												
France	27	70	18	72	10	74	7	76	4	79	4	80
United Kingdom	22	71	18	72	12	73	8	76	6	78	5	79
Sweden	17	73	11	75	7	75	6	77	3	80	3	80
Belgium	31	70	21	71	12	73	8	75	4	78	5	79

IM = Infant mortality rate per 1,000 live births.
LE = Life expectancy at birth (years, both sexes).
(a) Figures relate to 1988 (nationals only).

Sources: WB, *World Tables*, 1984–1995, various issues (Published for the WB by Johns Hopkins University Press); idem, *World Development Report*, 1978–2002, various issues (Published for the WB by Oxford University Press); ECWA/ESCWA, *Survey of the Economic Developments in the ECWA/ESCWA Region*, various issues (Baghdad, Amman and New York); idem, *Demographic and Related Socio-Economic Data Sheets for Countries of the Economic and Social Commission for Western Asia, 1978–2001*, various issues (Beirut, Baghdad and Amman); UNICEF, *The State of the World's Children*, various issues (Published for UNICEF by Oxford University Press); UNDP, *Human Development Report*, 1994–2006, various issues (Published for the UNDP by Oxford University Press); The US, Department of Commerce, US Census Bureau, *International Data Base*. Available at: http://www.census.gov/ipc/www/idbsum.html.

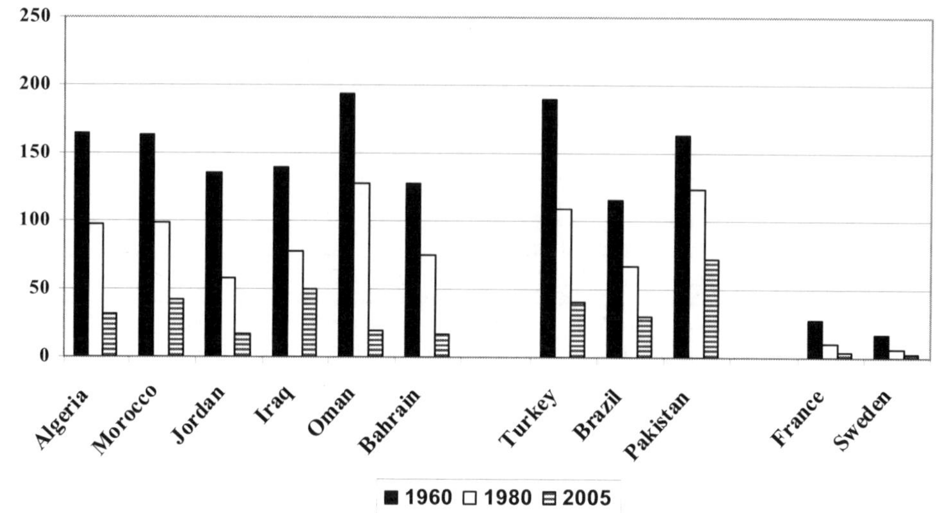

Figure 2.11 Infant Mortality Rates in some Arab Countries, non-Arab Developing Countries and Developed Countries, 1960–2005

average during the 1940–1942 period. In the Hashemite Emirate of Jordan, the life expectancy at birth in 1930 was only 38 years (for men and women).[151] Since then, the life expectancy at birth in all of the Arab countries has sharply increased, similar to many other developing societies worldwide, rising to 47 years in Iraq and Jordan, 48 in Tunisia, 50 in Syria, and 60 in Kuwait by 1960. By 2005, life expectancy at birth reached 71 years in Egypt and Morocco, 73 in Algeria, 75 in Tunisia, 77 in Kuwait and as high as 78 in Jordan – the highest of all the Arab countries. Thus, at the beginning of the twenty-first century, life expectancy in the Arab countries was approximately 25 years higher than it had been at mid-century and more than 30 years higher than during the Mandatory period.

(c) Young age structure A direct consequence of the prolonged high natural increase rates in the Arab countries was the creation of a very young age structure. This phenomenon will be examined in greater depth in Chapter 3. The implications of a wide-based age pyramid – namely, a high percentage of the young (under 20) population along with an extremely low percentage of an elderly population (over 65) – for the CDRs is a natural decline, given that the highest mortality rates are concentrated among the elderly population. The lowest worldwide CDRs in Kuwait since the early 1980s is a combined result of low infant and child mortality rates, high life expectancy, and above all, a wide-based age pyramid with an extremely small percentage of elderly population.

In addition to the overall improvement in the standard of living, the sharp decline in death rates among the Arab countries since the mid-twentieth century was the marked improvement in healthcare services. This was achieved mainly through the declining ratio of both physicians/population and hospital-beds/population,

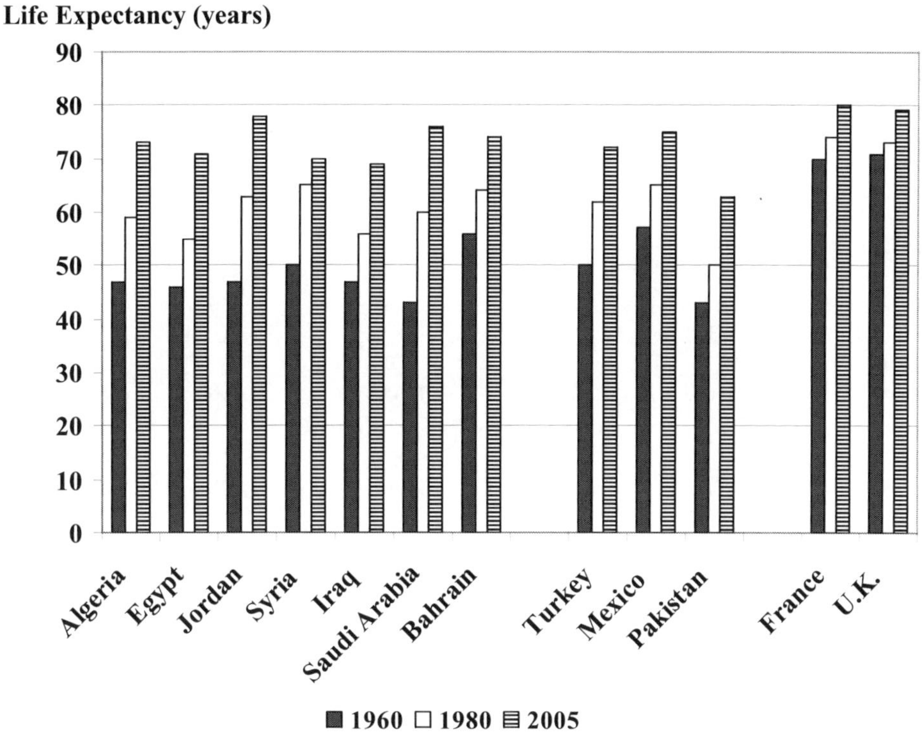

Figure 2.12 Life Expectancy at Birth (both sexes) in some Arab Countries, non-Arab Developing Countries and Developed Countries, 1960–2005

despite the rapid population growth. For example, by 1995 there was one physician for every 595 people in Egypt, compared to one for every 2,250 people in 1960. In Tunisia, the physician/population ratio improved from one physician for every 10,030 people in 1960 to one for every 1,429 people in 1998. As with the other socioeconomic indicators, the improvement of the healthcare services in the Gulf oil states was the most impressive of all of the Arab countries. The most dramatic improvement was in Oman, where the physician/population ratio declined from one physician for every 31,180 people in 1960 to one for every 1,900 people in 1980 and one for every 752 people in 1997. Kuwait, as in many other social indicators, in the area of healthcare services as well, achieved the lowest physician/population ratio, with one physician for every 529 people in 1998 (see Table 2.13).

As for the hospital-beds/population ratio, here too, the improvement was considerable, although less than in the physician/population ratio. In this respect, as in the others, the best achievement was in the Gulf oil countries. For example, there was only one hospital in Qatar in 1945 and two in Kuwait in 1949, and prior to the establishment of the UAE in 1971, healthcare services existed only in the cities of Abu Dhabi and Dubai.[152] By the end of the twentieth century, however, the indigenous GCC populations enjoyed one of the top healthcare services worldwide, with health centers spread throughout the area, including hospitals with the most advanced facilities. No less important is the wide coverage of healthcare services provided to the indigenous

Table 2.13 Average Number of Persons per Physician in some Arab Countries, non-Arab Developing Countries and Developed Countries, 1960–1998

Year	1960	1970	1980	1990	1998
		Arab Countries			
Egypt	2,250	1,900	970	1,320	595 (b)
Syria	4,630	3,860	2,270	1,160	694 (d)
Jordan	5,800	2,480	1,700	770	602
Tunisia	10,030	5,930	3,690	1,870	1,429
Morocco	9,410	13,090	10,750	4,840	2,174
Algeria	5,530	8,100	2,630	2,330	1,182 (b)
Saudi Arabia	16,370	7,460	1,670	660	602
Kuwait	1,210	1,050	570	—	529
Oman	31,180	8,380	1,900	1,060	752 (d)
		Non-Arab Developing Countries			
Iran	3,860	3,270	6,090	3,140	1,176 (c)
Turkey	2,800	5,930	1,630	1,870	826 (d)
Brazil	2,210	2,030	1,080 (a)	—	786 (c)
		Developed Countries			
France	930	750	580	350	330
Italy	640	550	340	210	181
Sweden	1,050	730	490	370	322
Belgium	780	650	400	310	253 (d)
United States	750	630	520	420	358 (b)
Canada	910	680	550	450	142 (b)

Notes: The data on physicians for the 1995-1998 period are taken from the WHO database, while the population data are taken from the US Census Bureau, *International Data Base*.

(a) Figure relates to 1984.
(b) Figures relate to 1995.
(c) Figures relate to 1996.
(d) Figures relate to 1997.

Sources: WB, *World Development Report, 1978–1999/2000*, various issues (Published for the WB by Oxford University Press); WHO, *WHO Statistics, Estimates for Health Personnel*. Available at: http://www3.who.int.

populations almost free of charge, including treatments abroad in cases where the necessary treatment can not be provided in local hospitals.

The process of declining CDRs in some of the Arab countries, however, somewhat halted during recent years as one can see in Table 2.4. This was a consequence of the declining fertility rates during the past two decades on the one hand, and increasing life expectancy on the other, which led to an increasing percentage of the elderly population within the total population. As mortality concentrates mainly among the elderly population, the increasing percentage of this age group affected the average CDRs.

5 Summary and Conclusions

The decline in the death rates since the nineteenth century along with the continuously high fertility rates led to the steady increase in the natural increase rates of the Arab societies since the late nineteenth century through the mid-1980s. Since then, however, the decline in the fertility rates in all of the Arab countries, even in Yemen and Sudan, has been sharper and faster than the decline in the CDRs, leading to a marked drop in the natural increase rates. Nevertheless, despite the considerable decline in fertility rates, at the dawn of the twenty-first century, Tunisia and Lebanon were the only Arab countries that succeeded in reaching a replacement-level fertility rate which ensure that in the future they will achieve a stable population. However, due to their current wide-based age pyramid, it will occur only in the late 2020s (see Chapter 3).

Therefore, while in the mid-twentieth century, there was a great similarity among all of the Arab countries in terms of their demographic characteristics – namely, high birth and death rates – with only minor differences from one country to another; two generations later, a huge demographic gap existed between them. At the beginning of the twenty-first century, as one can see in Figure 2.13, four different "demographic regimes" prevail in the Arab countries:

(a) The first group includes only Tunisia, Lebanon and recently also Algeria, which have indeed achieved the targeted replacement-level with a TFR of 1.8 children per woman in Tunisia and 1.9 in Lebanon and Algeria in 2005. From a purely demographic point of view, these countries function in a way which is similar to the worldwide developed countries although in the cases of Tunisia and Algeria, a major factor in the sharp fertility decline was the comprehensive national family planning programs carried out in these counties.

(b) The second and the largest group includes Egypt, Jordan, Syria, Morocco and Bahrain – countries that have succeeded in substantially lowering their TFR to 3–3.5 children per woman mainly through direct or indirect anti-natalist measures combined with macroeconomic policy changes which included reduced governmental subsidies on basic foodstuffs and public services. Thus, although the fertility rates of these countries indeed sharply declined during the past two decades, still, at the beginning of the twenty-first century, their TFR is much above the targeted replacement-level.

(c) The third group includes Sudan and Yemen, which are still characterized by high birth and death rates due to their poor socioeconomic condition. Therefore, for these countries, the future demographic trends are the darkest, as their population growth rates in the foreseeable future will continue to be extremely high, thus narrowing their ability to escape the "demographic trap syndrome." As the political instability continues, particularly in Sudan, the option for these countries to substantially reduce their fertility rates in order to achieve better economic performance is even more questionable.

(d) The fourth group includes the Gulf oil states (with the exception of Bahrain) which have created an unparalleled demographic pattern of extremely low CDRs and high fertility rates as a consequence of their unique socioeconomic and political *rentier* structure (see Chapter 4). In retrospect, it appears that these countries were rich enough to both reduce the death rates and preserve their traditional lifestyle – a lifestyle which does not encourage fertility decline. In recent years, however, even in these countries, the fertility rates are steadily declining – a direct consequence of an improvement in women's educational level. In Oman and Saudi Arabia in recent years the fertility decline is also welcomed by the authorities which has abandoned their traditional pro-natalist approach.

In retrospect, it appears that the "*rentier factor*" has had both a positive and negative impact on the fertility level of the indigenous Gulf women. On the positive side,

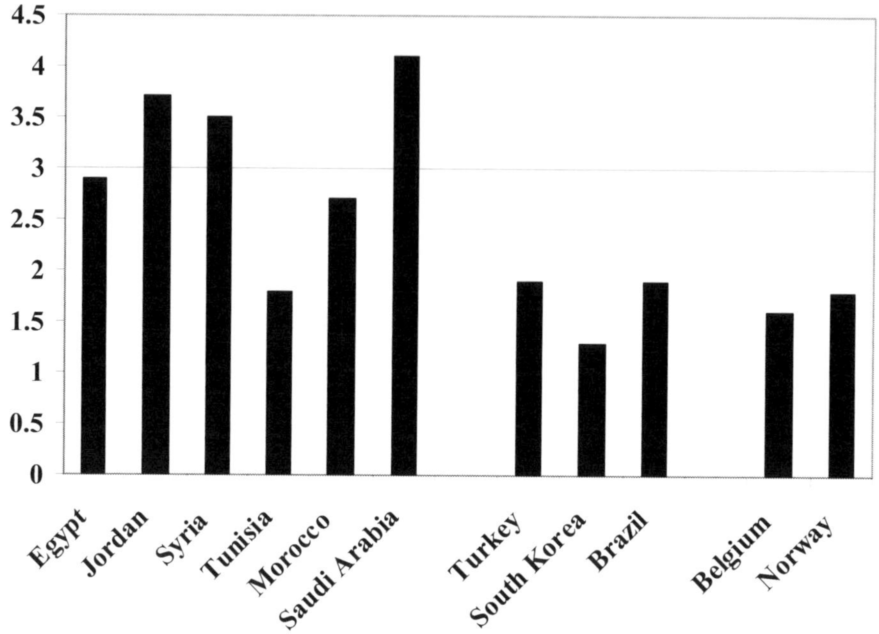

Figure 2.13 Total Fertility Rates in some Arab Countries, non-Arab Developing Countries and Developed Countries, 2005

preventing large-scale women employment outside the household, primarily in Saudi Arabia and Qatar, along with large-scale governmental subsidies on basic public services and products hindered the process of fertility decline. On the negative side, the rapid improvement of both healthcare and educational services promoted the process of fertility decline. However, despite the fertility decline, at the beginning of the twenty-first century, the fertility rates in these countries are still extremely high by any international comparison. Moreover, even if the process of fertility decline markedly accelerates in these countries in the coming years, their population growth rates will continue to be very high in the foreseeable future, as the wide-based age pyramid will dictate the continuation of extremely low CDRs.

In retrospect, three prominent differences in the course of the demographic transition can be identified between the developing countries, including the Arab countries, and the developed countries:

(a The period of the transition In the developed countries, the demographic transition "stretched" over two centuries, that is, from the late eighteenth century until the late 1960s. In contrast, among the developing countries the demographic transition only started in the mid-twentieth century; yet, some of the countries, such as the "Asian Tigers,"[153] had already reached the end of the third stage – namely, low natural increase rates due to both low fertility and mortality rates – by the mid-1980s, namely, in only one generation.

(b) The scale of the transition In none of the developed countries did the fertility rates ever reach as high a level as those prevailing in many developing countries, including all of the Arab countries, during the mid-twentieth century – namely, a CBR

of over 45 per 1,000 and a TFR of about 7 children per woman, and in some countries, such as Oman, Jordan and Syria, even higher. In the developed countries, the natural increase rate peaked at no more than 1.5%–1.6% in the two decades prior to the onset of World War I. This means that the natural increase rates of the Western European countries at the beginning of their third stage of the demographic transition were only half the natural increase rates which prevailed in the Arab countries in the early 1980s at the beginning of their third stage of the demographic transition process.

(c) Governmental involvement in family planning Generally speaking, in the developed countries worldwide, the Demographic Transition process has occurred without direct state intervention and in many cases even despite the implementation of various pro-natalist measures. It was a long and natural process, moving from one stage to the next one purely as a result of socioeconomic and political changes. In the developing countries, on the other hand, although the changes in socioeconomic conditions and policies greatly affected fertility patterns, a major contributor to the process of fertility decline during the past generation was the introduction of comprehensive national family planning programs aimed at accelerating the pace of the fertility decline.

In general, during the twentieth century, particularly in the second half of the century, all of the Arab countries underwent a profound "demographic revolution." This revolution had a tremendous impact on every aspect of life.

3 "Jobs for the Boys (and Girls)" *The Emergence of the Employment Dilemma*

Unemployment is a bomb that will explode sooner or later in the Arab region if we are not prepared to confront it now.

Husni Mubarak, March 2001[1]

Forget weapons of mass destruction: the biggest challenge to the Arab world is not to be found in the laboratories of evil scientists, but in countless cradles in the homes of Arab families.

John Martin, November 2003[2]

In terms of unemployment in the Arab countries, it is not hard to detect a common theme. As far back as the end of the nineteenth century, the Egyptian government considered bringing in Chinese workers to fill the agricultural labor shortage. Since its independence following World War II and until the mid-1970s, the Syrian authorities implemented a pro-natalist policy, due, at least in part, to a labor shortage. Likewise, from the October 1973 "oil boom" through the mid-1990s, the Gulf oil countries implemented a pro-natalist policy due to an extreme labor shortage which was dealt with through the import of millions of foreign workers. In the mid-1970s, unemployment in Jordan was less than 2%, and it became a labor-importer in order to avoid a labor shortage which would hinder its economic development. During the 1980s, both Iraq and Iran implemented pro-natalist policies, and Iraq also imported more than a million Egyptian workers due to its labor shortage.

Less than a generation later, by the end of the twentieth century, the open unemployment rate in each of the Arab countries, both the oil-based and the non-oil, was more than 15%, and in some countries even more than 20%. This does not take into consideration the huge disguised unemployment which prevails in all the Arab countries.

The emergence of the Arab employment dilemma can be traced to the high natural increase rates in the Arab countries during the second half of the twentieth century, with their tremendously devastating socioeconomic consequences. While these negative results primarily affected the poorer overpopulated non-oil Arab economies, from the late 1980s, the high natural increase rates became a socioeconomic problem in the

Arab oil-based economies as well, particularly in Saudi Arabia, Oman and Algeria.

By the beginning of the twenty-first century, it can be said that all of the Arab countries, with the sole exceptions of the tiny Gulf oil economies, namely, Qatar, Kuwait, and the UAE, were suffering to some extent from what has been called "the overpopulation syndrome" or "the overpopulation trap." This term refers to a situation in which rapid population growth hinders faster economic development. This has been the situation since the early 1980s in a considerable number of Arab countries, notably Egypt, Jordan, Syria, Yemen, Algeria, and Morocco.

The negative results of the rapid population growth in the overpopulated Arab countries were the main reasons for the creation of the "vicious circle of poverty" in these countries. The major links in this "vicious circle" are as follows: In a developing economy with high natural increase rates, the saving capability of the vast majority of the population is limited, due to a very low per capita income – in many cases only slightly above starvation level. The low income level is the consequence of a very low level of productivity in both the rural and the urban economies. The low productivity is the reflection of a low investments caused by low saving rates, which, in turn, leads to high fertility rates due to the low per capita income.[3]

The negative socioeconomic consequences of the rapid population growth in the Arab countries are many and varied. This chapter concentrates on the most devastating result: the emergence of a **structural unemployment problem**.

I The Consequences of the Young Age Structure

The result of the prolonged high natural increase rates was the creation of a wide-based age pyramid.[4] Already in 1960, the under-15 population constituted 42.8% of the total population in Egypt, 44.7% in Morocco, 46.3% in Syria, and 45.6% in Jordan in 1961. During the 1960s and 1970s, due to the rise in the natural increase rates as a result of the declining CDRs, the percentage of the young population within the total population increased in all of the Arab countries. For example, in 1979, the percentage of the under-15 population within the total population increased to 50.7% in Jordan compared to 45.6% in 1961. In the case of Egypt, the increase was even more dramatic. By 1980, Egypt's under-15 population made up as much as 50.8% of the total population compared to 42.8% in 1960. A similar process, as one can see in Table 3.1, occurred in the other Arab countries as well, with the sole exception of Tunisia.

In many non-Arab developing countries, the percentage of the young population within the total population had already started to decline in the 1960s and 1970s as their fertility rates started to drop during these two decades. The most profound decline in the under-15 percentage occurred in the "Asian Tigers." In the case of South Korea, for example, by 1983, the under-15 population constituted 32.3% of the total population, compared to 42.4% in 1962. In the other three "Asian Tigers," a similar decrease occurred as well.

In the developed countries, in contrast, the fertility rates were already very low in the 1960s and continued to drop to below replacement-level in the 1970s and 1980s. At the same time, life expectancy was steadily increasing. Consequently, the percentage of the young population within the total population has been gradually decreasing. Thus, for example, in Norway, the percentage of the under-15 population within the total population decreased from 25.8% in 1960 to 21.3% in 1982 and reached as low as

Table 3.1 The Age Structure of some Arab Countries, non-Arab Developing Countries and Western European Countries, 1960, 1980, 2004

Age Group Country	0–14	15–64	65+
	1960		
Egypt	42.8	53.7	3.5
Jordan (a)	45.6	50.6	3.8
Syria	46.3	48.9	4.8
Tunisia (c)	46.3	50.1	3.6
Morocco	44.7	51.1	4.2
Saudi Arabia	—	—	—
Oman	—	—	—
Iran (c)	46.1	50.0	3.9
Pakistan (a)	44.5	49.5 (1)	6.0 (2)
South Korea (b)	42.4	52.0 (1)	5.6 (2)
Denmark (b)	24.3	64.8	10.9
Norway	25.8	63.1	11.1
	1980		
Egypt (f)	50.8	45.6	3.6
Jordan (d)	50.7	46.6	2.7
Syria (e)	49.3	46.3	4.4
Tunisia (e)	41.8	53.8	4.4
Morocco (e)	45.6	51.7	2.7
Saudi Arabia	—	—	—
Oman	46.6	51.0	2.4
Iran (e)	43.2	52.7	4.1
Pakistan (e)	45.2	50.7	4.1
South Korea (g)	32.3	63.7	4.0
Denmark (f)	19.7	69.1	11.2
Norway (f)	21.3	63.6	15.1

19.8% in 2004. In Denmark, the decline was from 24.3% in 1962 to 18.8% in 2004 – one of the lowest worldwide. In the other EU countries, the same process has occurred.

Since the mid-1980s, the percentage of the young population within the total population in almost all of the Arab countries, as in many other developing countries worldwide, has steadily gone down as a result of a drop in the fertility rates. However, despite the declining percentage of the young population, they still remain the highest worldwide. Thus, for example, in 2004, the percentage of the under-15 population within the total population was 37.7% in Egypt, 37.8% in Jordan, 39.5% in Syria and 30.4% in Morocco in 2005. Tunisia achieved the lowest percentage of the under-15 population among all of the Arab countries at the beginning of the twenty-first century, with only 26.0% in 2004, due to its having the lowest fertility rates during the 1980s and 1990s (see Table 3.1). Overall, by 1998, the percentage of the under-18 population of all of the Middle Eastern populations (including Iran and Turkey) was 45.5%, compared to 22.4% among the industrialized countries.[5]

The combined result of the high natural increase rates, on the one hand, and a relatively low life expectancy, on the other, was the creation of age pyramids with a very narrow vertex in which the percentage of the elderly population in each of the

	2004		
Egypt (j)	37.7	56.5 (1)	5.8 (2)
Jordan	37.8	58.7	3.5
Syria	39.5	57.2	3.3
Tunisia	26.0	67.5	6.5
Morocco (i)	30.4	64.1	5.5
Saudi Arabia	49.3	47.7	3.0
Oman (i)	38.9	58.9	2.2
Iran	26.1	68.8	5.1
Pakistan (h)	42.2	54.4	3.4
South Korea	19.6	71.7	8.7
Denmark	18.8	66.2	15.0
Norway	19.8	65.5	14.7

— No available data.
(a) Figures relate to 1961.
(b) Figures relate to 1962.
(c) Figures relate to 1966.
(d) Figures relate to 1979.
(1) 15-60 years.
(e) Figures relate to 1981.
(f) Figures relate to 1982.
(g) Figures relate to 1983.
(2) 60 years and over.
(h) Figures relate to December 2003
(i) Figures relate to 2005.
(j) Figures relate to January 1, 2006.

Sources: Egypt, CAPMAS, *Statistical Yearbook*, various issues (Cairo); The Hashemite Kingdom of Jordan, Department of Statistics, *Statistical Abstract*, various issues (Amman); The Kingdom of Saudi Arabia, Ministry of Planning, Central Department of Statistics, *Statistical Yearbook*, various issues (Riyadh); Sultanate of Oman, Ministry of National Economy, *Statistical Yearbook*, various issues (Muscat); Syrian Arab Republic, Office of the Prime Minister, CBS, *Statistical Abstract*, various issues (Damascus); al-Mamlaka al-Maghribiyya, al-Mandubiyya al-Samiyya lil-Takhtit, Qisem al-Ihsaiyyat al-'Amma, *al-Nashra al-Ihsaiyya al-Sanawiyya lil-Maghrib*, various years (Rabat); al-Jumhuriyya al-Tunisiyya, Wizarat al-Tanmiyya, al-Ma'had al-Watani lil-Ihsa, *al-Nashriyya al-Ihsa al-Sanawiyya Li-Tunis*, various years (Tunis); UN, *Demographic Yearbook*, various issues (New York); ECWA/ESCWA, *Demographic and Related Socio-Economic Data Sheets for Countries of the Economic and Social Commission for Western Asia*, various issues (Beirut, Baghdad and Amman).

Arab countries, both the oil-based and the non-oil, was extremely low by any international comparison. In the case of Egypt, in January 2006, the 60 years and over population represented 5.8% of the total population. In Jordan and Syria, the percentage of the 65 and over population of the total population was 3.5% and 3.3% respectively, in 2004. The lowest percentage of the elderly population within the total population among the Arab countries was, of course, in the GCC countries as a result of their extremely high natural increase rates in the past three decades. Thus, by 2004, the percentage of the 65 and over population within the total population in Saudi Arabia was 3.0% and only 2.2% in Oman in 2005. The highest percentage of the 65 and over population among the Arab countries was in Tunisia, with 6.5% in 2004, as a result of its low fertility rates during the past generation.

In the developed European countries, in contrast, the combined result of very high life expectancy and extremely low fertility rates since the late 1960s has been a steady increase of the percentage of the elderly population. By the year 2004, the percentage of the 65 and over population within the total population was 14.7% in Norway and 15.0% in Denmark – almost fivefold greater than the prevailing rates in the Arab countries (see **Table 3.1**). In the late 1990s, Italy was the first EU country in which there were more people in the sixties age group than in the twenties.[6]

The end result of the extremely low fertility rate on the one hand and steadily increasing life expectancy on the other was a steady increase of the median age[7] in each of the European developed countries. Thus, for example, Austria's median age increased from 35.8 years in 1950 to 40.1 years in 2005. In Spain, the increase was from 27.7 years to 38.8 years during the corresponding period. In Italy, the country with the lowest fertility rates worldwide together with Russia, the increase of the median age was the highest among the European countries, from 29.0 years in 1950 to as high as 42.0 years in 2005 (see Table 3.2).

In the Arab countries as well, the median age of the population considerably increased during the past two decades due to the declining fertility rates along with increasing life expectancy. This rise, however, was at a much slower pace than in the

Table 3.2 The Percentage of the Population 60 Years and over of the Total Population in some Arab Countries, the "Asian Tigers" and some Developed European Countries, 1950, 2005, 2050

	1950		2005		2050*	
Country	60 years + (% of total population)	Median age (years)	60 years + (% of total population)	Median age (years)	60 years + (% of total population)	Median age (years)
			Arab Countries			
Egypt	5.1	20.0	7.2	22.9	19.3	36.1
Syria	6.8	19.4	4.7	20.6	19.8	37.1
Jordan	7.4	17.2	5.1	21.1	19.0	37.0
Algeria	6.8	19.9	6.5	24.0	24.3	39.4
Tunisia	8.0	20.9	8.7	26.7	28.1	42.5
Morocco	4.6	17.7	7.5	24.3	22.9	38.8
Saudi Arabia	5.6	19.0	4.2	23.3	18.0	36.0
Oman	5.0	19.8	4.3	22.5	20.4	37.2
			"Asian Tigers"			
Honk Kong	3.7	23.7	15.4	38.9	39.4	52.1
South Korea	5.4	19.1	13.7	35.0	42.2	54.9
Singapore	3.7	20.0	12.3	37.5	39.8	53.7
			European Countries			
Austria	15.4	35.8	21.9	40.1	35.3	48.0
Germany	14.6	35.4	25.1	42.1	29.4	49.4
Denmark	13.4	31.8	21.2	39.5	37.0	43.8
Sweden	14.9	34.3	23.4	40.2	30.3	43.3
Italy	12.2	29.0	25.3	42.0	38.6	50.5
UK	15.5	34.6	21.2	38.9	30.1	43.4
Spain	10.9	27.7	21.7	38.8	39.0	49.5
France	16.2	34.5	20.8	38.9	31.8	44.7
Belgium	16.0	35.5	22.1	40.3	33.2	46.2

* Medium variant projection.

Sources: UN, Population Division, *World Population Prospects: The 2006 Revision* (New York, 2007), pp. 59–64, 65–70; idem, *World Population Ageing: 1950–2050* (New York, 2002).

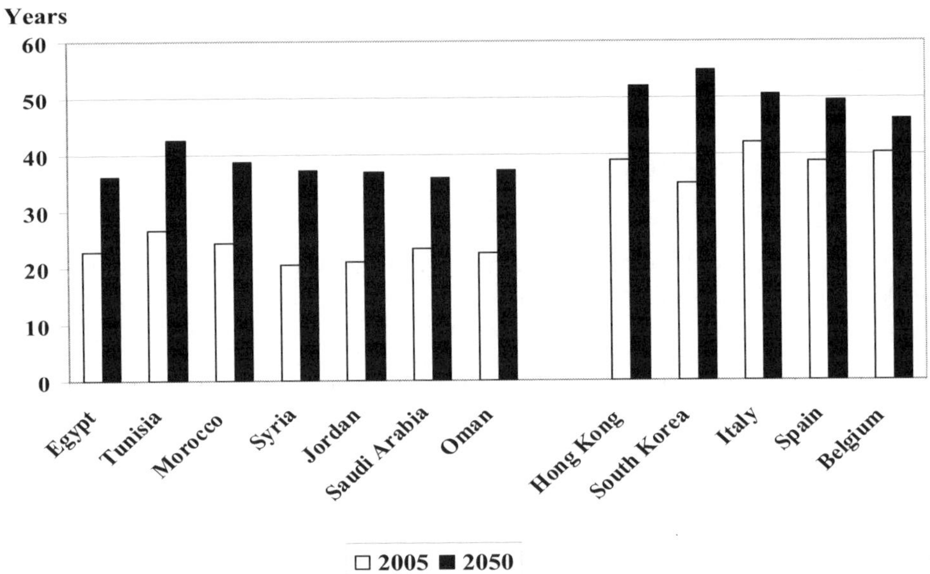

Figure 3.1 The Median age in some Arab Countries, Developed European Countries and the "Asian Tigers," 2005, 2050*

European developed countries. The highest increase was, of course, in Tunisia – from 20.9 years in 1950 to 26.7 years in 2005. The smallest increase among the Arab countries was in the GCC countries, as the fertility rates of their indigenous population was and still is the highest among the Arab countries (see Table 3.2).

1.1 The Short- and Long-term Implications of the Demographic Momentum

The end of the [demographic] transition is not the end of its consequences.

Jacques Vallin [8]

The long-term demographic implication of the wide-based age pyramid is that even if the fertility rates decline to replacement-level or even below it, the population will continue to grow. This is because the number of women of reproductive age will continue to increase for a number of decades before finally stabilizing. Only at that point will the population start to decline, in the case of below replacement-level fertility, or stabilize, in the case of replacement-level fertility. Thus, the younger the age pyramid, the longer the period between the achievement of replacement-level rate and the termination of population growth. This period is called the demographic momentum.

Therefore, if the world's fertility rate in the year 2000 was at replacement-level, the world's population would still grow by another 43% before stabilizing after 60 years due to the young age structure of the world's population in 2000.[9] According to UN forecasts, by the year 2050, the world's population will reach 9.2 billion (medium variant projection) compared to 6.7 billion in mid-2007. This means that during the first half of the twenty-first century, the number of people on earth will increase by 2.5 billion – equivalent to the world's total population in 1950. Thus, during the century between 1950 and 2050, the world's population will increase by 6.7 billion, equivalent to the total world's population in mid-2007. All of this increase will occur in the developing countries, particularly in the 50 least developed countries.[10] The real meaning of the demographic momentum, wrote Todaro, is that "every year that passes without a reduction in fertility means a larger multiple of the present total population size before it can eventually level off."[11]

Despite the marked fertility decline in most of the Arab countries since the mid-1980s, none of the Arab countries, with the exception of Tunisia, Lebanon and Algeria, are currently even close to replacement-level. In fact, in nominal numbers, their population growth during the 1990s was equal to or even higher than those of the 1980s, simply as a result of their wide-based age pyramids. For example, when Egypt's natural increase rate peaked at more than 3% in 1985, in nominal figures the net population growth was 1.466 million.[12] Two decades later, by the year 2005, Egypt's natural increase rate had declined to 1.9%. However, in nominal figures, the population increase was 1.364 million,[13] namely, a decline of only 7% in nominal figures in comparison to the net population increase in 1985, despite the decline of 37% in the natural increase rate.

In the Arab countries with a wider age pyramid than that of Egypt, not only did the population growth of recent years in nominal figures not decline, it rather increased. In the case of Syria, for example, during the year between mid-2005 and mid-2006, the population increased by 448,000 compared to an increase of 385,000 during the year between mid-1994 and mid-1995,[14] although the natural increase rate in 1994 was more than 1% higher than in 2005. One can find a similar process in Jordan, Algeria, and of course in the GCC countries where fertility decline during the past decade was the lowest among all the Arab countries.

In Tunisia and Morocco, due to their much larger fertility decline during the past two decades, the population increase in nominal figures in the early 2000s was indeed much smaller than in the 1980s. In the case of Morocco, in 2004 the population increased by 280,000 in nominal figures compared to an increase of 482,000 two decades earlier, in 1984.[15] In Tunisia in recent years, the annual nominal population growth declined to below the 100,000 mark. It was almost twice that number two decades earlier.[16]

Consequently, the population of the Arab countries will continue to increase rapidly during at least the first half of the twenty-first century, even if the current trend of declining fertility continues. According to the UN projection, by the year 2015, Egypt's population will number 86.2 million and will continue to increase to 98.5 million in 2025. During the 2007–2025 period, Egypt's population is projected to increase by 30.5%. In the Arab countries with younger age pyramids than that of Egypt and current higher natural increase rates, the population is projected to increase by much higher rates. Thus, for example, Syria's population is projected to reach 27.5 million in 2025, that is, to increase by as much as 38.1% during the 2007–2025 period. Jordan's population is projected to number 6.9 million in 2015 and to further increase to 8.0 million in 2025. The highest population growth rate is projected for Yemen whose current natural increase rate is higher than any of the other Arab countries. By 2025, Yemen's population will number 36.6 million, representing an increase of 63.3% during the 2007–2025 period.

Table 3.3 Demographic Projections for some Arab Countries, non-Arab Developing Countries, the "Asian Tigers" and some Developed European Countries, 2007–2025

Country	Population 1950 (millions)	Population 2007 (millions)	Population 2015 (millions)*	Population 2025 (millions)*	% Growth 1950–2007	% Growth 2007–2025
			Arab Countries			
Egypt	21.834	75.498	86.219	98.513	245.8	30.5
Syria	3.536	19.929	23.510	27.519	463.6	38.1
Jordan	0.472	5.924	6.923	8.029	1,155.1	35.5
Tunisia	3.530	10.327	11.204	12.170	192.5	17.8
Morocco	8.953	31.224	34.330	37.865	248.8	21.3
Algeria	8.753	33.858	38.088	42.882	286.8	26.6
Yemen	4.316	22.389	28.288	36.567	418.7	63.3
			Non-Arab Developing Countries			
Turkey	21.484	74.877	82.111	89.557	248.5	19.6
Iran	16.913	71.208	79.379	88.027	321.0	23.6
Brazil	53.975	191.791	210.048	228.883	255.3	19.3
Argentina	17.150	39.531	42.676	46.115	130.5	16.6
Thailand	20.607	63.884	66.763	68.803	210.0	7.7
			"Asian Tigers"			
South Korea	18.859	48.224	49.117	49.019	155.7	1.6
Singapore	1.022	4.436	4.809	5.104	334.1	15.1
Hong Kong	1.974	7.206	7.744	8.305	265.0	15.3
			Developed European countries			
France	41.829	61.647	63.746	65.769	47.4	6.7
Italy	47.104	58.877	59.001	58.079	25.0	-1.4
Belgium	8.628	10.457	10.613	10.742	21.2	2.7
Denmark	4.271	5.442	5.510	5.578	27.4	2.5
Austria	6.953	8.361	8.514	8.622	20.3	3.1
Germany	68.376	82.599	81.825	80.341	20.8	-2.7
Sweden	7.014	9.119	9.440	9.854	30.0	8.1
Norway	3.265	4.698	4.932	5.228	43.9	11.3

* Medium variant projection.

Source: UN, Population Division, *World Population Prospects: The 2006 Revision* (New York, 2007), pp. 43–47.

The lowest population growth rate among the Arab countries is projected in Tunisia, due to currently having the lowest fertility rate and the oldest age pyramid: 17.8% during the 2007–2025 period (see Table 3.3).[17] According to official Tunisian projections, by the year 2034, the country's total population will number 12.742 million compared to 9.932 million in 2004, representing an increase of 28.3% during these three decades.[18] According to this projection, by 2034, Tunisia's natural increase rate will only be 0.41%,[19] a result of a continuously declining CBRs and increasing CDRs due to the steady population ageing.

In the European developed countries, the population growth rates are currently already very low. In nominal figures, the natural increase of the EU population in 1999

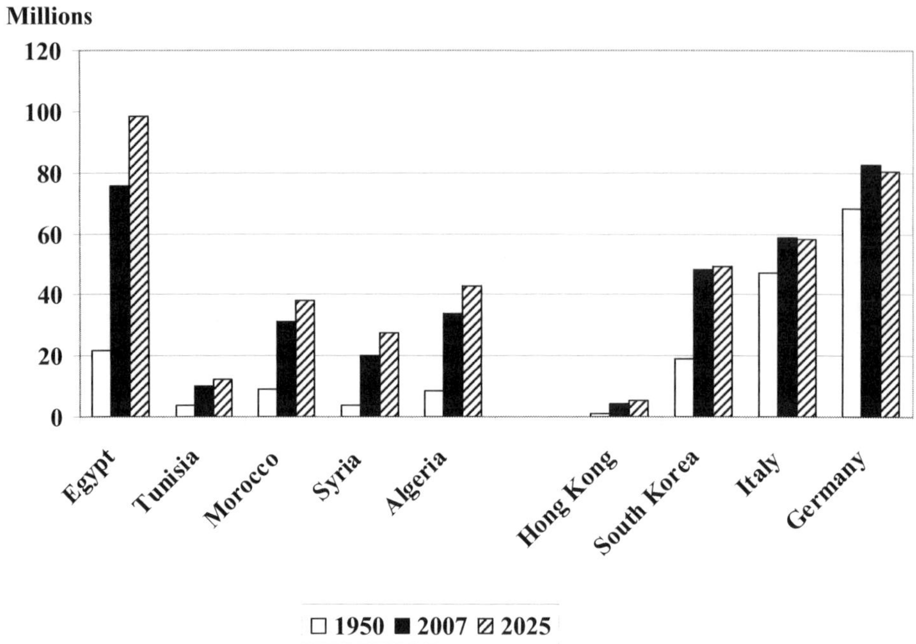

Figure 3.2 Demographic Projections for some Arab Countries, Developed European Countries and the "Asian Tigers," 2007–2025*
* Medium variant projection.

and 2000 amounted to only 966,000 and 1.05 million, respectively.[20] In 2002, the population of the EU increased by 0.3%, representing only 2% of the world's total population growth that year.[21] Overall, during the 1995–2004 decade, the population of the EU-25 countries increased by a mere 2.3%[22] – less than the average growth rate of the Arab countries in a single year! Italy is a good example for illustrating Europe's demographic situation in the past two decades. In 1991, the age group of 20–24, namely, those born between 1967 and 1971, numbered 4.7 million, while the age group of 0–4, that is, those born during the 1987–1991 period, numbered only 2.8 million.[23] By the year 2000, Europe's women under the age of 20 numbered 87 million, compared to 105 million in the age group of 20–40.[24] According to the latest available figures, in 2004, the share of the under-15 population within the total EU-25 countries population was 16.5%, compared to 18.8% in 1993. The percentage of the 15–24 age group also declined from 14.5% to 12.7% during the corresponding years.[25]

Thus, according to the calculations of Demeny, if Europe's fertility and mortality rates in the future were to remain the same as in the year 2000, "a generation of 1,000 persons would be replaced by a second generation of 645, followed by a third generation of 416, a fourth of 268, and so on."[26] Lutz and associates claimed that in the year 2000, Europe's population "began to generate negative momentum: a tendency to decline owing to shrinking cohorts of young people that was brought on by low fertility over the past three decades."[27] Currently, the negative effect of the demographic momentum is relatively small as it is only in its early stage. However, each year that the current below replacement-level fertility continues, the effect of the demographic momentum will intensify. In the countries that prevent large-scale immigration, the population increase will become negative in the very near future. Thus, for example, Belgium's population is projected to increase by a mere 2.7% during the 2007–2025 period, while Italy's population is projected to decrease by 1.4% during the corresponding years (see Table 3.3).

The implication of the almost-zero natural increase rates in the developed countries during the past four decades on the one hand, and the continuing rapid population growth in the developing countries on the other, is the steady decline in the share of the developed countries' population within the global population from 32.1% in 1950 to 18.3% in 2007 (see Table 3.4). During the 1990s, among the 81 million people that were added on annual average to the world's population, 91.4%, or 74 million people, were in the developing countries and a mere 7 million in the developed countries, which included the natural increase rate as well as the immigrants.[28] This trend is projected to continue during the first half of the twenty-first century as well. According to the UN medium variant projection, by the year 2050, the percentage of the developed countries within the total world's population will further shrink to only 13.5%. During the century of 1950–2050, the percentage of the developed countries within the worldwide population is projected to decline by more than 50%!

Thus, the only two options for the developed countries to overcome their expected negative population growth rates in the coming generation are either to encourage immigration through a liberal immigration policy or to achieve higher fertility rates through pro-natalist measures. Many of these countries, such as Sweden, France and Germany, have been trying for almost three decades to increase the fertility rates of their populations through substantial pro-natalist financial incentives,[29] but so far without much success. None of these countries has managed to achieve even the minimum of replacement-level fertility.

Therefore, the inescapable conclusion is that the only viable option for the developed countries to reverse their current demographic trends is to encourage large-scale immigration. This is precisely the approach taken in the EU countries during the past three decades. Thus, while in the 1960s net immigration accounted for less than 5% of the total population growth in the EU-15 counties, in the past decade, it was responsible for more than two-thirds of the EU net population growth, and its share is steadily increasing.[30] By the year 2002, net migration accounted for 75% of the EU

Table 3.4 World's Population, According to Level of Development, 1950–2050

	1950		1975		2007		2050*	
Development characteristic	Population (millions)	% world	Population (millions)	% world	Population (millions)	% world	Population (millions)	% world
Developed countries	814	32.1	1,048	25.7	1,223	18.3	1,245	13.5
Developing countries	1,721	67.9	3,028	74.3	5,448	81.7	7,946	86.5
World Total	2,535	100	4,076	100	6,671	100	9,191	100

* Medium variant projection.

Source: UN, Population Division, *World Population Prospects: The 2006 Revision* (New York, 2007), p. 1.

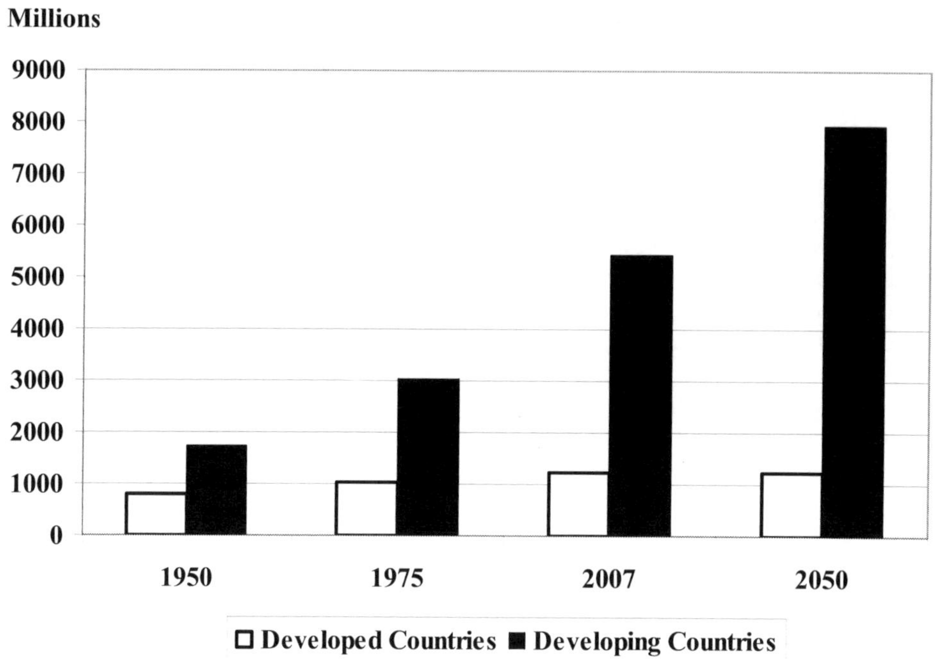

Figure 3.3 World's Population, According to Level of Development, 1950–2050

population increase, while the natural increase contributed only 25%.[31] In 2003, the net migration into the EU-25 member states amounted to 2.092 million.[32]

It should be emphasized, however, that the contribution of the immigration to the future population growth in the EU countries should not be considered only in terms of the nominal number of the immigrants. Even more important is the fact that the vast majority of the immigrants come from developing countries, with much higher fertility rates than those which prevail in the EU countries. Thus, for example, according to the 2001 Austrian census data, the TFR of the Muslim Austrian women was 2.3 children per woman, compared to 1.3 on average for Roman Catholic women which comprised 86% of the total Austrian women. In the case of France, the TFR during the years 1991–1998 averaged 3.2 for women born in Turkey and 2.9 for those born in Tunisia, compared to only 1.7 for those born in France. One can find a similar fertility differential according to country of origin in the Netherlands and Norway as well.[33]

The combined result of young immigrants and higher than national average fertility rate is a younger age pyramid of the minority communities in the developed EU countries. In the case of France, for example, by the early 2000s, as many as half of the Muslims were under the age of 24.[34] This means that the vast majority of French Muslims are either in their reproductive age or will be entering the reproductive age during the coming generation. Thus, already in the near future, the percentage of the first and second immigrant generations in the overall population of the host EU countries will be much higher than their current percentage. Given that a considerable percentage of the immigrants to the EU countries are Muslims, the percentage of non-

Christians in the EU countries will continue to rapidly increase in the foreseeable future.

Since the wave of immigration to developed European countries started four decades ago, this process has already had a profound effect on the ethnic composition of the European countries. For example, at the beginning of the twenty-first century, the percentage of Muslims within France's total population was estimated at 5% to 10%, and the percentage of non-Christians in Austria was estimated at 17%, the vast majority of whom were Muslims.[35] By the early 2000s, there were about 15 million Muslims in the EU developed countries.[36]

1.2 The Effects of the Young Age Structure on Labor Force Participation Rates

The age structure and fertility rates also have a direct impact on the labor force participation rate. In light of the young age pyramid which characterizes all the Arab countries, about 40% of the population is typically not included in the working age group (15–65). This means that *a priori* the potential labor force participation rate in the Arab countries is much smaller than that of the developed countries which have an older age structure.

The smallest number of working age population is of course in the countries with the widest age pyramid. For example, by 2005, the percentage of the working age population within Oman's total indigenous population was only 58.9%, whereas the corresponding figure was 65.5% in Norway and 66.2% in Denmark in 2004. The highest percentage worldwide of the working age population within the total population is in the "Asian Tigers." In South Korea, the working age population amounted to as much as 71.7% of the total population in 2004. The extremely high percentage of the working age population in these countries is a result of their sharp fertility decline of the past three decades. Thus, while the share of the under-15 population within the total population is currently small, the percentage of the 65 years and over population is still relatively low due to past high fertility rates. Among the Arab countries, Tunisia – the country with the lowest fertility rate during the past generation – currently has the highest percentage of the working age population with 67.7% in 2004 (see Table 3.1).

This period of an extremely high percentage of the working age population is called the demographic gift. It should be emphasized in this respect, however, that this "gift period" is not only a temporary one, stretching for no more than three decades, but also a "one time gift." After that, the share of the elderly population steadily increases due to the low fertility rates of the previous years. Thus, South Korean's 60 years and over population is projected to constitute 42.2% of the total population in 2050, compared to only 13.7% in 2005. In Hong Kong and Singapore as well, the percentage of the 60 years and over population is projected to be approximately 40% in 2050 compared to less than 15% in 2005 (see Table 3.2). As will be discussed in the concluding chapter of the book, the age structure is one of the most important factors which determine the pace of socioeconomic development.

In addition to the wide-based age pyramid, another factor which prevents high labor force participation rate in the Arab countries, both the oil-based and the non-oil alike, is the very low female labor force participation rate, a result of the high fertility rates as well as the traditional limitations on female employment. In the case of Algeria, for example, women constituted a mere 5.2% of the total labor force in 1966, rising slightly to 5.9% in 1977 and 7% in 1982.[37] In the other Arab countries, both the oil-based and the non-oil alike, female labor force participation rates in non-agricultural occupations were negligible as well during the 1960s and 1970s, amounting to no more than a few percent.

The low female labor force participation rates combined with the large percentage of the population outside the working age group translated into very low labor force participation rates in all the Arab countries. In the case of Egypt, for example, the 1986 population census recorded a labor force participation rate of only 27.7% (48.1% among males and as low as 6.2% among females). Jordan's labor force participation rate in 1991 was estimated to be even lower than Egypt's, with only 23.8% (39.9% among males and 6.6% among females).[38] The same phenomenon prevailed in the North African countries. In the case of Algeria, for example, the overall labor force participation rate in the early 1980s was less than 20%.[39]

Since the beginning of the "oil era," the lowest labor force participation rates among the Arab countries have been in the Gulf oil countries. In the case of Kuwait, for example, the labor force participation rate among the indigenous population in 1965 was recorded as being as low as 19.5% (37.2% among males and only 1% among women). The rate further declined to 18.8% in 1970 (36.1% among males and a mere 1.2% among females)[40] and remained at that level during the 1970s and the 1980s as well.[41] Likewise in Qatar, the labor force participation rate of the indigenous population was very low, amounting to only 19.0% in the mid-1980s.[42]

During the 1990s, the labor force participation rates of the GCC indigenous populations, with the exception of Bahrain (see below), continued to be the lowest among the Arab countries. For example, although the Saudi authorities do not publish complete employment data on a regular basis, according to the available data, the total number of Saudis employed in both the public and private sectors amounted to 3.2 million in 1999.[43] Considering the unemployment rate of 14% among the nationals (see below), the total Saudi labor force in 1999 was approximately 3.7 million, or at best 3.9 million, including the Saudi women working in the informal sector. This represents a labor force participation rate of only 22%–24%. This low labor force participation rate continued into the early 2000s as well. By 2002, the Saudi labor force participation rate was estimated at 19.0%,[44] and increased to 23.5% two years later, in 2004, according to SAMA figures.[45] Kuwait has a similar situation of low labor force participation rate, where, according to the 1995 population census, the national workforce numbered 147,768 while the total number of Kuwaiti citizens amounted to 653,616 – meaning a labor force participation rate of only 22.6%.[46]

It seems that the extremely low labor force participation rates of the indigenous GCC populations since the "oil boom" can mainly be attributed to the following four factors:

(a) An extremely wide-based age pyramid This was caused by high fertility rates, on the one hand, and very low infant and child mortality rates, on the other.

(b) A sharp increase in the educational system enrollment ratio The much higher enrollment at all educational levels among both males and females led to a short-term decrease in the labor force participation rates during the decade and a half following the October 1973 "oil boom." For example, despite Oman's rapid population growth, the indigenous labor force decreased from 137,000 in 1975 to 126,000 in 1985[47] – representing a decrease of more than 8% during one decade only.

(c) Early retirement One of the major tools used by the Gulf royal families to distribute the oil wealth among their citizens within the framework of the "*rentier*" socio-political formula was to employ the vast majority of the indigenous labor force in the public sector (see Chapter 4). Early retirement enabled the GCC authorities to employ new entrants into the labor market in the public sector and thus to increase the scale of the citizens who could enjoy public sector salaries. In the case of Saudi Arabia, for example, the official retirement age in the public sector is 55 years, 10 to 12 years earlier than in the developed countries.[48]

(d) Very low female labor force participation rates None of the GCC countries, other than Saudi Arabia, have explicit legislative restrictions on women's employment outside the household. Yet, in practice, a wide variety of occupations are considered "not suitable for women." In this regard, in an interview with the economic weekly *MEED* in 1979, the Qatari Education Under-Secretary, 'Abd al-'Aziz 'Abdallah al-Turki, said as follows:

> We make use of women here, but we are an Islamic country and we have special traditions. We find it very difficult, because of these traditions, to go into fields for the employment of women other than nursing and education.[49]

The lowest female labor force participation rate among the GCC indigenous women is in Saudi Arabia, although it has somewhat increased in recent years.[50] According to the latest available official Saudi data, by mid-2006, the Saudi female workforce amounted to 670,391, representing only 13.2% of the Saudi female working age population (15–64).[51] This low rate is due to the strict legislative restrictions on indigenous women employment, including prohibitions on women driving or mixing together with males in the workplace.

These severe limitations derive mainly from the fears of the *'ulama* (the Muslim clergy) that large-scale female employment will lead to cultural changes in male-female relationships and thus to a gradual change in the religious-cultural structure of Saudi society as a whole. The Saudi royal family prefers not to confront the *'ulama* on this issue in order to maintain the *status quo* between them. Indeed, the balance of power between the *'ulama* and the royal family is the most important criterion determining the overall position of women in each of the GCC societies. The greater the political power of the *'ulama*, the lower the position of women. The resistance of the Saudi *'ulama* to female employment is so great that in May 1993 they called for firing all the working women in Saudi Arabia, indigenous and foreigners alike.[52] Thus, as Wilson and Graham wrote: "women continue to serve as convenient scapegoats for the regime."[53]

Abdalla claims that: "The limited participation of [Gulf] women in the labor force is related to Arabian Gulf traditions and values which date back to the pre-oil era."[54] This is, of course, true, but the main question is why did these traditions norms and values not change following the massive socioeconomic development which occurred in these countries after the onset of the oil era. The answer to this question, paradoxically, is related directly to the oil era itself. The huge oil revenues enabled the Gulf oil countries to preserve their traditional norms in many aspects, including the traditional inferior attitude toward women. In other words, the Gulf oil countries had the sufficient financial resources to employ foreign women instead of employing their own indigenous women. Thus, while during the oil era, the Gulf women enjoyed free education, this education, in most cases, could not be translated into employment outside the households. The high salaries paid to male national employees in the public sector also hampered increasing women's participation in the labor force.[55]

In the late 1990s and the early 2000s, the Saudi authorities became more open toward the option of indigenous female employment outside the household in order to achieve both reduced dependence on foreign labor and lower fertility rates. Thus, for example, in the *SAMA 2000 Annual Report* it was written that: "It is important to expand Saudi female participation in the labor market . . . to take into consideration the high expenses incurred by the government for the education of Saudi females and the loss of economic returns . . . "[56] In order to balance between the need to increase female labor force participation rates, yet not withdraw from the tradition of segregation between males and females, in mid-2004 the Saudi authorities approved the establishment of an all-women industrial city, with the aim of employing about 10,000 Saudi women.[57] This is indeed a unique decision not only among all the Arab countries, but worldwide as well.

As in many other socioeconomic areas, in the area of female employment as well, Bahrain is unique among the Gulf oil countries. Not only are women not barred from employment outside their households, but they are actually encouraged to enter the labor market. According to official figures, female labor force participation increased from just 5% in 1971 to almost 40% in 2001. However, even in Bahrain national women represented less than 1% of the private sector workforce compared to more than 40% in the public sector.[58] The higher female labor force participation rate in Bahrain is attributed to the fact that Bahrain's per capita oil revenues are the lowest among the GCC countries.[59] Consequently, the salaries in Bahrain's public sector are also the lowest among the GCC countries. Hence, many women must work in order to contribute to the family income.

Since the early 1990s, the Omani authorities have also been trying to increase female labor force participation as part of their labor force nationalization policy (see Chapter 4). In addition to their ambition to reduce dependence on foreign labor, the Omani authorities aim to increase the indigenous female labor force participation rate as part of their anti-natalist policy (see Chapter 5). The intention of the Omani long-term socioeconomic development plan ("Oman 2020") in the area of female employment is to increase female labor force participation rates from 6% in 1995 to 12% in 2020.[60] Thus far, despite governmental efforts, the labor force participation rate of the indigenous Omani women remains quite low – no more than a few percent. In the richest GCC countries, namely, Qatar, Kuwait and UAE, women's labor force participation rates remained very low throughout the 1990s and early 2000s without any substantial change.[61]

Some researchers, such as Kapiszewski, have argued that the labor force participation rate of the indigenous GCC women is expected to increase in the near future.[62] However, the steady unemployment increase among GCC male nationals during the past decade (see Chapter 4) casts great doubt on this optimistic projection. This is because the paramount priority of the GCC royal families in the employment arena is to reduce the unemployment rates among male nationals and only then to increase female labor force participation rates. This, of course, is not a declared policy, but driven from an examination of the actual GCC employment policies which reveal a clear priority for male employment, even in Oman and Bahrain.

A major reason for the low priority of women employment in the GCC countries is that currently they are employed almost exclusively in the public sector. Thus, it is reasonable to expect that those who attempt to enter the labor force, at least in the short run, would also do so primarily through the public sector. This would only increase the employment pressure on the public sector, which already suffers from huge overstaffing.

In the non-oil Arab countries, there has been some increase in the labor force participation rates in the past two decades for two main reasons. The first is the increasing percentage of the working age group within the total population. The second reason is the increase in the female labor force participation rate itself, mainly in the 24–39 age group, as a consequence of the improvement in their educational level and the higher degree of openness toward women employment. Thus, for example, the female labor force participation rate in Egypt increased from 9% in 1981 to 17.6% in 1993, and in Syria from 9% in 1984 to 16% in 1994.[63]

According to the ILO figures, by 1997, the overall labor force participation rate was 37% in Egypt, 38.2% in Tunisia, and 39.1% in Morocco (15 years and over). The high labor force participation rates in the GCC countries, including 37.4% in Kuwait and 44.6% in Bahrain, can be explained by the fact that the ILO data include the

Table 3.5 Total Workforce and Labor Force Participation Rates in some Arab Countries, the "Asian Tigers" and some Developed European Countries, 1980 and 1997

Country	Labor force: Total 1997 (thousands)	Labor force: Annual growth % 1980–97	LFPR Total 1980	LFPR Total 1997	LFPR Male 1980	LFPR Male 1997	LFPR Female 1980	LFPR Female 1997
Arab Countries								
Egypt	23,817	2.6	35.0	37.0	50.7	51.4	18.9	22.1
Tunisia	3,562	2.9	34.3	38.2	48.0	52.2	20.1	23.9
Morocco	10,748	2.6	36.0	39.1	47.7	51.0	24.1	27.1
Syria	4,559	3.7	28.4	30.5	42.7	44.5	13.6	16.2
Jordan	1,671	5.3	23.8	28.9	39.2	43.8	7.2	13.4
Saudi Arabia	6,355	4.9	29.5	32.6	50.5	50.3	4.9	10.4
Kuwait	647	1.6	36.2	37.4	55.0	49.4	11.1	24.7
Bahrain	260	3.8	39.4	44.6	60.3	62.5	10.3	20.6
"Asian Tigers"								
South Korea	22,837	2.3	40.8	50.0	49.5	58.7	31.9	41.1
Singapore	1,731	2.6	46.3	50.3	59.3	61.0	32.7	39.5
Hong Kong	3,262	1.6	49.2	52.2	62.2	63.7	35.2	39.8
European Countries								
Germany	41,053	0.5	47.8	50.0	60.2	59.2	36.6	41.1
France	26,272	0.6	44.2	44.9	54.2	51.0	34.7	39.0
Italy	25,431	0.7	40.0	44.4	55.1	56.6	25.7	32.9
Belgium	4,225	0.4	40.1	41.5	54.2	50.4	26.6	32.9
Denmark	2,936	0.5	53.1	55.9	60.3	60.6	46.1	51.3

LFPR = defined as the ratio of the economically active population aged 15 years and over to the population of all ages.

Source: ILO, *World Employment Report, 1998–99* (Geneva, 1998), pp. 217–20, table 7.

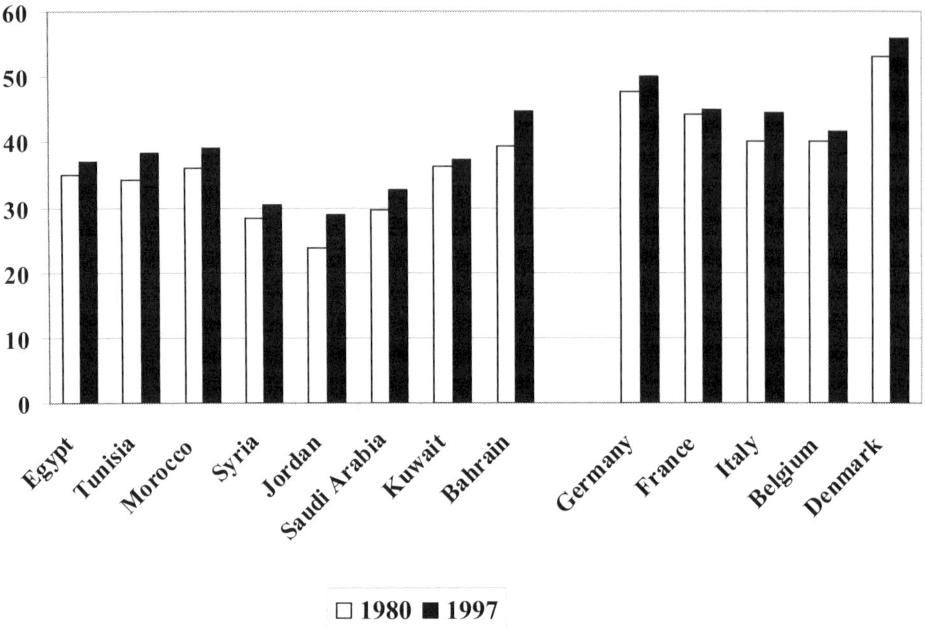

Figure 3.4 Labor Force Participation Rates in some Arab and European Countries, 1980 and 1997

foreign populations as well, with their extremely high labor force participation rates, estimated at 75%–85%. Even while recognizing the increase in the overall labor force participation rates of the non-oil Arab countries since the mid-1980s, the increases are not so impressive when viewed relative to those of the "Asian Tigers," not to mention the developed countries (see Table 3.5).

Despite the improving age structure toward a higher percentage of working age population, in the early 2000s, the dependency ratio[64] in the Arab countries are still among the highest worldwide, which together with the low female labor force participation rate produce the overall low labor force participation rate of no more than 27% in all of the Arab countries. Actually, during the 1990s, Arab women's share in the workforce was even lower than the situation which prevailed in the Sub-Saharan African countries. The low labor force participation rate is the core reason for the "low income trap" of the Arab countries.

In the "Asian Tigers," the Pacific countries and, of course, the developed countries, each worker supports less than one dependent, namely more than a half of their population is included in the workforce.[65] However, the long period of below replacement-level fertility, on the one hand, combined with the steadily increasing life expectancy, on the other, will serve to lower the dependency ratio and to create a "low income trap" in many developed countries, particularly the EU-15 countries, but in this case from the upper side of the age pyramid.

1.3 The Implications of the Young Age Pyramid for the Educational System

Following independence, all of the Arab countries without exception – both those that remained monarchies and those that came to be ruled by military officers – invested immense financial resources in education at all levels. Examination of the educational expenditure in the Arab countries reveals that each of them devoted a substantial percentage of their budgets to education. This was true even in periods of severe recession. Thus, for example, in 1985–1987, during the time of the lowest oil prices since the October 1973 "oil boom" (see Chapter 4), the outlay for education of the total governmental expenditure amounted to 15.8% in Jordan, 14.0% in Syria, 14.8% in Tunisia, and as much as 21.5% in Morocco. This outlay was considerably higher than in the "Asian Tigers" and in many worldwide developed countries. This high investment in education in the Arab countries continued into the 1990s and the early 2000s as well, despite the intensification of economic pressures. Therefore, during the years 2000–2002, the average public spending on education of the total governmental outlay

Table 3.6 Public Expenditure on Education in some Arab Countries, Developed Countries and the "Asian Tigers," 1985–2002

Country	Public expenditure on education as a percentage of governmental outlay			
	1985–87	***1991***	***1995–97***	***2002–2***
		Arab Countries		
Egypt	–	–	14.9	–
Tunisia	14.8	13.5	19.9	18.2
Morocco	21.5	26.1	24.9	26.4
Syria	14.0	17.3	13.6	–
Jordan	15.8	17.1	19.8	–
Saudi Arabia	13.6	17.8	22.8	–
Kuwait	13.4	–	14.0	17.4 (a)
Bahrain	12.3	14.6	12.0	–
		"Asian Tigers"		
South Korea	–	22.2	17.5	15.5
Singapore	11.5	18.2	23.3	–
Hong Kong	19.8	17.4	17.0	23.3
		Developed Countries		
The US	11.9	12.3	14.4	17.1
Australia	12.5	14.8	13.5	13.3
Canada	14.1	14.2	12.9	12.7
France	18.0	–	10.9	11.4
Belgium	14.3	–	6.0	–
Germany	–	–	9.6	9.5
Austria	7.8	7.6	10.4	11.1
Denmark	13.7	–	13.1	15.4
Sweden	12.8	13.8	12.2	12.8
Norway	14.7	14.6	16.8	16.2

– No data available.
(a) Figure relates to 2002–2004.

Sources: HNDP, *Human Development Report*, various years (New York: UNDP).

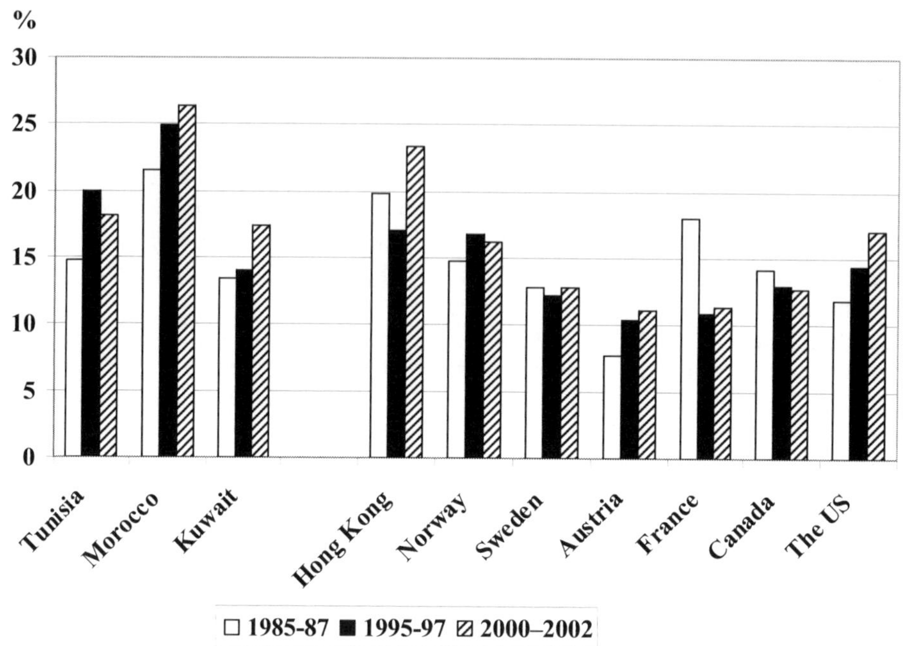

Figure 3.5 Public Expenditure on Education in some Arab and Developed Countries, 1985–2002

amounted, for example, to 18.2% in Tunisia and to as much as 26.4% in Morocco – more than twice as much as in many worldwide developed countries (see Table 3.6).

At first glance, these data are indeed impressive, indicating the immense importance of education in the Arab countries. One would expect that such a substantial investment in education would be translated into impressive educational and scientific achievements as well. In practice, however, this is not the case. This is because the huge investments in education were and still are "swallowed" by the rapid increase in the number of students as a result of the wide-based age pyramid. Consequently, the challenge of keeping pace with technological advances has become even more difficult for the non-oil Arab countries to meet. In the developed countries on the other hand, despite the fact that the educational outlay of the total governmental expenditure has not increased since the mid-1980s, and in many cases even decreased, the per capita educational investment has rather increased, given the low fertility rates of the past three decades.

Since human capital have become the paramount economic resource in the modern economy, one of the major factors accounting for the steady growth in the socioeconomic gap between the developed and the developing countries during the past generation is the increasing differential in per capita educational investment. The ESCWA report from 1997 noted in this regard as follows:

> Although investment in education was intensified during the past two decades, investments were concentrated on quantitative rather than qualitative growth . . . The net result was a

large supply of college graduates with qualifications that do not match the requirements of the labor markets in the 1990s.[66]

1.4 The Implications of the Young Age Pyramid for Future Employment Demands

Despite the low labor force participation rates, the nominal number of those entering the labor force in each of the Arab countries is steadily increasing as a consequence of the wide-based age pyramid. In the case of Syria, for example, during the 1960–1970 period, the working age population increased by 688,598, representing an increase of 68,860 on annual average.[67] During the 1991–2001 decade, however, the net increase in the Syrian working age population amounted to 3.630 million,[68] representing an increase of 363,000 on annual average, or 5.3 times the corresponding figure three decades earlier.

This trend, it should be emphasized, will continue well into the twenty-first century even if fertility rates sharply decline – a consequence of the "demographic momentum" phenomenon. For example, in mid-2001, the Syrian population in the age group of 0–4 numbered 2.1 million, while the age group of 40–44 numbered only 731,000.[69] This means that at a constant labor force participation rate, the number of those entering the labor force during the 2017–2021 period will be three times greater than the number of those retiring. Five years later, in mid-2006, the 40–44 age group numbered 883,000 while the 0–4 age group numbered 2.6 million.[70] Hence, in nominal figures, the gap between the 0–4 age group and the 40–44 age group increased from 1.369 million in 2001 to 1.717 million in 2006, representing an increase of 25% within only five years. In the case of Algeria, while the population growth rate is expected to decline to about 2% on annual average during the 2000–2015 period, the workforce is expected to increase by 3.7% on an annual average due to the extremely high fertility rates during the 1980s and the first half of the 1990s.[71] A similar process exists in all of the Arab countries, including Tunisia.

From a purely demographic viewpoint, the future employment dilemma of the Gaza Strip Palestinians is the most acute of all the Arab societies, as a result of their having the widest-base age pyramid. By mid-2000, the 0–4 age group numbered 231,392, compared to 41,235 in the 40–44 age group. This means that the number of those who enter the working age population in the 2016–2020 period will be as much as 5.6 times higher than the number of those retiring.[72] Thus, the argument of Shaban and associates that "over the coming two decades, demographic pressures on labor markets are expected to subside somewhat in countries that have already achieved substantial reductions in fertility, such as Egypt, Lebanon, Morocco, and Tunisia,"[73] is not correct.

According to the ALO, during the 1998–2000 years, the total Arab workforces grew by 3.3% annually, reaching 86.5 million in 2000.[74] According to ESCWA figures, by the early 2000s, the region's annual labor force growth rate reached 4.5% – the highest rate worldwide.[75] It is expected to increase annually by 4% in the coming decade and to reach 123 million by the year 2010, representing an increase of 36.5 million in nominal figures within a single decade.[76]

The prospect of an increase in employment demands casts a "heavy shadow" on the ability of the non-oil Arab economies to supply sufficient new work opportunities for their rapidly growing workforces. In the case of Jordan, for example, a World Bank

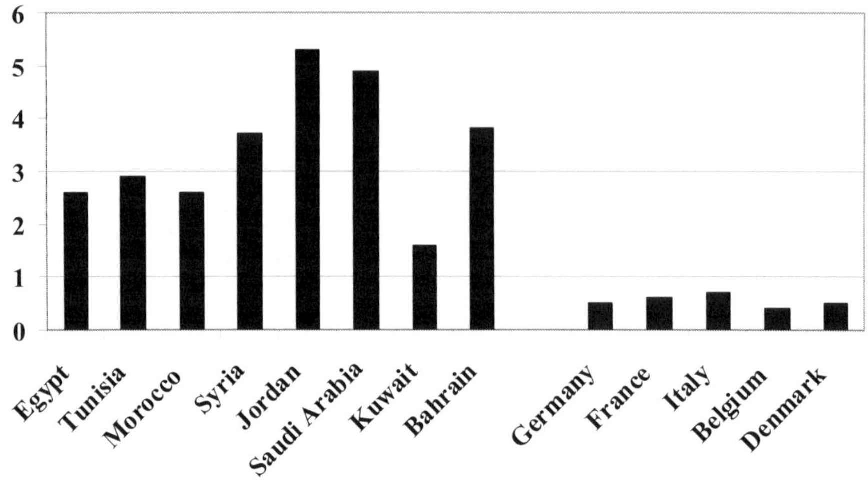

Figure 3.6 Annual Labor Force Growth Rates in some Arab and European Countries, 1980–1997 (%)

report from early 2003 specifically noted that, "with a labor force growing at 4%–5% per annum, Jordan needs at least 6% GDP growth to stabilize unemployment."[77] This means that each year that the Jordanian economy does not succeed in achieving this growth rate, which is considered very high by any international standard, unemployment will continue to increase. A similar growth rate is also needed in Egypt and Morocco in order to stabilize the unemployment level. An examination of the economic history of these countries during the past two decades reveals that neither has succeeded in achieving and maintaining this growth rate for more than a few years.

Thus, although many of the Arab countries succeeded in achieving remarkable economic growth rates during the past decade, mainly as a result of the implementation of structural economic reforms, this economic expansion was not enough to bring about a relief in the employment arena. Egypt's economic expansion, for example, amounted to 3.1% in 2001 and 3.5% in 2003[78] – almost twice the population growth rates in the corresponding years – the unemployment rate, however, did not even decline slightly (see below). In the North African countries, one can find a similar phenomenon of remarkable economic expansion which was not translated into unemployment reduction.[79] The end result has been a continuing increase in unemployment. This raises the question of whether the non-oil Arab economies are capable, under any circumstances, of maintaining an economic growth rate of approximately 7% on annual average.

2 Arab Employment Developments in Retrospect

In retrospect, it appears that the employment history of the Arab countries since the mid-twentieth century can broadly be divided into four main periods. As will be examined in Chapter 5, in each period there was a high correlation between the employment situation and the governmental family planning activities. The four periods are as follows:

2.1 Rapid Employment Expansion under Étatism

Some of the Arab countries were already plagued by high unemployment rates during the 1950s and 1960s, though short-lived in most cases, due to internal political instability, to wars or to a combination of these two factors. For example, in Jordan during the late 1960s and the early 1970s, the economy was forced to deal with both the severe economic consequences of the June 1967 War and the armed struggle between the Hashemite regime and the PLO. High unemployment rates also prevailed in Egypt in the 1966–1973 period as a result of the four wars in which Egypt was involved during that period (the War in Yemen, the June 1967 War, the War of Attrition and the October 1973 War). These cases, however, are the exceptions. They lasted for no more than a few years and were followed by economic expansion. Hence, during the 1950s and 1960s, unemployment in the vast majority of the Arab countries was quite low, a result of the following three factors:

(a) The low scale of labor forces The low scale of labor forces was due to the relatively small working age population in all of the Arab countries during that period with the sole exception of Egypt. Among all of the Arab countries, only Egypt, Morocco and Algeria had a population of more than 10 million in 1960. In Syria, for example, the total labor force, including those in the army and the various civilian security services, amounted to a little more than one million, with a labor force participation rate of 23%–25%. This means that the civilian labor force amounted to a maximum of 750,000. Among them, more than half were directly engaged in agriculture. In the case of Jordan, the labor force in 1970 amounted to less than half a million, including those in the army and the civilian security forces, representing a maximum civilian labor force of 400,000. Among them, approximately 100,000 were employed outside the Kingdom, the vast majority in the Gulf oil states (see Chapter 4). In Egypt, the labor force in 1960 amounted to approximately 7 million, namely one-fourth only of the current Egyptian labor force. Also in the case of Egypt a considerable percentage of the labor force was employed in the agricultural sector, the military and other security forces.

(b) The étatist economic approach One of the paramount aims of the étatist economic approach which was adopted by all of the army officers who seized power during the 1950s and 1960 was the elimination of unemployment as a measure to eradicate poverty and reduce the wide socioeconomic gaps. The *étatist* policy included massive employment of the urban labor force in the rapidly growing public sector (see below).

(c) The implementation of large-scale industrial and infrastructure projects These projects contributed to the rapid increase in employment opportunities not only in the major urban centers, but in the remote areas and the countryside as well, such as the Aswan High Dam in Egypt and the Tabaqa Dam on the Euphrates in Syria, both of which were accompanied by large-scale land reclamation. A similar macroeconomic policy and rapid expansion of public sector employment occurred in many other Arab countries during the 1950s and 1960s.

Consequently, the employment situation in the poorer Arab countries improved considerably during the 1960s. Within the framework of Egypt's First Five-Year

Development Plan for the period 1960–1965, more than one million new work opportunities were added[80] and "led to almost full employment in the 1960s . . . ," as claimed by El-Ghonemy.[81] According to one estimate, the number of unemployed in Egypt amounted to only 175,000 in the early 1960s.[82] Overall, according to El-Ghonemy, during the Nasserite period (1952–1970), the Egyptian economy achieved an average annual real growth rate of 5.7% – more than twice the population growth rate during the corresponding period.[83]

The Syrian economy also grew rapidly during the decade following its independence (1946), based on the rapid growth in the agricultural sector.[84] The 1955 IBRD report on Syria estimated that during the 1939–1955 period, Syria's national income almost doubled in real terms. Later, between 1954 and the collapse of the unification with Egypt in September 1961, Syrian economic expansion markedly slowed to an annual average of 3.2%, which was still higher than the population growth rate during the corresponding period.[85] In general, Syria's economic growth during the two decades of 1953–1973 was estimated at 4.5% on annual average,[86] namely, almost twice the population growth rate. Regarding that period, Sayigh wrote that: "Syria is one of the very few Arab economies which managed, on the whole, to achieve a reasonable rate of growth without the benefit of large petroleum resources and without the inflow of substantial foreign aid."[87]

In the Gulf countries, with the exception of Oman,[88] the overall economic situation largely improved during the 1950s and even more so during the 1960s and the early 1970s,[89] following the rapid increase of oil production.

2.2 The "Bonanza Oil Decade"

The October 1973 "oil boom" changed the socioeconomic situation in all of the Arab countries, but particularly in the oil economies, turning them, from the early 1980s, into some of the richest countries worldwide, with a per capita GNP well above most of the worldwide developed countries. By 1981, at the peak of the oil prices, Kuwait achieved a per capita GNP of $21,000 and Saudi Arabia of $16,010 compared to $13,290 in West Germany, $12,060 in Belgium, $9,280 in the UK, $8,040 in Italy and $5,630 in Spain (current prices).[90] The Gulf royal families now possessed the financial resources needed for the massive socioeconomic development plans that provided enormous employment opportunities for the indigenous and foreign labor forces, with the end result of negligible unemployment rates among the Gulf nationals (see Chapter 4).

In retrospect, the "oil decade" was the "bonanza period" not only for the Arab oil economies, but for the non-oil economies as well, when the vast majority of these countries achieved the highest economic growth rates ever in their modern history. Thus, for example, during the years 1973–1983, the annual average GDP growth rate amounted to 8.8% in Egypt, 8.0% in Syria, and reached as high as 11.1% in Jordan.[91] At the peak of the "oil decade," during the years 1976–1980, the Jordanian economy expanded by 62% in real terms[92] – higher than in any other period in its entire history.

The rapid expansion of the Arab non-oil economies during the "oil decade" was due mainly to the combined result of the following three factors:

***(a)* The surge of revenue from oil exports** of the smaller Arab oil-exporters, mainly Sudan, Egypt, and Syria, as a result of the overall increase in oil prices.

***(b)* The sharp rise in aid received from the Arab oil countries**, which dramatically increased after the Second Baghdad Arab Summit, held in late March 1979 (following the Egyptian-Israeli peace treaty), to the countries that did not enter into peace negotiations with Israel. In 1980, Arab aid to Jordan peaked at $1.3 billion,[93] representing one-fourth of the Jordanian GDP. The Arab aid to Syria in 1979 amounted to $1.85 billion, compared to $500-$600 million in the mid-1970s.[94]

(c) **The massive labor migration wave** from the poorer Arab countries to the Arab oil countries and, to a lesser extent, to Jordan. By 1973, on the eve of the "oil boom," the number of Egyptians working abroad was estimated at 160,000.[95] This number increased dramatically following the "oil boom," amounting to 1.365 million by the late 1970s.[96] Egypt's Foreign Minister estimated the number of Egyptians working in the Arab oil countries at 2.9 million in 1982,[97] representing approximately 15% of the total Egyptian labor force at that time. By mid-1983, the number of Egyptian workers in other Arab countries was estimated at approximately three million, more than a million of whom were in Iraq alone.[98] Although some estimations put the number of Egyptians working abroad in the mid-1980s far below the "conventional" figures (see Chapter 1), there is no doubt that the massive labor emigration wave from Egypt to the other Arab countries dramatically changed the Egyptian labor market.

Following the "oil boom," Jordan also became a major labor-exporter. According to Jordan's 1961 census, the number of Jordanian workers in other Arab countries was 15,901.[99] Their number dramatically increased following the October 1973 "oil boom," amounted to 139,000 (from the East Bank of the Jordan River only) in 1975[100] and reached as high as 250,000–300,000 in 1980, representing approximately 30% of the total Jordanian civilian labor force.[101] By 1983, according to official figures, the number of Jordanian workers in the other Arab countries was 271,200,[102] increasing to 328,000 in 1985,[103] namely, more than 40% of the total Jordanian civilian workforce – the highest rate among all of the Arab labor-exporting counties ever.

The third major Arab labor-exporter was North Yemen (YAR). By the mid-1980s, between 850,000 and 1.25 million North Yemenites were employed in the GCC countries, with the vast majority of them in Saudi Arabia.[104] Besides these three major Arab labor-exporting countries, other Arab countries also exported substantial numbers of workers. In the case of Syria, for example, by 1985 approximately 68,000 Syrians were working in Arab countries, mainly in Kuwait, Saudi Arabia and Jordan.[105]

Overall, from the labor-exporters' viewpoint, large-scale labor emigration had immense importance in four major areas:

(1) Large-scale labor emigration brought about considerable relief of employment pressures through both the emigration of a significant number of the local labor force, and the creation of a substantial number of work opportunities in the home countries driven by the workers' remittances.

(2) Massive financial aid from the rich Arab states enabled the non-oil Arab countries to absorb many additional employees into the public sector. For example, 44% of the new entrants into the labor force in Egypt during the 1976–1986 decade were absorbed into the public sector, and an additional 19% were absorbed into public enterprises. In Jordan, civil service employment grew by 9% on annual average during the 1970s and by 5% during the 1980s, reaching 50% of the total national labor force in 1987.[106]

(3) The surge in hard currency obtained through the workers' remittances and the financial aid from the Arab oil states led to substantial relief from the balance of payments deficits.

(4) The large-scale intra-Arab labor migration created a "mutual dependence" in the inter-Arab arena whereby the oil states needed the workers from the poorer countries, while the poorer countries needed both the financial aid and the numerous work opportunities provided by the oil states.[107]

The end result of the combined rapid economic expansion and the massive labor emigration was a sharp decline in unemployment rates in the poorer Arab countries. By 1982, Egypt's unemployment rate was estimated at only 5.7%,[108] declining from 8.4% in 1976.[109] Jordan's unemployment rate declined from 14% in 1972[110] to only 1.6% in 1976 and slightly increased to 3.9% in 1981.[111] Thus, in the mid-1970s, a new problem emerged in Jordan: a labor shortage that led the Jordanian authorities to permit labor immigration. By 1975, the number of foreign workers in Jordan was estimated at 32,800,[112] increasing to almost 140,000 by the end of 1984,[113] and reaching 186,506 in 1985, according to unofficial estimates.[114] Overall, the "oil decade" was "the bonanza decade" of the Arab countries from both economic and employment points of view.

2.3 Sobering Up from the "Oil boom" Illusion and Falling into a Deep Recession

The mode of production in the Arab countries is dominated by *rentier* economies and levels of economic performance marked by weak economic growth.

Arab Human Development Report–2005[115]

The Arab economies, both the oil-based and the non-oil alike, began to rapidly deteriorate following the end of the "bonanza oil decade," and even more so with the drop in oil prices to less than $10 per barrel in mid-1986, compared to $36 per barrel in 1980 (current prices). In constant 1990 prices, the decline in oil prices was from $49.6 in 1981 to $17.1 in 1986 (spot crude prices).[116] Generally speaking, the scale of the deterioration of the non-oil economies was a function of their dependence on the Arab oil economies.

Following the "oil boom," among the non-oil Arab countries, Jordan became the most dependent on the GCC countries. As Tayseer Abdel Jaber rightly noted, "Jordan became an oil economy without having oil."[117] Therefore, its economy experienced the worst deterioration as a result of the decline in aid given by the Arab oil states, from the peak of $1.3 billion in 1980 to only $600 million in 1987,[118] and the decline in the workers' remittances from more than $1 billion in the early 1980s to only $632 million in 1989.[119] The end of the Iran-Iraq War in September 1988 was also a major factor in Jordan's economic recession because during the war a considerable percentage of the activities in the 'Aqaba port were related to Iraq, while the Basra port was almost totally paralyzed. Moreover, during the war, a substantial portion of Jordan's export of goods was to Iraq.[120] According to an IMF report: "Real GDP declined at an average rate of 6.4% during 1986–1990, with the worst recession in the recent history of Jordan occurring in 1989 when real GDP contracted by 20.9%."[121] The severe recession was accompanied by a sharp increase in the external debt which reached as high as double the GDP and inflation intensified, climbing to 27% in 1989.[122] Naturally, the severe economic recession affected the unemployment rates, which sharply increased from 3% during the early 1980s to more than 10% by the end of the decade.[123]

The steady increase in unemployment rates in Jordan during the 1980s occurred along with the steady increase in the number of foreign workers in the Kingdom, estimated at 196,000 in early 1990.[124] The basic assumption of the Jordanian authorities had been that cheap foreign workers would replace the Jordanian nationals who had migrated to the Arab oil economies and that the Jordanian economy would benefit from the gap between the much higher remittances of the Jordanian workers abroad compared to the low salaries of the foreign workers in the Kingdom.[125] This assumption, however, collapsed in the mid-1980s, when the Jordanian migrants started returning from the GCC countries (see Chapter 4), while the foreign workers did not leave. Thus, in the late 1980s, a new employment situation emerged in Jordan: a parallel increase in the unemployment rates of the nationals and in the number of foreign workers.

The Syrian economy also greatly deteriorated during the second half of the 1980s as a combined result of the sharp drop in oil prices and political factors. The sharp drop in oil prices led to a parallel reduction in the aid received from the rich Arab oil countries, dropping to only $500 million on annual average during the years 1986–1988 – representing less than a third of the amount received in 1980.[126] In addition, Syria was by itself a smaller oil-exporter,[127] meaning that the overall decline in oil prices affected Syria's oil revenues as well. Although from 1982 until the end of the 1980s, Iran supplied Syria with oil, this assistance did not fully compensate for the decrease in Arab aid. Another factor contributing to the Syrian economic downturn was a marked reduction in workers' remittances. The final, and the most important, factor was the huge economic burden of the Strategic Balance Parity with Israel that Syria adopted following the Egyptian-Israeli peace treaty.[128] By the mid-1980s, Syria's military expenditures constituted between 50%–60% of the governmental budget (see Introduction).

The end result was that by 1989 the per capita GNP was $890 (in current prices) – almost half the amount of that in 1982.[129] The severe economic recession was accompanied by double-digit inflation[130] and chronic current account deficit.[131] In real terms, the Syrian average wage in 1986 was about one-quarter less than in 1982.[132] According to unofficial estimates, Syria's unemployment rate amounted to approximately 10% in the late 1980s.[133] The severe economic recession also began to have an impact on the stability of the Syrian regime. As Perthes claimed, "for the first time since coming to power in 1970, President Hafiz al-Asad and his regime were threatened by a loss of legitimacy as a result of economic rather than political problems."[134]

Egypt, like Jordan and Yemen, also suffered from the decline of the demand for Arab labor in the Gulf during the second half of the 1980s, particularly in Iraq. According to the UNDP estimate, in mid-1990, on the eve of the Iraqi invasion of Kuwait, the number of Egyptian workers in the other Arab countries was 1.96 million,[135]compared to approximately 3 million in the mid-1980s. It should be emphasized that the decline in the number of Egyptian workers in the Gulf countries during the second half of the 1980s had nothing to do with the boycott imposed on Egypt following its peace treaty with Israel.[136] Overall, during the years 1986–1989, Egypt's GDP declined by 6%. Due to the continuation of the rapid population growth, the decline was 14% in per capita terms.[137] Consequently, while in 1985/6 Egypt's per capita income was $750, it declined to only $600 in 1990.[138]

Egypt's economic recession was naturally manifested by an increase in unemployment. According to the 1986 census, the unemployment rate in Egypt was 14%,[139] while according to unofficial estimates the real unemployment rate in 1988 was as high as

20%, not including underemployment and hidden unemployment.[140] In addition to the economic recession, during the second half of the 1980s, the number of new entrants into the labor force remarkably increased as a result of the high natural increase rates of the past two decades, amounting to 450,000 on annual average.[141]

The economic recession of the 1980s affected the North African countries as well. Although the factors that led to the recession in the North African countries (with the exception of Libya, which is purely an oil economy) were quite different from those in the other Arab non-oil countries, the impact on the labor markets was the same – a steady unemployment increase. In the case of Morocco, the recession was the combined result of a decline in phosphate prices, droughts that hit North Africa first in the early 1980s and then again in the late 1980s, and increasing security expenditures due to the war in the Sahara.[142] The end result of the rapid growth in the labor force, on the one hand, and the shrinking economic activities on the other, was a rapid increase in unemployment, rising from 9% in 1980 to 14% in 1986 and 16% in 1989.[143] In Algeria, the unemployment rate in 1990 was estimated at 19.8%.[144]

The sharp drop in oil revenues during the second half of the 1980s had only a minor effect on the employment situation of the GCC nationals. The GCC governments exploited their huge financial reserves from the "oil decade"[145] to maintain the living standard of the indigenous population, including their employment in lucrative public sector positions. Although the number of foreign workers in the GCC countries did not decline during the second half of the 1980s, the number of new employment opportunities for foreign workers was considerably lower than that of the previous decade. At the same time, there was a shift from Arab to Asian workers in order to save expenditures. Thus, during the second half of the 1980s, the term "Arab solidarity" became meaningless, at least in the employment arena (see Chapter 4).

2.4 The Emergence of Structural Unemployment

> The [Moroccan] authorities . . . backed up by the security services and bureaucrats at the Interior Ministry are well aware that among the broad mass of the population, jobs, or rather lack of them, is the hottest political issue.
>
> Eileen Byrne, 2004[146]

> Nearly every macroeconomic indicator for the region exhibited healthy signs, except for employment.
>
> ESCWA *2004–2005 Socioeconomic Report*[147]

Why did the unemployment level in each of the Arab countries continue to increase during the past decade and a half despite the fact that the GDP growth rates were in most cases as much as twice the population growth rate? In other words, why was the relatively rapid economic expansion of the past decade not translated into unemployment decline?

The answer for this paradox lies in the new form of unemployment that emerged in all of the Arab countries, both the oil-based and the non-oil alike, since the early 1990s: structural unemployment. While in previous periods unemployment rates dropped in response to economic growth (mainly during the 1950s and the 1960s and again during the "oil decade"), since the early 1990s open unemployment, not to mention hidden unemployment and underemployment, continued to climb even in periods of high economic growth rates. The various components and aspects of this new unemployment pattern will be discussed below.

2.4.1 The "political connection" of the structural unemployment

During the 1970s and 1980s, the overall economic/employment situation had been quite similar in all of the non-oil Arab countries, namely, high growth rates which were followed by a recession due to changing oil prices. Since 1991, however, political factors, primarily the position toward the Kuwaiti crisis, were the most influential on the performances of the non-oil Arab economies.

Thus, in the early 1990s, Jordan, which did not support the anti-Iraqi coalition, was forced to deal with 350,000 returnees from the GCC countries (mainly from Kuwait and Saudi Arabia).[148] In addition, by 1991, Jordan's external debt amounted to $9.054 billion, of which $2.462 billion was a short-term debt,[149] while Jordan's total GDP that year was slightly above $4 billion.[150] This means that Jordan's external debt was more than twice the GDP. According to a study conducted by ESCWA, the cost of absorbing the returnees totaled $3.141 billion in the years 1992–1994 alone.[151] Jordan was not prepared to take in hundreds of thousands of returnees in the space of only a few months. Consequently, many of the socioeconomic problems that had been hidden during the "oil decade" rose to the surface, above all in the employment area. By late 1991, Jordan's official unemployment rate amounted to 22.9%. Many economists, however, believed that the Kingdom's actual unemployment rate, including those not registered with the authorities, was about 35%.[152]

Although the peace treaty with Israel did provide some major benefits for the Jordanian economy (see Introduction), it did not bring about an economic revolution and the Kingdom's economy continued to suffer from some basic shortcomings, the most serious being high unemployment. By 1998, Jordan's official unemployment rate was 15.2%, although according to unofficial estimates, the real rate was far above the official one.[153] According to an ESCWA estimate, in that year Jordan's real unemployment rate was 21%.[154] Although the Jordanian economy saw a remarkable growth of 6.2% on annual average during the 2001–2006 period, it was still not enough to bring about unemployment relief.[155]

However, the high unemployment rates among the Jordanian citizens during the 1990s did not bring about a reduction in the number of foreign workers. All of the attempts made by the Jordanian authorities to limit their number failed. According to the December 1994 census data, the number of foreigners in the Kingdom was 314,965,[156] which was almost twice their number prior to the Iraqi invasion of Kuwait. By 1995, the Ministry of Labor estimated the number of foreign workers in the Kingdom at 300,000.[157] During the second half of the 1990s, despite the various attempts of the Jordanian authorities to reduce the number of foreign workers, their number remained more or less stable at 250,000–300,000, the vast majority of whom were Egyptians.[158]

Hence, the Jordanian authorities failed to translate the various economic dividends of the peace treaty with Israel as well as the improved economic relationships with the GCC countries and the US since the mid-1990s into the creation of massive new job opportunities for their own citizens. It was a result of their failure to implement suitable labor immigration and employment policies, as will be examined in Chapter 4.

A similar process of economic recession during the early 1990s occurred in Yemen as well, due to its support of the Iraqis during the Kuwait crisis. Consequently, an estimated 800,000–900,000 Yemenites were forced to leave Saudi Arabia and return to Yemen.[159] The Yemenite authorities claimed that the number of returnees was actually much higher, amounting to one million, including both the workers and their accompanying family members.[160] As a result of this mass return of workers, Yemen was deprived of both workers' remittances and employment opportunities for its nationals. Thus, by 1992, Yemen's per capita GDP was only $464, compared to $692 in 1990.[161] Overall, during the years 1990–1994, Yemen's real GDP growth rate only reached 1.9% on annual average, equal to half of the population growth rate during the corresponding period.[162] Hence, by 1996, Yemen's unemployment rate climbed to 25% – the highest level of all the Arab countries[163] – and remained at that level during the second half of the 1990s and the early 2000s.[164]

The Iraqi invasion of Kuwait caused economic hardship even to the North African countries although they were not directly involved in the conflict. This came about mainly through the sharp recession of their tourism industry.[165] The reason for this is because one of the most prominent characteristics of the Middle Eastern tourism industry is its "regional form," namely, political tension in one country influences the tourism industry in the whole region. Hence, the combination of economic recession and a rapid increase in the employment demand was a steady increase in unemployment rates in all of the North African countries, without exception.

In the case of Tunisia, according to official figures, the average unemployment rate was more than 15% during the 1994–2000 period. In addition, large numbers of people were employed on a part-time, casual or seasonal basis, particularly in the agricultural sector.[166] In Morocco the unemployment rate was estimated at 17.8% in 1996[167] and increased to approximately 19% by the end of the decade.[168] In Algeria the unemployment rate was even higher than in Tunisia, climbing from 20.1% in 1991 to 28.0% in 1997,[169] and reaching approximately 30% in 2000.[170]

The countries that supported the anti-Iraqi coalition during the Kuwait crisis enjoyed many and varied financial benefits as a "reward" for their support. In the case of Egypt, these "rewards" mainly included a debt erasure of $7.5 billion to the US and massive recruitment of Egyptian labor to the GCC economies at the expense of workers from the Arab countries that did not join the anti-Iraqi coalition. According to the December 1996 census, 2.18 million Egyptian citizens temporarily migrated abroad.[171] By early 2001, the number of Egyptian workers abroad was estimated at 1.9 million.[172] In addition, during the first half of the 1990s, the Egyptian economy enjoyed tourism prosperity from tourists coming in from the GCC countries as well as from non-Arab countries. Overall, during the first half of the 1990s, the Egyptian GDP growth rate amounted to 18.7% in real terms – almost twice the population growth rate.[173] However, even these remarkable growth rates were not high enough to bring about unemployment decline which remained at the same level throughout the 1990s.

Among the non-oil Arab economies that supported the US-led anti-Iraqi coalition, Syria achieved the highest economic growth rates throughout the first half of the 1990s, amounting to almost 7% on annual average.[174] This rapid growth was the combined result of large-scale grants from the GCC countries, which amounted to more than $3 billion during the 1991–1993 period;[175] increasing oil production, from 200,000 b/d to 600,000 b/d;[176] a sharp rise in the number of Syrian workers abroad, mainly in Lebanon and the GCC countries;[177] and a marked increase in agricultural production due to the good weather in the early 1990s.[178]

However, starting in the mid-1990s, the Syrian economy began to deteriorate again as a result of two years of drought; low rates of private investments due to the slow privatization process; and, most importantly, the diminishing prospects for a Syrian-Israeli peace treaty. In per capita terms, the GDP growth rate was 1.8% in 1996, 1.3% in 1997, 1.5% 1998, and 0.6% in 1999.[179] The economic recession of the second half of the 1990s, combined with the inability to increase the number of workers abroad and the continued rapid expansion of the labor force led to an unemployment increase. According to official figures, by 2003, the unemployment rate was 11.7%, increasing from 9.5% in 2000 and 7.2% in 1995.[180] However, as in the cases of Egypt and Jordan, unofficial sources claimed a much higher unemployment rate, estimating it at 15%–20% in the late 1990s.[181]

Since the year 2000, however, Syrian economic performance has substantially improved, mainly due to an improved economic relationship with Iraq that contributed to the Syrian economy in two main areas: First, the export of goods to Iraq rose from only $200,000 in 1995[182] to as high as $3 billion in annual terms by the end of 2002.[183] Second, the flow of 180,000–200,000 b/d Iraqi oil through the Kirkuk-Banias pipeline enabled Syria to keep its oil exports at 400,000 b/d, bringing oil export revenues to a level of $1.8 billion by 2002.[184]

The increase in governmental revenues led the Syrian authorities to adopt an ambitious employment program with two major provisions: mandatory retirement from the public sector at the age of 60 and acceleration of the absorption of university graduates into the public sector.[185] However, the US invasion of Iraq in March 2003 ended the economic relationship between Syria and Iraq. Thus, there is no doubt that the end of Saddam Husayn's regime represented a turning point for Syria, not only from a political point of view but from an economic one as well.

2.4.2 The "demographic dimension" of the structural unemployment

Since the mid-1990s, although all of the Arab countries, almost without exception, have managed to achieve relatively high economic growth rates along with substantial fertility decline, unemployment has steadily increased or at least has not declined due to a surge in employment demand.

In the case of Egypt, during the second half of the 1990s, although the economy produced approximately 400,000 new jobs on annual average, the labor force increased by 500,000,[186] reflecting a 20% gap between the number of job opportunities and the expansion of the workforce. By the year 2000, while Egypt's official unemployment rate was 8%,[187] according to unofficial estimates the rate was more than double – approximately 15%–25%.[188] In 2002, the official number of the unemployed in Egypt was 1.9 million, while unofficial sources claimed a much higher number.[189] However, even according to the official Egyptian figures, the net number of unemployed jumped by 400,000 in 2000 alone. This means that despite the fact that during the 1990s Egypt achieved a remarkable GDP growth rate of 3.9% on annual average[190] – twice the population growth rate – unemployment did not decline.

This trend of relatively high economic growth rates along with climbing unemployment continued during the first half of the 2000s as well. During the fiscal years of 2004/5 and 2005/6, Egypt's real GDP growth rate amounted to 4.5% and 6.6%, respectively. However, the unemployment rate rather continued to increase as the number of new entrants into the workforce amounted to 650,000 annually,[191] compared to an average of 500,000 during the second half of the 1990s. More than anything else, these data represent "the demographic connection" of the Egyptian employment paradox. In the case of Syria, an annual average GDP growth rate of 3.3% during the 2001–2005 period, namely 1% higher than the population growth rate, was not enough to maintain the unemployment level which climbed to 20% in 2005 according to unofficial sources.[192]

A similar trend occurred in the North African countries. In the case of Morocco, although the economic expansion in 2003 and 2004 amounted to 6.1% and 5.4%, respectively,[193] namely three-times higher than the population growth rate, unemployment did not decline. In the case of Algeria, despite the continuation of rapid economic expansion in recent years,[194] unemployment continued to be very high, estimated by the IMF at approximately 21% in 2005,[195] a slight decline from 23.7% in 2004.[196] In the case of Tunisia, despite the strong GDP real growth rate of 5.4% in 2006, unemployment rate remained unchanged at 14.2%.[197]

Hence, during the past decade, the vast majority of the non-oil Arab countries have been forced to deal with an impossible situation: On the one hand, they have successfully implemented macroeconomic reforms which have indeed brought about impressive economic expansion, but on the other, even these high growth rates are lagging behind the rates needed in order to reduce unemployment.

2.4.3 The emergence of the severe "youth unemployment" problem

Unlike the Eastern European countries, whose recent adoption of the capitalist economic approach has led to the privatization of many governmental factories and establishments, including mass dismissal of employees, the major source of unemployment in the Arab countries is the inability of new entrants into the labor force to find employment in the first place. From an employment survey conducted in eleven Arab countries in the mid-1980s, it appears that 59% of the unemployed were first-time job seekers.[198] In 1989, while the overall unemployment in Tunisia was 14%, it was as high as 40% among the 18–26 age group.[199] In the same year, the unemployment rate among young urban Moroccans was 30% – almost twice the national average.[200] In the case of Saudi Arabia, in 1999, the unemployment rate among the 20–24 age group was 26.4%, while this rate was almost zero among the age group of 30 and above.[201]

A major component of urban unemployment during the 1980s, in both the oil and the non-oil Arab countries alike, was made up of young women who were first-time job seekers. Thus, it can be said that the highest unemployment rates in the Arab countries, without exception, were among women in the age group of 15–24.[202]

This trend of much higher unemployment rates among the younger age groups, particularly among first-time job seekers, was further exacerbated during the 1990s. By 1999, as many as 89.4% of the unemployed in Egypt were under the age of 30, and 60.1% were under the age of 25.[203] In the case of Syria, unemployment among the age group of 14–24 was estimated to be as high as 42.4% in 1999.[204] By 2003, about 80% of the unemployed in Algeria were under the age of 30.[205] Likewise, up to 60,000 Omanis under the age of 24 were unemployed in early 2003.[206]

2.4.4 The "educational dimension" of structural unemployment

Paradoxically, since the 1980s, the sector suffering the most from high unemployment in all of the Arab countries is that of young graduates from universities and other institutes of higher education. This trend was further exacerbated during the past decade. Azzam estimated that in Egypt, Syria and Jordan, more than 50% of the unemployed in the late 1990s were high school and higher education graduates.[207] In the case of Jordan, for example, by the end of 2002, according to official data, the unemployment rate among young university graduates was 32.1%. Unofficial sources claimed an even higher rate.[208] The worse situation existed in Egypt with an unemployment rate of 40% among male graduates and 50% among female graduates in 2005.[209]

One common argument for the high unemployment rates among the ranks of the young educated in the Arab countries is: "the educational system's failure to provide its students with the kinds of skills needed for private sector jobs."[210] While this argument is relevant to the Arab labor-importing countries, it is irrelevant in the cases of the poorer Arab countries, considering that in these countries, with the exception of Jordan, there are no foreign workers, at least not in considerable numbers.

It appears that the major factor which accounts for the increasing unemployment among young university graduates in the poorer Arab countries is the fact that among their four main labor-absorbing options – governmental employment, other public sector employment, migration to the Arab oil countries, and private sector employment – the number of new employment opportunities being created had been rapidly shrinking since the mid-1980s. At the same time, the number of "job seekers" had been steadily rising in line with the "demographic momentum" effects and the increase in women labor force participation rates.

3 The Increase in Disguised Unemployment and Underemployment

> The failure to use human capital, especially highly educated women, curbs economic development and squanders important energies and investments, which might otherwise contribute to greater economic development for all.
>
> *Arab Human Development Report–2005*[211]

A prominent phenomenon of the Arab labor markets found in the oil-based and the non-oil alike is that of huge disguised unemployment and, in the poorer Arab countries, underemployment as well.[212] One of the paramount aims of "Arab Socialism" – the Arab variety of the *étatism* of the developing countries in the 1950s and 1960s – was to narrow the huge socioeconomic gaps, primarily through eradicating unemployment and determining a minimum wage. The major tool for achieving this aim was to employ the vast majority of the urban workforce in the governmental bureaucracy and state-owned establishments and factories.

From a political viewpoint, the massive employment in the public sector, combined with the wide variety of subsidies on basic foodstuffs and social services promoted the identification of public sector employees with the authorities' ideologies and policies. This, it appears, was and still is one of the paramount factors contributing to the regime's stability in the non-oil Arab countries. Overall, in the early 1980s, 28% of the Egyptian workforce was employed in the public sector[213] – an extremely high percentage considering that 2.5–3 million Egyptians at that time were working abroad and approximately another 35% were working in agriculture. This means that private sector employment in the urban areas remained quite low, despite Sadat's *Infitah al-Iqtisadi* policy implemented since the mid-1970s.

Over time, however, this policy led to increasing disguised unemployment in the public sectors. As Wilson noted: "Underemployment remains, but in practice, employees receive what amounts to part-time pay for part-time work, though that is not the official job description."[214] For example, a labor survey conducted in Egypt in 1979 revealed that in Cairo alone there were 240,000 public sector employees "with nothing to do."[215] According to another estimate, the disguised unemployment in the Egyptian public sector in the late 1970s amounted to half a million employees.[216]

Despite the liberalization and privatization measures taken by many Arab countries during the 1990s, the public sector continued to be the larger employer for the urban workforces. In 1995, an estimated 35% of Egypt's total civilian workforce was employed by the public sector.[217] In 2001, the number of public sector employees in Egypt skyrocketed to 5.5 million.[218] By the year 2000, the Syrian workforce amounted to approximately 4 million, 1.4 million of whom were employed by the public sector.[219] By the end of 2003, almost one million Syrians were working in the civilian governmental ministries, of whom more than 100,000 in the Ministry of Economy alone![220] During the early 2000s, the Syrian authorities allocated a budget to absorb an additional 70,000 new employees into the public sector each year.[221] The aim of this policy was to prevent the increasing open unemployment, particularly among the educated young, to climb to a "politically dangerous" level.

Jordan is an example of a country that did not adopt the "Arab socialism" policy and has subsequently suffered from extremely high rates of disguised unemployment in the public sector. As the Jordanian Minister of Labor, 'Abd al-Hafez al-Shakhanbeh, acknowledged in April 1996:

> The administrative ranks in the government are highly bloated, as the number of civil servants totals 121,000, whereas in a country like Tunisia where the population is twice as much, the number of government workers is 50% less than in Jordan.[222]

Fahed al-Fanek estimated the number of governmental employees in Jordan in 1998 at 157,000. An additional 44,000 worked in other non-governmental public sector establishments and factories, and 85,000 were serving in the army.[223] Hence, in the late 1990s, even in Jordan, which had not adopted "the Arab socialism" policy, as much as 25% of its civilian workforce were employed in the public sector.

According to a World Bank study, the percentage of public sector employees among the total non-agricultural employees in the Middle East is the highest among the developing countries worldwide.[224] Thus, during the second half of the 1990s, public sector salaries in the Middle East represented 11% of the GDP – twice the average of the developing countries worldwide.[225] Richards and Waterbury argued that the reason a job in the public sector was and still is so attractive in the poorer Arab countries, despite its being low-paying, is that it "can easily be combined with a second job and provides a kind of 'income insurance.'"[226] Thus, in many cases, public sector employment is only a tool for achieving additional incomes through informal activities, legal and illegal alike. Equally destructive is the prevailing *baqshish* phenomenon. In the case of Syria, for example, Lesch wrote that:

> The first order of business . . . in Syria is to choose the right local broker . . . One cannot enter into a private or public sector business situation without a local mediator [*wasta*] because the vertical patronage networks that exist in the country require it . . . [227]

The sector that has suffered the most from disguised unemployment is that of higher education graduates. Since the late 1970s, however, and even earlier in Egypt, the balance between the supply and demand of university graduates in the Arab countries has been tipped in favor of the supply side. The major employer of graduates, that is, the public sector, could not continue to absorb additional employees. The levels of both disguised unemployment and underemployment were already high, and the governments of the non-oil Arab countries could no longer afford to increase salary expenditures, particularly since the end of the "oil decade." As a *FORBES* Magazine report on the Egyptian economy noted in late 1982:

> The government promises every college-educated Egyptian a job, and piles them into offices with little to do but complicate the ministries and public companies. Such employees are not paid much . . . but they cannot be fired, either. Many hold two jobs to make ends need. Others demand "lubrication" [*baqshish*] . . . for any effort.[228]

From a purely economic point of view, the public sector employment guarantee for every college and university graduate was very detrimental because rather than promote excellence in education, it discouraged competition between graduates. In any case, due to the rapid expansion of the labor force on the one hand, and the private sector weakness on the other, the Arab governments have not been able to live up to their promises. Hence, it is not surprising that in 2001, the waiting time required for higher education graduates for public sector employment in Egypt amounted to 11 years![229] One of the most devastating consequences of the large-scale disguised unemployment in the public sectors of the Arab countries is their low labor productivity.

Large-scale underemployment in the Arab countries prevails not only in the public sector but in the private sector as well, particularly among those who make their living in the agriculture and tourism sectors. The underemployment in the tourism industry and its related services and industries is attributable not only to the seasonal nature of this sector but also to the security-political instability affecting the number of tourists in the region. In the agriculture sector, the underemployment is concentrated mainly among those cultivating non-irrigated lands. This problem is particularly severe in Syria, where in the year 2000 only 22.6% of the total cultivated lands were irrigated.[230] During the first half of the 2000s, although the irrigated lands in Syria increased considerably from 1.210 million hectares[231] in 2000,[232] to 1.426 million hectares in 2005, still their percentage of the total cultivated lands was less than 30%.[233] Many of the Syrians who make their living from the non-irrigated lands were forced to work in neighboring Lebanon and Jordan during the intervening periods between the agricultural seasons.

4 Unemployment as a Differentiating Factor between the Arab Countries and the Developed Countries

The differences in the unemployment patterns between the Arab countries, particularly the non-oil, and the developed countries can be summarized according to the following six categories:

(a) The unemployment scale The open unemployment rate in each of the Arab countries in the early 2000s was at least 15%, and in many of the non-oil countries even higher, whereas in the developed countries the open unemployment rates were much lower, amounting in 2001 to 7.4% on average in the EU-15 countries and less than 6% in both Japan and the US.[234]

(b) "Unemployment by choice" In almost all of the developed countries worldwide, unemployment payments are provided by the government, thus allowing the labor forces in these countries, particularly the unmarried young, to be more selective in choosing work. Many jobs that are considered to be unattractive, due either to low social status or low wages, are in most cases filled by foreign workers, such as Turks in Germany, North Africans in France, Albanians in Italy, Indians and Pakistanis in the UK, and so forth. Thus, long-term unemployment[235] in the EU-15 countries in 2001 was as high as 45% of total unemployment,[236] with the labor market mismatch lying between the market demands on the one hand, and the desires and expectations of the indigenous labor forces on the other. However, in the non-oil Arab countries, the huge unemployment rate, particularly among the young, is a result of the mismatch between the number of new job opportunities and the number of new entrants into the labor force.

(c) The scale of disguised unemployment and underemployment In the Arab countries, in both the oil and the non-oil economies, the scale of disguised unemployment is far beyond that which is found in the developed countries, mainly due to two factors. First, the growth of the labor supply has greatly outpaced the creation of new job opportunities in productive areas. This has left the Arab governments with no other choice but to absorb a huge percentage of the urban surplus workforce into the public sector. A high rate of disguised unemployment, particularly in the poorer Arab countries, also prevails in the private sector due to low wages. In the developed countries, on the other hand, economic growth rates and the pace of creation of new work opportunities tend to be much higher than the growth of the labor force. Together with much higher salaries, this trend reduces the disguised unemployment level.

The second major factor is the differences in socioeconomic policies. As previously discussed, all of the Arab countries, with the exception of Lebanon, have adopted an *étatist* policy, with one of its main characteristics being wide-scale public sector employment. This is in contrast to the developed countries, where capitalism is the prevailing policy and thus the scale of public sector employment within the total employment is considerably lower. The fact that disguised unemployment prevails on a much larger scale in the public sector than in the private sector has contributed to the much higher disguised unemployment rates in the Arab countries.

(d) The age composition of the unemployed As previously discussed, the vast majority of the unemployed in both the oil and the non-oil Arab countries are young. In the developed countries, although the percentage of the young among the unemployed population is higher than their percentage in the labor force, it is still considerably lower than the corresponding percentage in the Arab countries. For example, in the year 2000, the percentage of the under-30 age group within the total unemployed population was 30.9% in Austria[237] and 43.4% in Belgium,[238] compared to more than 90% in the Arab countries.

This difference in the age composition of the unemployed population is mainly the result of three factors. Firstly, due to the wide-based age pyramid, the overall percentage of the young within the total labor force of the Arab countries is much higher than in the developed countries. Secondly, the already high female labor force participation rates in the developed countries contribute to preserving stable overall labor force participation rates. In the non-oil Arab countries, however, the steady increase in female labor force participation rates, particularly since the mid-1990s, is creating a situation in which the growth rates of the work force are far above the growth rates of the working age population. Lastly, despite privatization measures, the public sector is still the largest employer in the Arab countries, making it natural for unemployment to be more widespread among the young, many of whom are waiting for a job in the public sector. Since it is almost impossible to fire an employee from the public sector in the Arab countries, the percentage of unemployment in older ages is relatively small, particularly in the GCC countries (see Chapter 4). In contrast, a considerable number of the unemployed in the developed capitalist economies are older workers who have been laid off from the traditionally heavy labor-intensive industries (such as textile, wood, steel, etc.) and who are not equipped with the necessary skills to integrate into modern technological industries and services.

(e) The educational and professional levels of the unemployed In the Arab countries, a significant percentage of the unemployed are higher education graduates. In the developed economies, in contrast, the vast majority of the unemployed are uneducated, mainly due to the economic structure of these countries. In the case of the EU-15 countries, almost 90% of the new jobs created during the 1995–2001 period were in the high-tech sector (almost 20%) and the various knowledge-intensive services and industries (approximately 70%).[239] Thus, in 1999, in each of the EU-15 countries, the unemployment rate among those with a tertiary educational level was one-third that of those with less than a secondary educational level.[240] In other developed countries worldwide, one can find a similar trend of increasing unemployment in line with decreasing educational level. In the case of the US, for example, in 1997, the unemployment rates among those with a professional degree or a doctorate were 1.3% and 1.4%, respectively, whereas this rate sharply increased to 7.1% among those with less than a secondary educational level.[241]

Three main reasons have created the much higher unemployment rates among higher education graduates in the Arab countries: The first is a technical factor in which many higher education graduates are registered as unemployed in order to enter the waiting list for public sector employment while, during the waiting period, they are employed in various options in the informal sector. Unfortunately, as was examined in Chapter 1, there is no reliable method to measure the scale of this phenomenon. The second factor is the oversupply of higher education graduates in many fields as there is no matching between the labor market requirements and the field of study of the students. In addition, as higher education is free of charge in all of the Arab countries, paradoxically many of those who cannot find attractive private sector employment go to the universities in order to improve their chances of achieving public sector positions following graduation. The third factor is the small-scale of highly technological industries and services that require an educated and skilled workforce in the non-oil Arab countries.

(f) The geographical concentration of the unemployed While in the developed countries the unemployment rates, in most cases, are much higher in the remote areas than in the major urban centers, the opposite is true in the Arab countries where the unemployment rates in the major cities far exceed those in the countryside. In the case of Morocco, for example, the unemployment rate in the urban centers in recent years was

as much as 6% to 8% higher than in the rural areas.[242] In Tunisia one can find a similar pattern of considerably higher unemployment in the major urban centers compared to the countryside.[243]

The much higher unemployment rates in the major cities than in the rural areas in the non-oil Arab countries can be attributed to the following two factors: First, the agricultural employment pattern in the Arab countries is characterized in most cases by "household production," meaning that the entire family works together on cultivating the family fields. Thus, in effect, all of the family members are employed, including the women and children. Although this mode of employment creates large-scale disguised unemployment and underemployment, open unemployment in the rural areas is much lower than in the major cities. Second, there is an absence of employment opportunities in the countryside in the Arab countries other than in agriculture. Consequently, those who lose their means of livelihood as a result of scarcity in agricultural lands are forced to migrate to the major cities where employment opportunities, mainly in the informal sector, are much more varied. In the developed countries, on the other hand, the extremely high cost of living in the major cities, particularly housing, combined with the more flexible employment options available in the countryside and the remote areas, along with governmental allowances to the unemployed, "keep" many of the unemployed in the remote areas and the countryside.

More recently, however, there has also been further acceleration of economic hardships and unemployment in the peripheral areas in the poorer Arab countries. This is the case in Egypt, where the poorest areas are in Upper Egypt, as well as in Jordan, where the unemployment rates in the early 2000s in Ma'an, Tafila, Mafraq, and Madaba were considerably higher than in the capital, Amman.[244] The political implications of the deteriorating economic conditions in the Kingdom's southern region were manifested by the demonstrations against the Hashemite regime in this area, in which the Islamist opposition played a major part. Thus, whereas in the past, the main activities of Islamist opposition groups were concentrated in the major cities,[245] a new politically dangerous phenomenon is emerging in some of the non-oil Arab countries: that of increasing Islamist opposition activities in the remote and peripheral areas.

5 Summary and Conclusions

Until now, the non-oil Arab regimes have succeeded in avoiding a major political crisis on socioeconomic grounds through a series of temporary and unpredictable events leading to sharp economic growth and a rapid increase in job opportunities within a relatively short period of time. The first event was the October 1973 "oil boom," which led to rapid economic expansion until the mid-1980s. During that period, not only were millions of workers from the poorer Arab countries employed in the Arab oil countries, but the aid which was received from Arab oil countries was used, *inter alia*, to absorb many new employees, particularly higher education graduates, into the public sectors.

The second event was the Iraqi invasion of Kuwait, which served as an economic catalyst for the Arab countries that supported the anti-Iraqi coalition, primarily for Egypt and Syria. In the case of Egypt, a major part of the "reward" for its support of the anti-Iraqi coalition was the considerable increase in the number of Egyptians working in the GCC countries, in addition to the huge US financial aid and soft loans from the IMF. In the case of Syria, the "reward" was both in cash and soft loans from the GCC countries, in addition to acquiescence of the US and Israel to Syrian direct control over Lebanon, which led to the employment of hundreds of thousands of Syrians in Lebanon. Thus, the economies of these countries recovered during the first half of the 1990s after the deep recession of the second half of the 1980s.

The third event was the improvement in Arab–Israeli relations during the 1990s, which included the September 1993 Israeli-Palestinian Oslo Accords, the October 1994 Jordanian-Israeli peace agreement, and the Syrian-Israeli peace negotiations. These political developments led to a sharp growth in the tourism industry as well as the expansion of foreign investments in the region. In 1999, the number of tourists in Egypt climbed to 4.8 million, 66% of whom were Europeans. During the 1990s, the tourism industry became the largest private sector employer (direct and indirect) in Egypt,[246] and tourism receipts reached more than $4 billion in 2000 – higher than ever before.[247] In 1999, the number of tourists in Jordan reached 1.35 million, exceeding all previous record numbers.[248] In the North African countries, the tourism industry prospered during the 1990s and became a prominent factor for both hard currency and employment generation.[249]

The fourth event was the UN boycott on Iraq which led to an increase in Arab exports to Iraq. Thus, the Iraqi crisis actually benefited most of the non-oil Arab economies and more than compensated for the economic losses in tourism revenues and foreign investments caused by the Palestinian *Intifadat al-Aqsa* and the Iraqi crisis. Among all of the Arab countries, Syria was the greatest beneficiary from the Iraqi crisis in the forms of both massive exports to Iraq in addition to the 200,000 b/d of Iraqi oil which it received at very low prices. The surge in oil revenues since 2000 enabled the Syrian authorities to manage the economy almost without borrowing abroad. Thus, Syria was not subject to implementing IMF or World Bank reforms. However, all of these events led to temporary relief only. Following the removal of Saddam Husayn's regime in April 2003, the non-oil Arab countries had to find other sources for their exports, without which their economies would again deteriorate and unemployment surge even further.

Two decades ago, in late 1988, George Alan, a reporter of the monthly *The Middle East*, wrote an article about the Syrian economy entitled "An Economy Saved by Circumstances."[250] It seems that this title is also fitting for most of the non-oil Arab economies during the past three decades.

At the 91st Session of the ILO, held in Geneva on June 12, 2003, Jordan's King 'Abdallah, clearly underscored the connection between political stability and the employment situation by saying that: "Young people who desperately need opportunities and hope see themselves and their societies held back by poverty, health crises, illiteracy and more . . . Is it any surprise that these communities can become recruiting grounds for extremist ideologies?"[251]

4 The "New Arab Demographic Order"[1] *The Intra-Arab Labor Migration*

> If I have the choice between employing and paying a Saudi 4,000 riyals while I could pay a Filipino 1,000, of course I will employ the Filipino.
>
> Saudi businessman[2]

> Business visitors bringing new technology or foreign goods and services were regarded as something of a necessary evil, essential to the development of progress but a presence to be tolerated rather than encouraged.
>
> Pat Lancaster[3]

International migration is a relatively recent phenomenon, dating back to the emergence of nation states in Europe approximately 300 years ago. While much of twentieth century migration was brought about by political factors, such as internal (civil) and international wars, it is widely acknowledged that modern international migration, particularly since the 1950s, is characterized first and foremost by labor migration.[4] According to UN figures, by the year 2000, the numbers of international labor migrants amounted to 175 million (among them, 56 million went to European countries and 41 million to North American countries).[5]

I The Theoretical Framework of International Labor Migration[6]

The neo-classical economic interpretation treated international labor migration as a factor of production in line with Ricardo's International Trade Theory.[7] Hence, the basic assumption of the neo-classical International Labor Migration Theory is that labor is a kind of commodity and thus should be examined within the framework of "market" in which the forces of "demand" and "supply" interact and the price is determined according to the balance between them. In other words, workers are trading effort for income.

According to this perspective, uneven patterns of labor demand produce wage differentials, which, in turn, stimulate an increased labor supply through the mechanism of international migration. This produces a redistribution of human capital (workers) from areas of low salaries to areas of higher salaries. The motivation for emigration, according to the neo-classical perception, is a calculation of cost/benefit, that is, the prevailing wage in the home country versus the prospective wage in the migration destination minus the cost entailed by the emigration itself. Insofar as the gap is higher, the greater the motivation of the potential migrant. At the national level, through the international labor migration mechanism, countries can exchange labor services for capital (through workers' remittances) in the same way as exports of other goods and services. As such, both countries benefit – the labor-exporter and the labor-importer alike – making international migration a "win–win situation," similar to other forms of international trade.[8]

During the past two decades, in many developing countries worldwide, workers' remittances have become the most lucrative and stable source for hard currency,[9] as FDI (Foreign Direct Investments) "often move pro-cyclically, raising incomes during booms and depressing them during downturns."[10] Thus, according to the common perception, "remittances offset some of the output losses that a developing country may suffer from emigration of its highly skilled workers . . . Remittances also more than offset the loss of tax revenue in most developing countries."[11] In sum, through the workers' remittances, "an economy can spend more than it produces, import more than it exports or invest more than it saves."[12] In examining the issue of workers' remittances within the framework of both globalization and economic assistance given by developed countries to developing countries, Sander argued that: "Remittances are substantial and are becoming increasingly important as they continue to grow both nominally as well as compared to other transfers to developing countries."[13]

The common perception in the academic literature regarding the cost/benefit balance of labor immigration is also positive for several reasons. Firstly, labor immigration provides the host countries with the necessary workforce, in terms of both quantity and quality, at a much cheaper price than the local workforce. Moreover, it produces taxes, both direct and indirect, from the migrant workers that are, in most cases, much higher than the expenditures required to provide them with basic public services, such as healthcare and governmental subsidies. In addition, it contributes to raising the labor force participation rate and thereby improving the dependency ratio.

Thus, massive labor immigration has become a crucial factor in the development of many developed countries, particularly the EU countries, such as Germany, France and Belgium, where the dependency ratio has steadily decreased during the past three decades as a result of the population ageing phenomenon (see Chapter 3). Specifically regarding the inter-Arab labor migration, al-Yousif claimed that:

> Many expect globalization to lead to an increase in international migration, which like capital flows and trade offers potential gains to both the host country and the country of origin. This is so because the flow of labor improves the welfare of the migrants through higher earning income, their countries of origin through remittances, and the flow of labor benefits the host country by providing them with the skills they need at lower cost. The experience of the GCC countries during the last three decades is one example of this phenomenon.[14]

Was the intra-Arab labor migration indeed a "win–win situation"?

2 The GCC Development Strategy following the "Oil Boom"

> No region in the world economy has experienced more profound economic and social changes over the past half-century than the Arabian Peninsula.
>
> John Willoughby, 2005[15]

The socioeconomic developments that had occurred in the Middle East during the nineteenth century and the first half of the twentieth century did not affect the Gulf area which remained almost without any change compared to previous periods. At the end of World War I, the region's population continued to be very small, with approximately 1.5–2 million in the area of present day Saudi Arabia, about 175,000 in the area of present day Bahrain, Qatar, and Kuwait, and about half a million in present day Oman and the UAE.[16]

The economy of the Gulf area prior to the oil era was based mainly on pearl diving; subsistence agriculture in the coastal areas of Saudi Arabia and Oman; trade in the cities on the coasts, such as Manama of Bahrain, Kuwait city, Muscat of Oman, etc., and a traditional nomadic economy of raising camels and goats. In the early 1930s, however, the Gulf pearling industry collapsed as a result of the sharp decline in the worldwide demand for pearls due to the Great Depression and the development of Japanese cultured pearls which were considerably cheaper than natural pearls.[17] In addition, the number of the *Hajj* pilgrims markedly declined due to the Great Depression. Consequently, the Gulf region as a whole went into a severe recession, which lasted until the late 1940s. According to Saudi official sources, until the end of World War II, the Saudi government revenues were never higher than $4 million annually.[18] Consequently, until the mid-twentieth century, the Gulf region was the poorest area in the Middle East with the lowest per capita income, the highest death rates and the lowest life expectancy.

Oil was discovered in the Gulf region first in Bahrain in 1932, followed by Saudi Arabia in 1938, later by Kuwait, Qatar, the UAE and lastly by Oman in 1967. The next catalyst for the Gulf economy was the October 1973 "oil boom" which transformed the Gulf oil countries not only into the wealthiest in the Middle East region, but worldwide as well.

Following the October 1973 "oil boom," the Gulf oil countries have had to deal with the complicated dilemma of what to do with the sudden inflow of huge oil revenues. As oil is a depletable resource and its price fluctuates substantially, the development of alternative sources for both income and employment became the paramount aim of the GCC authorities. Thus, one of the three primary objectives of the Second Saudi Five-Year Development Plan for the 1975–1980 period was that of "diversifying sources of national income and reducing dependence on oil."[19] In later Saudi development plans, as in those of the other five Gulf oil countries, one can find a similar aim of economic diversification in order to reduce the dependence on oil incomes.[20] Among the Gulf leaders, Sultan Qabus of Oman was the most explicit. During the tenth anniversary of Oman's National Day on November 18, 1980, he made the following statement:

> Self-reliance is to be the keynote of all our plans for the future. Our first priority must therefore be the consolidation and expansion of our economy. It has long been our intension that our economy should be so diversified that our dependence on the one resource – oil – is

Table 4.1 Oil Production of the GCC Countries, 1970–2006 (thousand of b/d)

Year / Country	1970	1980	1990	2000	2001	2002	2004	2005	2006
Saudi Arabia	3,799	9,900	6,410	8,404	8,031	7,634	9,101	9,550	9,152
UAE	780	1,709	2,117	2,368	2,276	2,082	2,478	2,535	2,636
Kuwait	2,990	1,656	1,175	2,079	1,998	1,894	2,376	2,529	2,535
Qatar	362	472	406	737	714	679	818	835	850
Oman	332	282	685	970	960	897	751	774	738
Bahrain	67 (a)	48	42	38	35	35	35	35	35
Total GCC	**8,330**	**14,067**	**10,835**	**14,596**	**14,014**	**13,221**	**15,559**	**16,258**	**15,946**

(a) Figure relates to 1974.
Sources: EIA (Energy Information Administration, US Department of Energy), *International Petroleum Monthly*; idem, Table 1.1a and 11.1.a. Available at: http://www.eia.doe.gov.

reduced. To do this, we must exploit our country's other natural resources and our industrial potential to the full.[21]

In order to achieve the paramount goal of economic diversification, the GCC development plans following the October 1973 "oil boom" concentrated on two major arenas:

(a) **Rapid expansion of infrastructure facilities** which included everything from roads, highways, airports, seaports, telecommunication systems, and power stations as well as buildings of governmental ministries and other public services. The rapid expansion of the infrastructure facilities was the initial and pre-conditional step in the transformation from developing into developed economies.

(b) **Massive industrial development,** particularly oil-related ones, such as

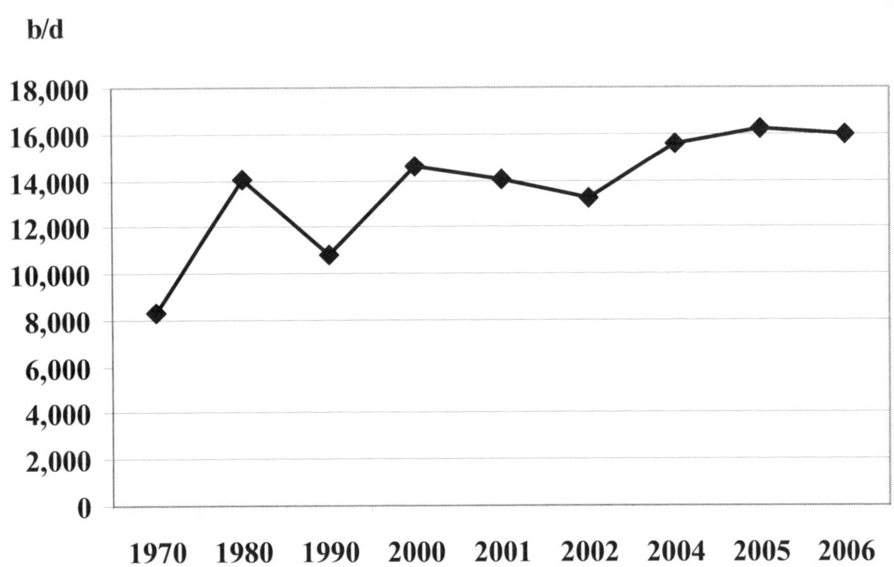

Figure 4.1 Oil Production of the GCC Countries, 1970–2006 (thousand of b/d)

Table 4.2 Crude Oil Prices, 1972–2007 (current prices, US$)

Year	US$/B	% change	Year	US$/B	% change
1972	1.9	--	1990	22.3	27.4
1973	2.8	47.4	1991	18.6	-16.6
1974	10.4	271.4	1992	18.4	-1.1
1975	10.7	2.9	1993	16.3	-11.4
1976	11.6	8.4	1994	15.5	-4.9
1977	12.4	6.9	1995	16.9	9.0
1978	13.0	4.8	1996	20.3	20.1
1979	29.8	129.2	1997	18.7	-7.9
1980	35.7	19.8	1998	12.3	-34.2
1981	34.3	-3.9	1999	17.5	42.3
1982	31.8	-7.3	2000	27.6	57.7
1983	28.8	-9.4	2001	23.1	-16.3
1984	28.1	-2.4	2002	24.4	5.6
1985	27.5	-2.1	2003	28.1	15.2
1986	13.0	-52.7	2004	36.1	28.5
1987	16.9	30.0	2005	50.6	40.2
1988	14.2	16.0	2006	61.1	20.8
1989	17.3	21.8	2007	69.1	13.1

1972–1987: Arabian Light/Dubai.
1888–2007: ORB

OPEC Reference Basket (ORB): From January 1, 1987 to June 15, 2005, OPEC calculated an arithmetic average of seven crude oil streams to estimate the OPEC basket price. Since June 16, 2005, OPEC decided to change the composition of the basket in order to better reflect the average quality of crude oil in OPEC member countries. The new basket is made up of 11 crude streams.

Sources: Paul Rivlin, *World Oil and Energy Trends: Strategic Implications for the Middle East*, Memorandum No. 57 (Tel Aviv University, Jaffee Center for Strategic Studies, September 2000), p. 17, table 1; OPEC website. Available at: http://www.opec.org; EIA website. Available at: http://www.eia.doe.gov; *MEES*, February 13, 1995; November 9, 1998; April 12, 2004.

petrochemicals, steel and aluminum, in which the Gulf oil economies have a clear comparative advantage of cheap energy. In this respect, Saad Eddin Ibrahim noted that in contrast to the developed countries which achieved their wealth through industrialization, "the GCC countries were trying to achieve industrialization through wealth."[22]

These large-scale development plans, however, required an extensive workforce of a size and quality that could not be supplied by local sources as the Gulf indigenous workforces were both small (see Table 4.5) and low-skilled.[23] In Saudi Arabia – the most populated among the Gulf countries – the illiteracy rate in 1974 was estimated to be 65% among males and as high as 98% among females. In the other Gulf oil countries, one can find similar high illiteracy rates.[24] As a result of these two basic labor limitations, the authorities of the Gulf oil countries decided that for the short-term, the necessary workforce would be supplied through immigration. For the longer run,

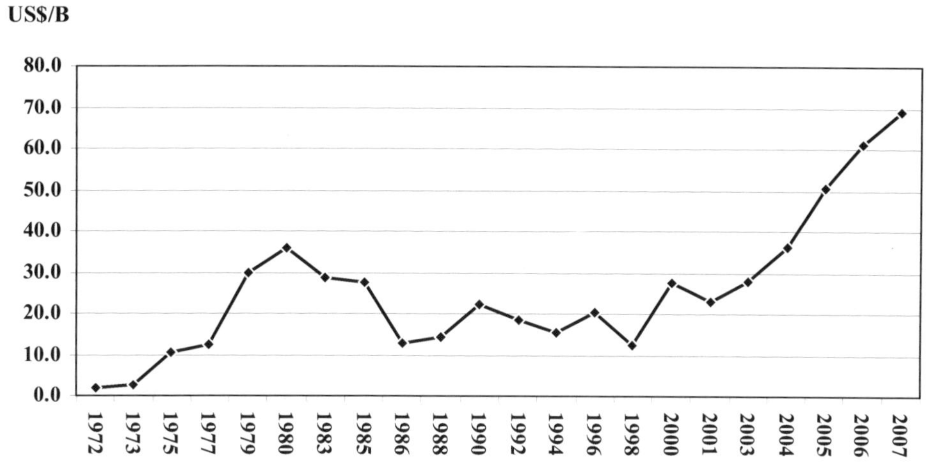

Figure 4.2 Crude Oil Prices, 1972–2007 (current prices, US$)

the required workforce, or at least its vast majority, would be supplied locally through massive investments in education and professional training on the one hand, and generous pro-natalist measures in order to maintain high fertility rates, on the other (see Chapter 5). It is important to emphasize, however, that the Gulf royal families never considered addressing the labor shortage through mass naturalization of foreign labor, *inter alia*, because of the large resistance from the local populations.[25]

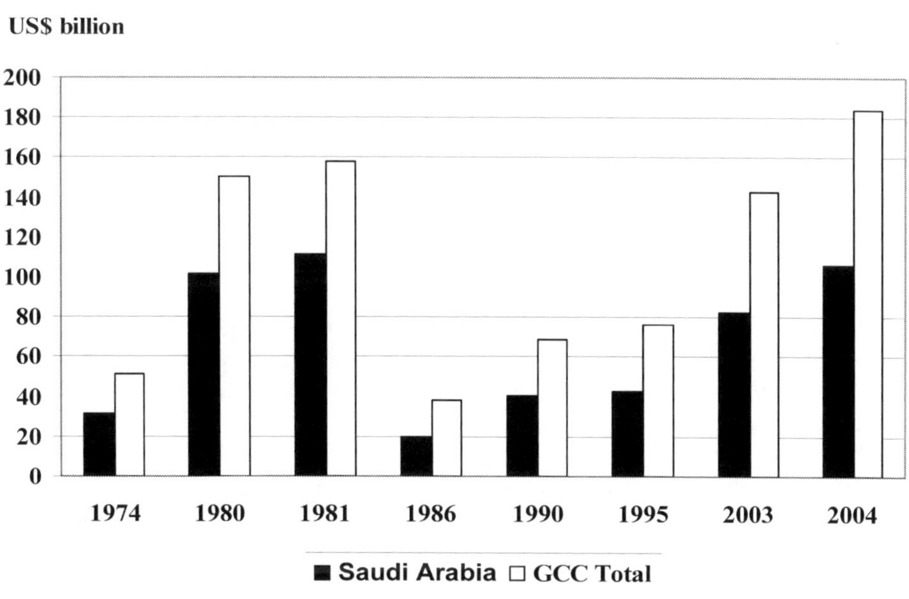

Figure 4.3 The GCC Oil Export Revenues, 1974–2004 (current prices, billions of US$)

Table 4.3 The GCC Oil Export Revenues, 1974–2004 (current prices, billions of US$)

Year	Total GCC	Saudi Arabia
1974	51.21	31.06
1975	46.18	27.62
1976	57.85	36.08
1977	63.82	41.11
1978	60.74	37.75
1979	93.82	57.15
1980	150.27	101.40
1981	157.80	111.50
1982	108.30	73.30
1983	76.10	44.80
1984	70.50	36.30
1985	60.00	27.50
1986	38.30	20.00
1987	45.60	22.70
1988	40.60	21.10
1989	50.78	24.09
1990	68.97	40.13
1991	64.74	43.31
1992	75.67	47.56
1993	71.32	41.35
1994	67.38	39.20
1995	76.30	42.70
1996	90.86	52.14
1997	85.92	48.90
1998	59.59	33.74
1999	76.08	43.19
2000	130.08	74.29
2001	109.42	59.61
2002	112.18	63.62
2003	142.81	82.07
2004	184.31	106.0

Sources: ESCWA, *Survey of Economic and Social Developments in the ESCWA Region, 1998–1999*, pp. 45-46; *Survey, 2000–2001*, p. 28, table 13; *Survey, 2003–2004,* p. 14, table 4; *Survey, 2004–2005*, p. 10, table 3.

3 The Subsequent Rapid Growth of Foreign Labor

Labor migration within the Arab region is not a new phenomenon; it had already started in the 1930s, following the discovery of oil in the Gulf area. However, until the early 1970s, the scale of labor migration in the Gulf oil states was relatively small mainly due to the low oil revenues. This also accounted for the slow pace of the socioeconomic development. In the early 1970s, prior to the "oil boom," the total number of foreigners in the Gulf oil countries was estimated to be between 800,000 and 1.25 million, including both workers and their accompanying family members.[26]

The unprecedented development projects following the "oil boom" led to an extremely rapid increase in the demand for foreign labor in the Gulf oil economies.

The enlistment of massive foreign labor following the "oil boom" did not demand substantial efforts on the part of the Gulf oil countries. This is because the foreigners were offered wages that were several times higher than the prevailing wages in their home countries. Thus, for example, according to a survey conducted in 1977, the wages for Egyptian construction labor in the Gulf were 780%–1,130% higher than those in Egypt.[27] In the late 1970s, while the annual wage of an Egyptian teacher was $600-$700 in Egypt, it was approximately $12,000 in Saudi Arabia.[28] Similar wage gaps also existed in comparison to the other non-oil Arab countries. For example, while the monthly wage for a non-skilled construction worker in Syria in the late 1970s was less than $70, he could earn about five-times that amount for the same work in any of the Gulf oil countries.[29] The combination of extremely high salaries, the liberal migration policy toward the family members of the foreign workers (see below), and the fact that for the Arab-Muslim migrants the religious-cultural life in the Gulf was quite similar to that in their home countries turned the Gulf into preferred migration destination.

In addition to the huge wage gaps between the Arab oil-based and the non-oil countries, two other major factors contributed to the massive intra-Arab labor migration following the "oil boom": The first and the most important factor was the substantial improvement of intra-Arab political relationships. During the Nasserite period, intra-Arab politics was characterized by a harsh struggle between "the revolutionary countries," namely those countries that were ruled by army officers, and those which were ruled by traditional monarchies, particularly those of the Gulf. However, following Egypt's June 1967 defeat, but more so following the death of 'Abd al-Nasser in late September 1970, this struggle ended, as Sadat's intra-Arab policy was that of cooperation and appeasement. The second factor was the adoption of encouraging labor emigration policy on the part of the over-populated Arab countries, the main ones being Egypt, Jordan, North Yemen and Sudan (see below).

Thus, in 1975, barely two years following the "oil boom," the total number of foreigners in the six Gulf oil countries climbed to 2.76 million, among whom 1.39 million were workers (50.4%) while the rest were accompanying family members. During the second half of the 1970s and the first half of the 1980s, the process of rapid increase in the number of foreign labor continued, simultaneous with the acceleration of development projects, first and foremost in the area of physical infrastructures and public services. Hence, by 1985, the foreign labor in the GCC countries numbered 4.37 million, representing an increase of more than threefold during the 1975–1985 decade (see Table 4.5).

In the mid-1980s, there was a widespread feeling that the process of rapid increase in the number of foreign labor in the GCC countries had ended and from that point on, their numbers would steadily decline.[30] This feeling was based on four fundamental factors: The first was the sharp decline of oil revenues, particularly following the collapse of oil prices in mid-1986 (see Table 4.3). The second factor was the adoption of labor force nationalization policies (sometimes called "indigenization"). The third factor was the rapid increase of the indigenous workforce due to the accelerated population growth along with the sharp improvement in its quality due to the huge investments in education and vocational training. The fourth factor was the completion of the major infrastructure projects.

This widespread concept is well illustrated in the GCC development plans from the mid-1980s when each of them, almost without exception, predicted a sharp decline in the number of foreign labor in the near future. For example, the Saudi Fourth Five-

Year Development Plan for the 1980–1985 years noted that: "For the first time since the First Plan [1970–1975], when rapid economic development began, not only the share, but also the absolute number of non-Saudi workers in the Kingdom will decline, while the economy will absorb substantial numbers of new Saudi entrants."[31] The aim of the plan in the labor force arena was to reduce the number of foreign workers by 22.6%; in nominal figures, from 2.66 million in 1985 to 2.06 in 1990.[32]

During the 1984–1987 period, in most of the GCC countries, some decline in the number of foreign labor occurred. The number of work permits granted to foreign workers by the Saudi authorities dropped by more than 10% in 1983 compared to the previous year.[33] In Oman the number of foreign labor declined by 27,000 in 1986 alone.[34] In the other GCC countries, the same trend occurred: The number of foreign workers declined or remained the same during the 1983–1987 period.

Table 4.4 Nationals and Expatriates in the GCC Populations, 1975–2005 ('000)

Country	Nationals	Foreigners	Total	% Foreigners
		1975		
Saudi Arabia	6,218 (a)	1,565	7,783	20.1
Kuwait	472	523	995	52.6
Bahrain	214	56	270	20.7
Oman	550	132	682	19.4
Qatar	60	97	157	61.8
UAE	170	388	558	69.5
Total	**7,684**	**2,761**	**10,445**	**26.4**
		1980		
Saudi Arabia	7,079	2,150	9,229	23.3
Kuwait	566	792	1,358	58.3
Bahrain (b)	239	112	351	31.9
Oman	805	179	984	18.2
Qatar	65	178	243	73.3
UAE	237	746	983	75.9
Total	**8,991**	**4,157**	**13,148**	**31.6**
		1986		
Saudi Arabia	7,849	2,314	10,163	22.8
Kuwait	750	1,072	1,822	58.8
Bahrain	295	140	435	32.2
Oman	816	494	1,310	37.7
Qatar	105	284	389	73.0
UAE	434	1,239	1,673	74.1
Total	**10,249**	**5,543**	**15,792**	**35.1**
		1990		
Saudi Arabia (c)	8,847	5,939	14,786	40.2
Kuwait	572	1,563	2,135	73.2
Bahrain	336	167	503	33.2
Oman	1,024	371	1,395	26.6
Qatar	100	350	450	77.8
UAE	531	1,014	1,545	65.6
Total	**11,410**	**9,404**	**20,814**	**45.2**

However, the recovery of oil prices after mid-1987, led to the reversal of the process and the number of foreign labor in each of the GCC countries, without exception, began to rise again, although at a slower pace than during the "oil decade." By mid-1990s, on the eve of the Iraqi invasion of Kuwait, the total number of foreigners in the GCC countries amounted to 9.4 million compared to 4.2 million in 1986. The number of foreign labor in the GCC countries in mid-1990 totaled 5.2 million compared to 4.4 million in 1985. The most dramatic increase was in Saudi Arabia whose foreign population more than doubled during the second half of the 1980s (see Tables 4.4 and 4.5).

The Iraqi invasion of Kuwait on August 1990 led to dramatic demographic changes in the GCC countries. In total contrast to Birks and Sinclair's projection that "massive returns of non-national Arab workers to their source countries from the GCC are unlikely,"[35] a large-scale departure of approximately two million Arabs and some hundreds of thousands of non-Arabs occurred. As was examined in Chapter 3, following Yemenite support of Iraq, about one million Yemenites were forced to leave Saudi Arabia and approximately 350,000 Jordanian citizens, the vast majority of

Table 4.4 (continued)

Country	Nationals	Foreigners	Total	% Foreigners
		1994		
Saudi Arabia	13,053	5,127	18,180	28.2
Kuwait	671	949	1,620	58.6
Bahrain	346	205	551	37.2
Oman	1,511	538	2,049	26.3
Qatar	129	403	532	75.8
UAE	629	1,522	2,151	70.8
Total	**16,339**	**8,744**	**25,083**	**34.9**
		2000		
Saudi Arabia	15,589	5,258	20,847	25.2
Kuwait	832	1,358	2,190	62.0
Bahrain	391	261	652	40.0
Oman	1,778	624	2,402	30.6
Qatar	152	428	580	73.8
UAE	703	2,187	2,890	75.7
Total	**19,445**	**10,116**	**29,561**	**34.2**
		2005		
Saudi Arabia (d)	16,529	6,144	22,673	27.1
Kuwait	881	1,332	2,213	60.2
Bahrain	438	269	707	38.0
Oman	1,842	666	2,508	26.5
Qatar (d)	172 (e)	572 (e)	744 (d)	76.9
UAE	825	2,944	3,769	78.1
Total	**20,687**	**11,927**	**32,614**	**36.6**

(a) Figure relates to 1974. (b) Figures relate to 1981. (c) Figures relate to 1988.
(d) Figures relate to 2004. (e) Author's calculation, based on 2004 Qatar's census data.

Sources: See Table 4.5.

whom were of Palestinian origin, were forced to leave Kuwait as a result of Yasir 'Arafat's and King Husayn's support of Iraq.

Following the large exodus of the foreigners, it was widely accepted among both researchers and politicians that the number of foreigners would never again reach the

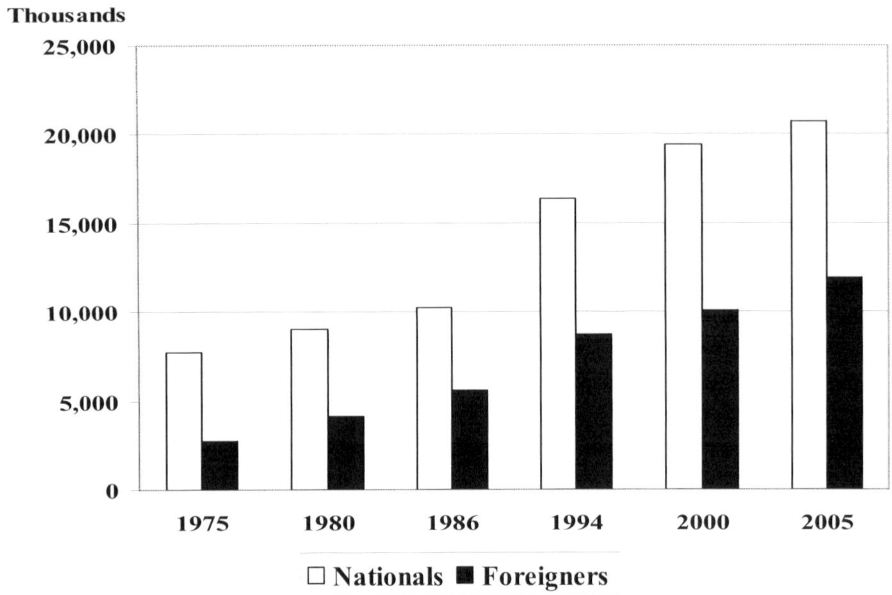

Figure 4.4 Nationals and Expatriates in the GCC Populations, 1975–2005 ('000)

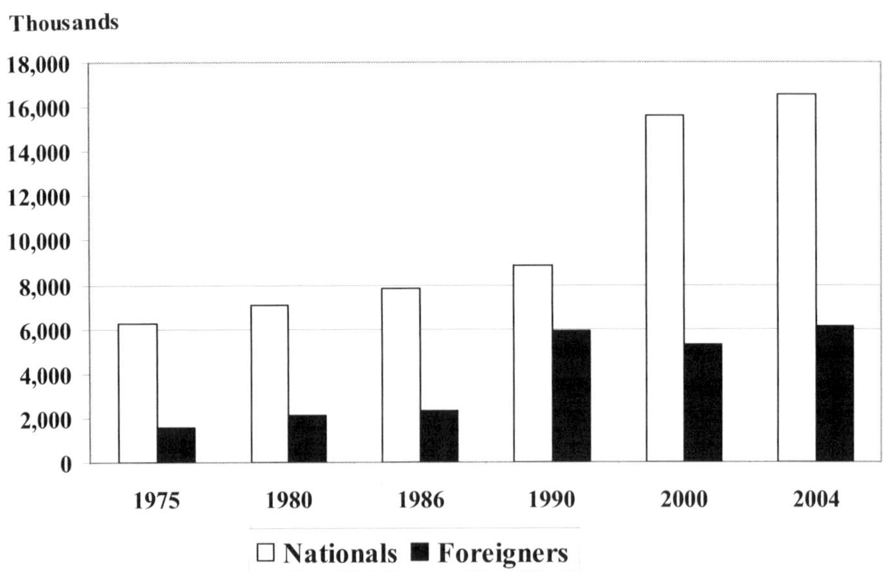

Figure 4.5 Nationals and Expatriates in the Saudi Arabian Population, 1975–2004 ('000)

numbers which had prevailed prior to the Iraqi invasion. This widely-held perception rested on four basic assumptions:

***(a)* There is a strong connection between oil prices and the number of foreign workers**, based on the belief that the number of foreign labor is a direct function of the scale of development projects. Due to the extreme financial damage to the

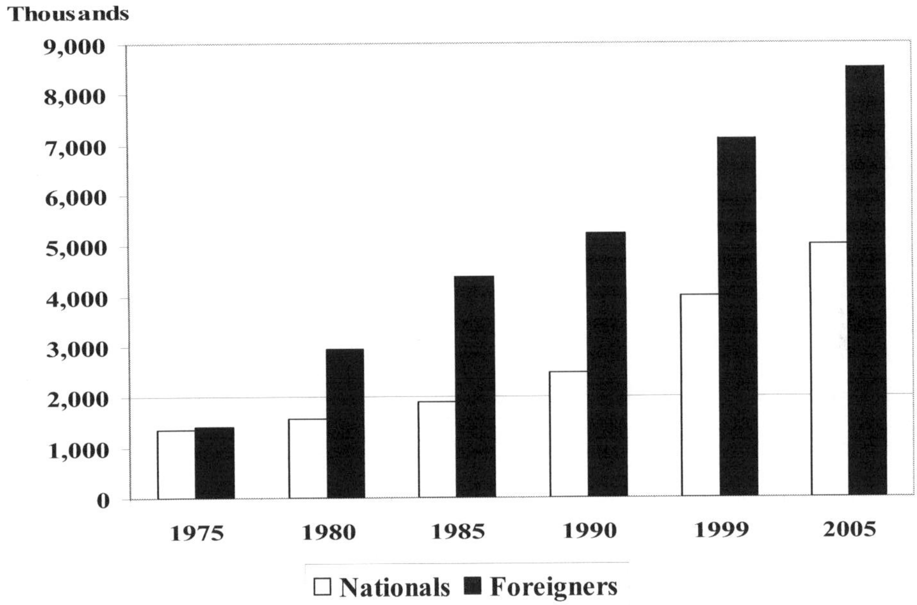

Figure 4.6 Nationals and Expatriates in the GCC Labor Forces, 1975–2005 ('000)

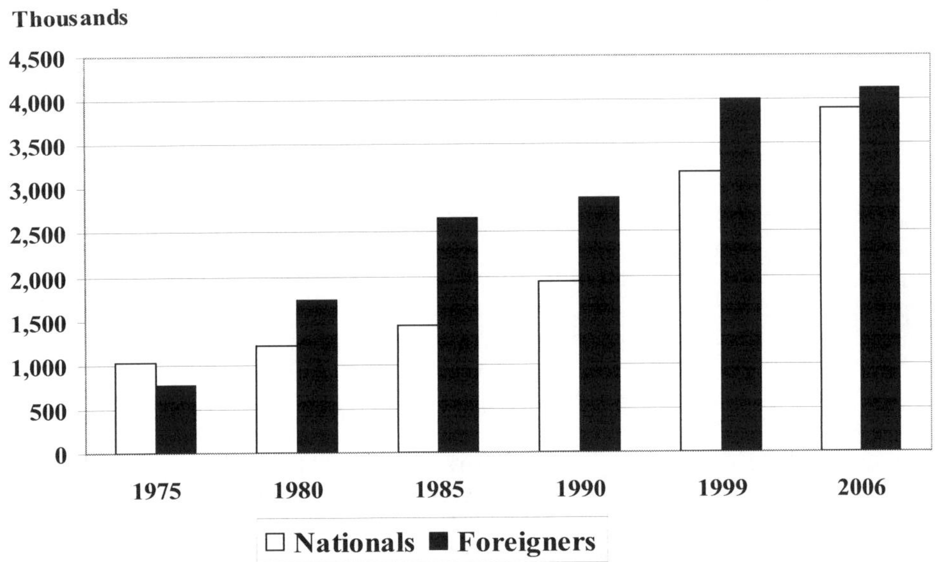

Figure 4.7 Nationals and Expatriates in the Saudi Arabian Labor Force, 1975–2006 ('000)

Table 4.5 Nationals and Expatriates in the GCC Labor Forces, 1975–2005 ('000)

Country	Nationals	Foreigners	Total	% Foreigners
		1975		
Saudi Arabia	1,027	773	1,800	42.9
Kuwait	92	213	305	69.8
Bahrain	46	30	76	39.5
Oman	137	71	208	34.1
Qatar	13	54	67	80.6
UAE	45	252	297	84.8
Total	**1,360**	**1,393**	**2,753**	**50.6**
		1980		
Saudi Arabia	1,220	1,734	2,954	58.7
Kuwait	108	384	492	78.0
Bahrain (a)	61	81	142	57.0
Oman	119	171	290	59.0
Qatar	15	106	121	87.6
UAE	54	471	525	89.7
Total	**1,577**	**2,947**	**4,524**	**65.1**
		1985		
Saudi Arabia	1,440	2,662	4,102	64.9
Kuwait	126	544	670	81.2
Bahrain	73	101	174	58.0
Oman (b)	167	300	467	64.2
Qatar	18	156	174	89.7
UAE	72	612	684	89.5
Total	**1,896**	**4,375**	**6,271**	**69.8**
		1990		
Saudi Arabia	1,934	2,878	4,812	59.8
Kuwait	118	731	849	86.1
Bahrain	127	132	259	51.0
Oman	189	442	631	70.0
Qatar	21	230	251	91.6
UAE	96	805	901	89.3
Total	**2,485**	**5,218**	**7,703**	**67.7**
		1999		
Saudi Arabia	3,173	4003	7,176	55.9
Kuwait	221	1,005	1,226	82.0
Bahrain	113	194	307	63.2
Oman	312 (d)	503	815	61.7
Qatar (c)	36	244	280	87.1
UAE (c)	124	1,165	1,289	90.4
Total	**3,979**	**7,114**	**11,093**	**64.1**
		2005		
Saudi Arabia (g)	3,901	4,124	8,025	51.4
Kuwait (g)	227	909	1,136	80.0
Bahrain (f)	144	192	336	57.1
Oman (e)	443	430	873	49.3
Qatar (f)	51	387	438	88.4
UAE	243	2,457	2,700	91.0
Total	**5,009**	**8,499**	**13,508**	**62.9**

GCC countries as a result of the Iraqi invasion, particularly to Kuwait and Saudi Arabia,[36] combined with the very low oil prices during the early 1990s (see Table 4.2), the scale of new development projects had dramatically decreased. Hence, the natural consequence would be a dramatic decline in the demand for foreign labor.

(b) **The large-scale departure of foreigners during the crisis created a great opportunity for the GCC authorities to regain their control over the number**

Table 4.5 (continued)

(a) Figures relate to 1981. (b) Figures relate to 1986. (c) Figures relate to 1997.
(d) Since the Omani authorities did not publish data on the scale of the Omani national workforce in 1999, only that of the foreign workforce, the data on the Omani national workforce in 1999 was calculated by the author on the basis of the 1995 data (270,000) and an average annual growth rate of 3.7% until 1999.
(e) Figures relate to December 2003. (f) Figures relate to 2004.
(g) Figures relate to 2006.

Sources for Tables 4.4 and 4.5: The State of Kuwait, Ministry of Planning, Central Statistical Office, *Annual Statistical Abstract*, various issues (Kuwait); Central Bank of Kuwait, *Economic Report*, various issues (Kuwait); The State (Kingdom) of Bahrain, Central Statistical Organization, *Statistical Abstract*, various issues (Manama); Dawlat al-Bahrayn, al-Jihaz al-Markazi lil-Ihsa, *al-Ta'adad al-'Amm lil-Sukan wal-Masakin wal-Mabani wal-Munsha'at-1991* (Manama, 1992); Bahrain Monetary Agency, *Annual Report*, various issues (Manama); Sultanate of Oman, Ministry of National Economy, *Statistical Yearbook*, various issues (Muscat); idem, Ministry of Development, *The Fifth Five-Year Development Plan, 1996–2000* (Muscat, July 1997); idem, Ministry of National Economy, *Selected Data and Indicators From the Results of General Populations, Housing Units and Establishments Censuses, 1993-2003* (Muscat, 2005); Central Bank of Oman, *Annual Report*, various issues (Muscat); The Kingdom of Saudi Arabia, Ministry of Planning, Central Department of Statistics, *Statistical Yearbook*, various issues (Riyadh); idem, *Seventh Development Plan, 1420/21-1424/25 A.H.* [2000–2004] (Riyadh, 2001); State of Qatar, Presidency of the Council of Ministers, Central Statistical Organization, *Annual Statistical Abstract*, various issues (Doha); idem, The Planning Council, *Qatar in Figures-2006* (Doha, October 2006); Qatar National Bank, *Qatar Economic Review*, various issues (Doha); ILO, *International Migration and Development in the Arab Region*, by J.S. Birks and C.A. Sinclair (Geneva, 1980); idem, *International Migration for Employment: Manpower and Population Evolution in the GCC and Libyan Arab Jamahiriya*, World Employment Programme Research, Working Paper, by J. S. Birks and C. A. Sinclair (Geneva, October 1989); ESCWA, *Demographic and Related Socio-Economic Data Sheets for Countries of the Economic and Social Commission for Western Asia*, various issues (Beirut, Baghdad and Amman); idem, *Population Situation in the ESCWA Region-1990* (Amman, May 1992); idem, League of Arab States and UNFPA, "Arab Labour Migration," Meeting of Senior Officials and Experts, Amman, April 4-6, 1993; US Department of State, Bureau of Near Eastern Affairs. Available at: http:///www.state.gov; HRD base Ltd., Lloyds Bank Chambers, *Socio-Demographic Profiles of Key Arab Countries* (Newcastle, May 1987); EIU, *Country Profile, Bahrain, Qatar, Oman, Saudi Arabia* and *the UAE*, various issues; Birks, Sinclair & Associates Ltd., *GCC Market Report*, 1990 and 1992 (Durham: Mountjoy Research Centre); "al-Simat al-Asasiyya li-Sukan al-Kuwayt wa-Kuwwat al-'Amal fi Nihayat 1994," *al-Iqtisadi al-Kuwayti*, No. 324 (May 1995); Andrzej Kapiszewski, *Nationals and Expatriates: Population and Labour Dilemmas of the Gulf Cooperation Council States* (Reading: Ithaca Press, 2001); idem, "Business Versus Politics: Local Versus Foreign Workforce in the GCC States," paper presented at the conference *Transnational Migration: Foreign Labor and its Impact in the Gulf*, Bellagio, Italy, 20-24 June 2005; The *NCB Economist*, Vol. 15, Issue 6 (April 26, 2005), p. 6, table 1; Human Right Watch, *Human Rights News*, "Population Statistics: Gulf Cooperation Council States." Available at: http://www.hrw.org.

of foreigners following two decades in which a huge number of illegal foreigners entered the GCC countries almost unrestrictedly (see below).

(c) The large-scale departure of foreign labor during the crisis emphasized to the GCC authorities how much their economies depended on foreign labor and how much this dependence was problematic, particularly in periods of political-security tensions. Thus, **following the end of the crisis, the GCC authorities repeated on many occasions that they would never let this situation of "being a minority in their own country" return**. Naturally, the Kuwaiti authorities were the most decisive on this issue. At the first National Council session following liberation, on July 9, 1991, the Kuwaiti Prime Minister, Sa'ad 'Abdalah al-Salim Al Sabah, announced that:

> Reaching the desired balance in the population composition is no longer considered to be a social objective and target; instead, it has become an inescapable necessity as a result of the limited financial resources caused by the occupiers' destruction of the oil wealth of the country . . .[37]

(d) In addition to the political aim of reducing the dependence on foreign labor, **since the mid-1980s, but more so during the 1990s, the GCC authorities implemented a labor force nationalization policy in order to replace foreign labor by nationals** (see below).

However, these optimistic projections did not materialize. In fact, the opposite was true. Throughout the 1990s, the number of foreign labor in each of the GCC countries substantially increased. By 1999, the number of foreign workers in all the GCC countries amounted to 7.1 million compared to 5.2 in 1990, representing an increase of almost 40%. As one can see in Table 4.5, the most substantial increase occurred in Saudi Arabia and the UAE. Hence, by the end of the twentieth century, almost three decades following the "oil boom," in each of the GCC countries, the foreigners represented more than half of the workforce. In Kuwait, Qatar and the UAE, the share of the nationals in the workforce declined to less than 20% and in many occupations national employees were not represented at all.

During the first half of the 2000s, not only did the number of foreign labor not decline, it rather continued to increase even more rapidly than during the 1990s. By 2005, the foreign labor in the GCC countries numbered 8.5 million, representing an increase of 20% within six years only. In Qatar and the UAE, the share of nationals in the workforce declined to only about 10%. If one includes both workers and their accompanying family members, the foreigners in the GCC countries in 2005 numbered almost 12 million, that is, more than four times their number in 1975 (see Tables 4.4 and 4.5).

4 The Unique Gulf Labor Migration Pattern[38]

A common approach taken in recent academic literature regarding the Gulf labor migration system is that it essentially resembles other global labor migration movements. Kapiszewski argued that:

> Only from a legal point of view, is the situation of foreign workers in the GCC countries different from that in most other states in the world as expatriates nowadays have practically no possibility of obtaining permanent residency or being eligible for citizenship. Otherwise,

> labor migration to the GCC states shares many characteristics with other movements of this kind, and the de facto transformation of temporary immigrants into settlers cannot be ruled out.[39]

As Kapiszewski further explained:

> Thus, GCC states have become mother countries for an increasing number of non-nationals, despite the objectives set up by the authorities . . . Thus, the development of modern societies in the GCC countries is already under way, although it is likely to take quite some time to develop all the bonds that a mature structure of this type requires.[40]

In another article, Kapiszewski argued that one of the paramount reasons for the preference given by the GCC authorities to Asian workers at the expense of Arab foreign labor was:

> [T]hey [the Asians] were used to leaving their families in their home countries, whereas Arab immigrants usually brought their families to the Gulf in the hope of settling there permanently.[41]

A similar view was expressed by Massey and associates who claimed that:

> [M]igrant networks and social institutions have nonetheless arisen to promote the perpetuation of migration and the emergence of settled communities, especially among migrants from the Arab world.[42]

However, some superficial similarities notwithstanding, the labor migration system in the GCC countries radically differs from that of other international labor migration systems in six distinct ways:

(a) The radical change in the employment pattern of the GCC nationals There is no equivalent anywhere for labor markets that changed so radically within the short period of less than two decades. Not only did the number of foreign labor increase by hundreds of percents, but the employment structure of the nationals also changed radically, from the traditional pre-industrial private sector occupations to predominantly public sector employment.

(b) The Gulf labor force structure There is no equivalent anywhere to the labor force structure that prevailed in the Gulf oil economies following the "oil boom." In the other major worldwide labor-importing countries, foreign labor serves as a complement to the local workforce, and, in the vast majority of cases, is employed in low status, low paying occupations. In general, in the more developed labor-importing countries, foreign labor represents less than 10% of the total workforce. For example, by 1997 within the total labor force, the foreign labor represented 9.9% in Austria, 9.1% in Germany, 6.1% in France and 5.2% in Sweden. Among the OECD countries, only in Luxemburg, Switzerland, Australia, Canada and the US, did foreign labor represent more than 10% of the total workforce.[43] In the Gulf oil economies, in contrast, not only has foreign labor represented more than half of the total workforce since the late 1970s, but in the richest oil-states, namely, the UAE, Qatar and Kuwait, foreign labor has made up the vast majority of the workforce while the national workforce has been "a complement to the foreign labor."[44] In many cases, it is an unnecessary complement which is employed almost exclusively in the public sector under lucrative work conditions and high salaries as part of the overall rentier

economic-political structure of these countries (see below). Paradoxically, foreign labor even makes up the vast majority of the security forces, one of their major roles being to enforce the labor and immigration regulations.

This being the case, it is necessary to reject the common notion of "integration" of foreign workers and their accompanying family members into the local GCC societies, where the indigenous population represents only a tiny fraction of the total workforce. Thus, large-scale naturalization would turn the indigenous population into a minority in their own countries. Moreover, since the early 1990s, as the vast majority of the foreign workers in these countries are not Arabs (see below), the actual meaning of large-scale naturalization is that these countries would loose their Arab identity. The situation in countries such as the US, Canada, Australia, New Zealand and even in the more developed EU countries is, of course, totally different, as the number of naturalized migrants is small in comparison to the indigenous population.

(c) Lack of employment stability In contrast to the common Western migration pattern, the position of foreign workers in the GCC countries is extremely unstable. According to the GCC migration rules, a foreign worker can be deported without prior notice. This shaky position was most evident during the Kuwait crisis when the vast majority of the Palestinians and the Jordanians in Kuwait and the Yemenites in Saudi Arabia were deported, despite the fact that they had been settled in these countries for decades. An ESCWA report on the returnees described the situation of the migrants who were forced to leave the GCC host countries as follows:

> The belief of some [Arab] emigrants that they would be able to settle forever in the host countries proved to be an illusion, revealing their unrealistic understanding of the conditions, principles and policies of emigration in these host countries.[45]

Two major factors account for the unstable position of the foreign workers in the GCC countries: First, in contrast to Western labor-importing countries, the GCC countries are not democratic. In democratic labor-importing countries, the legal system itself provides protection for the foreign workers through labor laws and regulations, civil rights, and the like. This, however, is not the case in the GCC countries. Second, while assorted NGOs in the democratic labor-importing countries protect the foreign workers from both the authorities and employers, such organizations do not exist in the Gulf.

(d) No citizenship option It is typical of the "Western-style migration chain" that after some time, in most cases usually no longer than a few years, migrants are joined by their family members. As such, the migration process often ends with the migrant and his family becoming citizens of the host country. This is the case in the US, Canada, Australia and the developed EU countries. In contrast, since the early 1980s, the GCC authorities have imposed strict limitations on the entrance of family members of the foreign workers (see below). Moreover, it is nearly impossible for migrant workers to receive citizenship in one of the GCC countries, be they Arabs or non-Arabs. The vast majority of those who nevertheless received citizenship in one of the GCC countries are females who married locals.[46]

(e) Permanent settlement is not desired by the foreign workers themselves Whereas the aim of the vast majority of migrant workers to the Western countries is to become a citizen of the host country, the typical labor migration scenario in the GCC countries

is that of a migrant worker who only comes for several years in order to earn as much money as possible before returning to his home country. As noted by Richards and Waterbury, "The vast majority of the migrants want to return home. Neither they nor the receiving countries view labor migration as permanent resettlement."[47] An Indian migrant worker, who was employed in the UAE together with his brother, described their employment motives in an interview for a field research project as follows: "Together, we decided to save some money and establish a small business in Kerala . . ."[48] Regarding the motivation of Egyptians to work in the Gulf, Roy noted that: "They may not like the conditions or the social values of the countries hosting them, but they are totally disinclined to jeopardize the opportunity to earn money . . . "[49] Rabo, who conducted an anthropological research project in the Syrian Euphrates Valley in the early 1980s, reached a similar conclusion:

> Young men may see migration to the Gulf as the only rapid means of gaining money to get married, to build a house, to buy a car or to invest in some business or other . . . Admittedly, those who have migrated . . . talk of the hardships in the Gulf . . . But they all say it is worthwhile since the pay is good.[50]

The initial aim of the GCC authorities was to prevent the settlement of foreign workers.[51] This attitude toward the foreign workers is also identified by Yamani, who noted that: "Most of the young [Saudi] people interviewed prefer to maintain a social distance from the foreigners . . . "[52] The attitude toward the foreign labor was and still is that they are "a necessary evil," and they are certainly not seen as a permanent element in the GCC societies.

(f) A wide interest in cheap foreign labor In developed labor-importing countries, the import of cheap foreign workers is mainly in the interest of the economic elite, but not in that of the whole population, due to the competition in the labor market, particularly in low wage occupations. In the GCC countries, however, the mass import of cheap foreign workers was, until recently, in the interest of both the economic elite and the middle class. The unlimited availability of cheap foreign workers enabled the GCC middle classes, which constituted the bulk of the GCC indigenous populations, to employ them in their small businesses and as domestic workers in their homes,[53] while their own employment was guaranteed in the public sector.

Moreover, since a foreigner was not allowed to work in the GCC countries without local sponsorship (*kafil*),[54] many nationals used the system for easy profit by serving as a sponsor for foreign workers without even employing them.[55] For example, the economic weekly *MEED* reported in late 1996 that a UAE citizen could earn AED5,000 ($1,360) just by supplying a visa and sponsoring a foreign worker.[56] The *kafala* system, labeled by Fred Halliday as "new slavery,"[57] produced a unique situation in which nationals could earn money strictly by virtue of their nationality. It should be taken into consideration that slavery was abolished in 1952 in Qatar, in 1962 in Saudi Arabia, in 1963 in the UAE and only in 1970 in Oman, namely, only a short period prior to the beginning of the mass labor migration to these countries.

4.1 The "Rentier Formula" in the GCC Unique Migration Pattern

The uniqueness of the GCC migration system is a direct function of the *sui generis structure* of the GCC societies, which are based on a kinship and tribal system.[58] In effect, these "intimate societies" prevent others from becoming members of this distinctive kinship-rentier system. This is because those outside the kinship networks would find themselves hard-pressed to integrate into what Beblawi has stressed as the "long tribal tradition of buying loyalty and allegiance . . . , distributing favors and benefits to its population."[59]

The term "rent" relates to "income derived from the gift of nature." Hence, the scale of the national income does not reflect the performance of the domestic economy, but is a function of the price of the rentier resource in the international market. The term "rentier state" refers to a situation in which the rent income, which predominates governmental revenues, is external to the domestic economy, and although only a few are involved in its generation, the majority of the population reaps the rental wealth.

At the national level, "as oil revenues increase to the point at which they dominate a government's revenues, the government evolves from an extractive state into a distributive one."[60] Thus, as claimed by Luciani, "The essential impact of oil production and exports is that they free the state from the need of raising income domestically."[61] This means that a clear distinction should be made between "rental-revenue states" and "tax-revenue states." The first type refers to "the allocation state" in the form of allocating the external rental revenues among the local population through both direct financial benefits and massive government subsidies on various public services and commodities. The latter type refers to "the production state," where taxes constitute the main financial source for the government's activities.[62] Hertog noted in this respect that:

> [T]he main political function of a commodity-rich state . . . is distribution of wealth, which implies that no effective political power-sharing is necessary . . . If certain groups may feel deprived, they have little bargaining leverage, not least as they have been formed, and their organization is controlled, by the state itself.[63]

Therefore, the rentier state broke the Gordian knot between "taxation" and "representation." As the rentier state authorities "have no need to extract, they have no need to represent."[64] Henry and Springborg noted that: "Oil rents . . . enabled regimes to seek legitimacy by distributing goods and services to people rather than through the more interactive, demanding, and risky approach of taxing them directly and being accountable to them."[65] The rentier state, according to Gause, has four political characteristics: First, due to the concentration of the rental incomes in the hand of the authorities, the government is also the dominant economic player. This enables the government to bestow privileges to allies and punish those who run afoul of it. Second, the government can provide a wide array of services to the citizens without the need of taxation. The third element is that the government is the prominent employer of the national workforces. The fourth element is weakening the potential opposition, such as labor unions and tribal elements. This weakening is done by buying the loyalty of the potential opposition by means of various financial benefits.[66] Indeed, the Gulf oil countries are perfectly suited to the above-mentioned elements of the "rentier state."

As such, while the basic political formula of the Western democratic countries is "no taxation without representation," in the GCC rentier states the political formula is "no taxation and no representation." In addition, the big merchants, which were the dominant political power in these societies in the pre-oil era, had become part of the "rentier relationship" system during the oil era. Ayubi claimed that:

> The transformation to a *rentier* political economy was accomplished . . . through a tacit deal between the *amir* and the merchant families in which power was traded for wealth. In return for receiving a sizable share of oil rents, the merchants by and large conceded their historical claim to participation in decision-making.[67]

Birks and Rimmer emphasized the continuation of the Gulf socio-political system prior to and into the oil era as well. They claimed that:

> Much of modern development is an extension of the traditional obligations between Shaikhs and their tributary populations, translated into modern form: thus it has become the obligation of the rulers to provide employment for their national populations, who accept it as a right in exchange for their loyalty and up-holding of the social norms[68]

In light of this *sui generis* rental political economy, it is understandable why a unique pattern of labor migration developed in this region. Since the 1970s, a dual society has been created in the Gulf: one consists of the lucky citizens which enjoy a high living standard in exchange for political loyalty toward the ruling families; the other is made up of foreigners who come for a limited period of time in order to earn as much money as possible and return to their homelands.

Thus, while the prime aim of the migrants in the Western labor-importing countries is to fully integrate into the host country and get citizenship for themselves and their family members, in the Gulf oil countries, in contrast, neither the migrants nor the indigenous populations have the ambition of mutual integration. The separation between nationals and foreigners in the GCC countries is so decisive that in many cases it also includes a physical separation in which many foreign workers are housed in work camps.

Under such different socioeconomic-political patterns, it is understandable why the labor migration pattern of the GCC countries was and still is so different from the Western one. A prominent distinction between the GCC migration pattern and that of the Western-democratic labor-importing countries is in the area of labor immigration policies as will be examined in the following section.

5 The GCC Labor and Immigration Policies: "From Encouragement through Limitation to Surrender"

The GCC labor and immigration policies should be examined in relation to three main parameters:

(a) **The need for foreign labor**, in terms of both quantity and quality, as a factor in the overall socioeconomic development programs.

(b) **The attitudes of the GCC authorities toward the various Middle Eastern political developments.**

(c) **The internal political situations in the GCC countries themselves.**

Taking the above-mentioned three parameters into consideration, the GCC labor and immigration policies since the October 1973 "oil boom" can broadly be divided into the following four periods:

5.1 Encouraging Labor Immigration during the "Oil Decade"

Following the October 1973 "oil boom," all of the Gulf oil countries, without exception, implemented a liberal labor immigration policy. The wish for rapid development suppressed any other considerations, including the security one.[69] Overall, during that period, the Gulf countries' unrestricted labor and immigration policies included the following measures:

(a) A liberal attitude toward accompanying family members Within the framework of the liberal labor immigration policies, the GCC authorities enabled almost free entrance for the accompanying family members of the foreign labor. Thus, by 1975, among the 2.76 million foreigners in the GCC countries, 1.39 million, namely, only 50% were workers while the other 50% were accompanying family members (see Tables 4.4 and 4.5). Within the framework of the liberal immigration policy, the GCC authorities subsidized education and healthcare services, as well as housing in many cases, for the foreign labor as well. Hence, the cost of living of the foreign workers and their accompanying family members during that period was relatively low.

(b) The cancellation of personal income tax for foreign labor In order to increase the attraction of the Gulf labor markets for foreign workers and companies, anyone who came to work in these countries was not subject to personal income tax.[70]

(c) Encouragement of foreign companies to import their own workers The need for rapid implementation of the major infrastructure projects led the GCC authorities to allow foreign companies to bring their own workers. In addition to saving time, this policy enabled the GCC authorities to impose the responsibility for the entry and exit of the foreign workers on the companies themselves as part of the contracts. In other words, many of the foreign workers in the Gulf countries were "an absent presence."

Beyond the purely socioeconomic factors, the liberal labor and immigration policies toward Arab foreigners had a clear political aim: To change the intra-Arab balance of power in their own favor through the employment of large numbers of workers from the poorer Arab countries, in addition to the financial aid given to these countries. Within the framework of this policy, in April 1975 the Saudi government announced an easing of entry requirements for Arab foreign labor and their accompanying family members.[71]

5.2 Limiting Foreign Labor Following the End of the "Oil Decade"

Since 1982, oil prices in the international market sharply declined. In 1983, the total GCC oil export revenues were only $76.1 billion and further declined to only $38.3 billion in 1986, compared to the peak of $157.8 billion in 1980 (see Table 4.3). The sharp decline in oil revenues led the GCC countries to change their macroeconomic policies accordingly. Generally speaking, the socioeconomic policy adopted by the GCC countries following the end of the "oil decade" rested on three main principles:

The first and most important was that despite the sharp decline in oil revenues, the living standard of the indigenous population should not be affected. The Iranian Islamic Revolution reinforced this decision.[72] Thus, while the "normal" reaction to a severe recession is to adopt a policy which on the one hand includes a sharp decline in government subsidies and allowances, and on the other directs the vast majority of the available financial resources to economic generation mechanisms, the GCC ruling families, with some minor differences among them, adopted a contradictory policy.

This included reducing public sector infrastructure investments,[73] while maintaining the various government subsidies and allowances. This policy was financed through increasing governmental budgetary deficits to levels of more than 10% of the GDP, something unfamiliar in developed economies. It seems that this kind of socioeconomic policy reflects, more than any other, the fundamental rentier nature of the GCC countries.

The second principle was to substantially cut the aid to the poorer Arab countries (see Chapter 3). Hence, the slogan of "*al-Wahda al-'Arabiyya*" ("Arab Unity") became even more questionable in the early 1980s.

The third principle was to decrease the numbers of the foreign labor through the nationalization policy. Although the unemployment rates among nationals in the early 1980s were still low, the GCC authorities realized that the former concept of absorbing almost the entire indigenous workforce in the public sector was no longer a viable option, certainly not in the longer run in light of the high natural increase rates.

Overall, the GCC labor force nationalization policy which was adopted following the "oil decade" included the following four measures:

(a) Deportation of illegal foreign workers Since the late 1970s, but more so during the early 1980s, a large number of illegal foreign workers were deported from the GCC countries.[74] The deportation of the illegal foreign workers was primarily aimed at opening up additional employment opportunities for nationals through the eradication of the "black labor market."

(b) Limitations on the entry of the foreign workers' accompanying family members A 1981 World Bank report concluded that due to the various subsidies on fuel, foodstuffs, electricity, water, education and healthcare, the actual cost of foreign labor is much higher than their wages.[75] Hence, imposing obligations on the entry of family members would not harm the economy but would save substantial financial resources.

(c) Limitation on the social services for the foreign labors In the case of the UAE, for example, the government decided in 1983 that from that point on, the foreigners would no longer receive free healthcare and education for their accompanying family members.[76] The aim of this measure was not only to save expenses, but also to substantially increase the cost of living for the foreign workers in order to reduce their motivation for bringing their families in the first place.[77]

(d) Adoption of a quota system for national The aim of this measure was to apply some of the costs of employing the national workforce on the private sector, rather than placing the entire burden on the public sector.

The first among the GCC countries to adopt a labor force nationalization policy as early as 1978 was Bahrain – the least rentier among the GCC countries. In 1985, the Kuwaiti authorities adopted a long-term nationalization policy aimed at equalizing the sizes of the national population and the foreign population by the year 2000. The Kuwaiti authorities hoped to accomplish this target through reducing the need for foreign labor with the introduction of advanced technology; scaling down labor-intensive projects that make little contribution to economic development; implementing stricter control over the entry of accompanying family members; and intensifying efforts to develop the national labor force. In order to promote the employment of nationals in the private sector, the Kuwaiti government imposed welfare service costs for foreign workers and their accompanying family members on employers rather than on the state.[78] In March 1985, the Kuwaiti Ministry of Labor and Social Affairs announced that "any non-Kuwaiti applying for a visa for his family must provide a statement to the effect that he has a minimum income of KD (Kuwaiti Dinar) 450 per month if employed by the government, or KD600 if employed in the private sector."[79] This policy of limiting the option of foreign labor of bringing their dependents through minimum income continues in Kuwait until the present.[80]

Likewise, the major aim of the Saudi Fourth Five-Year Development Plan (1985–1990) was to reduce the number of foreigners in the Kingdom by 1.2 million (of whom about 600,000 were workers) by the end of the plan.[81] In addition, from the mid-1980s, senior foreign workers were required to provide professional training to nationals as an integral part of their jobs so that nationals would be prepared to replace them in the future.[82] In order to increase the available job opportunities for Saudi nationals, in early 1988 the Saudi government adopted the principle of not approving the recruitment of any foreign worker for any position which could be filled by a Saudi national.[83]

In April 1987, the Omani Minister of Labor, Mustahil bin Ahmed al-Masheni, stated that foreign workers could no longer be hired in eleven job categories, including public relations personnel, Arabic typists, security officers, apprentices, drivers, fishermen, and shepherds.[84] As in the other GCC countries, the aim of this measure was to increase the available job opportunities for nationals, and to "share" the costs of employing nationals with the private employers.

In August 1989, the Bahraini government initiated an ambitious five-year labor force "Bahrainization" program by which it hoped to replace as many as one-third of foreigners with national employees. Letters were sent to most private sector companies directing them to increase the number of nationals they employed by 5% annually. Specific job categories were singled out for takeover by nationals, including senior administrative personnel, supervisors, engineers, technicians, computer operators, nurses, clerks, accountants, secretaries, sales and marketing personnel, and hotel and restaurant workers. The goal was that some 400 companies, employing approximately 60,000 foreign workers, would lay off 20,000 and replace them with nationals.[85]

Although during the second half of the 1980s the pace of the increase in the number of foreign labor in the GCC was much slower compared to the prior decade, the number of foreign labor in each of the GCC countries in 1990 was substantially higher than in 1985 (see Table 5.4). It should be emphasized that this increase in the number of foreign labor occurred despite the substantially lower oil revenues (see Table 4.3).

Why did this policy fail "to deliver the goods"? It seems that the following five factors constituted the main barriers to its success:

(a) The "no rush perception" Although the GCC authorities were fully aware of the importance of decreasing the dependence on foreign workforce, the prevailing feeling among the decision-making ranks was that the problem was not an immediate one, but rather one for the medium and longer run – something in line with the current attitude toward "global warming." Thus, for example, the Saudi Industry Minister, Ghazi al-Gosaybi, noted in mid-1979 in regard to the need for labor force Saudization that: "Some time in the future, be it in three, ten or fifteen years, there will no longer be such a surplus of wealth in the country – people [nationals] will welcome any work to earn a living . . . "[86] In this statement, attention should be focused on the phrase, "some time," that is, the threat of large-scale unemployment among nationals is not an immediate problem, but "a future one." The logical consequence is that there is no need to immediately enforce unpopular measures and thus to risk the Kingdom's "political order." In other words, from purely political calculations, it is not "worth" buying enemies now just for a threat in the future.

The "no rush" attitude prevented the GCC authorities from firmly implementing of their labor force nationalization policy. Thus, in practice, many of the former norms of the "bonanza oil decade" remained in force. According to a survey held by the Saudi newspaper *Ukaz* in mid-1990 on the subject of the implementation of the Saudization policy, it was viewed by many young Saudis as a "mere slogan." One Saudi graduate told the newspaper reporter that the Saudization advertisements were "nothing more than a meaningless routine . . . in fact, the positions went to expatriates."[87]

(b) Preference of the nationals for public sector employment In most cases, the nationals preferred employment in the public rather than in the private sector due to the more convenient working hours, job security, attractive wages and higher social status.[88] Looney noted in this regard as follows:

> Labor theory suggests that the unwillingness to accept socially undesirable jobs can be overcome by payment of higher wages than in desirable jobs. It appears, however, that in Saudi Arabia the social factors are so strong that . . . the wide gap is not large enough to draw Saudi workers into the formal sector. The extended family, subsidized loans, and the existence of the informal sector, enabling occasional work to supplement other income, allow Saudi workers to set a high reservation wage.[89]

Thus, by 1994, only 5.5% of the foreign workers in Saudi Arabia were employed by the public sector, while 94.5% were employed in the private sector.[90] On the other hand, the Saudi nationals employed by the industrial sector did not exceed 4% of the total employees.[91] In Kuwait, there was even a greater dichotomy in the labor market than in Saudi Arabia. By 1997, only 7% of the national workforce worked in the private sector while 93% were employed by the public sector.[92]

It should be noted that in practice, the GCC authorities themselves promoted the employment of nationals in the public sector as part of the rentier socioeconomic-political formula. Thus, for example, a report of Bahrain's National Economic Board noted that: "Bolstered by revenues from natural resources, the government has hired a large workforce, ensuring that many Bahrainis could find well-paying jobs in various public sector entities."[93] The most extreme example for this policy is the UAE in which almost the entire national workforce in the mid-1990s was employed by the public sector at unusually high salaries and excellent work conditions.[94]

(c) Preference of private employers to employ foreigners This preference was and still is a result of several factors, the most prominent being that the wages demanded by foreign workers are much lower than those demanded by nationals. In the case of Saudi Arabia, for example, a survey of the manufacturing industry in the early 1990s revealed that Saudi workers' wages were more than twice those of foreign workers while Saudi workers were only half as productive, making actual costs four times higher.[95] By the years 1996–1997, the monthly wage of Saudi nationals averaged SR (Saudi Riyal) 5,704 compared to SR1,901 for foreign labor. In many occupations, the wage of a Saudi national was as much as three-times higher than that of a foreign worker.[96] By the year 2001, while the monthly average wage for Saudi national males was SR6,684, it was only SR1,710 for male foreign labor.[97] A similar situation existed in Kuwait. In an interview with Kuwait Petroleum Corporation (KPC) managers, it was found that their failure to fill entry and mid-level positions with qualified Kuwaitis was driven by the ability of Kuwaiti nationals to get easier jobs, working fewer hours for the same pay in other governmental agencies.[98] In mid-1990, a Saudi governmental official commented on this subject as follows:

> The private sector demands from workers some qualities like patience and hard work, while Saudi youths are often running after comfort and salary increases. If they want to work at all in the private sector, they do so only until they get a government job.[99]

A similar observation was expressed in a mid-1995 NCB report:

> Aside from certain managerial and clerical jobs, the employment of nationals in private sector companies has been rather limited. Jobs in the public sector are still the first choice of employment for new graduates, not only because they are perceived to be more secure but also because they provide more convenient working hours, and have typically a more congenial work environment.[100]

(d) A lack of skilled workers in technical occupations Many employers blamed the educational system for failing to produce the kind of qualifications needed in the labor market.[101] Indeed, in the 1993/94 academic year, of the 153,780 students in the Saudi institutions of higher education, only 25,266 (16.4%) were enrolled in engineering, the exact sciences, agriculture and medicine, while the rest were studying arts and literature, education and *Shari'a*. In Qatar, in the 1995/96 academic year, of the 8,271 students, only 1,627, or less than 20%, were enrolled in science, engineering and technology programs.[102] In the other GCC countries one can find the same trend. Askari and associates presented this problem as follows:

> Unfortunately, by artificially creating employment opportunities for nationals in the public sector, governments have reduced the incentives to pursue courses of study that are in demand by private sector employers. The problem is not the quantity of education but rather its quality and its mix.[103]

The GCC rulers did not learn from 'Abd al-Nasser's mistake whose promise of public sector employment for every higher educational institution graduate had destroyed the merit for excellence and professionalism and just "dumped" the public sector with an increasing number of graduates until their marginal contribution had become negative. As public sector salaries of engineers and those in the exact science occupations were the same as those of graduates in the humanities and social sciences, the tendency of GCC students to concentrate on the humanities and social sciences was quite natural. Moreover, while graduates of the humanities and social sciences worked in government ministries side by side with the highest political ranks, those working in engineering and the exact science occupations were actually cut off from the political elite.[104]

(e) The "sponsorship system" The sponsorship system not only encouraged the expansion of the rentier mentality among GCC citizens, but also led to the import of additional foreign workers even if they were not really needed. Ramady noted in respect to Saudi Arabia as follows:

> The fact is that due to negative attitudes about certain types of work among Saudis, there are many expatriates in the Kingdom, even though it is the only country in the GCC with a large enough population to carry out the country's development on its own.[105]

Overall, during the 1970s and the 1980s, the GCC labor markets operated almost without regulations, quite similar to a free market without any customs duties. In this respect, the GCC labor markets were indeed unique. As rightly claimed by Said Abdullah al-Shaikh, the NCB Chief Economist, regarding the Saudi labor market:

> [T]he free labor-importing policy created a wage structure that reflected the flexibility of importing different skills and not the extent of searching domestically. The relative scarcities of local labor skills did not affect the wage structure [for nationals] since demand for all needed skills could be met through imports . . . Therefore, wages do not necessarily reflect the interaction of domestic labor supply and demand forces . . . The implication of this is that both the level and the structure of wages that prevailed in Saudi Arabia have been determined independently from the supply of Saudi local labor.[106]

Thus, during the two and a half decades following the "oil boom," a unique pattern of **dual labor market** – with the public sector almost exclusively for nationals and the private sector almost exclusively for foreigners – developed in each of the GCC countries. Beblawi noted in this regard: "Though utterly free enterprise-oriented, the number of government employees in the oil states is only matched by socialist-oriented states."[107] Consequently, the labor force nationalization policy was efficient only in the public sector in which the government, not the free market mechanism, determined both salaries and employment conditions.

During the 1990s, the inescapable consequence of the dual labor market on the one hand, and the rapid increase in the number of indigenous entrants into the labor markets on the other, was a sharp increase in unemployment among the GCC nationals. In 1993, the unemployment rate among Omani nationals amounted to 11.9%.[108] The unemployment rates of the nationals in Bahrain and the UAE was even higher than in Oman, amounting to 15% in early 1993.[109] In Saudi Arabia, the unemployment rate among nationals estimated at 20% in the mid-1990s.[110] Hence, the highest unemployment rate among the national workforce in the GCC countries paradoxically prevailed in the only country which potentially had the ability to run its economy without the need of foreign labor.

5.3 Strengthening Labor Force Nationalization Measures since the mid-1990s[111]

In the mid-1990s, the GCC authorities realized that two prominent employment issues had to be addressed: One involved narrowing the number of foreign workers in order to decrease the huge amounts of their remittances, which constituted a substantial percentage of the GCC oil revenues during the late 1980s and early 1990s. The second issue was to provide suitable job opportunities to the rapidly growing national workforces. Hence, during the 1990s, the GCC labor markets turned around 180 degrees from a "resource pressure on population," as Gilbar defined it during the "oil decade," (that is, the population was too small in proportion to the labor demands)[112] into a "demographic pressure on the economy," particularly in the employment arena. Consequently, since the mid-1990s the GCC countries, without exception, increased their efforts in the area of labor force nationalization which became their top socio-economic priority. This was particularly notable in Saudi Arabia and Oman – the two most populous GCC countries.

Since the mid-1990s, the migration and employment policies of the GCC countries have concentrated mainly on the following measures, with some of them representing a new approach and others constituting a continuation of previous policies:

(a) Tightening the rules regarding the employment of foreigners in the private sector Rules and regulations regarding employing foreigners in the private sector were tightened after the mid-1990s in order to eliminate the need of the nationals to compete with

foreign workers. Although all the GCC countries had taken steps in this direction already in the 1980s, since the mid-1990s two new mechanisms were added: The first was the wide use of a quota system, by which the government determined the minimum percentage of nationals to be employed in each sector. For example, Saudi Arabia's Resolution No. 50 of 1995 required every establishment which employs 20 or more workers to employ a minimum of 5% Saudis.[113] This minimum percentage increased to 25% in September 2000,[114] and again to 30% in 2002. Companies that failed to accomplish the minimum Saudization target would be penalized.[115] In order to enforce the Saudization regulations, the Saudi authorities established "Saudization committees" in the major regions of the Kingdom under the chairmanship of the region's governor.[116]

The second mechanism was to ban the employment of expatriates in specific job categories in which nationals could supply the demand. In the case of Oman, in 1995 the Central Bank stipulated that by the year 2000, Omanis should hold at least 75% of senior and middle management positions and 95% of clerical positions in each bank.[117] During the second half of the 1990s, the Omanization quota was expanded to other sectors. The new Omani labor law also stipulated that companies which do not comply with quota requirements would face fines and could not hire new foreign workers. More important than anything else, they would be barred from receiving government contracts.[118] During the mid-1990s, the Qatari authorities also adopted the quota mechanism in some occupations, although on a smaller scale than in Saudi Arabia and Oman,[119] as the unemployment rate among the Qatari nationals was much lower.

(b) Deportation of illegal foreign workers In order to stabilize the GCC labor markets, it was of paramount importance to sharply decrease the number of illegal foreign workers. To accomplish this aim, the GCC authorities implemented two major steps: The first was the announcement of an "amnesty period" during which illegal foreign workers could leave the country without any penalty. Those who would be caught following the end of the amnesty period would be sentenced to heavy penalties – up to $26,000 in the case of Saudi Arabia – and even imprisonment in some cases.[120] The second measure was increasing supervision on private employers in order to prevent them from employing illegal foreign workers. Indeed, since the mid-1990s, a substantial number of illegal foreign workers either left the GCC countries by themselves or were deported.[121] This policy of deporting illegal foreign labor continued in the early 2000s as well. In the case of Saudi Arabia, for example, during the four months from March to June 2005, in Jeddah alone, the police arrested 150,000 illegal foreigners.[122] In late 2007, the UAE authorities deported about 100,000 illegal Indian workers.[123]

(c) Training of nationals for certain private sector occupations Since the mid-1990s, the GCC authorities have been trying to enforce private labor employers to train nationals in order to give them the qualifications to replace foreign employees. The new Saudi Labor Law, issued in early 2006, specified that: "Every [private sector] employer should prepare the Saudi workforce and improve their standards in the technical, administrative and professional fields in order to gradually employ them in the jobs [currently] occupied by the non-Saudi workers."[124]

(d) Emphasizing technological education In order to reduce dependence on skilled foreign workers, more emphasis was placed on technological education at the secondary and university levels. Taking Saudi Arabia as an example, in the year 2000, only 6,000 of 31,000 physicians were Saudi nationals.[125] In this respect, Bahrain was the first among the GCC countries to change its educational and vocational training

system to suit it to the labor market demands. In 1996, the Bahraini Cabinet approved a national plan for preparing a well-educated and well-trained national workforce which would replace skilled foreign labor.[126] Two years earlier, in 1994, Oman had established a separate ministry for higher education.[127] Since then, promoting national professional education has received top governmental priority. Within the framework of Oman's Fifth Five-Year Development Plan (1996–2000), one of the paramount aims was "linking education and training policies with the requirements of the labor market."[128] This issue was also on the top priority list of the Saudi Seventh Five-Year Development Plan (2000–2004).[129]

(e) Directing new entrants into the labor market to the private sector The combination of the high percentage of salaries within the total government expenditures,[130] and the growing public sector disguised unemployment, led the GCC authorities to the conclusion that only the private sector has the ability to absorb new labor force entrants. In late 1998, when oil prices were the lowest ever (in real terms) since the "oil boom,"[131] the Bahraini Minister of Labor and Social Affairs, 'Abdul Nabi 'Abdallah al-Shuala, said:

> The private sector has to play a major role and share the responsibility of providing jobs to nationals. It is being done everywhere in the world and we want to do that as well.[132]

A *MEED* report on the Saudi economy from late 2000 noted in this regard: "The government has made clear through its words and actions that it sees private sector investment as the main driver of job creation."[133] To promote the employment of nationals in the private sector, the Saudi Seventh Five-Year Development Plan focused on improving the productivity of nationals, increasing the private sector's capacity to employ nationals, and establishing a comprehensive and reliable labor market database.[134] Among the GCC rulers, the most decisive in this direction, as in many other issues, was Sultan Qabus. Thus, for example, in his speech on the National Day of November 18, 1998, he said:

> We assert that it is important that citizens should be aware of their vital role in working for the success of the government's plan for private sector employment, and for the gradual replacement by Omanis of skilled and unskilled expatriates. There are abundant opportunities for honorable work in this sector."[135]

On many other occasions, Sultan Qabus spurred the nationals to stop waiting for public sector employment and to find jobs in the private sector. He was and still is the most straightforward with his citizens regarding the limited opportunities of public sector employment. This changing labor market mechanism is, in effect, a withdrawal from the traditional rentier formula: The private sector employers would be denied the previous lucrative option of employing extremely cheap foreign labor almost without any limitations, while the new entrants into the labor force would be denied the automatically public sector employment.

(f) Diminishing the cost gap between employing foreigners and nationals While the public sector can bear the gap between the costs of employing nationals and foreigners, the private sector acts in accordance with one rule only – being profitable to the greatest possible extent. Hence, the only way to overcome the natural preference of the private sector to employ cheap foreign workers is to diminish the huge wage gaps between nationals and foreigners. Indeed, all of the GCC countries have been actively addressing

this matter since the mid-1990s by increasing the costs of employing foreigners through taxation on the one hand, and by reducing the costs of employing nationals, mainly through government subsidies, on the other.

Oman was the first among the GCC countries to act in this direction. In 1995, the Omani authorities imposed a new tax on private employers of foreign workers (7.5% of their salaries) in order to finance vocational training for nationals.[136] Another major measure in this direction was the elimination of the *kafala* system. The new Omani Labor Law, enacted in May 2003, prohibits nationals from taking payment from a foreigner in exchange for employment.[137] In June 2000, the Saudi authorities established the Human Resources Development Fund (HRDF) in order to subsidize the training of nationals for employment in the private sector. In addition, the HRDF assumes payment of as much as 75% of the salaries of young Saudis employed in the private sector for their two first years of employment, up to a maximum of SR2,000 per month.[138]

(g) Religious justification for labor force nationalization Thus far, only Saudi Arabia has adopted this measure. One of the Saudization measures in the Seventh Five-Year Development Plan was that of "enlightening people through information media of the importance of work and its religious and social value."[139] The prime aim is to convince the masses that employment, in and of itself, has a great social and religious importance. It should be noted in this respect, however, that major changes in Saudi Arabia since its establishment were done through "religious justification," such as the introduction of radios and later television, etc.

(h) Preventing a rapid increase in female labor force participation rates Officially, since the early 1990s, all of the GCC countries have encouraged women employment. In practice, however, the social norms and, in the case of Saudi Arabia, the myriad of rules and regulations, limit the range of job opportunities actually available for national women. Thus, as noted in Chapter 3, the labor force participation rates of GCC women, with the sole exception of Bahrain, are among the lowest worldwide. SAMA's 2000 Annual Report noted in this respect that although the high cost of female education is not returned due to the limitations on female employment, such employment can only come about "in keeping with the conditions, characteristics and traditions of the [Saudi] society."[140] The same limitations are repeated in each of the ensuing SAMA annual reports as well as in many other Saudi official publications.[141]

While there is no doubt that increasing women's employment would contribute to the GCC economies and, at the same time bring about fertility decline, in the short run, raising female labor force participation rates would substantially increase the number of new entrants into the labor market and would further escalate the already high employment pressures. Moreover, since the vast majority of the GCC females are currently employed in public administration, healthcare and educational systems, the implication of increasing female labor force participation rates is to absorb them into the already bulging public sector.

(i) Using labor migration as a political tool During the 1980s, the GCC rulers made a clear distinction between their attitude toward a certain "regime" and its "citizens." The most prominent example of this was in regard to Egypt. While the GCC authorities officially boycotted the Egyptian government in keeping with the resolution of the second Baghdad Arab Summit, the number of Egyptian workers in each of the GCC countries, as well as in Iraq, which led the boycott of Egypt, substantially increased.

By mid-1990, prior to the Iraqi invasion of Kuwait, the number of Egyptian workers in the GCC countries was more than 600,000, that is, more than twice their number in 1979, prior to the boycott.[142] The official reason for this was that the Arab countries boycotted "the Egyptian government" but not "the Egyptian people." The real reason for continuing to employ Egyptians was that at that time the GCC countries were substantially dependent on them. It should be taken into account that the GCC educational and justice systems were adopted from Egypt. Thus, employing Egyptians in these systems was inevitable.

During the 1990s, however, the GCC nationals replaced the vast majority of the Arab foreign workers, including the Egyptians, in the public sector. In total contrast to the 1970s and the 1980s, during the 1990s the GCC authorities could use the migration option as an inter-Arab political tool. Hence, the citizens of countries that supported the anti-Iraqi coalition during the Kuwait crisis were welcomed; workers from countries that did not support the anti-Iraqi coalition were deported. Thus, during the 1990s, while the number of Egyptian and Syrian workers in the GCC countries substantially increased, the number of Yemenites, Sudanese, and Palestinians radically declined. With more than one million Egyptians working in Saudi Arabia and approximately half a million in the other GCC countries,[143] Mubarak's political maneuvering space in relation to the GCC countries, particularly toward Saudi Arabia, has indeed become limited.

5.4 The "Sobering Stage": Using Foreign Labor for Unemployment Eradication

> Economic success comes at a price. In the case of the UAE, that price is a growing demographic imbalance.
>
> *MEED*, September 2006[144]

In the late 1990s, the GCC authorities realized that large-scale replacement of foreigners by nationals in the private sector was not a viable option. The wage gaps as well as the *rentier* political formula, in practice, prevented the successful implementation of the previous labor policies. Consequently, the GCC authorities realized that in order to avoid "employment catastrophe" they had to place the creation of suitable employment options for nationals as the top priority of their labor policies and stop concentrating on the replacement of the foreign labor. The core of the new employment policy was to use cheap foreign labor as a tool to create suitable employment opportunities for nationals in the private sector. It could be said that the GCC countries moved from an "ideal policy" to a "practical policy."

This new policy, of course, is not an official one, as it represents a failure of the previous policy which was in force for more than two decades. However, a close examination of recent developments in each of the GCC labor markets illustrates the move in this new direction. Thus, for example, the number of Saudi nationals in the private sector increased dramatically from 485,726 in 2004 to 623,465 in 2005, an unprecedented growth of 28.4% within a single year. This increase, however, was not at the expense of foreign labor, but rather in line with the sharp increase in their number which climbed by 14% during that single year, from 4.163 million to 4.739 million.[145] This process continued in the following year as well. In 2006, the number of Saudi nationals employed in the private sector amounted to 710,000, namely, a further increase of almost 14%, while the number of foreign labor increased by an additional 130,000.[146] In Oman, too, one can find a similar "dual increase": Although the number of Omani nationals employed in the private sector increased by an impressive rate of 16% in 2006 alone, the number of the foreign workers employed by the private sector increased by an even higher rate of 20.2%.[147]

It seems that the most prominent sector that succeeded in increasing the number of employment opportunities for nationals through the massive use of cheap foreign workers is the tourism industry. During recent years, all of the GCC countries, including Saudi Arabia that had traditionally opposed any sort of tourism,[148] have devoted immense financial resources for the development of the tourism industry. This is mainly due to the fact that the tourism industry, by its basic nature, is heavily labor intensive. The official Saudi aim in this respect, as noted in early 2005 by Prince Sultan bin Salman, the Head of the Saudi Supreme Commission for Tourism, is "to Saudize 80% of the tourism sector."[149] In the case of Bahrain, the tourism industry was identified as one of the six key sectors targeted for leading the overall economic development.[150] In Oman as well, the tourism industry was recognized as one of the most promising sector in the area of employment generation.[151] Overall, during Oman's Sixth Five-Year Development Plan (2000–2005) the tourism industry expanded by an impressive rate of 9.9% on annual average.[152]

In the public sector, it should be emphasized, the previous policy of replacing the foreign workers by national employees continued as before. This is because government regulations, rather than free market forces, determine the rules and wages. In the case of Oman, for example, in 2006, while the number of foreign labor employed by the public sector declined by 2.1%, the number of Omani nationals increased by 6.4%, following an increase of 4.8% in 2004 and 6.1% in 2005.[153] In Saudi Arabia the same process has occurred. The number of public sector national employees increased from 631,024 in 2001 to 733,866 in 2006, while the number of foreign employees decreased from 79,835 to 69,797.[154] The huge increase of the oil export revenues since 2004 years has enabled the GCC government to finance this replacement process in the public sectors.

Therefore, while until the early 1990s the GCC countries promoted heavy-capital industries, aiming to reduce the dependence on foreign labor, since then, they have been promoting labor-intensive sectors. They realized that the only viable option for alleviating employment pressure among the indigenous workforce without changing the current rentier political formula is through adding substantial suitable job opportunities for nationals in the private sector through the use of massive cheap foreign labor. The choice of the tourism industry as the leading sector was driven by the fact that the tourism industry, more than any other economic sector, promotes local industries and services (food production, banking, construction, etc.),[155] which by themselves create a substantial number of job opportunities for nationals. In 2005, overall capital investments in the tourism industry in the GCC countries amounted to $19.7 billion – the highest amount ever.[156]

Among the GCC economies, Dubai is the best example of both the employment potential of the tourism industry on the one hand, and the "price" of the increased dependence on foreign workforce on the other. Overall, during the past two decades, the tourism industry became one of Dubai's paramount development "engines,"[157] achieving an impressive annual growth rate of 10% during the past decade – more than twice the worldwide average.[158] Indeed, the number of Dubai's nationals employed in the tourism industry itself as well as in its related industries and services substantially increased. The new job opportunities for Dubai's nationals constitute the most important factor for the fact that the unemployment rate among Dubai's nationals is the lowest among the indigenous Gulf workforces, amounting to only 5% in 2004.[159]

Easing the rules of private investments was the second side of the coin of the new employment policy. Private investments, both local and foreign, combined with massive governmental infrastructure investments, boosted Dubai's private sector activities. However, the "price" for this massive employment creation for Dubai's nationals was a sharp increase in the number of foreign labor. This phenomenon is not unique to the tourism industry alone and is a reality in other private sector industries and services. Consequently, according to the 2005 census data, among Dubai's 1.321 million inhabitants, 74.9% were males, the vast majority of whom were foreign workers.[160] In the other GCC countries one can find a similar situation, although on a smaller scale than in Dubai. The overall result, as illustrated in Table 4.5, was a massive increase in the number of foreign labor during the first half of the 2000s.

5.5 *Asians versus Arabs in the GCC Labor Markets*

Officially, all the GCC countries are obligated to employ nationals first, then non-national Arabs and only after that, non-national non-Arabs.[161] Moreover, at the Second Baghdad Arab Summit, all the Arab labor-importing countries agreed to give priority to workers from Arab countries in order to ensure that no other Arab countries would join Egypt in its peace treaty with Israel.

In reality, however, the opposite occurred. Since the early 1980s, following the end of the "oil decade," the share of Arabs within the total foreign workers in each of the GCC countries steadily declined, even in Kuwait which constituted the "fortress" of the Arab foreign labor since the 1950s. Thus, while in 1985 the percentage of Arabs of the total foreign workforce in Kuwait was 69.6%,[162] this percentage radically declined to 49.9% in 1994,[163] and further declined to as low as 40.9% in 1999.[164] In the other GCC countries, particularly in the UAE, Qatar and Oman, although the percentage of Asian workers within the total foreign workforce was already high during the 1970s, it sharply increased from the mid-1980s.[165] Overall, according to the various estimates, in 2004, the total number of non-national Arabs (including both workers and accompanying family members) in the GCC countries amounted to 3–3.5 million. This means that the number of Indians alone in the GCC countries in the early 2000s was higher than the total number of non-national Arabs.[166]

Why did the GCC authorities not accomplish their official policy of giving preference to non-national Arab workers? The common answer in the academic literature concentrates on two main reasons – political and economic: From the political viewpoint, the GCC rulers were afraid that Arab foreigners would spread "pan-Arab ideas" which the GCC rulers were opposed to.[167] However, it seems that if this argument is relevant, it applies to the 1970s alone. This is because since the early 1980s, it is quite meaningless to speak about any kind of "pan-Arab threat" regarding the GCC countries. Moreover, if the GCC rulers were indeed concerned about the spread of "pan-Arab ideas," Jordanians should have been preferred over Egyptians and Syrians – the two countries that led the pan-Arab ideology. In reality, however, as was previously examined, following the Kuwaiti crisis, while the Jordanian workers were deported from Kuwait and Saudi Arabia, Egyptian and Syrian workers were most welcome. In this respect, the indisputable factor for the preference of Asians at the expense of Arabs in the GCC countries was that the Asians were "passive observers," as they were defined by Choucri.[168]

The recent GCC preference for Asian workers is connected to the new employment policy: if massive foreign labor is a "necessary evil" not only for the short run, but for the longer run as well, a permanent settlement of the foreign workers should be more seriously addressed. Since the Asian workers not only tend to come alone to the Gulf,[169] but the salaries of their vast majority are extremely low, in reality they do not even have the option of settling permanently in the Gulf.

From a purely economic viewpoint, the Asian workers were willing to accept much lower salaries than the Arabs. For example, the data collected in 1987 from Saudi factories employing at least 100 employees, illustrates that the salaries of the non-national Arabs were twice that of the Asian employees. This gap increased to three-fold two years later, in 1989.[170]

5.6 The High Unemployment among the GCC Nationals: Is it "Real" or "Masked"?

Although there is no dispute about the fact that unemployment among the GCC nationals, particularly among the younger generation, has steadily increased during the past decade, many see this unemployment as "masked" rather than "real," due to the existence of the huge number of foreign labor. Thus, for example, Kapiszewski claimed that:

> The problem of unemployment of nationals in the GCC countries is, of course, different in nature from that in most other countries in the world. It is a "masked" unemployment, since millions of foreign workers have jobs in these countries. Thus, it is more a question of integrating the national workforce into the labor market than a question of expanding the economy to create new jobs.[171]

Girgis claimed that:

> While the unemployment problem is indeed a serious concern, the GCC, luckily, appears to have sufficient time to effectuate the envisioned transition. The number of foreigners is so large relative to the national population of labor force that nationals could **easily** [sic] replace foreigners if they had the requisite skills.[172]

These are only two of numerous examples of the prevailing attitudes regarding the unemployment nature among GCC nationals. Is the unemployment among the GCC nationals indeed only "masked," or is it a "real" problem? Is it practically possible to replace a large number of foreign workers by changing the immigration, educational and professional training policies? In order to answer this crucial question, we have first to define the occupational characteristics of the GCC foreign workers. Broadly speaking, during the past two decades, one can identify five major groups of foreign workers in the GCC countries:

(a) Domestic service workers The highly available cheap Asian foreign labor led to the widespread phenomenon of domestic employees. In 1999, for example, there were some 1.7 million foreign women employees in Saudi Arabia, a large percentage of

Cartoon 4.1
Source: *al-Watan*, July 7, 2004.

whom employed as housemaids.[173] In many cases, their wages were so low that "Some expatriates were even preparing to return to their homes in Pakistan and Bangladesh because they were no longer earning enough make their sacrifices worthwhile."[174] This high dependence on foreign labor for domestic purposes is well demonstrated in cartoon 4.1, published in the Kuwaiti newspaper *al-Watan*. It presents an Indian foreign worker scratching the nose of his Kuwaiti employer. At the top of the cartoon *al-Itakaliyya* – "dependence" – is written, namely, the GCC nationals use the foreigners even for scratching their noses.

From a purely economic viewpoint, it is obvious that these workers are not necessary for running the GCC economies. Their presence is due only to their extremely low cost.[175] Hence, these workers would not be replaced under any circumstances by GCC nationals. Cordesman noted in this regard that: "many of the non-Saudis are working in jobs . . . that often have little or no social value, and where the productivity is often so low that the jobs would not exist in their present form if the employer had to pay Saudi natives."[176]

(b) Unskilled and semi-skilled industrial workers Their share in the total foreign workforce is quite substantial. In the case of Saudi Arabia, in 1996–97, their share within the total foreign workforce amounted to 20%.[177] Their replacement by nationals, however, would be quite problematic since their salaries are relatively low and any legislated replacement through quotas would bring about an increase in production costs and consequently subsequent losses in profits. As the GCC economies become more integrated with the global economy, increased production costs could lead to the outsourcing of the production itself from the Gulf to countries with much lower salaries as is the case in many developed economies worldwide.[178]

(c) Highly skilled foreign workers This includes managers of large companies, particularly at the top managerial positions of the oil and gas companies, managers of larger hotels and many engineers and other highly skilled professional employees.

Although their importance to the GCC economies is as enormous as their salaries, their numbers are small and they do not have a significant impact on the overall GCC employment trends.

(d) Workers in the wholesale and retail trade These workers can be replaced relatively easily by nationals through legislation and regulations, as this area is not subject to international competition and does not suffer from a low social image.

(e) Construction workers Among all of the private sector activities, the percentage of indegenous employees in the construction sector is the lowest. For example, by 2005, the total number of employees in the Saudi Arabian construction and building sector was 1.943 million, among whom only 170,386, namely 8.8%, were Saudi nationals, the vast majority of them held medium and high managerial levels.[179] Among the low skilled construction workers, however, nationals were totally absent. Although at first glance the opportunity to replace a large amount of foreign workers by nationals is highest in this sector, as there is no international competition in this area, the construction industry suffers from a very low social image and thus would have to offer much higher salaries to nationals in order to attract them. In addition, while in Western developed countries the cost gap between the employment of locals and foreigners in the construction sector could be overcome through tax reduction in order to prevent cost increases, this is not an option in the GCC countries, since there is no taxation on housing. In fact, the GCC governments, not the citizen themselves, bear most of the housing costs through subsidized loans and generous grants.[180] Thus, the replacement of foreign labor by national employees in the construction sector would lead to a sharp increase in governmental expenditures on housing, not to mention the expected sharp rise in spending on infrastructure.

It appears that from a purely economic point of view, nationals cannot replace a large percentage of GCC foreign workers under the current economic structure and employment polices. Therefore, it is clear that the high unemployment rate among the GCC nationals, particularly the younger generation, constitutes "real unemployment" rather than "masked unemployment." It seems, however, that the core of the mistaken understanding of the nature of the unemployment among GCC nationals is a result of the basic failure to fully understand the nature of the GCC dual labor market mechanism. Thus, for example, in the 2004 IBRD report on the Middle Eastern employment situation, it was noted that: "Recently, even the oil-exporting countries that traditionally imported expatriate labor to supplement the national work force have witnessed rising rates of unemployment."[181] As the foreign workers are only a "supplement" to the national workforce, it is possible to replace them by unemployed nationals. This observation, however, is mistaken, as since the early 1970s the foreign workers in the GCC countries are not "a supplement for the national workforce," but rather the core of the workforce itself.

In the framework of this type of observation of the GCC labor markets, many claim that the strategy to alleviate unemployment among GCC nationals is through changing their educational and professional training. Thus, for example, an IMF report from 2003 argued that in order to ease indigenous employment pressure, "the long-term objective should be addressed by revamping educational and training policies and redirecting government expenditures toward building human capital."[182] Specifically regarding the UAE, the IMF recommended in 2004 that the UAE employment strategy should "continue to rely on raising the skills of nationals through better education and training programs geared toward private sector labor demands, while avoiding mandatory measures, such as quotas."[183] Likewise, Looney claimed that: "Enhancing the human capital of Saudis and the acquisition of skills that are valuable to the private sector is likely to increase demand and employment [of nationals]."[184]

However, the concentration of GCC students in the humanities and social sciences is only a reflection, and certainly not the cause of the GCC current dual labor market structure. In practice, as long as the GCC nationals are forced to compete with foreigners in the private sector, they will always lose – regardless of their educational level and professional skills. This is actually the case in any country worldwide. Foreigners will always be preferred by private employers not only due to their much lower costs, but because they are not organized and in most cases are not protected. Thus, relieving unemployment among GCC nationals through the replacement of foreigners in the private sector is not a viable option as long as foreign labor continues to be easily available.

6 Evaluating the GCC Immigration and Employment Policies

There is no doubt that the labor force nationalization policy in the public sector in all of the GCC countries succeeded to a great extent, primarily in Bahrain and Oman. By 1999, about 90% of Bahrain's public sector employees were nationals.[185] In the case of Oman, the number of foreign labor in the public sector declined from 35,812 in 1994 to 27,161 in 2001[186] and further to 22,990 in 2005. By 2005, the foreign workers constituted 17.4% of the total Omani public sector employees.[187] In the case of Saudi Arabia, by 2005, the Saudi nationals represented 91.0% of the total Saudi government employees, increasing from 85.3% in 1997.[188] Even in the UAE – the country with the highest percentage of foreign labor – by early 2004 the nationals constituted 85% of the total public sector employees.[189]

It should be taken into consideration, however, that a large proportion of the increase in the percentage of nationals within the public sector employees is meaningless from a productive viewpoint. This is because public sector employment of GCC nationals "can be thought of increasingly as a domestic subsidy, since marginal productivity in the public sector is very low and a large proportion of additions to the labor force in this sector are simply made to absorb new entrants into the job market."[190]

On many occasions, the Gulf newspapers themselves laugh at the widespread hidden unemployment of nationals in the public sector which has become so visible. Thus, for example, the following two cartoons demonstrate this prevalent phenomenon. Cartoon 4.2 presents a Kuwaiti national employed by the public sector, reading a newspaper. The only difference between working before the *Ramadan* and during the *Ramadan* is that during the *Ramadan* he is not drinking coffee and water due to the fast.

Cartoon 4.3 presents a Kuwaiti national who explains to his manager that he returned late from his break since he took a nap at home. The manager answered: "Up to now, I thought that you only slept at work. Now I realize that you also sleep at your home."

Thus, the real examination of the success of the GCC labor force nationalization policy should not concentrate on the public sector but rather on the private sector. In this respect, as the data reveals, the foreign workers continue to constitute the core of

Cartoon 4.2
Source: al-*Watan*, October 10, 2006.

the workforce in each of the GCC countries. In Kuwait, nationals made up only 2.8% of the total private sector employees in 2003.[191] In Saudi Arabia, by mid-2005, the nationals constituted only 11.6% of the total private sector employees.[192] In Oman, similar to Saudi Arabia, the nationals represented 11.3% of the total private sector employees in 2003.[193] In Bahrain – the least rentier among the GCC countries – the situation was much better and the percentage of nationals within the total private sector workforce was and still is much higher: As early as 1995, 29.3% of all the employees in Bahrain's private sector were nationals.[194] This percentage remained more or less stable in the decade which followed.[195]

In the areas of top managerial positions and highly skilled occupations, the labor force nationalization policy has failed almost totally. Almost all top jobs, such as hotel managers, engineers in high positions and so forth, are still occupied by foreign labor.[196] In mid-2004, for example, there were 40,000 Americans and 30,000 British foreign workers in Saudi Arabia alone.[197] One international contractor working in Saudi Arabia noted recently in this regard that: "There are simply not enough skilled nationals for the work available."[198]

The new employment policy has thus far succeeded to a large extent and in each of the GCC countries the number of nationals employed by the private sector has markedly increased in recent years. This success is clearest in the tourism industry, mainly in Bahrain and Oman. Thus, for example, most hotels in Muscat have an Omanization level of approximately 30%.[199] In the Golden Tulip Resort, nearly 50% of all the employees in late 2003 were Omanis.[200] The workforce at the Gulf Air call

Cartoon 4.3
Source: *al-Watan*, May 10, 2007.

center was 100% Omanis as early as 2004.[201] In the case of Bahrain, in early 2005, the labor force Bahranization rate in the tourism sector amounted to 44% – higher than in any other private sector field, with the exception of the banking sector.[202] Overall, by 2005, while the tourism industry contributed 5.4% of total Bahrain's GDP, it employed approximately 10% of the total workforce.[203] More than any others, these figures represent the huge employment potential the tourism industry has for GCC nationals.

However, although the "fourth stage" of the GCC labor force nationalization policy was more successful than the previous one, unemployment among the GCC nationals still remained high by any international standards. According to a high-level Saudi Arabian official, unemployment among nationals had climbed to 20% by 2001.[204] In November 2003, Walid bin Talal estimated that the unemployment rate among Saudi nationals had climbed to 30%, and that "we are creating an unlimited social problem."[205] The highest unemployment rate was measured among young first-time job seekers. According to official Saudi data, by the end of 1999, the unemployment rate of Saudi nationals aged 20–24 was 28% and 9.8% among those ages 25–29, while it was only 0.9% among those above 30,[206] workers who had entered into the public sector in "the good years" of the "oil decade." In recent years, the problem of young unemployment substantially increased. In 2004, unemployment among Saudis aged 20–24 was estimated to be as high as 35%.[207]

In the other GCC countries unemployment among nationals, particularly among the young, remained high as well. In the case of Bahrain, by early 2003, unemployment among Bahraini nationals was estimated at 15%,[208] increasing further to 20% in mid-2005.[209] In the UAE, although job creation was more than sufficient to absorb new entrants into the labor force, unemployment among nationals increased gradually from 7.6% in 1999 to 11.4% in 2004.[210]

The implications of the "fourth stage" of the GCC labor force nationalization policy are immense. Its actual meaning is that the GCC countries are sacrificing their future socio-demographic structure in order to solve their current unemployment problem. What will the political implications be when nationals, in cases like Qatar and the UAE, represent only a small percent of the total population? How much longer can this situation continue?

7 The Labor Emigration Policy of the Arab Labor-Exporting Countries

Generally speaking, the research on labor emigration policy, including in the Arab countries, has thus far not received sufficient academic attention. The main emphasis is, naturally, on the labor immigration policy which dictates the scale and direction of the international labor migration trends. However, in the case of the intra-Arab labor migration, although the labor-importing countries dictated the scale of the migrant workers, the labor emigration policy has had a great influence on the nationality composition of the migrant workers. A close examination of the labor emigration policy of the Arab labor-exporting countries reveals a distinct difference between two periods: prior to the oil price collapse in the mid-1980s and since then.

7.1 The Labor Emigration Policies of the non-oil Arab Countries until the mid-1980s

Seccombe and Lawless divided the labor migration policies of the non-oil Arab countries during the first period into the following four categories:[211]

(a) Preventive labor emigration policy The two countries that accomplished this policy of almost total preventive labor emigration were South Yemen and Algeria. In the case of Algeria, as will be examined in Chapter 5, the preventive labor emigration policy was part of the overall Algerian demographic approach since the early 1970s, which was based on the assumption that the country is under-populated. In the case of South Yemen, due to its small population in any case, the labor emigration potential of the country was quite insignificant.[212]

(b) Selective labor emigration policy This policy was implemented by Syria and by Egypt prior to the June 1967 War. In the early 1970s, the Syrian economy suffered from a scarcity of skilled labor, as a result of the huge "brain drain" of the 1960s, particularly following the adoption of the socialist socioeconomic policy of the Ba'th regime which seized power in March 1963.[213] Consequently, the Syrian authorities restricted labor emigration of public sector employees without prior approval from the authorities. Those who emigrated without prior approval were subject to severe penalties.[214] The second measure which aimed at preventing "brain drain" was a direct appeal of the Syrian authorities to the authorities of the Arab labor-importing countries not to employ Syrian citizens in certain occupations.[215] However, the labor

emigration of unskilled workers and *fellahin* was unregulated, and even encouraged.[216]

In the case of Egypt prior to the June 1967 War, the Egyptian authorities sent Egyptian teachers to work in other Arab countries, including in the Gulf states as part of Egypt's seniority status among the Arab countries at that time.[217] However, they prevented the emigration of necessary skilled and educated public sector employees.[218] By 1965, the number of Egyptian temporary labor emigrants was estimated at 100,000,[219] namely, only a few percents of the total Egyptian workforce at that time.

(c) Encouraging temporary labor emigration The countries that most implemented this policy were Egypt following the October 1973 War, Jordan, Tunisia and Sudan. The two fundamental aims of encouraging temporary labor emigration were to attract as many workers' remittances as possible and to alleviate employment pressure. The Egyptian supportive labor emigration policy since the early 1970s included the following three measures: (1) abolishing the previous restrictions on labor emigration. (2) signing contracts with the major labor-importing countries to which the Egyptian government would supply professional employees (teachers, physicians, etc.) (3) activating pressure on the labor-importing countries to employ Egyptians.[220]

Among the Arab labor-exporting countries, Jordan implemented the most supportive labor emigration policy. The core of the Jordanian labor emigration policy rested on two assumptions: The first was that without extensive labor emigration, the Jordanian economy would not be able to deal with the massive influx of Palestinian refugees. The second assumption was that the workers' remittances would be the most available option for hard currency.[221] Thus, by 1985, the number of Jordanian workers abroad was estimated at 328,000,[222] representing more than 40% of the total Jordanian civilian workforce – the highest rate among all of the Arab labor-exporting counties ever.

(d) Non-intervention labor emigration policy This policy, which was based on market forces, was implemented by Morocco, Lebanon and North Yemen. It should be emphasized, however, that in the case of Lebanon, in contrast to Morocco and North Yemen, the non-intervention policy was due to the weakness of the central regime that could not impose any other policy – neither restrictive nor supportive.

7.2 The Labor Emigration Policies of the non-oil Arab Countries since the mid-1980s

During the second half of the 1980s, all of the non-oil Arab countries adopted, in various degrees, a supportive labor emigration policy. The core reason for this changing policy was the intensification of the various socioeconomic constraints, primarily in the employment arena, following the collapse of the oil prices. The rulers of the non-oil Arab countries reached the conclusion that the structural unemployment required the adoption of this policy as all the other tools for alleviating the employment pressure were not bringing about sufficient relief.

The Arab country that changed its labor emigration policy the most was Syria. Within just a few years, its previous selective-preventive labor emigration policy was turned into a supportive labor emigration. In the late 1980s, Syria abolished all of the previous limitations on labor emigration. One of the prominent reasons that led the Syrian authorities to join the anti-Iraqi coalition during the Kuwait crisis was to facilitate a substantial increase in the number of Syrian labor in the GCC countries. By the late 1990s, the Syrian workers in the GCC countries numbered 265,000,[223] compared to only 53,000 in mid-1990.[224] In addition, Syrian politics of "digging in its heels" in Lebanon should be examined within the framework of its new labor emigration policy. The reconstruction of Lebanon following the October 1989 Ta'if Agreement and the direct Syrian control over Lebanon opened up the opportunity for hundred of thousands of Syrians to find employment there. By the late 1990s, approximately 800,000 Syrians were working in other Arab countries, representing 20% of the Syrian workforce and almost 30% of the civilian workforce – the highest rate among all of the Arab labor-exporting countries.

Egypt intensified its previous policy of encouraging labor emigration since the mid-1980s in line with its worsening employment situation. However, while until the late 1980s the GCC countries employed Egyptians for purely practical reasons, following the Kuwait crisis, the preference given to the Egyptian workers was mainly as a "gift" for Egypt's support of the anti-Iraqi coalition.

In retrospect, there is no doubt that in the labor migration arena, the most bizarre situation exits in Jordan. As was described in Chapter 3, during the 1990s, despite increasing unemployment, the number of foreign workers in Jordan rose rapidly. The end result was that by the early 2000s, the employment situation in the Kingdom was quite similar to the one that prevailed in the GCC countries, namely a large number of foreign workers despite high unemployment rates among the Jordanian citizens. The massive inflow of Iraqi refugees to Jordan after the Kuwait crisis only worsened Jordan's employment situation.[225] Therefore, the Jordanian authorities tried to alleviate the employment pressure by increasing job opportunities to Jordanians in the GCC countries.[226] Overall, by the year 2000, the number of Jordanian workers abroad amounted to 380,000.[227]

In retrospect, while the maneuvering space of Sadat and certainty Mubarak in the labor emigration policy was limited, in the case of Jordan, the current structural unemployment is a direct consequence of a mistaken "replacement labor migration policy" implemented until the late 1980s. Overall, Jordan is the best example of how a mistaken labor migration policy could "twist" the labor market with all its various socio-economic and political implications.

8 Was it Worth It? The Cost/Benefit Balance of the Intra-Arab Labor Migration for the Labor-Exporting Countries

What was the cost/benefit balance of the inter-Arab labor migration for the Arab labor-exporting countries? The prevailing perception in the academic literature is generally positive. Thus, for example, Richards and Waterbury wrote in the mid-1990s that:

> [T]he impact of emigration was on balance beneficial to the economies of the sending countries . . . [T]here is little reason to suppose that economic growth would have been more rapid in these countries had these workers remained at home . . . [228]

The basic assumption of these researchers was that the massive labor emigration only reduced the huge hidden unemployment and underemployment, particularly in the agricultural and the public sectors. Thus, not only was there a lack of evidence for a labor shortage in these fields, in many cases an increase in labor productivity seemed to emerge. The increases in real wages during the "oil decade" in many of the Arab labor-exporting countries support this assumption.

Other researchers who examined the process of inter-Arab labor migration within the framework of inter-Arab economic integration also agreed that the inter-Arab labor migration was beneficial to the labor-exporting and the labor-importing alike. They attributed this success to the fact that the inter-Arab labor migration brought together the financial resources of the Arab oil countries and the human capital of the non-oil Arab countries. For example, Tabbarah claimed in 1981 that the inter-Arab labor migration promoted "the social and economic integration of the Arab world."[229] Along the same line of thought, Sell noted in the late 1980s that "the Egyptian migration processes will promote economic and social integration in the region."[230]

There are other researchers who hold the opposite opinion toward the cost/benefit balance of the inter-Arab labor migration for the labor-exporting countries. Generally, their most common reservations are centered in two areas:

(a) **The minor contribution of the workers' remittances to the economic development of the labor-exporting countries**, given their sharp fluctuation, their uncertain nature, and the fact that a large proportion of the remittances are spent in unproductive areas, mainly on housing and consumer goods.[231] In addition, as the workers' remittances belong to the migrants themselves, the ability of the state to use these remittances is quite marginal.

(b) **The large-scale "brain drain"** hampers the economic development of the labor-exporting countries. Oweiss for example claimed that: "Unless there is compensation to Egyptian society as a whole, this migration can impede the economic and social development of Egypt."[232] Halliday argued that the overall cost/benefit balance of the inter-Arab labor migration for the labor-exporting countries was negative since the result was to:

> [d]epress local production, to reduce – through the loss of large numbers of skilled personnel – the countries' capacities to develop their own economies, and to increase dependency on external sources of finance, sources which are, at best, fluctuating and impossible to sustain.[233]

A similar argument was claimed by Nagi:

> Not only is the productive capacity of the migrants lost during their most active years, but, also, the process is selective and tends to draw away many of the most able members within each skill level of the labor force. Countries of origin are losing manpower from the very sectors that are most crucial to their development. Remittances . . . do not make up for this investment in labor which the poorer country has lost . . . [234]

Serageldin and associate also claimed that the contribution of the workers' remittances did not compensate on the manpower losses:

> [T]he countries supplying manpower have trained labor at considerable cost in the skills which the oil-rich countries attracted. Remittances, it is asserted, do not make up for this investment in labor which the poorer country has lost. [235]

In retrospect, however, it appears that these reservations were, in most cases, groundless, considering the lack of evidences that the productive sectors of the labor-exporting countries actually suffered from labor shortages, either in terms of quality or quantity. The few exceptions mentioned by some researchers were of agricultural labor shortage in North Yemen and Sudan when the vast majority of men from certain area or village emigrated abroad together.[236] These cases, however, were quite limited and certainly do not represent a widespread phenomenon. Overall, it is quite hard to talk about agricultural labor shortages in the 1970s and certainly not in the 1980s in any of the non-oil Arab countries. Moreover, the agricultural production growth rates in the major Arab labor-exporting countries during the "oil decade" were no lower than they were prior to the "oil boom." For example, Egypt's agricultural production growth rate averaged 3.0% annually during the 1970–1982 period compared to 2.9% during the years 1960–1970.[237]

Similarly, in the industrial sector, there is little, if any, evidence of labor shortages in any of the Arab labor-exporting countries. Egypt's industrial growth rate, for example, increased from 3.8% on annual average during the 1965–1973 period to as high as 10.6% on annual average during the years 1973–1983. In Jordan and North Yemen, the industrial production growth rate reached as high as 14.7% and 13.2%, respectively, on annual average during the 1973–1983 period.[238] Moreover, the large-scale workers' remittances, the "official" and the "unofficial" alike, raised local demand for goods and services and thus contributed to the economic expansion of the labor-exporting countries.[239] Thus, it appears that the massive labor emigration to the Arab oil countries was not only beneficial to the individual migrants but to their home countries as well, at least in the short run.

However, the more important question is: Was the inter-Arab labor migration indeed a "win–win situation" in the longer run as well? In the mid-1990s, Richards and Waterbury argued that: "The debate on the impact of [inter-Arab] labor migration is too often a clash of ignorant armies in the night."[240] One reason is the lack of consensus on the various aspects in which the labor-exporting countries have been affected as a result of the massive labor emigration. There has also been a lack of agreement on whether the many consequences of the labor emigration have been positive or negative. For example, there is disagreement as to whether an investment of workers' remittances in housing has had positive or negative effects on the construction sector of the labor-exporting countries. [241]

I fully agree with Richards and Waterbury regarding their claim that the current academic debate on the labor emigration cost/benefit balance is basically a "clash of ignorant armies in the night," but for a different reason. This is because the current academic debate largely concentrates on the short-term effects, while neglecting the medium and particularly the long-term effects. These long-term effects will be examined below regarding the two most crucial parameters:

(a) The effect on the labor market structure While there is no doubt that the short-term effect of the massive labor emigration was positive, in the longer run, it damaged the labor markets of the labor-exporting countries insofar as it created "an illusion" of relief from employment pressure. In practice, the two most promising employment options, particularly for first-time job seekers, were either entry into the public sector or emigration to one of the Arab labor-importing countries (see Chapter 3). Thus, the end result was only "more of the same" with no overall change in the options available for first-time job seekers. When these options were sharply reduced following the end of the "oil decade," the employment pressure resurfaced in full severity.

(b) The demographic effect Although it is clear that in the short run the massive labor emigration considerably reduced the demographic pressure in the major labor-exporting countries, in the longer run the consequence was extremely devastating. This is because, in total contrast to the worldwide trend of fertility decline following rapid socioeconomic development, in the major Arab labor-exporting countries, not only did

fertility decline not occur, but it even increased. In trying to explain the increase in Egypt's fertility rates during the "oil decade," Fargues argued that: "the migration itself contributed to the renewed rise in the birth rate because of the Egyptians' contact with the large family standard common in the Gulf."[242] I fully agree with Fargues that the "oil boom" indeed led to an increase in Egypt's fertility rates, but for a different reason. The real effect of the "oil boom" in the demographic arena was that the Egyptian government almost totally abandoned the issue of family planning – if not officially, at least in practice. In a similar manner, other Arab labor-exporting countries, such as Syria and Jordan, failed to adopt comprehensive family planning programs during the "oil decade" since labor emigration provided them with a temporary "shelter" from the deleterious consequences of the "demographic explosion" (see Chapter 5).

Thus, it appears that in contrast to the neo-classical economic interpretation on labor-exporting as an export of any other commodity or services, or the more recent approach that labor-exporting is a kind of FDI through the workers' remittances, in the case of the non-oil Arab countries, the massive labor emigration was similar to a huge loan. Although in the short run the economic situation largely improved, in the longer run these countries had to return this loan with extremely high interest rates in the form of the "demographic momentum" which dictates the continuation of rapid population growth for the foreseeable future. However, one should take into consideration that the massive labor emigration kept the non-oil Arab countries from becoming "Bangladesh," as was predicted by Boutros Boutros-Ghali regarding Egypt in light of its rapid population growth.[243]

9 Summary and Conclusions

It is a well-established fact that technology and a highly skilled workforce are the two most important assets for a modern economy, leading to both a high national income and economic diversification. However, by guaranteeing public sector employment for the indigenous workforce, with high salaries and luxurious work conditions, the GCC authorities in effect abolished the basic condition for free market capitalization, namely, labor market competition and the allocation of wages according to educational and skill levels. As such, although the GCC countries are basically capitalist economies, they certainly do not function as such when it comes to the labor market. Moreover, the low salaries of the foreign workers "favor the creation of output by adding more labor and less capital or new technology."[244] Thus, while in the rest of the labor-importing countries worldwide, massive labor immigration depressed national wages due to competition with foreign labor, particularly in the lower skill levels, in the GCC countries this did not happen. Instead, a unique employment pattern emerged: the dual labor market with a clear dichotomy between the nationals and the foreign labor.

As long as the economic expansion was rapid and the indigenous labor force was relatively small, the dual labor market structure constituted "a win–win situation" and worked to the benefit of both the indigenous as well as the foreign workers. The private sector employers, on the one hand, were allowed to recruit cheap foreign labor almost without any limitations, thereby maximizing their profits. The indigenous workforces, on their part, were guaranteed the luxury of public sector employment, regardless of their professional background and skill level.

Moreover, by not setting a minimum wage for foreign labor, the GCC royal families enabled the middle-class, the vast majority of whom were and still are public sector employees, to employ cheap foreign labor in domestic services. Through the adoption of this kind of employment policy, the GCC royal families guaranteed public compliance. However, the dual labor market mechanism prevented large-scale replacement of foreign labor by nationals in the private sector. Consequently, in recent years, the GCC authorities were forced to adopt even more liberal labor immigration policies which used huge numbers of cheap foreign labor in order to create work opportunities for nationals in the private sector.

In retrospect, it appears that whatever economic diversification has actually been achieved, it was done at the "price" of increasing dependence on foreign labor and not through developing industries in which nationals constituted the majority of the employees. The example of Dubai illustrates this phenomenon. In the early 2000s, three decades following the "oil boom," Dubai is indeed the most diverse among the GCC economies. However, Dubai's economic diversification was achieved through the rapid increase in the number of foreign workers, which still represents its most lucrative comparative advantage. The end result is that Dubai's nationals represent only 10% of the Emirate's population and an even smaller percentage in the workforce.

The political implication of the rentier system is no less crucial. Historically, the Gulf rulers were dependent on the big merchants and the Bedouin tribes. This dependence, however, also remained in force during the oil era. Although the Gulf rulers no longer need the taxes which the big merchants paid in the pre-oil era, they still need their political support. On the part of the big merchants, although they withdrew from their traditional claim for political participation, this withdrawal was in exchange for the continuation of their economic privileges, including the availability of almost unlimited cheap foreign labor. On many occasions, when the GCC authorities tried to narrow the scale of work permits for foreign workers, the big merchants "squeezed" the authorities to cancel this intention.[245] Hence, basically the GCC labor markets remained as before with nationals representing only a tiny percentage of the private sector workforce, despite two decades of the implementation of the labor force nationalization policy.

As for the Arab labor-exporting countries, their tragedy is that while during the "oil decade" the employment relationship between them and the GCC countries was characterized by "mutual dependence," in the mid-1980s this "mutual dependence" ended as a result of the sharp improvement in the educational level of the GCC nationals. However, instead of using "the amnesty period" of the "bonanza oil decade" and preparing their socioeconomic structure for the "post labor emigration era," the Arab labor-exporting countries chose the "easy way out" and did almost nothing. Consequently, although they have thus far avoided internal unrest on socioeconomic grounds, in the longer run they are faced with an employment problem without any solution at least in the foreseeable future.

5 Between Pro-Natalism and Anti-Natalism in the Arab Countries

[T]he demand for men, like that for any other commodity, necessarily regulates the production of men; quickens it when it goes on too slowly, and stops it when it advances too fast.

Adam Smith, *The Wealth of Nations*, 1776[1]

Man can undo himself with no other force than his own brutality. The roots of the brutality . . . are in the lack of population control.

Paul Erlich, 1968[2]

I The Attitude toward Population Growth in Historical Perspective

Todaro raised the basic demographic dilemma of the modern globalized world: "Is rapid population growth per se as serious a problem as many people believe, or is it a manifestation of more fundamental problems of underdevelopment and the unequal utilization of global resources between rich and poor nations, as others argue?"[3] The growing emphasis on "globalization," or "the new world economic order," on the one hand, and the steadily increasing socioeconomic gaps between the developed and the developing countries on the other, have only intensified the dispute over the issue of population growth and its socioeconomic effects in the developing countries.[4] At the heart of the debate, claimed Ali Mohammed, "is the fact that the causal links between population growth and economic growth are reciprocal and simultaneous."[5]

Until the mid-twentieth century, with very few exceptions, the conventional attitude toward the new phenomenon of accelerated population growth was positive and viewed as an important advantage from the perspectives of both political-security and economics, based on the assumption that a large nation is a strong nation and that rapid population growth would facilitate the adoption of modern mass production techniques and advanced technology.

In contrast to this conventional positive attitude were the few economists and philosophers, starting in the late eighteenth century, who argued that, in the long run, rapid population growth would have devastating economic and political consequences. As a result, this new phenomenon should be curbed or at least controlled.

The first among those few was Adam Smith who doubted the conventional attitude that rapid population growth is the most important indicator for the health situation, and thus also for the economic situation of any given society.[6] Smith's basic demographic attitude was that the desired population growth rate is not constant, but changes according to the labor market supply/demand balance. Thus, in his famous book, *The Wealth of Nations*, Smith claimed that: "Countries are populous, not in proportion to the number of people whom their produce can clothe and lodge, but in proportion to that of those whom it can feed. When food is provided, it is easy to find the necessary clothing and lodging."[7] Put simply, Smith was the first to claim that rapid population growth should not always be welcome, but should rather be regulated according to economic and employment conditions. Hence, Smith was the first to point out the need for a "population policy."

However, the most famous among those who opposed the conventional positive attitude toward rapid population growth was the English reverend and philosopher, Thomas Robert Malthus (1766–1834), who is considered the "father of the family planning policy." In 1798, Malthus published the book entitled *An Essay on the Principle of Population*. Malthus' basic argument was that while population increases in a geometric ratio,[8] the means of subsistence increases in an arithmetic ratio.[9] Thus, the inevitable result would be a steady decrease of per capita agricultural land and eventually a steady decrease in the marginal food production for every additional agricultural laborer, in line with the law of diminishing marginal productivity. The core of the Malthusian theory can be summarized as follows:

> [P]opulation is density-dependent. When population size exceeds the carrying capacity of its given resources base, feedback loops active checks that prevent further growth or even bring about a reduction in numbers.[10]

Malthus' conclusion was that in order to avoid conflicts over the means of production, people should voluntarily limit the number of their offspring. This theory was entitled "the Malthusian Population Trap," or "the Low Level Equilibrium Population Trap."[11] Immediately following the publication of the first version of *An Essay on the Principle of Population*, Malthus was harshly criticized by many. Eventually, the support for Malthus' theory came from an unexpected direction: from feminists and other organizations promoting the use of contraceptives. Thus, ironically, "the father" of modern family planning programs was a reverend who personally rejected the use of contraceptives from a religious point of view.

Since the 1960s, but more so since the early 1970s, when worldwide natural increase rates peaked at more than 2% annually, the "neo-Malthusians" warned of global catastrophe if the current population growth rates would not radically decrease. They pointed to the starvation epidemics and the overall poor socioeconomic conditions in sub-Saharan Africa as a direct consequence of the "Malthusian Population Trap." They advocated, in contrast to Malthus himself, the use of modern contraceptives, including free abortions in public hospitals, in order to bring about a rapid fertility decline.[12] Their basic argument was and still is that rapid population growth has a detrimental effect on environmental conditions, thereby "echoing Malthus' original concerns."[13] Thus, while until the 1960s the debate on the validity of Malthus' theory concentrated on the issue of the ability to produce sufficient food, since then, the debate has focused on the environmental and ecological consequences of the rapid population growth.

In contrast to Malthus' pessimistic attitude regarding the carrying-capacity limit of the planet was that of the French mathematician and philosopher, Marie Jean Antoine Nicolas Caritat, the Marquis de Condorcet (1743–1794). In a book entitled, *Esquisse d'un Tableau Historique des Progrès de l'Esprit Humain* [*Sketch for a Historical Picture of the Progress of the Human Mind*], published in 1795, Condorcet argued that modern technologies and new agricultural production methods would increase the level of food production. At the same time, educational reforms would bring education to the lower strata. Thus, fertility decline would ensue and the overpopulation problem would be solved naturally without the use of coercive means by the authorities.[14]

The modern criticism of Malthus' theory is that he disregarded the most important dimension of the Industrial Revolution – the huge technological progress that led to a steady increase in food availability. Overall, although the world's population increased fourfold during the twentieth century, the world's GDP increased 20 to 40 times during the corresponding period, leading to a sharp rise in living standards, even in the least developed sub-Saharan African countries.[15] During the second half of the twentieth century, the world economy performed better than at any time in human history with an annual GDP growth rate of 3.8% during the 1950–1998 period.[16] Thus, the highest economic growth rates occurred simultaneously with the highest population growth rates. Is there any connection between them? Did the rapid population growth serve as a catalyst for accelerated economic development?

In retrospect, it seems that the answer to this question is negative. This is because the economic development was much faster, particularly during the second half of the twentieth century, in the countries where the natural increase rates were quite low. As to the vast majority of the developing countries, although their socioeconomic situation at the end of the twentieth century was much better than in the mid-century, their economic growth rates were substantially lower than that of the developed countries. In general, during the past generation, across the world, the higher the natural increase rate, the lower the economic growth rate. Thus, it seems that there is a strong correlation between economic development and population growth, but this correlation is negative. It appears that the case of the non-oil Arab countries best illustrates this argument.

In any case, the dispute over the socioeconomic consequences of rapid population growth is still going on. As Wisensale and Khodair described it: "In many respects the echoes of Malthus' pessimism and Condorcet's optimism are heard clearly today as the great demographic debate of the twentieth century moves into the twenty-first."[17] However, many people, and not only those from the religious establishments, are not convinced that rapid population growth is by itself at the core of the poverty of the developing countries. Rather, they point to many other factors, mainly, the favorable conditions accorded to the developed countries in international trade as the core of poverty in the developing countries – a modern variant of the "Dependency Theory."[18]

In addition, the Marxist approach traditionally opposed the concept that the core of poverty in developing countries is the rapid population growth. The basic argument of the neo-Marxist economists during the 1960s and 1970s was that in many rural areas, mainly in sub-Saharan Africa, much arable land was left uncultivated due a labor shortage. Others adhered to the traditional argument that rapid population growth would promote technological developments and cost-saving production methods.[19] Some of those dealing with Middle Eastern economic development, although small in number, have argued along with the neo-Marxist approach, that the core of the Middle Eastern poverty is not the rapid population growth.[20] They point to the fact that although there was a seven-fold increase in Egypt's population during the twentieth century, the living standard of the Egyptian population considerably improved during this time, as manifested by the sharp rise in life expectancy, the marked reduction in infant and child mortality rates, the improvements in educational level, and above all, the substantial growth of per capita income.[21]

Thus, the debate about the socioeconomic consequences of rapid population growth is basically a "chicken and egg" question. Are the poor conditions of the sub-Saharan African countries, as well as other less developed countries, including the non-oil Arab countries, mainly the result of their high natural increase rates, or are the high natural increase rates only a natural outcome of their underdevelopment?

In recent years, however, it is increasingly clear that the answer to this debate is that the rapid population growth is one of, if not the most, important factor accounting for underdevelopment. At least in the case of the non-oil Arab countries, no one has succeeded in proving that rapid population growth has any economic advantage in and of itself. Moreover, in many countries with small populations, such as Norway and Sweden (4.5 million and 8.9 million, respectively, in 2000), the technological improvements since the mid-twentieth century were very impressive without the need for a large indigenous population, simply because the "market" for local products expanded from a local scale to an international one. A close examination on the composition of the more advanced economies reveals that at least 70% of their GDP is comprised of exports and imports.[22] Hence, removing barriers from international trade as part of the ongoing globalization process resulted in minimizing the significance of the size of the local population.

Overall, at the beginning of the twenty-first century, only religious clerics still support rapid population growth. This, it should be noted, is neither from socioeconomic nor from political-security viewpoints, but rather from cultural-religious points of view. Hence, Malthus "won the battle" although his basic assumption regarding the population/food balance proved to be mistaken.

2 The Various "Population Policy" Definitions

> Rulers of any political unit have a stake in the size and composition of the population over which they have authority, hence an incentive to try to influence demographic change in a desired direction.
>
> Paul Demeny, 2003[23]

What is the meaning of "population policy"? When can it be said that a government is implementing any kind of population policy and, even more importantly, how can it be clarified as to which policy is being implemented in cases when the policy is hidden due to the religious-cultural-political sensitive nature of the whole demographic issue? The US National Academy of Sciences defined the term "population policy" as "policies related to change in the quality and quantity of the population and its geographical distribution . . . "[24] According to the official definition of the UN Population Division, population policy includes "all policies and programs – including social and economic policies – concerned with the major population variables: fertility, mortality, internal migration and geographical distribution of population, and international migration."[25] Allan and Anne Findlay defined "population policy" as "those policies that seek in a deliberate way to change the size, growth, composition or distribution of a country's population."[26] From these and many other definitions, it appears that population policy, both pro- and anti-natalist alike, is a part of the broader socioeconomic policies of any given government.

In general, there are two components of "natalist policy." The first is that of responsive policy, which attempts to counter the negative consequences of rapid population growth, mainly in the areas of food supply, housing, employment opportunities, and basic public services, such as healthcare, education, transportation, sanitation, water and electricity. The second component is that of influencing policy, which aims to influence the fertility behavior itself, either through direct measures (such as family planning policy, child allowances, minimum age at first marriage, and a ban on polygamy), or through indirect measures (mainly by encouraging women's education and their employment outside the household, or by preventing their employment as a pro-natalist measure).[27]

It should be emphasized, however, that almost any government action has an influence of some kind, whether direct or indirect, on at least one of the demographic variables of any given population. For example, the provision of full government subsidies for education, particularly for women, has an immense influence on fertility patterns, as was illustrated in Chapter 2. However, during the past few decades, at least elementary and secondary education is universally provided almost free of charge, even in countries that are trying to promote higher fertility rates, such as the GCC oil countries, Israel, France, Belgium, Germany and Sweden. On the other hand, the provision of free or heavily subsidized healthcare services leads to a marked decline in infant and child mortality rates – a prominent factor contributing to fertility decline. Again, these services are highly subsidized in both anti- and pro-natalist countries.

As discussed in Chapter 2, the fertility rates in the Western countries have declined throughout the past two centuries without any direct governmental involvement. This begs the question as to why the developing countries, including the overpopulated Arab countries, would implement expensive direct anti-natalist measures if declining fertility occurs naturally in response to socioeconomic changes? Rather than concentrate on expensive direct anti-natalist measures, would it not be better to invest their limited resources in promoting the socioeconomic variables that eventually would lead to fertility decline? In other words, is it not more efficient to invest in education than in subsidizing contraceptives?

The answer to this crucial question is that the aim of direct anti-natalist policy is to speed up the process of fertility decline when the basic socioeconomic conditions, by themselves, are not in favor of lowering fertility. In other words, the aim of a family planning program is to overcome the "natural" barriers for fertility decline.[28] It is obvious, however, that if per capita income is high, infant and child mortality rates are low, female educational level and their labor force participation rates are high and social security for the elderly population is sufficient, fertility rates will be low, even in cases of the implementation of pro-natalist policies. This is best illustrated in the EU-15 countries during the past generation.

A pro-natalist policy can be direct, indirect, or a combination of both. Since any country which subsidizes public services, mainly, education and healthcare, not to mention basic foodstuffs and energy products, could be considered as "pro-natalist," we only define a country with a pro-natalist policy as one which implements direct measures aiming to increase or maintain high fertility rates, primarily through child allowances, marriage allowances and entitlement for housing according to the number of children.

3 An Historical Examination of the Western Natalist Perception until the Mid-Twentieth Century

Despite the rapid population growth in all the developed countries during the second half of the nineteenth century and the early twentieth century, none of them adopted an anti-natalist policy. The basic assumption of the Western European developed countries at that time was that they needed as large a labor force as possible in light of both the rapid industrial development plus the need for staff in their colonies around the world. This, in addition to the option of emigration to "the new world" in North America (see Chapter 2), eliminated the need to curb the rapid population growth.

This period of relatively rapid population growth, however, ended following World War I, when the developed countries entered into the third phase of the demographic transition. The Great Depression, which began in the late 1920s, "refueled" the already prevalent process of fertility decline (see Chapter 2). Consequently, many demographers realized that the fertility rates in some of the Western European countries had declined to such a low level that in the longer-term their natural increase rates would become negative, as the CDRs would exceed the CBRs.[29] As a reaction to this process, some of these countries adopted a pro-natalist approach. In the case of France, for example, in the early twentieth century, several laws were introduced in order to protect working mothers.[30]

All the dictatorships of the 1930s and the first half of the 1940s, of both right and left, without exception, adopted explicit pro-nataist policies due to their fear of loss of military manpower and national weakness as a result of the low fertility rates.[31] Under the Nazi regime, the fertility of the "superior" population in Germany and Austria was encouraged and the title of "Hero Mother" was conferred on fertile women.[32] Italy under the Dictatorship of Benito Mussolini also carried out a pro-natalist policy in an attempt to create an Italian "superior race" which included the taxation of bachelors and made abortion a crime.[33] Generally speaking, while in the European democratic countries the pro-natalist policy was involved with family welfare, in the dictatorships it was mainly a reaction to potential manpower for military and national strength.

The attitude of the European countries toward accelerating the population growth rates in their colonies was also positive as the implication of a larger population is higher consumption of imported goods and services.

Following World Word II, the attitude of the developed countries toward the rapid population growth in the developing countries radically changed in favor of fertility decline. This change was mainly due to two factors: First, the vast majority of them reached independence, freed from the rule of the Western European colonialist countries. The second factor was the acceleration of the natural increase rates to levels that never existed in any given society, in some cases even higher than 2.5% annually. Many of the developed countries leaders became worried from the socioeconomic and the political consequences of this new process not only in the developing countries themselves, but in the international arena as well.

The only viable solution that emerged in the developed countries for "the third world demographic problem" was to reduce the fertility rates through the adoption of family planning programs. These programs were initially based on the assumption that although "modernization" is indeed "the best contraceptive," the developing countries could not afford to wait until fertility rates would naturally decline in response to socioeconomic development. Hence, the process of fertility decline should be accelerated through "an outside intervention" in the form of a family planning programs.[34]

In order to promote family planning activities in developing countries, the International Planned Parenthood Federation (IPPF) was established in 1952 as an NGO with funding from private foundations as well as from some Western governments. The first members of the organization came from the US, the Netherlands, Sweden, West Germany, Singapore, and Hong Kong.[35] The aims of the IPPF were to increase awareness about the issue of family planning, to improve family education, and to support family planning services in developing countries. To achieve these goals, the IPPF encouraged the establishment of a parallel national association in each developing county that would pioneer family planning activities and bring about a favorable climate in public opinion toward the importance of fertility decline. The IPPF's basic assumptions were that knowledge of modern contraceptives is a basic human right and that a balance between worldwide population and natural resources is a preliminary condition for achieving economic prosperity, political stability and peace.[36]

4 An Historical Examination of the Natalist Policies of the Arab Countries

Since the mid-twentieth century, at the time that many of the Arab countries achieved independence, and until the present, the natalist approach of the Arab countries has changed in line with three variables: The first and the most important has been their economic growth rate; the second has been the change in both the internal and the intra-Arab politics; and the third has been the shift in the worldwide natalist perception. In the following sections, the natalist approach of the Arab countries, both the oil-based and the non-oil alike, will be examined according to the developments and changes in the above-mentioned three variables.

4.1 The 1950 and Early 1960s: "Population Growth is not the Core of Poverty"

At the beginning of the process of accelerated natural increase rates in the 1950s and early 1960s, the leaders of many developing countries perceived the concept that "population growth is not the core of poverty," in line with the traditional attitude toward population growth. Therefore, they made no attempts to limit it. The attempts made by Western leaders to convince them of the need to curb population growth were unsuccessful because the majority of the developing countries' regimes, as well as common public opinion, considered these Western attempts as an "imperialist conspiracy" and a variant of "neo-colonialism."[37] It should be taken into account, however, that many developing countries had received independence from the "West" only a decade earlier, following World War II, and that in many cases, this independence was achieved only after a long armed struggle. In addition, the Dependency Theory was widely accepted in the developing countries. Accordingly, it was widely believed by many that the end of Western colonialism, combined with the adoption of socialist-étatist socioeconomic policies, would bring about rapid socioeconomic development.

Furthermore, many in the developing countries believed that the core reason that the Western attempts to advocate fertility decline in the developing countries was not because of their care for the future socioeconomic prosperities of these newly independent countries, but rather because of their fear of changing the balance of power in the international political arena in favor of the developing countries through their much larger population.

Above all, at the very same time that the Western post-colonial countries were trying to advocate fertility decline in their former colonies, they were advocating higher fertility in their own countries. India was an exception as it adopted a national family planning policy as early as 1951.[38]

In line with the common approach among developing countries' during the 1950s and early 1960s, many Arab leaders also viewed the new phenomenon of rapid population growth as a blessing. From their perspective, the Malthusian Population Trap was not relevant.[39] Within the framework of the pro-natalist approach, in the former North African French colonies, the 1920 French law forbidding abortions and the promotion and use of contraceptives was still in force.[40]

Although the common approach was pro-natalist among the Arab countries at that time, in practice only Syria carried out specific pro-natalist measures. In 1949, the propaganda, distribution and the use of contraceptives was forbidden. Two additional regulations were ratified by the Syrian authorities in 1952: The first determined that families with more than three children would be granted discounts on pubic transportation; and the second was that these families would enjoy a special government bonus. Another decree in 1952 entitled state employees to a government subsidy in addition to their salary according to their number of children. Originally, this subsidy was meant to subsidize education costs for families with many children, but it soon became an instrument for encouraging higher fertility among state employees.[41] In 1956, Youssef Helbaoui, the head of economic analysis in Syria's Planning Department, noted that: "Malthus could not find any followers among us."[42]

It seems that the major reasons behind Syria's pro-natalist policy during that period were political and economic alike. From a political point of view, the feeling of the Syrian leadership was that the Syrian population was too small in comparison to the country's military needs. Economically, the massive agricultural development in the northern region (*al-Jazira*) needed a large workforce. By 1950, Syria's population totaled less than 3.3 million. Subtracting the under-15 population and the above-60 population left Syria with a potential workforce of no more than 750,000, taking into consideration the low female labor force participation rates.

In the case of Egypt, there were some who warned that the rapid population growth would lead to a Malthusian Population Trap. Following publication of the 1917 census results, Dr. Levi, the Chief of the Egyptian Department of Statistics, wrote that: "Given the state of its economic organization, the density of the population has reached a level that is only surpassed perhaps by China and certain parts of India."[43]

However, the most famous document published during the Monarch period that warned against the economic consequences of Egypt's rapid population growth was Wendell Cleland, *The Population Problem in Egypt*.[44] Despite these warnings, the Monarchy regime not only did not promote fertility decline, but actually adopted a pro-natalist approach. Muhammad al-Razaq, a senior official in the Ministry of Health, claimed in 1962 that under the Monarchy regime, he delivered a memo to the Minister of Health on the urgent need to narrow the fertility rates. In response, the Minister rebuked him, stating that: "the King [Faruq] wants to be a king of 100 million people regardless of whether they are naked or starving."[45] In contrast to Syria, however, the Egyptian authorities did not carry out specific pro-natalist measures, though contraceptives were not prohibited for distribution and use. In addition, the economic interests of the Egyptian industrialists and big landlords, who ruled not only the economy but politics as well, lay in the continued supply of cheap labor.[46]

The first among the Arab leaders to become aware of the devastating long-term results of rapid population growth was 'Abd al-Nasser. In early 1953, a short time after the "Free Officers" Revolution (July 23, 1952), a parliamentary committee for population affairs was established – a move that reflected official recognition of the existence of a demographic problem in Egypt.[47] At that time, the new regime began to operate in the area of demography in two directions: One was to encourage emigration of *fellahin* (peasants) from Egypt to other Arab countries;[48] and the second was to establish twenty experimental family planning clinics.[49] Additionally, a voluntary family planning association, the Egyptian Association for Population Studies, was established in 1953.[50] Muhammad Nagib, Egypt's first ruler following "the July Revolution," was also worried about Egypt's demographic pressure, arguing in 1955 that Egypt should act in two major areas: enlarging the cultivated area and narrowing the high fertility rates.[51]

Toward the end of the 1950s, however, 'Abd al-Nasser changed his basic demographic concept and started to advocate the approach that rapid economic development could raise the low living standard without the need for direct governmental family planning activities. This approach was evident in an interview he gave to the *Christian Science Monitor* in October 1959: "Instead of teaching people how to exercise birth control, we would do better to teach them how to increase their land production. . . . "[52]

'Abd al-Nasser himself never explained the reasons for the change in his demographic approach. Issawi claimed that this change was caused by an accelerating sense of nationalism in Egypt following the Suez War and the concept that a large population would provide a source of military strength for the continuing military conflict with Israel.[53] Abdel-Aziz Sayed argued that Egypt's unification with Syria in February 1958 raised strong feelings for an overall Arab unity, which included sharing the oil resources and redistributing the whole Arab population throughout the united Arab country that would be established.[54] Saad Eddin Ibrahim claimed that: "Some observers at the time suspected that Nasser, himself a father of five children, felt that a bigger population gave Egypt much greater weight in Arab, Middle Eastern, and international affairs."[55]

In addition to the above-mentioned factors, one might speculate that another purely political factor accounting for 'Abd al-Nasser's changing demographic concept during the late 1950s, was the struggle with Iraq for seniority in the Arab world.[56] Official adoption of a family planning program, aiming to reduce Egypt's fertility rates, could serve the Iraqi propaganda against 'Abd al-Nasser, accusing him, personally, of acting against the "Arab cause" and serving the "Western neo-colonialism" as well as the Zionist interests. Hence, 'Abd al-Nasser could not adopt an official anti-natalist policy, even if he was personally convinced of the need to reduce Egypt's fertility rates.

Although the twenty family planning clinics that were established in 1958 continued to operate, it was on an experimental basis only.[57] The overall approach of the Nasserite regime during the first decade of the Revolution was to leave the demographic issue to the public itself without any direct governmental involvement. Thus, we can conclude by saying that despite the awareness of the Nasserite regime of the devastating results of the rapid population growth, it preferred not to adopt a national family planning program and instead took "the economic approach," which, of course, did not arouse any opposition. From a short-term political viewpoint, this was the "easy way," but certainly not the best way, in light of Egypt's accelerating demographic pressures.

Moreover, 'Abd al-Nasser chose not to use his immense popularity following the Suez War to promote fertility decline. As part of his populist style of leadership,[58] 'Abd al-Nasser continued to operate within the broadest consensus possible, including in the demographic arena. In the words of Ajami: "Under Nasser . . . the state tried to be many things to many groups."[59] From 'Abd al-Nasser's point of view, implementing a declared family planning program was an admission that Egypt under his leadership could not achieve rapid economic development without marked fertility decline. This admission was, of course, totally opposed to his overall populist leadership nature.

In the other Arab countries, the issue of population pressure or the need for direct governmental family planning activities in order to curb the high fertility rates did not arise at all simply because, with the exception of Egypt, the population of the other Arab countries during the 1950s and early 1960s was quite low (see Table 2.3).

4.2 The Changing Approach in the mid-1960s: "Rapid Population Growth is the Core of Underdevelopment"

The results of the population censuses that were conducted in many developing countries in the late 1950s and early 1960s, including in many Arab countries, showed that the natural increase rates were actually higher than previously assumed. At the same time, many developing countries' leaders became increasingly aware of the negative correlation between economic development and population growth. In addition, the adoption of socialist-étatist policy, including a wide variety of subsidies, led to a steady increase in governmental spending in line with the population growth rate.

Thus, during the 1960s, some developing countries adopted a national family planning program in order to achieve two goals: first, a marked fertility decline; and second, a more balanced age pyramid in order to increase economic activity rates – the most important catalyst to overcome the "low income trap." The change in the demographic perception first began in Asia, with South Korea being the first to adopt a national family planning program as early as 1961, followed by Singapore in 1965, Indonesia and Taiwan in 1968, and Thailand and the Philippines in 1970.[60] It later moved to some South American countries as well as some, albeit very few, Arab countries (see below).

Following the election of John F. Kennedy as US President in 1961, the US began to be involved in worldwide demographic issues and became the largest donor to

UNFPA.[61] By channeling the funds through the UN and not directly to the countries themselves, the US administration was trying to avoid charges of "neo-imperialism," "racism," and "genocide," for which Western countries, particularly the US, were often accused.[62] In 1965, the USAID started to support demographic research and the implementation of family planning programs in some developing countries.[63]

In the early 1960s, the Catholic Church was also forced to change its traditional negative attitude toward contraceptives use due to two factors: The first was the rampant poverty in Latin America; and the second was the innovation of the birth control pill, which, from the beginning, was a cheap and easily used contraceptive method. Thus, in 1962, the Vatican Council decreed that "couples are autonomous in determining the number of their offspring."[64]

In the early 1960s, the traditional pro-natalist approach among some of the Arab countries began to change as well. The publication of the results of the censuses that were carried out in the late 1950s and early 1960s highlighted the trend of accelerating natural increase rates. The initiative for adopting family planning programs in the Arab countries, it should be emphasized, came from the political elite and not from "grassroots sources." In other words, it was not a natural reaction of the population to long-term socioeconomic changes, but purely a leadership initiative. Based on the results of a comparative study on the decision-making processes among the political elite on the issue of family planning in 17 countries, including Egypt, Thomas and Grindle reached the conclusion that: "Rarely, in fact, does population policy become an agenda item through social mobilization and pressure . . . "[65]

In the case of Egypt, this was clearly illustrated by the fact that women's organizations and physicians had been trying to promote family planning since the early 1930s but without much success. Although the family planning associations established in the Arab countries were formally NGOs, in practice they were governmental initiatives and enjoyed governmental financial support. The reason for this was the weakness of the "civil society" in the Arab countries – a direct consequence of their undemocratic political system.

Among the Arab leaders, the first to go beyond paying lip service on the subject of family planning was Tunisia's President, Habib Bourguiba. He realized that in order to substantially reduce fertility rates, direct anti-natalist measures would have to be taken.[66] Indeed, in 1961, Tunisia was the first among the former French North African colonies to repeal the 1920 French law forbidding abortions and the use of contraceptives.[67] In March 12, 1962, Bourguiba stated:

> With our rapidly growing population, the rising generations are exerting pressure on us. If we are not careful now, in ten to twenty years' time, there will be a marked disproportion between the national income and the number of people we have to feed. A race against the clock is going on between our economic development and the demographic increase. Unless we take, as of today, the necessary measures, the country in a few decades will experience convulsions.[68]

In June 1964, Tunisia officially adopted a national family planning program. The direct measures of the plan included the provision of family planning information and services within the existing network of the mother-and-child healthcare clinics, as well as sterilization procedures in public clinics and hospitals.[69] In contrast to 'Abd al-Nasser's concern about Egypt's rapid population growth, which was naturally due to Egypt's vast population, Bourguiba's anti-natalist perception already in the early

1960s is quite surprising, given the small size of Tunisia's population at that time – only 4.533 million in 1966.[70] Hence, despite Tunisia's small population, Bourguiba realized the true meaning of the long-term implications of the demographic momentum.

The Egyptian natalist concept changed in the early 1960s as well. On May 21, 1962, 'Abd al-Nasser presented the National Charter [*al-Mithaq al-Watani*] in which he stated that the population growth "constitutes the most dangerous obstacle that faces the Egyptian people in their drive toward raising the standard of production . . . Attempts at family planning deserve the most sincere efforts . . . "[71] It is widely accepted in the academic literature that the National Charter was "a turning point" in Egypt's natalist policy. This approach, however, should be re-examined. If the National Charter was indeed "a turning point," why, then, did it take three years, until mid-1965, for the Nasserite regime to actually start to implement a national family planning program? If the demographic pressure was so great and constituted "the most dangerous obstacle to further economic development," as 'Abd al-Nasser declared in the National Charter, then one would have expected the immediate implementation of an intensive anti-natalist policy.

It seems that one major factor accounting for the three year delay in carrying out the family planning program was the rapid economic growth achieved in the 1960–1963 period. This progress was reflected in the vast number of new employment opportunities created in Egypt: the construction of the Aswan High Dam; the establishment of heavy industries in Hilwan; and the rapid expansion of public services, primarily healthcare and education. These developments contributed to 'Abd al-Nasser's feelings that, at least for the moment, he could avoid implementing direct anti-natalist measures. To this "economic factor" one should also add a purely political one: the collapse of the union with Syria in September 1961, which was the first political defeat for 'Abd al-Nasser since he took power.[72] To a large extent, the collapse of the union cracked 'Abd al-Nasser's prestige among the masses. Thus, it is reasonable to believe that he preferred to avoid taking any controversial steps such a short time after the collapse of the union. Consequently, the declaration of the importance of the demographic issue in the National Charter did not translate into immediate action. 'Abd al-Nasser, it should be noted, was not unique in this respect. Thomas and Grindle observed that: "Periods of several years passed in many cases between a governmental decision to do something about population growth and the introduction of substantive measures to accomplish this goal."[73]

In the mid-1960s, it appeared that the socioeconomic problems caused by the rapid population growth had intensified even further. At the same time, it was quite clear that the Second Five-Year Development Plan for the years 1966–1970 would not even get off the ground due to the inability of the Egyptian authorities to raise the necessary capital. Robinson and El-Zanaty claimed that Egypt's drop of the "economic solution" for the demographic problem was "something approaching desperation."[74] Thus, in 1965, after 13 years in power, the "Free Officers" regime eventually adopted a national family planning program.[75] The short-term aim of the program was to reduce the CBR from 41 per 1,000 in 1966 to 30 in 1978.[76]

In 1966, Morocco also adopted a national family planning program, as the Moroccan government had come to realize the longer run demographic momentum effects. The IBRD report that was presented to the Moroccan government in that year clearly indicted this problem: "It is not so much the present density of population as its rate of growth which is so worrying . . . [T]he rapid population growth of recent years has meant that the proportion of the population which is necessarily non-productive has been growing, which places an increasing burden on those who are productive."[77] Another concern of the IBRD report was that the population growth rate would soon be higher than the economic expansion.[78]

A similar observation also appeared in the Moroccan Second Five-Year Development Plan for the years 1968–1972 which indicated the necessity of paying attention to the "unfavorable demographic situation, not only because of the rate of increase, but also because it results in an age pyramid in which the dependent population constitutes a large proportion of the total population."[79] However, despite the clear recommendation of the IBRD report "to adopt policies to encourage family limitation,"[80] the 1968–1972 Five-Year Development Plan lacked any practical family planning measure.[81] The solution for the intensified demographic problem within the framework of the 1968–1972 Plan was "to encourage labor emigration" in order to both reduce employment pressure and draw the workers' remittances.[82] Within the framework of the next Moroccan Five-Year Development Plan, covering the 1973–1977 period, the natalist policy which was adopted was to "inform, educate and motivate the population to practice voluntary family planning."[83] In practical terms, this means that although the Moroccan regime was fully aware of the demographic problem, it still chose to avoid taking any concrete anti-natalist measure.

It could be summarized by observing that during the 1960s the governments of the most populated Arab countries became worried not about the nominal number of their citizens, but about the long-term implications of the demographic momentum, primarily in the areas of supplying employment opportunities for the rapidly growing workforce and the increasing financial burden of the various governmental subsidies. It should be taken into consideration that the wide public support of the Arab regimes at that time, mainly the military regimes, rested largely on their socialist policy. Thus, uncontrolled population growth jeopardized the "core" of their socioeconomic policies, as in the longer run it would produce an unbearable financial burden.

However, at that stage, among the leaders of the Arab countries that officially adopted anti-natalist policy, Bourguiba was the only one to take the political risk of strongly supporting the implementation of an anti-natalist policy. In the case of King Hassan II of Morocco, Lapham wrote that: "It is not surprising that not much happened in terms of a vigorous family planning program, especially since in the background Hassan II remained silent on the question of family planning . . . "[84] As such, it is not surprising that the fact that King Hassan II signed the UN Declaration in support of family planning (see below) was not even reported in the Moroccan press, while the High Commission on Population was convened only twice between 1965 and 1975.[85] This "silence," it should be noted, was despite the clear recommendation of the 1966 IBRD report of the crucial need of "enthusiastic support from the highest levels of leadership"[86] for the success of the family planning program.

Overall, several patterns were common to the national family planning programs implemented in Tunisia, Egypt and Morocco during the 1960s. The first was that they emphasized the "supply side" so as to fulfill the perceived "unmet demand" for modern contraceptives among young couples. It was widely assumed at that time that the newly invented birth control pill and intrauterine device (IUD) would serve as "magic bullets" to bring about fertility decline.[87] These contraceptives and related medical services were distributed mainly through the existing mother-and-child clinics, which were already well established in these countries, even in the remote rural areas. Another prominent reason to use the mother-and-child clinics for providing family planning services was to use the confidence relationship between the community and the clinics' staff. These clinics generally consisted of a physician and a nurse who provided information and supplied contraceptives.[88]

The second common pattern was to mobilize the *'ulama* to support family planning policies in order to overcome the religious opposition of the Muslim Brothers to any kind of birth control. The authorities of Tunisia and Egypt made use of the most prominent official *Mufti*s to publish numerous *fatwa*s in the mass media, emphasizing that the use of contraceptives is not contradictory to the Islamic *Shari'a* [*halal*]. It was quite clear that without strong support of the *'ulama*, the programs would not succeed.

The third common pattern was the establishment of family planning associations as voluntary organizations in order to achieve three main goals: to coordinate between all the bodies involved in the various aspects of family planning; to promote co-operation with the IPPF; and to "somewhat cut" the direct relationship between the authorities and the family planning activities.

Although these three Arab countries were among the first developing countries worldwide to officially adopt family planning programs, only in Tunisia did the issue of fertility decline actually receive top governmental priority. In the case of Egypt, the program was practically abandoned following the June 1967 War along with other socioeconomic issues. During his last three years in power (1967–1970), 'Abd al-Nasser concentrated mainly on the ongoing military conflict with Israel and even initiated the War of Attrition in early 1969, which only ended in August 1970, just prior to his death on September 28, 1970. Other major obstacles to the successful implementation of the Egyptian family planning program during the late 1960s were: limited financial resources; lack of experience and knowledge among the plan's leaders in organizing and running such a program; frequent changes in the leadership of the Family Planning Executive Board; lack of coordination between the various bodies involved in the program; lack of medical staff training; and shortages of contraceptives.[89]

In the other Arab countries at that time, not only was family planning rejected, but in some of them active pro-natalist attitudes emerged. In the Algerian case, during the 1969–1983 period, the official policy was totally opposed to any kind of family planning, as it was perceived as a "false solution" for socioeconomic problems and a kind of "neo-colonialism."[90] In his Independence Day speech of 1972, Algeria's President, Houari Boumédiènne said that the country's population "is too small" in comparison to its large territory and natural resources and that increasing the size of the population "is a long-term investment."[91] Courbage claims that Boumédiènne's pro-natalist approach at that time was a result of the fact that: "It was commonly held that the power and glory of the Nation-State depended on the sheer weight of numbers, and President Boumédiènne set himself to forging a new African dragon which could feed 50 million people."[92]

Within this demographic concept, the Algerian authorities decided to discontinue the labor migration agreement with France, to encourage its expatriates to return to Algeria and denounced emigration as a form of post-colonial dependence.[93] Boumédiènne, as many other developing countries' leaders at that time, treated the high fertility rates as a reflection of underdevelopment rather than it cause. In 1974, Boumédiènne said in the UN General Assembly that: Algeria "refused [family planning] . . . as an alternative to development."[94] In a speech delivered on April 1978 at the Second Congress of the National Union of Algerian Peasants, Boumédiènne said that the two options to overcome the steady consumption increase as a result of the rapid population growth are "either by increased production or by importation."[95] As one can see, Boumédiènne did not even mention the possibility of limiting population growth rates in order to overcome the steady consumption increase.

In addition, as in many other developing countries, the Algerian opposition to family planning was also based on the fact that following independence, Algeria aligned itself with the Soviet Union and thus, naturally, rejected any Western idea, including in the family planning area.[96] Hence, it is not surprising that Algeria took the lead in the Bucharest Conference (see below) against the "imperialist conspiracy aimed at limiting the size of the Third World population."[97] In addition to the above-mentioned two "conventional" pro-natalist factors, which were not unique to Algeria alone, specifically in the case of Algeria, the pro-natalist approach was also driven by the feeling that rapid population growth is desirable in order to compensate for the numerous losses incurred during the War of Independence against France (1954–1962). It should be noted, however, that the crucial factor that enabled Algeria to maintain such a pro-natalist approach was the dramatic increase of its oil revenues following the "oil boom." In this respect, Algerian natalist policy should also be examined within the broader framework of the natalist concept of the Arab oil countries.

Overall, during the 1960s and early 1970s, the fertility rates in the Arab countries remained extremely high – with a CBR of around 40 per 1,000 (see Table 2.4) – even in the Arab countries that had officially adopted national family planning programs, with the exception of Egypt. However, in the case of Egypt, it is widely agreed that the fertility decline of the late 1960s and early 1970s was not brought about by the family planning program, but rather by the economic hardship endured in Egypt following the June 1967 War and the War of Attrition, combined with the fact that over one million Egyptians were in military service at that time.[98] This is actually also the official Egyptian explanation:

> The decline in birth rate in A.R.E. between 1966 and 1972 is due to the Arab–Israelian War and conscription of a large number of young adults for military services and consequently the postponement of their marriage. Beside, the economic problems that faced A.R.E. during this period and the commencement of the national family planning program have also contributed to the mentioned phenomenon.[99]

Hence, Egypt's fertility decline during the late 1960s and early 1970s was a result of 'Abd al-Nasser's failures in both the socioeconomic policy and the military conflicts and not as a result of a successful family planning policy. Thus, the increasing fertility rate following the October 1973 War, according to the official Egyptian explanation, was the result of "the accomplishment of many marriages which were previously postponed because the war."[100] This official stance should also be examined within the broader aspect of the de-Nasserization process which took place under Sadat's regime.

In 1966, twelve countries, including three Arab countries (Sweden, Columbia, Finland, Malaysia, Nepal, Singapore, South Korea, Yugoslavia, India, Egypt, Tunisia and Morocco) submitted a document to the UN calling for fertility reduction in the developing countries, giving its various devastating socioeconomic consequences. This document constitutes "a cornerstone" in the changing demographic approach of the major international organizations. On December 17, 1966, the UN General Assembly adopted resolution 2211, calling on the UN Secretary-General to intensify population programs in developing countries, to support demographic research, and to

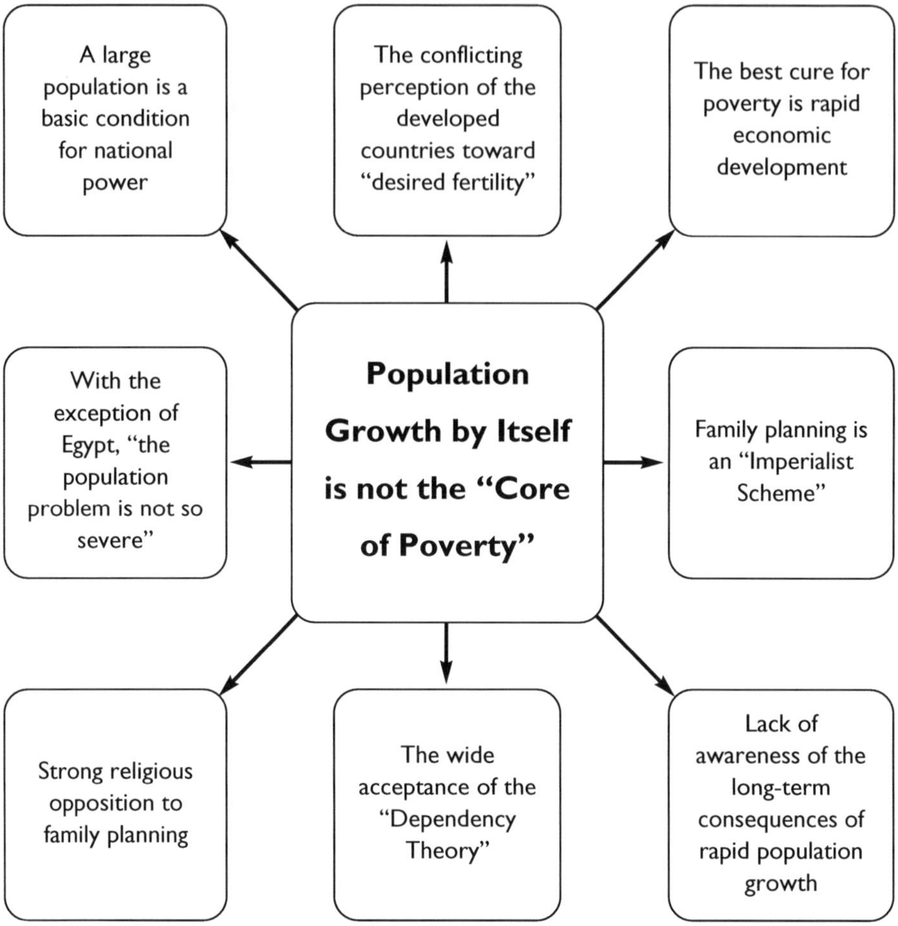

Chart 5.1 The Natalist Perception of the non-Oil Arab Countries until the early 1970s

disseminate demographic knowledge worldwide.[101] As a result, in 1967, UNFPA was established with the aims of assisting developing countries to implement family planning programs, expanding the overall activities of the UN on demographic issues and pursuing new anti-natalist programs for developing countries. Other UN agencies operating in the areas of labor, women, children and other related issues since the early 1970s include: the ILO, UNICEF, UNDP, FAO and WHO.

The population censuses that were conducted in many Arab countries during the late 1960s and early 1970s pointed to substantial increases in the natural increase rates. The first in many cases to become aware of the long-term implications of the continuing high natural increase rates were the professionals in the governmental branches dealing with demographic and related issues. Thus, for example, in a report of the Syrian CBS from 1973, it was written that:

> It seems that high population growth rates have adversely affected the efforts exerted for securing [a] better life for all members of the population. Despite the high economic development rates which were achieved during the last decade, such rates are still not sufficient to

> meet basic population needs . . . The high percentages of dependent children have led to increased consumer expenditure and a decreased volume of savings . . . [102]

Consequently, in the early 1970s, prior to the "oil boom," the Syrian traditional pro-natalist approach began to change. Although the Syrian population at that time was still quite small in number, amounting to 6.3 million in 1970, the Syrian authorities became aware of the long-term implications of the high natural increase rates, even though they did not implement any specific anti-natalist measures at that stage.

In the early 1970s, also the Jordanian authorities became aware of the severe consequences of high natural increase rates. In 1972, the Department of Statistics initiated a conference of demographic experts with the intention of drawing up a comprehensive demographic policy for the Kingdom.[103] Several months later, in 1973, the National Population Commission (NPC) was established, with the aim of advising the authorities in the area of population policies.[104] However, as in the Syrian case, this awareness did not translate into specific anti-natalist measures in Jordon either. In the *2002–JPFHS* it was written that:

> Because of the sensitive nature of the topic, the NPC took no distinct actions or steps. The Ministry of Health, through its Maternal and Child Health Centers, provided optional and predominantly free family planning services as an unofficial and indirect intervention in the population policy.[105]

Thus, although the vast majority of the non-oil Arab countries' leaders became aware of the devastating consequences of the rapid population growth, they still chose not to transform the demographic issue into a top governmental priority. The main reason for this inaction was purely political: While the benefits of fertility decline are only in the long run, the political risk is in the short run. Practically, the anti-natalist policy was hidden and the promotion of contraceptive use was done through the family planning associations, which allegedly were voluntary organizations, while the ministries of health provided family planning services as part of the wider range of healthcare services that was provided to the population free of charge. The most crucial element that was lacking in all of these plans (with the exception of Tunisia) was a declared responsibility of the authorities to the demographic issue.

During the early 1970s, due to the acceleration of the devastating results of the high natural increase rates in the developing countries, the international awareness of the crucial need to curb the high fertility rates moved forward. In 1973, of 117 developing countries worldwide, 32 countries implemented a national family planning program.[106] The most important indication of this increasing international awareness was the initiation of the First World Population Conference in Bucharest, Romania, in August 1974. It is widely acknowledged that this conference constituted a turning point in the world's family planning history. It was the first world conference to deal with population policy itself, rather than with demographic research as a whole, as did the first two UN demographic conferences (Rome in 1954 and Belgrade in 1965).[107] Moreover, the Bucharest Conference was extensively covered by the international media. This increasing awareness gave political legitimacy to many developing countries' leaders to start implementing declared national family planning programs.

During the conference itself, however, a crucial "chicken and egg" debate arose between the US and many developing countries regarding the role of family planning programs within the broader socioeconomic development approach. While the US suggested that the developing countries should implement comprehensive national family planning programs as a major tool for overcoming their socioeconomic problems, most developing countries, including China and India, argued that the better way to solve their socio-demographic problems was through changing the "world economic order" by improving the developing countries' ability to export their services and goods to the developed countries, rather than through aggressive family planning programs.[108]

Thus, during the conference, many developing countries' delegations argued that "instead of being a leading cause of underdevelopment, rapid population growth itself is a function of lack of development and that until couples experience the benefits of development, they will not be motivated to have smaller families."[109] Hence, the conference's slogan was that "development is the best contraceptive."[110] This new demographic perception was driven not only by new demographic knowledge, but rather by a clear political factor: the strive of many developing countries to change the international political and economic balance in favor of the developing countries by any means, including the demographic one. For example, in his statement to the 1984 Second World Population Conference, held in Mexico City (see below), Fidel Castro said:

> Uncontrolled population growth is not the result of biological factors; it is, above all, the result of the socioeconomic and cultural conditions to which these peoples were subjected throughout centuries of oppression and exploitation.[111]

Karim Lamrani, the Moroccan Prime Minister, also pointed in his statement to the 1984 Second World Population Conference to the worldwide population/resources imbalance, stating that:

> The unequal and unfair relations among nations have led, and will always lead, to a lack of balance between population density and the concentration of wealth. This is the tragic reality of our contemporary world . . . Therefore we should keep searching for a new international order . . . [112]

At the local level, the insistence of many developing countries' leaders, including the non-oil Arab countries, on the "indirect approach" was a result of the immense sensitivity of the family planning issue from both political and religious-cultural viewpoints. Donaldson noted that: "Third world leaders worry first about staying alive and in command and then, as time allows, about development."[113]

4.3 "Awareness without Action": The "Oil Boom" Illusion

The most prominent event that shaped the fertility approach of the Arab countries during the second half of the twentieth century – both the oil-based and the non-oil countries alike – was the October 1973 "oil boom." In retrospect, the "oil boom," more than any other factor, was responsible for the indirect anti-natalist approach of the non-oil Arab countries during the "oil decade." As a result of the high economic growth rates during the "oil decade," they were provided with a "shelter," albeit a temporary one, and could put off dealing with this politically sensitive issue.

Thus, although the Syrian authorities had already become aware of the long-term devastating consequences of the rapid population growth in the early 1970s, the tremendous improvement in the country's economic and employment conditions following the onset of the "oil boom" stopped this awareness from being translated into explicit anti-natalist measures. Furthermore, the "oil boom" was used as an excuse for the *Ba'thi-'Alawi* regime to avoid taking any unpopular socioeconomic measures in order to keep its legitimacy among the Muslim majority population. This was crucial, as since the mid-1970s, the Syrian regime and the Muslim Brothers had clashed over the control of the country.[114] Implementing a national family planning policy could have been used by the Muslim Brothers as a propaganda tool. Consequently, in their public expressions, the Syrian authorities tried to build a picture in which the increasing population growth rates was due to socioeconomic progress that had caused a decline in death rates. This meant that the country's demographic situation was an achievement rather than a failure of the regime. For example, in one of the few Hafiz al-Asad's demographic expressions in his statement to the 1984 World Population Conference, he said that the "mortality rate declined sharply . . . due to socioeconomic development, improvement of both preventive and clinical health services, expansion in potable water and drainage services, and improvement of the environment."[115]

In an attempt to maintain a low profile on the demographic issue, following the "oil boom" the Syrian authorities adopted an indirect anti-natalist approach. Thus, the Syrian Family Planning Association was established in 1974, not as a governmental organization but as a voluntary one, although, as in other Arab countries, it was financially supported by the government. Another indirect indicator was that the Syrian official press began to publish reports, articles, and cartoons about the socioeconomic consequences of the rapid population growth at the family rather than at the national level, as was the case in Egypt (see below). The aim was to connect the problem of large families to the socioeconomic situation of the families themselves, rather than to the national level. Thus, for example, Cartoon 5.1, published in mid-1984, shows a very

Cartoon 5.1
Source: *al-Thawra*, July 26, 1984.

Cartoon 5.2
Source: *al-Thawra*, May 28, 1987.

poor family with a large number of children, illustrating "the difficulty of bringing bread to a large family."

Cartoon 5.2, published three years later, in mid-1987, presents a pregnant woman with many children "threatening" her poor husband with her pregnancy.

The campaign to increase birth intervals was made to appear that the family planning services is only one among many other public services provided by the government for the welfare of mothers and their children.[116] This kind of policy is well illustrated in the interview given by Wahida al-'Azma, the Head of the Syrian branch of the IPPF, to the official *Tishrin* newspaper in 1982 in which she said that the aim of the family planning program is "to enable the parents to determine the timing of bringing children and their number according to the family's economic situation."[117] The following picture, published in the *Tishrin*, also illustrates the Syrian indirect approach. The picture presents a woman in a public health clinic receiving contraceptives as part of an overall medical treatment. The emphasis in the picture is not the family planning services themselves as a means to reduce fertility, but rather on the medical treatment that the woman receives from the government, free of charge, of course. As one can see, there is not even one sign in the picture that connects the medical treatments the woman is receiving and the anti-natalist campaign.

Another indicator for the Syrian indirect anti-natalist policy was the tendency of the regime not to deal with the high fertility rates as an isolated problem, but rather within the broader framework of the "population policy," including labor emigration and urbanization. As such, the financial pro-natal regulations were not cancelled.[118] Overall, during the "oil decade," the decline in Syrian fertility level was marginal. In 1986, Syria's CBR was 42.4 per 1,000 and the TFR was 7.1 children per woman,[119] compared to 48 and 7.6, respectively, in 1970 (see Table 2.4).

As in Syria, Jordan adopted an indirect approach to fertility decline for very similar reasons: on the one hand, the high economic growth rates and the substantial alleviation of employment pressures due to massive labor emigration following the "oil boom," and on the other, the escalation of Islamic opposition. As Susser noted, the Hashemite regime "strove to deepen its Islamic legitimacy in light of the new reality in the region."[120] In order to avoid further confrontation with the Islamic opposition, the Hashemite regime chose to implement the following indirect anti-natalist measures: First, financial assistance was provided for NGO activities in the family planning area. Second, family planning services were offered through the maternal and child health clinics. These clinics, it should be noted, did not actively promote the use of contraceptives, but rather supplied them upon request. Lastly, the option of sterilization was given as a legal method.[121]

A Syrian woman receives service in a public family planning clinic
Source: *Tishrin*, May 30, 1982.

It should be emphasized, however, that in contrast to Syria, the Hashemite regime neither financed active pro-natalist measures, nor prohibited the use of contraceptives. Thus, the transition from "the non-interfering natalist policy" to an unofficial anti-natalist policy did not involve any legislative changes. However, as in Syria, the effect of the Jordanian indirect anti-natalist measures was minor at best. In the late 1980s, Jordan's fertility rate remained very high by any international comparison, with a CBR of 38.7 per 1,000 and a TFR of 6.4 children per woman in 1988.[122]

Sadat also preferred the indirect family planning approach. In 1973, a new family planning program was initiated by the Supreme Council for Population and Family Planning [*al-Majlis al-A'la lil-Sukan wa-Tanzim al-Usra*] for a period of ten years, with the aim of reducing the CBR from 34 per 1,000 in 1973 to 24 in 1982 through an increase in the contraceptive prevalence rate from 16% to 35%. The plan's long-term goal was that Egypt's population would not exceed more than 60 million by the year 2000. In order to implement the new plan, in June 1973 a Department of Population was established in the Ministry of Health. The new plan emphasized indirect measures for fertility decline, mainly in the areas of improving women's educational level and employment opportunities; increasing agricultural mechanization in order to diminish the need for child employment; and reducing infant and child mortality rates in order to increase parents' confidence in the survival chances of their offspring. Within the framework of the new plan, in 1974, population concepts were introduced into intermediate and secondary school textbooks.[123] This trend of integrating the family planning issue within the broader aspect of socioeconomic and human resources development was clearly evident in the next Egyptian family planning program of

1980, entitled "National Strategy Framework for Population, Human Resource Development and the Family Planning Program." The plan's long-term goal was to reduce the CBR to 20 per 1,000 by the year 2000.[124]

Sadat's adoption of the indirect family planning approach was motivated by both political and economic considerations. From the political point of view, Sadat preferred to take the indirect approach as part of the overall policy of rapprochement toward the Muslim Brothers.[125] From the economic point of view, Sadat was "dazzled" by the rapid economic growth during the "oil decade" and the alleviation of employment pressure due to the large-scale labor emigration. Hence, he chose "the easy way." As Saad Eddin Ibrahim noted, Sadat "hardly paid any attention to the [demographic] problem."[126] Lippman wrote that: "Sadat and his prime ministers hardly even gave lip service to birth control, despite all their speeches about the demands posed by the rising population. They did not hide their embarrassment at the dogged, outspoken support for family planning by the only prominent figure to make that commitment – Sadat's wife, Jihan."[127]

During Sadat's eleven years in power (October 1970-October 1981), Egypt's fertility rates not only failed to decline, but rather started to increase again in 1974 with the improvement in both the economic and the political–security situations following the October 1973 War, climbing to a CBR of 37.0 per 1,000 in 1981 at the end of Sadat's period,[128] compared to 35.1 per 1,000 in 1971.[129] Overall, during Sadat's rule, Egypt's population increased from 33.807 million in 1971[130] to 43.322 million in 1981,[131] representing an increase of 28.1% within only ten years – a net increase of 9.5 million people. However, even more critical than the population growth itself was the widening of the age pyramid. By 1982, the percentage of the under-15 population within Egypt's total population amounted to almost 51%, compared to less than 43% in 1960 (see Table 3.1).

The ascendancy of Mubarak to the presidency following the murder of Sadat did not lead to a change in Egypt's family planning policy. In fact, during the first four years of his presidency, the demographic issue was almost totally ignored.[132] As in the case of Sadat, Mubarak also preferred not to confront the Muslim Brothers on the family planning issue. In addition, the rapid economic growth continued during the early 1980s, with the real GDP growth rate reaching 7.9% by the 1982/83 fiscal year, meaning an increase of 5% in per capita terms. At the same time, the current account deficit narrowed from over \$2 billion in the 1981/82 fiscal year to around \$1 billion in the 1983/84 fiscal year.[133] Like his two predecessors, Mubark decided to "sacrifice" Egypt's long-term socioeconomic development so as to avoid posing a threat to his regime in the short-term. Consequently, during the first half of the 1980s, Egypt's fertility rate continued to increase, amounting to a TFR of 6.9 children per woman in 1984,[134] and a CBR of 39.8 per 1,000 in 1985[135] – a higher rate than in the early 1960s – prior to the adoption of the first family planning program.

In addition to the rapid economic expansion, the high grants given by the Arab oil countries to the poorer Arab countries served to strengthen the feelings of "Arab Unity" [*al-Wahda al-'Arabiyya*], or at least "Arab Solidarity" [*al-Tadamun al-'Arabi*]. Accordingly, it was widely assumed by the non-oil Arab countries that the Arab oil countries would provide them with substantial economic assistance and employ their surplus workforce. These feelings were supported by a reduction in the tension between the "revolutionary" regimes and the Arab oil monarchies following the death of 'Abd al-Nasser. Tabbarah even used the term "The United Arab States":

> The area of this country is 14 million square kilometers; it is the second largest country in the world in area, after the Soviet Union . . . The per capita GNP was $2,000 in 1985, which means that the United Arab States is a developing country, but one which occupies a relatively high rank among those countries, similar to Mexico, Portugal or the Republic of Korea . . . [136]

Thus, following the "oil boom" the issue of rapid population growth in the non-oil Arab countries was viewed as posing a challenge, but only in the longer run. As Yousif and Hammouda noted: "population growth and its ramifications were seen as long-term problems which were undeniably important, but neither pressing nor urgent. Population issues were of secondary importance."[137] A major factor for this neglect was related to the overall "employment illusion" that prevailed due to the massive intra-Arab labor migration. As put it the 2004 MENA employment report: "It is not surprising that under those conditions [of low unemployment], earlier predictions of rising labor supplies because of population dynamics elicited little concern on the part of policymakers in the region."[138]

In addition to the "oil boom" effects, there was also a widespread feeling in the overpopulated Arab countries that the demographic trends for the short run, namely, for the coming generation, were already set and that the ability to change them, even through an extensive national family planning program, was very limited. As Hilmi 'Abd al-Rahman, the advisor to the Egyptian Prime Minister, stated in 1975:

> The development of the population for the next 25 years has already been determined . . . Our population will double in the next 25 years with only a 20% possibility of variation . . . Therefore, for the next 20 or 25 years the problem in Egypt is mainly to meet the requirements of an increase in population.[139]

Moreover, the World Bank staff that evaluated Egypt's demographic policy in August 1978 was optimistic regarding Egypt's future demographic characteristics and the successful outcome of the indirect family planning policy being carried out at that time. The World Bank staff projected that by the year 2000 Egypt's population would number 59.374 million, while during the second half of the 1990s the CBR would average 23.3 per 1,000 and the TFR would average 2.9.[140]

Following the election of Ronald Reagan in January 1981, who opposed abortions and family planning from a religious point of view, the US demographic concept radically changed. Instead of implementing family planning policies, the developing countries were encouraged to adopt a liberal economic policy that would bring about economic prosperity and thereby also bring about fertility decline without direct governmental involvement.[141] In his statement to the 1984 Second World Population Conference, Reagan said:

> Recognizing the seriousness of environmental and economic problems and their relationship to social realities, the US places a priority upon technological advancement and economic expansion which hold out the hope of prosperity and stability for a rapidly changing world.[142]

Reagan rejected the accusation that the "world economic order" was the cause for the underdevelopment of the developing countries. He claimed that a free market economy is the sole solution for the developing countries' socioeconomic problems, including the demographic issue. Hence, Reagan's demographic approach was reminiscent of the 1974 Population Conference slogan that "development is the best contraceptive." Indeed, at the Conference itself, the US delegation presented their platform that "the relationship between population growth and economic development is not necessarily a negative one" and that "government control of economies . . . had caused population growth in developing countries to change from an 'asset' to a 'peril.'"[143]

It is quite clear, however, that all of the above-mentioned factors for not implementing direct anti-natalist measures were only "excuses," aiming to avoid direct confrontation with the Islamist opposition. In retrospect, it is quite hard to believe that Sadat, Mubarak, Hafiz al-Asad and King Husayn of Jordan truly believed that the high fertility rates in their countries could substantially decline without direct governmental involvement or that the demographic problem was not severe.

Among the non-oil Arab countries, Tunisia was the only exception because even during the "oil decade" it did not abandon its direct family planning policy. This direct policy was expressed in all of the Tunisian public expressions. In his statement to the 1984 Second World Population Conference, the Tunisian Prime Minister, Mohamed Mzali, said:

> Since 1956 . . . our country has adopted sweeping legislation and bold measures in the areas of family planning, sexual equality and the protection of children and young people . . . A further step was taken this year when President Bourguiba set up the Ministry for the Family and the Promotion of Women.[144]

In contrast to the other overpopulated Arab countries, the Tunisian authorities neither tried to blame the "West" for the high fertility rates – although Tunisia was only released from French control in 1956 – nor to present the rapid population growth as "a governmental achievement" as did the Syrian authorities, but presented the demographic situation "as it actually was," without hiding the problem. A major factor for the Tunisian direct anti-natalist policy during the "oil decade" as well, was the relatively low amount of workers' remittances combined with the minor financial aid from the Arab oil countries.[145]

In sharp contrast to the overpopulated Arab countries, the family planning activities in many non-Arab developing countries during the late 1970s and the early 1980s were substantially expanded. This phenomenon was attributable to two main factors. First, the socioeconomic problems resulting from the high natural increase rates were steadily worsening, including employment pressures, inadequate public services, housing problems in the major cities, and above all, relatively low GDP growth rates due to the sharp increase in oil prices. The second factor was that the socioeconomic improvement of the 1960s and 1970s did not bring about substantial fertility decline. Hence, it became quite clear that indeed "the best contraceptive is development," but only for the longer run. In the short run, direct anti-natalist measures had to be carried out in order to rapidly curb the high fertility rates.

Regarding the demographic perception of the developing countries during the early 1980s, Finkle and Crane wrote that "They no longer spoke of international population assistance as racist, genocidal, or imperialistic, or accused Western nations of advocating population control as a substitute for foreign aid."[146] Thus, the demographic slogan of the 1980s returned to that of the late 1960s, namely, "the best contraceptive is a contraceptive." The practical meaning of the renewed slogan was the promotion of direct family planning activities in many developing countries. In 1983, 76% of the developing populations worldwide were living in countries that had an official family planning program aimed at curbing the high fertility rates, and an

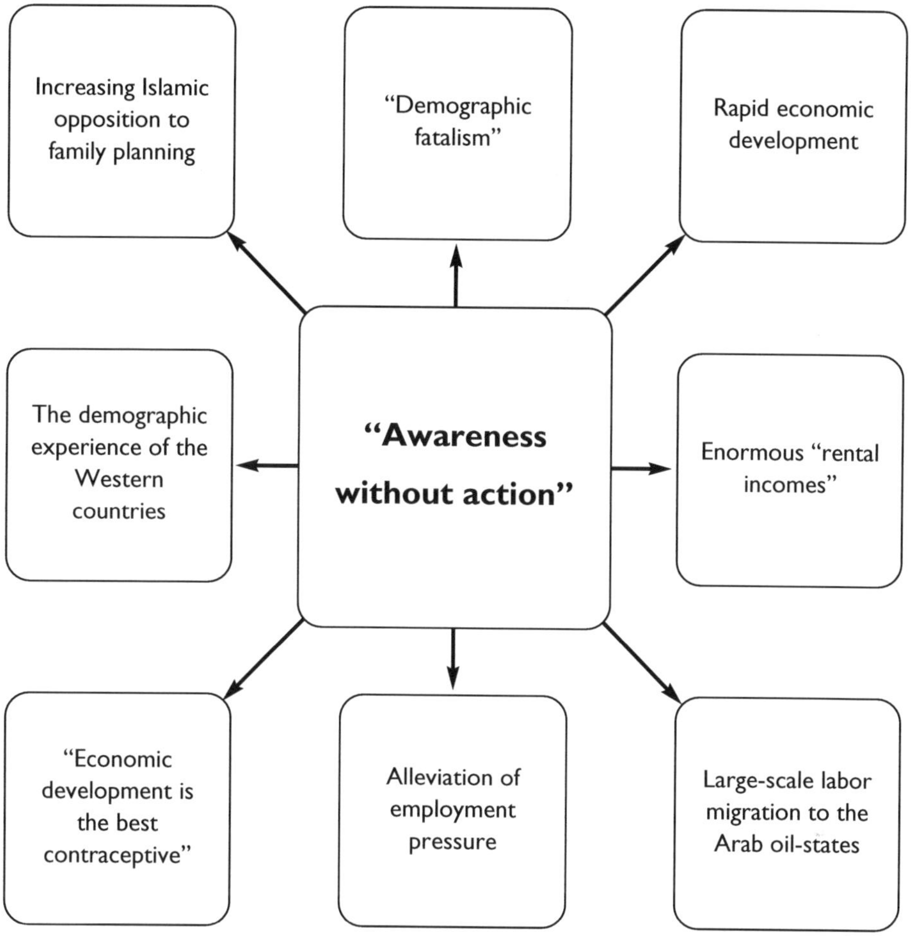

Chart 5.2 The Natalist Perception of the non-Oil Arab Countries during the "Oil Decade"

additional 17% were living in countries that supported family planning as a tool for healthcare and welfare improvement, but not as a direct anti-natalist tool.[147]

Without entering into the debate on the role of direct family planning activities in fertility decline (see below), one thing is indisputable: In many developing countries that adopted direct family planning programs, the fertility rates substantially declined. For example, by 1986, India's CBR was 29 per 1,000 compared to 42 in 1960. During the corresponding period, Indonesia's CBR declined from 44 to 29; in Brazil from 43 to 29; in the Philippines from 46 to 31; in Mexico from 54 to 32; and in South Korea from 43 to 23.[148] In contrast, in the overpopulated Arab countries, with the sole exception of Tunisia, the fertility rates had not declined during the 1970s and the first half of the 1980s, but rather had even increased or at least maintained their previous high levels. It can be said that from a purely demographic point of view, the "oil decade" was a "lost decade."

4.4 The Emergence of Pro-Natalism in the Arab Oil Countries

In the Arab oil countries, a new demographic situation emerged following the "oil boom." As was examined in Chapter 3, the short-term strategy adopted by these countries regarding the supply of labor was to import large numbers of temporary foreign workers, while the long-term goal was to supply the necessary workforce from local sources through a tremendous improvement in the educational and professional training systems, along with adopting pro-natalist policies. According to the Demographic Transition Theory, fertility rates would naturally decline without direct governmental involvement following a reduction in infant and child mortality rates, combined with a surge in economic development and women's educational level. Thus, the GCC pro-natalist policy was aimed at changing this natural demographic evolution and maintaining high fertility rates despite the tremendous socioeconomic development.

Overall, various direct pro-natalist measures were taken by the Gulf oil governments following the "oil boom" in order to maintain high fertility rates. The intensity of the measures varied from one country to another in line with the per capita oil revenues. The most intensive measures were taken by Kuwait and Qatar, the richest among the Gulf oil countries, and the least intensive measures were taken by Bahrain and Oman, the poorest among these countries. In retrospect, during the "oil decade," the GCC countries implemented the most extreme pro-natalist measures known worldwide during the second half of the twentieth century. The most prominent measures were the following:

(a) **The initiation of public housing projects** whereby the government sold housing at cost or provided land for building while offering loans at very low interest rates.[149] Besides encouraging high fertility rates, the policy of distributing land to the nationals also had a political target: to increase support for the royal families as part of the rentier system. In Kuwait, already in the 1950s, this policy constituted a major channel to distribute the oil revenues to the merchant elite and tribal notables. The regimes of Qatar and the UAE also adopted a similar policy, and in Saudi Arabia the system of land gifts has been in force since the beginning of the Ibn Sa'ud regime.[150]

(b) **The encouragement of early marriage through large marriage grants.** Despite the severe damage to the Kuwaiti economy caused by the Iraqi invasion, a large increase in the marriage grant to Kuwaiti nationals was approved by the Council of Ministers at the beginning of 1992. According to this decision, eligible Kuwaiti males were entitled to receive $14,000 (half as a grant and half as a loan) for their marriage to Kuwaiti women. This amount was twice the previous sum. The reason for such a large increase, according to the Kuwaiti Minister of Finance, Nasser 'Abdullah al-Roudhan, was "to encourage Kuwaiti youths to marry."[151]

(c) **Full governmental subsidies for education** (including books, clothing, etc.) provided from the first grade through university.

(d) **Child allowances for each child of nationals employed in the public sector.**[152]

In addition to the above-mentioned direct measures, a major indirect pro-natalist measure taken by the GCC countries (with the exception of Bahrain) was to maintain the low status of women. Generally speaking, pro-natalist policies related to women's status in three basic forms: First, a pro-natalist program could include the prohibition on contraceptive use and abortion. In 1975, following the publication of the September 1974 demographic census, the Saudi authorities banned the import, the distribution and use of contraceptives "as they contradict the teaching of Islam."[153] Second, since the most influential factor determining fertility behavior is women's economic activity rates, imposing various barriers on women's employment, legally or socially or both, as in the Saudi case, would eliminate the most influential factor for fertility decline. Finally, generous child allowances and subsidies on the one hand, and high salaries for nationals employed in the public sector on the other (with the exception of Bahrain), in practice eliminated the need for the "dual salary form" which was one of the prominent factors for the sharp fertility decline in the developed countries since the 1960s.

It should be noted, however, that with the exception of Saudi Arabia, the pro-natalist policies in the other GCC countries were carried out on a voluntary basis only. However, even in Saudi Arabia, despite the official restrictions on contraceptive use, in practice they were available during the 1970s, at least in the major cities.[154]

In retrospect, the GCC pro-natalist policy achieved its primary goal: While the educational level of the entire GCC indigenous women tremendously improved and the death rates radically declined, fertility levels remained extremely high. In 1985, the CBR and TFR were 44.7 per 1,000 and 5.9 children per woman, respectively, in Bahrain; 46.9 and 7.2, respectively, in Qatar; 46.3 and 7.5, respectively, in the UAE; and 46.0 and 7.5, respectively, in Saudi Arabia.[155] Fargues argued in this respect that "by giving them [to the citizens] more money so they could have large families with mothers staying at home, it has, in a way, funded the preservation of patriarchal society and delayed the onset of the demographic transition."[156]

4.5 "Demographic Sobriety": Direct Family Planning Programs is the Only Solution

The end of the "oil decade," and more so the drop in oil prices in 1986, led to a severe recession in all of the Arab economies, both the oil-based and non-oil alike (see Chapter 3). Consequently, the natalist approach of the overpopulated Arab countries dramatically changed, heralding a new period that can be called "Demographic Sobriety." In general, since the mid-1980s, the anti-natalist measures introduced in the over-populated Arab countries have been markedly intensified.

The first Arab country that changed its natalist perception following the end of the "oil decade" was Algeria. In 1983, under the rule of Chadli Bendjedid, Algeria adopted its first family planning program.[157] A year later, in 1984, the legal minimum age at first marriage was set at 18 years for women and 21 years for men. In 1985, the 1976 abortion law was substantially liberalized for the purpose of family planning.[158] As in the case of Syria, the Algerian family planning policy during the early 1980s was somewhat hidden, and emphasized the "birth spacing" for the benefit of the mothers and children, rather than as a national aim. In 1986, the National Committee on Population (Comité National de la Population) was established. The Algerian family planning policy found its legal basis in Act No. 85-05 of February 16, 1989. The law defined the framework for maternal and child protection, which consisted of a set of medical and social measures aimed at protecting the mother's health by offering medical and social conditions before, during and after pregnancy.[159] However, even this hidden policy was effective and the contraceptive prevalence rate substantially increased, amounting to 57.5% of the married women of childbearing age in 1992 in the urban centers compared to 17.5% in 1970, while in the countryside the increase was from barely 4% to 44.1% during the corresponding years.[160]

In the case of Egypt as well, the end of the "oil decade" led to a substantial revision in the family planning policy. In 1985, under Presidential Decree No. 18, the National Population Council was established, headed by Mubarak himself.[161] A year later, in 1986, a new family planning program was announced with the aim of reducing the natural increase rate from 2.8% in 1986 to 2.1% in 2001. There were two basic assumptions of the new plan: First, rapid population growth by itself constitutes a major socioeconomic problem, and thus a comprehensive national family planning program is necessary to reduce the high fertility levels in preparation for transforming the Egyptian society into an industrialized one. Second, a sharp fertility decline would bring about certain structural changes that would help raise the living standard.[162]

Although the new plan included many elements of previous ones, it reflected change in two critical areas. First, the demographic problem was given top governmental priority; and second, emphasis was placed on both the supply and the demand measures simultaneously.[163] On the "demand side," the new plan put particular emphasis on a strong mass media public information and education program conducted by the Egyptian State Information Service with technical assistance from the USAID.[164] A central part of the "demand side" was to convince the population that using contraceptives is permitted through numerous *fatwa*s issued by the most senior Islamic clerics.[165] Thus, for example, in early 1989, the Egyptian Grand Mufti, Muhammad Sayd Tantawi, said that the *Shari'a* allowed and even required the use of contraceptives in cases of a woman's weakness or illness as well as in cases of economic hardship.[166] In April 1990, in a seminar organized by the Women Secretariat of the National Party, Tantawi said that neither the *Quran* nor any other Islamic jurisprudence oppose family planning "as long as there was a need for it."[167] These are only two of numerous *fatwa*s issued by official Egyptian Islamic religious clerics permitting the use of contraceptives for the purpose of family planning. After focusing on the first stage of the "population issue" in general in order to enhance public awareness of the "demographic problem," the second phase of the new plan concentrated on providing more specific information on the various family planning options.[168]

In the area of the "supply side," the aim of the new plan was to eliminate the large-scale unmet need for contraceptives.[169] According to the 1984 Egypt Contraceptive Prevalence Survey, the desired number of children was 3.3, but the actual TFR was much higher as a result of the considerable unmet need for contraceptives.[170] Thus, in early 1987, the ministerial committee for social services decided to establish one family planning unit to serve every 2,000 families throughout the country.[171]

The anti-natalist activity was largely intensified in other Arab countries as well following the collapse of the oil prices in 1986. In 1987, the Tunisian authorities limited child allowances to families with a maximum of four children and one year later, in 1988, to only three children. A maternity leave of two months at full pay, followed by four months at half pay, was also limited in 1988 to the first three children.[172]

The year 1987 also marked a turning point in the Syrian natalist policy. In that year, the financial benefits given to large families were cancelled. At the same time, the Ministry of Health appealed to young families through the mass media to take family planning steps, while the range of activities of the Syrian Family Planning Association was markedly expanded.[173]

What were the major factors that led to intensifying family planning activities in many of the Arab countries starting in the mid-1980s?

(a) The collapse of the "economic solution" thesis In the mid-1980s, many leaders of the Arab overpopulated countries began to grasp the misguided nature of their belief that prolonged socioeconomic improvement would bring about fertility decline without direct governmental family planning activities. As previously noted, not only did fertility rates fail to decline, but in some countries, such as Jordan and Syria, they even increased, despite the substantial socioeconomic improvement.

(b) The collapse of the inter-Arab labor migration option The leaders of the largest Arab labor-exporting countries realized in the mid-1980s that alleviating the employment pressure through large-scale labor emigration to the Arab oil countries was no longer a realistic option, given the massive replacement of Arab by Asian workers (see Chapter 4).

(c) The sharp cut in the grants from the Arab oil countries Although even in the mid-1980s there were some who continued to believe in Arab unity, it was quite clear that the Arab oil countries would not continue to financially back the poorer Arab countries and that each country would have to operate according to its own interests. Thus, it became more expedient for these countries to promote direct and extensive family planning activities in order to compensate for the lack of financial backing from the Arab oil countries.

(d) The success of family planning programs in many non-Arab developing countries In the mid-1980s, it became clear that a growing number of developing countries, such as the "Asian Tigers," were successful at reducing their fertility rates through voluntary measures,[174] without the need of implementing the radical Chinese family planning measures.[175] This success led to an increase in the number of developing countries that implemented either direct or indirect anti-natalist measures.

(e) The change in the global political economy In the second half of the 1980s, an increasing number of developing countries worldwide fell into an economic recession and became increasingly dependent on aid from Western countries and international financial institutions, which forced them to adopt macroeconomic reforms that were more conducive to implementing national family planning programs.[176]

During the 1990s, there was a further increase in the direct anti-natalist activities in many Arab countries. In 1991, the government of Yemen[177] adopted a long-term family planning program aimed at reducing the TFR from 7 children per woman in 1990 to 4 in 2018[178] and raising the contraceptive prevalence rate to 50% so as to reach a natural increase rate of 2% by the year 2023.[179] The short-term aims were to reduce the TFR to 6 and to increase the contraceptive prevalence rate to 35% by the year 2000.[180] Actually, by 1997, the contraceptive prevalence rate in Yemen amounted to 21%, compared to only 10% in 1991/2.[181]

In Egypt, the family planning activities were also expanded during the 1990s. In 1991, the Egyptian government set two major demographic targets for the year 2007: The first was that the contraceptive prevalence rate would increase to 65% and that the CBR would decline to 25 per 1,000.[182] The increasing attention being devoted to the demographic issue within Egypt's overall socioeconomic development strategy was reflected in the fact that the Five-Year Development Plan for 1992/3–1996/7 period contained, for the first time ever, a separate chapter on the demographic challenge.[183]

Another important direct anti-natalist measure which started to be implemented in

Cartoon 5.3

the early 1990s, was that the cartoons which illustrated the devastating consequences of rapid population growth were appearing not only in the press, but in governmental publications as well, such as the Cartoons 5.3 and 5.4 that were published by the National Population Information Center in 1991.[184] The first cartoon presents a pregnant woman named, *al-Ziyada al-Sukaniyya* ["population growth"] hitting another woman, named, *al-Tanmiyya* ["economic development"] over the head with a pregnant woman which serve as a hammer. The second cartoon presents a dead tree, named, *Ziyadat al-Nasel* ["multiple children"] and the tree's branches are the most devastating consequences of rapid population growth, such as unemployment, ignorance, etc. The importance of these cartoons is far beyond the simple fact that they appeared in a governmental publication, but rather that they are openly presenting the most devastating consequences of the rapid population growth at the national level. The combination of the appearance of these cartoons in a governmental publication and their focusing on the national rather than the family level, as in the Syrian case, represent the move of the Egyptian government to an explicit and open family planning policy.

The setting of the 1994 World Population Conference in Cairo was an international acknowledgement of Egypt's successful family planning efforts. In January 1996, the Ministry of Health became the Ministry of Health and Population, reflecting the Ministry's increased responsibility for population policy activities. Within the framework of the new family planning policy, adopted in October 1995, the national family planning services were integrated into the broader mother-and-child healthcare services, and greater emphasis was placed on the rural areas, particularly those of Upper Egypt, where fertility rates were traditionally much higher than in the major cities.[185] Overall, by 1996 the number of family planning units operating throughout Egypt amounted to 4,733, of which 62.1% were located in the rural areas.[186]

Cartoon 5.4

In the year 2000, the Egyptian government adopted a new long-term demographic strategy, known as "vision 2017," covering the 2000–2017 period. The major aims of the new strategy were: reducing the fertility rate to replacement-level; achieving better spatial distribution of the population; improving the socioeconomic characteristics of the population; and reducing the socioeconomic and demographic gaps between Egypt's various regions.[187] Within the framework of the "vision 2017" strategy, the number of family planning units largely increased, amounting to 6,005 in 2005, representing an increase of 27% from their number in 1996.[188]

In addition to continuing the expansion of the "supply side," the Egyptian family planning policy proceeded to concentrate in the following three major parameters in order to maximize the "demand side" as well:

***(a)* Religious justification for contraceptive use** In recent years, it became an indisputable fact that in order to convince the population that contraceptive use is permitted (*halal*), the most senior clerics had to express it constantly and repeatedly in the various mass media, both written and electronic, something like the advertising of a commodity or a service. Thus, for example, the Egyptian Minister of *Awqaf* (religious endowments), Mahmud Hamdi Zakzouk, claimed in early 2004 that although there is no doubt as to the Islamic religious command on procreation, this command is conditional on the ability of the parents to support their offspring which is also an explicit Islamic command. The main aim of the national family planning policy, noted the Minister, is "to take care of the coming generation."[189]

***(b)* Convincing parents that a large number of children constitute the core reason for their poverty** The main message which the Egyptian government was trying to transfer was that the number of the children should be planned according to economic ability; otherwise the whole family would fall into a hopeless state of poverty.[190]

***(c)* Constant publication of cartoons in the various newspapers** which emphasize both the devastating consequences of the rapid population growth to Egypt as a country and to the parents themselves. This constant publication adopted the same principles as the publications of the *fatwa*s, namely, to keep the demographic issue constantly on the top public agenda. I only chose three cartoons which represent the two main demographic messages: The first two represents the devastating damage of rapid population growth to Egypt as a country and the latter one emphasize the conse-

Cartoon 5.5
Source: al-Ahram, December 8, 2002.

quences at the family level. In Cartoon 5.5, a frightening troll, named, *al-Ziyada al-Sukaniyya* ["population growth"] rapidly eats the earth with his two hands. "*Bidun ta'aliq*" ["without explanation"] is written at the bottom of the cartoon. Cartoon 5.6 presents a person who is standing on the roof and shouting at the birds, "in the name of your father, when you arrive safely [at your destination], please send me an employment contract;" that is, the unemployment problem is extremely severe due to the rapid population growth.

Cartoon 5.7 presents a pregnant woman who comes to the doctor and the doctor says to her: "Madam, you should go the explosives expert, not to someone like me." The meaning of the cartoon is that population growth is like explosives.

In Jordan, following the return of some 350,000 Jordanian citizens from the GCC countries, the authorities realized that the only viable option for reducing the socioeconomic burden, particularly the subsidy pressure in the short run and the employment pressure in the longer run, was through sharp fertility decline. Hence, in 1991, the NPC initiated the Birth Spacing National Program in an effort to promote fertility decline. In 1993, within the framework of the Five-Year Development Plan for the 1993–1997 period, the Jordanian government approved the program which was declared Jordan's official anti-natalist policy.[191] The plan contained very similar components, in terms of the characteristics of "supply" and "demand" to family planning programs implemented in other Arab countries.[192] The target set by the plan was to reduce the CBR by 1 point each year.[193]

In recent years, due to the increasing burden of the rapid population growth, the issue of family planning received higher governmental attention. In a meeting of the Jordanian Higher Population Council, held in May 26, 2003, Jordan's Prime Minister, 'Ali 'Abd al-Ragheb, called for initiating a detailed action program on demographic issues, claiming that Jordan's rapid population growth "has an adverse impact on various aspects of life since it is disproportionate to growth in the available national resources."[194] The *Jordan Times* reported in mid-2004 that: "Population challenges currently top the government's list of priorities . . . "[195]

Syria's family planning activities were also intensified during the 1990s, starting with the implementation of many conferences on the various demographic aspects. These conferences were designed to highlight the dangers of uncontrolled population growth to Syrian society as a whole and to convince the masses that there were no religious restrictions on contraceptives practice.[196] By mid-1993, the overall number of family planning clinics in Syria was 552, about two-thirds of which were in the rural areas.[197] It should be emphasized, however, that despite the cancellation of the financial benefits to large families, in contrast to Jordan, the Syrian anti-natalist approach during the 1990s continued to remain hidden. We cannot find any expression of Hafiz al-Asad himself or any other senior official publicly advocating an official and explicit family planning program. Thus, for example, in the conference "Economic and

Cartoon 5.6
Source: al-Ahram al-Iqtisadi, August 4, 2003.

Cartoon 5.7
Source: al-Ahram al-Iqtisadi, August 11, 2003.

Investment in Syria," held at the University of Damascus in March 1997, the Syrian Minister of Economy and Foreign Trade, Muhammad al-'Imadi, said that the demographic challenge of Syria "can only find its response in constant work, in the optimum use of the innovations of science and technology, and in a development policy that is compatible with the labor market."[198] The Minister did not even mention the need for a comprehensive family planning program in order to curb the high fertility rates.

It seems that the major factor for the Syrian hidden anti-natalist approach during the 1990s as well was that it had previously implemented explicit pro-natalist policy. Thus, while the Jordanian changing natalist policy was "smooth," as it had not previously implemented a pro-natalist policy, in the Syrian case, the actual meaning of changing from pro-natalist into anti-natalist was to admit that the previous policy was a mistaken one. Thus, during the 1990s, although the direct family planning measures taken by the authorities, primarily in terms of increasing accessibility to family planning services substantially expanded, the official anti-natalist policy remained largely hidden.

In May 2002, however, the Syrian authorities made a dramatic step toward promoting fertility decline by announcing that henceforth child allowances would be paid according to the number of children, rather than according to a fixed amount for each child, as had previously been the case. The highest allowance of 200 Syrian pound (S£) would be paid for the first child, S£150 for the second child, S£100 for the third child, and another S£25 for families with more than three children. The maximum for child allowances was set at S£475. Thus, the higher the number of children, the lower the average allowances paid for each child.[199] This change represents the transformation of the Syrian natalist policy from an indirect into a direct and explicit one.

Although Algeria succeeded in markedly reducing its fertility rates during the 1980s, by 1990, its natural increase rate was still as high as 2.8% – among the highest in the Arab countries. As examined in Chapter 3, during the 1990s, Algerian socioeconomic problems, above all, the steady unemployment increase, markedly intensified. Consequently, the Algerian authorities decided to strengthen its anti-natalist measures, concentrating on expanding family planning and reproductive health services. In March 1997, the Algerian authorities adopted a new family planning program with a target of achieving 60% contraceptive prevalence rate by the year 2000. The new plan mainly includes the following three measures:

(1) Provision of contraceptives free of charge through public healthcare facilities.
(2) Improving the quality of family planning services through advanced training of the medical staff in the clinics; upgrading the equipment in the clinics; and diversifying the available contraceptive methods.
(3) Developing information, education and communication activities in order to promote the awareness of the population as to the importance of fertility decline. [200]

A major characteristic of the anti-natalist measures implemented in the Arab countries since the early 1990s was that the activities, in contrast to the past, were carried out openly. Many Arab governments, particularly those of Syria, Jordan and Algeria, stopped trying to hide their ambitions to reduce fertility rates. This openness characterized the regional Arab organizations as well. Thus, for examples, the 2004 Regional Arab Population Forum recommended that: "Comprehensive reproductive health should be made generally available and include the provision of information and counselling on family planning . . . "[201] Hence, while the Arab organizations had previously examined the demographic issue in the broader context of the "Arab region," in recent years, the demographic issue was examined in the more practical terms of reducing fertility as an inescapable reaction to the socioeconomic problems of the poorer Arab countries.

It should be noted, however, that the change in approach of many Arab governments from hidden to open anti-natalist policy during the past decade was not unique. This was actually the trend in many non-Arab developing countries. The *2005 World Population Policies* noted that: "Unlike in the past, when perceptions of high fertility were usually not accompanied by policy intervention, virtually all countries which viewed fertility as too high in 2005 intervened to lower it."[202]

Overall, it seems that several factors contributed to make the anti-natalist policy an official policy or at least a "visible policy" among the non-oil Arab countries during the past decade:

(a) Worsening of the socioeconomic consequences of rapid population growth The severity of these socioeconomic consequences became overwhelming, even in countries that were relatively not so populous until the 1980s, such as Jordan, Syria and Yemen. The leaders of the non-oil Arab countries reached the inescapable conclusion that they would soon have to face a real political threat on socioeconomic grounds, as they could not "deliver the goods" anymore and live up their promises for "a better life." Hence, they were forced to make corresponding adjustments in their socioeconomic policies, including in the natalist policy, to the new demographic-economic situation. The paradox of this new situation was that while until the mid-1980s, the initiation of

official family planning policy had been considered politically dangerous, since then the greater political danger seemed to lie in the failure to implement such a policy. This realization, it should be emphasized, occurred at the same time as steadily increasing pressure from the IMF and the World Bank to implement economic reforms in line with the "Washington Consensus."[203]

(b) The "Iranian religious umbrella" In December 1988, Iran's High Judicial Council announced that "there is no Islamic barrier to family planning."[204] A year later, in December 1989, Iran officially declared the adoption of a national family planning program (see below). Thus, the adoption of a national family planning policy by the Iranian regime gave "a religious umbrella" to other Muslim countries to adopt a similar policy.

(c) The weakening of the Arab–Israeli conflict A major argument of those who were opposed to family planning in Egypt during the 1960s and 1970s was the continuation of the Arab–Israeli conflict. However, the diminishing of the conflict, starting with the March 1979 Egyptian-Israeli peace treaty and followed by the October 1991 Madrid Conference, the September 1993 Palestinian-Israeli Oslo Accords, the October 1994 Jordanian–Israeli peace treaty and the *de facto* peace with Morocco, Tunisia, Oman and Qatar since the mid-1990s, all contributed to reducing the level of the conflict from an overall Arab–Israeli conflict to a specific Palestinian-Israeli conflict. Thus, the Arab–Israeli conflict could no longer constitute an "excuse" not to implement anti-natalist policy.

(d) The collapse of the Soviet Union The demise of the Communist ideology in the late 1980s led to the creation of one superpower not only in the political realm but in the economic arena as well. This factor constituted a major lever for promoting family planning activities in many developing countries, including the overpopulated Arab countries. The collapse of the Soviet Union, it should be remembered, was brought about on purely economic grounds and was not the result of war or any other kind of international conflict. As such, the Communist ideology, which was opposed to family planning, was rendered irrelevant. It was quite apparent then that the only economic policy which could be of any use in the modern globalized economy was that of capitalism, which supported anti-natalist policy as the best option for curbing high fertility.

(e) The reversal in the US demographic policy Following the election of Bill Clinton to the office of US President in January 1993, the US reversed its demographic policy toward developing countries to that which had prevailed prior to the election of Ronald Reagan.[205] This renewed support also includes increasing financial aid to family planning programs in developing countries through the USAID.

(f) Easier access to the targeted population During the 1990s, it was much easier for the Arab governments to act in the area of family planning and related issues, mainly due to two factors: First, the sharp improvement in women's educational levels since the 1960s meant that the women who were the target of the family planning programs in the 1990s were much more educated than those of previous periods. Since women's educational level constitutes one of the most important factors shaping fertility rates, the likelihood of women availing themselves of the contraceptives being offered by the family planning programs in the 1990s was greater than ever before. Second, the widespread use of mass media, particularly electronic media, enabled the Arab governments to disseminate their messages on the subject of family planning more effectively than in the 1960s and 1970s, when such media were either scarce or not widely available.

(g) The weakening of the threat of the Islamic opposition During the 1990s, the leaders of the non-oil Arab countries were becoming more confident of the stability of their regime. Throughout the decades that these regimes existed, they built immense security forces whose only aim was to protect the regime's survival. The oil rental incomes enabled them to finance these huge security forces. Thus, paradoxically, the "oil boom" that was one of the paramount factors for strengthening the Islamic opposition, simultaneously served to finance the various security forces. The commanders of the security forces are, in most cases, relatives of the leaders themselves and the majority of their employees were either from the leader's tribe (in the case of Saddam Husayn's Iraq) or its religious sect (in the case of Syria since 1970). The hold of the security forces, in any circle – in both the army and civilian organizations – combined with technological improvements, enabled them to spy on potential opposition groups more easily than before. These developments practically eliminated any option of civilian or even army officers uprising. The case of Saddam Husayn illustrates just how stable these

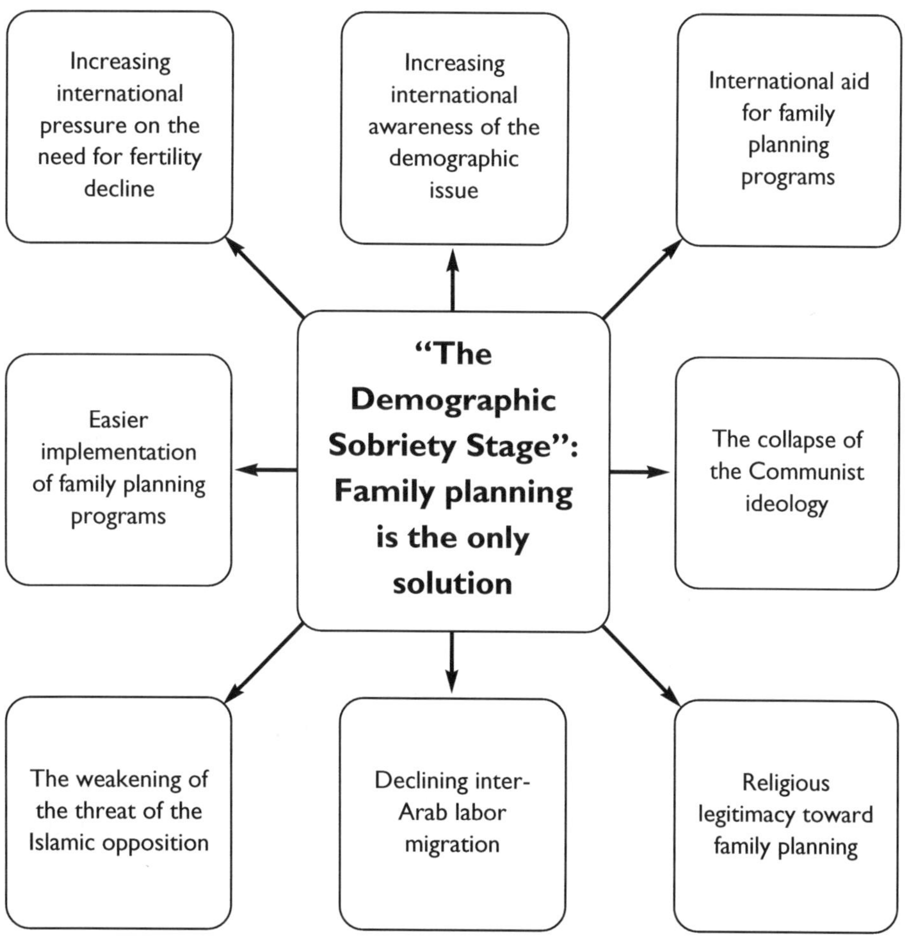

Chart 5.3 The Natalist Perception of the non-Oil Arab Countries following the "Oil Decade"

regimes were. Despite all the unimagined evils and mass murders conducted by Saddam Husayn's regime, it needed hundred of thousands of American soldiers with the most sophisticated weapons to eliminate it. The Syrian, Egyptian, and Jordanian regimes are no less stable. Thus, in total contrast to the situation in the 1950s and 1960s, the non-oil Arab regimes could implement a policy which is totally opposed by the Islamist opposition. It should be noted in this respect, however, that the Islamist oppositions are opposed not only to family planning, but also to the economic liberalization measures, both vigorously implemented since the early 1990s.

4.6 The Changing Natalist Policy of the GCC Countries during the 1990s

The most dramatic natalist perception change during the 1990s occurred in Oman and, to a lesser extent, in Saudi Arabia. These two countries gradually moved away from their traditional pro-natalist approach and started to advocate fertility decline. In the case of Oman, the natalist perception change was the outcome of several factors: First, the continued high natural increase rates combined with the increasing female labor force participation rates ensured a steady increase in the potential indigenous labor force. Hence, the most important factor for encouraging high fertility became irrelevant. The second factor was the prolonged low oil prices following the end of the "oil decade," which led to economic stagnation. The third factor was the growing unemployment problem among the nationals (see Chapter 4). Thus, following the publication of the 1993 census results, Sultan Qabus started to promote fertility decline. In January 1994, he said:

> We need to take another look at family planning. The recommended figure in the world as a whole is five members per family. When we see that the Omani family averages seven members, and that there is a strong belief that the creator will provide, we should also realize that almighty God has also given us intelligence and urged us to use it.[206]

Within the framework of "Oman 2020," the demographic issue was given high priority. The first aim of the Human Resource Development Strategy was: "To achieve a balance between population and economic growth by reducing the current population growth rate . . . "[207] Hence, Oman became the first among the GCC countries that started to promote fertility decline, not only practically but officially as well. In October 1994, the Birth Spacing Services Program was incorporated into the governmental maternal and child health clinics, where contraceptives are distributing free of charge.[208] In May 1999, the National Population Policy was officially declared and the National Population Committee (NPC) was established in order to implement the Sultanate's new demographic policy. The official goals of the NPC are "to channel economic and social development so that population growth matches available resources and to modify the administrative and geographical distribution of population where desirable."[209] Overall, by the year 2000, the percentage of married Omani women using family planning methods was 32%, compared to only 9% in the late 1980s.[210]

In the case of Saudi Arabia, it seems that the authorities eventually reached the inescapable conclusion that the high fertility rate of the indigenous population did not bring about a decline in the foreign labor dependence. Indeed, the Saudi Sixth Five-Year Development Plan for the years 1995–2000 acknowledged that: "Although the rapid growth of the Saudi population is not an entirely new phenomenon, it has now reached the stage of exerting considerable influence on many aspects of economic and social policy."[211] A clear indicator of the changing Saudi natalist approach was the repeal in 1996 of the law forbidding the promotion, distribution or use of contraceptives.[212] Another indicator of the Saudi changing natalist approach was their public admission of the existence of a demographic problem in the Kingdom, in contrast to their previous representation of the high fertility rates as an outcome of successful socioeconomic policy.[213] For example, the SAMA 2002 Annual Report noted:

> High population growth is straining public services such as education, health, municipalities, water, electricity, roads and housing with adverse effects on the standard of living and economic and social well-being.[214]

However, it should be emphasized that the change in the Saudi natalist approach was and still is very slow, in line with the overall "slow Saudi pace" – political and socioeconomic alike – aiming not to shake the Kingdom's "political order." In addition, in total contrast to Oman, the Saudi authorities still refuse to admit that their natalist approach changed into an anti-natalist one. Consequently, while in practice they began to implement some anti-natalist measures, in the public statements of high ranking politicians, they continued to ignore the Kingdom's demographic burden. For example, in response to a question by a *MEED* reporter in mid-2004 about the role of the tourism industry in generating employment to Saudi nationals, Prince Sultan bin Salman bin 'Abdulaziz Al Sa'ud, the Secretary-General of the Saudi Supreme Commission for Tourism (SCT), said as follows: "More than half of the people in the country are under 25. I do not see this as a problem. It is a problem if the majority of the population is older and needs . . . medical care. [The young population] is our biggest asset . . . "[215]

The indigenous populations of the other four GCC countries are very small and, with the exception of Bahrain, foreigners constitute more than 70% of the total population and more than 85% of the labor force. Given this demographic profile, the promotion of anti-natalist policy is not relevant in their case. However, although the basic fertility orientation of these countries, other than Bahrain,[216] remains pro-natalist, family planning services are available through the public healthcare clinics within the framework of the overall healthcare services offered to the indigenous populations free of charge. Thus, whereas in the 1970s and 1980s the GCC countries were all overtly pro-natalist, at the beginning of the twenty-first century only the three smallest remains pro-natalist, while the larger three promotes fertility decline in one way or another.

In an article published in 1988, Birks raised a question about whether it is possible that the GCC countries would implement anti-natalist measures in the future. His answer was definitively negative due to three main factors. First, the GCC rulers believed that the international and security positions of their countries would be too vulnerable as a result of their small indigenous populations. Second, the impact of family planning activities would be felt only after a period of at least a generation, and the perspective of the GCC rulers is much shorter. Third, the GCC rulers traditionally considered rapid population growth as a lever for enhancing economic development.[217] The reality, however, was quite the opposite and within less than a decade the natalist approach of the largest GCC countries radically changed in favor of anti-natalist.

5 Evaluation of the Family Planning Programs in the Arab Countries

As the data reveal, fertility rates in all of the Arab countries, even in the oil-countries, have substantially declined during the past two decades. This decline, however, started two decades after that of many other developing countries. Thus, while Turkey's TFR in 1960 was higher than Egypt's, in 2005 Turkey's TFR was 1.9 compared to 2.9 in Egypt and 3.5 in both Jordan and Syria. Many of the non-Middle Eastern developing countries achieved even lower TFR at the start of the twenty-first century, such as 1.3 in South Korea, 1.9 in Brazil, and 2.4 in Mexico in 2005 (see Table 2.4).

The common academic perception is that the current trend of fertility decline in the Arab countries will continue in the foreseeable future. The IBRD 2004 MENA report, for example, noted that: "It is safe to assume, however, that the era of high population growth is over. Evidence increasingly suggests that MENA is on a trajectory of declining population growth rates for the foreseeable future."[218] Robinson and El-Zanaty noted that: "Egypt is . . . well along in a 'transition' from high to low fertility and to ultimate stabilization."[219]

Is the Arab population growth indeed approaching "ultimate stabilization"? The demographic data of many Arab countries from recent years, however, are raising great doubt about the validity of these optimistic projections. Thus, for example, since the early 1990s Egypt's fertility rates have remained almost unchanged. Egypt's TFR averaged 3.1 children per woman according to the *2005–EDHS* (see Table 2.8), compared to 3.6 in the 1992–1995 period.[220] Hence, during the twelve years of 1992–2005, Egypt's TFR declined by 16% only, despite the continued efforts of the Egyptian government in the family planning area. Egypt's main demographic problem is in the rural areas of Upper Egypt, where the TFR remain very high at an average of 3.9 children per woman, namely, almost twice the replacement-level,[221] despite the fact that the *2003–EIDHS* indicated that 100% of the women who participated in the survey were aware of at least one modern birth control method.[222] The lack of success of the family planning program in the rural areas was identified as the main reason for the overall failure of the Egyptian family planning program thus far to reduce the country's average TFR to below 2.5 children per woman.[223] The results of the *2005-EDHS* led the USAID and the Egyptian Population Council to conduct research with the aim of exploring the factors behind this failure.[224]

Three factors can be identified as the main reasons for contributing to the high fertility rates in the rural areas of Upper Egypt: First, Upper Egypt is by far more traditional in comparison to other Egypt's regions.[225] Second, the availability of family planning services in this area does not approach the same standard as in Egypt's other areas, particularly in the major cities. Third, the indirect factors that contribute to lower fertility, mainly women's educational level and their employment opportunities, in addition to the enforcement of the prohibition on child labor, are not as strong as in the major cities and even in other rural areas. According to the *1995–EDHS* data, the mean age for first marriage of women aged 25–29 in Upper Egypt was only 17.8 years.[226] This means that a considerable percentage of women in this area are still getting married below the minimum legal age.

A similar pattern can be found in the other non-oil Arab countries as well. In the case of Syria, for example, since the mid-1980s and until the early 1990s, the fertility rate declined considerably. By 1993, Syria's CBR was 33.2 per 1,000,[227] compared to 42.4 in 1986.[228] The process of fertility decline, however, ended in the early 1990s.

According to the *1999 Multiple Survey*, Syrian TFR averaged 4.2 children per woman – the same rate as measured in the *1993–SMCHS*. According to the 2004 census results, the TFR declined to 3.6 children per woman, with 3.2 in the urban centers and 4.1 in the rural areas.[229] Thus, the changes made in the child allowances system in 2002 did not yet appear to be substantially affective.

In the case of Jordan, according to the *1997–JPFHS*, only 45.3% of the currently married women in the rural areas were using contraceptives (both modern and traditional), although almost 100% were knowledgeable about at least one modern contraceptive method.[230] This means that more than one half of the Jordanian rural married women chose not to use contraceptives despite being familiar with them. However, despite the fact that the "unmet need" for contraceptives in Jordan remained quite high in the early 2000s at the level of 11%,[231] the fertility rates continued to decline, amounting to a TFR of 3.7 in 2003,[232] compared to 4.4 according to the 1997–*JPFHS*.[233] The real Jordanian demographic challenge, however, will be to reduce the TFR further to below 2.5. Hence, although most Arab countries succeeded in reducing the fertility rate to below 4 children per woman, only a few succeeded in reducing it to below 3.

Tunisia is different from the rest of the Arab countries not only due to the fact that it achieved the lowest fertility rate at the start of the twenty-first century, but also due to the fact that the process of fertility decline continued without any fluctuation since the late 1960s.

The crucial demographic question, however, is why the fertility levels in all of the Arab countries (with the exception of Tunisia and Lebanon) remained much higher than in many non-Arab developing countries with similar socioeconomic characteristics?

Many researchers attribute this phenomenon to two main factors: Islam and the low status of women.[234] However, as rightly claimed by Olmsted, this conclusion is problematic for two major reasons: First, if Islam plays a major role in the high fertility rates of the Arab countries, how is it possible to explain the huge fertility dichotomy among the Arab countries themselves – Tunisia and Lebanon on the one hand, and the GCC countries and Yemen on the other? In addition, why have the fertility rates sharply declined in many non-Arab Muslim countries, such as Indonesia and Turkey, since the 1970s? The second reservation relating to the "Islamic factor" is that it presents Islam as a monolithic force, without taking into consideration "the various Islamic practices," not to mention the different views between the Shi'a and the Sunna.[235] In 1980, Allman noted in this regard that:

> Islam is rather more favorable to family planning than other religions, and that the obstacles to economic and social development that many Islamic countries face are the major determinants of their "traditional" demographic behavior.[236]

Thus, if Islam is not the core reason for the higher fertility rates of the Arab countries, what else could explain this phenomenon? Whereas the short-term factors have already been examined in Chapter 2, the long-term factors will be examined below:

***(a)* Low awareness of the important role played by fertility decline in accelerating economic development.** This low awareness not only led to delays in the implementation of family planning programs, but also to their marginality in the overall development strategy, even in those countries that adopted anti-natalist policy. The lack of awareness was typical not only of politicians but of academicians as well, as reflected in the total neglect of the family planning issue in the *Arab Human Development Reports*. Thus, for example, in the *2003 Arab Human Development Report*, the authors explained the socioeconomic gap between the Arab countries and the "Asian Tigers" through the gap in the per capita human capital investment, but they did not even mention the main factor for this gap, namely the different age structure:

> One of the most important lessons of the Asian experience is the critical role that early and intensive investment in human capital played as the foundation of development. Does the disparity in human capital formation between Arab and East Asian countries account for their divergent development fortunes?[237]

This is only one of numerous other examples. The overall result is that the most prestigious academic and research bodies concentrate their recommendations for accelerating socioeconomic development in the non-oil Arab countries in secondary areas, namely, the consequences of the rapid population growth, rather than dealing with the core of the Arab low socioeconomic performance, that is, the rapid population growth. Thus, by neglecting the family planning issue, these research bodies and individuals provided "shelter" for the non-oil Arab regimes not to intensify their family planning activities.

(b) **The prolonged Arab–Israeli conflict** also hampered the adoption of comprehensive family planning programs in the countries that were directly involved in the conflict. By devoting their attention and resources to the conflict itself, the leaders of the "confrontation states" neglected many socioeconomic issues, including the demographic issue. As Nonneman claimed, "a combination of political-economic and related political-cultural factors, added to by the Arab–Israeli conflict, continues to hamper political and economic development in the Middle East."[238]

(c) The Arab states, both the poorer and oil-based alike, were characterized by their **"soft state" nature** (see Introduction). This was reflected not only in the high subsidies on basic foodstuff, energy commodities and public services, but also in the low enforcement of basic laws that related to fertility patterns, mainly the minimum age at first marriage for women and restrictions on child employment. Khalid Muhi al-Din wrote that ‘Abd al-Nasser thought that he could raise sufficient financial resources for implementing the massive development plans, for improving and expanding public services and for increasing consumption by massive subsidies through the nationalization of the Suez Canal company and the nationalization of foreign assets.[239] In other words, it was a populist socioeconomic policy whereby the population was not forced to sacrifice by paying higher taxes or by shouldering any other personal economic burden in order to support the rapid population growth. In democratic countries, in contrast, as the public itself is forced to finance the economic burden of rapid population growth through higher taxation, the pressure for adopting anti-natalist measures is more likely to come from public organizations and political parties that oppose the prevailing pro-natalist policies.

(d) **The "Dutch Disease" Syndrome[240]** led many of the leaders of the non-oil Arab countries in the 1970s and 1980s to believe that they could succeed in achieving considerable economic expansion and substantial improvement in the living standard despite the rapid population growth. Lavy and Sheffer argued that the massive aid and the workers' remittances received by Jordan and Egypt had an overall negative effect on their economies insofar as they did not see the need to implement structural economic reforms in line with the changing world economic order.[241] The failure to adopt a comprehensive family planning program was part and parcel of this overall socioeconomic shortsightedness, as indicated by Richards:

> The worst legacy of the oil boom is not that the benefits were not widely shared but that they *were* widely shared: Labor exporters as well as oil producers caught the Dutch Disease, leaving the Arab world poorly equipped to face the challenge of an increasingly competitive international economy.[242]

Therefore, with the exception of Tunisia and Lebanon, not only are the actual fertility rates in the Arab countries remain much higher than the targeted replacement-level, but the desired number of children are also much higher than the replacement-level. According to the *2001-Syrian Family Health Survey*, the mean number of desired children was as high as 4.6,[243] 3.8 according to the *2002–Algerian Family Health Survey*,[244] and 3.2 according to the *2003/4–Moroccan Population Family Health Survey*.[245] This means that even if the Arab governments eventually achieve the goal of total elimination of unwanted pregnancies, the fertility rate will still remain much above the targeted replacement-level in the foreseeable future.

In addition, since the 1970s, in the developed countries there has been a steady increase in the percentage of childless women, which largely contributed to the sharp decline in the average fertility rates (see Chapter 2). In the Arab countries, in total contrast, the percentage of childless women remained insignificant. According to the *2003–EIDHS*, for example, it appears that "no women want to remain childless."[246] The childless phenomenon is so crucial for fertility decline that even if only 10% of the Egyptian women remain childless, Egypt's TFR would decline to 2.3 children per woman.[247] Hence, fertility decline in the Arab countries can be achieved only through less children per woman and not the same number of children for less women, as in the developed countries.

6 "Direct" or "Indirect"? The Contribution of Family Planning Programs to Fertility Decline

Chesnais argued in the late 1990s that: "Fertility is elastic; it can be reduced by family planning programs when it is considered too high; it can also be stimulated by social policies when it is considered too low."[248] Is it true? In the following section this crucial question will be examined first in the broader theoretical framework and later specifically in the case of the Middle East.

6.1 *The Efficacy of the Family Planning Programs: The Theoretical Framework*

The core question is whether the fertility decline which occurred in almost all of the developing countries worldwide during the past three decades was an outcome of the family planning programs carried out in many of these countries since the 1970s, or whether it was the outcome of prolonged socioeconomic development processes, similar to the fertility decline pattern which has occurred in the developed countries. The implication of the answer to this question is immense, as was examined in Chapter 2.

The indirect approach views fertility patterns primarily as determined by the desire for children, which is basically a function of their cost/benefit balance, the socio-cultural perceptions of the parents and women's status. Consequently, the access for contraceptives and their cost are not of much importance in determining fertility rates.[249] Therefore, as the core factor affecting fertility is the parents' decision, the technical supply of contraceptives provided by the government has for the most part only a limited impact on fertility behaviors.

The direct approach on the other hand, holds the view that a well-designed family planning program can effectively reduce fertility levels, particularly through preventing unwanted childbearing.[250] Based on the demographic surveys carried out in 93 developing countries in the early 1970s, Lapham and Mauldin noted that: "organized family planning programs affect demand, primarily by reducing the costs and increasing the availability of fertility regulation."[251] Also Todaro claimed that "family planning programs are needed to provide them [the parents] with the technological means to avoid unwanted pregnancies."[252] Ali claimed that "family planning programs do not just reduce the number of children and regulate reproduction. Rather, they also introduce or foster notions of individual choice and responsibility."[253] Hess argued that:

> Family planning services can reduce fertility in such circumstances by lowering the costs associated with using contraception. In particular, by providing information on modern contraceptive methods, by expanding the range of contraceptive techniques offered, by lowering the transaction costs involved in obtaining modern contraception, and by lending 'legitimacy' to the practice of birth control, organized family planning programs can make a significant contribution to a fertility transition.[254]

The 1994 World Bank demographic study presents the "integrative approach":

> The answer is not 'either/or' but rather 'both' and, even better, a balance of both that is responsive of the specific needs and conditions of different countries at different levels of the demographic transition and socioeconomic development.[255]

6.2 *The Efficacy of the Family Planning Programs: "The Middle Eastern Lesson"*

In the following section, the contribution of family planning programs in fertility decline will be examined in relation to the Middle Eastern experience.

The Middle Eastern "Direct" Approach

Analyzing Mubarak's family planning policy and based on Egypt's fertility decline since 1985, Gilbar reached the conclusion in 1993 that Mubarak's family planning policy was a major factor in Egypt's overall fertility decline during the second half of the 1980s and the early 1990s.[256] Saad Eddin Ibrahim also regarded Mubarak's family planning policy as a successful one. He claimed in 1995 that: "Despite the zigzagging and ambiguity, Egypt's population policy seems to be taking shape and proceeding on a well-defined track . . . While still short of the performance . . . , the results of the last five years are quite impressive."[257] Wisensale and Khodair argued in 1998 that Egypt's successful experience in family planning "represents one model from which other nations can learn."[258] In the case of Jordan, the *2004–JHDR* noted that the declining fertility of the recent decade, "can be largely attributed to the impact of considerable investment in family planning and reproductive health . . . combined with other socio-economic factors."[259]

The Middle Eastern "Indirect" Approach

The basic argument of those who support the indirect approach regarding Middle Eastern fertility decline is that this was mainly the result of both changing socio-economic policy and women educational improvement. Regarding Egypt's fertility reduction during the second half of the 1980s and the early 1990s, Fargues claimed in 1997 that:

> [N]o causal relationship has ever been established between the direct action of the Egyptian state to reduce the birth rate and its actual reduction . . . The lowering of the Egyptian birth rate is not a result of the systematic extension of family planning services . . . but rather a response to the country's changing economic, social, and political circumstances.[260]

According to Fargues, Egypt's fertility decline was a result of two paramount factors: First, the rapid improvement of female education; and second, the economic recession that started in the mid-1980s, following the end of the "oil decade," which by itself did not encourage higher fertility, combined with the decreasing governmental subsidies which led to increasing the child raising costs.[261] In another article, published in 1994, Fargues claimed that: "The next stage of the demographic transition [in the Arab countries], and particularly the fall in the birth rate, was instead a result of widening access to education . . . [I]t seems that state intervention has fuelled a trend which had already begun rather than initiating it."[262]

A similar argument was raised by Courbage who claimed that in the Arab countries "fertility transition is linked to the decline of the rent economy."[263] He explained the decline of Morocco's TFR from 7.4 children per woman in 1973 to 5.9 in 1977 through the increasing tax burden due to the sharp reduction in governmental rent revenues from phosphate exports. This increasing tax burden, "affected marriage and reproduction decisions . . . The opportunity cost of a birth became a factor in family strategies even amongst illiterate groups."[264] Also in the Syrian case, Courbage attributed the fertility decline of the late 1980s and early 1990s not to the changing natalist policy, but rather to the economic recession of the second half of the 1980s. This recession, according to Courbage, forced an increasing number of women to look to employment, as one salary became insufficient to support a family. Thus, without direct governmental intervention, Syria's fertility rates naturally declined in line with the increase in female labor force participation rates.[265]

6.3 The "Middle Eastern Lesson" under a Reality Examination

An examination of the "Middle Eastern lesson" reveals that there is no correlation between both economic situation and female educational level on the one hand, and fertility rates on the other. Thus, for example, although the female educational level in Jordan during the 1980s was much better than in both Egypt and Tunisia,[266] Jordan's fertility rate was much higher than in these two countries. In the case of the correlation between fertility rates and economic performances, one also cannot find a negative correlation: In the case of Syria, for example, fertility rates substantially declined during both periods of the deep economic recession of the second half of the 1980s as well as during the rapid economic expansion period of the first half of the 1990s. A similar inconsistency exists in many other Arab countries during the past generation.

On the other hand, one can find a high correlation between fertility decline and the intensity of the family planning programs. This high correlation can be found not only among Arab countries, but among non-Arab Islamic societies as well. A close examination of the Iranian fertility trends during the past four decades reveals a high correlation of the natalist policy in the form of decreasing fertility rates during "anti-natalist periods" and increasing fertility rates during the "pro-natalist period."[267] In 1966, prior to the implementation of the first family planning program, Iran's TFR was 7.7 children per woman,[268] declining to 6.5 in 1976 and increased again to 7.0 in 1980. In 1986, prior to the implementation of the national family planning program, Iran's TFR was measured at 6.3. Ten years later, in 1996, Iran's TFR declined to 2.8 and approached replacement-level at 2.2 in 2000.[269] According to the latest available data, by mid-2006, Iran's TFR declined to below-replacement level, averaging only 2.0 children per woman.[270] The socioeconomic changes in Iran during the past two decades were not so dramatic that they can, by themselves, provide sufficient explanation for this fertility decline. Thus, the only logical explanation for the Iranian unprecedented fertility decline since the early 1990s is the extensive implementation of a national family planning program.

The experience of Bangladesh also reveals a high correlation between national family planning program and fertility decline. Officially, Bangladesh, one of the poorest countries worldwide,[271] adopted a national family planning program in 1976.[272] By 1980, Bangladesh's TFR was 6.0 children per woman,[273] declining to 4.6 in 1990,[274] 3.3 in 1999/2000,[275] and reached as low as 3.0 by mid-2006.[276] Also in the case of Bangladesh, the socioeconomic indicators do not support such a rapid fertility decline. It was claimed by the CPD and UNFPA that Bangladesh's fertility decline "took place almost in the absence of concurrent improvement in income level and standards of living."[277] Thus, also in the case of Bangladesh the only logical explanation for the sharp fertility decline during the past two decades is the extensive anti-natalist measures taken by the government, which included financial benefits to those who followed the anti-natalist policy.

Hence, "the Middle Eastern lesson" is that in order to achieve rapid fertility decline, particularly in countries with low socioeconomic indicators, a direct and extensive governmental family planning program is an inevitable necessity. A crucial part of the anti-natalist policy, as was previously examined, is to change the traditional perception regarding both the desired number of children and the Islamic attitude toward the use of contraceptives. This changing attitude can only be done by the government as part of a national family planning campaign. This, however, is true not only in the Arab countries, but worldwide as well. Harbison and Robinson noted in this respect that: "Changed public opinion [regarding the desired number of children] was the most powerful and pervasive intervention of all."[278]

7 Why Tunisia and Lebanon?

As the data reveal, at the start of the twenty-first century, of all the Arab countries only Tunisia and Lebanon reached the desired replacement-level with a TFR of about 2 children per woman. Although the result was the same, the reasons for the sharp fertility decline in each of these two countries were totally different as will be examined below.

7.1 *Tunisia*[279]

Several factors were responsible for Tunisia's sharp fertility decline during the past three decades, the most important of which are as follows:

(a) **High governmental priority** was given to fertility decline since the mid-1960s, primarily by Bourguiba. The 2001 ECA Demographic Report noted that two of the main factors accounting for Tunisia's family planning success were "implication of a clear, well-designed and well-planned family planning and health program" and "political support for the population policy at the highest level."[280] Consequently, while the "demographic issue" was a central part in Tunisia's overall socioeconomic development plans, in the other non-oil Arab countries, the family planning issue received government attention only in periods of deep economic recession and was abandoned in periods of better economic performances. A central part of the top priority of the "population issue" in Tunisia was that since the 1960s Bourguiba did not try to "share" the responsibility of achieving the goal of fertility decline with others, but saw it as a sole governmental and even his personal responsibility.

(b) In contrast to the other Arab countries, the Tunisian anti-natalist measures were accompanied by **the promotion of women's status** through high enrollment rates in education, higher labor force participation rates, greater accessibility to legal abortion, and improved personal status in both the family itself and in overall public life.[281]

(c) Unlike many other Arab countries, whose long-standing political agenda included "Western hostility," **Tunisia maintained close relations with Western governments since gaining its independence.** Among the Arab countries, this "Western orientation" was unique to Tunisia and Lebanon alone. In the case of Egypt, for example, Ali noted that many Egyptians considered that the international aid for the Egyptian family planning program was "a Jewish-Christian conspiracy" aiming to weaken the Muslims in the world.[282]

(d) **The Islamic opposition in Tunisia never constituted a real political threat.** Thus, it was much easier for the Tunisian authorities to implement a comprehensive family planning policy without fear of the Islamic opposition.[283] A major factor of this was that following the election of Zine al-Abidine bin 'Ali in 1987 as the Tunisian President, political parties based on religion have been banned. Thus, while Egypt and Jordan "legalized" the political activities of the Islamic fundamentalists in order to appease them, the Tunisian authorities acted in the opposite direction and eradicated Islamic fundamentalism political activities. In retrospect, Tunisia became the only Arab country free from the "Islamic fundamentalist threat," which in turn, enabled it to implement a firm and successful family planning program as well as macroeconomic reforms.

7.2 Lebanon

The Lebanese low fertility rates, in total contrast to Tunisia, is attributed primarily to the following three factors: The most prominent is that Lebanon, in contrast to other Arab countries, was never a "soft state," meaning it never guaranteed public sector employment for its citizens and never offered a wide variety of free or even highly subsidized public services and basic foodstuffs. This was not only an outcome of the Lebanese "Western" culture, but also due to its political instability that prevented implementing large-scale socialist measures. Thus, in contrast to all of the other Arab countries, parents in Lebanon were forced to support their own children, rather than depend on massive governmental subsidies. This naturally led to lowering fertility. The second factor was the "shaky" political situation in the country since the onset of the second Civil War in 1975 which also did not encourage high fertility. The third factor was the massive emigration of young people of reproductive age. Thus, while in Tunisia the sharp fertility decline can be attributed to "good governance," in the case of Lebanon the low fertility rates should be attribute mainly to "no governance."

8 Summary and Conclusions

During the second half of the twentieth century, the demographic trends of the Arab countries were widely different from those which prevailed in most other developing countries worldwide. Thus, while in the early 1980s the fertility rates of Arab countries, both the oil-based and the non-oil alike, skyrocketed, many non-Arab developing countries were deep in the third stage of the demographic transition. It appears that two major barriers prevented implementation of declared and extensive family planning programs in the non-oil Arab countries until the mid-1980s. The primary barrier was the "oil effect" which "blinded" the leaders of the non-oil Arab countries in the arenas of both demography and socioeconomic policies. It was, it appears, "a period of false development," as the economic expansion and employment alleviation were based on rental sources rather than on internal production expansion. Thus, with the end of the "bonanza oil period" in the mid-1980s all the non-oil Arab countries, with the exception of Tunisia, found themselves in a situation of extremely high population growth rates on the one hand, and deep economic recession on the other.

The second barrier was the Islamic perception. As was examined previously, many attributed the high fertility rates in the Arab countries to the "Islamic factor," namely, that the Islamic culture, by definition, encourages high fertility. From the "Middle Eastern lesson," it appears that this common perception is a mistaken one. This is because during recent years, three Islamic Middle Eastern countries – Tunisia, Lebanon and Iran – achieved replacement fertility rate, while Turkey is rapidly approaching this target. Thus, it was not the "Islamic factor" that delayed fertility decline, but rather paralysis that "grabbed" the leaders of the non-oil Arab countries in regard to their willingness to confront the Islamic fundamentalist oppositions on the issue of family planning. Consequently, from a purely demographic point of view, the "oil period" was also "a lost period" in which although the leaders of the non-oil Arab countries were fully aware of the devastating consequences of the high fertility rates, in practice, they did not implement extensive anti-natalist measures and "hid behind the oil."

This hidden and wavering anti-natalist approach ended in the mid-1980s as a result of the collapse of both the "oil alternative" and the "pan-Arab ideology." The inescapable solution was radical socioeconomic changes, including the natalist policy. Thus, since the mid-1980s, the family planning activities of the non-oil Arab countries were greatly intensified. However, for some of these countries, this awakening was quite late, as they were forced to deal not only with a much larger population in nominal term, but also with a much younger population, dictating the demographic momentum consequences for the foreseeable future. Even in Egypt, the most populous Arab country, it was not until the mid-1980s that the demographic issue assumed high governmental priority.

In hindsight, if the non-oil Arab countries had initiated comprehensive anti-natalist measures in the 1960s instead of waiting until the late 1980s and in some cases until the mid-1990s, they could possibly have reached a stable population by the early 2020s. Egypt's population would then have numbered approximately 75 million in 2025, rather than more than 100 million as is estimated today. This is true in the case of the other Arab countries as well. One can conclude by stating that the failure of the leaders of the non-oil Arab countries to deal seriously with the demographic problem until very recently is responsible for prolonging the poverty and low living standards of their populations well into the twenty-first century.

Summary and Conclusions

The Emergence of the "Arab Demographic Catch 22"

The demographic and socioeconomic history of the Middle East during the twentieth century reveals that despite the unprecedented rapid population growth, the Malthusian Population Trap theory has proven to be a mistake. The last large-scale number of deaths due to starvation in the Middle East occurred in Iran during the years 1869–1871. Gilbar noted in this respect that: "specifically during the century that the natural increase rates increased the most, mass death from insufficient food stopped."[1] Generally speaking, it appears that in the parts of the world where starvation and epidemics did occur during the past century, mainly in the sub-Saharan African countries, they were caused by political-security instability that prevented socio-economic development, rather than by a limited amount of water or arable land, as the Malthusian Population Trap theory would explain it.

In retrospect, during the twentieth century, particularly in the second half, the increase in food production worldwide far exceeded the population growth rates as a direct result of technological development – namely, the "missing link" in the Malthusian Population Trap theory. Overall, the per capita food available for direct human consumption increased by as much as 24% during the 1961–1998 period. Consequently, since the 1960s, the prices of basic food items decreased steadily.

Moreover, as noted in Chapter 5, although the world's population increased four-fold during the twentieth century, the world's GDP increased 20 to 40 times during the corresponding period, leading to a sharp increase in the standard of living throughout the world, even in the least developed sub-Saharan African countries. Thus, the world's best economic achievements occurred precisely in the period that the global population growth rates were higher than ever before.

In this respect, the case of the Arab countries were no different and during the second half of the twentieth century, life expectancy at birth increased by as much as 25 years on average while the child mortality rate declined from almost one-third of live births to less than 4% and even 1% in the richest Gulf oil countries. These developments are indicative of the overall improvement in the standard of living in the Arab countries, even in the poorest two among them – Yemen and Sudan.

Indeed, the number of Arab countries that benefit from "self-sufficient food capacity,"[2] namely, countries that have the ability to produce their basic food needs in their own territory, steadily declined during the past two generations. This, however, is not a problem as long as the economy produces sufficient financial resources for the import of the foodstuffs needed. Allan noted in this respect that: "Having a strong and diverse economy is more important than being short of water . . . you can remedy a shortage of water through a diversified economy."[3] Hence, during the past two generations, despite the rapid population growth, none of the Arab countries, with the exception of Sudan (due to its prolonged civil war), failed to supply the basic foodstuffs needed.

Despite the refutation of the Malthusian Population Trap theory, however, the "mega-question" of the worldwide demographic carrying capacity has become the subject of debate between demographers, economists, sociologists, environmentalists and the like. On the one hand, the neo-Malthusian pessimists argue that the world is facing the threat of ecological catastrophe if the current population growth rates, and no less important, the intensified use of natural resources, are not controlled. The optimists, on the other hand, point to the sharp rise in the standard of living since the mid-twentieth century, despite the rapid population growth. From the optimistic viewpoint, the earth's carrying capacity is not static, but a function of technological development. As the technology steadily improves, the earth's carrying capacity increases accordingly.

The optimists also point to the fact that since the late 1970s, fertility rates are constantly declining in both the developed and the developing countries. Overall, at the beginning of the twenty-first century, the world's average natural increase rate is half of that which prevailed four decades ago, in the mid-1960s. Thus, future demographic pressure will gradually be relieved. In any case, they emphasize, it is impossible to predict future global demographic trends due to the enormous variables that are involved in this projection. The World Bank noted in 1994 that: "The long-run estimates for population show that there is little that can be said about the size of the population in the world in the distant future, other than that it could vary widely."[4]

Despite the continuing debate between "the optimists" and "the pessimists" regarding the earth's carrying capacity, the big change of the past generation in the area of demographic perception among the developing countries' leaders is that rapid population growth in and of itself is no longer considered a security-political asset or an engine for economic development. This changing perception, however, was the paramount lever that paved the way for the adoption of a more efficient family planning programs in developing countries since the 1980s, including in many of the non-oil Arab countries.

The end result of more effective family planning programs, combined with the marked improvement of women's educational level and gradual withdrawal from étatist-socialist policies, was a steady fertility decline. At the start of the twenty-first century, the TFR in the non-oil Arab countries was approximately half the level that prevailed three decades earlier, in the mid-1970s. In some of these countries, the reduction was more remarkable. Even in the Arab oil-based economies fertility rates have markedly declined during the past decade, mainly as a result of the women's educational improvement combined with some increase in their economically active rates. The most significant change in this respect has occurred in Bahrain, Saudi Arabia and Oman, although in the latter two to a lesser extent than in Bahrain.

Although fertility rates remarkably decreased in all the Arab countries during the past two decades, the economic performances of both the oil-based and the non-oil alike during that period were extremely poor by any international comparison. The most prominent expression for this poor performance was the stagnation, and in some countries even decline in real terms, of the per capita GDP.[5] In the cases of Syria and Jordan, as were examined in Chapter 3, the per capita GDP in the early 2000s did not even match the level in nominal figures which prevailed in these countries two decades earlier, in the early 1980s.[6] The crucial question, of course, is why were the economic performances of the Arab countries during the past generation so poor, despite the declining fertility rates and the various natural comparative advantages, not only as related to oil and gas, but transportation and tourism as well. What was wrong?

Broadly speaking, in explaining the poor economic performances of the Arab countries during the past generation, the academic literature concentrates on three main factors: The first is the political tension, both internally, mainly, the struggle between the regimes and the Islamist opposition, and internationally, primarily the Arab–Israeli conflict and the inter-Arab conflicts.[7] The second factor is the cultural-religious one, namely, the traditional Islamic perceptions that hindered globalization and human resources development. Kuran, for example, argued that: "The weakness of the region's private economic sectors and its deficiencies of human capital are among the lasting consequences of traditional Islamic law."[8] Murden also pointed to the Islamic culture and politics as the major barriers to improving economic performances and integration of the Arab countries in the global economy.[9] The third factor is, of course, the rapid population growth which "swallowed" the vast majority of the economic expansion.

A close examination of the socioeconomic policies of the Arab countries during the past three decades reveals, however, that all of the above-mentioned factors are consequences or reflections rather than the "core factors" of the poor economic performances of the Arab countries during the past generation. Overall, it seems that the same factors which hampered the implementation of an effective family planning policy in the non-oil Arab countries during the 1970s and most of the 1980s also prevented the adoption of the macroeconomic reforms needed for improving economic performances. Hence, avoiding the implementation of macroeconomic reforms and comprehensive family planning policies were "two sides of the same coin." As was examined in Chapter 3, during the "bonanza oil period," all of the Arab countries, with the exception of Tunisia and Lebanon, were Beblawi's "rentier states," and thus also Myrdal's "soft states" with no real change in their macroeconomic structure and natalist policies.

Indeed, there is no doubt that Rivlin and Even were right by claiming that: "Rental incomes play a key role throughout the [Middle East] region."[10] However, no less, and even more important than the rental incomes themselves, was their timing. The economic history of the Arab countries during the past four decades reveals that although there were periods of deep recession, they never lasted longer than a few years and were immediately followed by a sharp economic recovery. This was the case in the late 1960s and early 1970s when most of the non-oil Arab countries suffered from economic recession as a result of the June 1967 War and the War of Attrition combined with low oil prices. However, only few years later, this recession turned into extreme economic recovery as a result of the October 1973 "oil boom," opening the "bonanza oil decade" which stretched until the early 1980s. The "bonanza oil decade" again turned into a deep recession starting in 1985 as a result of the sharp decline in oil prices. However, this recession, also only lasted a few years and ended with the Iraqi invasion of Kuwait in August 1990. The non-oil Arab countries that joined the anti-Iraqi coalition benefited from relatively high economic growth rates during the early 1990s mainly as an outcome of the massive aid which they received as a "reward" for their support of the anti-Iraqi coalition as well as increasing employment opportunities for their surplus workforce in the Gulf oil states, mainly in Saudi Arabia and Kuwait. This was combined with the Arab–Israeli peace process which led to accelerated Western tourism in the Arab countries, increasing FDI in the region and massive US and international financial aid to the countries that were directly involved in the peace process.

The end of the peace process in the mid-1990s along with a sharp decline in oil prices again threw the region into a deep recession which, combined with the rapid population growth, led to a sharp decline in per capita GDP in most of the Arab countries, the oil-based and the non-oil alike.[11] However, this recession period also stretched only few years and ended in 1999, mainly due to the increasing oil prices, the rapid expansion of the tourism industry and the cancellation of the limit on the scale of Iraqi oil sales in December 1999[12] which led to a sharp increase of Iraqi imports of goods and services from other Arab countries.[13] Overall, one can conclude that during the past four decades, the most noticeable economic characteristic of the non-oil Arab countries was the fluctuation between rapid growth followed by a deep recession and vice versa.

Since the early 1970s, a prominent "rental factor" in the non-oil Arab countries was the massive intra-Arab labor migration. In retrospect, however, it appears that in the case of the non-oil Arab countries, the massive labor emigration was similar to a huge loan, in contrast to the classical perspective on labor-exporting as an export like any other commodity, in line with the Ricardian International Trade theory, or the recent approach that labor-exporting is a kind of FDI through the workers' remittances. Thus, although in the short run the economic situation largely improved, in the longer run, the contribution of the labor emigration to the macroeconomic development of the non-oil Arab countries was quite marginal.

Although from a purely political point of view, Susser is right in his claim that: "The Arab world, as such, no longer exists, any more than a Latin American world does,"[14] the economic ties between the Arab countries, in contrast to Aarts argument,[15] were rather markedly intensified following the October 1973 "oil boom." These intensified economic ties included not only massive intra-Arab labor migration, but also increased trade volumes, tourism and relatively large-scale aid to the poorer Arab countries. In the early 1980s, following the Second Baghdad Arab Summit, Arab aid amounted to about one-fourth of the Jordanian and Syrian GDP.

In the cases of Jordan and Egypt, the most important rental income source was, and still is, the "US economic umbrella." The massive US financial support to these two countries is not only as a reward for their peace treaties with Israel, but even more so because the US wants to "keep alive" these two regimes, as their alternative are the Islamic fundamentalist movements. This "economic umbrella" is manifested in various ways, but primarily through generous financial grants, soft loans and opening the US market for their goods through the QIZs.

In general, since the early 1970s, "the rental option" always constituted an alternative to both macroeconomic reforms and comprehensive anti-natalist policies. The history of the human race reveals that only in a few cases have regimes conducted harsh socioeconomic reforms when they had other options. Hence, harsh socioeconomic reforms, which would lead to deteriorating living standard in the short run and thus would certainly raise large-scale resistance, particularly of the lower classes, would be implemented only after the regime realized that there are no other options. In the Middle Eastern case, until the late 1980s, none of the recession periods was long enough to force the regimes to carry out these reforms. Therefore, although the performance of the non-oil Arab countries was poor by any international comparison, they were good enough through the various rental incomes to avoid political turmoil on socioeconomic grounds.

Laipson argued that the Middle Eastern rapid population growth "has taken place in circumstances of political distress and poor governance."[16] It seems that it was actually the opposite of Laipson's description. The continuation of rapid population growth in the non-oil Arab countries, with the exception of Yemen and Sudan, was because of the strength of the central regimes due to their massive rental incomes which enabled them to both avoid implementing the necessary socioeconomic reforms and establish huge security forces.[17] However, although the Arab regimes could guarantee their survival through the large-scale rental incomes, they were constantly forced to confront the Islamic fundamentalist opposition. The end result of the massive rental incomes on the one hand, and the severe resistance of the Islamic opposition to the implementation of anti-natalist and economic reforms on the other, was stagnant socioeconomic policies in the vast majority of the non-oil Arab countries throughout the 1970s and most of the 1980s. Thus, the most prominent political characteristic of these countries during the past generation was "stability within instability," namely, stable regimes that are constantly threatened by a strong opposition.

Only in the second half of the 1980s and more so during the 1990s when most of the "rental options" markedly declined, did it become clear, beyond any doubt, that the natalist approach and the macroeconomic policy alike must be radically changed in order to avoid socioeconomic catastrophe. Then, and only then, were some macroeconomic reforms and anti-natalist measures adopted almost simultaneously in the non-oil Arab countries in coordination with the IMF. However, large-scale demonstrations against the economic reforms were staged in many Arab countries, including the "food riots" in Egypt in January 1977,[18] in Morocco during the early 1980s,[19] in Jordan in April 1989 and again in August 1996,[20] and in Yemen in 1998.[21]

In retrospect, although the reforms were crucial in order to revive the non-oil Arab economies, they failed, at least until the present, to bring about relief in two paramount areas. The first is in the eradication of poverty. The initial assumption upon which the reforms were based was that economic liberalization would be for the benefit of all, including the lower strata, through job creation on the one hand, and increased competition which would bring about reduced prices of many commodities, on the other. This optimistic assumption, however, did not materialize. Hence, two decades later, at the beginning of the twenty-first century, the poverty scale in the entire non-oil Arab countries has remained extremely high, despite the fact that the economic performances of these countries largely improved.[22]

The only exception among the non-oil Arab countries is Tunisia, in which the damage from the liberalization measures to the lower strata was relatively minimized through governmental aid to poor families and support of the NGO activities among the lower strata.[23] Indeed, the latest available World Bank poverty indicators show that the incidence of extreme poverty in Tunisia declined from 8% in 1995 to 4% in 2000.[24] These indicators are likely to improve even further in the coming years as a result of Tunisia's acceleration economic growth rates. During the years 2000–2005,

Tunisia's per capita GDP increased by as much as 20% in real terms – higher than in any other non-oil Arab country.[25] On the other side of the poverty cycle is Yemen where 45.2% of the population lives below the income poverty line of $2 per capita per day and 15.7% below the abject poverty line[26] of $1 per day.[27] Even in Egypt, despite its tremendous economic development during the past decade, the percentage of the population living below the poverty line of $2 per day remained extremely high – 43.9% in 2003.[28] Tunisia, it should be noted, was able to achieve this low percentage of poor, due *inter alia*, to its considerably lower share of dependency population compared to the other non-oil Arab countries – a direct consequence of its successful anti-natalist policy in the 1970s and 1980s.

The second field in which the macroeconomic reforms did not bring relief was in unemployment. Whereas previously increases and decreases in unemployment had been a function of overall economic development, starting in the late 1980s, steady increases in unemployment rates occurred in all of the non-oil Arab countries even during periods of substantial economic expansion. This new phenomenon of structural unemployment developed when the number of new job opportunities could not match the number of new entrants into the labor forces. As described in the 2004 ESCWA socioeconomic report:

> The region now faces the highest global rate of new entrants into the labor market, the highest unemployment rate and, when calculated over the past two decades, the lowest global rate of per capita GDP growth.[29]

Moreover, a central part of the economic reforms carried out by the non-oil Arab countries was massive privatization of public sector companies. In the case of Egypt for example, the privatization scheme adopted in 1991, in coordination with the IMF, included 314 governmental companies, which employed over a million employees at that time. Ten years later, in 2001, the number of employees in these companies had been reduced to less than half a million.[30] Thus, at least in the short run, the process of privatization involved massive dismissal of employees due to previously huge hidden unemployment.

Hence, although during the past decade the percentage of the working age population within the total population in each of the Arab countries has substantially increased, due to the huge unemployment – both open and disguised – the actual meaning of a rapid increase of the working age population is rise in employment pressures rather than an increase in per capita income and savings. As Bloom, Canning and Sevilla noted, the demographic gift has to be earned. "Without the right policy environment, countries will be too slow to adapt to their changing age structure and, at best, will miss an opportunity to secure high growth."[31]

As the Asian Tigers simultaneously implemented both the macroeconomic reforms and comprehensive anti-natalist measures during the 1960s and 1970s, they could benefit from the improved dependency ratio during the 1980s and 1990s since the employment demand exceeded the workforce supply.[32] Consequently, the "demographic gift" constituted an engine to accelerate their economic performances through increasing labor productivity which, in turn, led to higher wages and savings. Results from various researches revealed that between 25% and 40% of "the East Asian economic miracle" should be attributed to the "demographic gift factor."[33] Overall, during the 1965–1990 period, the per capita income in the Asian Tigers increased by as much as 6% on annual average in real terms.[34] Thus, while in the Asian Tigers the availability of a larger workforce became an engine for accelerating economic growth rate during the past two decades, in the non-oil Arab countries, with the exception of Tunisia, the opposite occurred and the improving dependency ratio as a result of decreasing fertility rates was "wasted" due to the inability of the private sectors to absorb the bulging workforce.

Moreover, the non-Arab developing countries that adopted macroeconomic and demographic reforms during the 1960s and the 1970s, did it in a period when the international economic environment was much more in favor of increasing involvement of developing economies in the global economy than was the situation two decades later, in the 1980s and 1990s. This is because, the technological gap between the developed and the developing economies at the end of the twentieth century was already "too wide." Richards explains the main difference between the Asian Tigers and the Arab countries as follows: "Unlike the East Asian case, incomes in the Middle East grew for reasons which were fundamentally exogenous to the difficult process of structural transformation."[35] In other words, the rapid economic growth in the Arab countries during the 1970s and the first half of the 1980s was basically "a fabricated development," particularly in the technological and employment-generation areas, rather then "a real development," generated by endogenous engines.

Above all, due to the already extremely high employment pressure, the governments of the non-oil Arab countries could not seriously promote increasing female labor force participation, which, as was examined in Chapter 2, constitutes one of the two most important "fertility declining engines." Consequently, although there was some increase in the female economically active rates in the non-oil Arab countries during the past two decades, at the beginning of the twenty-first century this rate is still among the lowest worldwide.

Therefore, it seems that the worse legacy of the "oil booms" of 1973/74 and again in 1980/81 was not only the "Economic Dutch Disease" as claimed by Richards, but even more so a "Demographic Dutch Disease" that created a situation in which in order to reduce employment pressure, the non-oil Arab countries have to achieve an imaginary annual real GDP growth rate of more than 7%.[36] At the beginning of the twenty-first century, "the economic-demographic paradox" of the non-oil Arab countries is that although the economic growth rates are much above the population growth rates, in many cases even more than twice,[37] they are still not high enough to bring down unemployment. Hence, it appears that the developing countries that did not "jump on the bandwagon" for macroeconomic and demographic reforms during the 1960s and 1970s, in effect, "missed the boat," at least up to the present.

During the past decade, the most commonly recommended solutions for the current poor economic performances of the non-oil Arab countries concentrates in the areas of economic liberalization, exchange rate reforms, shrinking the public sector, reducing subsidies and promoting women economic participation in line with the "Washington Consensus." Yousef, for example, claimed that:

> [T]he Middle East requires a broad-based transformation of its economies to strengthen the core drivers of job creation and economic growth: greater entrepreneurship and private sector development; faster integration into global trade and investment flows; and less dependence on oil and greater economic diversification . . . Broad-based economic prosperity in the future requires greater attention to factors driving gender inequality [38]

In order to utilize the current Middle Eastern "demographic gift," Yousef claimed that:

> As East Asian's experience had shown, this differential – the so-called demographic gift – provides MENA with an opportunity to accelerate economic growth through faster accumulation of factors of production. Lower dependency ratios imply a potential for higher savings and investments. Rapid labor force growth, especially with increased education and longer life expectancy, provides economies with a larger pool of productive workers.[39]

Thus, according to Yousef, the combination of macroeconomic reforms and the current "demographic gift" period, have the potential to rescue the non-oil Arab countries from their current poor socioeconomic situation. His optimistic approach is also illustrated by the name of his book, *Unlocking the Employment Potential in the Middle East and North Africa,* published by the World Bank. Yousef's greatest mistake was in not realizing the basic difference between the non-oil Arab countries and the Asian Tigers. In the case of the Asian Tigers, as well as in some other worldwide developing economies, the changing age structure in favor of the working age population occurred simultaneously with macroeconomic reforms which produced various "endogenous development engines." In the non-oil Arab countries, in total contrast, since the "development engines" during the "bonanza oil decade" were exogenous, the current "demographic gift" period could not be utilized to promote per capita income and savings, as the labor markets do not have the ability to absorb the rapidly growing workforces.

Therefore, the "demographic gift" period of the non-oil Arab countries was actually "wasted" due to the mismatch between the labor supply and demand. Moreover, as higher education in the non-oil Arab countries did not develop in line with labor market demands, but rather as a target in and of itself, many of the university and other higher educational institutions graduates could not find suitable employment. This situation, of course, led to the creation of a whole generation, whose most prominent characteristic is "employment frustration."

Therefore, the non-oil Arab leaders are currently facing the most crucial dilemma ever: If they accelerate the pace of structural macroeconomic reforms and intensify the anti-natalist measures, they may succeed in alleviating some of the current socioeconomic pressures in the long run, but will almost certainly face intensified political unrest in the short run, as was the case in their previous attempts to cut subsidies on basic foodstuffs and services. On the other hand, if they choose to stick to their current stagnant socioeconomic policies, such as in the case of Syria, or to only partially implement the reforms, as in the cases of Egypt, Jordan and Morocco, they may avoid political unrest in the short run,[40] but in the longer run, their economies most certainly will collapse into a deep recession. As the Middle Eastern political history of the twentieth century reveals, a deep economic recession is "political dynamite" as it has thus far been the only motivator for large-scale spontaneous demonstrations against the regimes.

In retrospect, it appears that the main difference between the majority of the non-oil Arab countries and many of the developing countries worldwide is what Rivlin noted regarding the difference between Park's Korea and 'Abd al-Nasser's Egypt that "the leadership in South Korea gave priority to economic growth, while that in Egypt did not."[41] The core of this difference is that a considerable proportion of many non-oil Arab regimes' resources were directed toward "hate and hostility ideology," either toward "the Zionist entity" or toward "Western civilization." In the name of this "hate and hostility ideology," many leaders of the non-oil Arab countries, the most prominent of whom were 'Abd al-Nasser, Hafiz al-Asad and Saddam Husayn, and among the current leaders, Bashar al-Asad, realized that "their main task," other than, of course, continued control over their countries, was to "win this battle" even at the expense of socioeconomic achievements.

One might even say that in the case of the non-oil Arab countries, Malthus was so wrong until he was so right but not in the case of food scarcity but rather in the case of employment scarcity. It seems that at one point or other, already in the foreseeable future, "employment catastrophe" could not be avoided. Moreover, the Ricardian "Iron Law of Wages"[42] also proved to be true, not only in the case of agriculture, but rather across all economic sectors. Thus, although "Egyptians were guaranteed jobs, cheap food, free education . . . medical care, and low rents . . . for which they forfeited their political voice," as claimed by Brown,[43] they also lost the option of better socioeconomic conditions in the future. This analysis is valid in the cases of Syria, Morocco and Jordan as well, although to a lesser extent due to their smaller population.

Tunisia, on the other hand, which enjoyed the "oil boom effect" the least among the non-oil Arab countries, was the first to adopt macroeconomic reforms and an effective family planning policy already in the early 1970s. Consequently, its socioeconomic condition at the dawn of the twenty-first century was the best among all the non-oil Arab countries. By 2005, Tunisia's per capita GDP amounted to $7,768, compared to $4,688 in Jordan, $4,211 in Egypt and only $3,610 in Syria (in PPP terms, see Appendix 1). This means that at the start of the twenty-first century the living standard in Tunisia was twice as high as all the other non-oil Arab countries. A major pillar for current Tunisia's much better socioeconomic condition is its low fertility rates.

During the past two decades, the Gulf oil states have also been forced to confront a crucial "employment-development dilemma." Since the 1960s, when oil became their major financial resource, the development strategy of these countries rested on three major pillars: economic diversification, in order to create non-rental sources for both income and employment; pro-natalist policy aiming to reduce the dependence on foreign labor; and finally, improving educational and vocational training systems to enable the local workforces to replace the foreign workers in top managerial and skilled positions.

Four decades later, none of these three basic goals was actually achieved. As was examined in Chapter 4, the foreign workers in each of the Gulf oil states continue to regularly increase, even in Bahrain and Oman – the countries where the labor force nationalization policies are considered the most successful – while simultaneously the unemployment among nationals skyrocketed. As the previous labor policies largely failed, the Gulf authorities were recently forced to adopt a new employment strategy which has allowed for unlimited labor importation in order to create sufficient suitable job opportunities for the indigenous workforce. Thus, not only has the dependence on foreign labor not diminished, it has rather increased.

Therefore, while in the developed economies foreign workers constitute a supplement to the national workforce, in the Gulf oil economies, in total contrast, the indigenous workforces are a supplement, in many cases, even an unnecessary supplement, to the foreign workers. In Qatar, Abu Dhabi and Dubai, nationals represent only a few percents of the total workforce – no doubt a unique situation without even one similar case worldwide. At the top managerial positions as well, the Gulf oil countries have failed, at least so far, to replace the vast majority of foreign workers by nationals. It seems that even the Gulf authorities themselves do not really believe in their own labor and immigration policy. On the one hand, they continue to produce plans that were aimed at sharply cutting the number of the foreign labor, while simultaneously the official demographic and labor projections predict an increase rather than decrease in the number of foreign workers.[44]

Also in the area of economic diversification, the Gulf economies did not achieve their basic goal of reducing the oil income dependency. At the start of the twenty-first century, in each of these economies, oil and gas rental income still constitutes the vast majority of the governmental revenues and the main engine for socioeconomic development, particularly the services sectors, the most of which depend almost totally on governmental finance. In the developed economies, in total contrast, a considerable percentage of services sector activities are directed toward supplying services for local private sector industries and exporting services, such as IT (information technology) and research services, high-tech services, and the like. Thus, not only does the private services sector provide ongoing new job opportunities, ranging from top managerial positions to low-skilled jobs, but a considerable percentage of its activities do not depend on governmental funding.

The success of the UAE, particularly Dubai, in the area of economic diversification, was achieved only because the authorities removed almost all of the barriers to labor import and foreign investments. However, the "price" of the UAE's successful economic diversification was flooding the country with foreign workers while transforming the indigenous population into a tiny minority in their own country. Indeed, following the publication of the 2005 census results, the UAE Labor Minister warned that: "with population growth rates ranging from 10–15% a year,[45] nationals would comprise just 4% of the population in 2015."[46] A senior academic in Al-Ain University recently said that: "We are selling it [the country] like nobody else."[47]

Consequently, although there is no doubt that in each of the Gulf economies there was a tremendous development in the area of public services and infrastructure facilities, these developments, however, have not yet transformed these economies from a rentier-based into production-based. As Ayubi noted, "Economic expansion is not an economic development."[48] The continuing connection between oil prices and economic performances was highly illustrated during the late 1990s when oil prices were extremely low (see Table 4.2). Thus, in 1999, for example, the Saudi GDP shrank by 0.8% and that of Oman by 0.1%.[49] In the other four GCC countries, the trend was similar with negative or marginal GDP growth rates during the second half of the 1990s.

The huge oil revenues since 2004 enabled the Gulf royal families, in the meantime, to continue with their previous rentier socio-political formula. The political reforms that were carried out in these countries during the past decade were only limited to "surface reforms" with no real changes made in the form of public participation in the decision-making process.[50] As the political reforms were initiated by the authorities themselves, it is not surprising that the widest reforms were implemented by Al Thani royal family of Qatar – a country with no political opposition at all.[51] On the other hand, in Saudi Arabia, the country with the most dangerous opposition, no real political reform has been implemented yet. Ehteshami and Wright noted in this respect regarding the Gulf oil countries that: "While the elites hold power so tightly, change will come only if those in power choose to implement it."[52]

It seems that the failure of the GCC employment policies constituted the major factor for their relatively poor economic performances during the past generation. This is because while Adam Smith's growth theory mainly stressed the importance of free trade, the modern growth theories interpreted human capital as the most important economic tool.[53] In the Gulf oil economies, however, the human capital was and still is mainly imported. Moreover, as public sector employment was guaranteed almost to the entire indigenous workforce within the overall rentier socio-political framework, engineering, the exact sciences, etc. did not attract many of the young nationals who preferred the humanities and social sciences. Khan Zahid, the Chief Economist at Riyad Bank, recently said that: "The [Saudi] government and private sector took the easy option years ago and of course it is hard now to wean the economy off that dependence on cheap labor."[54] The end result of this process was the development of the "dual labor market trap." Hence, since the early 1980s, the GCC countries had become "rich developing economies" with all of the socio-political implications of this unique situation.

The intensification of youth frustration as a result of unemployment was one of the major catalysts for the expansion of Islamic radicalism in the Arab countries during the past generation. Richards noted that: "The mixture of regime incapacity, rising unemployment and poverty, and very young populations is politically highly volatile."[55] Specifically in the case of Saudi Arabia, Long wrote already in 1997, that is, four years prior to the September 11, 2001 al-Qa'ida attacks on the US, that:

> Increasing numbers of unemployed or underemployed young people – while their basic needs are being met by their families – are beginning to feel marginalized, frustrated, and resentful to the establishment, not for what it does but because they are not a part of it. It is such people who become willing listeners to the militant political message of the radical Islamists.[56]

The traditional academic assumption was that improvement in the educational level, combined with the sharp improvement in the living standard as a result of both increased public subsidies and massive public sector employment, would lead to greater secularization in the developing societies worldwide. In the case of the Arab counties, in the oil-based and the non-oil alike, in reality the opposite has occurred. The inability of the regimes to supply the needed employment opportunities and improved living standard, led many of the educated unemployed to support the Islamic opposition which promised them "a better life." This, it appears, is the core of the current "Arab Demographic Catch 22."

Appendix I
Key Economic Indicators for some Arab Countries, 2005

'Country	GDP (current $US, billions)	Per capita GNI (Atlas method, current $US)	Per capita GDP* (PPP $US)	HDI Rank*	Balance of trade (% of GDP)		Long-term debt current $US, (billions)
					Exports	Imports	
			Arab non-oil Countries				
Lebanon	21.9	6,320	5,837	78	19.3	44.3	18.9
Tunisia	28.7	2,880	7,768	87	48.0	50.6	14.7
Jordan	12.7	2,460	4,688	86	51.9	93.4	6.9
Syria	26.3	1,380	3,610	107	36.6	40.2	5.6
Egypt	89.4	1,260	4,211	111	30.5	32.7	28.1
Morocco	56.1	1,740	4,309	123	36.3	42.9	16.2
Sudan	27.5	640	1,949	141	18.1	28.0	11.7
Yemen	15.1	600	879	150	45.8	37.8	4.7
			Arab oil countries				
Kuwait	80.8	30,630	19,384	33	67.7	30.4	—
UAE	129.7	—	24,056	49	94.3	76.3	—
Qatar	42.5	—	19,844	46	68.3	33.5	—
Saudi Arabia	309.8	12,510	13,825	76	60.7	26.4	—
Libya	38.8	5,530	7,570	64	—	—	—
Algeria	102.3	2,730	6,603	102	47.6	23.5	16.4

— No data available.
* Data related to 2004.

GNI (Gross National Income). The sum of value added by all resident producers plus any product taxes (less subsidies) not included in the valuation of output plus net receipts of primary income (compensation of employees and property income) from abroad.

PPP (Purchasing Power Parity). A rate of exchange that accounts for different prices for goods and services in various countries worldwide, thus enabling an international comparison of real outputs and incomes.

HDI (Human Development Index).

Sources: UNDP, *Human Development Report–2006* (New York, 2006); World Bank, *World Development Indicators Database* (April 2007). Available online at: http://web.worldbank.org.

Notes

Introduction

1 On the definition of the term PPP, see Appendix 1. On the meaning of the PPP term regarding the Middle Eastern countries, see: Alan Richards and John Waterbury, *A Political Economy of the Middle East*, second edition (Boulder: Westview Press, 1996), pp. 11–13.

2 Kuwait and Libya were relatively rich countries already in the 1960s, with a per capita GNP of $3,650 in Kuwait and $1,490 in Libya in 1968 (current prices). This was due to their small indigenous populations on the one hand, and their relatively large oil exports on the other. See: The World Bank (WB), *World Tables, 1989–90 Edition* (Published for the WB by the Johns Hopkins University Press, 1990).

3 *Ibid.*

4 The two names common to this part of the Middle East are the "Arabian Gulf," used, naturally, by the Arabs, and the "Persian Gulf," used by the Persians. In order to avoid any political connotation, I decided to use the neutral name, the Gulf.

5 Gad G. Gilbar, *The Middle East Oil Decade and Beyond* (London and Portland: Frank Cass, 1997), p. 1.

6 WB, *World Tables, 1989–90 Edition.*

7 WB, *World Development Report–1983* (Published for the WB by Oxford University Press, 1983), pp. 148–49, table 1.

8 Eliyahu Kanovsky, *Economic Development of Jordan* (Tel Aviv University, The David Horovitz Institute for the Research of Developing Countries, 1974), p. 63.

9 On the economic damage to Egypt resulting from the June 1967 War, see: Eliyahu Kanovsky, *The Economic Impact of the Six-Day War: Israel, The Occupied Territories, Egypt, Jordan* (New York: Praeger Publishers, 1970), pp. 279–86.

10 Osama Hamed, "Egypt's Open Door Economic Policy: An Attempt at Economic Integration in the Middle East," *IJMES*, Vol. 13, No. 2 (1981), p. 1.

11 On the Syrian defence burden, see: Volker Perthes, *The Political Economy of Syria under Asad* (London and New York: I.B. Tauris, 1995), pp. 31–32; Paul Rivlin, "The Syrian Economy in the 1990s," *Data and Analysis* (Tel Aviv University, The Moshe Dayan Center, June 1999), pp. 53–54; Onn Winckler, "Hafiz al-Asad's Socio-Economic Legacy: The Balance of Achievements and Failures," *Orient*, Vol. 42, No. 3 (2001), p. 451.

12 Following the signing of the peace treaty with Israel, the tourism industry has become not only the most lucrative source of hard currency of Egypt – higher than Suez Canal revenues and the US financial aid together – but also the largest private sector employer. On the contribution of the tourism industry to the Egyptian economy, see: Yoel Mansfeld and Onn Winckler, "Options for Viable Economic Development through Tourism among the Non-Oil Arab Countries: The Egyptian Case," *Tourism Economics*, Vol. 10, No. 4 (2004), pp. 374–79.

13 On the contribution of the peace agreement with Israel to the Egyptian economy, see: Gad G. Gilbar and Onn Winckler, "The Economic Factor of the Arab–Israeli Peace Process: The Cases of Egypt, Jordan and Syria," in Elie Podeh and Asher Kaufman (eds.), *Arab–Jewish Relations: From Conflict to Reconciliation?* (Brighton and Portland: Sussex Academic Press, 2006), pp. 199–200.

14 By 2003, the total foreign grants which Jordan received amounted to JD682.6 million ($962 million), representing as high as 28.7% of the total governmental revenues, compared to JD415.9 million ($586 million) in 2002. See: Central Bank of Jordan, *Annual Report–2003* (Amman, 2004), p. 44. See also: *MEED*, July 22–28, 2005, p. 24.

15 *MEED*, September 10–16, 2004, pp. 28–29; July 22–28, 2005, pp. 28–29.

16 *MEED*, May 31, 2002, p. 25.

17 On the economic relationship between Egypt and Iraq until the collapse of Saddam Husayn regime, see: Onn Winckler, "The Economic Consequences of the Iraqi Crisis on the Mashreq Countries," *Mediterranean Politics*, Vol. 11, No. 3 (2006), pp. 406–7.

18 *MEED*, August 1, 2003, p. 6.

19 On the economic consequences of the collapse of oil prices in the mid-1980s, see Chapter 3.

20 Steven Heydemann, "Taxation without Representation: Authoritarianism and Economic Liberalization in Syria," in Ellis Goldberg, Reşat Kasaba and Joel Migdal (eds.), *Rules and Rights in the Middle East: Democracy, Law, and Society* (Seattle and London: University of Washington Press, 1993), pp. 69–80.

21 A "soft state," a term initiated by Gunnar Myrdal, refers to countries in which "policies decided on are often not enforced, if they are enforced at all, and in that the authorities, even when framing policies, are reluctant to place obligations on people." *Asian Drama: An Inquiry into the Poverty of Nations*, Vol. 1 (New York: Pantheon, Random House, 1968), p. 66. On the "soft state" Nasserism, see: Gad G. Gilbar, "Nasser's Soft Revolution," in his *Population Dilemmas in the Middle East* (London and Portland: Frank Cass, 1997), pp. 80–96; John Waterbury, "The 'Soft State' and the Open Door: Egypt Experience with Economic Liberalization, 1974–1984," *Comparative Politics*, Vol. 18, No. 1 (1985), pp. 65–83.

22 Iliya Harik, "Privatization: The Issue, the Prospects and the Fears," in Iliya Harik and Denis J. Sullivan (eds.), *Privatization and Liberalization in the Middle East* (Bloomington, IN: Indiana University Press, 1992), p. 16.

23 By the years 2000 and 2001, the FDI in Tunisia amounted to $1.265 billion – the highest among all the Arab countries in per capita terms. See: UNDP and AFESD, *Arab Human Development Report–2003* (Amman, 2003), p. 102, table 5.1.

24 Clement M. Henry and Robert Springborg, *Globalization and the Politics of Development in the Middle East* (Cambridge: Cambridge University Press, 2001), p. 99.

25 The replacement-level fertility rate is 2.1 children per woman. On this subject, see Chapter 2.

26 WB, *World Tables, 1995 Edition*, p. 648.

27 Philippe Fargues, "Demography and Politics in the Arab World," *Population: An English Selection*, Vol. 5 (1993), p. 1.

28 Charles B. Nam and Susan G. Philliber, *Population: A Basic Orientation*, second edition (Englewood Cliffs, New Jersey: Prentice-Hall, 1984), p. 2.

29 John Graunt along with William Petty, developed early human statistical and census methods which later provided a framework for modern demographic research.

30 John C. Caldwell, "Demography: Scope, Perspectives and Theory," pp. 1–2. Available at: http://cph.georgetown.edu/Conference.

31 On Graunt's research, see: D. V. Glass, "John Graunt and His Natural and Political Observations," *Proceedings of the Royal Society of London*, Vol. 159, No. 974 (1963), pp. 2–37.

32 The term demography itself started to be widely used in English-speaking countries only in the mid-twentieth century. Previously, the common term was "population study."

33 Caldwell, "Demography: Scope, Perspectives and Theory," p. 1.

34 On the development of the demographic discipline since Graunt, see: Frank Lorimer, "The Development of Demography," in Philip M. Hauser and Otis Dudley Duncan (eds.), *The Study of Population* (Chicago and London: The University of Chicago Press, 1959), pp. 124–79.

35 On the historian's view of demography, see: Dudley Kirk, "Demographic Transition Theory," *Population Studies*, Vol. 50, No. 3 (1996), pp. 373–75.

36 On the demographic approach of the PLO, see: Matti Steinberg, "Lir'ot et ha-Nolad: ha-Gorem ha-Demography be-Re'iyat Asha'f," in Ami Ayalon and Gad G. Gilbar (eds.), *Demographya ve-Politiqa be-Medinot 'Arav* (Tel Aviv: Hakibbutz Hameuchad, 1995), pp. 153–89 (Hebrew). On the Israeli pro-natalist policy, see: Onn Winckler, "The Failure of Pronatalism of the Developed States 'with Cultural-Ethnic Hegemony': The Israeli Lesson," *Population, Place and Space*, Vol. 14, No. 2 (2008), pp. 119–23.

37 André Burguière, "Demography," in Jacques Le Goff and Pierre Nora (eds.), *Constructing the Past: Essays in Historical Methodology* (Cambridge: Cambridge University Press, 1985), p. 99.

Chapter 1 *Sources for Demographic Research of the Arab States*

1 Pat Hudson, *History by Numbers: An Introduction to Quantitative Approaches* (London: Arnold, 2000), p. xvii.

2 On the history of demographic censuses, see: Australian Bureau of Statistics, "Census through the Ages." Available at: http://www.abs.gov.au.; Caldwell, "Demography: Scope, Perspectives and Theory," pp. 1, 4.

3 Michael Anderson, *Population Change in North-Western Europe, 1750–1850* (London: Macmillan Education, 1988), pp. 11–12.

4 On the Algerian censuses until independence (1962), see: Dorothy Good, "Notes on the Demography of Algeria," *Population Index*, Vol. 27, No. 1 (January 1961), p. 7, table 1.

5 Georges Sabagh, "The Demography of the Middle East," *Middle East Studies Association Bulletin*, Vol. 4, No. 2 (May 15, 1970), pp. 1–2.

6 The *Iltizam* system was based on renting the right of tax collection from a specific area on an annual basis in exchange for a fixed amount of tax that had to be delivered to the central authorities. The revenues of the tax collector, the *Multazim*, consisted of the gap between the amount that he succeeded in collecting and the amount that he was obligated to deliver to the regime.

7 Stanford J. Shaw, "The Ottoman Census System and Population, 1831–1914," *IJMES*, Vol. 9, No. 3 (1978), p. 325.

8 Haim Gerber, "The Population of Syria and Palestine in the Nineteenth Century," *Asian and African Studies*, Vol. 13, No. 1 (1979), p. 58.

9 Dominique Tabutin and Bruno Schoumaker, "The Demography of the Arab World and the Middle East from the 1950s to the 2000s," *Population*, Vol. 60, Nos. 5 & 6 (2005), p. 514.

10 Shaw, "The Ottoman Census," pp. 325–27; Bernard Lewis, *The Emergence of Modern Turkey*, second edition (Oxford and New York: Oxford University Press, 1968), p. 90.

11 Kemal H. Karpat, "Ottoman Population Records and the Census of 1881/82–1893," *IJMES*, Vol. 9, No. 3 (1978), p. 242.

12 Uri M. Kupferschmidt, "A Note on the Muslim Religions Hierarchy towards the End of the Ottoman Period," in David Kushner (ed.), *Palestine in the Late Ottoman Period* (Jerusalem: Yad Yizhak Ben-Zvi Press, 1986), p. 123.

13 M. A. Mekkawi for example, opened his essay, *The Population of Lebanon*, by stating: "The evolution of population information in Lebanon is thoroughly deceptive" (p. 1).

14 On the Pan Arab Project for Family Health, see the official website of the project at: http://www.papfam.org/papfam/indexEn.htm.

15 The GCC organization was established in 1981 and includes: Saudi Arabia, Kuwait, Oman, Qatar, Bahrain and the UAE.

16 Egypt, CAPMAS, *Statistical Yearbook, 1952–1992*, p. 3.

17 See the website of the DHS at: http://www.measuredhs.com.

18 ECWA, *The Population Situation in the ECWA Region-Jordan* (Beirut, 1979), p. 2.

19 According to UNRWA data, some 140,000 Palestinians already registered as refugees were part of the new exodus from the East Bank and Gaza Strip together with about 240,000 Jordanian citizens of the West Bank who are referred to as "displaced persons." See UNRWA website at: http://www.un.org/unrwa.

20 *Jordan Times*, December 29–30, 1994.

21 On the Jordanian 2004 census, see the official website of the Jordanian Department of Statistics at: http://www.dos.gov.jo/census2004/page1_e.htm

22 The Hashemite Kingdom of Jordan, Department of Statistics in collaboration with OPC Macro, *Jordan Population and Health Survey–2002* (Amman, June 2003). See also: "Jordan 2002: Results from the Population and Family Health Survey," *Studies in Family Planning*, Vol. 35, No. 4 (2004), pp. 291–95.

23 On the 1921–1922 census, see: Mohamed Chafic Dibbs, "The Relationship Between Censuses and Civil Registration in the Syrian Arab Republic," *Population Bulletin of ECWA*, No. 18 (June 1980), p. 82.

24 Robert Widmer, "Population," in Said B. Himadeh (ed.), *Economic Organization of Syria* (Beirut: The American University of Beirut Press, 1936), p. 3.

25 Bent Hansen, *Economic Development in Syria* (California: The Rand Corporation, 1969), p. 16.

26 Eliane Domschke and Doreen S. Goyer, *The Handbook of National Population Censuses, Africa and Asia* (New York, Westport, Connecticut and London: Greenwood Press, 1986), p. 835.

27 Egypt and Syria were unified during the period February 1958–September 1961.

28 Domschke and Goyer, *The Handbook of National Population Censuses, Africa and Asia*, p. 838; Syrian Arab Republic, State Planning Commission and CBS in collaboration with the Population Council, by Nader M. al-Hallak et al., *Composition and Growth of Population in the Syrian Arab Republic* (Damascus, September 1979), pp. 1–2.

29 ECWA, *The Population Situation in the ECWA Region-Syrian Arab Republic* (Beirut, 1980), p. 2.

30 Domschke and Goyer, *The Handbook of National Population Censuses, Africa and Asia*, p. 838.

31 Farid el-Boustani, "The levels of Demographic Data in the Syrian Arab Republic and Future Trends," in Syrian Arab Republic, Office of the Prime Minister, CBS, *Factors of Population Growth and Their Future Trends,* papers presented at a seminar held in Damascus, September 16–20, 1978, under the auspices of the Syrian CBS and UNFPA (Damascus, 1979), p. 5.

32 On the *2001–SFHS*, see: http://www.papfam.org/papfam/syria.htm.

33 See M. N. al-Hallak, "Demographic Situation in the Syrian Arab Republic," Expert Group Meeting on the Application of Demographic Data and Studies in Development Planning of the UN Economic and Social Office in Beirut, Beirut, December 7–12, 1970, pp. 7–8.

34 WB, *World Development Report–1990*, p. 231, table 27.

35 ESCWA, *Population Situation in the ESCWA Region–1990* (Amman, 1992), p. 112, table 6.7.

36 WB, *World Development Report–1990*, p. 231, table 27.

37 ESCWA, *Population Situation in the ESCWA Region–1990*, p. 200, table 12.3.

38 WB, *World Development Report–1996*, p. 199, table 6.

39 ESCWA, *Demographic and Related Socio-Economic Data Sheets for Countries of the Economic and Social Commission for Western Asia*, No. 8 (1995), p. 62, table 3.

40 *Ibid.*, p. 130, table 3.

41 Tabutin and Schoumaker, "The Demography of the Arab World and the Middle East," p. 522.

42 Ellen Laipson, "The Middle East's Demographic Transition: What Does It Mean?" *Journal of International Affairs*, Vol. 56, No. 1 (2002), pp. 177–78.

43 Dubai's total population, including both nationals and foreigners, increased from 689,420 in 1995 to 1,200,309 in 2005, namely an increase of 74% within only one decade. See the website of the UAE census at: http://www.tedad.ae. Dubai's GDP growth rate during the corresponding period was one of the highest worldwide, amounting in real terms to 13.4% on annual average during the 2000–2005 period.

44 On the collection of the demographic data in the Gulf countries during the 1970s and 1980s, see: 'Othman al-Hasan Muhammad Nur and Ziad Rashad al-Rawi, *al-Ihsa'at al-Sukaniyya fi Duwal al-Khalij al-'Arabiyya* (Riyadh: Arab Bureau of Education for the Gulf States, 1991).

45 UNDP, *Arab Human Development Report–2002* (New York, 2002), p. 99.

46 UNESCWA (hereafter: ESCWA) is a UN regional organization, currently based in Beirut, and its members include: Egypt, Syria, Lebanon, Iraq, Yemen, the Palestinians in the Occupied Territories and the GCC countries. The organization is part of the UN Secretariat and is one of the five regional commissions that report to the UN Economic and Social Council. The funding of the organization is mainly from the member states. In many cases, the data provided by ESCWA are either the only or the most lucrative source for GCC demographic data.

47 UN, Population Division and UNFPA, *Population Policy Compendium-Bahrain* (New York, 1981), p. 2; ESCWA, *Population Situation in the ESCWA Region–1990*, p. 25.

48 The *GFHS*, conducted in each of the GCC countries during the years 1995–1998, collected data in the fields of marriage patterns, fertility behaviors and contraceptive prevalence rates. On the *GFHS* framework, including the number of the surveyed population, their sex, age, spatial distribution and the like, see: al-Lajna al-Iqtisadiyya wal-Ijtima'iyya lil-Gharbi Asia (ESCWA), *al-Nashra al-Sukaniyya*, No. 49 (2000), p. 31, table 1.

49 *Kuwait Times,* at: http://www.kuwaittimes.net/business.asp?dismode=article&artid=1197920562.

50 Mustafa al-Shalkani, "A System for Collecting Vital Statistics in Gulf Cooperation Council Countries," *Population Bulletin of ESCWA*, Nos. 35–37 (December 1989–December 1990), p. 47.

51 [3] Allan G. Hill, "The Demography of the Kuwaiti Population of Kuwait," *Demography*, Vol. 12, No. 3 (1975), p. 537.

52 Al-Shalkani, "A System for Collecting Vital Statistics," pp. 49–50.

53 Dale F. Eickelman, *The Middle East: An Anthropological Approach*, second edition (Englewood Cliffs, N.J.: Prentice-Hall, 1989), p. 368. See also: John E. Peterson, *Oman in the Twentieth Century: Political Foundations of an Emerging State* (London: Croom Helm, 1978), p. 136.

54 ECWA, Technical Secretariat, "Achievements, Plans and Recommendations Relating to Population and Housing Censuses in the Sultanate of Oman," *ECWA Expert Group Meeting on Census Techniques*, Beirut, December 12–16, 1977, pp. 1–2.

55 By 1974, Oman's oil reserves estimated at 1.49 billion barrels. See PDO (Petroleum Development Oman) website at: http://www.pdo.co.om.

56 The website of the Omani Ministry of National Economy at: http://www.moneoman.gov.om.

57 The common definition of "workforce"/"labor force" is all those persons who "supply

labor," namely, all those persons who are defined during a specified period as employed and unemployed.

58 The Sultanate of Oman, Ministry of National Economy, *Statistical Yearbook–2001* (Muscat, 2002), pp. 416–17.

59 *Ibid.*, pp. 40–41, 47.

60 The British Embassy of Beirut, Middle East Development Division, by N. B. Hudson, *The First Population Census of Qatar*, April/May 1970 (Beirut, October 1970), pp. 3–4; ECWA, *The Population Situation in the ECWA Region-Qatar* (Beirut, 1980), p. 2.

61 Al-Shalkani, "A System for Collecting Vital Statistics," pp. 46, 53.

62 The website of Qatar's Planning Council at: http://www.planning.gov.qa/Qatar-Census–2004.

63 ECWA, *The Population Situation–Qatar*, p. 8.

64 Al-Shalkani, "A System for Collecting Vital Statistics," p. 48; ESCWA, *Population Situation in the ESCWA Region–1990*, p. 153.

65 State of Qatar, Presidency of the Council of Ministers, Central Statistical Organization, *Annual Statistical Abstract–1999* (Doha, 1999), p. 17, table 6.

66 The website of Qatar's Planning Council at: http://www.planning.gov.qa/Qatar-Census–2004.

67 Qatar, *Annual Statistical Abstract–2005*, tables 10 and 11.

68 The website of Qatar's Planning Council at: http://www.planning.gov.qa/Qatar-Census–2004

69 Qatar, *Annual Statistical Abstract–1999*, p. 66, table 37.

70 The UAE, previously known as the Trucial States, became independent in December 1971 with the termination of all existing treaties with the Trucial States. In February 1972, Ras al-Khaima joined the Union that since then has been made up of the seven independent emirates that merged into a federal state.

71 ECWA, *The Population Situation in the ECWA Region–United Arab Emirates* (Beirut, 1980), p. 2.

72 *Ibid.*

73 J. S. Birks and C. A. Sinclair, *International Migration Project: Country Case Study: The United Arab Emirates* (Durham: The University of Durham, Department of Economics, 1978), p. 3.

74 See, for example: UAE, Ministry of Planning, Central Statistical Department, *Annual Statistical Abstract, 1972–1976* (Abu Dhabi, 1977), p. 43, table 5.

75 UAE, Ministry of Economy, *Preliminary Results of Population, Housing and Establishments Census–2005* (Abu Dhabi, 2006).

76 UAE, Ministry of Information and Culture, *United Arab Emirates Yearbook–2006* (Abu Dhabi, 2006), p. 219.

77 Part of this section is based on my essay "The Surprising Results of the Saudi Arabian 2004 Demographic Census," *IJMES*, Vol. 40, No. 1 (January 2008), pp. 12–15.

78 Anthony H. Cordesman, *Saudi Arabia Enters the Twenty-First Century: The Political, Foreign Policy, Economic, and Energy Dimensions*, Vol. 2 (Westport: Praeger, 2003), p. 229.

79 George A. Lipsky, *Saudi Arabia: Its People, Its Society, Its Culture* (New Haven: HRAF Press, 1959), p. 24.

80 R. McGregor, "Saudi Arabia: Population and the Making of a Modern State," in J. I. Clarke and W. B. Fisher (eds.), *Populations of the Middle East and North Africa: A Geographical Approach* (London: University of London Press, 1972), p. 224. See also: al-Sayid Khalid al-Matri, *Sukan al-Mamlaka al-'Arabiyya al-Sa'udiyya* (Riyadh: Al-Dar al-Sau'diyya lil-Nasher wal-Tawzi', 1998), p. 16, table 1.

81 ECWA, *The Population Situation in the ECWA Region–Saudi Arabia* (Beirut, 1979), p. 2; Abdulla H. M. al-Khalifeh, "Population Spatial Distribution Policies in Saudi Arabia," in ESCWA, *Population Spatial Distribution* (Amman, 1993), p. 138.

82 ILO, *Migration for Employment Project: The Kingdom of Saudi Arabia and the Libyan Arab Jamahiriya: The Key Countries for Employment.* World Employment Programme Research, Working Paper, by J. S. Birks and C. A. Sinclair (Geneva, May 1979), p. 8.
83 ECWA, *The Population Situation–Saudi Arabia*, p. 2.
84 UN, Population Division and UNFPA, *Population Policy Compendium–Saudi Arabia* (New York, 1981), p. 2.
85 The Kingdom of Saudi Arabia, Central Planning Organization, *Development Plan, 1390 A.H.* (Riyadh, 1970), p. 50.
86 Muhammad Ahmad al-Ruythi, "Sukan al-Mamlaka al-'Arabiyya al-Sa'udiyya," in Muhammad Ahmad al-Ruythi (ed.), *Sukan al-'Alam al-'Arabi: al-Waqi' wal-Mustaqbal* (Riyadh: Maktabat al-'Abikan, 2003), p. 172, table 1.
87 ECWA, *The Population Situation–Saudi Arabia*, p. 2.
88 J.S. Birks and C.A. Sinclair, *International Migration Project, Country Case Study: The Kingdom of Saudi Arabia* (Durham: The University of Durham, Department of Economics, 1979), p. 4; MERI Report, *Saudi Arabia* (London: Croom Helm, 1985), p. 4; Richard F. Nyrop et al., *Area Handbook for Saudi Arabia*, third edition (Washington, D.C.: US Government Printing Office, 1977), p. 45.
89 The WB and the Ministry of Planning of Saudi Arabian, *Saudis in Transition: The Challenges of a Changing Labor Market*, by Ismail A. Sirageldin, Naiem A. Sherbiny and M. Ismail Serageldin (Published for the WB by Oxford University Press, 1984), p. 30.
90 Birks, Sinclair & Associates Ltd., *GCC Market Report–1992* (Durham: Mountjoy Research Centre, May 1992), p. 99, table 1.1.
91 Peter W. Wilson and Douglas F. Graham, *Saudi Arabia: The Coming Storm* (New York: M.E. Sharpe, 1994), p. 12.
92 *Ibid.*, p. 33, note 8.
93 The Kingdom of Saudi Arabia, Ministry of Planning, *Achievements of the Development Plans, 1390–1404A.H.* [1970–1984], (Riyadh, 1985), p. 118.
94 ILO, *Migration for Employment Project: The Kingdom of Saudi Arabia and the Libyan Arab Jamahiriya*, p. 3.
95 Gilbar, "Mavo: Beyn Demographya ve-Politiqa ba-Mizrah ha-Tikhon," in Ayalon and Gilbar (eds.), *Demographya ve-Politiqa be-Medinot 'Arav*, pp. 14–15 (Hebrew).
96 See, for example: EIU, *Country Profile–Saudi Arabia, 1987–88*, p. 7.
97 The Kingdom of Saudi Arabia, Ministry of Planning, Central Department of Statistics, *Statistical Yearbook–1416A.H.* [1996] (Riyadh, 1996), pp. 465–81.
98 Saudi Arabia, *Statistical Yearbook–1417A.H.* [1997]; *1418A.H.* [1998].
99 Al-Mamlaka al-'Arabiyya al-Sa'udiyya, Wizarat al-Iqtisad wal-Takhtit, *al-Nata'ij al-Awaliyya lil-Ta'dad al-'Amm lil-Sukan wal-Masakin–1425A.H.* [2004] (Riyadh, 2004), p. 3.
100 The *NCB Economist*, Vol. 15, Issue 6 (April 26, 2005), p. 6, table 1; Saudi Arabian Monetary Agency (SAMA), *Forty-First Annual Report–1426H.* [2005], p. 321, table 17.2.
101 Thus, for example, during the five years of 1994–1998, according to Saudi Ministry of Interior data, 22,065 foreigners obtained Saudi citizenship, 18,983 (86%) of whom were females. Source: *Saudi Economic Survey*, April 12, 2000, p. 11.
102 Federal Research Division, Library of Congress, *Saudi Arabia: A Country Study*, Fifth Edition (Washington, D.C.: Library of Congress, 1993), p. 59.
103 Cordesman, *Saudi Arabia Enters the Twenty-First Century*, Vol. 2, p. 230.
104 UN, Population Division, *Demographic Yearbook–2004* (New York, 2006).
105 SAMA, *Forty-Second Annual Report–1427H.* [2006], p. 275, table 18.2. See also: The Kingdom of Saudi Arabia, Ministry of Planning, *Eighth Development Plan, 1425/26–1429/30A.H.* [2005–2009] (Riyadh, 2004), chapter 17, table 17.1.
106 SAMA, *Forty-Third Annual Report–1428H.* [2007], p. 214, table 18.2.
107 See, for example: *The Middle East*, December 2005, p. 27; Saudi-American Bank (SAMBA), *The Saudi Economy at Mid-Year 2004* (Riyadh, 2004), p. 1.

108 Rshood M. Khraif, "Fertility in Saudi Arabia: Levels and Determinants," paper presented at: *XXIV General Population Conference*, Salvador, Brazil, August 18–24, 2001, p. 5. Available at: http://www.iussp.org/Brazil2001/s60/S62_03_khraif.pdf.

109 The *NCB Economist*, Vol. 15, Issue 6 (April 26, 2005), p. 5.

110 *Arab News*, April 24, 2003. Available online at: http://www.arabnews.com/?page=1&section=0&article=25558&d=24&m=4&y=2003.

111 The Kingdom of Saudi Arabia, Ministry of Planning, *Seventh Development Plan, 1420/21–1424/25A.H.* [2000–2004] (Riyadh, 1999), p. 162, table 6.3.

112 *Ibid*., p. 77; SAMA, *Thirty-Seventh Annual Report–1422H.* [2001], p. 270.

113 Mohamed A. Ramady, *The Saudi Arabian Economy: Policies, Achievements and Challenges* (New York: Springer, 2005), p. 354.

114 SAMA, *Forty-First Annual Report–1426H.* [2005], pp. 320–21; idem, *Forty-Second Annual Report–1427H.* [2006], pp. 271–72.

115 The NCB, also known as al-Ahli Bank, is the first Saudi bank, established in 1953.

116 The *NCB Economist*, Vol. 15, Issue 6 (April 26, 2005), pp. 5–7.

117 *Saudi Economic Survey*, December 1, 2004, p. 10.

118 Winckler, "The Economic Consequences of the Iraqi Crisis," pp. 410–12.

119 Saudi Arabia, *Eighth Development Plan, 2005–2009*, chapter 33.

120 EIU, *Country Profile–Saudi Arabia, 2006*, p. 21.

121 ILO, *International Migration and Development in the Arab Region*, by J. S. Birks and C. A. Sinclair (Geneva, 1980), p. 129, table 3.

122 See: Mark Brown, "Quantifying the Muslim Population in Europe: Conceptual and Data Issues," *International Journal of Social Research Methodology*, Vol. 3, No. 2 (2000), pp. 87–101.

123 Arnon Soffer, "Lebanon-Where Demography is the Core of Politics and Life," *Middle Eastern Studies*, Vol. 22, No. 2 (1986), p. 199, table 2.

124 On the Lebanese 1943 National Pact, see: Kamal S. Salibi, *The Modern History of Lebanon* (London: Weidenfeld and Nicolson, 1965), pp. 187–88; Itamar Rabinovich, *The War for Lebanon, 1970–1985* (Ithaca and London: Cornell University Press, 1985), pp. 24–26.

125 On the emigration of the Christian-Lebanese in the late nineteenth century and the early twentieth century, see: Akram Fouad Khater, *Inventing Home: Emigration, Gender, and the Middle Class in Lebanon, 1870–1920* (Berkeley: University of California Press, 2001).

126 Soffer noted in this regard that: "The Maronites left Lebanon in greater numbers than any other group throughout the years but especially at the outbreak of the civil war in 1975." Soffer, "Lebanon – Where Demography is the Core of Politics and Life," p. 200.

127 Philippe Fargues, "Demographic Islamization: Non-Muslims in Muslim Countries," *SAIS Review*, Vol. 21, No. 2 (2001), p. 113.

128 Colbert C. Held, *Middle East Patterns: Places, Peoples, and Politics*, second edition (Boulder: Westview Press, 1994), p. 221.

129 UNRWA's official data at: http://www.un.org/unrwa.

130 The Palestinian refugees in Lebanon, as in the other Arab countries, with the exception of Jordan, do not have the right of citizenship in the host countries.

131 Muhammad Faour, "The Demography of Lebanon: A Reappraisal," *Middle Eastern Studies*, Vol. 27, No. 4 (1991), p. 631.

132 On the socialist measures taken by the Nasserite and later by the Ba'thi regime, see: Ziad Keilany, "Socialism and Economic Change in Syria," *Middle Eastern Studies*, Vol. 9, No. 1 (1973), pp. 65–9.

133 M. E. Sales, *International Migration Project: Syrian Arab Republic* (Durham: The University of Durham, Department of Economics, 1978), p. 59; *al-Khalij*, January 11, 1985.

134 As will be examined in detail in Chapter 2, the average fertility rates of the urban dwellers, particularly that of the middle class, are markedly lower than those of the rural dwellers.

135 Syrian Arab Republic, Ministry of National Economy, Department of Statistics, *Statistical Abstract–1950* (Damascus, 1951), p. 17, table 3.
136 Mahmud A. Faksh, "The Alawi Community of Syria: A New Dominant Political Force," *Middle Eastern Studies*, Vol. 20, No. 2 (1984), p. 134, table 1.
137 The Yazidi religion has elements of Judaism, Christianity, and Islam, as well as of Paganism. The Bible and the Qur'an are both considered sacred. In 1964, there were approximately 10,000 Yazidis in Syria. Source: Library of Congress Country Studies. Available at: http://lcweb2loc.gov.
138 Held, *Middle East Patterns*, pp. 208–9; EIU, *Country Profile–Syria, 2000–2001*, p. 10.
139 CIA, *The World Factbook–2005*. Available at: http://www.cia.gov/publications/factbook.
140 Fargues, "Demographic Islamization: Non-Muslims in Muslim Countries," p. 106.
141 W. B. Fisher, "Jordan: A Demographic Shatter-Belt," in Clarke and Fisher (eds.), *Populations of the Middle East and North Africa*, pp. 211–12.
142 *Insight Guides*. Available at: http://www.insightguides.com; EIU, *Country Profile–Jordan, 1993–94*, p. 11.
143 UNRWA website at: http://www.un.org/unrwa. .
144 Peter Gubser, *Jordan: Crossroads of Middle Eastern Events* (Boulder: Westview Press, and London: Croom Helm, 1983), p. 12; Asher Susser, "Demographya ve-Politiqa be-Yarden," in Ayalon and Gilbar (eds.), *Demographya ve-Politiqa be-Medinot 'Arav*, p. 131 (Hebrew).
145 The Hashemite Kingdom of Jordan, Department of Statistics, *Statistical Yearbook–2002* (Amman, 2003), p. 5, table 2.1.
146 See also: *MEED*, September 10–16, 2004, p. 25.
147 EIU, *Country Profile–Egypt, 1999–2000*, p. 12.
148 A.S.M. Kashef, "Egypt," in John Dixon (ed.), *Social Welfare in the Middle East* (London: Croom Helm, 1987), p. 1.
149 See: Fargues, "Demography and Politics in the Arab World," p. 8.
150 CIA, *The World Factbook–2003*.
151 EIU, *Country Profile–Egypt, 1999–2000*, p. 12; Held, *Middle East Patterns*, p. 90; Ami Ayalon, "Egypt's Coptic Pandora's Box," in Ofra Bengio and Gabriel Ben-Dor (eds.), *Minorities and the State in the Arab World* (Boulder: Lynne Rienner Publishers, 1999), p. 53; Fargues, "Demographic Islamization," p. 106.
152 Under the name of the founder of this sect, Muhammad ibn 'Abd al-Wahhab (1703–1791), *Wahhabism* began in the Arabian Peninsula in the eighteenth century in reaction to the popular practice of *Sufism*. On the *Wahhabism*, see: Ewan W. Anderson, *The Middle East: Geography and Geopolitics* (London and New York: Routledge, 2000), p. 142.
153 Fouad al-Farsy, *Modernity and Tradition: The Saudi Equation* (London and New York: Kegan Paul International, 1990), p. 21.
154 *Gulf States Newsletter*, May 2, 2003, p. 6.
155 US Department of State, *International Religious Freedom Report–2002*, "Saudi Arabia." Available at: http://www.state.gov.
156 EIU, *Country Profile–Saudi Arabia, 2003*, p. 10; International Crisis Group, "The Shi'ite Question in Saudi Arabia," *Middle East Report*, No. 45 (September 19, 2005). Available at: http://merln.ndu.edu/archive/icg/shiitequestion.pdf., p. 1. With regard to the dispute on the number of Shi'is in Saudi Arabia, see also: Graham E. Fuller and Rend Rahim Francke, *The Arab Shi'a: The Forgotten Muslim*s (New York: St. Martin's Press, 1999), p. 180.
157 May Seikaly, "Women and Social Change in Bahrain," *IJMES*, Vol. 26, No. 3 (1994), p. 418; Fuller and Francke, *The Arab Shi'a*, p. 120.
158 On the clashes between the Shi'i activists and the Bahraini security forces, see: Dore Gold, "Bahrain," *MECS*, Vol. 18 (1994), pp. 253–56; Joshua Teitelbaum, "Bahrain," *MECS*, Vol. 20 (1996), pp. 250–53; Uzi Rabi and Joseph Kostiner, "The Shi'is in Bahrain: Class and Religious Protest," in Bengio and Ben-Dor (eds.), *Minorities and the State in the Arab World*, p. 172.

159 ESCWA, *Survey of Economic and Social Developments in the ESCWA Region, 2004–2005* (New York, 2005), p. 62.
160 Richards and Waterbury, *A Political Economy of the Middle East*, second edition, p. 134.
161 Rodney Wilson, *Economic Development in the Middle East* (London and New York: Routledge, 1995), p. 65.
162 *The Middle East*, February 2003, p. 47.
163 Eliyahu Kanovsky, "What's Behind Syria's Current Economic Problems?" *Occasional Papers* (Tel Aviv University, The Moshe Dayan Center, May 1985), p. 45. On the accuracy of the Syrian official economic data, see also: Perthes, *The Political Economy of Syria under Asad*, pp. 13–14.
164 ESCWA, *Survey, 2004–2005*, p. 20.
165 ESCWA, *Survey of Economic and Social Developments in the ESCWA Region–2004, Summary* (New York, 2004), pp. 7–8. See also: UNDP and the AFESD, *Arab Human Development Report–2005* (New York, 2006), pp. 65–66.
166 Dawn Chatty, "Women Working in Oman: Individual Choice and Cultural Constraints," *IJMES*, Vol. 32, No. 2 (2000), p. 251.
167 See, for example: Suliman S. al-Qudsi, "Labour Participation of Arab Women: Estimates of the Fertility to Labour Supply Link," *Applied Economics*, Vol. 30, No. 7 (1998), p. 932.
168 *Al-Sharq al-Awsat*, October 20, 1999, p. 7.
169 *MEED*, September 20, 2002, p. 39.
170 *MEED*, June 27, 2003, p. 7.
171 *MEED*, September 20, 2002, p. 39.
172 Saudi Arabia, *Seventh Development Plan*, p. 158.
173 ESCWA, *Survey, 2001–2002*, p. 19.
174 Ramady, *The Saudi Arabian Economy*, p. 365
175 SAMA, *Forty-Second Annual Report–1427H.* [2006], p. 280.
176 US, Department of State, *Country Reports on Human Rights Practices–2005*, "Saudi Arabia." Available at: http://www.state.gov/g/drl/rls/hrrpt/2005/61698.htm.
177 *MEED*, December 11, 1998, p. 31.
178 *MEED*, September 28, 2001, p. 28. In April 2001, the official unemployment rate among Bahraini nationals was 3.1%, increasing from 2.5% at the end of 1999. ESCWA, *Survey, 2001–2002*, p. 19.
179 *MEED*, September 28, 2001, p. 28.
180 EIU, *Country Profile–Bahrain, 2003*, p. 20.
181 *Jordan Times*, November 18, 1999; ESCWA, *Survey, 1998–1999*, p. 51.
182 ESCWA, *Survey, 2000–2001*, pp. 30–31; *MEED*, April 20, 2001, p. 28.
183 EIU, *Country Profile–Egypt, 2001*, p. 33.
184 *Al-Ahram Weekly*, February 27–March 5, 2002.
185 ESCWA, *Survey, 2001–2002*, p. 18.
186 Edward Gardner, "Wanted: More Jobs," *Finance & Development*, Vol. 40, No. 1 (March 2003). Available at: http://www.imf.org/external/pubs/ft/fandd/fda.
187 ILO, *World Employment Report–2001* (Geneva, 2001), p. 361, table 4.
188 Eliyahu Kanovsky, "Egypt's Troubled Economy: Mubarak's Inheritance," in *MECS, 1981–82*, p. 416.
189 See: *The Egyptian Gazette*, August 23, 1985. On the various estimates regarding the number of Egyptian workers in other Arab countries in the early 1980s, see: Gil Feiler, "The Number of Egyptian Workers in the Arab Oil Countries, 1974–1983: A Critical Discussion," *Occasional Papers* (Tel Aviv University, The Moshe Dayan Center, October 1986); Galal A. Amin and Elizabeth Awny, *International Migration of Egyptian Labor: A Review of the State of Art* (Ottawa: International Development Research Centre, May 1985), p. 25, table 6.
190 *MEED*, February 24, 1984, p. 55.

191 Egypt, CAPMAS, *External Migration As A Demographic Phenomenon* (Cairo, 1994), p. 14.

192 HRD Base Ltd., *Socio-Demographic Profiles of Key Arab Countries* (Newcastle: Lloyds Bank Chambers, May 1987).

193 EIU, QER, *Egypt*, No. 3 (1984), p. 10. See also: *Emirates News*, August 15, 1990.

194 Philippe Fargues, "International Migration in the Arab Region: Trends and Policies," paper presented at the *UN Expert Group Meeting on International Migration and Development in the Arab Region*. Beirut, May 15–17, 2006, p. 2. Available at: http://www.un.org/esa/population/migration/turin/Symposium_Turin_files/P09_Fargues.pdf.

195 See: ILO, *International Migration for Employment: Manpower and Population Evolution in the GCC and Libyan Arab Jamahiriya*, by J. S. Birks and C. A. Sinclair (Geneva, October 1989), p. 2.

196 "Kuwait: Expatriate Workers Outnumber Nationals," *The Arab Economist* (April 1979), p. 32.

197 According to a senior academic at the UAE University, the number of illegal foreign workers in the UAE in mid-2006 "could be as many as 500,000." *MEED*, September 8–14, 2006, p. 12.

198 See, for example: UN, Population Division, "Restrictive Labour Immigration Policies in the Oil-Rich Gulf: Effectiveness and Implications for Sending Asian Countries," by Nasra M. Shah (May 5, 2006), pp. 3–4. Available at: http://www.un.org/esa.

199 Michael E. Bonine, "Population Growth, the Labor Market and the Gulf Security," in David E. Long and Christian Koch (eds.), *Gulf Security in the Twenty-First Century* (Abu Dhabi: The Emirates Center for Strategic Studies and Research, 1997), p. 227.

200 Roger Owen and Şevket Pamuk, *A History of Middle East Economies in the Twentieth Century* (Cambridge, Mass.: Harvard University Press, 1999), p. 208.

201 On the informal economy in developing countries, see: Philip Harding and Richard Jenkins, *The Myth of the Hidden Economy: Towards a New Understanding of Informal Economic Activity* (Milton Keynes: Open University Press, 1989); Edgar L. Feige (ed.), *The Underground Economies: The Evasion and Information Distortion* (Cambridge: Cambridge University Press, 1989).

202 Delwin A. Roy, "The Hidden Economy in Egypt," *Middle Eastern Studies*, Vol. 28, No. 4 (1992), p. 689.

203 ILO, *International Migration for Employment: The Jordanian Migration System in Transition*, by Allan M. Findlay (Geneva, March 1987), p. 2.

204 WB, *World Tables*, various editions; idem, *World Development Report*, various issues; IMF, *International Financial Statistics Yearbook*, various issues.

205 In the case of Egypt, for example, while the official exchange rate in late 1983 was $1=£E (Egyptian Pound) 0.84, the unofficial rate was $1=£E1.12–1.20. In late 1985, the official exchange rate was $1=£E1.35 while the free market rate was $1=£E1.85. *MEED*, December 2, 1983, p. 11; December 7, 1985, p. 12; "MEED Special Report-Egypt," June 1986, p. 8.

206 Nazli Choucri, "The Hidden Economy: A New View of Remittances in the Arab World," *World Development*, Vol. 14, No. 6 (1986), p. 697. See also: Robert. E. Looney, "Patterns of Remittances and Labor Migration in the Arab World," *International Migration*, Vol. 24, No. 4 (1989), pp. 565–67.

207 By 1984, Egypt's recorded workers' remittances peaked at $3.93 billion (current prices). WB, *World Tables, 1995 Edition*, p. 259.

208 Nazli Choucri, "Migration in the Middle East: Old Economics or New Politics?" *Journal of Arab Affairs*, Vol. 7, No. 1 (1988), p. 12. On Egypt's real workers' remittances since the early 1970s, see: Elie Podeh and Onn Winckler, "The Boycott that Never Was: Egypt and the Arab System, 1979–1989," *Durham Middle East Papers*, No. 72 (December 2002), pp. 36–39; ESCWA, *Return Migration: Profiles, Impact and Absorption in Home Countries*

(New York, 1993), p. 36; Dan Tschirgi, "Egyptian Labor Migration: Social, Political and Economic Effects," in Mohammad Shtayyeh (ed.), *Labor Migration: Palestine, Jordan, Egypt and Israel* (Jerusalem: Palestine Center for Regional Studies, 1998), pp. 55–56.

209 WB, *World Tables, 1995 Edition*, pp. 258–59.

210 Roy, "The Hidden Economy in Egypt," p. 691.

211 Rodney Wilson, "Whither the Egyptian Economy?" *British Journal of Middle East Studies*, Vol. 20, No. 2 (1993), p. 211.

212 IMF, *Syrian Arab Republic: Staff Report for the 1987 Article IV Consultation* (February 18, 1988), p. 6c, chart 4.

213 WB, *World Tables, 1995 Edition*, p. 650.

214 See: Onn Winckler, *Demographic Developments and Population Policies in Ba'thist Syria* (Brighton and Portland: Sussex Academic Press, 1999), pp. 92–93, table 4.1.

215 *Emirates News*, July 25, 1983.

216 *MEED*, May 1, 1985, p. 34.

217 WB, *World Tables, 1995 Edition*, p. 386.

218 Musa Samha, "Population Spatial Distribution Policies in Jordan," in ESCWA, *Population Spatial Distribution*, p. 93

219 WB, *World Development Report–1996*, p. 218, table 16.

220 According to the 1996 census, the number of temporary Egyptian migrants was 2.18 million, which included both workers and accompanying family members. This means that the number of Egyptian workers abroad by the mid-1990s was only two-thirds their number in the mid-1980s. Source: Egypt, CAPMAS, *Statistical Yearbook, 1992–1998*, p. 11, table 1–15.

221 Paul Sullivan, "Contrary Views of Economic Diplomacy in the Arab World: Egypt," *Arab Studies Quarterly*, Vol. 21, No. 4 (1999), p. 67.

222 Richards and Waterbury, *A Political Economy of the Middle East*, second edition, p. 140.

223 WB, *Labor Market Reforms, Growth and Unemployment in Labor-Exporting MENA Countries*, by Pierre-Richard Agénor et al. (Washington, D.C., 2003), p. 6.

224 EIU, *Country Profile–Egypt, 2005*, p. 19.

225 EIU, *Country Profile–Egypt, 1989–90*, p. 16. According to other estimates, Egypt's hidden economy in 1988 was running between 35% and 55% of the recorded (official) GNP. See: Roy, "The Hidden Economy in Egypt," p. 707.

226 National Bank of Egypt, *The Underground Economy with Special Reference to the Case of Egypt*, by Ibrahim M. Oweiss (Cairo, December 1994), p. 21.

227 On this subject, see: ILO, *World Employment Report, 2004–2005* (Geneva, 2005), pp. 106–7.

Chapter 2 *Beyond Expectations: Arab Population Growth in Retrospect*

1 Cited from: Saad M. Gadalla, *Is There Hope? Fertility and Family Planning in a Rural Egyptian Community* (Cairo: American University in Cairo Press, 1978), p. 212.

2 Allan Findlay and Anne Findlay, *Population and Development in the Third World* (London and New York: Methuen, 1987), p. 1.

3 The Black Death was one of the worst natural disasters in world history, decimating about one-third of Europe's population. The total number of deaths from the pandemic is estimated to be 75 million people.

4 John Durand, "Historical Estimates of World Population: An Evaluation," *Population and Development Review*, Vol. 3, No. 3 (1977), p. 259, table 2.

5 On the various estimations of world's population growth rates during the first millennium, see: Angus Maddison, *The World Economy: A Millennium Perspective* (Paris: OECD, 2001), p. 231, table B–1.

6 WB, *World Development Report–1992*, p. 271, table 27.

7 See also: UN, Population Division, *World Population Prospects: The 2006 Revision* (New York, 2007), p. vii.

8 The replacement-level fertility rate is a function of age specific mortality rate, particularly that of infants and children. However, the minimum replacement-level fertility rate under the optimal conditions of low mortality as is the current situation in the developed countries worldwide is 2.1 children per woman rather than 2.0. This is due to two factors: First, in any given society (without migration), there are slightly more males than females; and second, because not all of the children survive up to the end of their childbearing period (normally age 45). Thus, a TFR of 2.1 children per woman corresponds to an NRR (Net Reproductive Rate) of 1.0. In developing countries, due to much higher infant and child mortality rates, the replacement-level fertility is higher than 2.1, varying from one society to another in accordance with the different specific death rates.

9 The academic literature on the Demographic Transition Theory is immense. A summary of the theory appears in John B. Casterline, "Demographic Transition," in Paul Demeny and Geoffery McNicoll (eds.), *Encyclopedia of Population* (New York: Macmillan Reference USA, 2003), pp. 210–16; Roland Pressat, *The Dictionary of Demography* (Oxford: Clarendon Press, 1985), pp. 52–55; Michael S. Teitelbaum, "Relevance of Demographic Transition Theory for Developing Countries," *Science*, Vol. 188 (May 2, 1975), p. 421; Ibrahim Bushnaf Bendardaf, *Socioeconomic Modernization and Demographic Changes in Syria* (Unpublished Ph.D. Thesis, University of Missouri, 1988), pp. 1–6.

10 Warren S. Thompson, "Population," *The American Journal of Sociology*, Vol. 34, No. 6 (1929), pp. 959–75. See the explanation of Kirk on Thompson's demographic classification of the world's countries: "Demographic Transition Theory," pp. 361–63.

11 Frank W. Notestein, "Population–The Long View," in Theodore W. Schultz (ed.), *Food for the World* (Chicago: University of Chicago Press, 1945), pp. 36–57.

12 An autarky economy refers to economic self-sufficiency with minimal trade at both the domestic and international levels.

13 Kirk, "Demographic Transition Theory," p. 369.

14 Notestein, "Population–The Long View," p. 40.

15 *Ibid.*, p. 41.

16 Jacques Vallin, "The End of the Demographic Transition: Relief or Concern?" *Population and Development Review*, Vol. 28, No. 1 (2002), p. 107.

17 Anderson, *Population Change in North-Western Europe, 1750–1850*, p. 31, figure 2.

18 Thus, for example, the life expectancy in England averaged 34.6 years (both sexes) during the years 1726–1751 and 37.8 years in Sweden during the period 1751–1755 (both sexes). In Japan the life expectancy during the first half of the nineteenth century averaged 33.7 years (both sexes). See: Maddison, *The World Economy*, p. 29, table 1–4.

19 Shirley Forster Hartley, *Population–Quantity vs. Quality: A Sociological Examination of the Causes and Consequences of the Population Explosion* (New Jersey: Prentice-Hall, Inc. Englewood Cliffs, 1972), p. 4.

20 *Ibid.*

21 Massimo Livi-Bacci, *The Population of Europe* (Oxford: Blackwell, 2000), p. 134, table 6.3.

22 Anderson, *Population Change in North-Western Europe, 1750–1850*, p. 31, figure 2.

23 Teitelbaum, "Relevance of Demographic Transition Theory for Developing Countries," p. 422.

24 Jean-Claude Chesnais, "Below-Replacement Fertility in the European Union (EU-15): Facts and Policies, 1960–1997," *Review of Population and Social Policy*, No. 7 (1998), p. 92, table 7.

25 *Ibid.*; Thompson, "Population," pp. 960–61, table 1.

26 Livi-Bacci, *The Population of Europe*, p. 134, table 3.6.

27 For example, during the period 1908–1913, the annual average natural increase rate was

1.3% in Germany, 1.2% in Italy, 1.1% in England and 1% in Switzerland and Spain. Source: Thompson, "Population," pp. 960–61, table 1.

28 Livi-Bacci, *The Population of Europe*, p. 126.

29 WB, *World Development Report–1995*, p. 213, table 26.

30 *Ibid.*

31 By 1933, for example, Britain's CBR measured 14.4 per 1,000. See: John Hobcraft, "Fertility in England and Wales: A Fifty-Year Perspective," *Population Studies*, Vol. 50, No. 3 (1996), p. 493.

32 The age-specific death rate is a CDR for a specific age group.

33 A discussion on the phenomenon of below replacement-level fertility and its factors in Western-European countries appears in: Dirk J. van de Kaa, *The Past of Europe's Demographic Future*, Uhlenbeck Lecture 17 (Wassenaar, 1999).

34 On the pro-natalist policy of the Western European developed countries, see: Paul Demeny, "Pronatalist Policies in Low-Fertility Countries: Patterns, Performance, and Prospects," *Population and Development Review*, Supplement to Vol. 12 (1986), pp. 335–58; Leslie King, "France Needs Children: Pronatalism, Nationalism and Women's Equity," *The Sociological Quarterly*, Vol. 39, No. 1 (1998), pp. 33–52.

35 The percentage of the urban population of Europe's total population increased from 52.4% in 1950 to 67.3% in 1975 and reached 73.4% in 2000. See: UN, Population Division, *World Urbanization Prospects: The 2001 Revision* (New York, March 2002), p. 5, table 2.

36 On this subject, see: John C. Caldwell, "Demographic Theory: A Long View," *Population and Development Review*, Vol. 30, No. 2 (2004), pp. 306–7.

37 Chesnais, "Below-Replacement Fertility in the European Union," p. 96.

38 See: Nadeya Sayed Ali Mohammed, *Population and Development in the Arab Gulf States: The Case of Bahrain, Oman and Kuwait* (Hampshire: Ashgate, 2003), pp. 40–62.

39 Maria Carmen Faus-Pujol, "Changes in the Fertility Rate and Age Structure of the Population of Europe," in Ray Hall and Paul White (eds.), *Europe's Population: Towards the Next Century* (London: UCL Press, 1995), p. 24, table 2.3.

40 Joshua Goldstein, Wolfgang Lutz and Maria Rita Testa, "The Emergence of Sub-Replacement Family Size Ideals in Europe," *Population Research and Policy Review*, Vol. 22, Nos. 5–6 (2003), pp. 479–96.

41 Rosangela Merlo and Don Rowland, "The Prevalence of Childlessness in Australia," *People and Place*, Vol. 8, No. 2 (2000), p. 21.

42 *The New York Times*, July 10, 1998.

43 *Ibid.*

44 Sarah F. Harbison and Warren C. Robinson, "Policy Implications of the Next World Demographic Transition," *Studies in Family Planning*, Vol. 33, No. 1 (2002), p. 37.

45 PRB, *Population Handbook*, fourth edition, by Arthur Haupt and Thomas T. Kane (New York, 1997), p. 49.

46 WB, W*orld Development Report–1978*, p. 105, table 15.

47 WB, W*orld Development Report–1982*, p. 145, table 18.

48 WB, W*orld Development Report–1992*, p. 271, table 27.

49 US Census Bureau, *International Data Base*.

50 "First Results of the Demographic Data Collection for 2002 in Europe," p. 3, table 1. Available at: http://europa.eu.int.

51 Gregg Eastebrook, "Overpopulation Is No Problem – In the Long Run," *New Republic*, October 11, 1999, p. 24.

52 Peter McDonald, "Low Fertility in Australia: Evidence, Causes and Policy Responses," *People and Place*, Vol. 8, No. 2 (2000), p. 7.

53 Chesnais, "Below-Replacement Fertility in the European Union," p. 86.

54 The EU-15 refers to the 15 countries of the EU before its expansion on May 1, 2004, when eight Central and Eastern European countries, as well as Cyprus and Malta joined the

organization. These countries are: Austria, Belgium, Denmark, Finland, France, Germany, Greece, the Republic of Ireland, Italy, Luxembourg, the Netherlands, Portugal, Spain, Sweden and the UK.

55 Chesnais, "Below-Replacement Fertility in the European Union," p. 87.

56 "First Results of the Demographic Data Collection for 2002 in Europe," p. 5, table 3.

57 Raluca Popescu, "Fertility and Social Policies in Europe," paper presented at the conference *European Integration Process from East to East: Civil Society and Ethnic Minorities in a Changing World*, Sibiu, Romania, December 2004, p. 1. Available at: http://www.iccv.ro/Nyess/Papers_Sibiu_2004/05.

58 Chesnais, "Below-Replacement Fertility in the European Union," p. 83.

59 *Ibid.*, p. 87.

60 Wolfgang Lutz, Vegard Skirbekk and Maria Rita Testa, "The Low Fertility Trap Hypothesis: Forces that May Lead to Further Postponement and Fewer Births in Europe," in Dimiter Philipov et al. (eds.), *Vienna Yearbook of Population Research–2006* (Vienna: Vienna Institute of Demography, 2006), pp. 167–92.

61 European Commission, Statistical Office of the European Union, *Eurostat Yearbook–2005* (Luxembourg, 2006), p. 62.

62 By 2005, while Russian's CBR was 9 per 1,000, the CDR was as high as 15 per 1,000, leading to a -0.6% natural increase rate. See: The US Census Bureau, *International Data Base.*

63 The data relate to North Yemen only. UNICEF, *The State of the World's Children–1988* (Published for UNICEF by Oxford University Press, 1998), p. 72, table 5. See also: Nam and Philliber, *Population*, p. 45.

64 ESCWA, *Demographic and Related Socio-Economic Data Sheets*, No. 11 (2001), p. 178, table 5.

65 The US Census Bureau, *International Data Base.*

66 See: Winckler, "The Failure of Pronatalism of the Developed States," pp. 123–24.

67 ECA, *The State of Demographic Transition in Africa* (Addis Ababa, December 2001), p. 1; Teitelbaum, "Relevance of Demographic Transition Theory for Developing Countries," p. 422; Peter N. Hess, *Population Growth and Socioeconomic Progress in Less Developed Countries: Determinants of Fertility Transition* (New York and London: Praeger, 1988), pp. 13–14.

68 John C. Caldwell, "The Global Fertility Transition: The Need for a Unifying Theory," *Population and Development Review*, Vol. 23, No. 4 (1997), pp. 803–12.

69 Kirk, "Demographic Transition Theory," p. 365.

70 Harbison and Robinson, "Policy Implications of the Next World Demographic Transition," p. 38.

71 Hartley, *Population*, p. 4.

72 US Census Bureau, *International Data Base.*

73 UNICEF, *The State of the World's Children–2000*, pp. 100–3, table 5.

74 Charles Issawi, *An Economic History of the Middle East and North Africa* (New York: Columbia University Press, 1982), p. 93.

75 *Ibid.* See also: Abdel R. Omran and Farzaneh Roudi, "The Middle East Population Puzzle," *Population Bulletin*, Vol. 48, No. 1 (1993), p. 5.

76 The data for the Arab labor-importing countries only refer to the indigenous populations. See: UNDP, *Human Development Report–2002*, pp. 162–65, table 5; ESCWA, *Demographic and Related Socio-Economic Data Sheets*, No. 11 (2001); Issawi, *An Economic History of the Middle East and North Africa*, p. 93, table 6.1.

77 A. M. Abdelghany, "Evaluating the Application of the Stable Population Model of the Population of Egypt," *Population Bulletin of ECWA*, No. 21 (December 1981), p. 109, table 3. See also: Robert Mabro, *The Egyptian Economy, 1952–1972* (Oxford: Clarendon Press, 1974), p. 29, table 2.2.

78 Warren C. Robinson and Fatma H. El-Zanaty, *The Demographic Revolution in Modern Egypt* (Boulder: Lexington Books, 2005), p.26, table 3.3.

79 The term "natural fertility" was proposed by Louis Henry in 1961 and describes the situation in a traditional society where fertility is basically "natural." This is because couples in developing societies tend to behave the same regardless of the current number of their descendants, namely, without any family planning. Among couples in modern societies, however, the current number of children is a determining factor for planning future births. See: Livi-Bacci, *The Population of Europe*, p. 108.

80 See: Robinson and El-Zanaty, *The Demographic Revolution in Modern Egypt*, p. 32.

81 See also: *al-Thawra*, June 16, 1988.

82 UN, *Demographic Yearbook–1963*, p. 495, table 19.

83 UN, *Demographic Yearbook–1984*, p. 288, table 9.

84 See: Omran and Roudi, "The Middle East Population Puzzle," p. 12.

85 On women's status in the Middle East, see: Dale F. Eickelman, *The Middle East and Central Asia: An Anthropological Approach*, fourth edition (Upper Saddle River, NJ.: Prentice-Hall, 2002), pp. 180–86.

86 In the case of the Arab countries, see: John R. Weeks, "The Demography of Islamic Nations," *Population Bulletin*, Vol. 43, No. 4 (1988), p. 25; Carla Makhlouf Obermeyer, "Islam, Women and Politics: The Demography of Arab Countries," *Population and Development Review*, Vol. 18, No. 1 (1992), pp. 45–56.

87 Laurie Ann Mazur, "Beyond the Numbers: An Introduction and Overview," in Laurie Ann Mazur (ed.), *Beyond the Numbers: A Reader on Population, Consumption, and Environment* (Washington, D.C.: Island Press, 1994), pp. 14–15.

88 By 2005, women comprised one-quarter of the total Tunisian labor force – the highest rate in the Middle East (with the exception of Israel). Source: EIU, *Country Profile–Tunisia, 2006*, p. 32.

89 Weeks, "The Demography of Islamic Nations," p. 21.

90 Valentine M. Moghadam, *Modernizing Women: Gender and Social Change in the Middle East* (Boulder and London: Lynne Rienner Publishers, 1993), p. 119. Specifically in the case of Egypt, see: Uri M. Kupferschmidt, "Nasserist and Post-Nasserist Elites in an Official Biographical Lexicon," in Elie Podeh and Onn Winckler (eds.), *Rethinking Nasserism: Revolution and Historical Memory in Modern Egypt* (Gainesville: University Press of Florida, 2004), p. 171.

91 Winckler, *Demographic Developments and Population Policies in Ba'thist Syria*, pp. 46–47.

92 Egypt Arab Republic, Ministry of Health and Population, National Population Council and Macro International Inc., *Egypt Interim Demographic and Health Survey–2003* (Cairo, Jsnuary 2004), p. 18, table 2.4.

93 In the early 1990s, 99% of the women in Yemen aged 15–19 were already married. Source: ESCWA, *Survey, 1996–1997*, p. 137.

94 Roderic Beaujot and Mongi Bchir, *Fertility in Tunisia: Traditional and Modern Contrasts* (Washington, D.C., PRB, 1984), p. 21, table 3.

95 ECA, *The State of Demographic Transition in Africa*, p. 36.

96 Syrian Arab Republic, Office of the Prime Minister, CBS and League of Arab States, Pan-Arab Project for Child Development, *Syrian Maternal and Child Health Survey–1993*, Principal Report (Damascus, 1999), p. 220.

97 UN, Social Development Division, Women Empowerment and Gender Mainstreaming, *Country Profile–Bahrain.*

98 *Syrian Maternal and Child Health Survey–1993*, p. 220.

99 *Egypt Interim Demographic and Health Survey–2003*, p. 18, table 2.4.

100 Al-Mamlaka al-Maghribiyya, al-Mandubiyya al-Samiyya lil-Takhtit, Qisem al-Ihsaiyyat al-'Amma, *al-Nashra al-Ihsaiyya al-Sanawiyya lil-Maghrib–2006* (Rabat, 2006), p. 28,

table 1–11. Age specific fertility rates are calculated by dividing the number of live births in each age group by the total female population (in thousands) in each age group.

101 Winckler, *Demographic Developments and Population Policies in Ba'thist Syria*, p. 49.

102 The Kingdom of Saudi Arabia, Ministry of Health, *Saudi Arabia Child Health Survey*, edited by Yagob al-Mazrou and Samir Farid (Riyadh, 1991), p. 269.

103 *Al-Lajna al-Iqtisadiyya wal-Ijtima'iyya lil-Gharbi Asia, al-Nashra al-Sukaniyya*, No. 49 (2000), p. 32.

104 On this subject, see: Mohammad Taghi Sheykhi, "The Socio-Psychological Factors of Family Planning with Special Reference to Iran: A Theoretical Appraisal," *International Sociology*, Vol. 10, No. 1 (1995), p. 72.

105 On this subject, see the Introduction of Joseph Kostiner to his edited volume, *Middle East Monarchies: The Challenge of Modernity* (Boulder: Lynne Rienner, 2001), pp. 2–5.

106 Peter J. Donaldson, *Nature Against Us: The United States and the World Population Crisis, 1965–1980* (Chapel Hill and London: The University of North Carolina Press, 1990), pp. 114–15.

107 Hess, *Population Growth and Socioeconomic Progress in Less Developed Countries*, p. 17.

108 UNDP, *The Arab Human Development Report–2002*, p. 39.

109 Moghadam, *Modernizing Women*, pp. 116–17.

110 Kirk, "Demographic Transition Theory," p. 370.

111 Sultanate of Oman, Ministry of Health, *Oman Child Health Survey*, edited by Murtadha J. Suleiman, Ahmed al-Ghassany and Samir Farid (Muscat, 1992), p. 203, table 11.4.

112 *Syrian Maternal and Child Health Survey–1993*, p. 169, table 12.11.

113 Syria, *Statistical Abstract–2006*, p. 68, table 8/2.

114 *Ibid.*

115 Al-Mamlaka al-Urduniyya al-Hashemiyya, *al-Itigahat al-Igtima'iyya fil-Urdun* (Amman, October 2006), p. 26.

116 Morocco, Ministry of Public Health, *National Survey on Population and Health–1992* (Rabat, 1992), figure 2 (no page). A similar trend appeared in the demographic survey conducted in the country in 1995. See: Royaume du Maroc, Ministère de la Santé Publique and Macro International Inc., *Enquête de Panel sur la Population et la Santé–1995* (Rabat, Janvier 1996), p. 24, table 3.1.

117 Al-Mamlaka al-Maghribiyya, *al-Nashra al-Ihsaiyya al-Sanawiyya lil-Maghrib–2006*, p. 28, table 1–12.

118 Hassan M. Yousif, Anne Goujon and Wolfgang Lutz, *Future Population and Education Trends in the Countries of North Africa* (Luxemburg: International Institute for Applied Systems Analysis, September 1996), pp. 10–13.

119 WB, *African Development Indicators–1998/99* (Washington D.C., 1998), p. 284, table 11–2. See also: Hayam El-Beblawi and Azza Mohamed Abedo, "Some Aspects of Child Labor in Egypt," *CDC Working Paper*, No. 41 (1999); Mohamed Abdel Rahman, "Socio-Demographic Aspects of Child Labor in Egypt," in CDC, *Population & Sustainable Development*, Research Monograph Series, No. 5 (Cairo, 1998), pp. 349–68.

120 *Gulf News*, November 13, 2003.

121 Yousif, Goujon and Lutz, *Future Population and Education Trends in the Countries of North Africa*, pp. 12–13.

122 Arab Republic of Egypt, Ministry of Health and Population, National Population Council and Macro International Inc., *Egypt Demographic and Health Survey–1995* (Cairo, September 1996), p. 39, table 3.2.

123 See: Anne Valia Goujon, "Population and Education Prospects in the Arab Region," in Ismail Sirageldin (ed.), *Human Capital: Population Economics in the Middle East* (Cairo: The American University in Cairo Press, 2002), p. 117, table 5.1.

124 State of Kuwait, Ministry of Health, *Kuwait Child Health Survey*, edited by Rashid al-Rashoud and Samir Farid (Kuwait, 1991), p. 216, table 11.4.

125 Mahmoud Farag, "Differences in Age at Marriage in Syria," in S. H. Huzayyin and G. T. Acsadi (eds.), *Family and Marriage in some African and Asiatic Countries*, Research Monograph Series, No. 6 (Cairo: CDC, 1976), p. 503, table 24.7.

126 Youssef Courbage, *New Demographic Scenarios in the Mediterranean Region* (Paris: National Institute of Demographic Studies) available at: http://www.ined.fr.

127 The Hashemite Kingdom of Jordan, Department of Statistics, *Jordan Population and Family Health Survey–1990* (Amman, 1992), p. 79, table 7.2.

128 *Egypt Demographic and Health Survey–2005*, p. 113, table 10.3.

129 On the connection between female education and fertility, see: Hamed Abu-Gamrah, "Fertility Levels and Differentials by Mother's Education in some Countries of the ECWA Region," in CDC, *Determinants of Fertility in some African and Asian Countries*, Research Monograph Series, No. 10 (Cairo, 1982), pp. 199–201; ESCWA, Population Section, *Gender and Population Dynamics in the ESCWA Region*, By Batool Shakoori (Beirut, 2000), pp. 6–7; Goujon, "Population and Education Prospects in the Arab Region," p. 118, figure 5.1; Richards and Waterbury, *A Political Economy of the Middle East*, second edition, p. 83; Courbage, *New Demographic Scenarios in the Mediterranean Region*, p. 14; Yousif, Goujon and Lutz, *Future Population and Education Trends in the Countries of North Africa*, pp. 13–15; al-Qudsi, "Labour Participation of Arab Women," p. 933.

130 ESCWA, *Demographic and Related Socio-Economic Data Sheets*, No. 11 (2001), pp. 102–3, tables 4 and 5.

131 ESCWA, *Social and Economic Situation of Palestinian Women, 2000–2006*, by Eileen Kuttab (Beirut, February 2007), p. 13.

132 Infant mortality rate among the Gaza Strip Palestinians declined from approximately 150 per 1,000 live births in 1967 to 20.5 in 2004. Among the West Bank Palestinians, the decline was from approximately 150 per 1,000 live births to 14 during the corresponding period. See: The Palestinian Ministry of Health website. Available at: http://www.moh.gov.ps.

133 PCBS, *The Demographic Survey in the West Bank and Gaza Strip*, Final Report (Ramallah, 1997).

134 Philippe Fargues, "Protracted National Conflict and Fertility Change: Palestinians and Israelis in the Twentieth Century," *Population and Development Review*, Vol. 26, No. 3 (2000), pp. 464–66.

135 *Ibid.*, p. 466, table 5. On the overall demographic developments of the Palestinians in the Occupied Territories since the Israeli occupation, see: Marwan Khawaja, "The Recent Rise in Palestinian Fertility: Permanent or Transient?" *Population Studies*, Vol. 54 (2000), pp. 331–46; idem, "The Fertility of Palestinian Women in Gaza, the West Bank, Jordan and Lebanon," *Population* (English Edition), Vol. 58, No. 3 (2003), pp. 273–302.

136 On the macroeconomic reforms implemented by the vast majority of the Arab countries since the 1970s, but more substantially since the early 1990s, see: Richards and Waterbury, *A Political Economy of the Middle East*, second edition, pp. 222–50; M. Riad El-Ghonemy, *Affluence and Poverty in the Middle East* (London and New York: Routledge, 1998), pp. 172–213.

137 Contraceptive prevalence rate is defined as the percentage of women between 15–49 years who practice, or whose sexual partners practice any form of contraception.

138 Israel, CBS, *Statistical Abstract of Israel–2006* (Jerusalem, 2007), pp. 192–93, table 3.9.

139 *Ibid.*, p. 200, table 3.12.

140 On the fertility pattern among the Israeli-Arabs and the connection between their fertility behavior and their socioeconomic condition, see: Winckler, "The Failure of Pronatalism of the Developed States," pp. 123–28.

141 See: Anthony H. Cordesman, *Bahrain, Oman, Qatar, and the UAE: Challenges of Security* (Boulder: Westview Press, 1997), pp. 78–79.

142 US Census Bureau, *International Data Base*.

143 In the case of Lebanese fertility differentials based on religion during the 1960s and 1970s,

see: James Allman, "The Demographic Transition in the Middle East and North Africa," *IJMES*, Vol. 12, No. 3 (1980), p. 287.

144 Gad Gilbar, *Kalkalat ha-Mizrah ha-Tikhon ba-'Et ha-Hadasha* (Tel Aviv: Ministry of Defense, 1990), pp. 30–31 (in Hebrew).

145 Abdelghany, "Evaluating the Application of the Stable Population Model of the Population of Egypt," p. 109, table 3.

146 UN, Population Division, "Mortality of Children Under Age 5: World Estimates and Projections, 1950–2025," *Population Studies*, No. 105 (New York, 1988), p. 32, table A.1.

147 WB, *World Development Report–2002*, pp. 232–33, table 1.

148 UNDP, *Human Development Report–2006*, pp. 315–18, table 10.

149 UN, "Mortality of Children Under Age 5," p. 38, table A.2.

150 On the increase of the death rates in Iraq, particularly infant and child mortality rates, following the sanctions imposed by the UN, see: Amatzia Baram, "The Effect of Iraqi Sanctions: Statistical Pitfalls and Responsibility," *The Middle East Journal*, Vol. 54, No. 2 (2000), pp. 194–223.

151 Allan G. Hill, "Population Growth in the Middle East since 1945 with Special Reference to the Arab Countries of West Asia," in John I. Clarke and Howard Bowen-Jones (eds.), *Change and Development in the Middle East* (London and New York: Methuen, 1981), p. 132, table 8.1.

152 K. L. Kohli and Musa'ad al-Omaim, "Mortality Levels, Trends and Differentials in Kuwait, 1957–1983," *Population Bulletin of ESCWA*, No. 28 (June 1986), p. 119; State of Qatar, Ministry of Information, *Qatar into the Seventies* (Doha, May 1973), p. 79; Jacqueline Ismael and Tareq Y. Ismael, "Social Policy in the Arab World," *Cairo Papers in Social Science*, Vol. 18, Monograph 1 (1995), p. 68.

153 The term "Asian Tigers" or the "East Asian Tigers" refers to Taiwan, South Korea, Hong Kong and Singapore which have maintained very high economic expansion and industrialization since the 1960s, thus transforming from developing into developed economies within the very short period of one generation only.

Chapter 3 *"Jobs for the Boys (and Girls)": The Emergence of the Employment Dilemma*

1 *Al-Ahram*, March 23, 2001. Quoted from: *MEED*, April 20, 2001, p. 24.

2 John Martin, "The Population Time Bomb," *The Middle East*, November 2003, p. 6.

3 Gilbar, *Kalkalat ha-Mizrah ha-Tikhon ba-'Et ha-Hadasha*, p. 40.

4 On the process of the development of a wide-based age pyramid due to high natural increase rates, see: Ismail Sirageldin, "Population Dynamics, Environment, and Conflict," in Ismail Sirageldin and Eqbal al-Rahmani (eds.), *Population and Development Transformations in the Arab World* (Greenwich: JAI Press, 1996), pp. 189–96.

5 UNICEF, *The State of the World's Children–2000*, p. 87, table 1; p.103, table 5.

6 *Ha'aretz,* July 22, 1998.

7 The median age divides the age distribution into two equal parts: one-half of the population falling below the median value and one-half above the median value.

8 Vallin, "The End of the Demographic Transition," p. 112.

9 John Knodel, "Deconstructing Population Momentum," *Population Today*, Vol. 27, No. 3 (March 1999), p. 2.

10 UN, *World Population Prospects: The 2006 Revision*, p. v.

11 Todaro, *Economic Development*, Seventh edition, p. 221.

12 Egypt, CAPMAS, *Statistical Yearbook, 1952–1992*, p. 28, table 1–18.

13 Egypt, CAPMAS, *Statistical Yearbook–2005*, p. 31, table 2–4.

14 Syria, *Statistical Abstract–2006*, p. 70, table 10/2.

15 Al-Mamlaka al-Maghribiyya, *al-Nashra al-Ihsaiyya al-Sanawiyya lil-Maghrib–2006*, p. 27, table 1–10.

16 Al-Jumhuriyya al-Tunisiyya, *al-Nashriyya al-Ihsaiyya al-Sanawiyya Li-Tunis–2005*, p. 29, table 2.1.
17 On the projected population growth rates in the Arab countries during the first half of the twenty-first century, see: Philippe Fargues, "Demographic Explosion or Social Upheaval?" in Ghassan Salamé (ed.), *Democracy without Democrats? The Renewal of Politics in the Muslim World* (London and New York: I.B. Tauris, 1994), pp. 157–65.
18 Al-Jumhuriyya al-Tunisiyya, Wizarat al-Tanmiyya wal-Ta'awun al-Dawli, *al-Isqatat al-Sukaniyya, 2004–2034* (Tunis, 2007), p. 22, table 15.
19 *Ibid.*, p. 23, table 16.
20 EU, *Eurostat Yearbook–2002*, p. 2.
21 Eurostat News Release, "European Population Trends in 2002," August 8, 2003. Available at: http://europa.eu.int/comm/eurostat.
22 EU, *Eurostat Yearbook–2005*, p. 62.
23 Jean-Claude Chesnais, "The Demographic Sunset of the West? *Population Today*, Vol. 25, No. 1 (January 1997), p. 5.
24 Paul Demeny, "Population Policy Dilemmas in Europe at the Dawn of the Twenty-First Century," *Population and Development Review*, Vol. 29, No. 1 (2003), p. 2.
25 EU, *Eurostat Yearbook–2005*, p. 64.
26 Demeny, "Population Policy Dilemmas in Europe," p. 3.
27 Wolfgang Lutz, Brian C. O'Neill and Sergei Scherbov, "Europe's Population at a Turning Point," *Science*, Vol. 299 (March 2003), p. 1991.
28 Todaro, *Economic Development*, seventh edition, p. 210.
29 See, for example: Ilona Ostner, Michael Reif and Hannu Turba, "Family Policies in Germany," third report for the project: *Welfare Policies and Employment in the Context of Family Change* (October 2003), p. 3. Available at: http://www.york.ac.uk/inst/spru/research/nordic/gerpoli.PDF. On France's pro-natalist policy, see: King, "France Needs Children," pp. 33–52.
30 EU, *Eurostat Yearbook–2002*, p. 2.
31 Eurostat News Release, "European Population Trends in 2002," August 8, 2003.
32 EU, *Eurostat Yearbook–2005*, p. 74.
33 Charles F. Westoff and Tomas Frejka, "Fertility and Religiousness Among European Muslims," paper presented at *the 2007 Annual Meeting of the Population Association of America*, New York, March 29–31, 2007, p. 3, table 2; pp. 5–6, table 3. Available at: http://paa2007.
34 Jonathan Laurence and Justin Vaisse, *Integrating Islam: Political and Religious Challenges in Contemporary France* (Washington, D.C.: Brookings Institution Press, 2006), p. 22.
35 CIA, *The World Factbook–2002*. Available at: http://www.cia.gov/cia/publications/factbook.
36 Laurence and Vaisse, *Integrating Islam*, pp. 24–25, table 1.6.
37 Mahfoud Bennoune, *The Making of Contemporary Algeria, 1830–1987: Colonial Upheavals and Post-Independence Development* (Cambridge: Cambridge University Press, 1988), p. 259.
38 ILO, *Yearbook of Labour Statistics*, various issues (Geneva).
39 Euromonitor Publications Limited, *Middle East Economic Handbook* (London: Euromonitor Publications Ltd., 1986), p. 81.
40 Shamlan Y. Alessa, *The Manpower Problem in Kuwait* (London and Boston: Kegan Paul International, 1981), p. 17, table 2.4.
41 See: ESCWA, *Survey of the Economic and Social Developments in the ESCWA Region–1995*, p. 40, table 12; Robert E. Looney, *Manpower Policies and Development in the Persian Gulf Region* (Westport and London: Praeger, 1994), p. 30, table 3.2.
42 *MEED*, January 27, 1989, p. 3; Looney, *Manpower Policies*, p. 30, table 3.2.
43 Saudi Arabia, *Seventh Development Plan*, p. 62, table 2.1.

44 ESCWA, *Survey, 2002–2003*, p. 16.
45 SAMA, *Fortieth Annual Report–1425H.* [2004], p. 305.
46 State of Kuwait, Ministry of Planning, Statistics and Information Center, *Annual Statistical Abstract–2000* (Kuwait, 2001), p. 91, table 76.
47 Onn Winckler, "The Challenge of Foreign Workers in the Persian/Arabian Gulf: The Case of Oman," *Immigrants & Minorities*, Vol. 18, No. 2 (2000), p. 28, table 2.
48 Rodney Wilson et al., *Economic Development in Saudi Arabia* (London and New York, RoutledgeCurzen, 2004), p. 97.
49 *MEED*, "Special Report-Qatar," November 1979, p. 11.
50 On the limitations on the Saudi women in the employment arena, see: Eleanor Abdella Doumato, "Women and Work in Saudi Arabia: How Flexible are Islamic Margins?" *The Middle East Journal*, Vol. 53, No. 4 (1999), pp. 568–83.
51 SAMA, *Forty-Third Annual Report–1428H.* [2007], p. 214, table 18.2.
52 Wilson and Graham, *Saudi Arabia*, p. 246.
53 *Ibid.*, p. 250.
54 Ikhlas A. Abdalla, "Attitudes Towards Women in the Arabian Gulf Region," *Women in Management Review*, Vol. 11, No. 1 (1996), p. 29.
55 Adil Osman Gebriel, "Overview of Major Issues in the Development of National Human Resources in the Gulf," in Abbas Abdelkarim (ed.), *Change and Development in the Gulf* (London: Macmillan Press, and New York: St. Martin's Press, 1999), pp. 152–53.
56 SAMA, *Thirty-Sixth Annual Report–1421H.* [2000], pp. 267–68.
57 *Saudi Economic Survey*, February 23, 2005, p. 5.
58 *The Middle East*, January 2003, p. 23.
59 By 2001, Bahrain's oil exports amounted to only 37,000 b/d and its oil revenues in that year amounted to $1.788 billion. See: The Cooperation Council of the Arab States of the Gulf (GCC), Statistical Department, *Statistical Bulletin*, No. 12 (2003), tables 144 and 148.
60 Sultanate of Oman, Ministry of Development, *The Fifth Five-Year Development Plan, 1996–2000* (Muscat, July 1997), p. 213. See also: Chatty, "Women Working in Oman," pp. 241–54.
61 See: Fatma al-Sayegh, "Domestic Politics in the United Arab Emirates: Social and Economic Policies, 1990–2000," in Joseph A. Kechichian (ed.), *Iran, Iraq, and the Arab Gulf States* (New York: Palgrave, 2001), pp. 172–73.
62 Andrzej Kapiszewski, *Nationals and Expatriates: Population and Labour Dilemmas of the Gulf Cooperation Council States* (Reading: Ithaca Press, 2001), p. 112.
63 ESCWA, *Survey, 1998–1999*, pp. 173–74.
64 The dependency ratio is the ratio of the economically dependent population (under 15 and over 64) to the productive population (aged 15–64). Hence, the dependency ratio is equal to the number of individuals aged below 15 or above 64 divided by the number of individuals aged 15–64.
65 UNDP, *Arab Human Development Report–2005*, p. 8; al-Qudsi, "Labour Participation of Arab Women," p. 931.
66 ESCWA, *Survey, 1996–1997*, p. 38, box 5.
67 UN, *Demographic Yearbook–1970*, pp. 296–97; *1975*, pp. 240–41.
68 Syria, *Statistical Abstract–1991*, p. 60, table 10.2; *2001*, p. 65, table 9/2.
69 Syria, *Statistical Abstract–2001*, p. 65, table 9/2.
70 Syria, *Statistical Abstract–2006*, p. 71, table 11/2.
71 The Economic Research Forum, *Economic Trends in the MENA Region–2002* (Cairo: The American University in Cairo Press, 2002), p. 88.
72 ESCWA, *Demographic and Related Socio-Economic Data Sheets*, No. 11 (2001), p. 99, table 1.
73 Radwan A. Shaban, Ragui Assaad and Sulayman S. al-Qudsi, "The Challenge of

Unemployment in the Arab Region," *International Labour Review*, Vol. 134, No. 1 (1995), p. 69.

74 Henry T. Azzam, *The Arab World Facing the Challenge of the New Millennium* (London and New York: I.B. Tauris, 2002), p. 5.

75 ESCWA, *Survey–2004, Summary*, p. 7.

76 Azzam, *The Arab World Facing the Challenge of the New Millennium*, p. 5.

77 WB, *The Hashemite Kingdom of Jordan*, A Quarterly Publication of the Jordan Country Unit, First Quarter 2003 (Washington, D.C., 2003), p. 8.

78 ESCWA, *Survey, 2003–2004*, p. 27.

79 *Africa Monitor*, July 2004, p. 3; *MEED*, January 9–15, 2004, p. 6; *Middle East International*, April 25, 2005, p. 24.

80 Moshe Efrat, "Tokhnit he-'Asor ve-Totzoteha," in Shimon Shamir (ed.), *Yeridat ha-Nasserism, 1965–1970: Shqi'ata shel Tenu'a Meshikhit* (Tel Aviv: Mif'alim Universitayim, 1978), p. 66 (Hebrew).

81 M. Riad El-Ghonemy, "An Assessment of Egypt's Development Strategy, 1952–1970," in Elie Podeh and Onn Winckler (eds.), *Rethinking Nasserism: Revolution and Historical Memory in Modern Egypt* (Gainesville: University Press of Florida, 2004), p. 258.

82 *Al-Mussawar*, No. 3377, June 30, 1989, p. 17.

83 El-Ghonemy, "An Assessment of Egypt's Development Strategy," p. 257.

84 Hansen, *Economic Development in Syria*, p. 13.

85 Foreign Areas Studies Division, *Area Handbook for Syria* (Washington, D.C.: The American University, July 1965), p. 236.

86 Yusif A. Sayigh, *The Economies of the Arab World: Development Since 1945* (London: Croom Helm, 1978), p. 229.

87 *Ibid.*

88 Oman remained a poor country during the 1960s as well, due both to the socioeconomic approach of the Sultan Sa'id bin Taymur and to the fact that oil export only started in 1967. Thus, Oman's per capita GNP in 1968 amounted to only $250. WB, *World Tables, 1989–90 Edition*, p. 432.

89 For example, Saudi Arabia's per capita GNP increased from $500 in 1968 to $830 in 1972, the year prior to the "oil boom," while that of Libya increased from $1,490 to $1,980 during the corresponding period. Kuwait's per capita GNP was already high in the early 1970s, amounting to $3,700 in 1972 (current prices). WB, *World Tables, 1989–90 Edition*, pp. 344, 356, 472. Accurate economic data for Bahrain, UAE, and Qatar during the late 1960s and early 1970s are not available.

90 WB, *World Tables, 1989–90 Edition.*

91 WB, *World Development Report–1985*, pp. 175–76, table 2.

92 *Middle East International*, February 22, 1985, p. 16.

93 Eliyahu Kanovsky, "Jordan's Economy: From Prosperity to Crisis," *Occasional Papers*, No. 106 (The Moshe Dayan Center, Tel Aviv University, May 1989), p. 41.

94 *MEED*, April 11, 1987, p. 36.

95 J. S. Birks, C. A. Sinclair and J. A. Socknat, "The Demand for Egyptian Labor Abroad," in Alan Richards and Philip L. Martin (eds.), *Migration, Mechanization, and Agricultural Labor Markets in Egypt* (Boulder: Westview Press, 1983), p. 118.

96 *The Arab Economist*, April 1980, p. 25; *al-Ahram*, January 14, 1980.

97 Ralph R. Sell, "Egyptian International Labor Migration and Social Processes: Toward Regional Integration," *International Migration Review*, Vol. 22, No. 3 (1988), p. 91.

98 *MEED*, September 16, 1983, p. 22; EIU, QER, *Egypt, Country Profile, 1986–87*, p. 8; Gil Feiler, "Migration and Recession: Arab Labor Mobility in the Middle East, 1982–1989," *Population and Development Review*, Vol. 17, No. 1 (1991), p. 136.

99 M. A. J. Share, "The Use of Jordanian Workers' Remittances," in Bichara Khader and

Adnan Badran (eds.), *The Economic Development of Jordan* (London: Croom Helm, 1987), p. 33, table 3.1.

100 J. S. Birks and C. A. Sinclair, *International Migration Project: Country Case Study: The Hashemite Kingdom of Jordan* (Durham: The University of Durham, Department of Economics, November 1978), p. 9, table. 3; Ian J. Seccombe, "Labour Emigration Policies and Economic Development in Jordan: From Unemployment to Labour Shortage," in Khader and Badran (eds.), *The Economic Development of Jordan*, p. 120.

101 J. S. Birks, I. Seragelding, C. A. Sinclair and J. A. Socknat, "Who is Migrating Where? An Overview of International Labor Migration in the Arab World," in Richards and Martin (eds.), *Migration, Mechanization, and Agricultural Labor Markets in Egypt*, p. 115, table 2; Share, "The Use of Jordanian Workers' Remittances," p. 34, table 3.2; *al-Dustur*, March 24, 1981.

102 Jordan, *Statistical Abstract–1989*, p. 83, table 4/2/3.

103 *Al-Ra'y*, July 14; July 29; November 27, 1986.

104 Allan M. Findlay, "Return to Yemen: The End of the Old Migration Order in the Arab World," in W. T. S. Gould and A. M. Findlay (eds.), *Population Migration and the Changing World Order* (Chichester: John Wiley & Sons, 1994), p. 214.

105 Winckler, *Demographic Developments and Population Policies in Ba'thist Syria*, p. 93, table 4.1.

106 Bayan Tabbara, "Labour Markets in the ESCWA Region During the Past 25 Years," in ESCWA, *Proceedings of the Expert Group Meeting on Assessment of Economic and Social Developments in the ESCWA Region During the Last 25 Years and Priorities for the Next Decade, 1999–2009* (New York, 1999), pp. 109–10.

107 On the development of the intra-Arab "mutual dependence" following the October 1973 "oil boom," see: Saad Eddin Ibrahim, "Oil, Migration and the New Arab Social Order," in Malcolm H. Kerr and El Sayed Yassin (eds.), *Rich and Poor States in the Middle East: Egypt and the New Arab Order* (Boulder: Westview Press, and Cairo: The American University in Cairo Press, 1982), pp. 17–70.

108 El-Ghonemy, *Affluence and Poverty in the Middle East*, p. 183.

109 Kashef, "Egypt," p. 26.

110 Tayseer Abdel Jaber, "Jordanian Labor Migration: Social, Political and Economic Effects," in Shtayyeh (ed.), *Labor Migration*, p. 85.

111 Muhammad Sa'ad 'Amirah, "Waqi' al-Bitala fil-Urdun wa-Nazara Nahwa al-Mustaqbal," in Mustafa al-Hamarneh (ed.), *al-Iqtisad al-Urduni: al-Mushkilat wal-Afaq* (Amman: Markaz al-Dirasat al-Istratigiyya, 1994), p. 224, table 2.

112 Birks and Sinclair, *International Migration and Development in the Arab Region*, p. 135, table 10.

113 *Al-Ra'y*, November 21, 1984.

114 HRD base Ltd., *Socio-Demographic Profiles of Key Arab Countries*, p. 44, table 3.2.

115 UNDP, *Arab Human Development Report–2005*, p. 20.

116 Paul Rivlin, *World Oil and Energy Trends: Strategic Implications for the Middle East*, Memorandum No. 57 (Tel Aviv University, Jaffee Center for Strategic Studies, September 2000), p. 17, table 1.

117 Abdel Jaber, "Jordanian Labor Migration," p. 83.

118 Kanovsky, "Jordan's Economy: From Prosperity to Crisis," p. 41.

119 WB, *World Tables, 1995 Edition*, pp. 386–87.

120 On the Jordanian-Iraqi economic relationship prior to the Iraqi invasion of Kuwait, see: Amatzia Baram, "Ba'thi Iraq and Hashemite Jordan: From Hostility to Alignment," *Middle East Journal*, Vol. 45, No. 1 (1991), pp. 56–58.

121 IMF, *Jordan: Background Information on Selected Aspects of Adjustment and Growth Strategy* (August 29, 1995), p. 16.

122 El-Ghonemy, *Affluence and Poverty in the Middle East*, p. 196.

123 ‘Amirah, “Waqi‘ al-Bitala fil-Urdun,” p. 224, table 2.
124 *Al-Dustur*, April 17, 1990.
125 On the Jordanian replacement labor migration policy, see: Ian J. Seccombe, “Immigrant Workers in an Emigrant Economy: An Examination of Replacement Migration in the Middle East,” *International Migration*, Vol. 24, No. 2 (1986), pp. 382–84.
126 Raymond A. Hinnebusch, “Syria,” in Tim Niblock and Emma Merphy (eds.), *Economic and Political Liberalization in the Middle East* (London and New York: British Academic Press, 1993), p. 188.
127 By 1985, Syria’s oil exports amounted to 150,000 b/d.
128 On the Syrian Strategic Balance Parity policy, see: Moshe Ma‘oz, *Syria and Israel: From War to Peace Making* (Oxford: Clarendon Press, 1995), pp. 183–200.
129 WB, *World Tables, 1995 Edition*, p. 648. On the deterioration of the Syrian economy during the second half of the 1980s, see: Eliyahu Kanovsky, “Middle East Economies and Arab–Israeli Peace Agreements,” *Israel Affairs*, Vol. 1, No. 4 (1995), pp. 28–29.
130 By 1986, the Syrian inflation rate amounted to 36% compared to 6%–19% during the first half of the 1980s. See: IMF, *Syrian Arab Republic: Staff Report for the 1987 Article IV Consultation* (February 18, 1988), p. 4.
131 *Al-Ittihad*, March 14, 1987; *al-Ahram al-Iqtisadi*, May 30, 1988.
132 IMF, *Syrian Arab Republic: Staff Report for the 1987 Article IV Consultation* (February 18, 1988), p. 4.
133 *Al-Hayat*, January 26, 1992.
134 Volker Perthes, “The Syrian Economy in the 1980s,” *The Middle East Journal*, Vol. 46, No. 1 (1992), p. 37.
135 ESCWA, *Return Migration*, p. 20, table 6.
136 See: Podeh and Winckler, “The Boycott that Never Was,” pp. 32–36.
137 WB, *World Tables, 1995 Edition*, pp. 4–5, table 2; pp. 28–29, table 7.
138 El-Ghonemy, *Affluence and Poverty in the Middle East*, p. 182.
139 *Al-Ahram al-Iqtisadi*, February 13, 1989; ESCWA, *Return Migration*, p. 17.
140 EIU, *Country Report-Egypt*, No. 4 (1988), p. 10.
141 *Al-Ahram*, February 11, 1990.
142 Bruce Maddy-Weitzman, “Masoret, Gidul Okhlosiya ve-Tikhnun Mishpaha be-Marocco,” in Ayalon and Gilbar (eds.), *Demographya ve-Politiqa be-Medinot ‘Arav*, p. 58 (Hebrew).
143 El-Ghonemy, *Affluence and Poverty in the Middle East*, p. 188.
144 EIU, *Country Profile–Algeria, 2004*, p. 36.
145 For example, the Saudi foreign currency reserves declined from $125 billion in 1980 to $65 billion in 1990. *Middle East International*, September 24, 1993, p. 20.
146 *Middle East International*, November 5, 2004.
147 ESCWA, *Survey, 2004–2005*, p. 29.
148 *MEED*, August 14, 1992, p. 19.
149 ESCWA, *Survey–1994*, p. 65, table 38.
150 WB, *World Tables, 1995 Edition*, p. 29, table 7.
151 *MEED*, November 8, 1991, p. 17.
152 *Jordan Times*, October 14, 1991.
153 *Jordan Times*, November 18, 1999.
154 ESCWA, *Survey, 1998–1999*, p. 51.
155 IMF, *Jordan: 2006 Article IV Consultation and Fourth Post*, Country Report No. 07/128 (March 2007), p. 6.
156 The Hashemite Kingdom of Jordan, Department of Statistics. Available at: http://www.dos.gov.jo.
157 *Jordan Times*, August 7, 1996.
158 ESCWA, *Survey, 2000–2001*, p. 31.

159 *The Middle East*, October 1991, p. 36; Nicholas Van Hear, *New Diaspora: The Mass Exodus, Dispersal, and Regrouping of Migrant Communities* (London: UCL Press, 1998), p. 87.
160 Findlay, "Return to Yemen," p. 218.
161 ESCWA, *National Accounts Studies of the ESCWA Region*, Bulletin No. 17 (1997), p. 9.
162 In regard to the overall impacts of the mass return on the Yemenite economy during the early 1990s, see: Nicholas Van Hear, "The Socio-Economic Impact of the Involuntary Mass Return to Yemen in 1990," *Journal of Refugee Studies*, Vol. 7, No. 1 (1994), pp. 18–38.
163 ESCWA, *Survey, 1996–1997*, p. 36.
164 *Gulf States Newsletter*, April 18, 2003, p. 19.
165 See, for example: *Middle East International*, May 3, 1991, p. 22.
166 EIU, *Country Profile–Tunisia, 1999–2000*, p. 22; p. 41, table 2; *Country Profile–Tunisia, 2001*, p. 25; IMF, *Tunisia: Recent Economic Developments*, Country Report No. 00/37 (March 2000), pp. 17–18.
167 IMF, *International Financial Statistics Yearbook–1999*, p. 665.
168 Nora Ann Colton, "The Maghrebi Economies as Emerging Markets?" in Yahia H. Zoubir (ed.), *North Africa in Transition: State, Society, and Economic Transformation in the 1990s* (Gainesville: University Press of Florida, 1999), p. 162; Azzam, *The Arab World Facing the Challenge of the New Millennium*, p. 118; ILO, *World Employment Report–2001*, p. 361, table 4.
169 IMF, *Algeria: Selected Economic Issues*, Country Report No. 98/87 (1998), p. 49, table 15; Country Report No. 96/71 (1996), p. 35, table 6.
170 EIU, *Country Profile–Algeria, 2001*, p. 32.
171 Egypt, CAPMAS, *Statistical Yearbook, 1992–1998*, p. 11, table 1–15.
172 EIU, *Country Profile–Egypt, 2001*, p. 15.
173 ESCWA, *National Accounts Studies of the ESCWA Region*, Bulletin No. 16 (1996), p. 3.
174 *MEED*, February 9, 1996, p. 2; EIU, *Country Profile–Syria, 2006*, p. 31.
175 *MEED,* November 18, 1994, p. 10.
176 ESCWA, *Survey–1995*, p. 159, table 81.
177 By the mid-1990s, the number of Syrian workers in other Arab countries was estimated at 800,000, namely, more than 15% of the total Syrian workforce and approximately 20% of the civilian workforce. (See Chapter 4)
178 By the early 1990s, the agricultural sector represented approximately 30% of the total Syrian GDP. Syria, *Statistical Abstract–2000*, pp. 536–37, table 29/16.
179 ESCWA, *National Accounts Studies of the ESCWA Region*, Bulletin No. 19 (1999), p. 6.
180 ESCWA, *Survey, 2001–2002*, p. 17; The Economic Research Forum, *Syria Country Profile: The Road Ahead for Syria* (Cairo, February 2005), p. 11.
181 EIU, *Country Profile–Syria, 2000–2001*, p. 20.
182 ESCWA, *External Trade Bulletin of the ESCWA Region*, eleventh edition (2002), pp. 84–86, table II–4.
183 Eyal Zisser, *Be-Shem ha-Av: Bashar al-Asad: Shanim Rishonot ba-Shilton* (Tel Aviv: Tel Aviv University Press, 2004), p. 200 (Hebrew); ESCWA, "Oil for Food: Impact on Iraq and its Main Arab Trading Partners," p. 6. Available at: http://www.escwa.org.
184 EIA, "Major Non-OPEC Countries Oil Revenues" (June 2003), *EIA website.*
185 ESCWA, *Survey, 2001–2002*, p. 18.
186 EIU, *Country Profile–Egypt, 1999–2000*, p. 28.
187 ESCWA, *Survey, 2000–2001*, pp. 30–31; *MEED*, April 20, 2001, p. 28.
188 EIU, *Country Profile–Egypt, 2001*, p. 33.
189 *Al-Ahram Weekly*, February 27-March 5, 2003.
190 IMF, *Arab Republic of Egypt: Selected Issues*, Country Report No. 05/179 (June 2005), p. 15, table 1.

191 *MEED*, April 13–19, 2007, pp. 29–30.
192 EIU, *Country Profile–Syria, 2006*, p. 32.
193 IMF, *Morocco: 2007 Article IV Consultation*, Country Report No. 07/323 (September 2007), p. 16, table 1.
194 By 2005, Algeria's GDP growth rate amounted to 5.5% in real terms. EIU, *Country Profile–Algeria, 2006*, p. 33.
195 IMF, *Algeria: 2006 Article IV Consultation*, Country Report No. 07/72 (February 2007), p. 5, footnote 1.
196 *WB, Middle East and North Africa: Economic Developments and Prospects–2005*, p. 6.
197 IMF, *Tunisia: 2007 Article IV Consultation*, Country Report No. 07/302 (August 2007), p. 5; EIU, *Country Profile–Tunisia, 2006*, p. 33.
198 Kashef, "Egypt," p. 26; Shaban, Ragui and al-Qudsi, "The Challenge of Unemployment in the Arab Region," p. 75.
199 EIU, *Country Profile–Tunisia, 1989–90*, p. 10. See also: Euromonitor Publications Limited, *Middle East Economic Handbook*, p. 381.
200 Mohamed Farid Azzi, "Maghrebi Youth: Between Alienation and Integration," in Zoubir (ed.), *North Africa in Transition*, pp. 113–14.
201 SAMBA, "Saudi Arabia's Employment Profile," October 8, 2000, p. 3; Wilson et al., *Economic Development in Saudi Arabia*, p. 98.
202 Shaban, Ragui and al-Qudsi, "The Challenge of Unemployment in the Arab Region," p. 75; Richards and Waterbury, *A Political Economy of the Middle East*, second edition, pp. 136–38.
203 ILO, *Yearbook of Labour Statistics–2002*, pp. 487–88, table 3B.
204 The Economic Research Forum, *Economic Trends in the MENA Region–2002*, p. 91.
205 EIU, *Country Profile–Algeria, 2004*, pp. 36–37.
206 *MEED*, May 2, 2003, p. 23.
207 Azzam, *The Arab World Facing the Challenge of the New Millennium*, p. 11.
208 *Jordan Times*, July 10, 2003.
209 EIU, *Country Profile–Egypt, 2005*, p. 40.
210 See, for example, Gardner, "Wanted: More Jobs."
211 UNDP, *Arab Human Development Report–2005*, p. 9.
212 The term "underemployment" refers to a situation in which a worker is employed, but not in the desired capacity, whether in terms of wage, hours or level of skill and experience.
213 EIU, QER, *Egypt-Annual Supplement, 1985*, p. 30.
214 Wilson, *Economic Development in the Middle East*, p. 65.
215 Henry J. Bruton, "Egypt's Development in the Seventies," *Economic Development and Cultural Change*, Vol. 33, No. 4 (1983), p. 690.
216 *Ibid.*
217 ESCWA, *Survey, 1998–1999*, pp. 174–75.
218 EIU, *Country Profile–Egypt, 2001*, p. 14; *Ha'aretz*, May 1, 2002.
219 ESCWA, *Survey, 2000–2001*, p. 23.
220 Syria, *Statistical Abstract–2004*, p. 92, table 9/3.
221 *Ha'aretz*, May 1, 2002.
222 *Jordan Times*, April 20, 1996.
223 *Jordan Times*, February 21, 1999.
224 WB, *Labor Market Reforms, Growth and Unemployment in Labor-Exporting MENA Countries*, p. 6.
225 Adam Bennett, "Failed Legacies," *Finance & Development*, Vol. 40, No. 1 (March 2003).
226 Richards and Waterbury, *A Political Economy of the Middle East*, second edition, p. 120.
227 David W. Lesch, "History and Political Culture in Syria: Obstacles to Integration in the Global Economy After the Gulf War," in Moshe Ma'oz, Joseph Ginat and Onn Winckler (eds.), *Modern Syria: From Ottoman Rule to Pivotal Role in the Middle East* (Brighton and

Portland: Sussex Academic Press, 1999), pp. 57–58. See also the report of Cowell on the *baqshish* phenomenon in Syria: *The New York Times Magazine* (April 1, 1990), p. 33; EIU, *Country Profile–Syria, 2006*, p. 32.

228 *FORBES*, October 25, 1982, p. 48.

229 EIU, *Country Profile–Egypt, 2001*, p. 33.

230 Syria, *Statistical Abstract–2001*, p. 109, table 6/4.

231 One hectare is equal to 10,000 square meters, that is, 10 dunams.

232 Syria, *Statistical Abstract–2001*, p. 109, table 6/4.

233 Syria, *Statistical Abstract–2006*, p. 115, table 6/4.

234 European Commission, Directorate-General for Employment and Social Affairs, *Employment in Europe 2002: Recent Trends and Prospects* (Luxembourg, July 2002), p. 16.

235 Long-term unemployment is defined as the state of being unemployed for one year or more and looking for a job.

236 EU, *Eurostat Yearbook–2002*, p. 17.

237 ILO, *Yearbook of Labour Statistics–2002*, pp. 509–10, table 3B.

238 *Ibid.*, pp. 510–11, table 3B.

239 European Commission, *Employment in Europe–2002*, p. 29.

240 The European Commission website. Available at http://europa.eu.int/comm/regional_policy.

241 US Department of Labor, Bureau of Labor Statistics. Available at: http://www.bls.gov/opub/ooq/1999/Fall/oochart/pdf.

242 IMF, *Morocco: 2007 Article IV Consultation*, Country Report No. 07/323 (September 2007), p. 6.

243 The Economic Research Forum, *Economic Trends in the MENA Region–2002*, p. 91.

244 *Jordan Times*, July 10, 2003.

245 See, for example: Kirk S. Bowman and Jerrold D. Green, "Urbanization and Political Instability in the Middle East," in Michael E. Bonine (ed.), *Population, Poverty, and Politics in Middle East Cities* (Gainesville: University Press of Florida, 1997), pp. 237–55.

246 Cassandra, "The Impending Crisis in Egypt," *The Middle East Journal*, Vol. 49, No. 1 (1995), p. 19.

247 The National Bank of Egypt, *The Egyptian Economy in Brief–2000* (Cairo, 2001).

248 *The Middle East*, March 2000, p. 21.

249 On the North African tourism industry, see: Matthew Gray, "The Political Economy of Tourism in North Africa: Comparative Perspectives," *Thunderbird International Business Review*, Vol. 42, No. 4 (2000), pp. 393–408; Robert A. Poirier, "Tourism and Development in Tunisia," *Annals of Tourism Research*, Vol. 22, No. 1 (1995), pp. 157–71; Scott Youngstedt, "Tourism in Morocco: Opportunities, Challenges and Threats," *Africa Insight*, Vol. 33, No. 1 (2003), pp. 61–68.

250 George Alan, "Syria: An Economy Saved by Circumstances," *The Middle East*, December 1988, pp. 27–29.

251 The official website of the ILO, Press Release. Available at: http://www.ilo.org.

Chapter 4 *The "New Arab Demographic Order": The Intra-Arab Labor Migration*

1 Due to the enormous importance of the intra-Arab labor migration, Georges Sabagh entitled this phenomenon "the new demographic order": See his "Migration and Social Mobility in Egypt," in Kerr and Yassin (eds.), *Rich and Poor States in the Middle East*, p. 71.

2 Mai Yamani, "Health, Education, Gender and the Security of the Gulf in the Twenty-First Century," in Long and Koch (eds.), *Gulf Security in the Twenty-First Century*, p. 274.

3 Pat Lancaster, "Gulf Tourism – Lifting the Lid on a Well-kept Secret," *The Middle East*, April 1995, p. 25.

4 M. G. Quibria, "Migrant Workers and Remittances: Issues for Asian Developing Countries," *Asian Development Review*, Vol. 4, No. 1 (1986), p. 79.
5 IOM, "Facts and Figures on International Migration," *Migration Policy Issues*, No. 2 (March 2003). Available at: http://www.iom.int.
6 This section is based on my article: "Was it Worth It? A Reexamination of the Cost/Benefit Balance of the Inter-Arab Labor Migration," *Journal of South Asian and Middle Eastern Studies*, Vol. 29, No. 4 (2006), pp. 38–59.
7 The International Trade theory, developed by David Ricardo in the early nineteenth century, was a logical consequence of Ricardo's Comparative Advantage Theory which explains why it can be beneficial for two parties to trade without barriers if one is more efficient at producing goods or services needed by the other side. In that case, free trade, both locally and internationally, is a "win–win situation" for the benefit of both trading partners. On Ricardo's International Trade theory, see: Andrea Maneschi, "Ricardo's International Trade Theory: Beyond the Comparative Cost Example," *Cambridge Journal of Economics*, Vol. 16 (1992), pp. 421–37.
8 Findlay, "Return to Yemen," p. 206; Douglas S. Massey et al., "An Evaluation of International Migration Theory: The North American Case," *Population and Development Review*, Vol. 20, No. 4 (1994), p. 701.
9 By 2003, workers' remittances worldwide amounted to $150 billion – three times the development aid given by the developed countries to the developing countries. *The New York Times*, June 6, 2004.
10 Dilip Ratha, "Workers' Remittances: An Important and Stable Source of External Finance," in IBRD, *Global Development Finance: Striving for Stability in Development Finance* (Washington, D.C., 2003), p. 157.
11 *Ibid.*, p. 164.
12 Claudia M. Buch and Anja Kuckulenz, "Worker Remittances and Capital Flows to Developing Countries," Center for European Economic Research (ZEW), Discussion Paper No. 04–31 (2004), p. 3. Available at: http://ftp.zew.de/pub/zew-docs/dp/dp0431.pdf.
13 Cerstin Sander, "Migrant Remittances to Developing Countries," prepared for the *UK Department of International Development* (June 2003), pp. 5–6. Available at: http://www.dai.com/publications/other.php.
14 Yousif Khalifa al-Yousif, "Oil Economies and Globalization: The Case of the GCC Countries," p. 9. Available at: http://www.sba.luc.edu/orgs/meea/volume6/al-yousif.htm.
15 John Willoughby, "Ambivalent Anxieties of the South Asian-Gulf Arab Labor Exchange," American University, Washington, D.C., Department of Economics, Working Paper Series No. 2005-02 (March 2005), p. 1. Available at: http://www.american.edu/cas/econ/workingpapers/2005-02.pdf.
16 Owen and Pamuk, *A History of Middle East Economies*, p. 76. Lorimer estimated that Oman's population in 1907 numbered approximately half a million. See: Muhammad Zahra, "Sukan Sultanat Uman," in al-Ruythi (ed.), *Sukan al-'Alam al-'Arabi*, p. 358, table 2.
17 Rodney Wilson, *The Economies of the Middle East* (London: Macmillan Press, 1979), pp. 74–75. On the pearl industry in the Gulf during the nineteenth century and early twentieth century, see: Mohamed G. Rumaihi, "The Mode of Production in the Arab Gulf Before the Discovery of Oil," in Tim Niblock (ed.), *Social and Economic Development in the Arab Gulf* (London: Croom Helm, 1980), pp. 50–60.
18 The Kingdom of Saudi Arabia, Ministry of Planning, *Third Development Plan, 1400–1405 A.H.* [1980–1985] (Riyadh, 1980), p. 8.
19 The Kingdom of Saudi Arabia, Ministry of Planning, *Second Development Plan, 1395–1340 A.H.* [1975–1980] (Riyadh, 1975), p. 20.
20 On this subject, see: ESCWA, *Economic Diversification in the Oil-Producing Countries: The*

Case of the Gulf Cooperation Council Economies (New York, 2001), p. 1; Wilson et al., *Economic Development in Saudi Arabia*, pp. 20–21.

21 Sultanate of Oman, Ministry of Information, *The Speeches of H.M. Sultan Qaboos bin Said, 1970–1990* (Muscat, n.d), p. 78.

22 Quoted from: Douglas S. Massey, et al., *Worlds in Motion: Understanding International Migration at the End of the Millennium* (Oxford: Clarendon Press, 1998), p. 134.

23 See: Nader Fergany, "Manpower Problems and Projections in the Gulf," in M. S. El-Azhary (ed.), *The Impact of Oil Revenues on Arab Gulf Development* (London: Croom Helm, and Boulder: Westview Press, 1984), pp. 157–59; Richards and Waterbury, *A Political Economy of the Middle East*, second edition, p. 369.

24 ECWA, *Demographic and Related Socio-Economic Data sheets*, No. 2 (1978), country pages.

25 Baquer Salman al-Najjar "Population Policies in the Countries of the Gulf Co-operation Council," in Abdelkarim (ed.), *Change and Development in the Gulf*, pp. 138–39.

26 Abbas Abdelkarim, "Oil, Population Change and Social Development in the Gulf: Some Major Trends and Indicators," in Abdelkarim (ed.), *Change and Development in the Gulf*, p. 33; Sharon Stanton Russell, "International Migration and Political Turmoil in the Middle East," *Population and Development Review*, Vol. 18, No. 4 (1992), p. 720; Birks and Sinclair, *International Migration and Development in the Arab Region*, p. 26.

27 ILO, *Employment Opportunities and Equity in a Changing Economy: Egypt in the 1980's. A Labour Market Approach*, by Bent Hansen and Samir Radwan (Geneva, 1982), p. 91, table 34.

28 Roger Owen, *Migrant Workers in the Gulf* (London: The Minority Rights Group, 1985), p. 4.

29 *Nidhal al-Falahin*, July 12, 1978; *al-Thawra* (Damascus), January 23, 1980.

30 See, for example: Alan Richards and Philip L. Martin, "The Laissez-Faire Approach to International Labor Migration," *Economic Development and Cultural Change*, Vol. 31, No. 3 (1983), p. 465; Feiler, "Migration and Recession," p. 137; Sell, "Egyptian International Labor Migration and Social Processes," p. 101; Ann M. Lesch, "Egyptian Labor Migration," in Ibrahim M. Oweiss (ed.), *The Political Economy of Contemporary Egypt* (Washington, D.C.: Center for Contemporary Arab Studies, Georgetown University, 1990), pp. 90–91.

31 The Kingdom of Saudi Arabia, Ministry of Planning, *Fourth Development Plan, 1405–1410 A.H.* [1985–1990] (Riyadh, 1985), p. 50.

32 *Ibid.*, pp. 50–51.

33 *Al-Bayan*, August 13, 1984.

34 EIU, *Country Profile–Oman, 1992/93*, p. 13.

35 J. S. Birks and C. A. Sinclair, "Repatriation, Remittances and Reunions: What is Really at Stake for Arab Countries Supplying Labour to the Gulf Co-Operation Council States," in Charles E. Davies (ed.), *Global Interests in the Arab Gulf* (New York: St. Martin's Press, 1992), p. 105.

36 See: Winckler, "The Economic Consequences of the Iraqi Crisis," pp. 396–97.

37 Muhammad Ali al-Ramadhan, "New Population Policy in Kuwait: The Quest for a Balance in the Population Composition," *Population Bulletin of ESCWA*, No. 43 (1995), p. 39.

38 This paragraph is based on my article "Labor and Liberalization: The Decline of the GCC *Rentier* System," in Joshua Teitelbaum (ed.), *Political Liberalization in the Persian Gulf* (New York: Columbia University Press, forthcoming 2009).

39 Kapiszewski, *Nationals and Expatriates*, p. 193.

40 *Ibid.*, pp. 197–98.

41 Andrzej Kapiszewski, "Arab Labor Migration to the GCC States," in IOM and League of Arab States, *Arab Migration in a Globalized World* (Cairo, May 2004), p. 120.

42 Massey et al., *Worlds in Motion*, p. 159.
43 ILO, *World Employment Report–2001* (Geneva, 2001), p. 19, table 1.5.
44 Owen, *Migrant Workers in the Gulf*, p. 4.
45 ESCWA, *Return Migration*, p. 10.
46 Thus, for example, in 1989, of the 3,759 foreigners who obtained Saudi nationality, 2,995 (80%) were females. *Saudi Economic Survey*, September 9, 1992, p. 17. In 1997, among 4,413 foreigners who received Saudi citizenship, 3,576 were females. *Saudi Economic Survey*, April 12, 2000, p. 11.
47 Richards and Waterbury, *A Political Economy of the Middle East*, second edition, p. 384.
48 Sulayman Khalaf and Saad al-Kobaisi, "Migrants' Strategies of Coping and Patterns of Accommodation in the Oil-Rich Gulf Societies: Evidence from the UAE," *British Journal of Middle Eastern Studies*, Vol. 26, No. 2 (1999), p. 282.
49 Delwin A. Roy, "Egyptian Emigrant Labor: Domestic Consequences," *Middle Eastern Studies*, Vol. 27, No. 3 (1991), p. 574.
50 Annika Rabo, *Change on the Euphrates: Villagers, Townsmen and Employees in Northern Syria* (University of Stockholm, Department of Social Anthropology, 1986), p. 101.
51 See, for example: Peter N. Woodward, *Oil and Labor in the Middle East: Saudi Arabia and the Oil Boom* (New York: Praeger, 1988), p. 26.
52 Mai Yamani, *Changed Identities: The Challenge of the New Generation in Saudi Arabia* (London: The Royal Institute of International Affairs, 2000), p. 81.
53 According to the various estimates, by late 2004 some two million Asian maids were working in the GCC countries, representing more than 20% of the total foreign labor in these countries. Source: *Middle East Online*, updated October 18, 2004. Available at: http://www.middle-east-online.com.
54 The origin of the *kafala* system is in the Bedouin tradition which requires that a foreigner who wants to pass in the territory of a certain tribe pays one of the tribe members for protection while traveling through the tribe's territory.
55 Owen, *Migrant Workers in the Gulf*, p. 8; "Gulf Population and Labour Force Structure," *The NCB* [National Commercial Bank] *Economist*, Vol. 5, No. 4 (June/July 1995), p. 10.
56 *MEED*, December 6, 1996, p. 34.
57 Quoted in: Nazih N. Ayubi, *Over-stating the Arab State: Politics and Society in the Middle East* (London and New York: I.B. Tauris, 1995), p. 227.
58 On the kinship and tribal system of the Gulf societies, see the Introduction in Philip Khoury and Joseph Kostiner (eds.), *Tribes and State Formation in the Middle East* (London and New York: I.B. Tauris, 1991), pp. 1–21.
59 Hazem Beblawi, "The Rentier State in the Arab World," in Giacomo Luciani (ed.), *The Arab State* (London: Routledge, 1990), p. 89.
60 Benjamin Smith, "Oil Wealth and Regime Survival in the Developing World, 1960–1999," *American Journal of Political Science*, Vol. 48, No. 2 (2004), p. 233.
61 Giacomo Luciani, "Allocation vs. Production States: A Theoretical Framework," in Luciani (ed.), *The Arab State*, p. 71.
62 *Ibid.*
63 Steffen Hertog, "Segmented Clientelism: The Political Economy of Saudi Economic Reform Efforts," in Paul Aarts and Gred Nonneman (eds.), *Saudi Arabia in the Balance* (London: Hurst & Company, 2005), pp. 112–13.
64 Smith, "Oil Wealth and Regime Survival in the Developing World," p. 233.
65 Henry and Springborg, *Globalization and the Politics of Development in the Middle East*, p. 8.
66 Gregory Gause III, *Oil Monarchies, Domestic and Security Challenges in the Arab Gulf States* (New York: Council on Foreign Relations, 1994), p. 43.
67 Ayubi, *Over-stating the Arab States*, pp. 251–52.
68 J. S. Birks and J. A. Rimmer, *Developing Education Systems in the Oil States of Arabia:*

Conflicts of Purpose and Focus (University of Durham: Centre for Middle Eastern and Islamic Studies, 1984), p. 4.

69 Sharon Stanton Russell, "Politics and Ideology in Migration Policy Formulation: The Case of Kuwait," *International Migration Review*, Vol. 23, No. 1 (1989), p. 36.

70 For example, in April 1975, the Saudi authorities abolished income tax for foreign labor. See: EIU, QER, *Saudi Arabia, Jordan*, No. 2 (1975), p. 5.

71 UN, *Population Policy Compendium-Saudi Arabia*, p. 5.

72 A prominent factor in the Islamic revolution in Iran was a mistaken socioeconomic policy implemented by the Shah, in which the oil wealth was concentrated in the hands of a few, while the vast majority of the population not only did not enjoy the oil wealth but rather suffered greatly from the consequences of hyperinflation.

73 In the case of the UAE, for example, development expenditures declined by more than half in 1983 compared to the previous year, the last one of the "oil decade." See: *Al-Bayan*, August 15, 1984.

74 J. S Birks, I. J. Seccombe and C. A. Sinclair, "Labour Migration in the Arab Gulf States: Patterns, Trends and Prospects," *International Migration*, Vol. 26, No. 3 (1988), p. 270.

75 "Growing Concern Over Dependence on Foreign Labor," *Arab Oil*, Vol. 13, No. 9 (1983), p. 28.

76 MERI Report, *United Arab Emirates* (London: Croom Helm, 1985), p. 46.

77 Shah, "Restrictive Labour Immigration Policies in the Oil-Rich Gulf," p. 4.

78 K. L. Kohli and Musa'ad al-Omaim, "Changing Patterns of Migration in Kuwait," *Population Bulletin of ESCWA*, No. 32 (June 1988), p. 92; UN, Population Division, *Case Studies in Population Policy: Kuwait*, Population Policy Paper No. 15 (New York, 1988), p. 51.

79 The difference in the required minimum income was due to the fact that government employees, including foreigners, enjoyed the privilege of certain services while those employed in the private sector did not. UN, *Case Studies in Population Policy: Kuwait*, p. 38.

80 Shah, "Restrictive Labour Immigration Policies in the Oil-Rich Gulf," p. 1.

81 Saudi Arabia, *Fourth Development Plan, 1405–1410 A.H.* [1985–1990], pp. 50–51.

82 *MEED*, March 29, 1986, p. 8.

83 *Saudi Economic Survey*, March 16, 1988, p. 8.

84 *Middle East Newsletters, Gulf States,* April 20, 1987, pp. 11–12.

85 *Gulf States Newsletter*, August 21, 1989, p. 13; EIU, *Country Report, Bahrain, Qatar*, No. 2 (1993), p. 10.

86 *MEED*, "Special Report–Saudi Arabia," June 1979, p. 8.

87 *Gulf States Newsletter*, July 9, 1990, p. 14.

88 See, for example: *Gulf States Newsletter,* November 20, 1995; Rob Franklin, "Migrant Labor and the Politics of Development in Bahrain," *MERIP Reports*, Vol. 15, No. 4 (May 1985), p. 10; Kapiszewski, *Nationals and Expatriates*, p. 5.

89 Robert E. Looney, *The Economic Development of Saudi Arabia: Consequences of the Oil Prices Decline* (Greenwich and London: JAI Press, 1990), p. 80.

90 *Saudi Economic Survey*, December 13, 1995, p. 6.

91 *Saudi Economic Survey*, December 6, 1995, p. 5.

92 *MEED*, August 14, 1998, p. 2; Azzam, *The Arab World Facing the Challenge of the New Millennium*, p. 176.

93 Bahrain Economic Development Board, *Reforming Bahrain's Labour Market* (Manama, 2004), p. 2.

94 By 1996, for example, the average government salary was as high as AED107,600 (about $30,000) annually. In addition to these high salaries, the UAE citizens were entitled to various financial benefits, including housing and various government allowances and subsidies. Source: Willoughby, "Ambivalent Anxieties of the South Asian-Gulf Arab

Labor Exchange," p. 7. See also: IMF, *United Arab Emirates: 2004 Article IV Consultation*, Country Report No. 04/175 (June 2004), p. 25.

95 Masao Endo, "Saudization: Development in the Early 1990's and Prospects for the Rest of the Decade", *JIME REVIEW* (Winter 1996), p. 79. See also: *The NCB, Economist*, Vol. 5, Issue 4 (June/July 1995), p. 8; Ramady, *The Saudi Arabian Economy*, p. 361, table 12.4.

96 Said Abdullah al-Shaikh, "Demographic Transitions in Saudi Arabia and Their Impact on Economic Growth and the Labor Market," *Saudi Economic Survey*, September 13, 2000, p. 20, tables 3 and 4; Ishac Diwan and Maurice Girgis, "Labor Force and Development in Saudi Arabia," paper presented at the symposium *Future Vision for the Saudi Economy*, Riyadh, September 2002, p. 14, figure 15.

97 SAMA, *Thirty-Eighth Annual Report–1423H.* [2002], p. 321, table 18.9.

98 Mary Ann Tetreault, "Kuwait's Economic Prospects", *Middle East Executive Report* (January 1993), p. 12.

99 *Gulf States Newsletter*, July 9, 1990, pp. 14–15. See also: *MEED*, March 12, 1993, p. 46.

100 "Gulf Population and Labour Force Structure," *The NCB Economist*, Vol. 5, Issue 6 (June/July 1995), p. 8.

101 *Ibid.*, p. 7; *Gulf States Newsletter*, November 20, 1995, p. 10.

102 ESCWA, *Statistical Abstract*, Sixteenth Issue, pp. 145–46.

103 Hossein Askari, Vahid Nowshirvani and Mohamed Jaber, *Economic Development in the GCC: The Blessing and the Curse of Oil* (Greenwich and London: JAI Press, 1997), pp. 71–72.

104 Specifically in the case of Qatar, see: Ahmad Mohammed Nama, *Human Resources Development: The Case of Qatar* (Unpublished Ph.D. Thesis, Claremont Graduate School, 1983), p. 83.

105 Ramady, *The Saudi Arabian Economy*, p. 360.

106 Al-Shaikh, "Demographic Transitions in Saudi Arabia," pp. 15, 19, 21.

107 Beblawi, "The Rentier State," p. 91. See also: Woodward, *Oil and Labor in the Middle East*, p. 19.

108 Sultanate of Oman, Ministry of Development, *General Census of Population, Housing and Establishments–1993* (Muscat 1995), p. 55.

109 *MEED*, March 12, 1993, p. 8; *Gulf States Newsletter*, April 8, 1996, p. 13.

110 Kapiszewski, *Nationals and Expatriates*, p. 233.

111 This section is based on my article "Labor and Liberalization: The Decline of the GCC *Rentier* System," in Joshua Teitelbaum (ed.), *Political Liberalization in the Persian Gulf* (New York: Columbia Universty Press, forthcoming 2009).

112 Gilbar, "Mavo: Beyn Demographya ve-Politiqa ba-Mizrah ha-Tikhon," p. 4.

113 EIU, *Country Profile–Saudi Arabia, 2003*, p. 19; *The Middle East*, December 2005, pp. 27–28; Cordesman, *Saudi Arabia Enters the Twenty-First Century*, Vol. 2, pp. 273–74.

114 ESCWA, *Survey, 2000–2001*, p. 35.

115 ESCWA, *Survey, 1996–1997*, p. 37.

116 SAMA, *Thirty-Eighth Annual Report–1423H.* [2002], p. 324.

117 EIU, *Country Profile–Oman, 2003*, p. 23; *MEED*, May 4, 2001, p. 24.

118 *The Middle East*, November 1996, p. 28; EIU, *Country Profile–Oman, 2005*, p. 23.

119 EIU, *Country Profile–Bahrain, Qatar, 1996–97*, p. 37; Europa Publications, *The Middle East and North Africa–1998*, Forty-Fourth Edition (London, 1998), p. 869.

120 Nasra M. Shah, "Arab Migration Patterns in the Gulf," in IOM and League of Arab States, *Arab Migration in a Globalized World*, p. 107.

121 See, for example: *Saudi Economic Survey*, February 15, 1995, p. 8; Yamani, *Changed Identities*, p. 83; Shah, "Arab Migration Patterns in the Gulf," p. 107; Sultanate of Oman, Ministry of Information, "Oman 2000." Available at: http://www.omanet.com; EIU, *Country Profile–Bahrain, 2004*, p. 22.

122 Shah, "Restrictive Labour Immigration Policies in the Oil-Rich Gulf," pp. 5–6.

123 *Akhbar al-Khalij*, November 16, 2007.
124 *Saudi Economic Survey*, February 8, 2006, p. 19.
125 *Saudi Economic Survey*, February 21, 2001, p. 7.
126 Hamad Al-Sulayti, "Education and Training in GCC Countries: Some Issues of Concern," in The Emirates Center for Strategic Studies and Research, *Education and the Arab World: Challenges of the Next Millennium* (Abu Dhabi, 1999), p. 272.
127 Mohamed El-Shibiny, "Higher Education in Oman: Its Development and Prospects," in K. E. Shaw (ed.), *Higher Education in the Gulf: Problems and Prospects* (Exeter: University of Exeter Press, 1997), pp. 156–57.
128 Oman, *The Fifth Five-Year Development Plan*, p. 112.
129 Saudi Arabia, *Seventh Development Plan*, p. 116.
130 In 1994, for example, salaries for public sector employees constituted about half of the total Bahraini governmental expenditures. *MEED*, November 24, 1995, p. 26. By 2002, public sector salaries amounted to as much as 40% of the total Kuwaiti governmental expenditures. *MEED*, October 10–16, 2003, p. 33.
131 In December 1998, OPEC Reference Basket price was $9.7 per barrel (current prices). See: *OAPEC Monthly Bulletin*, August-September 2003, p. 17, table 4.
132 *MEED*, December 11, 1998, p. 22.
133 *MEED*, December 1, 2000, p. 38.
134 Saudi Arabia, *Seventh Development Plan*, p. 157.
135 *Times of Oman*, November 19, 1998.
136 EIU, *Country Profile–Oman, Yemen, 1998–99*, p. 11.
137 Sultanate of Oman, Ministry of Information, "Oman Labour Law." Available at: http://www.omanet.com.
138 *Saudi Economic Survey*, August 30, 2000, p. 7; Ramady, *The Saudi Arabian Economy*, p. 359.
139 SAMA, *Thirty-Eighth Annual Report–1423H.* [2002], p. 319.
140 SAMA, *Thirty-Sixth Annual Report–1421H.* [2000], p. 267.
141 In SAMA's 2006 report, for example, it was written that the Saudi authorities are operating in order to increase employment opportunities for Saudi women, but "without contravention of Islamic Shari'a." SAMA, *Forty-Second Annual Report–1427H.* [2006], p. 276.
142 Podeh and Winckler, "The Boycott that Never Was," pp. 32–36.
143 ESCWA, *Survey, 1998–1999*, p. 51.
144 *MEED*, September 8–14, 2006, p. 12.
145 SAMA, *Forty-Second Annual Report–1427H.* [2006], p. 281, table 18.6.
146 SAMA, *Forty-Third Annual Report–1428H.* [2007], p. 219, table 18.7.
147 Central Bank of Oman, *Annual Report–2006* (Muscat, 2007), p. 8.
148 On the development of the GCC tourism industry, see: Yoel Mansfeld and Onn Winckler, "The Tourism Industry as an Alternative for the GCC Oil-Based *Rentier* Economy," *Tourism Economics*, Vol. 13, No. 3 (2007), pp. 333–60.
149 *Saudi Economic Survey*, February 23, 2005, p. 5.
150 *MEED*, March 31-April 6, 2006, p. 8.
151 On the development of the Omani tourism industry, see: Onn Winckler, "The Birth of Oman's Tourism Industry," *Tourism*, Vol. 55, No. 2 (2007), pp. 221–34.
152 Central Bank of Oman, *Annual Report–2006*, p. 7.
153 *Ibid.*, p. 8.
154 SAMA, *Forty-Third Annual Report–1428H.* [2007], p. 218, table 18.5.
155 The academic literature on the contribution of the tourism industry to the development of related services and industries is vast. See, for example: Timothy J. Tyrrell and Robert J. Johnston, "A Framework for Assessing Direct Economic Impacts of Tourist Events:

Distinguishing Origins, Destinations and Causes of Expenditure," *Journal of Travel Research*, Vol. 40, No. 1 (2001), pp. 94–101.

156 MEED, *Gulf Economic Review–2006*, p. 68.

157 On the attitude of Dubai's authorities toward the tourism industry since the mid-1980s, see: *al-Ittihad*, July 4, 1988; *al-Majalla*, February 6; March 20, 1994; *The Middle East*, March 1994, p. 29; *International Herald Tribune*, June 10, 1993; IMF, *United Arab Emirates: 2004 Article IV Consultation*, Country Report No. 04/175 (June 2004), p. 7, box 1.

158 During the years 1995–2003, the number of hotel-beds in Dubai increased from 22,846 to 41,226, while the number of tourist hotel nights increased from 3,968,207 to 10,290,709 during the corresponding period. Source: Government of Dubai, Department of Economic Development, *Dubai Economic Statistics–2005*, p. 114, table 4–3–5; p. 117, table 4–3–5. By 2007, the number of tourist hotel nights in Dubai skyrocketed to 15,865,557, namely, a further increase of more than 50% over the 2003 figure. See: Government of Dubai, Department of Economic Development, *Hotel Statistics Summary, 1998–2007* (Dubai, 2008), p. 73.

159 Afshin Molavi, "Dubai Dispatch City on a Hall," *The New Republic Online Edition*, February 2, 2004. Available at: http://www.tnr.com; al-Abbas al-Luwati and Wafa Issa, "Finding Jobs for UAE Nationals," *Gulfnews.com*, December 8, 2006. Available at: http://archive.gulfnews.com.

160 K.T. Abdurab, "Dubai Population Hits 1.3 Million," *Arab News*, December 8, 2006.

161 See, for example, the Qatari labor law from 1962 in Emile A. Nakhleh, "Labor Markets and Citizenship in Bahrayn and Qatar," *The Middle East Journal*, Vol. 31, No. 2 (1977), p. 149; Qatar, *Qatar into the Seventies*, p. 77.

162 Al-Ramadhan, "New Population Policy in Kuwait," p. 31, table 1.

163 "Al-Simat al-Asasiyya li-Sukan al-Kuwayt wa-Kuwwat al-'Amal fi Nihayat 1994," *al-Iqtisadi al-Kuwayti*, No. 324 (May 1995), p. 25, table 1.

164 EIU, *Country Profile–Kuwait, 1999–2000*, p. 11.

165 Thus, for example, in April 2000, the Arab foreign workers represented less than 11% of the total foreign workers in the UAE. See: ESCWA, *Survey, 2000–2001*, p. 35.

166 *Middle East International*, January 21, 2005, p. 23.

167 See, for example: Kapiszewski, *Nationals and Expatriates*, p. 59; Abdelkarim, "Oil, Population Change and Social Development in the Gulf," pp. 36–37.

168 Nazli Choucri, "Asians in the Arab World: Labor Migration and Public Policy," *Middle Eastern Studies*, Vol. 22, No. 2 (1986), p. 252.

169 See, for example: ESCWA, *Survey, 1992*, p. 120; Massey et al., *Worlds in Motion*, p. 142.

170 ESCWA, League of Arab States and UNFPA, "Arab Labour Migration," *Meeting of Senior Officials and Experts*. Amman, April 4–6, 1993, p. 7.

171 Kapiszewski, *Nationals and Expatriates*, pp. 210–11.

172 Maurice Girgis, "National Versus Migrant Workers in the GCC: Coping with Change," in Heba Handoussa and Zafiris Tzannatos (eds.), *Employment Creation and Social Protection in the Middle East and North Africa* (Cairo: The American University in Cairo Press, 2002), p. 102.

173 Ramady, *The Saudi Arabian Economy*, p. 361.

174 Daryl Champion, "The Kingdom of Saudi Arabia: Elements of Instability within Stability," *Middle East Review of International Affairs*, Vol. 3, No. 4 (1999), p. 4.

175 Ugo Fasano and Rishi Goyal, "Emerging Strains in GCC Labor Markets," IMF Working Paper No. 04/71 (April 2004). Available at: http://www.imf.org/external/pubs/ft/wp/2004/wp0471.pdf.

176 Cordesman, *Saudi Arabia Enters the Twenty-First Century*, Vol. 2, p. 271.

177 Al-Shaikh, "Demographic Transitions in Saudi Arabia," p. 20, table 5.

178 With regard to the Saudi Arabian dilemma on this issue, see: Wilson et al., *Economic Development in Saudi Arabia*, pp. 105–6.

179 SAMA, *Forty-Second Annual Report–1427H.* [2006], p. 281, table 18.6; *MEED*, March 16–22, 2007, p. 5.

180 In the case of the UAE, see, for example: *Gulf News*, October 23, 1984; *al-Khalij*, June 17, 1983; *al-Bayan*, August 31; September 1, 1983; March 28, 1984.

181 IBRD, *Unlocking the Employment Potential in the Middle East and North Africa: Toward A New Social Contract*, by Tarik Yousef et al., MENA Development Report (Washington, D.C., 2004), p. 5.

182 Ugo Fasano and Zubair Iqbal, "GCC Countries: From Oil Dependence to Diversification," IMF Working Paper, 2003, p. 6. Available at: http://www.imf.org/external/pubs/ft/med/2003/eng/fasano.

183 IMF, *United Arab Emirates: 2004 Article IV Consultation*, Country Report No. 04/175 (June 2004), p. 32.

184 Robert E. Looney, "Saudization and Sound Economic Reforms: Are the Two Compatible?" *Strategic Insights*, Volume III, Issue 2 (February 2004). Available at: http://www.ccc.nps.navy.mil/si/2005.

185 ESCWA, *Survey, 1998–1999*, p. 53. See also: EIU, *Country Profile–Bahrain, 2001–2002*, p. 19.

186 Central Bank of Oman, *Annual Report–2001*, p. 17.

187 Central Bank of Oman, *Annual Report–2005*, p. 25, table 2.5.

188 SAMA, *Forty-Second Annual Report–1427H.* [2006], p. 276, table 18.3.

189 Emiratisation.org., April 6, 2004. Available at: http://emiratisation.org]; *UAE INTERACT*, May 2, 2005. Available at: http://www.uaeinteract.com.

190 ESCWA, *Economic Diversification in the Oil-Producing Countries*, p. 38.

191 EIU, *Country Report–Kuwait*, June 2005, p. 20.

192 *MEED*, March 16–22, 2007, p. 5.

193 *The Middle East*, June 2004, p. 53.

194 ESCWA, *Survey, 1998–1999*, p. 53; EIU, *Country Profile–Bahrain, 2001–2002*, p. 19.

195 Bahrain Monetary Agency, *Economic Indicators*, No. 5 (September 2004), p. 4.

196 *MEED*, March 16–22, 2007, p. 4.

197 *MEED*, September 17–23, 2004, p. 40.

198 *MEED*, March 16–22, 2007, p. 4.

199 Oman Information Center, "Is Oman Doing Enough to Put Itself on the Tourism Map?," August 5, 2003. Available at: http://www.omaninfo.com/cgi-bin/journal/DocView.asp?DocumentID=88.

200 *Times of Oman*, December 21, 2003.

201 *The Middle East*, June 2004, p. 50.

202 *Bahrain Tribune*, April, 7; August 13, 2005.

203 *MEED*, March 31-April 6, 2006, p. 8.

204 ESCWA, *Survey, 2001–2002*, p. 19.

205 *MEES*, February 2, 2004.

206 Cordesman, *Saudi Arabia Enters the Twenty-First Century*, Vol. 2, p. 278.

207 Shah, "Restrictive Labour Immigration Policies in the Oil-Rich Gulf," p. 3.

208 *Ibid.*

209 *MEED*, May 6–12, 2005, p. 30.

210 IMF, *United Arab Emirates: Selected Issues and Statistical Appendix*, Country Report No. 05/268 (August 2005), p. 27.

211 Ian J. Seccombe and Richard I. Lawless, "State Intervention and the International Labour Market: A Review of Labour Emigration Policies in the Arab World," in Reginald Appleyard (ed.), *The Impact of International Migration on Developing Countries* (Paris:

Development Centre of the Organization for Economic Co-Operation and Development, 1989), pp. 69–78.

212 By 1978, South Yemen's population numbered 1.8 million. See: ECWA and League of Arab States, *Statistical Indicators of the Arab World for the Period of 1970–1979* (Beirut, 1981), p. 4, table I–1.

213 Winckler, *Demographic Developments and Population Policies in Ba'thist Syria*, p. 87.

214 ESCWA, *Population Situation–1990*, p. 192.

215 Thus, for example, in March 1979 the Syrian Minister of Education approached the Saudi Arabian authorities with the request not to renew the contracts of Syrian teachers. See: *MEED*, May 29, 1979, p. 47.

216 Sales, *International Migration Project, Country Case Study: Syrian Arab Republic*, pp. 63–64.

217 On the "export" of Egyptian teachers to other Arab countries during the Nasserite period, see: S. A. Messiha, "The Export of Egyptian School Teachers," *Cairo Papers in Social Science*, Vol. 3, No. 4 (1983).

218 On the Egyptian labor emigration policy prior to the June 1967 War, see: Ali E. Hillal Dessouki, "The Shift in Egypt's Migration Policy: 1952–1978," *Middle Eastern Studies*, Vol. 18, No. 1 (1982), pp. 55–56.

219 Ralph R. Sell, "Gone For Good?" *Cairo Papers in Social Science*, Vol. 10, No. 2 (Summer 1987), p. 28; "Employment Opportunities and Equity in Egypt," Part III, *MEN Economic Weekly*, November 25, 1983, p. 10.

220 On the Egyptian supportive labor emigration policy since the late 1960s, see: Lesch, "Egyptian Labor Migration," pp. 102–6.

221 John M. Wardwell, "Jordan," in William J. Serow et al. (eds.), *Handbook of International Migration* (New York and London: Greenwood Press, 1990), p. 168.

222 *Al-Ra'y*, July 14; July 29; November 27, 1986.

223 Kapiszewski, *Nationals and Expatriates*, p. 65, table 3.3.

224 Birks, Sinclair & Associates Ltd., *GCC Market Report–1990*.

225 According to prevailing estimates, by early 2007, the number of Iraqi refugees in Jordan amounted to one million. See: *The Guardian*, January 24, 2007.

226 *Jordan Times*, March 23, 2000.

227 *Ibid.*

228 Richards and Waterbury, *A Political Economy of the Middle East*, second edition, p. 378. A similar view was presented by Shafik, who claimed that the large-scale inter-Arab labor migration was to the benefit of Egypt, Jordan and Yemen in light of their surplus workforces. See: Nemat Shafik, "Has Labor Migration Promoted Economic Integration in the Middle East?" in Sirageldin and al-Rahmani (eds.), *Population and Development Transformations in the Arab World*, p. 178.

229 Quoted from: Georges Sabagh, "Immigrants in the Arab Gulf Countries: 'Sojourners' or 'Settlers"? in Luciani (ed.), *The Arab State*, p. 350.

230 Sell, "Egyptian International Labor Migration and Social Processes," p. 87.

231 See, for example: Nasrah M. Shah, "Arab Labour Migration: A Review of Trends and Issues," *International Migration*, Vol. 32, No. 1 (1994), pp. 10–11; UNDP, *Jordan Human Development Report–2004* (Amman, 2004), p. 36.

232 Ibrahim M. Oweiss, "Migration of Egyptians," *L'Égypte Contemporaine*, No. 381 (July 1980), p. 6. See also: Wilson, "Whither the Egyptian Economy?" pp. 211–12.

233 Fred Halliday, "Labor Migration in the Arab World," *Merip Reports* (May 1984), p. 8.

234 Mostafa H. Nagi, "Labor Immigration and Development in the Middle East: Patterns, Problems, and Policies," *International Review of Modern Sociology*, Vol. 12, No. 2 (1982), pp. 204–5.

235 WB, *Manpower and International Labor Migration in the Middle East and North Africa*, by Ismail Serageldin et al. (Published for the WB by Oxford University Press, 1983), p. 68.

236 In many cases, migrants in the GCC countries "pull" other family members or friends from their villages to come to work in the Gulf. This phenomenon of a migrant who attracts other relatives or friends to follow him in the host country is very common in international labor migration and is not restricted to the Middle East alone.

237 In the other non-oil Arab economies, one can find a similar trend. See: WB, *World Development Report–1984*, pp. 220–21, table 2.

238 WB, *World Development Report–1985*, pp. 176–77, table 2.

239 On the discussion of the contribution of the workers' remittances to the Arab labor-exporting countries, see: Kapiszewski, "Arab Labor Migration to the GCC Countries," pp. 126–29.

240 Richards and Waterbury, *A Political Economy of the Middle East*, second edition, p. 376.

241 See, for example: Roy, "Egyptian Emigrant Labor," pp. 561–62.

242 Fargues, "Demographic Explosion or Social Upheaval?," p. 166.

243 In the late 1980s, Boutros Boutros-Ghali said regarding Egypt's demographic burden that: "Egypt with 20 million people could have been a Mediterranean country, a Greece or Portugal. Egypt with 70 million people will be Bangladesh." Thomas W. Lippman, *Egypt After Nasser: Sadat, Peace and the Mirage of Prosperity* (New York: Paragon House, 1989), p. 164.

244 ESCWA, *Survey, 2003–2004*, p. 44.

245 See, for example: Kapiszewski, *Nationals and Expatriates*, p. 208.

Chapter 5 *Between Pro-Natalism and Anti-Natalism in the Arab Countries*

1 Adam Smith, *An Inquiry into the Nature and the Cause of the Wealth of Nations*, third edition with notes by J. R. McCulloch (London: Ward, Lock & Co., Limited, 1812), p. 77.

2 Paul Erlich, *The Population Bomb* (New York, Ballantine Books, 1971), p. xiii.

3 Todaro, *Economic Development*, seventh edition, p. 209.

4 According to UN data from the early 1990s, the developed countries, populated by only 25% of the total worldwide population, were responsible for 85% of all forest products consumed, 72% of steel products, and 75% of worldwide energy used. See: Mazur, "Beyond the Numbers," p. 3.

5 Mohammed, *Population and Development in the Arab Gulf States*, p. xi.

6 William Petersen, *Founder of Modern Demography: Malthus* (New Brunswick and London: Transaction Publishers, 1999), p. 40.

7 *Ibid.*, p. 143.

8 Geometric ratio: 1, 2, 4, 8, 16, 32 etc.

9 Arithmetic ratio: 2, 4, 6, 8, 10, etc.

10 Harbison and Robinson, "Policy Implications of the Next Demographic Transition," p. 38.

11 The academic literature on Malthus' demographic perception is enormous. See, for example: John Avery, *Progress, Poverty and Population: Re-reading Condorcet, Godwin and Malthus* (London and Portland: Frank Cass, 1997), pp. 55–75; John C. Caldwell, "Malthus and the Less Developed World: The Pivotal Role of India," *Population and Development Review*, Vol. 24, No. 4 (1998), pp. 675–96; Todaro, *Economic Development*, seventh edition, pp. 224–26; Nam and Philliber, *Population*, pp. 38–40.

12 On the neo-Malthusianism doctrine, see: Pressat, *The Dictionary of Demography*, pp. 157–58.

13 UN, Population Division, *World Population Monitoring–2001: Population, Environment and Development* (New York, 2001), p. 28.

14 On Condorcet's demographic perception, see: Steven K. Wisensale and Amany A. Khodair, "The Two-child Family: The Egyptian Model of Family Planning," *Journal of Comparative Family Studies*, Vol. 29, No. 3 (1998), p. 503; Nam and Philliber, *Population*, p. 38; Avery, *Progress, Poverty and Population*, pp. 1–12.

15 UN, *World Population Monitoring–2001*, p. 1.
16 Maddison, *The World Economy*, p. 125.
17 Wisensale and Khodair, "The Two-child Family," p. 503.
18 The Dependency Theory maintains that the increasing economic gap between the "central countries," i.e., the Western developed countries, and the "peripheral countries," i.e., the developing countries, was caused by the former's use of the latter's natural resources during the colonial period and the unequal terms of international trade between the developed and the developing countries in favor of the former since the end of the colonial period. On the Dependency Theory, see: J. Samuel Valenzuela and Arthuro Valenzuela, "Modernization and Dependency: Alternative Perspectives in the Study of Latin American Underdevelopment," *Comparative Politics*, Vol. 10, No. 4 (1978), pp. 535–57.
19 Todaro, *Economic Development*, seventh edition, pp. 234–38; "Links between Population and Economic Growth," *Population Today*, Vol. 14, No. 2 (March 1986), pp. 3, 8.
20 See, for example: *al-Ahram al-Iqtisadi*, September 1, 1980.
21 See: Richards and Waterbury, *A Political Economy of the Middle East*, second edition, p. 89.
22 In the case of Germany, for example, by 2006 the foreign trade made up as much as 75.2% of the total GDP. See: WB, *Country Profile*. Available at: http://web.worldbank.org.
23 Paul Demeny, "Population Policy: A Concise Summary," The Population Council, Policy Research Division Working Paper No. 173 (New York, 2003), p. 4.
24 National Academy of Sciences, *Rapid Population Growth: Consequences and Policy Implications* (Baltimore and London: The Johns Hopkins University Press, 1971), p. 70.
25 UN, Population Division, *National Population Policies* (New York, 1998), p. 1.
26 Findlay and Findlay, *Population and Development in the Third World*, p. 67. Another two definitions, one of a UN demographic expert group and the second of Bernard R. Berelson, the President of the Population Council (1968–1974), appear in Hanna Rizk, "Population Policies: Scope, Goals, Means, and Problems," *Population Bulletin of ECWA*, No. 7 (July 1974), pp. 132–34.
27 National Academy of Sciences, *Rapid Population Growth*, p. 70.
28 See, for example: UN, Population Division, *Fertility, Contraception and Population Policies* (New York, 2003), p. 7.
29 Demeny, "Population Policy: A Concise Summary," pp. 9–10.
30 Marie-Thérèse Letablier, "Fertility and Family Policies in France," *Journal of Population and Social Security*, supplement to Vol. 1 (2003), pp. 245–46; King, "France Needs Children," p. 39.
31 John C. Caldwell, Pat Caldwell and Peter McDonald, "Policy Responses to Low Fertility and Its Consequences: A Global Survey," *Journal of Population Research*, Vol. 19, No. 1 (2002), p. 7.
32 Stephen Pollock, "Fertility, Mortality and Disease," *Interdisciplinary Science Reviews*, Vol. 31, No. 1 (2006), p. 9.
33 Elizabeth L. Krause, "Forward vs. Reverse Gear: The Politics of Proliferation and Resistance in the Italian Fascist State," *Journal of Historical Sociology*, Vol. 7, No. 3 (1994), p. 269.
34 See, for example: Dov Friedlander, Barbara S. Okun and Sharon Segal, "The Demographic Transition Then and Now: Process, Perspectives, and Analyses," *Journal of Family History*, Vol. 24, No. 4 (1999), pp. 496–97.
35 Peter J. Donaldson and Amy Ong Tsui, "The International Family Planning Movement," *Population Bulletin*, Vol. 45, No. 3 (1990), pp. 9–10.
36 Stanley P. Johnson, *World Population – Turning the Tide: Three Decades of Progress* (London: Graham & Trotman/Martinus Nijhoff, 1994), pp. 103–4.
37 "Neo-Colonialism" is a political term that was widely used during the 1950s and 1960s by

which the Western political-military dominance over the developing countries was simply replaced by economic dominance.

38 See: Joseph Chamie, "Trends, Variations, and Contradictions in National Policies to Influence Fertility," in Jason L. Finkle and C. Alison McIntosh (eds.), *The New Politics of Population: Conflict and Consensus in Family Planning*, Supplement to Vol. 20 of *Population and Development Review* (New York: The Population Council, 1994), p. 37; Kelley Lee and Gill Walt, "Linking National and Global Population Agendas: Case Studies From Eight Developing Countries," *Third World Quarterly*, Vol. 16, No. 2 (1995), p. 259.

39 Gabriel Baer, *'Arviyey ha-Mizrah ha-Tikhon*, second edition (Tel Aviv: Hakibbutz Hameuchad, 1973), p. 39 (Hebrew).

40 UN, *Fertility, Contraception and Population Policies*, p. 20.

41 Adnan Habbab, "Family Planning in the Syrian Arab Republic," paper presented at the *First Regional Population Conference of ECWA*, Beirut, February 18–March 1, 1974, pp. 5–6.

42 Quoted from: Youssef Courbage, "Fertility Transition in Syria: From Implicit Population Policy to Explicit Economic Crisis," *International Family Planning Perspectives*, Vol. 20, No. 4 (1994), p. 142.

43 I. Lévi, "Le Recensement de la Population de l'Egypte de 1917," *L'Égypte Contemporaine*, Vol. 13, No. 67 (1922). Quoted from: Philippe Fargues, "State Policies and the Birth Rate in Egypt: From Socialism to Liberalism," *Population and Development Review*, Vol. 23, No. 1 (1997), p. 116.

44 Wendell Cleland, *The Population Problem in Egypt* (Lancaster, PA: Science Press Printing Company, 1936).

45 Azriel Karni, "Temurot be-Yahas la-Piquah 'al ha-Yeluda ba-Mizrah ha-Tikhon," *Hamizrah Hehadash*, Vol. 17 (1967), p. 230 (Hebrew).

46 Baer, *'Arviyey ha-Mizrah ha-Tikhon*, p. 39.

47 *Al-Ahram al-Iqtisadi*, June 5, 1989.

48 Karni, "Temurot be-Yahas la-Piquah 'al ha-Yeluda ba-Mizrah ha-Tikhon," p. 231.

49 J. Mayone Stycos et al., *Community Development and Family Planning: An Egyptian Experiment* (Boulder and London: Westview Press, 1988), p. 14.

50 Khalid Ikram, *Egypt: Economic Management in a Period of Transition*, A World Bank Country Economic Report (Baltimore and London: The Johns Hopkins University Press, 1980), p. 110.

51 Mohammed Neguib, *Egypt's Destiny* (London: Victor Gollancz Ltd., 1955), pp. 158–62; Nazek Nosseir, "Egypt: Population, Urbanization, and Development," in Dan Tschirgi (ed.), *Development in the Age of Liberalization: Egypt and Mexico* (Cairo: The American University in Cairo Press, 1996), p. 191.

52 Quoted from: Gadalla, *Is There Hope?* p. 212.

53 Charles Issawi, *Egypt in Revolution* (London: Oxford University Press, 1963), p. 302.

54 Hussein Abdel-Aziz Sayed, "The Population Family Planning Program in Egypt: Structure and Performance," *Population Studies*, Vol. 11, No. 70 (July-September 1984), p. 7.

55 Saad Eddin Ibrahim, "State, Women, and Civil Society: An Evaluation of Egypt's Population Policy," in Carla Makhlouf Obermeyer (ed.), *Family, Gender, and Population in the Middle East* (Cairo: The American University in Cairo Press, 1995), pp. 59–60.

56 Though I did not find official evidence to support this factor.

57 Stycos et al., *Community Development and Family Planning*, p. 14; Sayed, "The Population Family Planning Program in Egypt," p. 7.

58 On 'Abd al-Nasser's populist leadership style, see: Elie Podeh and Onn Winckler, "Introduction: Nasserism as a Form of Populism," in Podeh and Winckler (eds.), *Rethinking Nasserism*, pp. 18–28.

59 Fouad Ajami quoted in the Preface of Gouda Abdel-Khalek and Robert Tignor (eds.), *The*

Political Economy of Income Distribution in Egypt (New York: Holmes and Meier, 1982), p. 9.

60 Donaldson, *Nature Against Us*, p. 117.

61 Other major donors to the UNFPA were Japan and Sweden.

62 Jason L. Finkle and C. Alison McIntosh, "The New Politics of Population," in Finkle and McIntosh (eds.), *The New Politics of Population*, pp. 8–9.

63 Donaldson, *Nature Against Us*, p. 42; p. 48, table 3.1.

64 Nam and Philliber, *Population*, p. 299.

65 John W. Thomas and Merilee S. Grindle, "Political Leadership and Policy Characteristics in Population Policy Reform," in Finkle and McIntosh (eds.), *The New Politics of Population*, p. 53.

66 G. M. Stubbs, "Population Policy in the Arab Countries," in Abdel-Rahim Omran, *Population in the Arab World: Problems and Prospects* (London: Croom Helm, 1980), p. 181.

67 UN, *Fertility, Contraception and Population Policies*, p. 20.

68 IBRD, *The Population Program of the Government of Tunisia: A Second Review*, Report No. 651-TUN (February 27, 1975), p. 6.

69 On the earlier stages of the Tunisian family planning program, see: IPPF-Middle East and North Africa Region, "Family Planning and Population Policies in the Middle East and North Africa," in James Allman (ed.), *Women's Status and Fertility in the Muslim World* (New York and London: Praeger, 1978), pp. 42–43; Robert J. Lapham, "Population Policies in the Middle East and North Africa," *Middle East Studies Association Bulletin*, Vol. 11, No. 2 (May 1, 1977), pp. 7–8.

70 IBRD, *The Population Program of the Government of Tunisia*, p. 3.

71 *Al-Ahram*, May 22, 1962. The English translation appears in: Nissim Rejwan, *Nasserist Ideology: Its Exponents and Critics* (New York: John Wiley & Sons, 1974), pp. 195–265.

72 On the factors for the collapse of the unification between Egypt and Syria, see: Elie Podeh, *The Decline of Arab Unity: The Rise and Fall of the United Arab Republic* (Brighton and Portland: Sussex Academic Press, 1999), pp. 110–58.

73 Thomas and Grindle, "Political Leadership and Policy Characteristics in Population Policy Reform," p. 60.

74 Robinson and El-Zanaty, *The Demographic Revolution in Modern Egypt*, p. 43.

75 On Egypt's family planning program during the second half of the 1960s, see: Gad G. Gilbar, "Family Planning Under Mubarak," in his *Population Dilemmas in the Middle East*, pp. 117–19; Gadalla, *Is There Hope?* pp. 213–19.

76 Wisensale and Khodair, "The Two-child Family," p. 505.

77 IBRD, *The Economic Development of Morocco* (Published for IBRD by The Johns Hopkins University Press, 1966), pp. 10–11.

78 *Ibid.*, p. 91.

79 IPPF-Middle East and North Africa Region, "Family Planning and Population Policies in the Middle East and North Africa," p. 37.

80 IBRD, *The Economic Development of Morocco*, p. 94.

81 Farzaneh (Nazi) Roudi, "Fertility Policies in the Middle East and North Africa," paper presented at the *Second Mediterranean Social and Political Research Meeting*, Florence, March 21–25, 2001, p. 22.

82 Fargues, "International Migration in the Arab Region: Trends and Policies," p. 15.

83 Allman, "The Demographic Transition in the Middle East and North Africa," p. 292.

84 Lapham, "Population Policies in the Middle East and North Africa," p. 6.

85 Scott D. Grosse, "The Politics of Family Planning in the Maghrib," *Studies in Comparative International Development*, Vol. 17, No. 1 (1982), p. 28.

86 IBRD, *The Economic Development of Morocco*, p. 94.

87 Muhammad Faour, "Fertility Policy and Family Planning in the Arab Countries," *Studies in Family Planning*, Vol. 20, No. 5 (1989), p. 256; Mazur, "Beyond the Numbers," p. 11.

88 Sayed, "The Population Family Planning Program in Egypt," pp. 9–12. See also: WB, *Egypt: Staff Appraisal of a Second Population Project* (Washington, D.C., August 14, 1978), p. 4.

89 On the problems with the implementation of the Egyptian family planning program during the second half of the 1960s, see: Gadalla, *Is there Hope?* pp. 215–19; Mahasen Mostafa Hassanin, Amany Mousa Mohamed and Galaa Helmy Selem, "Estimating Family Planning Target Population of Egypt in 1997," in *CDC 24th Annual Seminar on Population Issues and the Challenges of the 21st Century in the Middle East, Africa and Asia*, Research Monograph Series No. 24 (Cairo, 1995), p. 441; Robinson and El-Zanaty, *The Demographic Revolution in Modern Egypt*, pp. 46–47.

90 Fargues, "Demographic Explosion or Social Upheaval?" p. 165.

91 Chamie, "Trends, Variations, and Contradictions," p. 37.

92 Youssef Courbage, "Economic and Political Issues of Fertility Transition in the Arab World: Answers and Open Questions," *Population and Environment*, Vol. 20, No. 4 (1999), p. 370.

93 Fargues, "International Migration in the Arab Region: Trends and Policies," p. 16.

94 London School of Hygiene & Tropical Medicine and the UNPF, by Kelley Lee et al., *Population Policies and Programmes: Determinants and Consequences in Eight Developing Countries* (London, 1995), p. 20.

95 *Population and Development Review*, Vol. 4, No. 2 (1978), p. 373.

96 Lee and Walt, "Linking National and Global Population Agendas," p. 259.

97 Roudi, "Fertility Policies in the Middle East and North Africa," p. 14.

98 Gilbar, "Nasser's Soft Revolution," pp. 84–85.

99 Egypt, CAPMAS, *Statistical Yearbook, 1952–1984*, p. 3.

100 *Ibid.*

101 Hartley, *Population: Quantity vs. Quality*, pp. 310–11; Johnson, *World Population*, p. 93.

102 Syrian Arab Republic, Office of the Prime Minister, CBS, *Socio-Economic Development in Syria, 1960–1970*, Studies Series No. 73 (Damascus, 1973), p. 47.

103 Charles W. Warren et al., "Fertility and Family Planning in Jordan: Results from the 1985 Jordan Husbands' Fertility Survey," *Studies in Family Planning*, Vol. 21, No. 1 (1990), pp. 33–34.

104 ESCWA, *Population Situation–1990*, p. 101.

105 *Jordan Population and Family Health Survey–2002*, p. 3.

106 Ronald Freedman and Bernard Berelson, "The Record of Family Planning Programs," *Studies in Family Planning*, Vol. 7, No. 1 (1976), p. 5.

107 UN, *Fertility, Contraception and Population Policies*, p. 16.

108 Donaldson and Tsui, "The International Family Planning Movement," p. 11; Godfrey Roberts, "Population Policy Issues in Selected Asian Countries," in Godfrey Roberts (ed.), *Population Policy: Contemporary Issues* (New York: Praeger, 1990), p. 86.

109 ECA, Food Security and Sustainable Development Division, "Population Policies, Environment and Sustainable Development in the ECA Region," paper presented at *Nexus Seminar*, North Africa sub-Regional development Center, Tangier, June 26–29, 1998, pp. 2–3.

110 WB, *Population and Development: Implications for the World Bank* (Washington, D.C., 1994), pp. 51–52.

111 UNFPA, *Population Perspectives: Statements by World Leaders* (New York, 1984), p. 31.

112 *Ibid.*, p. 100.

113 Donaldson, *Nature Against Us*, p. 114.

114 On the confrontation between the *Ba'thi-'Alawi* regime and the Muslim Brothers since the mid-1970s, see: Raymond A. Hinnebusch, *Authoritarian Power and State Formation in*

Ba'thist Syria (Boulder: Westview Press, 1990), pp. 291–99; Moshe Ma'oz, *Asad: The Sphinx of Damascus: A Political Biography* (New York: Weidenfeld & Nicholson, 1988), pp. 159–63.

115 UNFPA, *Population Perspectives: Statements by World Leaders*, p. 145.

116 See, for example: *Tishrin*, June 22, 1980.

117 *Tishrin*, May 30, 1982.

118 A broader discussion on the Syrian natalist policy during the "oil decade," appears in: Winckler, *Demographic Developments and Population Policies in Ba'thist Syria*, pp. 111–14.

119 ESCWA, *Demographic and Related Socio-Economic Data Sheets*, No. 5 (1987), p. 204, table 2.

120 Asher Susser, "ha-Ahim ha-Muslemim be-Yarden: Du-Qiyum ve-'Imut Mevuqar," in Meir Litvak (ed.), *Islam ve-Demoqratyya ba-'Olam ha-'Aravi* (Tel Aviv: Hakibbutz Hameuchad, 1997), pp. 125–26 (Hebrew).

121 On the Jordanian anti-natalist measures, see: Gad G. Gilbar, "Jordan's Road to Family Planning Policy," in his *Population Dilemmas*, pp. 73–76; Onn Winckler, *Population Growth and Migration in Jordan, 1950–1994* (Brighton and Portland: Sussex Academic Press, 1997), pp. 82–84.

122 ESCWA, *Population Situation–1990*, p. 94, table 5.4.

123 On the new Egyptian family planning program, see: Charles F. Gallagher, "Population and Development in Egypt, Part 1: Birth and Death on the Nile," *American University Field Staff Report*, No. 31 (1981), p. 11; Robinson and El-Zanaty, *The Demographic Revolution in Modern Egypt*, pp. 53–59; Allen C. Kelley, Atef M. Khalifa and M. Nabil El-Khorazaty, *Population and Development in Rural Egypt* (Durham, N.C.: Duke Press Policy Studies, 1982), pp. 40–41; *Egypt Demographic and Health Survey–2005*, p. 3; Sayed, "The Population Family Planning Program in Egypt," p. 19; WB, *Egypt: Staff Appraisal of a Second Population Project* (August 14, 1978), p. 5; Stycos et al., *Community Development*, p. 15; *al-Ahram al-Iqtisadi*, June 21, 1982; June 5, 1989; June 12, 1989.

124 Roudi, "Fertility Policies in the Middle East and North Africa," p. 16; *Egypt Demographic and Health Survey–2005*, p. 3; *al-Ahram al-Iqtisadi*, February 6, 1982.

125 On the relationship between Sadat and the Islamic opposition, see: Raymond A. Hinnebusch, *Egyptian Politics under Sadat: The Post-Populist Development of an Authoritarian-Modernizing State* (Cambridge: Cambridge University Press, 1985), pp. 206–8.

126 Saad Eddin Ibrahim, "State, Women, and Civil Society," p. 65.

127 Lippman, *Egypt After Nasser*, p. 162.

128 Egypt, CAPMAS, *Statistical Yearbook, 1952–1992*, p. 28, table 1–18.

129 Egypt, CAPMAS, *Statistical Yearbook, 1952–1984*, p. 30.

130 *Ibid.*, p. 8.

131 Egypt, CAPMAS, *Statistical Yearbook, 1952–1992*, p. 28, table 1–18.

132 Ami Ayalon, "Demographya, Politiqa, ve-Masoret be-Mitzrayim shel Mubarak," in Ayalon and Gilbar (eds.), *Demographya ve-Politiqa be-Medinot 'Arav*, p. 32 (Hebrew).

133 *MEED*, December 2, 1983, p. 10; August 10, 1984, p. 10.

134 *Population Today*, Vol. 15, No. 5 (May 1987), p. 5.

135 Egypt, CAPMAS, *Statistical Yearbook, 1952–1992*, p. 28, table 1–18.

136 Riad Tabbarah, "Challenges in Arab Demography," *Population Bulletin of ESCWA*, No. 33 (December 1988), pp. 3–4.

137 Hassan M. Yousif and Ahmad A. Hammouda, "Alternative Population Projection Scenarios by Education Attainment for Egypt, the Sudan and Tunisia," *Population Bulletin of ESCWA*, No. 43 (1995), p. 68. See also: Jeffrey G. Williamson and Tarik M. Yousef, "Demographic Transitions and Economic Performance in the Middle East and North Africa," in Sirageldin (ed.), *Human Capital*, p. 17.

138 IBRD, *Unlocking the Employment Potential in the Middle East and North Africa*, p. 17.

139 Cited from: John Waterbury, *The Egypt of Nasser and Sadat: The Political Economy of Two Regimes* (Princeton: Princeton University Press, 1983), p. 44. See also: *al-Ahram al-Iqtisadi*, December 20, 1982.
140 WB, *Egypt: Staff Appraisal of a Second Population Project* (August 14, 1978), p. 4, table 2.
141 On the change in the US demographic approach following the ascendancy of Ronald Reagan, see: Jason L. Finkle and Barbara B. Crane, "Ideology and Politics at Mexico City: The United States at the 1984 International Conference on Population," *Population and Development Review*, Vol. 11, No. 1 (1985), pp. 11–16; Donaldson and Tsui, "The International Family Planning Movement," pp. 12–14.
142 UNFPA, *Population Perspectives: Statements by World Leaders*, p. 159.
143 Finkle and Crane, "Ideology and Politics at Mexico City," p. 11.
144 UNFPA, *Population Perspectives: Statements by World Leaders*, pp. 151–52.
145 During the 1965–1973 period, Tunisia's GDP growth rate was 6.5% on annual average, compared to 4.1% during the 1973–1983 decade.
146 Finkle and Crane, "Ideology and Politics at Mexico City," p. 1.
147 Ronald Freedman, "Family Planning Programs in the Third World," *The Annals of the American Academy*, No. 510 (July 1990), p. 34.
148 UNICEF, *The State of the World's Children–1988*, pp. 72–73, table 5.
149 Baquer Salman al-Najjar, "Population Policies in the Countries of the Gulf Co-operation Council: Politics and Society," *Immigrants & Minorities*, Vol. 12, No. 2 (1993), p. 212.
150 Gause, *Oil Monarchies*, p. 54.
151 *Gulf States Newsletter,* April 6, 1992, p. 5.
152 UN, Population Division, "Qatar," *World Population Policies*, Vol. III (1990), pp. 39–40; Gause, *Oil Monarchies*, pp. 60–61; al-Najjar, "Population Policies in the Countries of the Gulf Co-operation Council," p. 212.
153 See: Allan G. Hill, "Population Growth in the Middle East and North Africa: Selected Policy Issues," in A. L. Udovich (ed.), *The Middle East: Oil, Conflict and Hope* (Lexington: Lexington Books, 1976), p. 36; Allman "The Demographic Transition in the Middle East and North Africa," pp. 24–25.
154 Shirley Kay, "Social Change in Modern Saudi Arabia," in Tim Niblock (ed.), *State, Society and Economy in Saudi Arabia* (London: Croom Helm, 1982), p. 180.
155 ESCWA, *Demographic and Related Socio-Economic Data Sheets*, No. 5 (1987), p. 4, table 2; p. 164, table 2; p. 184, table 2; p. 224, table 2.
156 Fargues, "Demography and Politics in the Arab World," p. 5.
157 Lee and Walt, "Linking National and Global Population Agendas," p. 264.
158 Louisiana Lush et al., "Politics and Fertility: A New Approach to Population Policy Analysis," *Population Research and Policy Review*, Vol. 19, No. 1 (2000), p. 9.
159 Report submitted by the Algerian government to the UN under Article 18 of the Convention on the Elimination of all Forms of Discrimination against Women, September 1, 1998. Available at: http://www.algeria-un.org/default.asp?doc=1426.
160 *Ibid.*
161 Gilbar, "Family Planning Under Mubarak," p. 120; ESCWA, *Population Situation–1990*, p. 96.
162 Kamran Asdar Ali, *Planning the Family in Egypt: New Bodies, New Selves* (Austin: University of Texas Press, 2002), pp. 30–31.
163 Mona A. Khalifa, "Family Planning and Sustainable Development in Egypt," *CDC Series on Population and Development*, No. 5 (Cairo, 1994), pp. 4–5; Gilbar, "Family Planning Under Mubarak," p. 120.
164 *Egypt Interim Demographic and Health Survey–2003*, p. 41.
165 *Al-Ahram al-Iqtisadi*, February 24, 1988.
166 *Al-Ahram*, February 7, 1989. See also Tantawi's other speech in the issue of family planning in *al-Ahram*, October 22, 1989.

167 *Al-Ahram*, April 20, 1990.
168 *Egypt Interim Demographic and Health Survey–2003*, p. 41.
169 Ali, *Planning the Family in Egypt*, p. 33; Khalifa, "Family Planning and Sustainable Development in Egypt," pp. 12–13.
170 *Population Today*, Vol. 15, No, 5 (May 1987), p. 5.
171 *The Egyptian Gazette*, February 11; July 23, 1987.
172 UN, Population Division, "Tunisia," *World Population Policies*, Vol. III (1990), pp. 159–60; Faour, "Fertility Policy and Family Planning in the Arab Countries," p. 260.
173 ESCWA, *Population Situation–1990*, p. 192.
174 During the 1980s, the fertility rates of both Singapore and South Korea had rapidly declined and reached below replacement-level in 1990. WB, W*orld Development Report–1992*, pp. 271–72, table 27.
175 The Chinese family planning slogan was: "One is best, at most two, never a third." On the Chinese "one-child policy," see: UN, Population Division, *Case Studies in Population Policy: China*, Population Policy Paper No. 20 (New York, 1989), pp. 37–45; Susan E. Short and Fengying Zhai, "Looking Locally at China's 'One-child Policy," *Studies in Family Planning*, Vol. 29, No. 4 (1998), pp. 373–85; Edwin A. Winckler, "Chinese Reproductive Policy at the Turn of the Millennium: Dynamic Stability," *Population and Development Review*, Vol. 28, No. 3 (2001), pp. 379–418. On Singapore's family planning program, see: UNFPA, *Singapore*, Population Profile No. 1 (New York, 1977); John J. Palen, "Population Policy: Singapore," in Roberts (ed.), *Population Policy*, pp. 168–69.
176 See, for example: Lee and Walt, "Linking National and Global Population Agendas," p. 264.
177 In May 1990, North and South Yemen were again united into one country.
178 Nazy Roudi, "Population Policies Vary in Middle East," *Population Today*, Vol. 21 (April 1993), p. 10.
179 Gihan A. Shawky, "Detecting Changes in Fertility in Algeria, Egypt and Yemen," *CDC Working Paper* No. 42 (Cairo, 1999), pp. 36–37; ESCWA, "Population Policies and Programmes in the Arab World," by Hussein A. Sayed, *Arab Population Conference*, Amman, April 4–8, 1993, p. 5.
180 UN, Population Division, "Levels and Trends in Fertility in Oman and Yemen," by Eltigani E. Eltigani, workshop on *Prospects for Fertility Decline in High Fertility Countries*, New York, July 9–11, 2001, p. 9.
181 *Ibid.*, p. 5.
182 Mohamed Kamel Marwan, "Population Strategy, 1992/2007," *Population Studies*, Vol. 14, No. 75 (July–September 1992), pp. 113–15.
183 Hassanin et al., "Estimating Family Planning Target Population of Egypt in 1997," p. 442; Saad Eddin Ibrahim, "State, Women, and Civil Society," p. 62.
184 Arab Republic of Egypt, National Population Information Center, special issue, October 14, 1991.
185 *Egypt Demographic and Health Survey–2000*, p. 4; *Egypt Demographic and Health Survey–2005*, pp. 3–4.
186 Naguib Ghita, "A Seminar on the Preliminary Results of the 1996 Census on Population, Housing and Establishments in the Light of the National Population Strategy," *Population Studies*, Vol. 16, No. 81 (January–March 1998), p. 103.
187 Robinson and El-Zanaty, *The Demographic Revolution in Modern Egypt*, p. 115.
188 USAID, *Egypt's Population Program: Assessing 25 Years of Family Planning*, by Scott Moreland (New York, March 2006), p. v.
189 *Al-Ahram*, 6 March 2004.
190 See, for example: *al-Ahram*, September 11, 2002.
191 *Jordan Population and Family Health Survey–2002*, p. 3; The Hashemite Kingdom of

Jordan, Ministry of Planning, *Plan for Economic and Social Development, 1993–1997* (Amman, 1993), p. 155.

192 *Jordan Population and Family Health Survey–1997*, pp. 2–3.

193 The Hashemite Kingdom of Jordan, Ministry of Planning, Economic Aid Coordination Unit, *Partners in Development*, No. 31 (December 1999), p. 5.

194 *Jordan Times*, May 27, 2003.

195 *Jordan Times*, July 23–24, 2004.

196 See: Eyal Zisser, "Syria," *MECS*, Vol. 18 (1994), p. 619.

197 *Syrian Maternal and Child Health Survey–1993*, p. 177.

198 Mohammed al-Imadi, "The Economic and Investment Policies in Syria," in Hans Hopfinger and Raslan Khadour (eds.), *Economic Development and Investment Policies in Syria* (Neustadt an der Aisch: Verlagsdrucherei Schmidt, 1998), p. 22.

199 *Tishrin*, May 19, 2002.

200 Report submitted by Algeria to the UN under Article 18 of the Convention on the Elimination of all Forms of Discrimination against Women, September 1, 1998.

201 ESCWA, *Regional Arab Population Forum*, Beirut, November 19–21, 2004 (Beirut, March, 2005), p. 6.

202 UN, Population Division, *World Population Policies–2005* (New York, 2006), p. 13.

203 The "Washington Consensus," which emerged in the early 1980s during Reagan's term, maintained that only private sector-led export-oriented economies, based on governmental budgetary balance, low inflation, market determined prices and reduced governmental regulations, have the ability to promote economic performances and job creation in developing economies. See: Alan Richards, "The Political Economy of Economic Reform in the Middle East: The Challenge to Governance," prepared for the RAND Project: *The Future of Middle East Security–2001*, p. 4. Available at: http://sccie.ucsc.edu/documents/working_papers/2001/challenge_econreform.pdf.

204 Roudi, "Fertility Policies in the Middle East and North Africa," p. 19.

205 McIntosh and Finkle, "The Cairo Conference," p. 240; Mazur, "Beyond the Numbers," pp. 12–13.

206 International Republican Institute, *Oman: Political Development & the Maglis Ash'Shura* (Washington, D. C., July 1995), pp. 26–27. See also the speech of Sultan Qabus in his annual meet-the-people tour of January 1994 in *al-Wasat*, January 24, 1994.

207 Oman, *The Fifth Five-Year Development Plan, 1996–2000*, p. 192. See also: *The Middle East*, November 1997, p. 26.

208 ESCWA, *Survey, 1996–1997*, p. 133; Eltigani, "Levels and Trends in Fertility in Oman and Yemen," p. 9.

209 Sultanate of Oman, Ministry of National Economy, *Oman 2003–2004*. Available at: http://www.omanet.om; *al-Khalij*, April 28, 2007.

210 Eltigani, "Levels and Trends in Fertility in Oman and Yemen," p. 5.

211 Saudi Arabia, *Sixth Development Plan*, p. 89.

212 UN, *Fertility, Contraception and Population Policies*, p. 23.

213 See, for example: SAMA, *Thirty-Sixth Annual Report–1421H.* [2000], p. 261.

214 SAMA, *Thirty-Eighth Annual Report–1423 H.* [2002], p. 56.

215 *MEED*, July 23–29, 2004, p. 6.

216 During the past two decades, the fertility rates of the indigenous Bahraini population have been the lowest among the GCC countries.

217 J. S. Birks, "The Demographic Challenge in the Arab Gulf," in B. R. Pridham (ed.), *The Arab Gulf and the Arab World* (London: Croom Helm, 1988), pp. 136–37.

218 IBRD, *Unlocking the Employment Potential in the Middle East and North Africa*, p. 4.

219 Robinson and El-Zanaty, *The Demographic Revolution in Modern Egypt*, p. 3.

220 *Egypt Demographic and Health Survey–2000*, p. 48, table 4.4.

221 *Egypt Demographic and Health Survey–2005*, p. 44, table 4.1.

222 *Egypt Interim Demographic and Health Survey–2003*, p. 29, table 3.1.
223 *Al-Ahram*, September 19, 2007.
224 USAID and Egypt Population Council, *Achieving Replacement-Level Fertility in Egypt: Challenges and Potential Opportunities*, by John B. Casterline and Ronia Roushdy (New York, October 2006).
225 See, for example: Ali, *Planning the Family in Egypt*, pp. 42–43.
226 ECA, *The State of Demographic Transition in Africa*, p. 40.
227 UN, *Demographic Yearbook–1996*, p. 323.
228 ESCWA, *Demographic and Related Socio-Economic Data Sheets*, No. 5 (1987), p. 204, table 2.
229 Syria, *Statistical Abstract–2006*, p. 68, table 8/2.
230 *Jordan Population and Family Health Survey–1997*, p. 36, table 4.2; p. 41, table 4.7.
231 *Jordan Times*, August 4, 2004.
232 *Jordan Times*, July 7, 2004.
233 *Jordan Population and Family Health Survey–1997*, p. 28, table 3.3.
234 See, for example: Obermeyer, "Islam, Women and Politics," p. 33.
235 Jennifer Olmsted, "Reexamining the Fertility Puzzle in MENA," in Eleanor Abdella Doumato and Marsha Pripstein Posusney (eds.), *Women and Globalization in the Arab Middle East: Gender, Economy & Society* (Boulder and London: Lynne Rienner Publishers, 2003), pp. 86–87.
236 Allman, "The Demographic Transition in the Middle East and North Africa," p. 296.
237 UNDP and AFESD, *Arab Human Development Report–2003*, pp. 90–91.
238 Gred Nonneman, "Rentiers and Autocrats, Monarchs and Democrats, State and Society: The Middle East Between Globalization, Human 'Agency,' and Europe," *International Affairs*, Vol. 77, No. 1 (2001), p. 159.
239 Leonard Binder, "Gamal 'Abd al-Nasser: Iconology, Ideology and Demonology," in Podeh and Winckler (eds.), *Rethinking Nasserism*, p. 57.
240 The term Dutch Disease is connected to the term "rentier state" and refers to a situation in which a country enjoys large revenues from the export of a natural resource and then deteriorates into a deep recession following a sharp decline in the export revenues of that particular natural resource. This economic phenomenon is known as the "Dutch Disease" because its existence was first noted in the Netherlands in the 1960s following the discovery of North Sea gas. After a relatively short period of high revenues from gas exports, the Dutch economy deteriorated into a deep recession.
241 Victor Lavy and Eliezer Sheffer, *Foreign Aid and Economic Development in the Middle East: Egypt, Syria, and Jordan* (New York: Praeger Publishers, 1991).
242 Alan Richards, "Oil Wealth in the Arab World: Whence, to Whom, and Whither?" in Dan Tschirgi (ed.), *The Arab World Today* (Boulder and London: Lynne Rienner Publishers, 1994), p. 68.
243 The *2001-Syrian Family Health Survey*. Available at: http://www.papfam.org/papfam/syriatable.htm.
244 The *2002-Algerian Family Health Survey*. Available at: http://www.papfam.org/papfam/algeria.htm
245 The *2003/4-Moroccan Family Health Survey*. Available at: http://www.papfam.org/papfam/moroccotable.htm
246 USAID and Egypt Population Council, *Achieving Replacement-Level Fertility in Egypt*, p. 2.
247 *Ibid.*
248 Chesnais, "Below-Replacement Fertility in the European Union," p. 85.
249 See, for example: Lant H. Pritchett, "Desired Fertility and the Impact of Population Policies," *Population and Development Review*, Vol. 20, No. 1 (1994), pp. 1–55.
250 In the early 1990s, it was estimated that in the developing countries (excluding China), as

much as a quarter of the pregnancies were unwanted and an even higher percentage were unplanned. See: Mazur, "Beyond the Numbers," p. 16; David Bloom et al., "Economic Growth and the Demographic Transition," NBER (National Bureau of Economic Research) Working Paper No. 8685 (Cambridge, December 2001), p. 52. Available at: http://www.nber.org/papers/w8685.

251 Robert J. Lapham and W. Parker Mauldin, "Family Planning Program Effort and Birthrate Decline in Developing Countries," *International Family Planning Perspectives*, Vol. 10, No. 4 (1984), p. 110.

252 Todaro, *Economic Development*, seventh edition, p. 240.

253 Ali, *Planning the Family in Egypt*, p. 1.

254 Hess, *Population Growth and Socioeconomic Progress in Less Developed Countries*, p. 20.

255 WB, *Population and Development*, pp. 2, 6. See also: Susan H. Cochrane and David K. Guilkey, "The Effects of Fertility Intensions and Access to Services on Contraceptive Use in Tunisia," *Economic Development and Cultural Change*, Vol. 43, No. 4 (1995), pp. 779–804.

256 Gilbar, "Family Planning Under Mubarak," pp. 132–33.

257 Saad Eddin Ibrahim, "State, Women, and Civil Society," p. 77.

258 Wisensale and Khodair, "The Two-child Family," p. 513.

259 UNDP, *Jordan Human Development Report–2004*, p. 18.

260 Fargues, "State Policies and the Birth Rate in Egypt," p. 115.

261 *Ibid.*, pp. 127–28.

262 Fargues, "Demographic Explosion or Social Upheaval?" pp. 157, 165.

263 Youssef Courbage, "Issues in Fertility Transition in the Middle East and North Africa," *Economic Research Forum*, Working Paper No. 9903 (Cairo, 1999), p. 7. Available at: http://www.erf.org.eg/uploadpath/pdf/9903.pdf.

264 *Ibid.*, pp. 8–9.

265 Courbage, "Fertility Transition in Syria," p. 145.

266 ESCWA, *Arab Women in ESCWA Member States* (New York, 1994), p. 78, table 8.

267 On the Iranian natalist policies since the 1960s, see: WB, *Fertility and Family Planning in Iran*, by Rodolfo A. Bulatao and Gail Richardson, Discussion Paper Series No. 13 (December 1994); Homa Hoodfar and Samad Assadpour, "The Politics of Population Policy in the Islamic Republic of Iran," *Studies in Family Planning*, Vol. 31, No. 1 (2000), pp. 19–34; Yasmin L. Mossavar-Rahmani, "Family Planning in Post-Revolutionary Iran," in Guity Nashat (ed.), *Women and Revolution in Iran* (Boulder: Westview Press, 1983), pp. 253–62; Mohammad Jalal Abbasi et al., "Revolution, War and Modernization: Population Policy and Fertility Change in Iran," *Journal of Population Research*, Vol. 19, No. 1 (2002), pp. 25–46.

268 Abbasi et al., "Revolution, War and Modernization," p. 26.

269 Mohammad Jalal Abbasi-Shavazi and Peter McDonald, "National and Provincial-Level Fertility Trends in Iran, 1972–2000," The Australian National University, *Working Paper in Demography* No. 94 (February 2005), p. 4.

270 PRB, *World Population Data Sheet–2006* (New York, 2006), p. 5.

271 By 2004, Bangladesh's per capita GDP (PPP terms) was $1,870 and it was ranked 137 in the HDI. See: UNDP, *Human Development Report–2006*, p. 285, table 1.

272 On Bangladesh's family planning policy, see: John C. Caldwell et al., "The Bangladesh Fertility Decline: An Interpretation," *Population and Development Review*, Vol. 25, No. 1 (1999), pp. 67–84; UN, "Bangladesh," *World Population Policies*, Vol. 1 (1987), p. 44; *Population Today*, Vol. 26, No. 1 (January 1998), p. 7.

273 WB, *World Development Report–1982*, p. 144, table 18.

274 WB, *World Development Report–1992*, p. 270, table 1; UNICEF, *The State of the World's Childrem–2005*, p. 142, table 10.

275 Carl Haub, "Flat Birth Rates in Bangladesh and Egypt Challenge Demographers' Projections," *Population Today*, Vol. 28, No. 7 (October 2000), p. 4.

276 PRB, *World Population Data Sheet–2006*, p. 5.

277 Center for Policy Dialogue (CPD) Bangladesh and UNFPA, "Re-thinking Population Policy in Bangladesh," *CPD-UNFPA Paper Series* No. 24 (June 2003), p. 1. Available at: http://www.cpd-bangladesh.org/publications/cpdunfpa/unfpa24.PDF.

278 Harbison and Robinson, "Policy Implications of the Next Demographic Transition," p. 43.

279 The following section dealing with the uniqueness of Tunisia family planning policy is based on: Gad G. Gilbar and Onn Winckler, "Nasser's Family Planning Policy in Perspective," in Podeh and Winckler (eds.), *Rethinking Nasserism*, pp. 296–98.

280 ECA, *The State of Demographic Transition in Africa*, p. 3.

281 See: London School of Hygiene & Tropical Medicine and UNPF, *Population Policies and Programmes*, p. 41; Foreign Area Studies, the American University, edited by Harold D. Nelson, *Tunisia: A Country Study* (Washington, D.C., 1979), p. 86.

282 Ali, *Planning the Family in Egypt*, p. 154.

283 On this subject, see: K. L. Brown, "The Campaign to Encourage Family Planning in Tunisia and some Responses at the Village Level, "*Middle Eastern Studies*, Vol. 17, No. 1 (1981), p. 82; Beaujot and Bchir, *Fertility in Tunisia*, pp. 36–37.

Summary and Conclusions

1 Gilbar, *Kalkalat ha-Mizrah ha-Tikhon*, pp. 40–41.

2 On the definition of "sufficient water" and "food security" in general and in the Middle East in particular, see: Tony Allan, *The Middle East Water Question: Hydropolitics and the Global Economy* (London: I.B. Tauris, 2000), pp. 3–40.

3 *MEED*, February 9, 2001, p. 31.

4 Quoted from: Dermot Grenham, "Demography: The Effects of Changing Population Profiles," paper presented to *the Staple Inn Actuarial Society*, January 24, 1995, p. 4. Available at: http://www.actuaries.org.uk/files/pdf/library/SIAS–1995/demography.pdf.

5 UNDP, *Arab Human Development Report–2002*, p. 88.

6 See, for example, The Economic Research Forum, *Syria Country Profile*, pp. 7–8.

7 See, for example, ESCWA, *Survey, 2003–2004*, p. 22, box 5; Clement Henry, "A Clash of Globalization: Obstacles to Development in the Middle East," *Harvard International Review*, Vol. 25, No. 1 (2003), p. 3. Available at: http://hir.harvard.edu/articles/1101.

8 Timur Kuran, "Why the Middle East Is Economically Underdeveloped: Historical Mechanisms of International Stagnation," paper presented in the conference *Institutional Barriers to Economic Change: Cases Considered*, George Mason University, June 24, 2003. Available at: http://www.international.ucla.edu/cms/files/kuran.0130.pdf.

9 Simon W. Murden, *Islam, the Middle East, and the New Global Hegemony* (Boulder and London: Lynne Rienner Publishers, 2002), p. 95.

10 Paul Rivlin and Shmuel Even, *Political Stability in the Arab States: Economic Causes and Consequences*, Memorandum No. 74 (Tel Aviv University, Jaffee Center for Strategic Studies, December 2004), p. 9.

11 ESCWA, *Survey, 1998–1999*, pp. 24–25, table 8.

12 The "oil-for-food agreement," signed between the UN and Iraq in May 1996 enabled Iraq to export oil in exchange for food and medical supplies. Initially, Iraq was permitted to sell oil in the amount of $2 billion every six months. In 1998, the amount was raised to $5.26 billion for every six-month period. In December 1999, however, due to the rapid increase of oil prices, the limit on Iraq's oil exports was abolished.

13 Winckler, "The Economic Consequences of the Iraqi Crisis on the Mashreq Countries," pp. 400–7.

14 Asher Susser, "The Decline of the Arabs", *Middle East Quarterly*, Vol. 10, No. 4 (2003), p. 4.
15 Paul Aarts claimed that: "[the Middle East] economic integration has hardly moved beyond the stage of rhetoric." See: Paul Aarts, "The Middle East: A Region without Regionalism or the End of Exceptionalism?" *Third Word Quarterly*, Vol. 20, No. 5 (1999), p. 911.
16 Laipson, "The Middle East's Demographic Transition," p. 177.
17 On the tight connection between rental income, regime survival and democracy, see: Michael L. Ross, "Does Oil Hinder Democracy?" *World Politics*, Vol. 53, No. 3 (2001), pp. 325–61.
18 Gilbar, *Kalkalat ha-Mizrah ha-Tikhon*, p. 201.
19 Colton, "The Maghrebi Economies as Emerging Markets?" p. 160.
20 Asher Susser, "Jordan," *MECS*, Vol. 20 (1996), pp. 425–32.
21 Joseph Kostiner, "Yemen," *MECS*, Vol. 22 (1998), pp. 664–65.
22 UNDP, *Human Development Report–2006*, pp. 292–94, table 3.
23 El-Ghonemy, *Affluence and Poverty in the Middle East*, pp. 178–80; 200–5; *MEED*, June 30, 2005, pp. 4–5.
24 IMF, *Tunisia: Staff Report for the 1987 Article IV Consultation*, Country Report No. 06/207 (June 2006), p. 4.
25 IMF, *Tunisia: 2005 Article IV Consultation, Preliminary Conclusions of the IMF Mission* (January 20, 2006). See also: *MEED*, June 24–30, 2005, p. 4.
26 The abject poverty (or destitution) line refers to a minimum level of subsistence of approximately 2,150 calories per person per day.
27 EIU, *Country Profile–Yemen, 2006*, p. 21.
28 *MEED*, April 13–19, 2007, p. 30. See also: The Economic Research Forum, *Economic Trends in the MENA Region–2002*, p. 100, box 5.3.
29 ESCWA, *Survey, 2004, Summary*, p. 1.
30 *The Middle East*, April 2003, pp. 54–55.
31 Bloom, Canning and Sevilla, "Economic Growth and the Demographic Transition," p. 20.
32 See: UN, Population Division, *Population Growth and Economic Development*. Report on the Consultative Meeting of Economists Convened by the UNPF, New York, September 28–29, 1992, p. 9.
33 On the demographic factor of "the East Asian economic miracle," see: WB, *The East Asian Miracle: Economic Growth and Public Policy* (Published for the WB by Oxford University Press, 1993), pp. 38–40; Geoffrey McNicoll, *Policy Lessons of the East Asian Demographic Transition*, Population Council Working Paper No. 210 (New York, 2006).
34 Bloom, Canning and Sevilla, "Economic Growth and the Demographic Transition," pp. 26–27. On the pattern of the rapid economic expansion of South Korea and Taiwan see: Dani Rodrik, "Getting Interventions Right: How South Korea and Taiwan Grew Rich," *Economic Policy*, Vol. 10, No. 2 (1995), pp. 55–107.
35 Richards, "The Political Economy of Economic Reform in the Middle East," p. 7.
36 See: The Economic Research Forum, *Economic Trends in the MENA Region–2002*, p. 88.
37 In 2005, for example, the real GDP growth rate amounted to 5.4% in Egypt and 3.9% in Yemen. ESCWA, *Survey of Economic and Social Developments in the ESCWA Region, 2006–2007, Summary* (New York, April 2007), p. 3.
38 Tarik M. Yousef, "Development, Growth and Policy Reform in the Middle East and North Africa since 1950," *Journal of Economic Perspectives*, Vol. 18, No. 3 (2004), pp. 108–9.
39 IBRD, *Unlocking the Employment Potential in the Middle East and North Africa*, p. 4.
40 Indeed, in order to avoid political unrest, the Egyptian government chose not to implement its commitment to the IMF to raise energy prices to market level. See: EIU, *Country Profile–Egypt, 2005*, p. 39.

41 Paul Rivlin, "Nasser's Egypt and Park's Korea: A Comparison of their Economic Achievements," in Podeh and Winckler (eds.), *Rethinking Naserrism*, p. 278.

42 The basic assumption of Ricardo's "Iron Law of Wages" is that any commodity reflects its cost of production. Thus, "the labor price," namely, the wage, is a function of the supply/demand balance, as in any other commodity. Hence, in an economy with a substantial labor surplus, wages will always remain low and thus the production level as well. On Ricardo's "Iron Law of Wages," see: Henry William Spiegel, *The Growth of Economic Thought* (Englewood Cliffs, N.J.: Prentice-Hall, 1971), pp. 325–26; Charles E. Staley, *A History of Economic Thought* (Cambridge: Basil Blackwell Inc., 1989), pp. 81–84.

43 Nathan B. Brown, "Nasserism's Legal Legacy," in Podeh and Winckler (eds.), *Rethinking Nasserism*, p. 129.

44 See, for example, Ramady, *The Saudi Arabian Economy*, p. 356.

45 During the 2001–2006 period, Dubai's population increased by an enormous rate of 44.6% – higher than in any other Arab country.

46 *MEED*, September 8–14, 2006, p. 12.

47 *Ibid.*

48 Ayubi, *Over-stating the Arab State*, p. 248.

49 *Gulf States Newsletter*, February 6, 2002, p. 11; *MEED*, May 4, 2001, p. 22.

50 On the political reforms in the GCC countries since the early 1990s, see: Andrzej Kapiszewski, "Elections and Parliamentary Activity in the GCC States: Broadening Political Participation in the Gulf Monarchies since the 1990s," paper presented at the *Sixth Mediterranean Social and Political Research Meeting,* Montecatini, March 16–20, 2005.

51 EIU, *Country Profile–Qatar, 2005*, p. 10.

52 Anoushiravan Ehteshami and Steven Wright, "Political Change in the Arab Oil Monarchies: From Liberalization to Enfranchisement," *International Affairs*, Vol. 83, No. 5 (2007), p. 915.

53 James Gwartney, Robert Lawson and Ralph Holcombe, "Economic Freedom and the Environment for Economic Growth," *Journal of Institutional and Theoretical Economics*, Vol. 155, No. 4 (1999), p. 643.

54 *MEED*, March 16–22, 2007, p. 5.

55 Richards, "The Political Economy of Economic Reform in the Middle East," p. 3.

56 David. E. Long, *The Kingdom of Saudi Arabia* (Gainesville: University Press of Florida, 1997), p. 16.

Bibliography

Official Publications

The State (Kingdom) of Bahrain

Central Statistics Organization, Directorate of Statistics. *Statistical Abstract*, various issues. Manama.

Al-Jihaz al-Markazi lil-Ihsa. *Al-Ta'dad al-'Amm lil-Sukan wal-Masakin wal-Mabani wal-Munsha'at–1991*. Manama, 1992 (Arabic).

Ministry of Health. *Bahrain Child Health Survey–1989*. Edited by Samir Farid et al. Manama, 1992.

Bahrain Economic Development Board. *Reforming Bahrain's Labour Market*. Manama, 2004.

Bahrain Monetary Agency. *Annual Report*, various issues. Manama.

—— *Economic Indicators*, various issues. Manama.

Arab Republic of Egypt

CAPMAS (Central Agency for Public Mobilisation and Statistics). *Statistical Yearbook*, various Issues, Cairo.

—— *Population, Housing, and Establishments Census–1986*, Preliminary Results. Cairo, June 1987.

—— *External Migration As A Demographic Phenomenon*. Cairo, 1994.

Ministry of Health and Population, National Population Council and Macro International Inc. *Egypt Demographic and Health Survey–1995*. Cairo, September 1996.

—— *Egypt Demographic and Health Survey–2000*. Cairo, January 2001.

—— *Egypt Interim Demographic and Health Survey–2003*. Cairo, January 2004.

—— *Egypt Demographic and Health Survey–2005*. Cairo, March 2006.

Supreme Council for Family Planning and Population. "National Strategy Framework of Population, Human Resource Development and the Family Planning Program." *Population Studies*, No. 56 (January–March 1981).

National Bank of Egypt. *The Underground Economy with Special Reference to the Case of Egypt*. By Ibrahim M. Oweiss. Cairo, December 1994.

—— *The Egyptian Economy in Brief–2000*. Cairo, 2001.

—— *Egypt in Figures–2006*. Cairo, June 2007.

National Population Information Center. Special Issue, October 14, 1991. Cairo.

The European Union (EU)

Statistical Office of the European Union. *Eurostat Yearbook*, various issues. Luxembourg.

European Commission, Directorate-General for Employment and Social Affairs. *Employment in Europe 2002: Recent Trends and Prospects*. Luxembourg, July 2002.

The Islamic Republic of Iran

National Report on Population: The Islamic Republic of Iran. Submitted to the International Conference on Population and Development, Cairo, 1994.

The State of Israel

Central Bureau of Statistics. *Statistical Abstract of Israel*, various issues. Jerusalem.

The Hashemite Kingdom of Jordan

Department of Statistics. *Statistical Yearbook*, various issues. Amman.
—— *Jordan Population and Family Health Survey–1990.* Amman, 1992.
—— *Al-Ta'dad al-'Amm lil-Sukan wal-Masakin–1994.* Amman, 1995 (Arabic).
—— *Jordan Population and Health Survey–1997.* Amman, 1998.
—— *Jordan Population and Health Survey–2002.* Amman, June 2003.
—— *Employment and Unemployment Survey.* February 2001, Principal Report. Amman, April 2001.
—— *Al-Itigahat al-Igtima'iyya fil-Urdun.* Amman, October 2006 (Arabic).
Ministry of Planning. *Plan for Economic and Social Development, 1993–1997.* Amman, 1993.
——, Economic Aid Coordination Unit. *Partners in Development*, No. 31, December 1999.
Central Bank of Jordan. *Annual Report*, various issues. Amman.

The State of Kuwait

Ministry of Planning. Statistics and Information Center. *Annual Statistical Abstract*, various issues. Kuwait.
Ministry of Health. *Kuwait Child Health Survey.* Edited by Rashid al-Rashoud and Samir Farid. Kuwait, 1991.
Central Bank of Kuwait. *Economic Report*, various issues. Kuwait.

Kingdom of Morocco

Al-Mandubiyya al-Samiyya lil-Takhtit, Qisem al-Ihsaiyyat al-'Amma. *Al-Nashra al-Ihsaiyya al-Sanawiyya lil-Maghrib*, various years. Rabat.
Ministry of Public Health. *National Survey on Population and Health–1992.* Rabat, 1992.
—— *Enquête de Panel sur la Population et la Santé* (EPPS)–*1995.* Rabat, Janvier 1996.

Sultanate of Oman

Ministry of National Economy. *Statistical Yearbook*, various issues. Muscat.
—— *Facts & Figures on Development Efforts, 1970–2000.* Muscat, November 2000.
Development Council. *The Second Five-Year Development Plan, 1981–1985.* Muscat, 1981.
Ministry of Development. *The Fifth Five-Year Development Plan, 1996–2000.* Muscat, July 1997.
—, National Statistical Department. *General Census of Population, Housing, and Establishments–1993.* Muscat, 1995.
Ministry of National Economy. *Oman 2003–2004.* Available at: http://www.omanet.om.
—— *Selected Data and Indicators From the Results of General Populations, Housing Units and Establishments Censuses, 1993–2003.* Muscat, 2005.
Ministry of Health. *Oman Child Health Survey.* Edited by Murtadha J. Suleiman, Ahmed al-Ghassany and Samir Farid. Muscat, 1992.
—— *Oman Family Health Survey–1995.* Edited by Ali J.M. Sulaiman, Asya al-Riyami and Samir Farid. Muscat, 1996.
Ministry of Information. *The Speeches of HM. Sultan Qaboos bin Said, 1970–1990.* Muscat, n.d.
Central Bank of Oman. *Annual Report*, various issues. Muscat.

Palestinian National Authority (PNA)

Ministry of Health. *Health Indicators*, various issues. Ramallah.

Central Bureau of Statistics. *The Demographic Survey in the West Bank and Gaza Strip*, Final Report. Ramallah, 1997.

—— *Al-Maseh al-Sihi al-Dimughrapi–2004*. Ramallah, 2004 (Arabic).

State of Qatar

Presidency of the Council of Ministers, Central Statistical Organization. *Annual Statistical Abstract*, various issues. Doha.

Ministry of Health. *Qatar Child Health Survey*. Edited by Abdul-Jalil Salman, Khalifa al-Jaber and Samir Farid. Doha, 1991.

Ministry of Information. *Qatar into the Seventies*. Doha, May 1973.

The Planning Council, the General Secretariat. *Qatar in Figures–2006*. Doha, October 2006.

Qatar National Bank. *Qatar Economic Review*, various issues. Doha.

The Kingdom of Saudi Arabia

Ministry of Planning, Central Department of Statistics. *Statistical Yearbook*, various issues. Riyadh.

—— *Development Plan, 1390 A.H.* Riyadh, 1970.

—— *Second Development Plan, 1395–1340A.H.* [1975–1980]. Riyadh, 1975.

—— *Third Development Plan, 1400–1405A.H.* [1980–1985]. Riyadh, 1980.

—— *Fourth Development Plan, 1405–1410A.H.* [1985–1990]. Riyadh, 1985.

—— *Achievements of the Development Plans, 1390–1404A.H.* [1970–1984]. Riyadh, 1985.

—— *Fifth Development Plan, 1410–1415A.H.* [1990–1995]. Riyadh, 1990.

—— *Sixth Development Plan, 1415–1420A.H.* [1995–2000]. Riyadh, 1996.

—— *Seventh Development Plan, 1420/21–1424/25A.H.* [2000–2004]. Riyadh, 1999.

—— *Eighth Development Plan, 1425/26–1429/30A.H.* [2005–2009]. Riyadh, 2004.

Al-Nata'ij al-Awaliyya lil-Ta'dad al-'Amm lil-Sukan wal-Masakin 1425A.H. Riyadh, 2004 (Arabic).

Ministry of Health. *Saudi Arabia Child Health Survey*. Edited by Yagob al-Mazrou and Samir Farid. Riyadh, 1991.

Saudi Arabian Monetary Agency (SAMA). *Annual Report*, various issues. Riyadh.

Syrian Arab Republic

Office of the Prime Minister, CBS. *Statistical Abstract*, various issues. Damascus.

—— *Socio-Economic Development in Syria, 1960–1970*, Studies Series No. 73. Damascus, 1973.

—— and State Planning Commission in collaboration with the Population Council. *Composition and Growth of Population in the Syrian Arab Republic*. By M. Nader al-Hallak et al. Damascus, September 1979.

—— *Factors of Population Growth and Their Future Trends*. Papers presented at a seminar under the auspices of the Syrian CBS and UNFPA, Damascus, September 16–20, 1978. Damascus, 1979.

—— and League of Arab States, Pan-Arab Project for Child Development. *Syrian Maternal and Child Health Survey*–1993. Principal Report. Damascus, 1999.

Tunisian Republic

Wizarat al-Tanmiyya wal-Ta'awun al-Dawli, al-Ma'had al-Watani lil-Ihsa. *Al-Nashriyya al-Ihsa al-Sanawiyya Li-Tunis*, various years. Tunis (Arabic).

—— *Al-Isqatat al-Sukaniyya, 2004–2034*. Tunis, 2007 (Arabic).

United Arab Emirates (UAE)

Ministry of Planning, Central Statistical Department. *Annual Statistical Abstract*, various issues. Abu Dhabi.

Ministry of Economy. *Preliminary Results of Population, Housing and Establishments Census–2005*. Abu Dhabi, 2006.

Ministry of Health. *United Arab Emirates Child Health Survey*. Edited by Abdul-Wahab al-Muhaideb, Abdul-Ghaffar Abdul-Ghafour and Smir Farid. Abu Dhabi, 1991.
Ministry of Information and Culture. *United Arab Emirates Yearbook–2006*. Abu Dhabi, 2006.
Government of Dubai, Department of Economic Development. *Dubai Economic Statistics*, various issues. Dubai.
—— *Hotel Statistics Summary, 1998–2007*. Dubai, 2008.

United Kingdom (UK)

The British Embassy of Beirut, Middle East Development Division. By N. B. Hudson. *The First Population Census of Qatar*. April/May 1970. Beirut, October 1970.

United States (US)

USAID. *Egypt's Population Program: Assessing 25 Years of Family Planning*. By Scott Moreland. New York, March 2006.
—— and Egypt Population Council. *Achieving Replacement-Level Fertility in Egypt: Challenges and Potential Opportunities*. By John B. Casterline and Ronia Roushdy. New York, October 2006.

Yemen

Ministry of Planning and International Cooperation. *Statistical Yearbook*, various issues. Sana'a.

The Cooperation Council of the Arab States of the Gulf (GCC)

Secretarial General, Statistical Department. *Statistical Bulletin*, No. 12, 2003.

Publications of Official International Organizations

The World Bank (WB)

World Development Report, various issues. Published for the World Bank by Oxford University Press, Oxford and New York.
W*orld Tables*, various issues. Published for the World Bank by Johns Hopkins University Press, Baltimore and London.
African Development Indicators, various issues. Washington, D.C.
Egypt: Staff Appraisal of a Second Population Project. Washington, D.C., August 14, 1978.
Manpower and International Labor Migration in the Middle East and North Africa. By Ismail Serageldin et al. Published for the World Bank by Oxford University Press, Oxford and New York, 1983.
—— and the Ministry of Planning of Saudi Arabia. *Saudis in Transition: The Challenges of a Changing Labor Market*. By Ismail A. Sirageldin, Naiem A. Sherbiny and M. Ismail Serageldin. Published for the World Bank by Oxford University Press, Oxford and New York, 1984.
The East Asian Miracle: Economic Growth and Public Policy. Published for the World Bank by Oxford University Press, Oxford and New York, 1993.
Population and Development: Implications for the World Bank. Washington, D.C., 1994.
Fertility and Family Planning in Iran. By Rodolfo A. Bulatao and Gail Richardson. Discussion Paper Series No. 13. Washington, D.C., December 1994.
[The] *Hashemite Kingdom of Jordan*. A Quarterly Publication of the Jordan Country Unit, First Quarter 2003. Washington, D.C., 2003.
Labor Market Reforms, Growth and Unemployment in Labor-Exporting MENA Countries. By Pierre-Richard Agénor et al. Washington, D.C., 2003.

Middle East and North Africa: Economic Developments and Prospects–2005. Washington, D.C., 2005.

International Bank for Reconstruction and Development (IBRD)

The Economic development of Libya. Published for IBRD by The Johns Hopkins University Press, Baltimore and London, 1960.
The Economic Development of Morocco. Published for IBRD by The Johns Hopkins University Press, Baltimore and London, 1966.
The Population Program of the Government of Tunisia: A Second Review. Report No. 651-TUN. Washington, D.C., February 27, 1975.
Global Development Finance: Striving for Stability in Development Finance. Washington, D.C., 2003.
Unlocking the Employment Potential in the Middle East and North Africa: Toward A New Social Contract. By Tarik Yousef et al. MENA Development Report. Washington, D.C., 2004.

International Monetary Fund (IMF)

International Financial Statistics Yearbook, various issues. Washington, D.C.
Syrian Arab Republic: Staff Report for the 1987 Article IV Consultation. February 18, 1988.
Jordan: Background Information on Selected Aspects of Adjustment and Growth Strategy. August 29, 1995.
Algeria: Selected Economic Issues. Country Report No. 96/71. 1996.
Demography, Capital Dependency and Growth in MENA. By Tarik M. Yousef, African Department. January 31, 1998.
Algeria: Selected Economic Issues. Country Report No. 98/87. 1998.
Tunisia: Recent Economic Developments. Country Report No. 00/37. March 2000.
"GCC Countries: From Oil Dependence to Diversification." By Ugo Fasano and Zubair Iqbal. *IMF Working Paper*, 2003. Available at: http://www.imf.org/external/pubs/ft/med/2003/eng/fasano.
"Emerging Strains in GCC Labor Markets." By Ugo Fasano and Rishi Goyal. *IMF Working Paper* No. 04/71, April 2004. Available at: http://www.imf.org/external/pubs/ft/wp/2004/wp0471.pdf.
United Arab Emirates: 2004 Article IV Consultation. Country Report No. 04/175. June 2004.
Arab Republic of Egypt: Selected Issues. Country Report No. 05/179. June 2005.
United Arab Emirates: Selected Issues and Statistical Appendix. Country Report No. 05/268. August 2005.
Tunisia: 2005 Article IV Consultation, Preliminary Conclusions of the IMF Mission. January 20, 2006.
Tunisia: Staff Report for the 1987 Article IV Consultation. Country Report No. 06/207. June 2006.
Algeria: 2006 Article IV Consultation. Country Report No. 07/72. February 2007.
Jordan: 2006 Article IV Consultation and Fourth Post. Country Report No. 07/128. March 2007.
Tunisia: 2007 Article IV Consultation. Country Report No. 07/302. August 2007.
Morocco: 2007 Article IV Consultation. Country Report No. 07/323. September 2007.
United Arab Emirates: Statistical Appendix. Country Report No. 07/348. October 2007.

The United Nations (UN)

Department of Economic and Social Affairs, Population Division

Demographic Yearbook, various issues. New York: UN Publications.
World Urbanization Prospects, various issues. New York.
—— and UNFPA. *Population Policy Compendium–Bahrain*. New York, 1981.
—— and UNFPA. *Population Policy Compendium–Saudi Arabia*. New York, 1981.

Case Studies in Population Policy: Kuwait. Population Policy Paper No. 15. New York, 1988.

"Mortality of Children Under Age 5: World Estimates and Projections, 1950–2025." *Population Studies*, No. 105. New York, 1988.

Case Studies in Population Policy: China. Population Policy Paper No. 20. New York, 1989.

"World Population Policies." *Population Studies*, 3 Vols. New York, 1990.

Population Growth and Economic Development. Report on the Consultative Meeting of Economics Converted by the UNPF. New York, September 28–29, 1992.

National Population Policies. New York, 1998.

World Population Monitoring–2001: Population, Environment and Development. New York, 2001.

"Levels and Trends in Fertility in Oman and Yemen." By Eltigani E. Eltigani. Workshop on *Prospects for Fertility Decline in High Fertility Countries*. New York, July 9–11, 2001.

International Migration Report–2002. New York, 2002.

World Population Ageing: 1950–2050. New York, 2002.

Fertility, Contraception and Population Policies. New York, 2003.

Operational Aspects of Census Taking in the ESCWA Region: Results of ESCWA Questionnaire. By Ahmed Hussein. New York, August 12, 2005.

World Population Policies–2005. New York, 2006.

"Restrictive Labour Immigration Policies in the Oil-Rich Gulf: Effectiveness and Implications for Sending Asian Countries." By Nasra M. Shah. May 5, 2006. Available at: http://www.un.org/esa.

World Population Prospects: The 2006 Revision. New York, 2007.

United Nations Economic Commission for Africa (ECA)

Food Security and Sustainable Development Division. "Population Policies, Environment and Sustainable Development in the ECA Region." Paper presented at *Nexus Seminar*, North Africa sub-Regional Development Center, Tangier, June 26–29, 1998.

The State of Demographic Transition in Africa. Addis Ababa, December 2001.

Economic and Social Conditions in North Africa: A Mid-Decade Assessment. Addis Ababa, April 2006.

United Nations Development Programme (UNDP)

Human Development Report, various issues. Published for the UNDP by Oxford University Press, Oxford and New York.

Arab Human Development Report–2002. Published for the UNDP by Oxford University Press, Oxford and New York, 2002.

—— and AFESD. *Arab Human Development Report*–2003. Amman, 2003.

—— and the Jordanian Ministry of Planning and International Cooperation. *Jordan Human Development Report–2004*. Amman, 2004.

—— and AFESD. *Arab Human Development Report–2005*. New York, 2006.

United Nations Educational, Scientific, and Cultural Organization (UNESCO)

Statistical Yearbook, various issues. Paris.

United Nations Economic and Social Office in Beirut (UNESOB)

"Demographic Situation in the Syrian Arab Republic." By M. N. al-Hallak. Expert Group Meeting on the Application of Demographic Data and Studies in Development Planning of the UN Economic and Social Office in Beirut. Beirut, December 7–12, 1970.

UN Economic (and Social) Commission for Western Asia (ECWA/ESCWA)

Demographic and Related Socio-Economic Data Sheets for Countries of the Economic and Social Commission for Western Asia, various issues. Beirut, Baghdad and Amman.

External Trade Bulletin of the ESCWA Region, various issues. New York.

National Accounts Studies of the ESCWA Region, various issues. New York.
Statistical Abstract of the ESCWA Region, various issues. New York.
Survey of Economic and Social Developments in the ECWA/ESCWA Region, various issues. New York.
Habbab, Adnan. "Family Planning in the Syrian Arab Republic." Paper presented at the *First Regional Population Conference of ECWA*. Beirut, February 18–March 1, 1974.
Technical Secretariat. "Achievements, Plans and Recommendations Relating to Population and Housing Censuses in the Sultanate of Oman." *ECWA Expert Group Meeting on Census Techniques*. Beirut, December 12–16, 1977.
The Population Situation in the ECWA Region–Jordan. Beirut, 1979.
The Population Situation in the ECWA Region–Saudi Arabia. Beirut, 1979.
The Population Situation in the ECWA Region–Qatar. Beirut, 1980.
The Population Situation in the ECWA Region–Syrian Arab Republic. Beirut, 1980.
The Population Situation in the ECWA Region–United Arab Emirates. Beirut, 1980.
—— and League of Arab States. *Statistical Indicators of the Arab World for the Period of 1970–1979*. Beirut, 1981.
Population Situation in the ESCWA Region–1990. Amman, May 1992.
"Population Policies and Programmes in the Arab World." By Hussein A. Sayed. *Arab Population Conference*. Amman, April 4–8, 1993.
—, League of Arab States and UNFPA. "Arab Labour Migration." *Meeting of Senior Officials and Experts*. Amman, April 4–6, 1993.
Population Spatial Distribution. Amman, 1993.
Compendium of Social Statistics and Indicators, third issue. New York, December 1993.
Return Migration: Profiles, Impact and Absorption in Home Countries. New York, 1993.
Arab Women in ESCWA Member States. New York, 1994.
Social Impact of Reconstructing with Special Reference to Employment. New York, 1999.
Proceedings of the Expert Group Meeting on Assessment of Economic and Social Developments in the ESCWA Region During the Last 25 Years and Priorities for the Next Decade, 1999–2009. New York, 1999.
Population Section. *Gender and Population Dynamics in the ESCWA Region*. By Batool Shakoori. Beirut, 2000.
Al-Nashra al-Sukaniyya [*Population Bulletin of ESCWA*], No. 49, 2000 (Arabic).
Economic Diversification in the Oil-Producing Countries: The Case of the Gulf Cooperation Council Economies. New York, 2001.
Regional Arab Population Forum. Beirut, November 19–21, 2004. Beirut, March 2005.
Social and Economic Situation of Palestinian Women, 2000–2006. By Eileen Kuttab. Beirut, February 2007.

United Nations Funds for Population Activities (UNFPA)

Singapore. Population Profile No. 1. New York, 1977.
Population Perspectives: Statements by World Leaders. New York, 1984.

United Nations Children's Fund (UNICEF)

The State of the World's Children, various issues. New York.

International Labour Office (ILO)

Yearbook of Labour Statistics, various issues. Geneva.
World Employment Report, various issues. Geneva.
Migration for Employment Project: The Kingdom of Saudi Arabia and the Libyan Arab Jamahiriya: The Key Countries for Employment. World Employment Programme Research, Working Paper. By J. S. Birks and C. A. Sinclair. Geneva, May 1979.
International Migration and Development in the Arab Region. By J. S. Birks and C. A. Sinclair. Geneva, 1980.

Employment Opportunities and Equity in A Changing Economy: Egypt in the 1980's. A Labour Market Approach. By Bent Hansen and Samir Radwan. Geneva, 1982.

International Migration for Employment: The Jordanian Migration System in Transition. By Allan M. Findlay. Geneva, March 1987.

International Migration for Employment: Manpower and Population Evolution in the GCC and Libyan Arab Jamahiriya. World Employment Programme Research, Working Paper. By J. S. Birks and C. A. Sinclair. Geneva, October 1989.

United Nations Statistics Division

"Population and Housing Censuses." October 5, 2005. Available at: http://unstats.un.org.

World Tourism Organization (WTO)

Yearbook of Tourism Statistics, various issues. Madrid.

Dissertations (Ph.D Thesis)

Bendardaf, Ibrahim Bushnaf. *Socioeconomic Modernization and Demographic Changes in Syria.* Unpublished Ph.D. Thesis, University of Missouri, 1988.

Nama, Ahmad Mohammed. *Human Resources Development: The Case of Qatar.* Unpublished Ph.D. Thesis, Claremont Graduate School, 1983.

Publications of Commercial Companies and Banks

Birks, Sinclair & Associates Ltd. *GCC Market Report*, 1990 and 1992. Durham: Mountjoy Research Centre.

Euromonitor Publications Limited. *Middle East Economic Handbook.* London: Euromonitor Publications Ltd., 1986.

HRD base Ltd., Lloyds Bank Chambers. *Socio-Demographic Profiles of Key Arab Countries.* Newcastle, May 1987.

MERI Report. *Saudi Arabia.* London: Croom Helm, 1985.

—— *United Arab Emirates.* London: Croom Helm, 1985.

The NCB Economist (National Commercial Bank-Saudi Arabia), various issues. Riyadh.

Saudi-American Bank (SAMBA). *The Saudi Economy*, various issues. Riyadh.

Books

Arabic and Hebrew

Ayalon, Ami and Gad G. Gilbar (eds.). *Demographya ve-Politiqa be-Medinot 'Arav* [Demography and Politics in the Arab States]. Tel Aviv: Hakibbutz Hameuchad, 1995 (Hebrew).

Baer, Gabriel. *'Arviyey ha-Mizrah ha-Tikhon* [The Arabs of the Middle East], second edition. Tel Aviv: Hakibbutz Hameuchad, 1973 (Hebrew).

Gilbar, Gad G. *Kalkalat ha-Mizrah ha-Tikhon ba-'Et ha-Hadasha* [The Economic Development of the Middle East in Modern Times]. Tel Aviv: Ministry of Defense, 1990 (Hebrew).

Al-Hamarneh, Mustafa (ed.). *Al-Iqtisad al-Urduni: al-Mushkilat wal-Afaqa* [The Problems and Horizons of the Jordanian Economy]. Amman: Markaz al-Dirasat al-Istratigiyya, 1994 (Arabic).

Litvak, Meir (ed.). *Islam ve-Demoqratyya ba-'Olam ha-'Aravi* [Islam and Democracy in the Arab World]. Tel Aviv: Hakibbutz Hameuchad, 1997 (Hebrew).

Al-Matri, al-Sayid Khalid. *Sukan al-Mamlaka al-'Arabiyya al-Sa'udiyya.* Riyadh: Al-Dar al-Sa'udiyya lil-Nasher wal-Tawzi', 1998 (Arabic).

Nur, 'Othman al-Hasan Muhammad and Ziad Rashad al-Rawi. *Al-Ihsa'at al-Sukaniyya fi Duwal al-Khalij al-'Arabiyya.* Riyadh: Arab Bureau of Education for the Gulf States, 1991 (Arabic).

Al-Ruythi, Muhammad Ahmad (ed.). *Sukan al-'Alam al-'Arabi: al-Waqi' wal-Mustaqbal*, 2 Vols. Riyadh: Maktabat al-'Abikan, 2003 (Arabic).

Shamir, Shimon (ed.). *Yeridat ha-Nasserism, 1965–1970: Shqi'ata shel Tenu'a Meshihit* [The Decline of Nasserism 1965–1970: The Waning of a Messianic Movement]. Tel Aviv: Mif'alim Universitayim, 1978 (Hebrew).

Zisser, Eyal. *Be-Shem ha-Av: Bashar al-Asad: Shanim Rishonot ba-Shilton*. Tel Aviv: Tel Aviv University Press, 2004 (Hebrew).

English

Aarts, Paul and Gred Nonneman (eds.). *Saudi Arabia in the Balance*. London: Hurst & Company, 2005.

Abdelkarim, Abbas (ed.). *Change and Development in the Gulf*. London: Macmillan Press, and New York: St. Martin's Press, 1999.

Abdel-Khalek, Gouda and Robert Tignor (eds.). *The Political Economy of Income Distribution in Egypt*. New York: Holmes and Meier, 1982.

Alessa, Shamlan Y. *The Manpower Problem in Kuwait*. London and Boston: Kegan Paul International, 1981.

Ali, Kamran Asdar. *Planning the Family in Egypt: New Bodies, New Selves*. Austin: University of Texas Press, 2002.

Allan, Tony. *The Middle East Water Question: Hydropolitics and the Global Economy*. London: I.B. Tauris, 2000.

Allen, Calvin H. and W. Lynn Rigsbee. *Oman Under Qaboos: From Coup to Constitution, 1970–1996*. London and Portland: Frank Cass, 2000.

Allman, James (ed.). *Women's Status and Fertility in the Muslim World*. New York and London: Praeger Publishers, 1978.

Amin, Galal A. *Egypt's Economic Predicament: A Study in the Interaction of External Pressure, Political Folly and Social Tension in Egypt, 1960–1990*. Leiden: Brill, 1995.

—— and Elizabeth Awny. *International Migration of Egyptian Labour: A Review of the State of Art*. Ottawa: International Development Research Centre, May 1985.

Anderson, Ewan W. *The Middle East: Geography and Geopolitics*. London and New York: Routledge, 2000.

Anderson, Michael. *Population Change in North-Western Europe, 1750–1850*. London: Macmillan Education, 1988.

Appleyard, Reginald (ed.). *The Impact of International Migration on Developing Countries*. Paris: Development Centre of the Organization for Economic Co-Operation and Development, 1989.

Askari, Hossein. *Saudi Arabia's Economy: Oil and the Search for Economic Development*. Greenwich and London: JAI Press, 1990.

—, Vahid Nowshirvani and Mohamed Jaber. *Economic Development in the GCC: The Blessing and the Curse of Oil*. Greenwich and London: JAI Press, 1997.

Avery, John. *Progress, Poverty and Population: Re-reading Condorcet, Godwin and Malthus*. London and Portland: Frank Cass, 1997.

Ayubi, Nazih N. *Over-stating the Arab State: Politics and Society in the Middle East*. London and New York: I.B. Tauris, 1995.

El-Azhary, M. S. (ed.). *The Impact of Oil Revenues on Arab Gulf Development*. London: Croom Helm, and Boulder: Westview Press, 1984.

Azzam, Henry T. *The Arab World Facing the Challenge of the New Millennium*. London and New York: I.B. Tauris, 2002.

Beaujot, Roderic and Mongi Bchir. *Fertility in Tunisia: Traditional and Modern Contrasts*. Washington, D.C.: PRB, 1984.

Beblawi, Hazem and Giacomo Luciani (eds.). *The Rentier State*, 2 Vols. London: Croom Helm, 1987.

Bengio, Ofra and Gabriel Ben-Dor (eds.). *Minorities and the State in the Arab World*. Boulder: Lynne Rienner Publishers, 1999.

Bennoune, Mahfoud. *The Making of Contemporary Algeria, 1830–1987: Colonial Upheavals and Post-Independence Development*. Cambridge: Cambridge University Press, 1988.

Birdsall, Nancy, Allen C. Kelley and Steven W. Sinding (eds.). *Population Matters: Demographic Change, Economic Growth, and Poverty in the Developing World*. Oxford: Oxford University Press, 2000.

Birks, J. S. and C. A. Sinclair. *International Migration Project: Country Case Study: The United Arab Emirates*. Durham: The University of Durham, Department of Economics, 1978.

—— *International Migration Project: Country Case Study: The Hashemite Kingdom of Jordan*. Durham: The University of Durham, Department of Economics, 1978.

—— *International Migration Project, Country Case Study: The Kingdom of Saudi Arabia*. Durham: The University of Durham, Department of Economics, 1979.

Birks, J. S. and J. A. Rimmer. *Developing Education Systems in the Oil States of Arabia: Conflicts of Purpose and Focus*. The University of Durham, Centre for Middle Eastern and Islamic Studies, 1984.

Bonine, Michael E. (ed.). *Population, Poverty, and Politics in Middle East Cities*. Gainesville: University Press of Florida, 1997.

Cairo Demographic Center (CDC). *Demographic Aspects of Socio-Economic Development in some Arab and African Countries*. Edited by S. A. Huzayyin and T. E. Smith. Research Monograph Series, No. 5. Cairo, 1974.

—— *Family and Marriage in some African and Asiatic Countries*. Edited by S. A. Huzayyin and G. T. Acsadi. Research Monograph Series, No. 6. Cairo, 1976.

—— *Determinants of Fertility in some African and Asian Countries*. Research Monograph Series, No. 10. Cairo, 1982.

—— *Population & Development*. Population & Development Research Monograph Series, No. 1. Cairo, 1994.

—— *Population & Development*. Research Monograph Series, No. 2. Cairo, 1995.

—— *CDC 24th Annual Seminar on Population Issues and the Challenges of the 21st Century in the Middle East, Africa and Asia*. Research Monograph Series, No. 24. Cairo, 1995.

—— *Population & Sustainable Development*. Research Monograph Series, No. 5. Cairo, 1998.

—— *CDC 28th Annual Seminar on Population Issues in the Middle East, Africa and Asia*. Research Monograph Series, No. 28. Cairo, 1999.

—— *CDC 35th Annual Conference on Population and Development*. Monograph Series, No. 35. Cairo, 2005.

—— *CDC 36th Annual Conference on Population and Development*. Monograph Series, No. 36. Cairo, 2006.

Charles, Enid. *The Menace of Under-Population*. London: Watts, 1936.

Clarke, J. I. and W. B. Fisher (eds.). *Populations of the Middle East and North Africa: A Geographical Approach*. London: University of London Press, 1972.

Clarke, John I. and Howard Bowen-Jones (eds.). *Change and Development in the Middle East*. London and New York: Methuen, 1981.

Cleland, John and John Hobcraft (eds.). *Reproductive Change in Developing Countries: Insights from the World Fertility Survey*. Oxford: Oxford University Press, 1985.

Cleland, Wendell. *The Population Problem in Egypt*. Lancaster, PA: Science Press Printing Company, 1936.

Cordesman, Anthony H. *Bahrain, Oman, Qatar, and the UAE: Challenges of Security*. Boulder: Westview Press, 1997.

—— *Saudi Arabia Enters the Twenty-First Century: the Political, Foreign Policy, Economic, and Energy Dimensions*, Vol. 2. Westport: Praeger, 2003.

Courbage, Youssef. *New Demographic Scenarios in the Mediterranean Region*. Paris: National Institute of Demographic Studies. Available at: http://www.ined.fr.

Davies, Charles E. (ed.). *Global Interests in the Arab Gulf*. New York: St. Martin's Press, 1992.

Demeny, Paul and Geoffrey McNicoll (eds.). *Encyclopedia of Population*. New York: Macmillan Reference USA, 2003.

Dixon, John (ed.). *Social Welfare in the Middle East*. London: Croom Helm, 1987.

Domschke, Eliane and Doreen S. Goyer. *The Handbook of National Population Censuses: Africa and Asia*. New York, Westport and London: Greenwood Press, 1986.

Donaldson, Peter J. *Nature Against Us: The United States and the World Population Crisis, 1965–1980*. Chapel Hill and London: The University of North Carolina Press, 1990.

Doumato, Eleanor Abdella and Marsha Pripstein Posusney (eds.). *Women and Globalization in the Arab Middle East: Gender, Economy & Society*. Boulder and London: Lynne Rienner Publishers, 2003.

[The] Economic Research Forum. *Economic Trends in the MENA Region–2002*. Cairo: The American University in Cairo Press, 2002.

—— *Syria Country Profile: The Road Ahead for Syria*. Cairo, February 2005.

Eickelman, Dale F. *The Middle East: An Anthropological Approach*, second edition. Englewood Cliffs, N.J.: Prentice-Hall, 1989.

—— *The Middle East and Central Asia: An Anthropological Approach*, fourth edition. Upper Saddle River, N.J.: Prentice-Hall, 2002.

[The] Emirates Center for Strategic Studies and Research. *Education and the Arab World: Challenges of the Next Millennium*. Abu Dhabi, 1999.

Erlich, Paul. *The Population Bomb*. New York, Ballantine Books, 1971.

Fargues, Philippe (ed.). *Mediterranean Migration–2005 Report*. Florence: European University Institute, 2005.

Al-Farsy, Fouad. *Modernity and Tradition: The Saudi Equation*. London and New York: Kegan Paul International, 1990.

Feige, Edgar L. (ed.). *The Underground Economies: The Evasion and Information Distortion*. Cambridge: Cambridge University Press, 1989.

Feiler, Gil. *Economic Relations between Egypt and the Gulf Oil States, 1967–2000*. Brighton and Portland: Sussex Academic Press, 2004.

Findlay, Allan and Anne Findlay. *Population and Development in the Third World*. London and New York: Methuen, 1987.

Finkle, Jason L. and C. Alison McIntosh (eds.). *The New Politics of Population: Conflict and Consensus in Family Planning*. Supplement to Vol. 20 of *Population and Development Review*. New York: The Population Council, 1994.

Foreign Areas Studies Division. *Area Handbook for Syria*. Washington, D.C.: The American University, July 1965.

—— *Tunisia: A Country Study*. Edited by Harold D. Nelson. Washington, D.C., 1979.

Fuller, Graham E. and Rend Rahim Francke. *The Arab Shi'a: The Forgotten Muslims*. New York: St. Martin's Press, 1999.

Gadalla, Saad M. *Is there Hope? Fertility and Family Planning in a Rural Egyptian Community*. Cairo: American University in Cairo Press, 1978.

Gause, Gregory III. *Oil Monarchies: Domestic and Security Challenges in the Arab Gulf States*. New York: Council on Foreign Relations, 1994.

El-Ghonemy, M. Riad. *Affluence and Poverty in the Middle East*. London and New York: Routledge, 1998.

Gilbar, Gad G. *The Middle East Oil Decade and Beyond*. London and Portland: Frank Cass, 1997.

—— *Population Dilemmas in the Middle East*. London and Portland: Frank Cass, 1997.

Le Goff, Jacques and Pierre Nora (eds.). *Constructing the Past: Essays in Historical Methodology*. Cambridge: Cambridge University Press, 1985.

Goldberg, Ellis, Reşat Kasaba and Joel Migdal (eds.). *Rules and Rights in the Middle East: Democracy, Law and Society*. Seattle and London: University of Washington Press, 1993.

Gould, W. T. S. and A. M. Findlay (eds.). *Population Migration and the Changing World Order*. Chichester: John Wiley & Sons, 1994.

Gubser, Peter. *Jordan: Crossroads of Middle Eastern Events*. Boulder: Westview Press, and London: Croom Helm, 1983.

Hall, Ray and Paul White (eds.). *Europe's Population: Towards the Next Century*. London: UCL Press, 1995.

Handoussa, Heba and Zafiris Tzannatos (eds.). *Employment Creation and Social Protection in the Middle East and North Africa*. Cairo: The American University in Cairo Press, 2002.

Hansen, Bent. *Economic Development in Syria*. California: The Rand Corporation, 1969.

Harding, Philip and Richard Jenkins. *The Myth of the Hidden Economy: Towards a New Understanding of Informal Economic Activity*. Milton Keynes: Open University Press, 1989.

Harik, Iliya and Denis J. Sullivan (eds.). *Privatization and Liberalization in the Middle East*. Bloomington, IN: Indiana University Press, 1992.

Hartley, Shirley Forster. *Population–Quantity vs. Quality: A Sociological Examination of the Causes and Consequences of the Population Explosion*. New Jersey: Prentice-Hall Inc., Englewood Cliffs, 1972.

Hauser, Philip M. and Otis Dudley Duncan (eds.). *The Study of Population*. Chicago and London: The University of Chicago Press, 1959.

Held, Colbert C. *Middle East Patterns: Places, Peoples, and Politics*, second edition. Boulder: Westview Press, 1994.

Henry, Clement M. and Robert Springborg. *Globalization and the Politics of Development in the Middle East*. Cambridge: Cambridge University Press, 2001.

Hess, Peter N. *Population Growth and Socioeconomic Progress in Less Developed Countries: Determinants of Fertility Transition*. New York and London: Praeger, 1988.

Himadeh, Said B. (ed.). *Economic Organization of Syria*. Beirut: The American University of Beirut Press, 1936.

Hinnebusch, Raymond A. *Egyptian Politics under Sadat: The Post-Populist Development of an Authoritarian-Modernizing State*. Cambridge: Cambridge University Press, 1985.

—— *Authoritarian Power and State Formation in Ba'thist Syria*. Boulder: Westview Press, 1990.

Hopfinger, Hans and Raslan Khadour (eds.). *Economic Development and Investment Policies in Syria*. Neustadt an der Aisch: Verlagsdrucherei Schmidt, 1998.

Hopkins, Nicholas S. and Saad Eddin Inrahim (eds.). *Arab Society: Class, Gender, Power, and Development*, third edition. Cairo: The American University in Cairo Press, 1997.

Hudson, Pat. *History by Numbers: An Introduction to Quantitative Approaches*. London: Arnold, 2000.

Ibrahim, Saad Eddin. *The New Arab Social Order: A Study of the Social Impact of the Oil Wealth*. Boulder: Westview Press and London: Croom Helm, 1982.

Ikram, Khalid. *Egypt: Economic Management in a Period of Transition*, A World Bank Country Economic Report. Baltimore and London: The Johns Hopkins University Press, 1980.

International Organization for Migration (IOM) and League of Arab States. *Arab Migration in a Globalized World*. Cairo, May 2004.

International Republican Institute. *Oman: Political Development & the Maglis Ash-Shura*. Washington, D.C., July 1995.

Ismael, Jacqueline S. *Kuwait: Social Change in Historical Perspective*. Syracuse: Syracuse University Press, 1982.

Issawi, Charles. *Egypt in Revolution*. London: Oxford University Press, 1963.

—— *An Economic History of the Middle East and North Africa*. New York: Columbia University Press, 1982.

Johnson, Stanley P. *World Population–Turning the Tide: Three Decades of Progress*. London: Graham & Trotman/ Martinus Nijhoff, 1994.

van de Kaa, Dirk J. *The Past of Europe's Demographic Future*, Uhlenbeck Lecture 17. Wassenaar, 1999.

Kanovsky, Eliyahu. *The Economic Impact of the Six-Day War: Israel, The Occupied Territories, Egypt, Jordan*. New York: Praeger Publishers, 1970.

—— *Economic Development of Jordan*. Tel Aviv University, The David Horovitz Institute for the Research of Developing Countries, 1974.

Kapiszewski, Andrzej. *Nationals and Expatriates: Population and Labour Dilemmas of the Gulf Cooperation Council States*. Reading: Ithaca Press, 2001.

Kechichian, Joseph A. (ed). *Iran, Iraq, and the Arab Gulf States*. New York: Palgrave, 2001.

Kelley, Allen C., Atef M. Khalifa and M. Nabil El-Khorazaty. *Population and Development in Rural Egypt*. Durham, N.C.: Duke Press Policy Studies, 1982.

Kerr, Malcolm H. and El Sayed Yassin (eds.). *Rich and Poor States in the Middle East: Egypt and the New Arab Order*. Boulder: Westview Press, and Cairo: The American University in Cairo Press, 1982.

Khader, Bichara and Adnan Badran (eds.). *The Economic Development of Jordan*. London: Croom Helm, 1987.

Khater, Akram Fouad. *Inventing Home: Emigration, Gender, and the Middle Class in Lebanon, 1870–1920*. Berkeley: University of California Press, 2001.

Khoury, Philip and Joseph Kostiner (eds.). *Tribes and State Formation in the Middle East*. London and New York: I.B. Tauris, 1991.

Kostiner, Joseph (ed.). *Middle East Monarchies: The Challenge of Modernity*. Boulder: Lynne Rienner, 2001.

Kushner, David (ed.). *Palestine in the Late Ottoman Period*. Jerusalem: Yad Yizhak Ben-Zvi Press, 1986.

Laurence, Jonathan and Justin Vaisse. *Integrating Islam: Political and Religious Challenges in Contemporary France*. Washington, D.C.: Brookings Institution Press, 2006.

Lavy, Victor and Eliezer Sheffer. *Foreign Aid and Economic Development in the Middle East: Egypt, Syria, and Jordan*. New York: Praeger Publishers, 1991.

Lewis, Bernard. *The Emergence of Modern Turkey*, second edition. Oxford and New York: Oxford University Press, 1968.

Lippman, Thomas W. *Egypt After Nasser: Sadat, Peace and the Mirage of Prosperity*. New York: Paragon House, 1989.

Lipsky, George A. *Saudi Arabia: Its People, Its Society, Its Culture*. New Haven: HRAF Press, 1959.

Livi-Bacci, Massimo. *The Population of Europe*. Oxford: Blackwell, 2000.

London School of Hygiene & Tropical Medicine and the UNPF. *Population Policies and Programmes: Determinants and Consequences in Eight Developing Countries*. By Kelley Lee et al. London, 1995.

Long, David. E. *The Kingdom of Saudi Arabia*. Gainesville: University Press of Florida, 1997.

—— and Christian Koch (eds.). *Gulf Security in the Twenty-First Century*. Abu Dhabi: The Emirates Center for Strategic Studies and Research, 1997.

Looney, Robert E. *The Economic Development of Saudi Arabia: Consequences of the Oil Prices Decline*. Greenwich and London: JAI Press, 1990.

—— *Manpower Policies and Development in the Persian Gulf Region*. Westport and London: Praeger, 1994.

Luciani, Giacomo (ed.). *The Arab State*. London: Routledge, 1990.

Mabro, Robert. *The Egyptian Economy, 1952–1972*. Oxford: Clarendon Press, 1974.

Maddison, Angus. *The World Economy: A Millennium Perspective*. Paris: OECD, 2001.

Malthus, Thomas Robert. *An Essay on the Principle of Population*. Edited by Philip Appleman. New York: W. W. Norton, 1976.

Ma'oz, Moshe. *Asad: The Sphinx of Damascus: A Political Biography*. New York: Weidenfeld & Nicholson, 1988.

—— *Syria and Israel: From War to Peace Making*. Oxford: Clarendon Press, 1995.

—, Joseph Ginat and Onn Winckler (eds.). *Modern Syria: From Ottoman Rule to Pivotal Role in the Middle East*. Brighton and Portland: Sussex Academic Press, 1999.

Massey, Douglas S. et al. *Worlds in Motion: Understanding International Migration at the End of the Millennium*. Oxford: Clarendon Press, 1998.

Mazur, Laurie Ann (ed.). *Beyond the Numbers: A Reader on Population, Consumption, and Environment*. Washington, D.C.: Island Press, 1994.

McNicoll, Geoffrey. *Policy Lessons of the East Asian Demographic Transition*. Population Council Working Paper No. 210. New York, 2006.

Mekkawi, M. A. *The Population of Lebanon*. Beirut, January 1970.

Moghadam, Valentine M. *Modernizing Women: Gender and Social Change in the Middle East*. Boulder and London: Lynne Rienner Publishers, 1993.

Mohammed, Nadeya Sayed Ali. *Population and Development in the Arab Gulf States: The Case of Bahrain, Oman and Kuwait*. Hampshire: Ashgate, 2003.

Murden, Simon W. *Islam, the Middle East, and the New Global Hegemony*. Boulder and London: Lynne Rienner Publishers, 2002.

Myrdal, Gunnar. *Asian Drama: An Inquiry into the Poverty of Nations*, 2 Vols. New York: Pantheon, Random House, 1968.

Nam, Charles B. and Susan G. Philliber. *Population: A Basic Orientation*, second edition. Englewood Cliffs, New Jersey: Prentice-Hall, 1984.

Nashat, Guity (ed.). *Women and Revolution in Iran*. Boulder: Westview Press, 1983.

National Academy of Sciences. *Rapid Population Growth: Consequences and Policy Implications*. Baltimore and London: The Johns Hopkins University Press, 1971.

Neguib, Mohammed. *Egypt's Destiny*. London: Victor Gollancz Ltd., 1955.

Niblock, Tim (ed.). *Social and Economic Development in the Arab Gulf*. London: Croom Helm, 1980.

—— (ed.). *State, Society and Economy in Saudi Arabia*. London: Croom Helm, 1982.

—— *Saudi Arabia: Power, Legitimacy and Survival*. London and New York: Routledge, 2006.

—— and Emma Merphy (eds.). *Economic and Political Liberalization in the Middle East*. London and New York: British Academic Press, 1993.

—— and Rodney Wilson (eds.). *The Political Economy of the Middle East*, 6 Vols. Cheltenham, K: Edward Elgar, 1999.

Nyrop, Richard F. et al. *Area Handbook for Saudi Arabia*, third edition. Washington, D.C.: US Government Printing Office, 1977.

Obermeyer, Carla Makhlouf (ed.). *Family, Gender, and Population in the Middle East*. Cairo: The American University in Cairo Press, 1995.

Omran, Abdel-Rahim. *Population in the Arab World: Problems and Prospects*. London: Croom Helm, 1980.

—— *Family Planning in the Legacy of Islam*. London and New York: Routledge, 1992.

Oweiss, Ibrahim M. (ed.). *The Political Economy of Contemporary Egypt*. Washington, D.C.: Center for Contemporary Arab Studies, Georgetown University, 1990.

Owen, Roger. *Migrant Workers in the Gulf*. London: Minority Rights Group, 1985.

—— and Şevket Pamuk. *A History of Middle East Economies in the Twentieth Century*. Cambridge, Mass.: Harvard University Press, 1999.

Perthes, Volker. *The Political Economy of Syria under Asad*. London and New York: I.B. Tauris, 1995.

Petersen, William. *Founder of Modern Demography: Malthus*. New Brunswick and London: Transaction Publishers, 1999.

Peterson, John E. *Oman in the Twentieth Century: Political Foundations of an Emerging State*. London: Croom Helm, 1978.

Philipov, Dimiter et al. (eds.). *Vienna Yearbook of Population Research–2006*. Vienna: Vienna Institute of Demography, 2006.

Podeh, Elie. *The Decline of Arab Unity: The Rise and Fall of the United Arab Republic*. Brighton and Portland: Sussex Academic Press, 1999.

—— and Onn Winckler (eds.). *Rethinking Nasserism: Revolution and Historical Memory in Modern Egypt*. Gainesville: University Press of Florida, 2004.

—— and Asher Kaufman (eds.). *Arab–Jewish Relations: From Conflict to Reconciliation?* Brighton and Portland: Sussex Academic Press, 2006.

[The] Population Reference Bureau. *Population Handbook*, fourth edition. By Arthur Haupt and Thomas T. Kane. New York, 1997.

—— *World Population Data Sheets*, various issues. New York.

—— *Family Planning Worldwide*. New York, 2002.

Pressat, Roland. *The Dictionary of Demography*. Oxford: Clarendon Press, 1985.

Pridham, B. R. (ed.). *The Arab Gulf and the Arab World*. London: Croom Helm, 1988.

Rabinovich, Itamar. *The War for Lebanon, 1970–1985*. Ithaca and London: Cornell University Press, 1985.

Rabo, Annika. *Change on the Euphrates: Villagers, Townsmen and Employees in Northern Syria*. University of Stockholm, Department of Social Anthropology, 1986.

Radwan, Samir. *Towards Full Employment: Egypt into the 21st Century*. Cairo: Egyptian Center for Economic Studies, 1998.

Ramady, Mohamed A. *The Saudi Arabian Economy: Policies, Achievements and Challenges*. New York: Springer, 2005.

Al-Rasheed, Madawi. *A History of Saudi Arabia*. Cambridge: Cambridge University Press, 2002.

Rejwan, Nissim. *Nasserist Ideology: Its Exponents and Critics*. New York: John Wiley & Sons, 1974.

Richards, Alan and Philip L. Martin (eds.). *Migration, Mechanization, and Agricultural Labor Markets in Egypt*. Boulder: Westwiew Press, 1983.

Richards, Alan and John Waterbury. *A Political Economy of the Middle East*, second edition. Boulder: Westview Press, 1996.

Rivlin, Paul. *World Oil and Energy Trends: Strategic Implications for the Middle East*. Memorandum No. 57. Tel Aviv University, Jaffee Center for Strategic Studies, September 2000.

—— *Economic Policy and Performance in the Arab World*. Boulder and London: Lynne Rienner Publishers, 2001.

—— and Shmuel Even. *Political Stability in the Arab States: Economic Causes and Consequences*. Memorandum No. 74. Tel Aviv University, Jaffee Center for Strategic Studies, December 2004.

Roberts, Godfrey (ed.). *Population Policy: Contemporary Issues*. New York: Praeger, 1990.

Robinson, Warren C. and Fatma H. El-Zanaty. *The Demographic Revolution in Modern Egypt*. Boulder: Lexington Books, 2005.

Salamé, Ghassan (ed.). *Democracy without Democrats? The Renewal of Politics in the Muslim World*. London and New York: I.B. Tauris, 1994.

Sales, M. E. *International Migration Project: Syrian Arab Republic*. Durham: The University of Durham, Department of Economics, 1978.

Salibi, Kamal S. *The Modern History of Lebanon*. London: Weidenfeld and Nicolson, 1965.

Sayigh, Yusif A. *The Economies of the Arab World: Development Since 1945*. London: Croom Helm, 1978.

Schultz, Theodore W. (ed.). *Food for the World*. Chicago: University of Chicago Press, 1945.

Serow, William J. et al. (eds.). *Handbook of International Migration*. New York and London: Greenwood Press, 1990.

Shaw, K. E. (ed.). *Higher Education in the Gulf: Problems and Prospects*. Exeter: University of Exeter Press, 1997.

Shaw, Paul R. *Mobilizing Human Resources in the Arab World*. London: Kegan Paul International, 1983.

Shtayyeh, Mohammad (ed.). *Labor Migration: Palestine, Jordan, Egypt and Israel*. Jerusalem: Palestine Center for Regional Studies, 1998.

Sick, Gary G. and Lawrence G. Potter (eds.). *The Persian Gulf at the Millennium: Essays in Politics, Economy, Security, and Religion*. New York: St. Martin's Press, 1999.

Sirageldin, Ismail. (ed.). *Human Capital: Population Economics in the Middle East*. Cairo: The American University in Cairo Press, 2002.

—— and Eqbal al-Rahmani (eds.). *Population and Development Transformations in the Arab World*. Greenwich: JAI Press, 1996.
Soliman, Salwa et al. *Population and Development in Egypt*. Cairo: CDC, 1994.
Smith, Adam. *An Inquiry into the Nature and the Cause of the Wealth of Nations*, third edition with notes by J. R. McCulloch. London: Ward, Lock & Co., Limited, 1812.
Spiegel, Henry William. *The Growth of Economic Thought*. Englewood Cliffs, N.J.: Prentice-Hall, 1971.
Staley, Charles E. *A History of Economic Thought*. Cambridge: Basil Blackwell Inc., 1989.
Stycos, J. Mayone et al. *Community Development and Family Planning: An Egyptian Experiment*. Boulder and London: Westview Press, 1988.
Todaro, Michael P. *Economic Development*, seventh edition. Reading, Mass.: Addison-Wesley, 1999.
Tschirgi, Dan (ed.). *The Arab World Today*. Boulder and London: Lynne Rienner Publishers, 1994.
—— (ed.). *Development in the Age of Liberalization: Egypt and Mexico*. Cairo: The American University in Cairo Press, 1996.
Udovich, A. L. (ed.). *The Middle East: Oil, Conflict and Hope*. Lexington: Lexington Books, 1976.
Van Hear, Nicholas. *New Diaspora: The Mass Exodus, Dispersal, and Regrouping of Migrant Communities*. London: UCL Press, 1998.
Waterbury, John. *Egypt: Burdens of the Past – Options for the Future*. Indiana: American University Field Staff, 1978.
—— *The Egypt of Nasser and Sadat: The Political Economy of Two Regimes*. Princeton: Princeton University Press, 1983.
Wilson, Peter W. and Douglas F. Graham. *Saudi Arabia: The Coming Storm*. New York: M.E. Sharpe, 1994.
Wilson, Rodney. *The Economies of the Middle East*. London: Macmillan Press, 1979.
—— *Economic Development in the Middle East*. London and New York: Routledge, 1995.
—— et al. *Economic Development in Saudi Arabia*. London and New York, RoutledgeCurzon, 2004.
Winckler, Onn. *Population Growth and Migration in Jordan, 1950–1994*. Brighton and Portland: Sussex Academic Press, 1997.
—— *Demographic Developments and Population Policies in Ba'thist Syria*. Brighton and Portland: Sussex Academic Press, 1999.
Woodward, Peter N. *Oil and Labor in the Middle East: Saudi Arabia and the Oil Boom*. New York: Praeger, 1988.
Yamani, Mai. *Changed Identities: The Challenge of the New Generation in Saudi Arabia*. London: The Royal Institute of International Affairs, 2000.
Yousif, Hassan M., Anne Goujon and Wolfgang Lutz. *Future Population and Education Trends in the Countries of North Africa*. Luxemburg: International Institute for Applied Systems Analysis, September 1996.
Zoubir, Yahia H. (ed.). *North Africa in Transition: State, Society, and Economic Transformation in the 1990s*. Gainesville: University Press of Florida, 1999.

Articles

Arabic and Hebrew

'Amirah, Muhammad Sa'ad. "Waqi' al-Bitala fil-Urdun wa-Nazara Nahwa al-Mustaqbal." [The Unemployment Situation in Jordan and its Future Prospect]. In Mustafa al-Hamarneh (ed.), *Al-Iqtisad al-Urduni: al-Mushkilat wal-Afaq*. Amman: Markaz al-Dirasat al-Istratigiyya, 1994, pp. 206–26 (Arabic).

Ayalon, Ami. "Demographya, Politiqa, ve-Masoret be-Mitzrayim shel Mubarak" [Demography, Politics and Tradition in Mubarak's Egypt]. In Ami Ayalon and Gad G. Gilbar (eds.), *Demographya ve-Politiqa be-Medinot 'Arav*. Tel Aviv: Hakibbutz Hameuchad, 1995, pp. 29–50 (Hebrew).

Efrat, Moshe. "Tokhnit ha-'Asor ve-Totzoteha" [The Ten-Year Plan and its Consequences] in Shimon Shamir (ed.), *Yeridat ha-Nasserism, 1965–1970: Shqi'ata shel Tenu'a Meshikhit*. Tel Aviv: Mif'alim Universitayim, 1978, pp. 61–78 (Hebrew).

Gilbar, Gad G. "Mavo: Beyn Demographya ve-Politiqa ba-Mizrah ha-Tikhon" [Introduction: Between Demography and Politics in the Middle East]. In Ami Ayalon and Gad G. Gilbar (eds.), *Demographya ve-Politiqa be-Medinot 'Arav*. Tel Aviv: Hakibbutz Hameuchad, 1995, pp. 11–28 (Hebrew).

Karni, Azriel. "Temurot be-Yahas la-Piquah 'al ha-Yeluda ba-Mizrah ha-Tikhon" [Trends in Fertility Control in the Middle East]. *Hamizrah Hehadash*, Vol. 17 (1967), pp. 222–41 (Hebrew).

Maddy-Weitzman, Bruce. "Masoret, Gidul Okhlosiya ve-Tikhnun Mishpaha Be-Marocco" [Tradition, Population Growth and Family Planning in Morocco]. In Ami Ayalon and Gad G. Gilbar (eds.), *Demographya ve-Politiqa be-Medinot 'Arav*. Tel Aviv: Hakibbutz Hameuchad, 1995, pp. 51–67 (Hebrew).

Al-Ruythi, Muhammad Ahmad. "Sukan al-Mamlaka al-'Arabiyya al-Sa'udiyya." In Muhammad Ahmad al-Ruythi (ed.), *Sukan al-'Alam al-'Arabi: al-Waqi' wal-Mustaqbal*. Riyadh: Maktabat al-'Abikan, 2003, pp. 165–212 (Arabic).

"Al-Simat al-Asasiyya li-Sukan al-Kuwayt wa-Kuwwat al-'Amal fi Nihayat 1994." *Al-Iqtisadi al- Kuwayti*, No. 324 (May 1995), pp. 24–30 (Arabic).

Steinberg, Matti. "Lir'ot et ha-Nolad: ha-Gorem ha-Demography be-Re'iyat Asha"f" [To Foresee the Events: The Demographic Factor in the PLO Perception]. In Ami Ayalon and Gad G. Gilbar (eds.), *Demographya ve-Politiqa be-Medinot 'Arav*. Tel Aviv: Hakibbutz Hameuchad, 1995, pp. 153-89 (Hebrew).

Susser, Asher. "Demographya ve-Politiqa be-Yarden" [Demography and Politics in Jordan]. In Ami Ayalon and Gad G. Gilbar (eds.), *Demographya ve-Politiqa be-Medinot 'Arav*. Tel Aviv: Hakibbutz Hameuchad, 1995, pp. 131–51 (Hebrew).

—— "ha-Ahim ha-Muslemim be-Yarden: Du-Qiyum ve-'Imut Mevuqar" [The Muslim Brothers in Jordan: Coexistence and Controlled Confrontation]. In Meir Litvak (ed.), *Islam ve-Demoqratyya ba-'Olam ha-'Aravi*. Tel Aviv: Hakibbutz Hameuchad, 1997, pp. 123–46 (Hebrew).

Zahra, Muhammad. "Sukan Sultanat Uman." In Muhammad Ahmad al-Ruythi (ed.), *Sukan al-'Alam al-'Arabi: al-Waqi' wal-Mustaqbal*. Riyadh: Maktabat al-'Abikan, 2003, pp. 347–412 (Arabic).

—— "Sukan al-Imarat al-'Arabiyya al-Mutahida." In Muhammad Ahmad al-Ruythi (ed.), *Sukan al-'Alam al-'Arabi: al-Waqi' wal-Mustaqbal*. Riyadh: Maktabat al-'Abikan, 2003, pp. 53–119 (Arabic).

English and French

Aarts, Paul. "The Middle East: A Region without Regionalism or the End of Exceptionalism?" *Third Word Quarterly*, Vol. 20, No. 5 (1999), pp. 911–25.

Abbasi, Mohammad Jalal et al. "Revolution, War and Modernization: Population Policy and Fertility Change in Iran." *Journal of Population Research*, Vol. 19, No. 1 (2002), pp. 25–46.

Abbasi-Shavazi, Mohammad Jalal and Peter McDonald. "National and Provincial-Level Fertility Trends in Iran, 1972–2000." The Australian National University, *Working Paper in Demography* No. 94. February 2005.

Abdalla, A. Ikhlas, "Attitudes Towards Women in the Arabian Gulf Region." *Women in Management Review*, Vol. 11, No. 1 (1996), pp. 29–39.

Abdelkarim, Abbas. "Oil, Population Change and Social Development in the Gulf: Some Major

Trends and Indicators." In Abbas Abdelkarim (ed.), *Change and Development in the Gulf*. London: Macmillan Press, and New York: St. Martin's Press, 1999, pp. 25–48.

Abdel-Fadil, Mahmoud. "The Macro-Behaviour of Oil-Rentier States in the Arab Region." In Hazem Beblawi and Giacomo Luciani (eds.), *The Rentier State*, Vol. II. London: Croom Helm, 1987, pp. 83–107.

Abdelghany, A. M. "Evaluating the Application of the Stable Population Model of the Population of Egypt." *Population Bulletin of ECWA*, No. 21 (December 1981), pp. 105–16.

Abdel Jaber, Tayseer. "Jordanian Labor Migration: Social, Political and Economic Effects." In Mohammad Shtayyeh (ed.), *Labor Migration: Palestine, Jordan, Egypt and Israel*. Jerusalem: Palestine Center for Regional Studies, 1998, pp. 81–105.

Abdel Rahman, Mohamed. "Socio-Demographic Aspects of Child Labor in Egypt." In CDC, *Population & Sustainable Development*. Research Monograph Series, No. 5. Cairo, 1998, pp. 49–68.

Abu-Gamrah, Hamed. "Fertility Levels and Differentials by Mother's Education in some Countries of the ECWA Region." In CDC, *Determinants of Fertility in some African and Asian Countries*. Research Monograph Series, No. 10. Cairo, 1982, pp. 191–211.

Addleton, J. "The Impact of the Gulf War on Migration and Remittances in Asia and the Middle East." *International Migration*, Vol. 29, No. 4 (1991), pp. 509–26.

Allman, James. "The Demographic Transition in the Middle East and North Africa." In James Allman (ed.), *Women's Status and Fertility in the Muslim World*. New York and London: Praeger Publishers, 1978, pp. 3–32.

—— "The Demographic Transition in the Middle East and North Africa." *IJMES*, Vol. 12, No. 3 (1980), pp. 277–301.

Ayalon, Ami. "Egypt's Coptic Pandora's Box." In Ofra Bengio and Gabriel Ben-Dor (eds.), *Minorities and the State in the Arab World*. Boulder: Lynne Rienner Publishers, 1999, pp. 53–71.

Azzi, Mohamed Farid. "Maghrebi Youth: Between Alienation and Integration." In Yahia H. Zoubir (ed.), *North Africa in Transition: State, Society, and Economic Transformation in the 1990s*. Gainesville: University Press of Florida, 1999, pp. 109–26.

Baram, Amatzia. Ba'thi Iraq and Hashemite Jordan: From Hostility to Alignment." *The Middle East Journal*, Vol. 45, No. 1 (1991), pp. 51–70.

—— "The Effect of Iraqi Sanctions: Statistical Pitfalls and Responsibility." *The Middle East Journal*, Vol. 54, No. 2 (2000), pp. 194–223.

Beaujot, Roderic. "Attitudes Among Tunisians Toward Family Planning." *International Family Planning Perspectives*, Vol. 14, No. 2 (1988), pp. 54–60.

El-Beblawi, Hayam and Azza Mohamed Abedo. "Some Aspects of Child Labor in Egypt." *CDC Working Paper*, No. 41. 1999.

Beblawi, Hazem. "The Rentier State in the Arab World." In Giacomo Luciani (ed.), *The Arab State*. London: Routledge, 1990, pp. 85–98.

Bennett, Adam. "Failed Legacies." *Finance & Development*, Vol. 40, No. 1 (March 2003). Available at: http://www.imf.org/external/pubs/ft/fandd/2003/03/benn.htm.

Binder, Leonard. "Gamal 'Abd al-Nasser: Iconology, Ideology and Demonology." In Elie Podeh and Onn Winckler (eds.), *Rethinking Nasserism: Revolution and Historical Memory in Modern Egypt*. Gainesville: University Press of Florida, 2004, pp. 45–71.

Birks, J. S. "The Demographic Challenge in the Arab Gulf." In B. R. Pridham (ed.), *The Arab Gulf and the Arab World*. London: Croom Helm, 1988, pp. 131–52.

Birks, J. S., I. Seragelding, C. A. Sinclair and J. A. Socknat. "Who is Migrating Where? An Overview of International Labor Migration in the Arab World." In Alan Richards and Philip L. Martin (eds.), *Migration, Mechanization, and Agricultural Labor Markets in Egypt*. Boulder: Westview Press, 1983, pp. 103–16.

Birks, J. S., C. A. Sinclair and J. A. Socknat. "The Demand for Egyptian Labor Abroad." In Alan Richards and Philip L. Martin (eds.), *Migration, Mechanization, and Agricultural Labor Markets in Egypt*. Boulder: Westview Press, 1983, pp. 117–34.

Birks, J. S. and C. A. Sinclair. "Repatriation, Remittances and Reunions: What is Really at Stake for Arab Countries Supplying Labour to the Gulf Co-Operation Council States." In Charles E. Davies (ed.), *Global Interests in the Arab Gulf*. New York: St. Martin's Press, 1992, pp. 86–116.

Birks, J. S., I. J. Seccombe and C. A. Sinclair. "Labour Migration in the Arab Gulf States: Patterns, Trends and Prospects." *International Migration*, Vol. 26, No. 3 (1988), pp. 267-86.

Bloom, David, David Canning and Jaypee Sevilla. "Economic Growth and the Demographic Transition." NBER (National Bureau of Economic Research) Working Paper No. 8685. Cambridge, December 2001. Available at: http://www.nber.org/papers/w8685.

Bonine, Michael E. "Population Growth, the Labor Market and the Gulf Security." In David E. Long and Christian Koch (eds.), *Gulf Security in the Twenty-First Century*. Abu Dhabi: The Emirates Center for Strategic Studies and Research, 1997, pp. 226–64.

Bowman, Kirk S. and Jerrold D. Green. "Urbanization and Political Instability in the Middle East." In Michael E. Bonine (ed.), *Population, Poverty, and Politics in Middle East Cities*. Gainesville: University Press of Florida, 1997, pp. 237–55.

Brand, Laurie A. "Economic and Political Liberalization in a Rentier Economy: The Case of the Hashemite Kingdom of Jordan." In Iliya Harik and Denis J. Sullivan (eds.), *Privatization and Liberalization in the Middle East*. Bloomington, IN: Indiana University Press, 1992, pp. 167-88.

Brown, K. L. "The Campaign to Encourage Family Planning in Tunisia and some Responses at the Village Level." *Middle Eastern Studies*, Vol. 17, No. 1 (1981), pp. 64-83.

Brown, Mark. "Quantifying the Muslim Population in Europe: Conceptual and Data Issues." *International Journal of Social Research Methodology*, Vol. 3, No. 2 (2000), pp. 87–101.

Brown, Nathan B. "Nasserism's Legal Legacy." In Elie Podeh and Onn Winckler (eds.), *Rethinking Nasserism: Revolution and Historical Memory in Modern Egypt*. Gainesville: University Press of Florida, 2004, pp. 127–43.

Bruton, Henry J. "Egypt's Development in the Seventies." *Economic Development and Cultural Change*, Vol. 33, No. 4 (1983), pp. 675–704.

Buch, Claudia M. and Anja Kuckulenz. "Worker Remittances and Capital Flows to Developing Countries." Center for European Economic Research (ZEW), Discussion Paper No. 04–31. 2004. Available at: http://ftp.zew.de/pub/zew-docs/dp/dp0431.pdf.

Burguière, André. "Demography." In Jacques Le Goff and Pierre Nora (eds.), *Constructing the Past: Essays in Historical Methodology*. Cambridge: Cambridge University Press, 1985, pp. 99–122.

Caldwell, John C. "The Global Fertility Transition: The Need for a Unifying Theory." *Population and Development Review*, Vol. 23, No. 4 (1997), pp. 803–12.

—— "Malthus and the Less Developed World: The Pivotal Role of India." *Population and Development Review*, Vol. 24, No. 4 (1998), pp. 675–96.

—— "Demography: Scope, Perspectives and Theory." Available at: http://cph.georgetown.edu/Conference.

—— "Demographic Theory: A Long View." *Population and Development Review*, Vol. 30, No. 2 (2004), pp. 297–316.

—— et al. "The Bangladesh Fertility Decline: An Interpretation." *Population and Development Review*, Vol. 25, No. 1 (1999), pp. 67-84.

—, Pat Caldwell and Peter McDonald. "Policy Responses to Low Fertility and Its Consequences: A Global Survey." *Journal of Population Research*, Vol. 19, No. 1 (2002), pp. 1–24.

Cassandra. "The Impending Crisis in Egypt." *The Middle East Journal*, Vol. 49, No. 1 (1995), pp. 9–27.

Center for Policy Dialogue (CPD) Bangladesh and UNFPA. "Re-thinking Population Policy in Bangladesh." *CPD-UNFPA Paper Series* No. 24 (June 2003). Available at: http://www.cpd-bangladesh.org/publications/cpdunfpa/unfpa24.PDF.

Chamie, Joseph. "Trends, Variations, and Contradictions in National Policies to Influence Fertility." In Jason L. Finkle and C. Alison McIntosh (eds.), *The New Politics of Population: Conflict and Consensus in Family Planning*. Supplement to Vol. 20 of *Population and Development Review*. New York: The Population Council, 1994, pp. 37–50.

Champion, Daryl. "The Kingdom of Saudi Arabia: Elements of Instability within Stability." *Middle East Review of International Affairs*, Vol. 3, No. 4 (1999), pp. 1–23.

Chatty, Dawn. "Women Working in Oman: Individual Choice and Cultural Constrains." *IJMES*, Vol. 32, No. 2 (2000), pp. 241–54.

Chesnais, Jean-Claude. "Below-Replacement Fertility in the European Union (EU–15): Facts and Policies, 1960–1997." *Review of Population and Social Policy*, No. 7 (1998), pp. 83–101.

Choucri, Nazli. "The Hidden Economy: A New View of Remittances in the Arab World." *World Development*, Vol. 14, No. 6 (1986), pp. 697–712.

—— "Asians in the Arab World: Labor Migration and Public Policy." *Middle Eastern Studies*, Vol. 22, No. 2 (1986), pp. 252–73.

—— "Migration in the Middle East: Old Economics Or New Politics?" *Journal of Arab Affairs*, Vol. 7, No. 1 (1988), pp. 1–15.

Cleland, John. "Marital Fertility Decline in Developing Countries: Theories and the Evidence." In John Cleland and John Hobcraft (eds.), *Reproductive Change in Developing Countries*. Oxford: Oxford University Press, 1985, pp. 223–52.

Cochrane, Susan H. and David K. Guilkey. "The Effects of Fertility Intensions and Access to Services on Contraceptive Use in Tunisia." *Economic Development and Cultural Change*, Vol. 43, No. 4 (1995), pp. 779-804.

Colton, Nora Ann. "The Maghrebi Economies as Emerging Markets?" In Yahia H. Zoubir (ed.), *North Africa in Transition: State, Society, and Economic Transformation in the 1990s*. Gainesville: University Press of Florida, 1999, pp. 159–76.

Courbage, Youssef. "Fertility Transition in Syria: From Implicit Population Policy to Explicit Economic Crisis." *International Family Planning Perspectives*, Vol. 20, No. 4 (1994), pp. 142–46.

—— "Issues in Fertility Transition in the Middle East and North Africa." *Economic Research Forum*, Working Paper No. 9903. Cairo, 1999. Available at: http://www.erf.org.eg/uploadpath/pdf/9903.pdf.

—— "Economic and Political Issues of Fertility Transition in the Arab World: Answers and Open Questions." *Population and Environment*, Vol. 20, No. 4 (1999), pp. 353-80.

Demeny, Paul. "Pronatalist Policies in Low-Fertility Countries: Patterns, Performance, and Prospects." *Population and Development Review*, Supplement to Vol. 12 (1986), pp. 335–58.

—— "Population Policy Dilemmas in Europe at the Dawn of the Twenty-First Century." *Population and Development Review*, Vol. 29, No. 1 (2003), pp. 1–28.

—— "Population Policy: A Concise Summary." The Population Council, Policy Research Division, Working Paper No. 173. New York, 2003.

Dessouki, Ali E. Hillal. "The Shift in Egypt's Migration Policy: 1952–1978." *Middle Eastern Studies*, Vol. 18, No. 1 (1982), pp. 53–68.

Dibbs, Mohamed Chafic. "The Relationship Between Censuses and Civil Registration in the Syrian Arab Republic." *Population Bulletin of ECWA*, No. 18 (June 1980), pp. 81–101.

Diwan, Ishac and Maurice Girgis. "Labor Force and Development in Saudi Arabia." Paper presented at the symposium *Future Vision for the Saudi Economy*. Riyadh, September 2002.

Donaldson, Peter J. and Amy Ong Tsui. "The International Family Planning Movement." *Population Bulletin*, Vol. 45, No. 3 (1990), pp. 1–44.

Doumato, Eleanor Abdella. "Women and Work in Saudi Arabia: How Flexible are Islamic Margins?" *The Middle East Journal*, Vol. 53, No. 4 (1999), pp. 568-83.

Durand, John. "Historical Estimates of World Population: An Evaluation." *Population and Development Review*, Vol. 3, No. 3 (1977), pp. 253–96.

Ehteshami, Anoushiravan and Steven Wright. "Political Change in the Arab Oil Monarchies:

From Liberalization to Enfranchisement." *International Affairs*, Vol. 83, No. 5 (2007), pp. 913–32.
Eickelman, Christine. "Fertility and Social Change in Oman: Women's Perspectives." *The Middle East Journal*, Vol. 47, No. 4 (1993), pp. 652–66.
Endo, Masao. "Saudization: Development in the Early 1990s and Prospects for the Rest of the Decade." *JIME REVIEW* (Winter 1996), pp. 75–92.
"L'Explosion Démographique en Syrie." *Syrie & Monde Arabe*, Vol. 12, No. 253 (1975), pp. 4–11.
Faksh, Mahmud A. "The Alawi Community of Syria: A New Dominant Political Force." *Middle Eastern Studies*, Vol. 20, No. 2 (1984), pp. 133–53.
Faour, Muhammad. "Fertility Policy and Family Planning in the Arab Countries. *Studies in Family Planning*, Vol. 20, No. 5 (1989), pp. 254–63.
—— "The Demography of Lebanon: A Reappraisal." *Middle Eastern Studies*, Vol. 27, No. 4 (1991), pp. 631–41.
Farag, Mahmoud. "Differences in Age at Marriage in Syria." In S. H. Huzayyin and G. T. Acsadi (eds.), *Family and Marriage in some African and Asiatic Countries*, Research Monograph Series, No. 6. Cairo: CDC, 1976, pp. 493–504.
Fargues, Philippe. "Demography and Politics in the Arab World." *Population: An English Selection*, Vol. 5 (1993), pp. 1–20.
—— "Demographic Explosion or Social Upheaval?" In Ghassan Salamé (ed.), *Democracy Without Democrats? The Renewal of Politics in the Muslim World*. London and New York: I.B. Tauris, 1994, pp. 156–79.
—— "State Policies and the Birth Rate in Egypt: From Socialism to Liberalism." *Population and Development Review*, Vol. 23, No. 1 (1997), pp. 115–38.
—— "Protracted National Conflict and Fertility Change: Palestinians and Israelis in the Twentieth Century." *Population and Development Review*, Vol. 26, No. 3 (2000), pp. 441-82.
—— "Demographic Islamization: Non-Muslims in Muslim Countries." *SAIS Review*, Vol. 21, No. 2 (2001), pp. 103–16.
—— "International Migration in the Arab Region: Trends and Policies." Paper presented at the *UN Expert Group Meeting on International Migration and Development in the Arab Region*. Beirut, May 15–17, 2006. Available at: http://www.un.org/esa/population/migration/turin/Symposium.
Farid, Samir. "Fertility Patterns in the Arab Region." *International Family Planning Perspectives*, Vol. 10, No. 4 (1984), pp. 119–24.
Faus-Pujol, Maria Carmen. "Changes in the Fertility Rate and Age Structure of the Population of Europe." In Ray Hall and Paul White (eds.), *Europe's Population: Ttowards the Next Century*. London: UCL Press, 1995, pp. 17–33.
Feiler, Gil. "The Number of Egyptian Workers in the Arab Oil Countries, 1974–1983: A Critical Discussion." *Occasional Papers*. Tel Aviv University, The Moshe Dayan Center, October 1986.
—— "Scope and Some Effects of Remittances of Egyptian Migrant Workers in the Arab Oil-Producing Countries, 1973–1984." *Asian and African Studies*, Vol. 21 (1987), pp. 305–25.
—— "Migration and Recession: Arab Labor Mobility in the Middle East, 1982–1989." *Population and Development Review*, Vol. 17, No. 1 (1991), pp. 134–55.
Fergany, Nader. "Manpower Problems and Projections in the Gulf." In M. S. El-Azhary (ed.), *The Impact of Oil Revenues on Arab Gulf Development*. London: Croom Helm, and Boulder: Westview Press, 1984, pp. 155–69.
Findlay, Allan M. "Return to Yemen: The End of the Old Migration Order in the Arab World." In W. T. S. Gould and A. M. Findlay (eds.), *Population Migration and the Changing World Order*. Chichester: John Wiley & Sons, 1994, pp. 205–23.
Finkle, Jason L. and Barbara B. Crane. "Ideology and Politics at Mexico City: The United States at the 1984 International Conference on Population." *Population and Development Review*, Vol. 11, No. 1 (1985), pp. 1–28.

Finkle, Jason L. and C. Alison McIntosh. "The New Politics of Population." In Jason L. Finkle and C. Alison McIntosh (eds.), *The New Politics of Population: Conflict and Consensus in Family Planning*. Supplement to Vol. 20 of *Population and Development Review*. New York: The Population Council, 1994, pp. 3–34.

Fisher, W. B. "Jordan: A Demographic Shatter-Belt." In J. I. Clarke and W. B. Fisher (eds.), *Populations of the Middle East and North Africa: A Geographical Approach*. London: University of London Press, 1972, pp. 202–19.

Franklin, Rob. "Migrant Labor and the Politics of Development in Bahrain." *MERIP Reports*, Vol. 15, No. 4 (May 1985), pp. 7–13, 32.

Freedman, Ronald. "Family Planning Programs in the Third World." *The Annals of the American Academy*, No. 510 (July 1990), pp. 33–43.

—— and Bernard Berelson. "The Record of Family Planning Programs." *Studies in Family Planning*, Vol. 7, No. 1 (1976), pp. 1–40.

Friedlander, Dov, Barbara S. Okun and Sharon Segal. "The Demographic Transition Then and Now: Process, Perspectives, and Analyses." *Journal of Family History*, Vol. 24, No. 4 (1999), pp. 493–533.

Gallagher, Charles F. "Population and Development in Egypt, Part I: Birth and Death on the Nile." *American University Field Staff Report*, No. 31 (1981).

Gardner, Edward. "Wanted: More Jobs." *Finance & Development*, Vol. 40, No. 1 (March 2003). Available at: http://www.imf.org/external/pubs/ft/fandd/2003/03/gard.htm.

Gebriel, Adil Osman. "Overview of Major Issues in the Development of National Human Resources in the Gulf." In Abbas Abdelkarim (ed.), *Change and Development in the Gulf*. London: Macmillan Press, and New York: St. Martin's Press, 1999, pp. 151–63.

Gerber, Haim. "The Population of Syria and Palestine in the Nineteenth Century." *Asian and African Studies*, Vol. 13, No. 1 (1979), pp. 58-80.

Ghita, Naguib. "A Seminar on the Preliminary Results of the 1996 Census on Population, Housing and Establishments in the Light of the National Population Strategy." *Population Studies*, Vol. 16, No. 81 (January–March 1998), pp. 99–109.

El-Ghonemy, M. Riad. "An Assessment of Egypt's Development Strategy, 1952–1970." In Elie Podeh and Onn Winckler (eds.), *Rethinking Nasserism: Revolution and Historical Memory in Modern Egypt*. Gainesville: University Press of Florida, 2004, pp. 253–63.

Gilbar, Gad G. "Family Planning Under Mubarak." In his *Population Dilemmas in the Middle East*. London and Portland: Frank Cass, 1997, pp. 113–36.

—— "Jordan's Road to Family Planning Policy." In his *Population Dilemmas in the Middle East*. London and Portland: Frank Cass, 1997, pp. 67–79.

—— "Nasser's Soft Revolution." In his *Population Dilemmas in the Middle East*. London and Portland: Frank Cass, 1997, pp. 80–96.

—— and Onn Winckler. "Nasser's Family Planning Policy in Perspective." In Elie Podeh and Onn Winckler (eds.), *Rethinking Nasserism: Revolution and Historical Memory in Modern Egypt*. Gainesville: University Press of Florida, 2004, pp. 282–304.

—— "The Economic Factor of the Arab–Israeli Peace Process: The Cases of Egypt, Jordan and Syria." In Elie Podeh and Asher Kaufman (eds.), *Arab–Jewish Relations: From Conflict to Reconciliation?* Brighton and Portland: Sussex Academic Press, 2006, pp. 190–209.

Girgis, Maurice. "National Versus Migrant Workers in the GCC: Coping with Change." In Heba Handoussa and Zafiris Tzannatos (eds.), *Employment Creation and Social Protection in the Middle East and North Africa*. Cairo: The American University in Cairo Press, 2002, pp. 95–120.

Glass, D. V. "John Graunt and His Natural and Political Observations." *Proceedings of the Royal Society of London*, Vol. 159, No. 974 (1963), pp. 2–37.

Goldstein, Joshua, Wolfgang Lutz and Maria Rita Testa. "The Emergence of Sub-Replacement Family Size Ideals in Europe." *Population Research and Policy Review*, Vol. 22, Nos. 5–6 (2003), pp. 479–96.

Good, Dorothy. "Notes on the Demography of Algeria." *Population Index*, Vol. 27, No. 1 (January, 1961), pp. 3–32.

Goujon, Anne Valia. "Population and Education Prospects in the Arab Region." In Ismail Sirageldin (ed.), *Human Capital: Population Economics in the Middle East*. Cairo: The American University in Cairo Press, 2002, pp. 116–40.

Gray, Matthew. "The Political Economy of Tourism in North Africa: Comparative Perspectives." *Thunderbird International Business Review*, Vol. 42, No. 4 (2000), pp. 393–408.

Grenham, Dermot. "Demography: The Effects of Changing Population Profiles." Paper presented to *the Staple Inn Actuarial Society*, January 24, 1995. Available at: http://www.actuaries.org.uk/files/pdf.

Grosse, Scott D. "The Politics of Family Planning in the Maghrib." *Studies in Comparative International Development*, Vol. 17, No. 1 (1982), pp. 22–48.

Gwartney, James, Robert Lawson and Ralph Holcombe. "Economic Freedom and the Environment for Economic Growth." *Journal of Institutional and Theoretical Economics*, Vol. 155, No. 4 (1999), pp. 643–63.

Halliday, Fred. "Labor Migration in the Arab World." *Merip Reports* (May 1984), pp. 3–10.

Hamed, Osama. "Egypt's Open Door Economic Policy: An Attempt at Economic Integration in the Middle East." *IJMES*, Vol. 13, No. 2 (1981), pp. 1–9.

Harbison, Sarah F. and Warren C. Robinson. "Policy Implications of the Next World Demographic Transition." *Studies in Family Planning*, Vol. 33, No. 1 (2002), pp. 37–48.

Harik, Iliya. "Privatization: The Issue, the Prospects and the Fears." In Iliya Harik and Denis J. Sullivan (eds.), *Privatization and Liberalization in the Middle East*. Bloomington, IN: Indiana University Press, 1992, pp. 1–23.

Hassanin, Mahasen Mostafa, Amany Mousa Mohamed and Galaa Helmy Selem. "Estimating Family Planning Target Population of Egypt in 1997." In *CDC 24th Annual Seminar on Population Issues and the Challenges of the 21st Century in the Middle East, Africa and Asia*. Research Monograph Series, No. 24. Cairo, 1995, pp. 440–55.

Heeren, Henk. J. "Pronatalist Population Policies in some Western European Countries." *Population Research and Policy Review*, Vol. 1, No. 2 (1982), pp. 137–52.

Henry, Clement. "A Clash of Globalization: Obstacles to Development in the Middle East." *Harvard International Review*, Vol. 25, No. 1 (2003), p. 3. Available at: http://hir.harvard.edu/articles/1101.

Hertog, Steffen. "Segmented Clientelism: The Political Economy of Saudi Economic Reform Efforts." In Paul Aarts and Gred Nonneman (eds.), *Saudi Arabia in the Balance*. London: Hurst & Company, 2005, pp. 111–43.

Heydemann, Steven. "Taxation without Representation: Authoritarianism and Economic Liberalization in Syria." In Ellis Goldberg, Reşat Kasaba and Joel Migdal (eds.), *Rules and Rights in the Middle East: Democracy, Law, and Society*. Seattle and London: University of Washington Press, 1993, pp. 69–101.

Hill, Allan G. "The Gulf States: Petroleum and Population Growth." In J. I. Clarke and W. B. Fiecher (eds.), *Populations of the Middle East and North Africa: A Geographical Approach*. London: University of London Press, 1972, pp. 242–73.

—— "The Demography of the Kuwaiti Population of Kuwait." *Demography*, Vol. 12, No. 3 (1975), pp. 37–48.

—— "Population Growth in the Middle East and North Africa: Selected Policy Issues." In A. L. Udovich (ed.), *The Middle East: Oil, Conflict and Hope*. Lexington: Lexington Books, 1976, pp. 7–57.

—— "Population Growth in the Middle East since 1945 with Special Reference to the Arab Countries of West Asia." In John I. Clarke and Howard Bowen-Jones (eds.), *Change and Development in the Middle East*. London and New York: Methuen, 1981, pp. 130–53.

Hinnebusch, Raymond A. "Syria." In Tim Niblock and Emma Merphy (eds.), *Economic and Political Liberalization in the Middle East*. London and New York: British Academic Press, 1993, pp. 177–202.

Hobcraft, John. "Fertility in England and Wales: A Fifty-Year Perspective." *Population Studies*, Vol. 50, No. 3 (1996), pp. 485–524.

Hoodfar, Homa and Samad Assadpour. "The Politics of Population Policy in the Islamic Republic of Iran." *Studies in Family Planning*, Vol. 31, No. 1 (2000), pp. 19–34.

Ibrahim, Saad Eddin. "Oil, Migration and the New Arab Social Order." In Malcolm H. Kerr and El Sayed Yassin (eds.), *Rich and Poor States in the Middle East: Egypt and the New Arab Order*. Boulder: Westview Press and Cairo: The American University in Cairo Press, 1982, pp. 17–70.

—— "State, Women, and Civil Society: An Evaluation of Egypt's Population Policy." In Carla Makhlouf Obermeyer (ed.), *Family, Gender, and Population in the Middle East*. Cairo: The American University in Cairo Press, 1995, pp. 57–79.

Al-Imadi, Mohammed. "The Economic and Investment Policies in Syria." In Hans Hopfinger and Raslan Khadour (eds.), *Economic Development and Investment Policies in Syria*. Neustadt an der Aisch: Verlagsdrucherei Schmidt, 1998, pp. 3–33.

International Crisis Group. "The Shi'ite Question in Saudi Arabia." *Middle East Report*, No. 45 (September 19, 2005). Available at: http://merln.ndu.edu/archive/icg/shiitequestion.pdf.

International Planned Parenthood Federation (IPPF)-Middle East and North Africa Region. "Family Planning and Population Policies in the Middle East and North Africa." In James Allman (ed.), *Women's Status and Fertility in the Muslim World*. New York and London: Praeger, 1978, pp. 33–53.

Ismael, Jacqueline and Tareq Y. Ismael. "Social Policy in the Arab World." *Cairo Papers in Social Science*, Vol. 18, Monograph 1 (1995).

Kanovsky, Eliyahu. "What's Behind Syria's Current Economic Problems?" *Occasional Papers*. The Moshe Dayan Center, Tel Aviv University, May 1985.

—— "Jordan's Economy: From Prosperity to Crisis." *Occasional Papers* No. 106. The Moshe Dayan Center, Tel Aviv University, May 1989.

—— "Middle East Economies and Arab–Israeli Peace Agreements." *Israel Affairs*, Vol. 1, No. 4 (1995), pp. 22–39.

Kapiszewski, Andrzej. "Arab Labor Migration to the GCC Countries." In IOM and League of Arab States. *Arab Migration in a Globalized World*. Cairo, May 2004, pp. 115–33.

—— "Elections and Parliamentary Activity in the GCC States: Broadening Political Participation in the Gulf Monarchies since the 1990s." Paper presented at the *Sixth Mediterranean Social and Political Research Meeting*, Montecatini, March 16–20, 2005.

—— "Business Versus Politics: Local Versus Foreign Workforce in the GCC States." Paper presented at the conference *Transnational Migration: Foreign Labor and its Impact in the Gulf*. Bellagio, Italy, June 20–24, 2005.

Karpat, Kemal H. "Ottoman Population Records and the Census of 1881/82–1893." *IJMES*, Vol. 9, No. 3 (1978), pp. 237–74.

Kashef, A. S. M. "Egypt." In John Dixon (ed.), *Social Welfare in the Middle East*. London: Croom Helm, 1987, pp. 1–31.

Kay, Shirley. "Social Change in Modern Saudi Arabia." In Tim Niblock (ed.), *State, Society and Economy in Saudi Arabia*. London: Croom Helm, 1982, pp. 171-85.

Keilany, Ziad. "Socialism and Economic Change in Syria." *Middle Eastern Studies*, Vol. 9, No. 1 (1973), pp. 61–72.

Khalaf, Abdulhadi. "What the Gulf Ruling Families Do when They Rule." *Orient*, Vol. 44, No. 4 (2003), pp. 537–54.

Khalaf, Sulayman and Saad al-Kobaisi. "Migrants' Strategies of Coping and Patterns of Accommodation in the Oil-Rich Gulf Societies: Evidence from the UAE." *British Journal of Middle Eastern Studies*, Vol. 26, No. 2 (1999), pp. 271–98.

Khalifa, Mona A. "Family Planning and Sustainable Development in Egypt." *CDC Series on Population and Development*, No. 5. Cairo, 1994.

Khawaja, Marwan. "The Recent Rise in Palestinian Fertility: Permanent or Transient?" *Population Studies*, Vol. 54 (2000), pp. 331–46.

—— "The Fertility of Palestinian Women in Gaza, the West Bank, Jordan and Lebanon." *Population* (English Edition), Vol. 58, No. 3 (2003), pp. 273–302.

Khoury, Nabeel A. "The Politics of Intra-Regional Migration in the Arab World." *Journal of South Asian and Middle Eastern Studies*, Vol. 11, No. 2 (1982), pp. 3–20.

Khraif, Rshood M. "Fertility in Saudi Arabia: Levels and Determinants." Paper presented at *XXIV General Population Conference*, Salvador, Brazil, August 18–24, 2001. Available at: http://www.iussp.org/Brazil2001/s60/S62_03_khraif.pdf.

King, Leslie. "France Needs Children: Pronatalism, Nationalism and Women's Equity." *The Sociological Quarterly*, Vol. 39, No. 1 (1998), pp. 33–52.

Kirk, Dudley. "Demographic Transition Theory." *Population Studies*, Vol. 50, No. 3 (1996), pp. 361-87.

Kohli, K. L. and Musa'ad al-Omaim. "Mortality Levels, Trends and Differentials in Kuwait, 1957–1983." *Population Bulletin of ESCWA*, No. 28 (June 1986), pp. 91–123.

—— "Changing Patterns of Migration in Kuwait." *Population Bulletin of ESCWA*, No. 32 (June 1988), pp. 75–94.

Krause, Elizabeth L. "Forward vs. Reverse Gear: The Politics of Proliferation and Resistance in the Italian Fascist State." *Journal of Historical Sociology*, Vol. 7, No. 3 (1994), pp. 261-88.

Kupferschmidt, Uri M. "A Note on the Muslim Religions Hierarchy towards the End of the Ottoman Period." In David Kushner (ed.), *Palestine in the Late Ottoman Period*. Jerusalem: Yad Yizhak Ben-Zvi Press, 1986, pp. 123–29.

—— "Nasserist and Post-Nasserist Elites in an Official Biographical Lexicon." In Elie Podeh and Onn Winckler (eds.), *Rethinking Nasserism: Revolution and Historical Memory in Modern Egypt*. Gainesville: University Press of Florida, 2004, pp. 163–76.

Kuran, Timur. "Why the Middle East Is Economically Underdeveloped: Historical Mechanisms of International Stagnation." Paper presented at the conference *Institutional Barriers to Economic Change: Cases Considered*, George Mason University, June 24, 2003. Available at: http://www.international.ucla.edu/cms/files/kuran.0130.pdf.

Laipson, Ellen. "The Middle East's Demographic Transition: What Does It Mean?" *Journal of International Affairs*, Vol. 56, No. 1 (2002), pp. 175-88.

Lapham, Robert J. "Population Policies in the Middle East and North Africa." *Middle East Studies Association Bulletin*, Vol. 11, No. 2 (May 1, 1977), pp. 1–30.

—— and W. Parker Mauldin. "Family Planning Program Effort and Birthrate Decline in Developing Countries." *International Family Planning Perspectives*, Vol. 10, No. 4 (1984), pp. 109–18.

Lee, Kelley and Gill Walt. "Linking National and Global Population Agendas: Case Studies From Eight Developing Countries." *Third World Quarterly*, Vol. 16, No. 2 (1995), pp. 257–72.

Leete, Richard and Iqbal Alam. "Asia's Demographic Miracle: 50 Years of Unprecedented Change." *Asia-Pacific Population Journal*, Vol. 14 No. 4 (1999), pp. 9–20.

Lesch, Ann M. "Egyptian Labor Migration." In Ibrahim M. Oweiss (ed.), *The Political Economy of Contemporary Egypt*. Washington, D.C.: Center for Contemporary Arab Studies, Georgetown University, 1990, pp. 90–108.

Lesch, David W. "History and Political Culture in Syria: Obstacles to Integration in the Global Economy After the Gulf War." In Moshe Ma'oz, Joseph Ginat and Onn Winckler (eds.), *Modern Syria: From Ottoman Rule to Pivotal Role in the Middle East*. Brighton and Portland: Sussex Academic Press, 1999, pp. 57–78.

Letablier, Marie-Thérèse. "Fertility and Family Policies in France." *Journal of Population and Social Security*, supplement to Vol. 1 (2003), pp. 245–61.

Looney, Robert E. "Patterns of Remittances and Labor Migration in the Arab World." *International Migration*, Vol. 24, No. 4 (1989), pp. 563-80.

—— "Structural Change in the Arabian Gulf: Impact of the Foreign Workforce." *Population Bulletin of ESCWA*, Vols. 35–37 (December 1989-December 1990), pp. 129–59.

—— "Saudization and Sound Economic Reforms: Are the Two Compatible?" *Strategic*

Insights, Volume III, Issue 2 (February 2004). Available at: http://www.ccc.nps.navy .mil/si/2005.

Lorimer, Frank. "The Development of Demography." In Philip M. Hauser and Otis Dudley Duncan (eds.), *The Study of Population*. Chicago and London: The University of Chicago Press, 1959, pp. 124-79.

Luciani, Giacomo. "Allocation vs. Production States: A Theoretical Framework." In Giacomo Luciani (ed.), *The Arab State*. London: Routledge, 1990, pp. 65-84.

Lush, Louisiana et al. "Politics and Fertility: A New Approach to Population Policy Analysis." *Population Research and Policy Review*, Vol. 19, No. 1 (2000), pp. 1–28.

Lutz, Wolfgang. "The Future of World Population." *Population Bulletin*, Vol. 49, No. 1 (June 1994).

——, Brian C. O'Neill and Sergei Scherbov. "Europe's Population at a Turning Point." *Science*, Vol. 299 (March 2003), pp. 1991–92.

——, Vegard Skirbekk and Maria Rita Testa. "The Low Fertility Trap Hypothesis: Forces that May Lead to Further Postponement and Fewer Births in Europe." In Dimiter Philipov et al. (eds.), *Vienna Yearbook of Population Research–2006*. Vienna: Vienna Institute of Demography, 2006), pp. 167–92.

Maddy-Weitzman, Bruce. "The Berber Question in Algeria: Nationalism in the Making?" In Ofra Bengio and Gabriel Ben-Dor (eds.), *Minorities and the State in the Arab World*. Boulder: Lynne Rienner Publishers, 1999, pp. 31–52.

Mahdi, Saleh T. and Armando Barrientos. "Saudisation and Employment in Saudi Arabia." *Career Development International*, Vol. 8, No. 2 (2003), pp. 70–77.

Malecki, Edward J. and Michael C. Ewers. "Labor Migration to World Cities: With a Research Agenda for the Arab Gulf." *Progress in Human Geography*, Vol. 31, No. 4 (2007), pp. 467-84.

Malik, Monica and Tim Niblock. "Saudi Arabia's Economy: the Challenge of Reform." In Paul Aarts and Gred Nonneman (eds.), *Saudi Arabia in the Balance*. London: Hurst & Company, 2005, pp. 85–110.

Maneschi, Andrea. "Ricardo's International Trade Theory: Beyond the Comparative Cost Example." *Cambridge Journal of Economics*, Vol. 16 (1992), pp. 421–37.

Mansfeld, Yoel and Onn Winckler. "Options for Viable Economic Development through Tourism among the Non-Oil Arab Countries: The Egyptian Case." *Tourism Economics*, Vol. 10, No. 4 (2004), pp. 365- 88.

——, "The Tourism Industry as an Alternative for the GCC Oil-Based *Rentier* Economy," *Tourism Economics*, Vol. 13, No. 3 (2007), pp. 333–60.

——, "The Role of the Tourism Industry in Transforming a *Rentier* to a Long-Term Viable Economy: The Case of Bahrain." *Current Issues in Tourism*, Vol. 11, No. 3 (2008), pp.237–67.

Marwan, Kamel Mohamed. "Population Strategy, 1992/2007." *Population Studies*, Vol. 14, No. 75 (July–September 1992), pp. 113–15.

Massey, Douglas S. et al. "An Evaluation of International Migration Theory: The North American Case." *Population and Development Review*, Vol. 20, No. 4 (1994), p. 699–751.

Mazur, Laurie Ann. "Beyond the Numbers: An Introduction and Overview." In Laurie Ann Mazur (ed.), *Beyond the Numbers: A Reader on Population, Consumption, and Environment*. Washington, D.C.: Island Press, 1994, pp. 1–20.

McCarthy, Justin A. "Nineteenth Century Egyptian Population." *Middle Eastern Studies*, Vol. 12, No. 3 (1976), pp. 1–39.

McDonald, Peter. "Low Fertility in Australia: Evidence, Causes and Policy Responses." *People and Place*, Vol. 8, No. 2 (2000), pp. 6–21.

McGregor, R. "Saudi Arabia: Population and the Making of a Modern State." In J. I. Clarke and W. B. Fisher (eds.), *Populations of the Middle East and North Africa: A Geographical Approach*. London: University of London Press, 1972, pp. 220–41.

McIntosh, Alison and Jason L. Finkle. "The Cairo Conference on Population and

Development: A New Paradigm?" *Population and Development Review*, Vol. 21, No. 2 (1995), pp. 223–60.

Merlo, Rosangela and Don Rowland. "The Prevalence of Childlessness in Australia." *People and Place*, Vol. 8, No. 2 (2000), pp. 21–32.

Messiha, S. A. "The Export of Egyptian School Teachers." *Cairo Papers in Social Science*, Vol. 3, No. 4 (1983).

Mossavar-Rahmani, Yasmin L. "Family Planning in Post-Revolutionary Iran." In Guity Nashat (ed.), *Women and Revolution in Iran*. Boulder: Westview Press, 1983, pp. 253–62.

Nagi, Mustafa H. "Labor Immigration and Development in the Middle East: Patterns, Problems, and Policies." *International Review of Modern Sociology*, Vol. 12, No. 2 (1982), pp. 185–40.

Al-Najjar, Baquer Salman. "Population Policies in the Countries of the Gulf Co-operation Council: Politics and Society." *Immigrants & Minorities*, Vol. 12, No. 2 (1993), pp. 200–18.

—— "Population Policies in the Countries of the Gulf Cooperation Council." In Abbas Abdelkarim (ed.), *Change and Development in the Gulf*. London: Macmillan Press, and New York: St. Martin's Press, 1999, pp. 133–50.

Nakhleh, Emile A. "Labor Markets and Citizenship in Bahrayn and Qatar." *The Middle East Journal*, Vol. 31, No. 2 (1977), pp. 143–56.

Nonneman, Gred. "Rentiers and Autocrats, Monarchs and Democrats, State and Society: The Middle East Between Globalization, Human 'Agency,' and Europe." *International Affairs*, Vol. 77, No. 1 (2001), pp. 141–62.

Nosseir, Nazek. "Egypt: Population, Urbanization, and Development." In Dan Tschirgi (ed.), *Development in the Age of Liberalization: Egypt and Mexico*. Cairo: The American University in Cairo Press, 1996, pp. 187–197.

Notestein, Frank W. "Population–The Long View." In Theodore W. Schultz (ed.), *Food for the World*. Chicago: University of Chicago Press, 1945, pp. 36–57.

Obermeyer, Carla Makhlouf. "Islam, Women and Politics: The Demography of Arab Countries." *Population and Development Review*, Vol. 18, No. 1 (1992), pp. 33–60.

Olmsted, Jennifer. "Reexamining the Fertility Puzzle in MENA." In Eleanor Abdella Doumato and Marsha Pripstein Posusney (eds.), *Women and Globalization in the Arab Middle East: Gender, Economy & Society*. Boulder and London: Lynne Rienner Publishers, 2003, pp. 73–92.

Omran, Abdel Rahim and Farzaneh Roudi. "The Middle East Population Puzzle." *Population Bulletin*, Vol. 48, No. 1 (1993), pp. 1–40.

Ostner, Ilona, Michael Reif and Hannu Turba. "Family Policies in Germany." Third report for the project: *Welfare Policies and Employment in the Context of Family Change* (October 2003). Available at: http://www.york.ac.uk/inst/spru/research/nordic/gerpoli.PDF.

Oweiss, Ibrahim M. "Migration of Egyptians." *L'Égypte Contemporaine*, No. 381 (July 1980), pp. 5–16.

Palen, John J. "Population Policy: Singapore." In Godfrey Roberts (ed.), *Population Policy: Contemporary Issues*. New York: Praeger, 1990, pp. 167–78.

Panzac, Daniel. "The Population of Egypt in the Nineteenth Century." *Asian and African Studies*, Vol. 21, No. 1 (1987), pp. 11–32.

Patterson, John G. and Nanda R. Shrestha. "Population Growth and Development in the Third World: The Neocolonial Context." *Studies in Comparative International Development*, Vol. 23, No. 2 (1988), pp. 3–32.

Perthes, Volker. "The Syrian Economy in the 1980s." *The Middle East Journal*, Vol. 46, No. 1 (1992), pp. 37–58.

Podeh, Eile and Onn Winckler. "The Boycott that Never Was: Egypt and the Arab System, 1979–1989." *Durham Middle East Papers*, No. 72 (December 2002).

—— "Introduction: Nasserism as a Form of Populism." In Elie Podeh and Onn Winckler (eds.), *Rethinking Nasserism: Revolution and Historical Memory in Modern Egypt*. Gainesville: University Press of Florida, 2004, pp. 1–42.

Poirier, Robert A. "Tourism and Development in Tunisia." *Annals of Tourism Research*, Vol. 22, No. 1 (1995), pp. 157–71.

Pollock, Stephen. "Fertility, Mortality and Disease." *Interdisciplinary Science Reviews*, Vol. 31, No. 1 (2006), pp. 9–18.

Popescu, Raluca. "Fertility and Social Policies in Europe." Paper presented at the conference *European Integration Process from East to East: Civil Society and Ethnic Minorities in a Changing World*. Sibiu, Romania, December 2004. Available at: http://www.iccv.ro/Nyess/Papers_Sibiu_2004/05.

Pritchett, Lant H. "Desired Fertility and the Impact of Population Policies." *Population and Development Review*, Vol. 20, No. 1 (1994), pp. 1–55.

Al-Qudsi, Suliman S. "Labour Participation of Arab Women: Estimates of the Fertility to Labour Supply Link." *Applied Economics*, Vol. 30, No. 7 (1998), pp. 931–41.

Quibria, M. G. "Migrant Workers and Remittances: Issues for Asian Developing Countries." *Asian Development Review*, Vol. 4, No. 1 (1986), pp. 78–99.

Rabi, Uzi and Joseph Kostiner. "The Shi'is in Bahrain: Class and Religious Protest." In Ofra Bengio and Gabriel Ben-Dor (eds.), *Minorities and the State in the Arab World*. Boulder: Lynne Rienner Publishers, 1999, pp. 171-88.

Al-Ramadhan, Muhammad Ali. "New Population Policy in Kuwait: The Quest for a Balance in the Population Composition." *Population Bulletin of ESCWA*, No. 43 (1995), pp. 29–53.

Richards, Alan. "Oil Wealth in the Arab World: Whence, to Whom, and Whither?" In Dan Tschirgi (ed.), *The Arab World Today*. Boulder and London: Lynne Rienner Publishers, 1994, pp. 67–76.

—— "The Political Economy of Economic Reform in the Middle East: The Challenge to Governance." Prepared for the RAND Project: *The Future of Middle East Security*–2001. Available at: http://sccie.ucsc.edu/documents/working_papers/2001/challenge_econreform.pdf.

—— and Philip L. Martin. "The Laissez-Faire Approach to International Labor Migration." *Economic Development and Cultural Change*, Vol. 31, No. 3 (1983), pp. 451–74.

Rivlin, Paul. "The Syrian Economy in the 1990s." *Data and Analysis*. Tel Aviv University, The Moshe Dayan Center, June 1999.

—— "Nasser's Egypt and Park's Korea: A Comparison of their Economic Achievements." In Elie Podeh and Onn Winckler (eds.), *Rethinking Nasserism: Revolution and Historical Memory in Modern Egypt*. Gainesville: University Press of Florida, 2004, pp. 264-81.

Rizk, Hanna. "Population Policies: Scope, Goals, Means, and Problems." *Population Bulletin of ECWA*, No. 7 (July 1974), pp. 132–55.

—— "Trends in Fertility and Family Planning in Jordan." *Studies in Family Planning*, Vol. 8, No. 4 (1977), pp. 91–99.

Roberts, Godfrey. "Population Policy Issues in Selected Asian Countries." In Godfrey Roberts (ed.), *Population Policy: Contemporary Issues*. New York: Praeger, 1990, pp. 85–97.

Rodrik, Dani. "Getting Interventions Right: How South Korea and Taiwan Grew Rich." *Economic Policy*, Vol. 10, No. 2 (1995), pp. 55–107.

Ross, Michael L. "Does Oil Hinder Democracy?" *World Politics*, Vol. 53, No. 3 (2001), pp. 325–61.

Roudi, Farzaneh (Nazi). "Fertility Policies in the Middle East and North Africa." Paper presented at the *Second Mediterranean Social and Political Research Meeting*, Florence, March 21–25, 2001.

Roy, Delwin A. "Egyptian Emigrant Labor: Domestic Consequences." *Middle Eastern Studies*, Vol. 27, No. 3 (1991), pp. 551-82.

—— "The Hidden Economy in Egypt." *Middle Eastern Studies*, Vol. 28, No. 4 (1992), pp. 689–711.

Russell, Sharon Stanton. "Politics and Ideology in Migration Policy Formulation: The Case of Kuwait." *International Migration Review*, Vol. 23, No. 1 (1989), pp. 24–47.

—— "International Migration and Political Turmoil in the Middle East." *Population and Development Review*, Vol. 18, No. 4 (1992), pp. 719–27.

—— and Muhammad Ali Al-Ramadhan. "Kuwait's Migration Policy since the Gulf Crisis." *IJMES*, Vol. 26, No. 4 (1994), pp. 569-87.

Rumaihi, Mohamed G. "The Mode of Production in the Arab Gulf Before the Discovery of Oil." In Tim Niblock (ed.), *Social and Economic Development in the Arab Gulf*. London: Croom Helm, 1980, pp. 49–60.

Sabagh, Georges. "The Demography of the Middle East." *Middle East Studies Association Bulletin*, Vol. 4, No. 2 (May 15, 1970), pp. 1–19.

—— "Migration and Social Mobility in Egypt." In Malcolm H. Kerr and El Sayed Yassin (eds.), *Rich and Poor States in the Middle East: Egypt and the New Arab Order*. Boulder: Westview Press, and Cairo: The American University in Cairo Press, 1982, pp. 71–95.

—— "Immigrants in the Arab Gulf Countries: 'Sojourners' or 'Settlers"? In Giacomo Luciani (ed.), *The Arab State*. London: Routledge, 1990, pp. 349–72.

Sander, Cerstin. "Migrant Remittances to Developing Countries." Prepared for the *UK Department of International Development*, June 2003. Available at: http://www.dai.com/publications/other.php.

Sayed, Hussein Abdel-Aziz. "The Population Family Planning Program in Egypt: Structure and Performance." *Population Studies*, Vol. 11, No. 70 (July–September 1984), pp. 3–38.

Al-Sayegh, Fatma. "Domestic Politics in the United Arab Emirates: Social and Economic Policies, 1990–2000." In Joseph A. Kechichian (ed.), *Iran, Iraq, and the Arab Gulf States* (New York: Palgrave, 2001), pp. 161–75.

Seccombe, Ian J. "Immigrant Workers in an Emigrant Economy: An Examination of Replacement Migration in the Middle East." *International Migration*, Vol. 24, No. 2 (1986), pp. 377–96.

—— "Labour Emigration Policies and Economic Development in Jordan: From Unemployment to Labour Shortage." In Bichara Khader and Adnan Badran (eds.), *The Economic Development of Jordan*. London: Croom Helm, 1987, pp. 118–32.

—— and Richard I. Lawless. "State Intervention and the International Labour Market: A Review of Labour Emigration Policies in the Arab World." In Reginald Appleyard (ed.), *The Impact of International Migration on Developing Countries*. Paris: Development Centre of the Organization for Economic Co-Operation and Development, 1989, pp. 69-89.

Seikaly, May. "Women and Social Change in Bahrain." *IJMES*, Vol. 26, No. 3 (1994), pp. 415–26.

Sell, Ralph R. "Gone For Good?" *Cairo Papers in Social Science*, Vol. 10, No. 2 (Summer 1987).

—— "Egyptian International Labor Migration and Social Processes: Toward Regional Integration." *International Migration Review*, Vol. 22, No. 3 (1988), pp. 87–108.

Shaban, Radwan A., Ragui Assaad and Sulayman S. al-Qudsi. "The Challenge of Unemployment in the Arab Region." *International Labour Review*, Vol. 134, No. 1 (1995), pp. 65-81.

Shafik, Nemat. "Has Labor Migration Promoted Economic Integration in the Middle East?" In Ismail Sirageldin and Eqbal al-Rahmani (eds.), *Population and Development Transformations in the Arab World*. Greenwich: JAI Press, 1996, pp. 163-81.

Shah, Nasra M. "Arab Labour Migration: A Review of Trends and Issues." *International Migration*, Vol. 32, No. 1 (1994), pp. 3–27.

—— "Arab Migration Patterns in the Gulf." In IOM and League of Arab States. *Arab Migration in a Globalized World*. Cairo, May 2004, pp. 91–113.

Al-Shalkani, Mustafa. "A System for Collecting Vital Statistics in Gulf Cooperation Council Countries." *Population Bulletin of ESCWA*, Nos. 35–37 (December 1989-December 1990), pp. 43–97.

Share, M. A. J. "The Use of Jordanian Workers' Remittances." In Bichara Khader and Adnan Badran (eds.), *The Economic Development of Jordan*. London: Croom Helm, 1987, pp. 32–44.

Shaw, Stanford J. "The Ottoman Census System and Population, 1831–1914." *IJMES*, Vol. 9, No. 3 (1978), pp. 325–38.

Shawky, Gihan A. "Detecting Changes in Fertility in Algeria, Egypt and Yemen." *CDC Working Paper*, No. 42. Cairo, 1999.

Sheykhi, Mohammad Taghi. "The Socio-Psychological Factors of Family Planning with Special Reference to Iran: A Theoretical Appraisal." *International Sociology*, Vol. 10, No. 1 (1995), pp. 71-82.

El-Shibiny, Mohamed. "Higher Education in Oman: Its Development and Prospects." In K. E. Shaw (ed.), *Higher Education in the Gulf: Problems and Prospects*. Exeter: University of Exeter Press, 1997, pp. 150-81.

Short, Susan E. and Fengying Zhai. "Looking Locally at China's One-child Policy." *Studies in Family Planning*, Vol. 29, No. 4 (1998), pp. 373–85.

Sirageldin, Ismail. "Population Dynamics, Environment, and Conflict." In Ismail Sirageldin and Eqbal al-Rahmani (eds.), *Population and Development Transformations in the Arab World*. Greenwich: JAI Press, 1996, pp. 185–218.

Smith, Benjamin. "Oil Wealth and Regime Survival in the Developing World, 1960–1999." *American Journal of Political Science*, Vol. 48, No. 2 (2004), pp. 232–46.

Soffer, Arnon. "Lebanon – Where Demography is the Core of Politics and Life." *Middle Eastern Studies*, Vol. 22, No. 2 (1986), pp. 197–205.

Al-Sulayti, Hamad. "Education and Training in GCC Countries: Some Issues of Concern." In The Emirates Center for Strategic Studies and Research. *Education and the Arab World: Challenges of the Next Millennium*. Abu Dhabi, 1999, pp. 271–78.

Sullivan, Paul. "Contrary Views of Economic Diplomacy in the Arab World: Egypt." *Arab Studies Quarterly*, Vol. 21, No. 4 (1999), pp. 65–93.

Susser, Asher. "The Decline of the Arabs." *Middle East Quarterly*, Vol. 10, No. 4 (2003), pp. 3–16.

Tabbarah, Riad. "Challenges in Arab Demography." *Population Bulletin of ESCWA*, No. 33 (December 1988), pp. 3–16.

Tabutin, Dominique and Bruno Schoumaker. "The Demography of the Arab World and the Middle East from the 1950s to the 2000s." *Population*, Vol. 60, Nos. 5 & 6 (2005), pp. 505–616.

Teitelbaum, Michael S. "Relevance of Demographic Transition Theory for Developing Countries." *Science*, Vol. 188 (May 2, 1975), pp. 420–25.

Thomas, John W. and Merilee S. Grindle. "Political Leadership and Policy Characteristics in Population Policy Reform." In Jason L. Finkle and C. Alison McIntosh (eds.), *The New Politics of Population: Conflict and Consensus in Family Planning*. Supplement to Vol. 20 of *Population and Development Review*. New York: The Population Council, 1994, pp. 51–70.

Thompson, Warren S. "Population." *The American Journal of Sociology*, Vol. 34, No. 6 (1929), pp. 959–75.

Tschirgi, Dan. "Egyptian Labor Migration: Social, Political and Economic Effects." In Mohammad Shtayyeh (ed.), *Labor Migration: Palestine, Jordan, Egypt and Israel*. Jerusalem: Palestine Center for Regional Studies, 1998, pp. 45–77.

Tyrrell, Timothy J. and Robert J. Johnston. "A Framework for Assessing Direct Economic Impacts of Tourist Events: Distinguishing Origins, Destinations and Causes of Expenditure." *Journal of Travel Research*, Vol. 40, No. 1 (2001), pp. 94–101.

Valenzuela, J. Samuel and Arthuro Valenzuela. "Modernization and Dependency: Alternative Perspectives in the Study of Latin American Underdevelopment." *Comparative Politics*, Vol. 10, No. 4 (1978), pp. 535–557.

Vallin, Jacques. "The End of the Demographic Transition: Relief or Concern?" *Population and Development Review*, Vol. 28, No. 1 (2002), pp. 105–20.

Van Hear, Nicholas. "The Socio-Economic Impact of the Involuntary Mass Return to Yemen in 1990." *Journal of Refugee Studies*, Vol. 7, No. 1 (1994), pp. 18–38.

Wardwell, John M. "Jordan." In William J. Serow et al. (eds.), *Handbook of International Migration*. New York and London: Greenwood Press, 1990, pp. 167–87.

Warren, Charles W. et al. "Fertility and Family Planning in Jordan: Results from the 1985 Jordan Husbands' Fertility Survey." *Studies in Family Planning*, Vol. 21, No. 1 (1990), pp. 33–39.

Waterbury, John. "The 'Soft State' and the Open Door: Egypt Experience with Economic Liberalization, 1974–1984." *Comparative Politics*, Vol. 18, No. 1 (1985), pp. 65–83.

Weeks, John R. "The Demography of Islamic Nations." *Population Bulletin*, Vol. 43, No. 4 (1988).

Westoff, Charles F. and Tomas Frejka. "Fertility and Religiousness Among European Muslims." Paper presented at the *2007 Annual Meeting of the Population Association of America*, New York, March 29–31, 2007. Available at: http://paa2007.princeton.edu/download.aspx?submissionId=70869.

Widmer, Robert. "Population." In Said B. Himadeh (ed.), *Economic Organization of Syria*. Beirut: The American University of Beirut Press, 1936, pp. 3–26.

Williamson, Jeffrey G. and Tarik M. Yousef. "Demographic Transitions and Economic Performance in the Middle East and North Africa." In Ismail Sirageldin (ed.), *Human Capital: Population Economics in the Middle East*. Cairo: The American University in Cairo Press, 2002, pp. 16–36.

Willoughby, John. "Ambivalent Anxieties of the South Asian-Gulf Arab Labor Exchange." American University, Washington, D.C., Department of Economics, Working Paper Series No. 2005-02 (March 2005). Available at: http://www.american.edu/cas/econ/workingpapers/2005-02.pdf.

Wilson, Rodney. "Whither the Egyptian Economy?" *British Journal of Middle East Studies*, Vol. 20, No. 2 (1993), pp. 204–13.

Winckler, Edwin A. "Chinese Reproductive Policy at the Turn of the Millennium: Dynamic Stability." *Population and Development Review*, Vol. 28, No. 3 (2001), pp. 379–418.

Winckler, Onn. "The Challenge of Foreign Workers in the Persian/Arabian Gulf: The Case of Oman." *Immigrants & Minorities*, Vol. 18, No. 2 (2000), pp. 23–52.

—— "Hafiz al-Asad's Socio-Economic Legacy: The Balance of Achievements and Failures." *Orient*, Vol. 42, No. 3 (2001), pp. 449–67.

—— "The Demographic Dilemma of the Arab World: The Employment Aspect." *Journal of Contemporary History*, Vol. 37, No. 4 (2002), pp. 617–36.

—— "The Economic Consequences of the Iraqi Crisis on the Mashreq Countries." *Mediterranean Politics*, Vol. 11, No. 3 (2006), pp. 395–417.

—— "Was it Worth It? A Reexamination of the Cost/Benefit Balance of the Inter-Arab Labor Migration." *Journal of South Asian and Middle Eastern Studies*, Vol. 29, No. 4 (2006), pp. 38–59.

—— "The Birth of Oman's Tourism Industry." *Tourism*, Vol. 55, No. 2 (2007), pp. 221–34.

—— "The Surprising Results of the Saudi Arabian 2004 Demographic Census." *IJMES*, Vol. 40, No. 1 (January 2008), pp. 12–15.

—— "The Failure of Pronatalism of the Developed States 'with Cultural-Ethnic Hegemony': The Israeli Lesson." *Population, Place and Space*, Vol. 14, No. 2 (2008), pp. 119–34.

Wisensale, Steven K. and Amany A. Khodair. "The Two-child Family: The Egyptian Model of Family Planning." *Journal of Comparative Family Studies*, Vol. 29, No. 3 (1998), pp. 503–16.

Yamani, Mai. "Health, Education, Gender and the Security of the Gulf in the Twenty-First Century." In David. E. Long and Christian Koch (eds.), *Gulf Security in the Twenty-First Century*. Abu Dhabi: The Emirates Center for Strategic Studies and Research, 1997, pp. 265–79.

Zohry, Ayman Gaafar and Lee L. Been. "Infant Mortality and Health Care in the Arabian Gulf Region." In *CDC 24th Annual Seminar on Population Issues and the Challenges of the 21st Century in the Middle East, Africa, and Asia*. Research Monograph Series, No. 24. Cairo, 1995, pp. 487- 507.

Youngstedt, Scott. "Tourism in Morocco: Opportunities, Challenges and Threats." *Africa Insight*, Vol. 33, No. 1 (2003), pp. 61–68.

Yousef. Tarik M. "Development, Growth and Policy Reform in the Middle East and North Africa since 1950." *Journal of Economic Perspectives*, Vol. 18, No. 3 (2004), pp. 91–116.

Yousif, Hassan M. and Ahmad A. Hammouda. "Alternative Population Projection Scenarios by Education Attainment for Egypt, the Sudan and Tunisia." *Population Bulletin of ESCWA*, No. 43 (1995), pp. 55–98.

Al-Yousif, Yousif Khalifa. "Oil Economies and Globalization: The Case of the GCC Countries." Available at: http://www.sba.luc.edu/orgs/meea/volume6/al-yousif.htm.

Daily Newspapers

Arabic and Hebrew

Al-Ahram (Cairo, Arabic).
Akhbar al-Khalij (Manama, Arabic).
Al-Bayan (Dubai, Arabic).
Al-Dustur (Amman, Arabic).
Ha'aretz (Tel Aviv, Hebrew).
Al-Hayat (London, Arabic).
Al-Ittihad (Abu Dhabi, Arabic).
Al-Khalij (Sharja, Arabic).
Al-Ra'y (Amman, Arabic).
Al-Sharq al-Awsat (London, Arabic).
Al-Thawra (Damascus, Arabic).
Tishrin (Damascus, Arabic).
Al-Watan (Kuwait, Arabic).

English

Arab Times (Montgomery).
Bahrain Tribune (Manama).
The Egyptian Gazette (Cairo).
Emirates News (Abu Dhabi).
Financial Times (London).
The Guardian (London).
Gulf News (Dubai).
International Herald Tribune (Paris).
Jordan Times (Amman).
Kuwait Times (Kuwait).
The New York Times (New York).
Times of Oman (Muscat)

Weeklies and Monthlies

Arabic

Al-Ahram al-Iqtisadi (Weekly, Cairo).
Al-Majalla (London, weekly).
Al-Mussawar (Weekly, Cairo).
Nidhal al-Falahin (Damascus).
Al-Wasat (Weekly, London).

English

Africa Monitor (Monthly, London).
Al-Ahram Weekly (Weekly, Cairo).
The Arab Economist (Monthly, London).

EIA, *International Petroleum Monthly* (Washington, D.C.).
Gulf States Newsletter (bi-weekly, West Sussex).
MEED (Middle East Economic Digest, Weekly, London).
MEES (Middle East Economic Survey, Weekly, Beirut).
MEN Economic Weekly (weekly, Cairo).
The Middle East (Monthly, London).
Middle East International (Weekly, London).
The New Republic (bi-weekly, New York).
Population Today (Monthly, New York).
Saudi Economic Survey (Weekly, Riyadh).

Quarterlies and Annuals

EIU (Economist intelligence Unit). *Country Report and Profile*, Algeria, Bahrain, Egypt, Jordan, Kuwait, Morocco, Oman, Qatar, Saudi Arabia, Syria, Tunisia, UAE (Quarterly and Annual Profile, London).
Middle East Contemporary Survey (MECS). (Annual, The Moshe Dayan Center, Tel Aviv University).
The Middle East and North Africa (Annual, Europa Publications, London).

Internet Websites and Databases

1. The Australian Bureau of Statistics [http://www.abs.gov.au].
2. The European Union (EU) Official Website [http://europa.eu.int].
3. The Hashemite Kingdom of Jordan, Department of Statistics [http://www.dos.gov.jo].
4. Sultanate of Oman, Ministry of National Economy [http://www.moneoman.gov.om].
5. Sultanate of Oman, Ministry of Information [http://www.omanet.com].
6. Oman Information Center (Omaninfo) [http://www.omaninfo.com].
7. PDO (Petroleum Development Oman) website [http://www.pdo.co.om].
8. The Palestinian Ministry of Health [http://www.moh.gov.ps].
9. State of Qatar, The Planning Council [http://www.planning.gov.qa].
10. The US Department of Commerce, US Census Bureau [http:/www.census.gov].
11. The US Ministry of Energy, EIA [http://www.eia.doe.gov].
12. The US Department of State, Bureau of Near Eastern Affairs [http://www.state.gov].
13. US Department of Labor, Bureau of Labor Statistics [http://www.bls.gov].
14. CIA (Central Intelligence Agency). *The World Factbook* [http://www.cia.gov/publications].
15. Population Reference Bureau. *Bureau Data Finder* [http://www.prb.worldpop.org/datafinder.htm].
16. The Pan Arab Project for Family Health of the Arab League Website [http://www.papfam.org].
17. UNRWA website [http://www.un.org/unrwa].
18. ECA [http://www.uneca.org].
19. WHO. *Estimates for Health Personnel* [http://www3.who.int].
20. ILO (International Labour Organization) [http://www.ilo.org].
21. International Organization for Migration (IOM) [http://www.iom.int].
22. The World Bank Group, International Database [http://www.worldbank.org/data.]
23. OAPEC (Organization of Arab Petroleum Exporting Countries) [http://www.opec.org/home].
24. *OPEC Monthly Bulletin* [http://www.oapecorg.org/Publications.htm].
25. *Arab News Online* [http://www.arabnews.com].
26. *Insight Guides* [http://www.insightguides.com].
27. Human Right Watch. *Human Rights News* [http://www.hrw.org].
28. Library of Congress, *Country Studies* [http://lcweb2loc.gov].
29. *Gulfnews.com* [http://archive.gulfnews.com].

Index